# The Norton
# Introduction to Literature

# The Norton
# Introduction to Literature

BAIN · BEATY · HUNTER

# Poetry

EDITED BY

## J. PAUL HUNTER

*Emory University*

W · W · NORTON & COMPANY · INC.

NEW YORK

COPYRIGHT © 1973 BY W. W. NORTON & COMPANY, INC.

## First Edition

Library of Congress Cataloging in Publication Data

Hunter, J.   Paul, 1934–   comp.
Poetry.

(The Norton introduction to literature)
1. Poetry—Collections.  I. Title.  II.  Series.
PN6101.H85                821'.008                72–14191
ISBN 0–393–09380–8

Since this page cannot legibly accommodate all the copyright notices, the four pages following constitute an extension of the copyright page.

Samuel Allen: "American Gothic" reprinted by permission of the author.
A. R. Ammons: From *Uplands, New Poems,* copyright © 1970 by A. R. Ammons, and *Briefings,* copyright © 1971 by A. R. Ammons. Selections reprinted by permission of W. W. Norton & Company, Inc.
Brother Antoninus: From *The Rose of Solitude,* copyright © 1967 by Doubleday & Company, Inc. Reprinted by permission of the publisher.
Richard Armour: From *Light Armour,* copyright 1954 by Richard Armour. Reprinted by permission of McGraw-Hill Book Company.
John Ashbery: From *Rivers and Mountains,* copyright © 1962, 1963, 1964, 1966 by John Ashbery. Reprinted by permission of Holt, Rinehart and Winston, Inc.
W. H. Auden: From *Collected Shorter Poems 1927–1957,* copyright 1940, renewed 1968 by W. H. Auden. Reprinted by permission of Random House, Inc. and Faber and Faber Limited. "Hammerfest" from *About the House,* copyright © 1962 by W. H. Auden. Reprinted by permission of Random House, Inc.
Hilaire Belloc: From *Sonnets and Verse,* published by Gerald Duckworth & Co. Ltd. Reprinted by permission of A. D. Peters and Company.
John Berryman: From *Short Poems,* copyright 1948 by John Berryman. Reprinted by permission of Farrar, Straus & Giroux, Inc.
John Betjeman: From *Collected Poems* published by John Murray (Publishers) Ltd. and Houghton Mifflin Co. Selections reprinted by permission of John Murray Ltd.
Earle Birney: From *Selected Poems.* Reprinted by permission of The Canadian Publishers, McClelland and Stewart Limited, Toronto.
J. P. Bishop: From *Now With His Love,* copyright 1933 by Charles Scribner's Sons; renewal copyright © 1961 Margaret M. Bronson. Reprinted by permission of Charles Scribner's Sons.
Louise Bogan: From *The Blue Estuaries,* copyright 1936, 1954, 1968 by Louise Bogan; copyright renewed 1964 by Louise Bogan. Reprinted by permission of Farrar, Straus & Giroux, Inc.
Julian Bond: Selections reprinted by permission of the author.
Gwendolyn Brooks: From *The World of Gwendolyn Brooks,* copyright 1949 by Gwendolyn Brooks Blakely. Reprinted by permission of Harper & Row, Publishers, Inc.
A. J. Butler: "Naked I Came" from *Amaranth and Asphodel.* Reprinted by permission of Basil Blackwell Publisher.
Turner Cassity: From *Watchboy, What of the Night?,* copyright © 1962 by Turner Cassity. Reprinted by permission of Wesleyan University Press. "Calvin in the Casino" first appeared in *Poetry.*
Helen Chasin: From *Coming Close and Other Poems,* copyright © 1968 by Yale University. Reprinted by permission of Yale University Press.
Leonard Cohen: "Suzanne," words and music by Leonard Cohen. Reprinted by permission of Continental Total Media Project, Inc.
Frances Cornford: From *Collected Poems* (1954). Reprinted by permission of Dufour Editions, Inc.
Hart Crane: From *The Collected Poems and Selected Letters and Prose of Hart Crane,* copyright © 1933, 1958, 1966 by Liveright Publishing Corporation. Reprinted by permission of Liveright, Publishers, New York.
Countee Cullen: From *On These I Stand,* copyright 1925 by Harper & Row, Publishers, Inc.; renewed 1953 by Ida M. Cullen. Reprinted by permission of the publishers.
E. E. Cummings: From *Poems 1923–1954.* "Buffalo Bill's," "In Just," and "the rose is dying" copyright 1923, 1951 by E. E. Cummings. "the season 'tis, my lovely lambs,"

PRINTED IN THE UNITED STATES OF AMERICA

1 2 3 4 5 6 7 8 9 0

# Copyrights vii

# Contents

## I. The Poem in Focus: Subject and Tone

## II. The Middle Distance: Craft, Form, and Kind

* French original

* Italian original

* Latin original

## III. The Larger Frame: Poems in Contexts

# Foreword

## Using This Book

This book is an anthology: a generous collection of what the editors think are, for the most part, enjoyable, stimulating, and significant literary works. With all literature to choose from, the editors had to use additional criteria to limit the selection. Among these criteria are the type of audience, considerations of similarity and variety, and illustrative utility.

We assume an audience of English-speaking, reasonably literate, late-20th-century readers with some experience of literature but not necessarily with specific literary or other background in common. Judging in purely qualitative terms, we have perhaps "over-represented" 20th-century, especially recent-20th-century works, but we feel these are the most readily enjoyable and comprehensible works, requiring intelligence and awareness but not necessarily as much specific information and experience. We have tried to include some works that are familiar to at least some students and to many instructors. We have also tried to include the excellent but unfamiliar, the forgotten, undiscovered, or new, the seldom if ever anthologized, for surely one of the pleasures of reading is the joy of discovery.

We have also tried to include a wide variety of works—in subject matter, in form, in tone, in attitude, in effect. Yet, where offered a choice among equally excellent possibilities, we have chosen works that interact with each other by comparability of subject matter, form, tone, or effect; for reading, like other experiences, is in large measure comparative. Some even say that one can have a pure experience—feeling fur, for example—only once, and that all subsequent fur-feelings are comparisons with the first one. Any alert reader will find multiple instances of comparable works, not only those deliberately juxtaposed by the editors but works from widely separated sections and even from different genres.

Where other considerations—excellence, appropriateness to audience, variety, and comparability—have been satisfied, we have chosen from among works that best illustrate an appropriate and appropriately timed critical or pedagogical point. This is not only an anthology but a textbook; the works are not only selected but arranged or ordered to introduce the reader to the serious study of literature. Any selection of excellent literary works may be read in many meaningful orders, and this anthology is, we trust, no exception, but in a bound book some one order is fixed. We divide literature into genres—fiction, drama, poetry —and within each genre proceed in a pattern as parallel as the nature and exigencies of the genres permit. Each begins with works to be read, or "closely read" discretely and analytically as suggested below, but all or many of them are also grouped by subject matter or theme—

elements readily accessible to all regardless of past reading experience. The early subject matter groupings of stories and plays also introduce and incorporate matters of structure; since the formal elements in poems are more complex, fixed, and defined, these are introduced in groups separate from and subsequent to the subject-matter groups. The second major section of each collection specifically addresses itself to some secondary ways of understanding a literary work in the genre: the relation of a short story to rites and patterns of initiation, the specific elements of language, meter, and forms in a poem, and the relation between a play as a literary work and its actualization upon the stage. The final major section within each genre presents works in biographical or historical contexts: works by a single author, works from a historical period or contiguous periods, and so on.

The arrangement is not meant to classify the works. What it does suggest is a method for introducing students to the serious study of literature. It begins with considerations that assume no specific literary method or experience but assume expectations aroused by certain human situations—subject matter or theme; it builds toward making conscious certain literary expectations, those of form and kind; and finally it introduces contextual expectations—those created by the author's other works, by the norms of a period or a tradition, the historical realities. All these elements and expectations operate simultaneously and interact, of course, and it would be not only possible but desirable to return to works placed early in the selections with the accumulated experience of having read through the entire anthology to discover just what has been gained by heightened awareness of form, kind, and context.

The pattern of arrangement and implied method here described is followed in general within each genre. More specific and detailed description of the order within each genre, with variations and varied emphases necessitated by the inherent differences between genres, appears in sections called "Note on Arrangement" at the end of each separate preface. Since one of our principles—indeed, perhaps, our first principle—is that the study of literature is the reading of literature, we have preferred to fill the pages available to us with literary works, and to let understanding, awareness, and engagement grow out of that reading. At the same time, we recognize the necessity of some assistance. The works are annotated—as is customary in Norton anthologies—in order to free the instructor from spending valuable class time in glossing the texts. Each genre is preceded by a preface, which is designed to raise some general questions about how to expect. Each genre is followed by a section entitled "The Elements of Fiction," "The Elements of Poetry," or "The Elements of Drama," which contain brief essays on such topics as, for example, "Audience," "Tone," or "Metaphor": these essays may be read as introductory chapters to sections of the anthology, as a glossary of literary terms and the necessary technical vocabulary, or ignored. Finally, the teachers' manuals may be drawn on for classroom questions or writing topics.

## Studying Literature

Questions of definition and theory are apt to become, over the years, central for a teacher, but for a student the central questions are, at the beginning, practical: how to read literature with enjoyment, interest, and understanding and how to relate it to life beyond the classroom. Of course, no universal how-to formula exists, not only because all individual readers differ from one another but also because different works of literature demand different approaches. Still, there are common grounds among readers and common grounds among works, for although every work is *in a sense* unique, many things about it are not unique at all, and in approaching any work of literature a reader may save himself many difficulties by using some common tools. Ultimately, one's experience with a work is very personal—and at its furthest reaches private—but the experience begins communally. No private insight occurs if the reader does not first participate in a sharing with the writer, and that sharing depends upon uses of language which are agreed on and discoverable. The classroom and the textbook represent places and ways of delineating and articulating what is public and shareable.

But where does one begin? "Read, read, read, read, my unlearned reader" is the advice *Tristram Shandy* offers, and the literal and intense following of that advice is assumed by nearly every college teacher. For almost half a century the *close reading* approach to literature has dominated the college classroom, asking that each student read completely, carefully, analytically each individual literary work, making sure to know exactly the significance of each word, each phrase, each part, each transition. Over the years this approach has undergone many variations and shifts of emphasis and has been known by many names ("the new criticism" and "formalism" are two of the most popular and lasting), but its premises remain fairly constant: that any literary work is a self-existent whole which will reveal its own laws, meanings, and implications if it is approached intensely and sensitively. "Close reading" emphasizes the knowledge of basic tools and the asking of basic questions: What, literally, does each line, or sentence, or unit of dialogue say? What kind of vocabulary (or "diction") does the work use, and how specialized is it? What images does it use, and what are their emotional connotations? How does the setting contribute to the total effect? Who is telling the story, or speaking the dialogue, or addressing us in the poem, and how does knowledge of that speaker color our responses to what he or she says? All such questions mean to get at the work's final effect, helping to explain not only what the work "says" but what responses it evokes, intellectual and emotional, and they articulate both what a reader first feels impressionistically and point toward new areas of feeling and response, extending the range of the work's effect.

A second popular approach to literature is *generic*, and in classroom practice the generic and close-reading approaches often quietly merge. The generic approach assumes that each genre (in the sense that we are using the term to distinguish fiction, poetry, and drama) has some identifying characteristics which may be usefully isolated—that, for example, all plays have some elements in common which differentiate them from stories and poems—and that a reader who knows these characteristics may test an individual work against them to evaluate the work, to clarify it, and to learn at the same time more about the genre as a genre. The generic approach assumes that the writer and reader both approach a work in a certain genre with specific—if not always fully conscious—expectations and that part of the effect depends on whether, and how, those expectations are satisfied. Knowing what to expect, even when one's expectation is not fulfilled—in fact, especially when one's expectation is not fulfilled—puts the reader on a common ground with the author. The writer may, and often does, re-contour that ground quickly, but for a moment at least the commonness of ground allows communication to begin. Writers who choose to write drama rather than fiction commit themselves to the materials and possibilities of the dramatic genre, and this commitment enables the reader to concentrate on terms, problems, and questions that relate especially to drama. The generic approach is primarily an admission that *groups* of works have something in common and that recognizing the *nature* of the grouping provides the basis for further study and consideration.

Some generic critics believe that there are "essential" characteristics of each genre and that the differences between genres are deeply rooted in the ultimate order of the world or of human nature. Others simply find genres a convenient way of describing tendencies. Either group may use the generic approach as a tool for reading individual works, and either may extend the genre distinction to smaller units. Distinctive groups within genres, sometimes called subgenres or types or kinds, often have specific characteristics. Drama is, for example, traditionally divided into comedy and tragedy, each with characteristics which can be described, and many smaller groups are also recognized as having clear group identity: romantic comedy, black comedy, tragicomedy, melodrama, revenge plays, heroic plays, absurd plays are a few of the kinds of drama which provide expectations more specific than those of drama itself. Similarly there are many kinds of fiction (mystery stories, for example, or initiation stories, as well as novels, romances, and novellas) and of poetry (epic, pastoral, satiric, confessional, etc.); writers often choose their kind with great care and precision, to impose specific tasks upon themselves and to guarantee communication with the reader through a well defined common area of expectation. Even when the writer's choice of kind is arbitrary, capricious, or unconscious, the reader can profit from sensible comparisons and contrasts between an individual work and the norm of the group, and when a writer sets out deliberately to make his own unique kind the reader who knows the conventions of the other kinds will see more clearly what is going on.

Other classroom approaches to literature have gone in and out of fashion: the *biographical* approach (which emphasizes the relation of a work to the events and psychological patterns of an author's life), the *historical* approach (which emphasizes the development of forms and strategies and the passing on of techniques from one writer to another), and the *thematic* approach (which groups works by the subjects that they deal with or ideas that they present, rather than by genre, form, or style) have been among the more popular ones. The close-reading and generic approaches—often modified to fit the special interests or needs of a particular moment or a particular instructor—have, however, dominated the literature classroom for many years, and whatever concessions to fashion are made usually occur within the general framework of the close-reading and generic approaches. The selections in Sections I and II of the Norton Introduction to each genre are arranged so as to be especially convenient for these approaches.

In the last few years there has been a growing restlessness about these traditional approaches, and many attempts at experimentation reflect uncertainty about classroom method. The uncertainty is not so much disillusionment with what the close-reading and generic approaches can do, but a worry about what they cannot do; it is not so much a matter of replacing traditional methods as of supplementing them so that literature may seem more integrally related to other things. Students and teachers alike often weary of tool-sharpening, especially if they are not sure what larger tasks the tools are good for; most actors, athletes, and lovers can put up with strenuous discipline if they have a performance in view, but few are enchanted by practice for its own sake.

Seeing the relation of literature to other art and to the larger culture of which it is part is largely a matter of thinking about literature in context, related to a specific time and place—besides having "universal" and "timeless" aspects. Students who insist on knowing how a work relates to political or social or moral questions are, in an important sense, addressing the same issues as scholars trying to "place" a work in its whole cultural setting. (All of the more important critical and scholarly movements of the last few years—phenomenology, structuralism, psychological criticism, contextualism, neo-historicism—share the concern with literature as existing in time and having a specific relationship to the immediate cultural context which it reflects and addresses.) Seeing how one work of an author relates to other works, how specific events shape and control both the theme and the form of a work, how persuasive devices work upon a reader or audience in a specific emotional context, how the ideas of one time may be translated into a world with different assumptions and pressures—all these possibilities represent attempts to expand beyond the self-existent world of an individual work and the galaxy of a particular genre or kind. And such larger concerns often correct and clarify as well as expand, for reading many works by one writer (or knowing more about events to which the author refers) often corrects mistakes or reveals resonances which are not discoverable when one reads the work in isolation. Section III of the Norton Introduction to each genre is arranged to facilitate the investigation of such temporal and cultural matters. As editors, we have tried to arrange this book so that students and teachers can take advantage of classroom procedures already in use and adventure a little beyond what is already familiar or what they already do well.

C. E. B.
J. B.
J. P. H.

# A Preface to Poetry

Reading a poem is one thing. Experiencing it is something else. And experiencing it fully depends not merely on a reader's willingness, but on his readiness to cope with a poem's richness, resonance, and complication. Look, for example, at this poem—one of the most famous in the English language:

## To His Coy Mistress

Had we but world enough, and time,
This coyness, lady, were no crime.
We would sit down, and think which way
To walk, and pass our long love's day.
Thou by the Indian Ganges' side                    5
Shouldst rubies find: I by the tide
Of Humber would complain. I would
Love you ten years before the Flood,
And you should if you please refuse
Till the conversion of the Jews.                    10
My vegetable love should grow
Vaster than empires, and more slow;
An hundred years should go to praise
Thine eyes, and on thy forehead gaze;
Two hundred to adore each breast;                   15
But thirty thousand to the rest.
An age at least to every part,
And the last age should show your heart.
For, lady, you deserve this state;
Nor would I love at lower rate.                      20
    But at my back I always hear
Time's wingéd chariot hurrying near;
And yonder all before us lie
Deserts of vast eternity.
Thy beauty shall no more be found,                  25
Nor, in thy marble vault, shall sound
My echoing song; then worms shall try
That long preserved virginity,
And your quaint honor turn to dust,
And into ashes all my lust:                         30
The grave's a fine and private place,
But none, I think, do there embrace.
    Now therefore, while the youthful hue
Sits on thy skin like morning dew,
And while thy willing soul transpires               35
At every pore with instant fires,
Now let us sport us while we may,
And now, like am'rous birds of prey,

Rather at once our time devour,
Than languish in his slow-chapped pow'r.          40
Let us roll all our strength and all
Our sweetness up into one ball,
And tear our pleasures with rough strife
Thorough the iron gates of life.
Thus, though we cannot make our sun               45
Stand still, yet we will make him run.

The title suggests the situation—a man is speaking to his beloved—and before we are far into the poem we recognize his familiar argument: let's not wait, let's make love now. But much more is going on in the poem than this simple "message."

Seduction is a promising subject, but it is nearly as easy to be dull on this subject as on less fascinating ones, and the subject has inspired some very dreary poetry. The interest and power of this poem depend on more than the choice of subject, however useful that subject is in whetting a reader's expectations. No reader is likely to use the poem as a handbook for his own life, and few readers are likely to read it at a moment when their own lives parallel precisely the poem's situation. Its relevance is of a larger kind: it portrays vividly and forcefully a recognizable situation, saying something *about* that situation but (more important) making us react to the situation and feel something about it. Experiencing a poem involves not only knowing what it says but also feeling the pleasures provided by its clever management of our own ideas and emotions. All poems have a design on us—they try to make us feel certain things—and a full experience of a poem requires full recognition of the complexities of design so that we can feel specific emotions and pleasures—not only the general ones of contemplating seduction.

Let's begin at the beginning. What do you expect of a poem about a would-be seduction? One thing you can be almost certain of is that it will contain attractive images of physical enjoyment. The first verse-paragraph (lines 1–20) contains such images, and so does the third (especially lines 33–38). The first set of images suggest the languorous, lazy appeal of a timeless world where physical enjoyment seems to fill all time and all space. First are images of rich sensuousness; the leisurely contemplation of enjoyment, the timeless walks in exotic lands, the finding of precious stones, the luxury of delaying the supreme moment. Gradually sensuousness becomes sensuality, and the speaker imagines himself praising various parts of the girl's body. In line 33, the poem returns to sexual contemplation but with much more intensity. Now the girl seems to be not only a passive object of admiration but a live, breathing, perspiring, passionate respondent. And a moment later, the speaker projects the beauty and energy of the love act itself. He suggests something of his anticipation of supreme ecstasy by the vividness and intensity of the images and language he uses: from the languid, flowing, floating suggestions of the early lines through the breathless anticipation of lines 33–37 to the violence of lines 41–44 with their explicit visualization of the union, the rolling into one, of "strength" and "sweetness."

But not all the poem portrays glorious pleasure. The second verse paragraph (lines 21–32) contains some pretty grim stuff. Instead of the endless languor of unhurried walks and exotic places in the early lines, we have anxiety and consciousness of time—a hurrying chariot, moving up fast from behind. And instead of the centuries of body-worship, eternity consists of vast deserts. Grimmest of all is the image of a different kind of fall than the one the speaker desires; the carefully preserved virginity of the girl, the speaker imagines, will be tested and destroyed in the grave by worms. The speaker summarizes with gross understatement and macabre humor in lines 31–32:

> The grave's a fine and private place,
> But none, I think, do there embrace.

The contrast of all that grimness of future dryness and death empha-sizes (first) the unreal romanticism of the timeless world which, according to the speaker, the girl seems to want, and (second) the vividly portrayed sensual pleasures of a potential moment right now. Such contrasts work for us as well as for the presumed girl; in fact, they are part of a carefully contrived argument that organizes the poem. We might well have expected, just from the title and the opening lines, that the poem would be organized as a formal argument. The first words of each paragraph clearly show the outlines: (1) "Had we . . . " (If we had no limits of time or space); (2) "But . . . " (But we do have such limits); (3) "Now, therefore . . . ." The poem is cast as a long, detailed hypothetical syllogism; it uses the form of a standard argument, with vivid examples and carefully contrived rhetoric, to sug-gest the urgency of enjoying the moment. It is a specious argument, of course, but real people have fallen for worse ones. But this isn't "real life"; the story doesn't even end. As in most other poems (and unlike most drama and fiction), the "plot" and its resolution have little to do with the final effect. Part of the point here is to notice the flaw in the argument. A good logician could show you that the speaker commits the fallacy of the "denied antecedent," that is, he proves what cannot happen but fails to prove what can. Seduction seldom, of course, gets worked out in purely logical terms, and so in one sense the logic of the argument doesn't matter—any more than whether the speaker finally seduces the girl. But in another sense it matters a great deal and con-tributes to our complex experience of the poem. For if we spot the illogic and find it amusing (since the argument is obviously an effective one, logical or not), we not only feel the accuracy of the poem's ob-servation about seduction but we experience something important about the way words work. Often their effect is more far-reaching than what they say on a literal level, just as this poem reaches much further than any literal statement of its "message" or "meaning." Poetry often exploits the fact that words work in such mysterious ways; in fact, most poems, in one way or another, are concerned with the fact that words may be used suggestively to open out on horizons beyond logical and syntactical categories.

Reading a poem about seduction is hardly the same thing as getting seduced, and only a very peculiar poet or reader would expect it to be, though some of the censorship controversies over the teaching of poems like this may sometimes imply that life and art are the same thing. Anyone who thinks they are is bound to be disappointed by a poem about seduction, or about anything else. One does not go to a poem instead of being seduced, or as a sublimation, or as a guide. A poem about anything does not intend to be the thing itself, or even to recreate it precisely. Poetry, like other literature, is an ordered imitation of perceived reality expressed in words. By definition, by intention, and by practice, poetry modifies life to its own artistic ends, "ordering" —that is, making meaningful—what is only a version in any case. What poetry offers us is not life itself, naked and available, but a perspective (*perceived* reality) on some recognizable situations or ideas; not Truth with a capital T, but interpretations and stances; not passion itself, but words that evoke associations and memories and feelings. A poem can provide an angle of vision which in "real life" is often blurred through our closeness to experience. And just as the poet fictionalizes—whether he begins with a real event or not—we as readers end with his version, which exists in tension with other things we know, about words, about poetry, about argument, about seduction, about everything. That tension tests not the "truth" of the poet's vision but the effects produced by the poem; the more we know, the richer these effects are likely to be.

Anyone with developed sensitivities and a modest amount of knowledge of the suggestiveness of words can find the crucial words that express and evoke the sensual appeal. The devices of contrast (the flowing Ganges flanked by rubies vs. vast deserts; the spacious wandering vs. the confinement of a marble vault; eternal adoration vs. those traditional symbols of mortality, ashes and dust) may be readily seen by anyone willing to look at the poem carefully. In short, much of the poem is readily available to almost any reader who looks carefully; much of its power is right there on the page, and a reader need make only a minimal effort to experience it.

But a number of things in the poem require special skill or knowledge. The poem's parody of a hypothetical syllogism is only available to those who can recognize a hypothetical syllogism and see the distortion in this one. Of course, not recognizing the syllogism is not too serious, as long as the reader "senses" the falsity of the argument and finds the incongruity in its effectiveness; he simply misses a joke which is part of the poem's complexity. But some other matters in the poem are more crucial, for lack of knowledge about them would not only drain the poem of some of its richness but might even force a misunderstanding of what the poem says on its most literal level.

Look, for instance, at the following words: "coy" (title) and "coyness" (line 2); "mistress" (title); "complain" (line 7); "vegetable" (line 11); "adore" (line 15). All of these words are common enough, but each offers a problem in interpretation because of changes in meaning. The poem was written more than three hundred years ago, in the mid-17th century, and many words used in a specific way then have changed over the years. Words are, in a sense, alive and ever-changing; change is a part of the excitement of language as well as a potential frustration, and if we construe each of these words exactly as it is construed now we will be badly misled. The most obvious change in meaning is in the word "mistress," for to us it implies a specific sexual relationship, one that would make the elaborate seduction plea here seem a little late. The most common 17th-century meaning of "mistress" was simply "a woman who has command over a man's heart; a woman who is loved and courted by a man; a sweetheart, lady-love." This definition comes from the *Oxford English Dictionary*, a valuable reference guide that lists historical as well as modern meanings, with detailed examples of usages. The *OED* can also show us that the new meaning of "mistress" was coming into use when this poem was written, and perhaps the meanings are played off against each other, as a kind of false lead; such false leads are common in poetry, for poets often like to toy with our expectations and surprise us.

"Coy" and "coyness" offer a similar problem; in modern usage they usually suggest playful teasing, affectation, coquettishness. But originally they suggested shyness, modesty, reluctance, reserve, not simply the affectation of those things. Of course, we find out very little about the girl herself in this poem (except what we can infer from the things the speaker says to her and the way he says them), but we are not led to think of her as sly and affected in her hesitancy to receive her lover's advances.

"Complain" and "adore" are more technical. The former indicates a lover going through the ritual of composing a "complaint"—a poem which bewails his misery because of a lady's disdain. Thus, the speaker here self-deprecatingly (but comically) imagines himself (in the unreal, timeless world of the first verse paragraph) as a pining swain, while his love is luxuriating half-across the earth, oblivious to his pain. Obviously, the speaker wants no part of such sado-masochistic romantic nonsense; he prefers sexual pleasure to poetic posing. "Adore" technically means to worship as a deity; there is a certain irony in regarding the girl's body as an object of religious worship, but this speaker carries through his version of the girl's fantasy, modestly refusing to name those parts he wishes to devote thirty thousand years to, and regarding her "heart" (usually synonymous with soul in the Renaissance) as the ultimate conquest for the last age.

The term "vegetable" is even more complex, for it depends on a whole set of physiological/psychological doctrines in the Renaissance. According to those doctrines, the human soul was made up of three souls which corresponded to the different levels of living matter. The Vegetable Soul man possessed in common with plants and animals; the Sensible Soul he possessed in common with animals; the Rational Soul was possessed by man alone. The Vegetable Soul was the lowest and had only the powers of reproduction, nourishment, and growth. The sense, the passions, and the imagination were under the power of the

Sensible Soul. A "vegetable love" would be without feeling or passion, appropriate to the lowest forms of life. The speaker thus reduces the notion of timeless, romantic nonphysical love to what he considers its proper level—a subhuman, absurd one. He pictures love without physical involvement not as a higher spiritual attraction but rather as a lower, nonsentient one.

Several other parts of the poem similarly require historical knowledge. Lines 33–36 depend upon Renaissance love psychology which considered physiological reactions (the rosy skin, perspiration) to be stimulated by the release of "animal spirits" in the blood. This release happened when the emotions were heightened by sight of the beloved; phantasms from the eye descended to the soul and released the animal spirits. The soul was thus "present" in the physiological response (the animal spirits), and the speaker pictures it here as involved in the very moment of desire, trying to unite—through the body—with the soul of the beloved. This love psychology may seem somewhat naive, but it is a humbling experience to try to explain our modern notions of how eyes and emotions relate to bodily processes.

The final two lines of the poem depend heavily upon specific knowledge. First there is an allusion to Greek mythology—an allusion which actually began several lines before the end with the reference to Time's slow-chapped (i.e., slow-jawed) power. According to the myth, Chronos (Time) ate all his children except Zeus (who had been hidden by Rhea), and Zeus afterward seized Chronos' power as chief of the gods. Zeus later made the sun stand still to lengthen his love night with Alcmene. We cannot, the speaker says, make time stand still as Zeus did, but we can speed it up. His argument assumes the 17th-century belief that each sex act made a person's life one day shorter. The speaker keeps insisting that the coming of death—time's end—is easier to cope with if you have something interesting to do while you wait.

Up to now we have not even mentioned the man who wrote the poem, Andrew Marvell. Whether Marvell ever had such a coy friend as this poem implies is not very important to us (though it may have been very important to him). For us, the relevant point is the fiction of the poem—regardless of whether that fiction is based on actual fact. But some facts about authorship may be very useful to us as readers of the poem, as long as we *use* them to help us with the poem and do not simply engage in biographical speculation. In many cases, knowledge about the author is likely to help us recognize the poet's distinctive strategies, and reading other poems by him often reveals his attitudes or devices so that we can read any one poem with more clarity, security, and depth; the index can guide you to other poems by Marvell.

A reader may experience a poem in a satisfactory way without all of the special knowledge I have been describing, but additional knowledge and developed skill can heighten the experience of almost any poem. Poems do not "hide" their meaning, and good poets usually communicate rather quickly in some basic way. Rereadings, reconsiderations, and the application of additional knowledge allow us to hear resonances built into the poem, qualities that make it enjoyable to

experience again and again. We have really only begun to look closely
at this particular poem, and if you were to continue to reread it carefully, you would very likely discover richnesses which this brief discussion has not even suggested. The route to meaning is often clear on
first reading a poem, but the full possibilities of experience may require
more time, energy, and knowledge of the right questions to ask.

Now look at this 20th-century poem:

## (ponder,darling,these busted statues

(ponder,darling,these busted statues
of yon motheaten forum be aware
notice what hath remained
—the stone cringes
clinging to the stone, how obsolete                                    5

lips utter their extant smile. . . .
remark

a few deleted of texture
of meaning monuments and dolls

resist Them Greediest Paws of careful                                 10
time all of which is extremely
unimportant)whereas Life

matters if or

when the your-and-my-
idle vertical worthless                                               15
self unite in peculiarly
momentary

partnership (to instigate
constructive
                  Horizontal
business. . . . even so, let us make haste                           20
—consider well this ruined aqueduct

lady,
which used to lead something into somewhere)

Here are some questions about the poem:

1. In what ways is this poem easier to read after having analyzed
*To His Coy Mistress?* What specific evidence can you find that the
author of (*ponder,darling*) had *Coy Mistress* in mind?

2. Why are the first and last parts of the poem in parentheses? In
what way does the nonparenthesized section differ from the parenthe-
sized sections? What other devices of contrast do you find?

3. Why are such formal and archaic words as "ponder" and "yon"
juxtaposed with slang such as "busted" and "motheaten"?

4. How do the ravages of time in this poem differ from those in *Coy Mistress?*

5. The argument used in *Coy Mistress* is called the *carpe diem* argument; *carpe diem* is Latin for "seize the day," that is, live for the immediate moment. How does this poem vary from the basic *carpe diem* pattern? Could you tell, from the language of the poem itself, that it was not written in the 17th century, when the *carpe diem* motif flourished?

6. What is the setting of the poem? How is the setting important? How does the aqueduct unite the setting with the theme of the poem? Try to explain the speaker's habit of associating what he looks at with the argument he is trying to construct.

7. Why are the stanzas divided as they are?

8. Other poems by e.e. cummings (he insisted on spelling his own name without capitals) are *chanson innocente* (p. 259), *the season tis my lovely lambs* (p. 233), *portrait* (p. 32), *l(a* (p. 382). Do you see any pattern in his uses of horizontal and vertical movement? Does the spacing affect the rhythm and pace as you read the poem?

The preceding discussion and questions may make it seem as if you need to know a lot to read a poem intelligently and experience it fully. You do. The more you know, the better a reader of poems you are likely to be; the more practice you have had in reading other poems, the more likely you are to be able to experience a poem new to you. But knowing facts is not by itself enough; willingness to discover something new is a crucial quality of mind for reading poems well, and being willing to let the poem itself dictate which questions to ask is important to locating the right facts and discovering the right way of putting them together. Most readers can find out what they need to know for most poems if they figure out what questions to ask.

Poetry reading has many hazards, and almost as many of them result from overeagerness as from apathy; many people who read poetry enthusiastically do not read it well, just as many poems that mean well do not mean much. The questions you ask of poetry should channel your enthusiasm and direct it toward meaningful experience, but they should not destroy it. Some people are rather protective about poetry, and think it shouldn't be analyzed lest it shrivel or collapse. But such an attitude toward the "poor little poem" is finally rather patronizing; good poems are hardy, and they won't disintegrate when confronted with difficult questions. The techniques of analysis mean to make you both tougher-minded (less subject to gimmicks and quackery) and more sensitive (to the nuances and depths of good poems), and they also aim to allow the poem to open itself to you.

No one can give you a method that will offer you total experience of all poems. But because many characteristics of an individual poem are characteristics that one poem shares with other poems, there are guidelines which can prompt you to ask the right questions. Here is a checklist of some things to remember:

1. *Identify the poem's situation.* What is said is often conditioned by where it is said and by whom. Identifying the speaker and his place in the situation puts what he says in perspective.

2. *Read the syntax literally.* What the words say literally in normal sentences is only a starting point, but it is the place to start. Not all poems use normal prose syntax, but most of them do, and you can save yourself embarrassment by paraphrasing accurately (that is, rephrasing what the poem literally says, in plain prose) and not simply free-associating from an isolated word or phrase.

3. *Articulate for yourself what the title, subject, and situation make you expect.* Poets often use false leads and try to surprise you by doing shocking things, but defining expectation lets you be conscious of where you are when you begin.

4. *Be willing to be surprised.* Things often happen in poems that turn them around. A poem may seem to suggest one thing at first, then persuade you to its opposite, or at least to a significant qualification or variation.

5. *Find out what is implied by the traditions behind the poem.* Verse forms, poetic kinds, and metrical patterns all have a frame of reference, traditions of the way they are usually used and for what. For example, the anapest is usually used for comic poems, and if a poet uses it "straight" he is aware of his "departure" and is probably making a point by doing it.

6. *Remember that poems exist in time, and times change.* Not only the meanings of words, but whole ways of looking at the universe and man's role vary in different ages. Consciousness of time works two ways: your knowledge of history provides a context for reading the poem, and the poem's *use* of a word or idea may modify your notion of a particular age.

7. *Bother the reference librarian.* Look up anything you don't understand: an unfamiliar word (or an ordinary word used in an unfamiliar way), a place, a person, a myth, an idea—anything the poem uses.

8. *Take a poem on its own terms.* Adjust to the poem; don't make the poem adjust to you. Be prepared to hear things you do not want to hear. Not all poems are about your ideas, nor will they always present emotions you want to feel. But be tolerant and listen to the poem's ideas, not only to your desire to revise them for yourself.

9. *Argue.* Discussion usually results in clarification and keeps you from being too dependent on personal biases and preoccupations which sometimes mislead even the best readers. Talking a poem over with someone else (especially someone very different) can expand the limits of a too narrow perspective.

10. *Assume there is a reason for everything.* Poets do make mistakes, but in poems that show some degree of verbal control it is usually safest to assume that the poet chose each word carefully; if the choice seems peculiar to us, it is usually *we* who are missing something. Craftsmanship obliges us to try to account for the specific choices and only settle for conclusions of ineptitude if no hypothetical explanation will make sense.

These guidelines are built into the arrangement of this book so that it will be easier for you to ask the right questions. Most beginning readers have better instincts than they think they have and already

know many things that can be useful in reading poetry; the arrangement is designed to begin where beginning readers are and make use
of what they already have. Poems are arranged in groups so that you
will find, side by side, poems that invite comparisons—because they
treat the same subject in different ways, because they use the same
device for different ends, because they share a form but have different
content, different moods, etc. (Of course, any one poem may profitably
be compared with other poems too, and many readers will want to
construct their own groupings.)

The groups are progressive and cumulative too; the early groups
invite questions that a beginning reader of poetry can readily handle,
and the later groups assume some accretion of knowledge and sophistication. This does not mean that all the poems in the early groups are
simple and all the later ones difficult; rather it means that the group—
as group—invites questions which increasingly imply some familiar-
ity with poetry. The early groupings are by subject matter; here you
will find within an individual subject group widely different poems
which invite you to find what artistic aims and choices brought the
differences about. The groupings in Section II invite you to confront
the many strategies and forms and inheritances that poets work from.
The groupings in the last section suggest the problems of passing time
and the questions these problems raise about the "present" of each
poem—questions which are sometimes nearly as hard to answer for last
week's poetry as for that of the Middle Ages. The groupings are identified in the Note on Arrangement, below. Many teachers and students
will, of course, want to use the groups in a different order or ignore
the grouping idea entirely; the editor does not claim to have discovered
the best possible order for all possible readers or that any order or
method will work for all students. And the book contains many more
poems than most teachers would wish to assign in an introductory
course; the groupings simply provide a suggestive framework for good
teaching and good reading, and they are meant to stimulate questions
and provoke discussion. At the end of the book are more conventional
indices (by author, title, and first line) for users of the text who may
wish to move from poem to poem in a different way.

The poems selected for this book are of many kinds, representing
most of the major directions of poetry through the ages and including
most of the classics usually taught in undergraduate courses. But I have
placed more than the usual emphasis on new poems, especially by
younger writers, for it seems to me that a knowledge of poetry demands
not only a knowledge of what has been written but of what is being
written now, and that the easiest access to older poems is, for students,
often through the new. I have also tried to provide an appropriate context for much of this newness by choosing old poems that place it in
focus; the "Protest and Satire" selection reminds us, for example, that
poems addressed to the moment have long been a part of the poetic
tradition—that, in fact, "occasional" poetry is in the mainstream of the
tradition. I have included some lyrics from popular songs (the Beatles,
Pete Seeger, Paul Simon, Bob Dylan, Leonard Cohen), many poems by

black poets (though not all on blackness itself), and poems based on non-Western traditions and forms. In short, experienced teachers of poetry will find most of their favorites here, but they will also find some surprises. Beginning readers will find enough variety to introduce them to most of the problems, and pleasures, they can find in poetry elsewhere.

The best way to learn about poetry is by reading poems. There is nothing magic about the arrangement of poems, or about any "method" in approaching them. At best, analysis is only a means to an end, not a value in itself. But careful attention to the issues suggested by arrangement and analysis is a way of getting access to poetry and what it offers. Having a finely developed skill may be a pleasure in itself, but the feel of it in action provides the real experience. And the best test of a method, or a course, or a textbook is what happens when its limits are transcended: if, when all is said and analyzed, you can experience more fully the next poem you read beyond the covers of this book, you will have begun to approach the worlds that offer themselves through poetry.

## Note on Arrangement

The poems in this anthology are arranged in groups designed to suggest comparisons and stimulate classroom discussion. The groupings are of several kinds, gradually moving toward more difficult and complex questions. Those in Section I are by subject matter:

Love—from *They Flee from Me* through *Politics*
War—*There Died a Myriad* through *Kilroy*
Death—*A Litany in Time of Plague* through *Arrangements with Earth for Three Dead Friends*
Poetry and the Arts—*In Memory of W. B. Yeats* through *The Living Values*
The Simple Life—*My Mind to Me a Kingdom Is* through *Not Leaving the House*
The Golden Age—*The Golden Age Was When the World Was Young* through *In California*
Sensuous and Sensual Experience—*After Great Pain* through *The Crossed Apple*

Subject labels do justice to very few of the poems, of course, and one of the major values in reading poems grouped by subject is in recognizing how varied poems on traditional subjects may be: the poems here very often surprise the expectations readers bring to such subjects. The next group (beginning with *Auto Wreck*) contains poems on subjects which in some ages have been considered "unpoetic," but the poems themselves suggest that poetry's range is not to be circumscribed by artificial limits of subject matter. The final group in Section I further tests such limits by presenting a series of attitudes sometimes thought to be "unpoetic"—even though poetry of satire and protest has flourished in almost all ages and cultures. Many of the groups contain subgroups (such as the poems describing Brueghel paintings) and "bridge" poems which connect different groups.

The groupings in Section II are more complex and raise a series of technical problems:

Speaker—*Channel Firing* through *A Widow in Wintertime*
Setting and Situation—*Sunday Morning* through *The Garden*
Connotation—*Still to Be Neat* through *Meditation on Statistical Method*
Metaphor and Symbolism—*That Time of Year* through *MacFlecknoe*
Structure—*Frankie and Johnny* through *Inviting a Friend to Supper*

The poems in each group illustrate a range of possibilities and suggest the many different uses of poetic devices. The "structure" group, for example, contains subgroups structured by narrative, dramatic, and descriptive strategies, and the final few poems in the group suggest other varieties of structure and structural problems.

The next few groups suggest the various effects of different systems of belief and frames of reference, illustrating how individual poems make different degrees of demand:

Judeo-Christian Tradition—*Hymn to God My God, in My Sickness* through *The Ache of Marriage*
Classical History and Myth—*To Helen* through *chanson innocente*
Non-Western Cultural Traditions—*I Am a Cowboy in the Boat of Ra* through *Night in the House by the River*
Private Myth (example: Yeats)—*Easter 1916* through *The Circus Animals' Desertion*

The next group (from *Thomas Rymer* through *Opening the Cage*) presents a variety of stanza and verse forms, and the following one (beginning with *Amor Che*) illustrates in detail one form, the sonnet. The poems from *The Lamb* to *At Barstow* illustrate some of the standard poetic kinds, and those from *You've Told Me, Maro* through *As the Spring Rains Fall* present one kind (the epigram) and, at the end of the group, add some other short poems to test the validity of definitions by kind.

Coleridge's *Metrical Feet* exemplifies (and names) the most common poetic rhythms, and the poems which follow (from *A Visit from St. Nicholas* through *Ah Sunflower*) demonstrate the varied tones possible within one meter, the anapest. The group beginning with Pope's famous "Sound and Sense" passage and ending with *To the memory of Mr. Oldham* demonstrates various imitative sound effects, and the poems from *Break, Break, Break* to *Jabberwocky* exemplify other possibilities of pause, rhythm, and sound. The final group in Section II (from *This Cross-Tree Here* through *l(a* suggests how visual effects are sometimes used.

Section III groups poems according to various problems of history and context. The first group (from *Though Amaryllis Dance in Green* through Hall's *Satire III*) presents poems written within a limited period of time, the late Elizabethan era. The second, from *To the Virgins, to Make Much of Time* to (*ponder,darling,these busted statues,* samples variations in *carpe diem* poetry from the Renaissance to modern times, and the next (beginning with *To Roses in the Bosom of Castara*) suggests some other traditional uses of the rose (the central symbol of *carpe diem* poetry), ending with several poems about the nature of traditional symbolism. The next three groups exemplify various cultural assumptions about the idea of order and suggest how those assumptions relate to recurrent metaphors (the world as stage, for example). The group from *1 September 1939* through *The Second-Best Bed* suggests a variety of problems in factual knowledge about context; the poems in this group have been left unannotated to emphasize informational demands that poems may make. The final two sections, illustrating problems and possibilities of interpreting an authorial context, present generous selections from two poets, John Keats and Adrienne Rich. Both groups are supplemented by prose passages in which the authors discuss their own work.

The groupings are, of course, merely for convenience of study; they are not relief maps of the poetic universe. Imaginative and sensible use of them may raise useful questions about poetry, as well as enrich one's experience of individual poems, but no arrangement (and no book) is an adequate substitute for a good teacher, and many teachers will think of other useful ways to approach the poems. Every classroom situation is unique in its demands and possibilities, and the aim of this book is to provide the teacher with a generous selection of poems from which to choose, a series of suggestive issues, and a convenient structure for moving toward increasingly complex critical problems. The arrangement assumes the need for close analysis and technical knowledge, but teachers will need to decide—on the basis of their own interests and the needs of individual classes—when and how to introduce specific problems and terms. Beyond the provocation of the groupings themselves, the book provides ten short essays ("The Elements of Poetry") which discuss technical problems and define terms. These essays may be used to introduce such topics as "Figurative Language" or "Prosody," or they may be consulted for definitions that, in context, provide a fuller sense of meaning than glossaries arranged in a series of isolated one-sentence units.

The texts of the poems have been carefully chosen and edited; poems which use older conventions of capitalization, spelling and punctuation have been modernized except where (as in Emily Dickinson or Spenser's *The Faerie Queene*) unique authorial habits would have been obscured or linguistic patterns distorted (as in the passage from Chaucer). Each poem is dated. Dates of publication appear below the poem on the right; the date is that of first volume publication (or, in the case of poems taken from plays, of performance), unless otherwise indicated. When periodical or anthology publication substantially preceded volume publication, that earlier date is given instead and preceded by a *p.* When the date of composition is known to differ substantially from the publication date, that date is given instead and appears on the *left.*

# Acknowledgments

If you are old enough to edit a textbook, you are indebted to literally hundreds of people, family, colleagues, teachers, and students. We are. If you cannot thank them wittily, it is more important anyway to thank them sincerely. We do.

In the preparation of this book we have acquired many new indebtednesses which should be acknowledged. Our colleagues at Emory University, especially in the Department of English and the University Library, continue to be lodes of information, encouragement, and wisdom. Special thanks are due to Debbie Hunter for many hours of capable assistance. A place of honor was earned by Mrs. Carolyn Breecher, formerly of the Emory University English Department, for many services and for the engaging wit with which they were performed.

On several occasions during the preparation of this work a retreat from everyday was needed. The Ossabaw Island Project provided it, and we wish to thank the Ossabaw Island Foundation and particularly Mr. and Mrs. Clifford B. West and Mr. and Mrs. Charles B. Wood for the provision and for the grace with which it was offered.

At W. W. Norton & Company, Ann Holler, Carol Paradis, Mill Jonakait, Calvin Towle, and John Benedict have provided assistance and encouragement in many ways and on many occasions.

Arrangements have been made for suitable expressions of gratitude for the assistance and encouragement of our wives at a more appropriate time and place.

# The Norton
# Introduction to Literature

# I

SIR THOMAS WYATT

## They Flee from Me

They flee from me, that sometime did me seek,
With naked foot stalking in my chamber.
I have seen them, gentle, tame, and meek,
That now are wild, and do not remember
That sometime they put themselves in danger      5
To take bread at my hand; and now they range,
Busily seeking with a continual change.

Thankéd be Fortune it hath been otherwise,
Twenty times better; but once in special,
In thin array, after a pleasant guise,      10
When her loose gown from her shoulders did fall,
And she me caught in her arms long and small.[1]
And therewith all sweetly did me kiss
And softly said, "Dear heart, how like you this?"

It was no dream, I lay broad waking.      15
But all is turned, thorough[2] my gentleness,
Into a strange fashion of forsaking;
And I have leave to go, of her goodness,
And she also to use newfangleness.[3]
But since that I so kindely[4] am servéd,      20
I fain[5] would know what she hath deservéd.

1557

EZRA POUND

## A Virginal

No, no! Go from me. I have left her lately.
I will not spoil my sheath with lesser brightness,
For my surrounding air hath a new lightness;
Slight are her arms, yet they have bound me straitly
And left me cloaked as with a gauze of æther;      5
As with sweet leaves; as with a subtle clearness.
Oh, I have picked up magic in her nearness
To sheathe me half in half the things that sheathe her.
No, no! Go from me, I have still the flavor,
Soft as spring wind that's come from birchen bowers.      10
Green come the shoots, aye April in the branches,

1. Slender.
2. Through.
3. Fondness for novelty.
4. In a way natural to women.
5. Eagerly.

As winter's wound with her sleight hand she staunches,
Hath of the trees a likeness of the savor:
As white their bark, so white this lady's hours.

                                                    1912


WILLIAM SHAKESPEARE

## Th' Expense of Spirit

Th' expense[1] of spirit in a waste[2] of shame
Is lust in action; and, till action, lust
Is perjured, murderous, bloody, full of blame,
Savage, extreme, rude, cruel, not to trust;
Enjoyed no sooner but despiséd straight:                5
Past reason hunted; and no sooner had,
Past reason hated, as a swallowed bait,
On purpose laid to make the taker mad:
Mad in pursuit, and in possession so;
Had, having, and in quest to have, extreme;            10
A bliss in proof;[3] and proved, a very woe;
Before, a joy proposed; behind, a dream.
All this the world well knows; yet none knows well
To shun the heaven that leads men to this hell.

                                                    1609


R. LYNCHE

## What Sugared Terms

What sugared terms, what all-persuading art,
What sweet mellifluous words, what wounding looks
Love used for his admittance to my heart!
Such eloquence was never read in books.
He promised pleasure, rest, and endless joy,           5
Fruition of the fairest she alive.
His pleasure, pain; rest, trouble; joy, annoy,
Have I since found, which me of bliss deprive.
The Trojan horse thus have I now let in,
Wherein enclosed these arméd men were placed—          10
Bright eyes, fair cheeks, sweet lips, and milk-white skin;
These foes my life have overthrown and razed.
Fair outward shows prove inwardly the worst:
Love looketh fair, but lovers are accurst.

                                                    1596


SIR PHILIP SIDNEY

## Leave Me, O Love

Leave me, O Love, which reachest but to dust,
And thou, my mind, aspire to higher things;

---

1. Expending.                          3. In the act.
2. Using up; also, desert.

Grow rich in that which never taketh rust:[1]
Whatever fades but fading pleasure brings.
   Draw in thy beams, and humble all thy might                     5
To that sweet yoke where lasting freedoms be;
Which breaks the clouds and opens forth the light
That doth both shine and give us sight to see.
   O take fast hold; let that light be thy guide
In this small course which birth draws out to death,                     10
And think how evil becometh him[2] to slide,
Who seeketh heav'n, and comes of heav'nly breath.
   Then farewell, world, thy uttermost I see;
Eternal Love, maintain thy life in me.

1581

JONATHAN SWIFT

## Lesbia for Ever on Me Rails[3]

Lesbia for ever on me rails;
   To talk on me she never fails:
Yet, hang me, but for all her art;
   I find that I have gained her heart:
My proof is this: I plainly see                     5
   The case is just the same with me:
I curse her ev'ry hour sincerely;
   Yet, hang me, but I love her dearly.

1736

GEORGE MEREDITH

## By This He Knew She Wept[1]

By this he knew she wept with waking eyes:
That, at his hand's light quiver by her head,
The strange low sobs that shook their common bed
Were called into her with a sharp surprise,
And strangled mute, like little gaping snakes,                     5
Dreadfully venomous to him. She lay
Stone-still, and the long darkness flowed away
With muffled pulses. Then, as midnight makes
Her giant heart of Memory and Tears
Drink the pale drug of silence, and so beat                     10
Sleep's heavy measure, they from head to feet
Were moveless, looking through their dead black years,
By vain regret scrawled over the blank wall.
Like sculptured effigies they might be seen

---

1. According to *Matthew* 6:19–20, the difference between heavenly and earthly treasures is that in heaven "neither moth nor rust doth corrupt, and . . . thieves do not break through nor steal."
2. How badly it suits him. (In the 16th century evil was usually pronounced as one syllable, e'il.)

3. A version of Catullus, 92: "Lesbia mi dicit male." Lesbia was Catullus's name for a woman his poems frequently celebrated, a woman irresistible but difficult.
1. The first poem in the sequence, *Modern Love*. Each "sonnet" in the group has 16 lines.

Upon their marriage-tomb, the sword between;[2]                    15
Each wishing for the sword that severs all.

1862

DONALD J. LLOYD

# Bridal Couch

Follows this a narrower bed,
Wood at feet, wood at head;
Follows this a sounder sleep,
Somewhat longer and too deep.

All too meanly and too soon                                        5
Waxes once and wanes our moon;
All too swiftly for each one
Falls to dark our winter sun.

Let us here then wrestle death,
Intermingled limb and breath,                                      10
Conscious both that we beget
End of rest, endless fret,

And come at last to permanence,
Tired dancers from a dance,
Yawning, and content to fall                                       15
Into any bed at all.

1956

JAMES DICKEY

# Cherrylog Road

Off Highway 106[1]
At Cherrylog Road I entered
The '34 Ford without wheels,
Smothered in kudzu,[2]
With a seat pulled out to run                                      5
Corn whiskey down from the hills,

And then from the other side
Crept into an Essex
With a rumble seat of red leather
And then out again, aboard                                         10
A blue Chevrolet, releasing
The rust from its other color,

Reared up on three building blocks.
None had the same body heat;
I changed with them inward, toward                                 15
The weedy heart of the junkyard,

2. According to medieval custom, a sword placed between lovers was supposed to guarantee chastity.
1. The poem is set in the mountains of North Georgia.
2. A rapidly growing vine, introduced from Japan to combat erosion but now covering whole fields and groves of trees.

For I knew that Doris Holbrook
Would escape from her father at noon

And would come from the farm
To seek parts owned by the sun                                    20
Among the abandoned chassis,
Sitting in each in turn
As I did, leaning forward
As in a wild stock-car race

In the parking lot of the dead.                                   25
Time after time, I climbed in
And out the other side, like
An envoy or movie star
Met at the station by crickets.
A radiator cap raised its head,                                   30

Become a real toad or a kingsnake
As I neared the hub of the yard,
Passing through many states,
Many lives, to reach
Some grandmother's long Pierce-Arrow                              35
Sending platters of blindness forth

From its nickel hubcaps
And spilling its tender upholstery
On sleepy roaches,
The glass panel in between                                        40
Lady and colored driver
Not all the way broken out,

The back-seat phone
Still on its hook.
I got in as though to exclaim,                                    45
"Let us go to the orphan asylum,
John; I have some old toys
For children who say their prayers."

I popped with sweat as I thought
I heard Doris Holbrook scrape                                     50
Like a mouse in the southern-state sun
That was eating the paint in blisters
From a hundred car tops and hoods.
She was tapping like code,

Loosening the screws,                                             55
Carrying off headlights,
Sparkplugs, bumpers,
Cracked mirrors and gear-knobs,
Getting ready, already,
To go back with something to show                                 60

Other than her lips' new trembling
I would hold to me soon, soon,

Where I sat in the ripped back seat
Talking over the interphone,
Praying for Doris Holbrook                                    65
To come from her father's farm

And to get back there
With no trace of me on her face
To be seen by her red-haired father
Who would change, in the squalling barn,        70
Her back's pale skin with a strop,
Then lay for me

In a bootlegger's roasting car
With a string-triggered 12-gauge shotgun
To blast the breath from the air.                            75
Not cut by the jagged windshields,
Through the acres of wrecks she came
With a wrench in her hand,

Through dust where the blacksnake dies
Of boredom, and the beetle knows                          80
The compost has no more life.
Someone outside would have seen
The oldest car's door inexplicably
Close from within:

I held her and held her and held her,            85
Convoyed at terrific speed
By the stalled, dreaming traffic around us,
So the blacksnake, stiff
With inaction, curved back
Into life, and hunted the mouse                              90

With deadly overexcitement,
The beetles reclaimed their field
As we clung, glued together,
With the hooks of the seat springs
Working through to catch us red-handed          95
Amidst the gray breathless batting

That burst from the seat at our backs.
We left by separate doors
Into the changed, other bodies
Of cars, she down Cherrylog Road                        100
And I to my motorcycle
Parked like the soul of the junkyard

Restored, a bicycle fleshed
With power, and tore off
Up Highway 106, continually                               105
Drunk on the wind in my mouth,
Wringing the handlebar for speed,
Wild to be wreckage forever.

1964

JOHN ASHBERY

## Civilization and Its Discontents[1]

A people chained to aurora[2]
I alone disarming you

Millions of facts of distributed light

Helping myself with some big boxes
Up the steps, then turning to no neighborhood;                    5
The child's psalm, slightly sung
In the hall rushing into the small room.
Such fire! leading away from destruction.
Somewhere in outer ether I glimpsed you
Coming at me, the solo barrier did it this time.                  10
Guessing us staying, true to be at the blue mark
Of the threshold. Tired of planning it again and again.
The cool boy distant, and the soaked-up
Afterthought, like so much rain, or roof.

The miracle took you in beside him.                               15
Leaves rushed the window, there was clear water and the sound of a lock.
Now I never see you much anymore.
The summers are much colder than they used to be
In that other time, when you and I were young.
I miss the human truth of your smile,                             20
The halfhearted gaze of your palms,
And all things together, but there is no comic reign
Only the facts you put to me. You must not, then,
Be very surprised if I am alone: it is all for you,
The night, and the stars, and the way we used to be.             25

There is no longer any use in harping on
The incredible principle of daylong silence, the dark sunlight
As only the grass is beginning to know it,
The wreath of the north pole,
Festoons for the late return, the shy pensioners               30
Agasp on the lamplit air. What is agreeable
Is to hold your hand. The gravel
Underfoot. The time is for coming close. Useless
Verbs shooting the other words far away.

I had already swallowed the poison                               35
And could only gaze into the distance at my life
Like a saint's with each day distinct.
No heaviness in the upland pastures. Nothing
In the forest. Only life under the huge trees
Like a coat that has grown too big, moving far away,            40
Cutting swamps for men like lapdogs, holding its own,
Performing once again, for you and for me.

1965

1. The title of a book, by Freud, which     2. Dawn.
deals with the demands of instinct and the
restrictions of civilization.

ERNEST DOWSON

## Non Sum Qualis Eram Bonae sub Regno Cynarae[1]

Last night, ah, yesternight, betwixt her lips and mine
There fell thy shadow, Cynara! thy breath was shed
Upon my soul between the kisses and the wine;
And I was desolate and sick of an old passion,
    Yea, I was desolate and bowed my head:     5
I have been faithful to thee, Cynara! in my fashion.

All night upon mine heart I felt her warm heart beat,
Night-long within mine arms in love and sleep she lay;
Surely the kisses of her bought red mouth were sweet;
But I was desolate and sick of an old passion,     10
    When I awoke and found the dawn was gray:
I have been faithful to thee, Cynara! in my fashion.

I have forgot much, Cynara! gone with the wind,
Flung roses, roses riotously with the throng,
Dancing, to put thy pale, lost lilies out of mind;     15
But I was desolate and sick of an old passion,
    Yea, all the time, because the dance was long:
I have been faithful to thee, Cynara! in my fashion.

I cried for madder music and for stronger wine,
But when the feast is finished and the lamps expire,     20
Then falls thy shadow, Cynara! the night is thine;
And I am desolate and sick of an old passion,
    Yea hungry for the lips of my desire:
I have been faithful to thee, Cynara! in my fashion.

                          p. 1891

JOHN DRYDEN

## Why Should a Foolish Marriage Vow[2]

Why should a foolish marriage vow,
    Which long ago was made,
Oblige us to each other now
    When passion is decayed?
We loved, and we loved, as long as we could,     5
    Till our love was loved out in us both;
But our marriage is dead when the pleasure is fled:
    'Twas pleasure first made it an oath.

If I have pleasures for a friend,
    And farther love in store,     10
What wrong has he whose joys did end,
    And who could give no more?

---

   1. Horace, Odes, IV, i, lines 3–4: "I am not as I was under the reign of the kindly Cynara."        2. A song from Dryden's play, *Marriage a la Mode.*

'Tis a madness that he should be jealous of me,
Or that I should bar him of another:
For all we can gain is to give ourselves pain,    15
When neither can hinder the other.

1671

ANONYMOUS

## Western Wind

Western wind, when wilt thou blow,
The small rain down can rain?
Christ, if my love were in my arms
And I in my bed again!

ca. 1300

W. B. YEATS

## Politics

*"In our time the destiny of man presents its meaning in political terms."*
—THOMAS MANN

How can I, that girl standing there,
My attention fix
On Roman or on Russian
Or on Spanish politics?
Yet here's a traveled man that knows    5
What he talks about,
And there's a politician
That has read and thought,
And maybe what they say is true
Of war and war's alarms,    10
But O that I were young again
And held her in my arms!

1939

EZRA POUND

## There Died a Myriad[1]

There died a myriad,
And of the best, among them,
For an old bitch gone in the teeth,
For a botched civilization,

Charm, smiling at the good mouth,    5
Quick eyes gone under earth's lid,

For two gross of broken statues,
For a few thousand battered books.

1920

1. Section V of "E. P. Ode pour L'Élection de Son Sépulcre."

HENRY REED

# Lessons of the War

## *Judging Distances*

Not only far away, but the way that you say it
Is very important. Perhaps you may never get
The knack of judging a distance, but at least you know
How to report on a landscape: the central sector,
The right of arc and that, which we had last Tuesday,          5
    And at least you know

That maps are of time, not place, so far as the army
Happens to be concerned—the reason being,
Is one which need not delay us. Again, you know
There are three kinds of tree, three only, the fir and the poplar,          10
And those which have bushy tops to; and lastly
    That things only seem to be things.

A barn is not called a barn, to put it more plainly,
Or a field in the distance, where sheep may be safely grazing.
You must never be over-sure. You must say, when reporting:          15
At five o'clock in the central sector is a dozen
Of what appear to be animals; whatever you do,
    Don't call the bleeders *sheep.*

I am sure that's quite clear; and suppose, for the sake of example,
The one at the end, asleep, endeavors to tell us          20
What he sees over there to the west, and how far away,
After first having come to attention. There to the west,
On the fields of summer the sun and the shadows bestow
    Vestments of purple and gold.

The still white dwellings are like a mirage in the heat,          25
And under the swaying elms a man and a woman
Lie gently together. Which is, perhaps, only to say
That there is a row of houses to the left of arc,
And that under some poplars a pair of what appear to be humans
    Appear to be loving.          30

Well that, for an answer, is what we might rightly call
Moderately satisfactory only, the reason being,
Is that two things have been omitted, and those are important.
The human beings, now: in what direction are they,
And how far away, would you say? And do not forget          35
    There may be dead ground in between.

There may be dead ground in between; and I may not have got
The knack of judging a distance; I will only venture
A guess that perhaps between me and the apparent lovers,
(Who, incidentally, appear by now to have finished,)          40
At seven o'clock from the houses, is roughly a distance
    Of about one year and a half.

MARIANNE MOORE

# In Distrust of Merits

Strengthened to live, strengthened to die for
    medals and positioned victories?
They're fighting, fighting, fighting the blind
    man who thinks he sees—
who cannot see that the enslaver is                                    5
enslaved; the hater, harmed. O shining O
        firm star, O tumultous
            ocean lashed till small things go
        as they will, the mountainous
            wave makes us who look, know                             10

depth. Lost at sea before they fought! O
        star of David, star of Bethlehem,
O black imperial lion
        of the Lord[1]—emblem
of a risen world—be joined at last, be                               15
joined. There is hate's crown beneath which all is
        death; there's love's without which none
            is king; the blessed deed bless
        the halo. As contagion
            of sickness makes sickness,                              20

contagion of trust can make trust. They're
        fighting in deserts and caves, one by
one, in battalions and squadrons;
        they're fighting that I
may yet recover from the disease. My                                 25
Self; some have it lightly; some will die. "Man's
        wolf to man" and we devour
            ourselves. The enemy could not
        have made a greater breach in our
            defenses. One pilot-                                      30

ing a blind man can escape him, but
        Job disheartened by false comfort[2] knew
that nothing can be so defeating
        as a blind man who
can see. O alive who are dead, who are                               35
proud not to see, A small dust of the earth
        that walks so arrogantly
            trust begets power and faith is
        an affectionate thing. We
            vow, we make this promise                                40

to the fighting—it's a promise—"We'll
        never hate black, white, red, yellow, Jew,
Gentile, Untouchable." We are
        not competent to

1. The symbols of Judaism, Christianity, and Islam.
2. Divinely afflicted as a trial of faith,
Job was "comforted" by friends who assured him that he was being punished for sinning.

make our vows. With set jaw they are fighting,                    45
fighting, fighting—some we love whom we know,
    some we love but know not—that
        hearts may feel and not be numb.
It cures me; or am I what
    I can't believe in? Some                                    50

in snow, some on crags, some in quicksands,
    little by little, much by much, they
are fighting fighting fighting that where
    there was death there may
be life. "When a man is prey to anger,                          55
he is moved by outside things; when he holds
    his ground in patience patience
        patience, that is action or
        beauty," the soldier's defense
            and hardest armor for                               60

the fight. The world's an orphans' home. Shall
    we never have peace without sorrow?
without pleas of the dying for
    help that won't come? O
quiet form upon the dust, I cannot                              65
look and yet I must. If these great patient
        dyings—all these agonies
            and wound-bearings and bloodshed—
        can teach us how to live, these
            dyings were not wasted.                             70

Hate-hardened heart, O heart of iron,
    iron is iron till it is rust.
There never was a war that was
    not inward; I must
fight till I have conquered in myself what                      75
causes war, but I would not believe it.
        I inwardly did nothing.
            O Iscariot-like crime!
        Beauty is everlasting
            and dust is for a time.                             80

                                                              1944

RICHARD LOVELACE

## To Lucasta, Going to the Wars

Tell me not, sweet, I am unkind
    That from the nunnery
Of thy chaste breast and quiet mind,
    To war and arms I fly.

True, a new mistress now I chase,                                5
    The first foe in the field;
And with a stronger faith embrace
    A sword, a horse, a shield.

Yet this inconstancy is such
   As you too shall adore;                                    10
I could not love thee, dear, so much,
   Loved I not Honor more.

1649

JOHN SCOTT

## I Hate That Drum's Discordant Sound

I hate that drum's discordant sound,
Parading round, and round, and round:
To thoughtless youth it pleasure yields,
And lures from cities and from fields,
To sell their liberty for charms                                 5
Of tawdry lace, and glittering arms;
And when Ambition's voice commands,
To march, and fight, and fall, in foreign lands.

I hate that drum's discordant sound,
Parading round, and round, and round:                            10
To me it talks of ravaged plains,
And burning towns, and ruined swains,[1]
And mangled limbs, and dying groans,
The widows' tears, and orphans' moans;
And all that Misery's hand bestows,                              15
To fill the catalogue of human woes.

1782

DENISE LEVERTOV

## What Were They Like?

1) Did the people of Viet Nam
   use lanterns of stone?
2) Did they hold ceremonies
   to reverence the opening of buds?
3) Were they inclined to rippling laughter?                      5
4) Did they use bone and ivory,
   jade and silver, for ornament?
5) Had they an epic poem?
6) Did they distinguish between speech and singing?

1) Sir, their light hearts turned to stone.                      10
   It is not remembered whether in gardens
   stone lanterns illumined pleasant ways.
2) Perhaps they gathered once to delight in blossom,
   but after the children were killed
   there were no more buds.                                 15
3) Sir, laughter is bitter to the burned mouth.
4) A dream ago, perhaps. Ornament is for joy.
   All the bones were charred.

1. Youths.

5) It is not remembered. Remember,
   most were peasants; their life    20
   was in rice and bamboo.
   When peaceful clouds were reflected in the paddies
   and the water buffalo stepped surely along terraces,
   maybe fathers told their sons old tales.
   When bombs smashed the mirrors    25
   there was time only to scream.
6) There is an echo yet, it is said,
   of their speech which was like a song.
   It is reported their singing resembled
   the flight of moths in moonlight.    30
   Who can say? It is silent now.

                                          1966


WILFRED OWEN

# Dulce Et Decorum Est[1]

Bent double, like old beggars under sacks,
Knock-kneed, coughing like hags, we cursed through sludge,
Till on the haunting flares we turned our backs
And towards our distant rest began to trudge.
Men marched asleep. Many had lost their boots    5
But limped on, blood-shod. All went lame; all blind;
Drunk with fatigue; deaf even to the hoots
Of disappointed shells that dropped behind.

Gas! Gas! Quick, boys!—An ecstasy of fumbling,
Fitting the clumsy helmets just in time;    10
But someone still was yelling out and stumbling
And floundering like a man in fire or lime.—
Dim, through the misty panes and thick green light
As under a green sea, I saw him drowning.

In all my dreams, before my helpless sight,    15
He plunges at me, guttering, choking, drowning.

If in some smothering dreams you too could pace
Behind the wagon that we flung him in,
And watch the white eyes writhing in his face,
His hanging face, like a devil's sick of sin;    20
If you could hear, at every jolt, the blood
Come gargling from the froth-corrupted lungs,
Obscene as cancer, bitter as the cud
Of vile, incurable sores on innocent tongues,—
My friend, you would not tell with such high zest    25
To children ardent for some desperate glory,
The old Lie: Dulce et decorum est
Pro patria mori.

1917

1. Part of a phrase from Horace, quoted in full in the last lines: "It is sweet and proper to die for one's country."

EZRA POUND

# These Fought in Any Case[1]

These fought in any case,
and some believing,
      pro domo,[2] in any case . . .

Some quick to arm,
some for adventure,
some from fear of weakness,                                        5
some from fear of censure,
some for love of slaughter, in imagination,
learning later . . .
some in fear, learning love of slaughter;                          10

Died some, pro patria,
      non "dulce" non "et decor"[3] . . .
walked eye-deep in hell
believing in old men's lies, then unbelieving
came home, home to a lie,                                          15
home to many deceits,
home to old lies and new infamy;
usury age-old and age-thick
and liars in public places.

Daring as never before, wastage as never before.                  20
Young blood and high blood,
fair cheeks, and fine bodies;

fortitude as never before

frankness as never before,
disillusions as never told in the old days,                        25
hysterias, trench confessions,
laughter out of dead bellies.

                                 1920

A. E. HOUSMAN

# Epitaph on an Army of Mercenaries

These, in the day when heaven was falling,
   The hour when earth's foundations fled,
Followed their mercenary calling
   And took their wages and are dead.

Their shoulders held the sky suspended;                            5
   They stood, and earth's foundations stay;
What God abandoned, these defended,
   And saved the sum of things for pay.

                            p. 1917

---

1. Section IV from "E. P. Ode pour L'Élection de Son Sépulcre."
2. For the homeland.
3. According to the Roman poet Horace: *Dulce et decorum est pro patria mori* ("It is sweet and proper to die for one's country"). Pound says "not sweet" and "not proper."

A. E. HOUSMAN

# 1887[1]

From Clee[2] to heaven the beacon burns,[3]
    The shires[4] have seen it plain,
From north and south the sign returns
    And beacons burn again.

Look left, look right, the hills are bright,       5
    The dales are light between,
Because 'tis fifty years tonight
    That God has saved the Queen.

Now, when the flame they watch not towers
    About the soil they trod,       10
Lads, we'll remember friends of ours
    Who shared the work with God.

To skies that knit their heartstrings right,
    To fields that bred them brave,
The saviors come not home tonight:       15
    Themselves they could not save.[5]

It dawns in Asia, tombstones show
    And Shropshire[6] names are read;
And the Nile spills his overflow
    Beside the Severn's dead.[7]       20

We pledge in peace by farm and town
    The Queen they served in war,
And fire the beacons up and down
    The land they perished for.

"God save the Queen" we living sing,       25
    From height to height 'tis heard;
And with the rest your voices ring,
    Lads of the Fifty-third.[8]

Oh, God will save her, fear you not:
    Be you the men you've been,       30
Get you the sons your fathers got,
    And God will save the Queen.

1896

---

1. Queen Victoria's golden jubilee.
2. A small town in Shropshire.
3. Fires were lighted all over England in honor of the jubilee.
4. The provinces. ("The shires" was applied to other parts of England by the inhabitants of the London area.)
5. According to *Matthew* 25:42 and *Mark* 15:31, the scribes and elders or chief priests said of the crucified Jesus: "He saved others; himself he cannot save."
6. The volume containing this poem was entitled *A Shropshire Lad.*
7. The Severn is the chief river through Shropshire.
8. A Shropshire regiment.

FRANCIS SCOTT KEY

## The Star-Spangled Banner[1]

O say, can you see, by the dawn's early light,
    What so proudly we hailed at the twilight's last gleaming—
Whose broad stripes and bright stars, through the perilous fight
    O'er the ramparts[2] we watched were so gallantly streaming!
And the rockets' red glare, the bombs[3] bursting in air,        5
Gave proof through the night that our flag was still there;
O! say, does that star-spangled banner yet wave
O'er the land of the free, and the home of the brave?

On that shore dimly seen through the mists of the deep,
    Where the foe's haughty host in dread silence reposes,        10
What is that which the breeze, o'er the towering steep,
    As it fitfully blows, half conceals, half discloses?
Now it catches the gleam of the morning's first beam,
In full glory reflected now shines on the stream;
'Tis the star-spangled banner; O long may it wave        15
O'er the land of the free, and the home of the brave!

And where is that band who so vauntingly[4] swore
    That the havoc of war and the battle's confusion
A home and a country should leave us no more?
    Their blood has washed out their foul footsteps' pollution.        20
No refuge could save the hireling and slave
From the terror of flight, or the gloom of the grave;
And the star-spangled banner in triumph doth wave
O'er the land of the free and the home of the brave.

O! thus be it ever, when freemen[5] shall stand        25
    Between their loved homes and the war's desolation!
Blest with vict'ry and peace, may the heav'n-rescued land
    Praise the Power that hath made and preserved us a nation.
Then conquer we must, when our cause it is just,
And this be our motto—*"In God is our trust"*:[6]        30
And the star-spangled banner in triumph shall wave
O'er the land of the free, and the home of the brave.

        1814

RANDALL JARRELL

## Eighth Air Force[1]

If, in an odd angle of the hutment,[2]
A puppy laps the water from a can
Of flowers, and the drunk sergeant shaving

---

1. Written during the battle of Fort McHenry, September 14, 1814, to be sung to the tune "To Anacreon in Heaven."
2. Broad embankments, part of a fortification.
3. Mortar shells.
4. Boastfully.
5. Full citizens.
6. This motto was not used on U. S. coins until 1864.

1. Jarrell wrote that this poem is "about the air force which bombed the continent from England. The man who lies counting missions has one to go before being sent home. The phrases from the Gospels compare such criminals and scapegoats as these with that earlier criminal and scapegoat about whom the Gospels were written."
2. Military camp.

Whistles *O Paradiso!*[3]—shall I say that man
Is not as men have said: a wolf to man?                    5

The other murderers troop in yawning;
Three of them play Pitch,[4] one sleeps, and one
Lies counting missions, lies there sweating
Till even his heart beats: One; One; One.
*O murderers!* . . . Still, this is how it's done:          10

This is a war. . . . But since these play, before they die,
Like puppies with their puppy; since, a man,
I did as these have done, but did not die—
I will content the people as I can
And give up these to them: Behold the man![5]              15

I have suffered, in a dream, because of him,
Many things; for this last savior, man,
I have lied as I lie now. But what is lying?
Men wash their hands, in blood, as best they can:
I find no fault in this just man.[6]                        20

1948

JOHN PICKERING

## Farewell, Adieu, That Courtly Life[1]

Farewell, adieu, that courtly life,
To war we tend to go;
It is good sport to see the strife
Of soldiers in a row.
   How merrily they forward march            5
   These enemies to slay,
   With hey, trim, and trixie[2] too,
   Their banners they display.

Now shall we have the golden cheats,[3]
When others want[4] the same;                               10
And soldiers have full many feats
Their enemies to tame;
   With cocking[5] here, and booming there,
   They break their foe's array;
   And lusty lads amid the fields                    15
   Their ensigns do display.

The drum and flute play lustily,
The trumpet blows amain,[6]
And venturous knights courageously
Do march before their train                                 20

3. A once popular tenor aria from Meyerbeer's *L'Africaine.*
4. A card game, a variety of all-fours.
5. Pilate's words to the multitude. See *John* 19:5.
6. See *Matthew* 27, *Luke* 23, and *John* 18 and 19.
1. From *A New Interlude of Vice.* Directions say it should be sung to the tune of "Have over the water to Floride [sic]" or "Selenger's Round."
2. Nonsense words.
3. Booty.
4. Lack.
5. Fighting.
6. Loudly.

With spears in rest, so lively dressed
In armor bright and gay;
With hey, trim, and trixie too,
Their banners they display.

                                                    1567

ALFRED, LORD TENNYSON

## The Charge of the Light Brigade[1]

### I

Half a league, half a league,
Half a league onward,
All in the valley of Death
    Rode the six hundred.[2]
"Forward the Light Brigade!                         5
Charge for the guns!" he said.
Into the valley of Death
    Rode the six hundred.

### II

"Forward, the Light Brigade!"
Was there a man dismayed?                           10
Not though the soldier knew
    Someone had blundered.
Theirs not to make reply,
Theirs not to reason why,
Theirs but to do and die.                           15
Into the valley of Death
    Rode the six hundred.

### III

Cannon to right of them,
Cannon to left of them,
Cannon in front of them                             20
    Volleyed and thundered;
Stormed at with shot and shell,
Boldly they rode and well,
Into the jaws of Death,
Into the mouth of hell                              25
    Rode the six hundred.

### IV

Flashed all their sabres bare,
Flashed as they turned in air
Sabring the gunners there,
Charging an army, while                             30
    All the world wondered.

1. The Crimean charge took place on October 25, 1854; nearly half the officers and men were wounded or killed, and immediate reports suggested even heavier casualties. Legend says Tennyson took the rhythm of the poem from an item in the London *Times* which contained the phrase "Someone had blundered" (but the phrase doesn't actually occur in the item).
2. Pronounced "hunderd" in Tennyson's native Lincolnshire.

Plunged in the battery-smoke
Right through the line they broke;
Cossack and Russian
Reeled from the sabre-stroke                    35
    Shattered and sundered.
Then they rode back, but not,
    Not the six hundred.

V

Cannon to right of them,
Cannon to left of them,                         40
Cannon behind them
    Volleyed and thundered;
Stormed at with shot and shell,
While horse and hero fell.
They that had fought so well                     45
Came through the jaws of Death,
Back from the mouth of hell,
All that was left of them,
    Left of six hundred.

VI

When can their glory fade?                       50
O the wild charge they made!
    All the world wondered.
Honor the charge they made!
Honor the Light Brigade,
    Noble six hundred!                           55

p. 1854


WILLIAM COLLINS

## Ode Written in the Beginning of the Year 1746

How sleep the brave[1] who sink to rest
By all their country's wishes blest!
When Spring, with dewy fingers cold,
Returns to deck their hallowed mold,
She these shall dress a sweeter sod              5
Than Fancy's feet have ever trod.

By fairy hands their knell is rung,
By forms unseen their dirge is sung;
There Honor comes, a pilgrim gray,
To bless the turf that wraps their clay,         10
And Freedom shall awhile repair,
To dwell a weeping hermit there!

1746

1. Soldiers who died supporting the king in the Jacobite rebellion of 1745.

RAYMOND R. PATTERSON

## You Are the Brave

You are the brave who do not break
In the grip of the mob when the blow comes straight
To the shattered bone; when the sockets shriek;
When your arms lie twisted under your back.

Good men holding their courage slack                                    5
In their frightened pockets see how weak
The work that is done; and feel the weight
Of your blood on the ground for their spirits' sake;

And build their anger, stone on stone;
Each silently, but not alone.                                           10

1962

ARCHIBALD MACLEISH

## The Silent Slain

We too, we too, descending once again
The hills of our own land, we too have heard
Far off—Ah, que ce cor a longue haleine[1]—
The horn of Roland[2] in the passages of Spain,
The first, the second blast, the failing third,                        5
And with the third turned back and climbed once more
The steep road southward, and heard faint the sound
Of swords, of horses, the disastrous war,
And crossed the dark defile[3] at last, and found
At Roncevaux[4] upon the darkening plain
The dead against the dead and on the silent ground
The silent slain—

1926

EDGAR A. GUEST

## The Things that Make a Soldier Great

The things that make a soldier great and send him out to die,
To face the flaming cannon's mouth, nor ever question why,
Are lilacs by a little porch, the row of tulips red,
The peonies and pansies, too, the old petunia bed,
The grass plot where his children play, the roses on the wall:       5
'Tis these that make a soldier great. He's fighting for them all.

'Tis not the pomp and pride of kings that make a soldier brave;
'Tis not allegiance to the flag that over him may wave;

1. Charlemagne, on hearing the third and final blast of Roland's horn: "Ah, this horn has long breath."
2. The French epic hero.
3. A narrow gorge or other natural barrier that restricts lateral troop movement.
4. A village in northern Spain, site of Charlemagne's defeat and Roland's death in 778.

For soldiers never fight so well on land or on the foam
As when behind the cause they see the little place called home.    10
Endanger but that humble street whereon his children run—
You make a soldier of the man who never bore a gun.

What is it through the battle smoke the valiant soldier sees?
The little garden far away, the budding apple trees,
The little patch of ground back there, the children at their play,    15
Perhaps a tiny mound behind the simple church of gray.
The golden thread of courage isn't linked to castle dome
But to the spot, where'er it be—the humble spot called home.

And now the lilacs bud again and all is lovely there,
And homesick soldiers far away know spring is in the air;    20
The tulips come to bloom again, the grass once more is green,
And every man can see the spot where all his joys have been.
He sees his children smile at him, he hears the bugle call,
And only death can stop him now—he's fighting for them all.

1918

SIEGFRIED SASSOON

# Base Details

If I were fierce, and bald, and short of breath,
    I'd live with scarlet Majors at the Base,
And speed glum heroes up the line to death.
    You'd see me with my puffy petulant face,
Guzzling and gulping in the best hotel,    5
    Reading the Roll of Honor.[1] "Poor young chap,"
I'd say—"I used to know his father well;
    Yes, we've lost heavily in this last scrap."
And when the war is done and youth stone dead,
I'd toddle safely home and die—in bed.    10

1918

LARRY RUBIN

# The Draft Dodger

The poets who are veterans of the wars
Know what to love: they have seen their lines
Crumble, and watched their ink run red from wells
Below the veins. The works of death bloom
In bursts above the trench; unchained from grief    5
This soldier's pen is splintered from the sword
He wields, a blade of blindness to protect
The poems unborn. Apocalypse glistens like peace
In his vision; past the void, the lines
Re-form. The bombardier goes home, and beauty    10
Suppurates[2] from wounds.

---

1. List of dead.                    2. Festers.

My draft board
Was most kind, surmising, perhaps, an old
Embarrassment, the beauty of the guns,
The danger in the love of enemies.

1967

ROY FULLER

## The Fifties

The wretched summers start again
With lies and armies ready for
Advancing on that fast terrain.

Like those of China, Poland, Spain,
With twenty territories more,                    5
The wretched summers start again.

The rumors and betrayals stain
The helpless millions of the poor
Advancing on that fast terrain.

Asian and European rain                          10
Falls from between the blue of yore:
The wretched summers start again.

And rubble and the jungle gain
A foothold on the cultured shore,
Advancing on that fast terrain.                  15

Short youth was shortened by the pain
Of seasons suitable for war:
The wretched summers start again,
Advancing on that fast terrain.

1954

RICHARD EBERHART

## The Fury of Aerial Bombardment

You would think the fury of aerial bombardment
Would rouse God to relent; the infinite spaces
Are still silent. He looks on shock-pried faces.
History, even, does not know what is meant.

You would feel that after so many centuries       5
God would give man to repent; yet he can kill
As Cain could, but with multitudinous will,
No farther advanced than in his ancient furies.

Was man made stupid to see his own stupidity?
Is God by definition indifferent, beyond us all?  10
Is the eternal truth man's fighting soul
Wherein the Beast ravens in its own avidity?

Of Van Wettering I speak, and Averill,
Names on a list, whose faces I do not recall
But they are gone to early death, who late in school                15
Distinguished the belt feed lever from the belt holding pawl.[1]

1947

ANONYMOUS

## The Soldier's Song

I sing the praise of honored wars,
The glory of well-gotten scars,
The bravery of glittering shields,
Of lusty hearts and famous fields;
For that is music worth the ear of Jove,                5
A sight for kings, and still the soldier's love.

Look! Oh, methinks I see
The grace of chivalry;
The colors are displayed,
The captains bright arrayed.                10
See now the battle's ranged,
Bullets now thick are 'changed.

Hark! shots and wounds abound,
The drums alarum sound.
The captains cry: Za-za!                15
The trumpets sound ta-ra!
Oh, this is music worth the ear of Jove,
A sight for kings, and still the soldier's love.

1605

RANDALL JARRELL

## The Death of the Ball Turret Gunner[2]

From my mother's sleep I fell into the State,
And I hunched in its belly till my wet fur froze.
Six miles from earth, loosed from its dream of life,
I woke to black flak and the nightmare fighters.
When I died they washed me out of the turret with a hose.                5

1945

W. B. YEATS

## On Being Asked for a War Poem

I think it better that in times like these
A poet's mouth be silent, for in truth

1. Machine-gun parts.
2. "A ball turret was a plexiglass sphere set into the belly of a B-17 or B-24 and inhabited by two .50 caliber machine-guns and one man, a short, small man. When this gunner tracked with his machine-guns a fighter attacking his bomber from below, he revolved with the turret; hunched upside-down in his little sphere, he looked like the foetus in the womb. The fighters which attacked him were armed with cannon firing explosive shells. The hose was a steam hose." (Jarrell's note)

We have no gift to set a statesman right;
He has had enough of meddling who can please
A young girl in the indolence of her youth,                    5
Or an old man upon a winter's night.

p. 1915

LI PO

# Fighting South of the Ramparts[1]

Last year we were fighting at the source of the Sang-kan;[2]
This year we are fighting on the Onion River road.[3]
We have washed our swords in the surf of Parthian seas;
We have pastured our horses among the snows of the T'ien Shan,
The King's armies have grown grey and old                      5
Fighting ten thousand leagues away from home.
The Huns have no trade but battle and carnage;
They have no fields or ploughlands,
But only wastes where white bones lie among yellow sands.
Where the House of Ch'in built the great wall that was to keep away
    the Tartars.                                               10
There, in its turn, the House of Han lit beacons of war.
The beacons are always alight, fighting and marching never stop.
Men die in the field, slashing sword to sword;
The horses of the conquered neigh piteously to Heaven.
Crows and hawks peck for human guts,                           15
Carry them in their beaks and hang them on the branches of withered
    trees.
Captains and soldiers are smeared on the bushes and grass;
The General schemed in vain.
Know therefore that the sword is a cursed thing
Which the wise man uses only if he must.[4]                    20

ca. 750

ROBERT GRAVES

# The Persian Version

Truth-loving Persians do not dwell upon
The trivial skirmish fought near Marathon.[1]
As for the Greek theatrical tradition
Which represents that summer's expedition
Not as a mere reconnaissance in force                          5
By three brigades of foot and one of horse
(Their left flank covered by some obsolete
Light craft detached from the main Persian fleet)
But as a grandiose, ill-starred attempt
To conquer Greece—they treat it with contempt;                10

1. Translated by Arthur Waley. All the
notes to this poem are Waley's.
2. "Runs west to east through northern
Shansi and Hopei, north of the Great
Wall."
3. "The Kashgar-darya, in Turkestan."
4. "Quotation from the *Tao Te Ching*."

1. Badly outnumbered, and awaiting
support from the Spartans, the Athenians
killed 6,400 Persians while losing 192 of
their own number. The Persians were ultimately rescued by the fleet. The battle
occurred in 490 B.C.

And only incidentally refute
Major Greek claims, by stressing what repute
The Persian monarch and the Persian nation
Won by this salutary demonstration:
Despite a strong defense and adverse weather                    15
All arms combined magnificently together.

                                                        p. 1943

EUGENE MCCARTHY

## Kilroy[1]

Kilroy is gone,
the word is out,
absent without leave
from Vietnam.

Kilroy                                                          5
who wrote his name
in every can
from Poland to Japan
and places in between
like Sheboygan and Racine                                      10
is gone
absent without leave
from Vietnam.

Kilroy
who kept the dice                                              15
and stole the ice
out of the BOQ[2]
Kilroy
whose name was good
on every IOU                                                   20
in World War II
and even in Korea
is gone
absent without leave
from Vietnam.                                                  25

Kilroy
the unknown soldier
who was the first to land
the last to leave,
with his own hand                                              30
has taken his good name
from all the walls
and toilet stalls.
Kilroy
whose name around the world                                    35

---

1. A legendary "hero" of World War II. American soldiers then and since scribbled "Kilroy was here" everywhere—to suggest that no task was too great nor place too remote for American fighting spirit.
2. Bachelor Officers' Quarters.

was like the flag unfurled
has run it down
and left Saigon
and the Mekong
without a hero or a song                    40
and gone
absent without leave
from Vietnam.

1968

THOMAS NASHE

## A Litany in Time of Plague[1]

Adieu, farewell, earth's bliss;
This world uncertain is;
Fond[2] are life's lustful joys;
Death proves them all but toys;[3]
None from his darts can fly;                    5
I am sick, I must die.
    Lord, have mercy on us!

Rich men, trust not in wealth,
Gold cannot buy you health;
Physic[4] himself must fade.                    10
All things to end are made,
The plague full swift goes by;
I am sick, I must die.
    Lord, have mercy on us!

Beauty is but a flower                    15
Which wrinkles will devour;
Brightness falls from the air;
Queens have died young and fair;
Dust hath closed Helen's[5] eye.
I am sick, I must die.                    20
    Lord, have mercy on us!

Strength stoops unto the grave,
Worms feed on Hector[6] brave;
Swords may not fight with fate,
Earth still holds ope her gate.                    25
"Come, come!" the bells[7] do cry.
I am sick, I must die.
    Lord, have mercy on us.

Wit with his wantonness
Tasteth death's bitterness;                    30
Hell's executioner

1. England was ravaged by bubonic plague in 1592.
2. Foolish.
3. Trifles.
4. Restorative powers, personified.
5. Helen of Troy, a traditional type of beauty.
6. The bravest Trojan, a traditional type of strength.
7. Church bells which toll for deaths.

Hath no ears for to hear
What vain art can reply.
I am sick, I must die.
    Lord, have mercy on us.                                            35

Haste, therefore, each degree,
To welcome destiny;
Heaven is our heritage,
Earth but a player's stage;
Mount we unto the sky.                                                 40
I am sick, I must die.
    Lord, have mercy on us.

1592

JAMES SHIRLEY

## The Glories of Our Blood and State

The glories of our blood[1] and state[2]
    Are shadows, not substantial things;
There is no armor against fate,
    Death lays his icy hand on kings:
        Scepter and crown                                              5
        Must tumble down,
And in the dust be equal made
With the poor crooked scythe and spade.

Some men with swords may reap the field,
    And plant fresh laurels where they kill;                           10
But their strong nerves at last must yield,
    They tame but one another still:
        Early or late,
        They stoop to fate,
And must give up their murmuring breath,                               15
When they, pale captives, creep to death.

The garlands wither on your brow,
    Then boast no more your mighty deeds;
Upon Death's purple altar now,
    See where the victor-victim bleeds:                                20
        Your heads must come
        To the cold tomb;
Only the actions of the just
Smell sweet, and blossom in their dust.

1659

JOHN DONNE

## Death Be Not Proud

Death be not proud, though some have calléd thee
Mighty and dreadful, for thou art not so;

1. Ancestry.                        2. Social position.

For those whom thou think'st thou dost overthrow
Die not, poor Death, nor yet canst thou kill me.
From rest and sleep, which but thy pictures[1] be,      5
Much pleasure; then from thee much more must flow,
And soonest[2] our best men with thee do go,
· Rest of their bones, and soul's delivery.[3]
Thou art slave to Fate, Chance, kings, and desperate men,
And dost with Poison, War, and Sickness dwell;          10
And poppy or charms can make us sleep as well,
And better than thy stroke; why swell'st[4] thou then?
One short sleep past, we wake eternally
And death shall be no more; Death, thou shalt die.

1633

WILLIAM CARLOS WILLIAMS

# Tract

I will teach you my townspeople
how to perform a funeral
for you have it over a troop
of artists—
unless one should scour the world—          5
you have the ground sense necessary.

See! the hearse leads.
I begin with a design for a hearse.
For Christ's sake not black—
nor white either—and not polished!          10
Let it be weathered—like a farm wagon—
with gilt wheels (this could be
applied fresh at small expense)
or no wheels at all:
a rough dray to drag over the ground.          15

Knock the glass out!
My God—glass, my townspeople!
For what purpose? Is it for the dead
to look out or for us to see
how well he is housed or to see          20
the flowers or the lack of them—
or what?
To keep the rain and snow from him?
He will have a heavier rain soon:
pebbles and dirt and what not.          25
Let there be no glass—
and no upholstery, phew!
and no little brass rollers
and small easy wheels on the bottom—
my townspeople what are you thinking of?          30

1. Likenesses.          3. Deliverance.
2. Most willingly.      4. Puff with pride.

A rough plain hearse then
with gilt wheels and no top at all.
On this the coffin lies
by its own weight.
               No wreaths please—      35
especially no hot house flowers.
Some common memento is better,
something he prized and is known by:
his old clothes—a few books perhaps—
God knows what! You realize      40
how we are about these things
my townspeople—
something will be found—anything
even flowers if he had come to that.
So much for the hearse.      45

For heaven's sake though see to the driver!
Take off the silk hat! In fact
that's no place at all for him—
up there unceremoniously
dragging our friend out to his own dignity!      50
Bring him down—bring him down!
Low and inconspicuous! I'd not have him ride
on the wagon at all—damn him—
the undertaker's understrapper!
Let him hold the reins      55
and walk at the side
and inconspicuously too!

Then briefly as to yourselves:
Walk behind—as they do in France,
seventh class, or if you ride      60
Hell take curtains! Go with some show
of inconvenience; sit openly—
to the weather as to grief.
Or do you think you can shut grief in?
What—from us? We who have perhaps      65
nothing to lose? Share with us
share with us—it will be money
in your pockets.
           Go now
I think you are ready.      70

                  1917

ROBERT FROST

# Provide, Provide

The witch that came (the withered hag)
To wash the steps with pail and rag,
Was once the beauty Abishag,[1]

---

1. In *1 Kings* 1, a beautiful young woman named Abishag is brought to the aged King David.

The picture pride of Hollywood.
Too many fall from great and good                    5
For you to doubt the likelihood.

Die early and avoid the fate.
Or if predestined to die late,
Make up your mind to die in state.[2]

Make the whole stock exchange your own!          10
If need be occupy a throne,
Where nobody can call *you* crone.

Some have relied on what they knew,
Others on being simply true.
What worked for them might work for you.          15

No memory of having starred
Atones for later disregard
Or keeps the end from being hard.

Better to go down dignified
With boughten friendship at your side           20
Than none at all. Provide, provide!

                                                              1936

A. E. HOUSMAN

## To an Athlete Dying Young

The time you won your town the race
We chaired[1] you through the marketplace;
Man and boy stood cheering by,
And home we brought you shoulder-high.

Today, the road all runners come,                     5
Shoulder-high we bring you home,
And set you at your threshold down,
Townsman of a stiller town.

Smart lad, to slip betimes away
From fields where glory does not stay,               10
And early though the laurel[2] grows
It withers quicker than the rose.

Eyes the shady night has shut
Cannot see the record cut,
And silence sounds no worse than cheers            15
After earth has stopped the ears:

Now you will not swell the rout
Of lads that wore their honors out,

2. Ceremoniously, with official honor.      2. Wreath of honor.
1. Carried aloft in triumph.

Runners whom renown outran
And the name died before the man.                    20

So set, before its echoes fade,
The fleet foot on the sill of shade,
And hold to the low lintel[3] up
The still-defended challenge-cup.

And round that early-laureled head                   25
Will flock to gaze the strengthless dead,
And find unwithered on its curls
The garland[4] briefer than a girl's.

1896

## e. e. cummings

### portrait

Buffalo Bill's
defunct
        who used to
        ride a watersmooth-silver
                                stallion              5
and break onetwothreefourfive pigeonsjustlikethat
                                        Jesus
he was a handsome man
                and what i want to know is
how do you like your blueeyed boy                     10
Mister Death

1923

JAMES WORLEY

### De Gustibus[1]

Think how many men have bluntly died
With the good, familiar taste of bread
Recent on their lips. Stricken at table,
Executed unexpectedly
Following a seeming sustenant meal,                   5
Downed by a sudden gulp or hungry battle—
That chronic disrespecter of digestion—
How quickly the dis-gusting smack of death
Slipped to salute their savoring mouths
And whittle away the staff of life                    10
With an unobtrusive blade of cold.
Then think of the bitter bread you've known.
Be glad. Better bitter, and aware,
Than savory, and lulled by fickle breath.

1965

---

3. Upper part of a door frame.
4. Wreath of flowers.
1. "De gustibus non est disputandum," Latin proverb: "There is no disputing about taste." The "occasion" of the poem was the assassination of Malcolm X.

ETHERIDGE KNIGHT

# For Malcolm, a Year After

Compose for Red[1] a proper verse;
Adhere to foot and strict iamb,[2]
Control the burst of angry words
Or they might boil and break the dam.
Or they might boil and overflow                          5
And drench me, drown me, drive me mad.
So swear no oath, so shed no tear,
And sing no song blue Baptist sad.
Evoke no image, stir no flame,
And spin no yarn across the air.                         10
Make empty anglo tea lace words—
Make them dead white and dry bone bare.

Compose a verse for Malcolm man,[3]
And make it rime and make it prim.
The verse will die—as all men do—                       15
But not the memory of him!
Death might come singing sweet like C,
Or knocking like the old folk say,
The moon and stars may pass away,
But not the anger of that day.                           20

1966

BEN JONSON

# On My First Son

Farewell, thou child of my right hand,[1] and joy;
My sin was too much hope of thee, loved boy:
Seven years thou'wert lent to me, and I thee pay,
Exacted by thy fate, on the just[2] day.
O could I lose all father now! for why                   5
Will man lament the state he should envý,
To have so soon 'scaped world's and flesh's rage,
And, if no other misery, yet age?
Rest in soft peace, and asked, say, "Here doth lie
Ben Jonson his[3] best piece of poetry."                 10
For whose sake henceforth all his vows be such
As what he loves may never like too much.

1616

---

1. "Detroit Red" was one of the names of Malcolm X.
2. Metrical terms; see the glossary.
3. "No, I didn't mean for 'man' to be a vocative. Rather I meant for 'man' to be a term of endearment, an affectionate attachment to Malcolm. You know like 'ito & ita' is in Spanish? To me, 'man' & 'boy' serve the same purpose—like: Charlie boy, Sonny man, etc. Also, without the comma, the reader is less likely to make the mistake of thinking that I'm addressing him—which I am not. Further, 'man' simply for what it means literally and visually shows the inseparateness of the two, Malcolm & man." (Knight's note)

1. A literal translation of the son's name, Benjamin.
2. Exact; the son died on his seventh birthday, in 1603.
3. Ben Jonson's (a common Renaissance form of the possessive).

DYLAN THOMAS

# A Refusal to Mourn the Death, by Fire, of a Child in London

Never until the mankind making
Bird beast and flower
Fathering and all humbling darkness
Tells with silence the last light breaking
And the still hour                                         5
Is come of the sea tumbling in harness

And I must enter again the round
Zion of the water bead
And the synagogue of the ear of corn
Shall I let pray the shadow of a sound                     10
Or sow my salt seed
In the least valley of sackcloth to mourn

The majesty and burning of the child's death.
I shall not murder
The mankind of her going with a grave truth               15
Nor blaspheme down the stations of the breath
With any further
Elegy of innocence and youth.
Deep with the first dead lies London's daughter,
Robed in the long friends,                                 20
The grains beyond age, the dark veins of her mother,
Secret by the unmourning water
Of the riding Thames.
After the first death, there is no other.

1945

JOHN CROWE RANSOM

# Bells for John Whiteside's Daughter

There was such speed in her little body,
And such lightness in her footfall,
It is no wonder her brown study[1]
Astonishes us all.

Her wars were bruited in our high window.             5
We looked among orchard trees and beyond
Where she took arms against her shadow,
Or harried unto the pond

The lazy geese, like a snow cloud
Dripping their snow on the green grass,               10
Tricking and stopping, sleepy and proud,
Who cried in goose, Alas,

1. Stillness, as if in meditation or deep thought.

For the tireless heart within the little
Lady with rod that made them rise
From their noon apple-dreams and scuttle          15
Goose-fashion under the skies!

But now go the bells, and we are ready,
In one house we are sternly stopped
To say we are vexed at her brown study,
Lying so primly propped.                          20

1924

MARK TWAIN

## Ode to Stephen Dowling Bots, Dec'd[1]

And did young Stephen sicken,
    And did young Stephen die?
And did the sad hearts thicken,
    And did the mourners cry?

No; such was not the fate of                      5
    Young Stephen Dowling Bots;
Though sad hearts round him thickened,
    'Twas not from sickness' shots.

No whooping-cough did rack his frame,
    Nor measles drear with spots;                 10
Not these impaired the sacred name
    Of Stephen Dowling Bots.

Despised love struck not with woe
    That head of curly knots,
Nor stomach troubles laid him low,                15
    Young Stephen Dowling Bots.

O no. Then list with tearful eye,
    Whilst I his fate do tell.
His soul did from this cold world fly,
    By falling down a well.                        20

They got him out and emptied him;
    Alas it was too late;
His spirit was gone for to sport aloft
    In the realms of the good and great.

1884

1. The ode is supposedly written by Emmeline Grangerford, the 13-year-old daughter of one of the feuding families in *Huckleberry Finn.* Huck says, "She could write about anything you choose [sic] to give her to write about just so it was sadful. Every time a man died, or a woman died, or a child died, she would be on hand with her 'tribute' before he was cold."

WILLIAM WORDSWORTH

# A Slumber Did My Spirit Seal

A slumber did my spirit seal;
  I had no human fears:
She seemed a thing that could not feel
  The touch of earthly years.

No motion has she now, no force:           5
  She neither hears nor sees;
Rolled round in earth's diurnal[1] course,
  With rocks, and stones, and trees.

                        1800

WALTER SAVAGE LANDOR

# Rose Aylmer[2]

Ah what avails the sceptered race,
  Ah what the form divine!
What every virtue, every grace!
  Rose Aylmer, all were thine.
Rose Aylmer, whom these wakeful eyes      5
  May weep, but never see,
A night of memories and of sighs
  I consecrate to thee.

                        1806

SYLVIA PLATH

# Lady Lazarus[3]

I have done it again.
One year in every ten
I manage it——

A sort of walking miracle, my skin
Bright as a Nazi lampshade,          5
My right foot

A paperweight,
My face a featureless, fine
Jew linen.

Peel off the napkin          10
O my enemy.
Do I terrify?——

1. Daily.
2. Daughter of the fourth Baron Aylmer, she became a friend of Landor's when she was 17. She died suddenly at 20.

3. According to *John* 11, Jesus raised Lazarus, the brother of Mary and Martha, from the dead.

The nose, the eye pits, the full set of teeth?
The sour breath
Will vanish in a day.                                          15

Soon, soon the flesh
The grave cave ate will be
At home on me

And I a smiling woman.
I am only thirty.                                              20
And like the cat I have nine times to die.

This is Number Three.
What a trash
To annihilate each decade.

What a million filaments.                                      25
The peanut-crunching crowd
Shoves in to see

Them unwrap me hand and foot——
The big strip tease.
Gentlemen, ladies                                             30

These are my hands
My knees.
I may be skin and bone,

Nevertheless, I am the same, identical woman.
The first time it happened I was ten.                          35
It was an accident.

The second time I meant
To last it out and not come back at all.
I rocked shut

As a seashell.                                                 40
They had to call and call
And pick the worms off me like sticky pearls.

Dying
Is an art, like everything else.
I do it exceptionally well.                                    45

I do it so it feels like hell.
I do it so it feels real.
I guess you could say I've a call.

It's easy enough to do it in a cell.
It's easy enough to do it and stay put.                        50
It's the theatrical

Comeback in broad day
To the same place, the same face, the same brute
Amused shout:

"A miracle!"                                                   55
That knocks me out.
There is a charge

For the eyeing of my scars, there is a charge
For the hearing of my heart——
It really goes.                                               60

And there is a charge, a very large charge
For a word or a touch
Or a bit of blood

Or a piece of my hair or my clothes.
So, so, Herr Doktor.                                          65
So, Herr Enemy.

I am your opus,
I am your valuable,
The pure gold baby

That melts to a shriek.                                       70
I turn and burn.
Do not think I underestimate your great concern.

Ash, ash—
You poke and stir.
Flesh, bone, there is nothing there——                        75

A cake of soap,
A wedding ring,
A gold filling.

Herr God, Herr Lucifer
Beware                                                        80
Beware.

Out of the ash
I rise with my red hair
And I eat men like air.

                                                          1965

THOMAS CAREW

# Epitaph on the Lady Mary Villiers[1]

This little vault, this narrow room,
Of Love, and Beauty is the tomb;

1. The 2½-year-old daughter of Carew's patron.

The dawning beam that 'gan to clear
Our clouded sky, lies darkened here,
For ever set to us, by death                                          5
Sent to enflame the world beneath;
'Twas but a bud, yet did contain
More sweetness than shall spring again,
A budding star that might have grown
Into a Sun, when it had blown.                                        10
This hopeful beauty, did create
New life in Love's declining state;
But now his Empire ends, and we
From fire, and wounding darts are free:
His brand, his bow, let no man fear,                                  15
The flames, the arrows, all lie here.

                                                                    1640


EMILY DICKINSON

## Because I Could Not Stop for Death

Because I could not stop for Death—
He kindly stopped for me—
The Carriage held by just Ourselves—
And Immortality.

We slowly drove—He knew no haste                                     5
And I had put away
My labor and my leisure too,
For His Civility—

We passed the School, where Children strove
At Recess—in the Ring—                                               10
We passed the Fields of Gazing Grain—
We passed the Setting Sun—

Or rather—He passed Us—
The Dews drew quivering and chill—
For only Gossamer,[1] my Gown—                                        15
My Tippet[2]—only Tulle[3]—

We paused before a House that seemed
A Swelling of the Ground—
The Roof was scarcely visible—
The Cornice—in the Ground—                                           20

Since then—'tis Centuries—and yet
Feels shorter than the Day
I first surmised the Horses' Heads
Were toward Eternity—

ca. 1863

---

1. A soft sheer fabric.                    3. A fine net fabric.
2. Scarf.

JAMES WRIGHT

## Arrangements with Earth for Three Dead Friends

Sweet earth, he ran and changed his shoes to go
Outside with other children through the fields.
He panted up the hills and swung from trees
Wild as a beast but for the human laughter
That tumbled like a cider down his cheeks.                    5
Sweet earth, the summer has been gone for weeks,
And weary fish already sleeping under water
Below the banks where early acorns freeze.
Receive his flesh and keep it cured of colds.
Button his coat and scarf his throat from snow.               10

And now, bright earth, this other is out of place
In what, awake, we speak about as tombs.
He sang in houses when the birds were still
And friends of his were huddled round till dawn
After the many nights to hear him sing.                       15
Bright earth, his friends remember how he sang
Voices of night away when wind was one.
Lonely the neighborhood beneath your hill
Where he is waved away through silent rooms.
Listen for music, earth, and human ways.                      20

Dark earth, there is another gone away,
But she was not inclined to beg of you
Relief from water falling or the storm.
She was aware of scavengers in holes
Of stone, she knew the loosened stones that fell              25
Indifferently as pebbles plunging down a well
And broke for the sake of nothing human souls.
Earth, hide your face from her where dark is warm.
She does not beg for anything, who knew
The change of tone, the human hope gone gray.                 30

1957

W. H. AUDEN

## In Memory of W. B. Yeats

(*d. January, 1939*)

I

He disappeared in the dead of winter:
The brooks were frozen, the airports almost deserted,
And snow disfigured the public statues;
The mercury sank in the mouth of the dying day.
What instruments we have agree                                5
The day of his death was a dark cold day.

Far from his illness
The wolves ran on through the evergreen forests,
The peasant river was untempted by the fashionable quays;

By mourning tongues                                                                    10
The death of the poet was kept from his poems.

But for him it was his last afternoon as himself,
An afternoon of nurses and rumors;
The provinces of his body revolted,
The squares of his mind were empty,                                                    15
Silence invaded the suburbs,
The current of his feeling failed; he became his admirers.

Now he is scattered among a hundred cities
And wholly given over to unfamiliar affections,
To find his happiness in another kind of wood                                          20
And be punished under a foreign code of conscience.
The words of a dead man
Are modified in the guts of the living.

But in the importance and noise of tomorrow
When the brokers are roaring like beasts on the floor of the Bourse,[1]   25
And the poor have the sufferings to which they are fairly accustomed,
And each in the cell of himself is almost convinced of his freedom,
A few thousand will think of this day
As one thinks of a day when one did something slightly unusual.
What instruments we have agree                                                         30
The day of his death was a dark cold day.

## II

You were silly like us; your gift survived it all:
The parish of rich women, physical decay,
Yourself. Mad Ireland hurt you into poetry.
Now Ireland has her madness and her weather still,                                     35
For poetry makes nothing happen: it survives
In the valley of its making where executives
Would never want to tamper, flows on south
From ranches of isolation and the busy griefs,
Raw towns that we believe and die in; it survives,                                     40
A way of happening, a mouth.

## III

Earth, receive an honored guest:
William Yeats is laid to rest.
Let the Irish vessel lie
Emptied of its poetry.                                                                 45

In the nightmare of the dark
All the dogs of Europe bark,
And the living nations wait,
Each sequestered in its hate;

Intellectual disgrace                                                                  50
Stares from every human face,
And the seas of pity lie
Locked and frozen in each eye.

1. The Paris stock exchange.

Follow, poet, follow right
To the bottom of the night,                               55
With your unconstraining voice
Still persuade us to rejoice;

With the farming of a verse
Make a vineyard of the curse,
Sing of human unsuccess                                   60
In a rapture of distress;

In the deserts of the heart
Let the healing fountain start,
In the prison of his days
Teach the free man how to praise.                         65

1939

MATTHEW ARNOLD

# Memorial Verses

*April 27, 1850*[1]

Goethe in Weimar sleeps,[2] and Greece,
Long since, saw Byron's struggle cease.[3]
But one such death remained to come;
The last poetic voice is dumb—
We stand today by Wordsworth's tomb.                      5

When Byron's eyes were shut in death,
We bowed our head and held our breath.
He taught us little; but our soul
Had *felt* him like the thunder's roll.
With shivering heart the strife we saw                    10
Of passion with eternal law;
And yet with reverential awe
We watched the fount of fiery life
Which served for that Titanic[4] strife.
    When Goethe's death was told, we said:                15
Sunk, then, is Europe's sagest head.
Physician of the iron age,
Goethe has done his pilgrimage.
He took the suffering human race,
He read each wound, each weakness clear;                  20
And struck his finger on the place,
And said: *Thou ailest here, and here!*
He looked on Europe's dying hour
Of fitful dream and feverish power;
His eye plunged down the weltering strife,                25
The turmoil of expiring life—
He said: *The end is everywhere,*

---

1. The day William Wordsworth died.
2. Goethe had died in 1832.
3. Byron died in the Greek civil war in 1824.

4. Colossal. The Titans, in Greek myth, were the ruling family of gods until overthrown by the Olympians.

*Art still has truth, take refuge there!*
And he was happy, if to know
Causes of things, and far below                    30
His feet to see the lurid flow
Of terror, and insane distress,
And headlong fate, be happiness.

And Wordsworth!—Ah, pale ghosts, rejoice!
For never has such soothing voice                   35
Been to your shadowy world conveyed,
Since erst, at morn, some wandering shade
Heard the clear song of Orpheus come
Through Hades, and the mournful gloom.
Wordsworth has gone from us—and ye,                 40
Ah, may ye feel his voice as we!
He too upon a wintry clime
Had fallen—on this iron time
Of doubts, disputes, distractions, fears.
He found us when the age had bound                  45
Our souls in its benumbing round;
He spoke, and loosed our heart in tears.
He laid us as we lay at birth
On the cool flowery lap of earth,
Smiles broke from us and we had ease;               50
The hills were round us, and the breeze
Went o'er the sun-lit fields again;
Our foreheads felt the wind and rain.
Our youth returned; for there was shed
On spirits that had long been dead,                 55
Spirits dried up and closely furled,
The freshness of the early world.

Ah! since dark days still bring to light
Man's prudence and man's fiery might,
Time may restore us in his course                   60
Goethe's sage mind and Byron's force;
But where will Europe's latter hour
Again find Wordsworth's healing power?
Others will teach us how to dare,
And against fear our breast to steel;               65
Others will strengthen us to bear—
But who, ah! who, will make us feel?
The cloud of mortal destiny,
Others will front it fearlessly—
But who, like him, will put it by?                  70

Keep fresh the grass upon his grave
O Rotha,[5] with thy living wave!
Sing him thy best! for few or none
Hears thy voice right, now he is gone.

1850

5. The small stream, uniting Lake Grasmere and Lake Windermere, near which Wordsworth was buried.

DAVID FERRY

# Johnson on Pope

*from* The Lives of the Poets[1]

He was protuberant behind, before;
Born beautiful, he had grown up a spider;
Stature so low, he could not sit at table
Like taller men; in middle life so feeble
He could not dress himself, nor stand upright                    5
Without a canvas bodice; in the long night
Made servants peevish with his demands for coffee;
Trying to make his spider's legs less skinny,
He wore three pair of stockings, which a maid
Had to draw on and off; one side was contracted.               10
But his face was not displeasing, his eyes were vivid.

He found it very difficult to be clean
Of unappeasable malignity;
But in his eyes the shapeless vicious scene
Composed itself; of folly he made beauty.                      15

                                                              1960


ALLEN TATE

# Mr. Pope

When Alexander Pope strolled in the city
Strict was the glint of pearl and gold sedans.[2]
Ladies leaned out more out of fear than pity
For Pope's tight back was rather a goat's than man's.

Often one thinks the urn should have more bones            5
Than skeletons provide for speedy dust,
The urn gets hollow, cobwebs brittle as stones
Weave to the funeral shell a frivolous rust.

---

1. "The person of Pope is well known not to have been formed by the nicest model. He has, in his account of the 'Little Club,' compared himself to a spider, and by another is described as protuberant behind and before. . . . His stature was so low that, to bring him to a level with common tables, it was necessary to raise his seat. But his face was not displeasing, and his eyes were animated and vivid.

By natural deformity or accidental distortion his vital functions were so much disordered that his life was a 'long disease.' His most frequent assailant was the headach, which he used to relieve by inhaling the steam of coffee, which he very frequently required. . . . When he rose he was invested in boddice made of stiff canvass, being scarce able to hold himself erect till they were laced, and he then put on a flannel waistcoat. One side was contracted. His legs were so slender that he enlarged their bulk with three pair of stockings, which were drawn on and off by the maid; for he was not able to dress or undress himself, and neither went to bed nor rose without help. His weakness made it very difficult for him to be clean. . . . The reputation which his friendship gave procured him many invitations; but he was a very troublesome inmate. He brought no servant, and had so many wants that a numerous attendance was scarcely able to supply them. . . . One of his constant demands was of coffee in the night, and to the woman that waited on him in his chamber he was very burthensome; but he was careful to recompense her want of sleep, and Lord Oxford's servant declared that in a house where her business was to answer his call she would not ask for wages."—Samuel Johnson, *Life of Pope,* 1781.

2. Sedan chairs.

And he who dribbled couplets like a snake
Coiled to a lithe precision in the sun      10
Is missing. The jar is empty; you may break
It only to find that Mr. Pope is gone.

What requisitions of a verity
Prompted the wit and rage between his teeth
One cannot say. Around a crooked tree      15
A moral climbs whose name should be a wreath.

                            1928

A. E. HOUSMAN

# Terence, This Is Stupid Stuff

"Terence,[1] this is stupid stuff:
You eat your victuals fast enough;
There can't be much amiss, 'tis clear,
To see the rate you drink your beer.
But oh, good Lord, the verse you make,      5
It gives a chap the belly-ache.
The cow, the old cow, she is dead;
It sleeps well, the horned head:
We poor lads, 'tis our turn now
To hear such tunes as killed the cow.      10
Pretty friendship 'tis to rhyme
Your friends to death before their time
Moping melancholy mad:
Come, pipe a tune to dance to, lad."

     Why, if 'tis dancing you would be,      15
There's brisker pipes than poetry.
Say, for what were hop-yards meant,
Or why was Burton built on Trent?[2]
Oh many a peer of England brews
Livelier liquor than the Muse,      20
And malt does more than Milton can
To justify God's ways to man.[3]
Ale, man, ale's the stuff to drink
For fellows whom it hurts to think:
Look into the pewter pot      25
To see the world as the world's not.
And faith, 'tis pleasant till 'tis past:
The mischief is that 'twill not last.
Oh I have been to Ludlow fair[4]
And left my necktie God knows where,      30
And carried half-way home, or near,
Pints and quarts of Ludlow beer:

1. Housman originally titled the volume in which this poem appeared "The Poems of Terence Hearsay."
2. Burton was famous for its ales, originally brewed from special springs there.
3. Milton said his purpose in *Paradise Lost* was to "justify the ways of God to men."
4. Ludlow was a market town in Shropshire, and its town fair would be a social high point for a youth growing up in the county.

Then the world seemed none so bad,
And I myself a sterling lad;
And down in lovely muck I've lain,                         35
Happy till I woke again.
Then I saw the morning sky:
Heigho, the tale was all a lie;
The world, it was the old world yet,
I was I, my things were wet,                               40
And nothing now remained to do
But begin the game anew.

　　Therefore, since the world has still
Much good, but much less good than ill,
And while the sun and moon endure                          45
Luck's a chance, but trouble's sure,
I'd face it as a wise man would,
And train for ill and not for good.
'Tis true, the stuff I bring for sale
Is not so brisk a brew as ale:                             50
Out of a stem that scored the hand
I wrung it in a weary land.
But take it: if the smack is sour,
The better for the embittered hour;
It should do good to heart and head                        55
When your soul is in my soul's stead;
And I will friend you, if I may,
In the dark and cloudy day.

　　There was a king reigned in the East:
There, when kings will sit to feast,                       60
They get their fill before they think
With poisoned meat and poisoned drink.
He gathered all that springs to birth
From the many-venomed earth;
First a little, thence to more,                            65
He sampled all her killing store;
And easy, smiling, seasoned sound,
Sate the king when healths went round.
They put arsenic in his meat
And stared aghast to watch him eat;                        70
They poured strychnine in his cup
And shook to see him drink it up:
They shook, they stared as white's their shirt:
Them it was their poison hurt.
—I tell the tale that I heard told.                        75
Mithridates,[5] he died old.

1896

5. The king of Pontus, he was said to have developed a tolerance of poison by taking gradually increasing quantities.

MARIANNE MOORE

# Poetry

I, too, dislike it: there are things that are important beyond all this
    fiddle.
Reading it, however, with a perfect contempt for it, one discovers in
it after all, a place for the genuine.
    Hands that can grasp, eyes
    that can dilate, hair that can rise                                5
        if it must, these things are important not because a

high-sounding interpretation can be put upon them but because they
        are
useful. When they become so derivative as to become unintelligible,
the same thing may be said for all of us, that we
    do not admire what                                                10
    we cannot understand: the bat
        holding on upside down or in quest of something to

eat, elephants pushing, a wild horse taking a roll, a tireless wolf under
a tree, the immovable critic twitching his skin like a horse that feels
        a flea, the base-
    ball fan, the statistician—                                       15
    nor is it valid
        to discriminate against "business documents and

school-books"[1]; all these phenomena are important. One must make a
        distinction
however: when dragged into prominence by half poets, the result is
        not poetry,
nor till the poets among us can be                                    20
    "literalists of
    the imagination"[2]—above
        insolence and triviality and can present

for inspection, "imaginary gardens with real toads in them," shall we
        have
it. In the meantime, if you demand on the one hand,                   25
    the raw material of poetry in
    all its rawness and
    that which is on the other hand
        genuine, you are interested in poetry.

1921

1. *"Diary of Tolstoy,* p. 84: 'Where the boundary between prose and poetry lies, I shall never be able to understand. The question is raised in manuals of style, yet the answer to it lies beyond me. Poetry is verse: prose is not verse. Or else poetry is everything with the exception of business documents and school books.' " (Moore's note)
2. " 'Literalists of the imagination.' Yeats, *Ideas of Good and Evil* (A. H. Bullen, 1903), p. 182. 'The limitation of his view was from the very intensity of his vision; he was a too literal realist of imagination, as others are of nature; and because he believed that the figures seen by the mind's eye, when exalted by inspiration, were "eternal existences," symbols of divine essences, he hated every grace of style that might obscure their lineaments.' " (Moore's note)

ARCHIBALD MACLEISH

# Ars Poetica[1]

A poem should be palpable and mute
As a globed fruit,

Dumb
As old medallions to the thumb,

Silent as the sleeve-worn stone                               5
Of casement ledges where the moss has grown—

A poem should be wordless
As the flight of birds.

A poem should be motionless in time
As the moon climbs,                                          10

Leaving, as the moon releases
Twig by twig the night-entangled trees,

Leaving, as the moon behind the winter leaves,
Memory by memory the mind—

A poem should be motionless in time                          15
As the moon climbs.

A poem should be equal to:
Not true.

For all the history of grief
An empty doorway and a maple leaf.                           20

For love
The leaning grasses and two lights above the sea—

A poem should not mean
But be.

                                                         1926

X. J. KENNEDY

## Ars Poetica

The goose that laid the golden egg
Died looking up its crotch
To find out how its sphincter worked.

Would you lay well? Don't watch.

                                                         1961

1. "The Art of Poetry," title of a poetical treatise by the Roman poet Horace
(65–8 B.C.).

GEORGE HERBERT

# Jordan[1]

Who says that fictions only and false hair
Become[2] a verse? Is there in truth no beauty?
Is all good structure in a winding stair?
May no lines pass, except they do their duty[3]
  Not to a true, but painted chair?                               5

Is it no verse, except enchanted groves
And sudden arbors shadow coarse-spun lines?
Must purling streams refresh a lover's loves?
Must all be veiled while he that reads, divines,
  Catching the sense at two removes?                             10

Shepherds are honest people; let them sing:
Riddle who list, for me, and pull for prime[4]:
I envy no man's nightingale or spring;
Nor let them punish me with loss of rhyme,
  Who plainly say, *My God, My King*.                            15

1633

ROBERT HERRICK

# I Sing of Brooks[1]

I sing of brooks, of blossoms, birds, and bowers,
Of April, May, of June, and July flowers.
I sing of Maypoles, hock carts, wassails, wakes,[2]
Of bridegrooms, brides, and of their bridal cakes.
I write of youth, of love, and have access                        5
By these to sing of cleanly wantonness.
I sing of dews, of rains, and, piece by piece,
Of balm, of oil, of spice, and ambergris.[3]
I sing of times trans shifting, and I write
How roses first came red, and lilies white.                      10
I write of groves, of twilights, and I sing
The court of Mab, and of the fairy king.[4]
I write of Hell; I sing (and ever shall)
Of Heaven, and hope to have it after all.

1648

1. A river in the Holy Land which
meanders 120 miles to cover 60.
2. Befit.
3. Bow in obeisance, as to a throne.
4. A metaphor from primero: Shuffle
for me, whoever wants to, and draw for
the winning card.
1. This poem serves as the introduction
or "argument" to Herrick's volume *Hes-*

*perides.*
2. Hock carts brought in the last of the
harvest; wakes were not only night watches
for the dead, but also vigils on the eve of
a religious festival.
3. An ingredient in perfume, taken from
whales.
4. Mab was the fairy queen and Oberon
the king.

ALEXANDER POPE

# [Why Did I Write?][1]

Why did I write? what sin to me unknown                125
Dipped me in ink, my parents', or my own?
As yet a child, nor yet a fool to fame,
I lisped in numbers,[2] for the numbers came.
I left no calling for this idle trade,
No duty broke, no father disobeyed.                    130
The Muse but served to ease some friend, not wife,
To help me through this long disease, my life,
To second, Arbuthnot! thy art and care,
And teach, the being you preserved, to bear.
   But why then publish? Granville the polite,    135
And knowing Walsh, would tell me I could write;
Well-natured Garth inflamed with early praise,
And Congreve loved, and Swift endured my lays;
The courtly Talbot, Somers, Sheffield read,
Ev'n mitred Rochester would nod the head,              140
And St. John's self (great Dryden's friends before)[3]
With open arms received one poet more.
Happy my studies, when by these approved!
Happier their author, when by these beloved!
From these the world will judge of men and books,      145
Not from the Burnets, Oldmixons, and Cooks.[4]
   Soft were my numbers; who could take offense
While pure description held the place of sense?
Like gentle Fanny's was my flow'ry theme,
A painted mistress, or a purling stream.               150
Yet then did Gildon[5] draw his venal quill;
I wished the man a dinner, and sate still:
Yet then did Dennis[6] rave in furious fret;
I never answered, I was not in debt:
If want provoked, or madness made them print,          155
I waged no war with Bedlam or the Mint.[7]
   Did some more sober critic come abroad?
If wrong, I smiled; if right, I kissed the rod.
Pains, reading, study, are their just pretense,
And all they want[8] is spirit, taste, and sense.      160
Commas and points they set exactly right,
And 'twere a sin to rob them of their mite.
Yet ne'er one sprig of laurel graced these ribalds,
From slashing Bentley down to pidling Tibalds.[9]

1. From *An Epistle to Dr. Arbuthnot*, addressed to Pope's physician friend. The poem is Pope's "apologia" (explanation) for his poetic career.
2. Regular metrical units.
3. "All these were Patrons or Admirers of Mr. Dryden" (Pope's note), and early encouragers of Pope himself.
4. "Authors of secret and scandalous History." (Pope's note)
5. Charles Gildon, a hack writer who frequently attacked Pope.
6. John Dennis, a talented but irascible critic with whom Pope quarreled often.
7. Bedlam is Bethlehem Hospital for the insane; the "Mint" was a "liberty" where fugitives could not be arrested. Many debtors lived there.
8. Lack.
9. Talented but pedantic scholars. Richard Bentley is "slashing" because of the many bracketed passages in his Milton edition, passages which Bentley thought Milton didn't write; Lewis Theobald (pronounced Tibald) fastidiously edited Shakespeare.

Each wight who reads not, and but scans and spells,                165
Each word-catcher that lives on syllables,
Ev'n such small critics some regard may claim,
Preserved in Milton's or in Shakespear's name.
Pretty! in amber[1] to observe the forms
Of hairs, or straws, or dirt, or grubs, or worms!                 170
The things, we know, are neither rich nor rare,
But wonder how the devil they got there?
    Were others angry? I excused them too;
Well might they rage, I gave them but their due.
A man's true merit 'tis not hard to find,                         175
But each man's secret standard in his mind,
That casting-weight[2] pride adds to emptiness,
This, who can gratify? for who can *guess?*
The bard whom pilfered pastorals renown,
Who turns[3] a Persian tale for half a crown,[4]                  180
Just writes to make his barrenness appear,
And strains from hard-bound brains, eight lines a year;
He, who still wanting, though he lives on theft,
Steals much, spends little, yet has nothing left:
And he, who now to sense, now nonsense leaning,                   185
Means not, but blunders round about a meaning:
And he, whose fustian's so sublimely bad,
It is not poetry, but prose run mad:
All these, my modest satire bade *translate,*
And owned that nine such poets made a Tate.[5]                    190
How did they fume, and stamp, and roar, and chafe!
And swear, not Addison[6] himself was safe.

1735

WILLIAM WORDSWORTH

## A *Poet!*—He Hath Put His Heart to School

A *Poet!*—He hath put his heart to school,
Nor dares to move unpropped upon the staff
Which Art hath lodged within his hand—must laugh
By precept only, and shed tears by rule.
Thy Art be Nature; the live current quaff,                         5
And let the groveler sip his stagnant pool,
In fear that else, when Critics grave and cool
Have killed him, Scorn should write his epitaph.
How does the Meadow-flower its bloom unfold?
Because the lovely little flower is free                           10
Down to its root, and, in that freedom, bold;
And so the grandeur of the Forest-tree
Comes not by casting in a formal mould,
But from its *own* divine vitality.

1842

1. Small objects were often preserved in translucent amber.
2. A weight added to make the scales balance.
3. Translates.
4. "Ambrose Philips translated a book called the *Persian Tales*." (Pope's note)

5. Nahum Tate, poet laureate from 1692 to 1715.
6. Joseph Addison, journalist and man of letters who incurred Pope's displeasure by comparing some of Pope's early poems unfavorably with those of Ambrose Philips, a justly neglected poet.

JAMES WELDON JOHNSON

## O Black and Unknown Bards

O black and unknown bards of long ago,
How came your lips to touch the sacred fire?
How, in your darkness, did you come to know
The power and beauty of the minstrel's lyre?
Who first from midst his bonds lifted his eyes?                5
Who first from out the still watch, lone and long,
Feeling the ancient faith of prophets rise
Within his dark-kept soul, burst into song?

Heart of what slave poured out such melody
As "Steal away to Jesus"? On its strains                       10
His spirit must have nightly floated free,
Though still about his hands he felt his chains.
Who heard great "Jordan roll"? Whose starward eye
Saw chariot "swing low"? And who was he
That breathed that comforting, melodic sigh,                    15
"Nobody knows de trouble I see"?[1]

What merely living clod, what captive thing,
Could up toward God through all its darkness grope,
And find within its deadened heart to sing
These songs of sorrow, love and faith, and hope?               20
How did it catch that subtle undertone,
That note in music heard not with the ears?
How sound the elusive reed so seldom blown,
Which stirs the soul or melts the heart to tears?

Not that great German master[2] in his dream                   25
Of harmonies that thundered amongst the stars
At the creation, ever heard a theme
Nobler than "Go down, Moses."[3] Mark its bars,
How like a mighty trumpet-call they stir
The blood. Such are the notes that men have sung               30
Going to valorous deeds; such tones there were
That helped make history when Time was young.

There is a wide, wide wonder in it all,
That from degraded rest and servile toil
The fiery spirit of the seer should call                       35
These simple children of the sun and soil.
O black slave singers, gone, forgot, unfamed,
You—you alone, of all the long, long line
Of those who've sung untaught, unknown, unnamed,
Have stretched out upward, seeking the divine.                 40

1. Titles and phrases from Negro spiri-    2. Beethoven.
tuals.                                      3. A Negro spiritual.

You sang not deeds of heroes or of kings;
No chant of bloody war, no exulting paean
Of arms-won triumphs; but your humble strings
You touched in chord with music empyrean.
You sang far better than you knew; the songs          45
That for your listeners' hungry hearts sufficed
Still live—but more than this to you belongs:
You sang a race from wood and stone to Christ.

                                               1917


WALLACE STEVENS

## Of Modern Poetry

The poem of the mind in the act of finding
What will suffice. It has not always had
To find: the scene was set; it repeated what
Was in the script.
                    Then the theatre was changed          5
To something else. Its past was a souvenir.

It has to be living, to learn the speech of the place.
It has to face the men of the time and to meet
The women of the time. It has to think about war
And it has to find what will suffice. It has          10
To construct a new stage. It has to be on that stage
And, like an insatiable actor,    slowly    and
With meditation, speak words that in the ear,
In the delicatest ear of the mind,    repeat,
Exactly, that which it wants to hear, at the sound          15
Of which, an invisible audience listens,
Not to the play, but to itself, expressed
In an emotion as of two people, as of two
Emotions becoming one. The actor is
A metaphysician in the dark, twanging          20
An instrument, twanging a wiry string that gives
Sounds passing through sudden rightnesses, wholly
Containing the mind, below which it cannot descend,
Beyond which it has no will to rise.
                              It must          25
Be the finding of a satisfaction, and may
Be of a man skating, a woman dancing, a woman
Combing. The poem of the act of the mind.

                                          p. 1940


CHARLES OLSON

## A B C s

The word forms
on the left: you must
stand in line. Speech

is as swift as synapse[1]
but the acquisition of same                                  5
is as long
as I am old

    rat  on the first floor landing of the three-decker
          (grey)
  black  eat a peck of storage batteries 'fore            10
          I die
cabbage  my friend Cabbage, with whom to bake potatoes up
          Fisher's Hill

    rust  in the bed of Beaver Brook—from the junk in it
          And the iris ("flags," we called 'em)            15
          And the turtle I was surprised by

up to last night's dream, the long brown body pleased
I kissed her buttock curve

Interiors,
and their registration                                       20

Words, form
but the extension of
content

Style, est verbum[2]

The word                                                     25
is image, and the reverend reverse is
Eliot

Pound[3]
is verse

AMIRI BARAKA (LEROI JONES)

# Black Art

Poems are bullshit unless they are
teeth or trees or lemons piled
on a step. Or black ladies dying
of men leaving nickel hearts
beating them down. Fuck poems                                5
and they are useful, they shoot
come at you, love what you are,
breathe like wrestlers, or shudder
strangely after pissing. We want live
words of the hip world live flesh &                          10

1. The junction between nerve cells.          exponents of different kinds of modern
2. Is the Word.                               poetry.
3. T. S. Eliot and Ezra Pound, leading

coursing blood. Hearts Brains
Souls splintering fire. We want poems
like fists beating niggers out of Jocks
or dagger poems in the slimy bellies
of the owner-jews. Black poems to                               15
smear on girdlemamma mulatto bitches
whose brains are red jelly stuck
between 'lizabeth taylor's toes. Stinking
Whores! We want "poems that kill."
Assassin poems, Poems that shoot                               20
guns. Poems that wrestle cops into alleys
and take their weapons leaving them dead
with tongues pulled out and sent to Ireland. Knockoff
poems for dope selling wops or slick halfwhite
politicians. Airplane poems. rrrrrrrrrrrrrrrrrrr              25
rrrrrrrrrr. . . . tuhtuhtuhtuhtuhtuhtuhtuhtuhtuh
. . . . rrrrrrrrrrrrrr. . . Setting fire and death to
whities ass. Look at the Liberal
Spokesman for the jews clutch his throat
& puke himself into eternity. . . rrrrrrrrrr               30
There's a negroleader pinned to
a bar stool in Sardi's[1] eyeballs melting
in hot flame. Another negroleader
on the steps of the white house one
kneeling between the sheriff's thighs                          35
negotiating cooly for his people.
Aggh . . . stumbles across the room . . .
Put it on him, poem. Strip him naked
to the world! Another bad poem cracking
steel knuckles in a jewlady's mouth                            40
Poem scream poison gas on beasts in green berets
Clean out the world for virtue and love,
Let there be no love poems written
until love can exist freely and
cleanly. Let Black People understand                          45
that they are the lovers and the sons
of lovers and warriors and sons
of warriors Are poems & poets &
all the loveliness here in the world.

We want a black poem. And a                                    50
Black World.
Let the world be a Black Poem
And Let All Black People Speak This Poem
Silently

or LOUD                                                        55

                                                             1966

---

1. A fashionable New York bar and restaurant.

WILLIAM SHAKESPEARE

## Shall I Compare Thee to a Summer's Day?

Shall I compare thee to a summer's day?
Thou art more lovely and more temperate:
Rough winds do shake the darling buds of May,
And summer's lease hath all too short a date:
Sometimes too hot the eye of heaven shines,                     5
And often is his gold complexion dimmed;
And every fair from fair sometimes declines,
By chance or nature's changing course untrimmed;[1]
But thy eternal summer shall not fade,
Nor lose possession of that fair thou ow'st;[2]                 10
Nor shall Death brag thou wander'st in his shade,
When in eternal lines to time thou grow'st:
So long as men can breathe, or eyes can see,
So long lives this, and this gives life to thee.

                                                        1609

MICHAEL DRAYTON

## How Many Paltry, Foolish, Painted Things

How many paltry, foolish, painted things,
That now in coaches trouble every street,
Shall be forgotten, whom no poet sings,
Ere they be well wrapped in their winding sheet![1]
Where I to thee eternity shall give,                            5
When nothing else remaineth of these days,
And queens hereafter shall be glad to live
Upon the alms of thy superfluous praise.
Virgins and matrons, reading these my rhymes,
Shall be so much delighted with thy story                       10
That they shall grieve they lived not in these times,
To have seen thee, their sex's only glory.
So shalt thou fly above the vulgar throng,
Still to survive in my immortal song.

                                                        1619

DYLAN THOMAS

## In My Craft or Sullen Art

In my craft or sullen art
Exercised in the still night
When only the moon rages
And the lovers lie abed
With all their griefs in their arms,                            5
I labor by singing light

---

1. Disordered.                          1. Shroud.
2. Ownest.

Not for ambition or bread
Or the strut and trade of charms
On the ivory stages
But for the common wages                                    10
Of their most secret heart.

Not for the proud man apart
From the raging moon I write
On these spindrift[1] pages
Nor for the towering dead                                   15
With their nightingales and psalms
But for the lovers, their arms
Round the griefs of the ages,
Who pay no praise or wages
Nor heed my craft or art.                                   20
1946

WILLIAM SHAKESPEARE

## Not Marble, Nor the Gilded Monuments

Not marble, nor the gilded monuments
Of princes, shall outlive this powerful rhyme;
But you shall shine more bright in these conténts
Than unswept stone, besmeared with sluttish time.
When wasteful war shall statues overturn,                   5
And broils root out the work of masonry,
Nor Mars his[2] sword nor war's quick fire shall burn
The living record of your memory.
'Gainst death and all-oblivious enmity
Shall you pace forth; your praise shall still find room     10
Even in the eyes of all posterity
That wear this world out to the ending doom.[3]
So, till the judgment that yourself arise,
You live in this, and dwell in lovers' eyes.
1609

ARCHIBALD MACLEISH

## "Not Marble Nor the Gilded Monuments"

### *for Adele*

The praisers of women in their proud and beautiful poems,
Naming the grave mouth and the hair and the eyes,
Boasted those they loved should be forever remembered:
These were lies.

---

1. Literally, wind-driven sea spray.
2. Mars's (a common Renaissance form

of the possessive). "Nor . . . nor": neither
. . . nor.
3. Judgment Day.

The words sound but the face in the Istrian sun is forgotten.                     5
The poet speaks but to her dead ears no more.
The sleek throat is gone—and the breast that was troubled to listen:
Shadow from door.

Therefore I will not praise your knees nor your fine walking
Telling you men shall remember your name as long                                 10
As lips move or breath is spent or the iron of English
Rings from a tongue.

I shall say you were young, and your arms straight, and your mouth
          scarlet:
I shall say you will die and none will remember you:
Your arms change, and none remember the swish of your garments,               15
Nor the click of your shoe.

Not with my hand's strength, not with difficult labor
Springing the obstinate words to the bones of your breast
And the stubborn line to your young stride and the breath to your
          breathing
And the beat to your haste                                                        20
Shall I prevail on the hearts of unborn men to remember.

(What is a dead girl but a shadowy ghost
Or a dead man's voice but a distant and vain affirmation
Like dream words most)

Therefore I will not speak of the undying glory of women.                        25
I will say you were young and straight and your skin fair
And you stood in the door and the sun was a shadow of leaves on your
          shoulders
And a leaf on your hair—

I will not speak of the famous beauty of dead women:
I will say the shape of a leaf lay once on your hair.                            30
Till the world ends and the eyes are out and the mouths broken
Look! It is there!

                                                                      1930

# To the Stone-Cutters

Stone-cutters fighting time with marble, you foredefeated
Challengers of oblivion
Eat cynical earnings, knowing rock splits, records fall down,
The square-limbed Roman letters
Scale in the thaws, wear in the rain. The poet as well                            5
Builds his monument mockingly;
For the man will be blotted out, the blithe earth die, the brave sun
Die blind and blacken to the heart:
Yet stones have stood for a thousand years, and pained thoughts found
The honey of peace in old poems.                                                 10

                                                                      1924

W. H. AUDEN

# Musée des Beaux Arts[1]

About suffering they were never wrong,
The Old Masters: how well they understood
Its human position; how it takes place
While someone else is eating or opening a window or just walking dully
    along;
How, when the aged are reverently, passionately waiting         5
For the miraculous birth, there always must be
Children who did not specially want it to happen, skating
On a pond at the edge of the wood:
They never forgot
That even the dreadful martyrdom must run its course         10
Anyhow in a corner, some untidy spot
Where the dogs go on with their doggy life and the torturer's horse
Scratches its innocent behind on a tree.

In Brueghel's *Icarus*,[2] for instance: how everything turns away
Quite leisurely from the disaster; the plowman may         15
Have heard the splash, the forsaken cry,
But for him it was not an important failure; the sun shone
As it had to on the white legs disappearing into the green
Water; and the expensive delicate ship that must have seen
Something amazing, a boy falling out of the sky,         20
Had somewhere to get to and sailed calmly on.
1938

WILLIAM CARLOS WILLIAMS

# Landscape with the Fall of Icarus[1]

According to Brueghel
when Icarus fell
it was spring

a farmer was plowing
his field         5
the whole pageantry

of the year was
awake tingling
near

1. The Museum of the Fine Arts, in Brussels.
2. "Landscape with the Fall of Icarus," by Pieter Brueghel the elder, located in the Brussels Museum. According to Greek myth, Daedalus and his son Icarus escaped from imprisonment by using home-made wings of wax; but Icarus flew too near the sun, the wax melted, and he drowned. In the Brueghel painting the central figure is a peasant plowing, and several other figures are more immediately noticeable than Icarus who, disappearing into the sea, is easy to miss in the lower right-hand corner. Equally ignored by the figures is a dead body in the woods.
1. See the notes to the poem above.

                    the edge of the sea                    10
                    concerned
                    with itself

                    sweating in the sun
                    that melted
                    the wings' wax                         15

                    unsignificantly
                    off the coast
                    there was

                    a splash quite unnoticed
                    this was                               20
                    Icarus drowning

                                                    1962

MICHAEL HAMBURGER

# Lines on Brueghel's *Icarus*[1]

The plowman plows, the fisherman dreams of fish;
Aloft, the sailor through a world of ropes
Guides tangled meditations, feverish
With memories of girls forsaken, hopes
Of brief reunions, new discoveries,                        5
Past rum consumed, rum promised, rum potential.
Sheep crop the grass, lift up their heads and gaze
Into a sheepish present: the essential,
Illimitable juiciness of things,
Greens, yellows, browns are what they see.                 10
Churlish and slow, the shepherd, hearing wings—
Perhaps an eagle's—gapes uncertainly.

Too late. The worst had happened: lost to man
The angel, Icarus, for ever failed,
Fallen with melted wings when, near the sun                15
He scorned the ordering planet, which prevailed
And, jeering, now slinks off, to rise once more.
But he—his damaged purpose drags him down—
Too far from his half-brothers on the shore,
Hardly conceivable, is left to drown.                      20

                                                    1952

JOHN BERRYMAN

# Winter Landscape[2]

The three men coming down the winter hill
In brown, with tall poles and a pack of hounds

1. See notes to Auden's "Musée des Beaux Arts."
2. Berryman once wrote that if he annotated his own poems he would say of this one that "the subject . . . is not really the painting by the elder Brueghel to which from the start to finish the poem refers." The painting is Brueghel's "Hunters in the Snow."

At heel, through the arrangement of the trees,
Past the five figures at the burning straw,
Returning cold and silent to their town,                    5

Returning to the drifted snow, the rink
Lively with children, to the older men,
The long companions they can never reach,
The blue light, men with ladders, by the church
The sledge and shadow in the twilit street,                 10

Are not aware that in the sandy time
To come, the evil waste of history
Outstretched, they will be seen upon the brow
Of that same hill: when all their company
Will have been irrecoverably lost,                          15

These men, this particular three in brown
Witnessed by birds will keep the scene and say
By their configuration with the trees,
The small bridge, the red houses and the fire,
What place, what time, what morning occasion               20

Sent them into the wood, a pack of hounds
At heel and the tall poles upon their shoulders,
Thence to return as now we see them and
Ankle-deep in snow down the winter hill
Descend, while three birds watch and the fourth flies.      25

1948

WILLIAM  CARLOS  WILLIAMS

## The Dance

In Brueghel's great picture, The Kermess,[1]
the dancers go round, they go round and
around, the squeal and the blare and the
tweedle of bagpipes, a bugle and fiddles
tipping their bellies (round as the thick-                  5
sided glasses whose wash they impound)
their hips and their bellies off balance
to turn them. Kicking and rolling about
the Fair Grounds, swinging their butts, those
shanks must be sound to bear up under such                  10
rollicking measures, prance as they dance
in Brueghel's great picture, The Kermess.

1944

1.  A drawing by Pieter Brueghel the elder.

WILLIAM  CARLOS  WILLIAMS

# Children's Games[1]

### I

This is a schoolyard
crowded
with children

of all ages near a village
on a small stream                                        5
meandering by

where some boys
are swimming
bare-ass

or climbing a tree in leaf                               10
everything
is motion

elder women are looking
after the small
fry                                                      15

a play wedding a
christening
nearby one leans

hollering
into                                                     20
an empty hogshead

### II

Little girls
whirling their skirts about
until they stand out flat

tops pinwheels                                           25
to run in the wind with
or a toy in 3 tiers to spin

with a piece
of twine to make it go
blindman's-buff  follow  the                             30

leader stilts
high and low tipcat jacks
bowls hanging by the knees

standing on your head
run the gauntlet                                         35
a dozen on their backs

1. The title of a painting (by Pieter Brueghel the elder) which the poem describes.

feet together kicking
through which a boy must pass
roll the hoop or a

construction                                        40
made of bricks
some mason has abandoned

III
The desperate toys
of children
their                                                45

imagination equilibrium
and rocks
which are to be

found
everywhere                                           50
and games to drag

the other down
blindfold
to make use of

a swinging                                           55
weight
with which

at random
to bash in the
heads about                                          60

them
Brueghel saw it all
and with his grim

humor faithfully
recorded                                             65
it

                                                    1962


RICHARD  WILBUR

## Museum Piece

The good gray guardians of art
Patrol the halls on spongy shoes,
Impartially protective, though
Perhaps suspicious of Toulouse.[1]

---

1. Toulouse-Lautrec, 19th-century French painter famous for his posters, drawings, and
paintings of singers, dancers, and actresses.

Here dozes one against the wall,                              5
Disposed upon a funeral chair.
A Degas[2] dancer pirouettes
Upon the parting of his hair.

See how she spins! The grace is there,
But strain as well is plain to see.                          10
Degas loved the two together:
Beauty joined to energy.

Edgar Degas purchased once
A fine El Greco,[3] which he kept
Against the wall beside his bed                              15
To hang his pants on while he slept.

                                                          1950

STEPHEN SPENDER

## The Living Values

Alas for the sad standards
In the eyes of the Old Masters
Sprouting through glaze of their pictures!

Images we watch through glass
Look back on us, intruding on our time:                      5
As Nature, spread before the summer mansion,
Butts through windows in on our dimension.

To airman over continental ranges,
Propellor's stiff and glassy flicker
Between him and the map below                               10
Spells dynamics of this invisible
Age of invention, that whirls out of sight.

Varnish over paint, and dust over glass!
Stares back, remote, the drummer's static drum;
The locked ripeness of the Centaurs' feast;[1]              15
The blowing flags, frozen stiff
Under cracked varnish, and the facing
Reproach of Rembrandt's self-Rembrandt.[2]

Alas for the sad standards
In the eyes of the new-dead young                           20
Sprawled in the mud of battle.
Stare back, stare back, with dust over glazed
Eyes, their gaze at partridges,

---

2. Degas, a 19th-century French impressionist, usually considered the master of the human figure in movement.
3. El Greco, a 16th-century Spanish painter, known for the mannered disproportion of his figures.
1. The Centaurs, half horse and half man, were invited to a wedding feast, where they became drunk and treated the women rudely, according to Greek myth. The episode has been a favorite for many artists.
2. Rembrandt's famous self-portraits emphasize self-revelation and detailed psychological analysis. More than 60 of them are extant.

Their dreams of nudes, and their collected
Hearts wound up with love, like little watch springs.    25

To ram them outside Time, violence
Of wills that ride this cresting day
Struck them with lead so swift
They look at us through its glass trajectory
And we, living, look back at them through glass,    30
Their bodies now sunk inch-deep in gold frames.

Through the invisible they look at us,
Like values of Old Masters
That mock us with strange peace!

1939

SIR EDWARD DYER

## My Mind to Me a Kingdom Is

My mind to me a kingdom is;
    Such present joys therein I find
That it excels all other bliss
    That earth affords or grows by kind.[1]
Though much I want[2] which most would have,    5
Yet still my mind forbids to crave.

No princely pomp, no wealthy store,
    No force to win the victory,
No wily wit to salve a sore,
    No shape to feed a loving eye;    10
To none of these I yield as thrall.
For why[3] my mind doth serve for all.

I see how plenty suffers oft,
    And hasty climbers soon do fall;
I see that those which are aloft    15
    Mishap doth threaten most of all:
They get with toil, they keep with fear.
Such cares my mind could never bear.

Content I live, this is my stay;
    I seek no more than may suffice;    20
I press to bear no haughty sway;
    Look, what I lack my mind supplies;
Lo, thus I triumph like a king,
Content with that my mind doth bring.

Some have too much, yet still do crave;    25
    I little have, and seek no more.
They are but poor, though much they have,
    And I am rich with little store.

1. Naturally.                    3. Because.
2. Lack.

They poor, I rich; they beg, I give;
They lack, I leave; they pine, I live.          30

I laugh not at another's loss;
    I grudge not at another's gain;
No worldly waves my mind can toss;
    My state at one doth still remain.
I fear no foe, I fawn no friend;               35
I loathe not life, nor dread my end.

Some weigh their pleasure by their lust,
    Their wisdom by their rage of will;
Their treasure is their only trust;
    A cloakéd craft their store of skill.       40
But all the pleasure that I find
Is to maintain a quiet mind.

My wealth is health and perfect ease;
    My conscience clear my choice defense;
I neither seek by bribes to please,            45
    Nor by deceit to breed offense.
Thus do I live; thus will I die.
Would all did so as well as I!

                                        1588

SAMUEL TAYLOR COLERIDGE

## This Lime-Tree Bower My Prison[1]

Well, they are gone, and here must I remain,
This lime-tree bower my prison! I have lost
Beauties and feelings, such as would have been
Most sweet to my remembrance even when age
Had dimmed mine eyes to blindness! They, meanwhile,   5
Friends, whom I never more may meet again,
On springy[2] heath, along the hilltop edge,
Wander in gladness, and wind down, perchance,
To that still roaring dell, of which I told;
The roaring dell, o'erwooded, narrow, deep,          10
And only speckled by the midday sun;
Where its slim trunk the ash from rock to rock
Flings arching like a bridge;—that branchless ash,
Unsunned and damp, whose few poor yellow leaves
Ne'er tremble in the gale, yet tremble still,        15
Fanned by the waterfall! and there my friends
Behold the dark green file of long lank weeds,[3]
That all at once (a most fantastic sight!)
Still nod and drip beneath the dripping edge
Of the blue clay-stone.

---

1. Coleridge wrote the poem during a visit to his cottage by some friends; an accident on the way of their arrival prevented him from accompanying them on walks, during one of which the poem is set.
2. "Elastic, I mean." (Coleridge's note)
3. Plants usually called adder's tongue or hart's tongue.

                    Now, my friends emerge                        20
Beneath the wide wide Heaven—and view again
The many-steepled tract magnificent
Of hilly fields and meadows, and the sea,
With some fair bark, perhaps, whose sails light up
The slip of smooth clear blue betwixt two Isles          25
Of purple shadow! Yes! they wander on
In gladness all; but thou, methinks, most glad,
My gentle-hearted Charles![4] for thou hast pined
And hungered after Nature, many a year,
In the great City pent,[5] winning thy way               30
With sad yet patient soul, through evil and pain
And strange calamity! Ah! slowly sink
Behind the western ridge, thou glorious Sun!
Shine in the slant beams of the sinking orb,
Ye purple heath-flowers! richlier burn, ye clouds!       35
Live in the yellow light, ye distant groves!
And kindle, thou blue Ocean! So my friend
Struck with deep joy may stand, as I have stood,
Silent with swimming sense; yea, gazing round
On the wide landscape, gaze till all doth seem           40
Less gross than bodily; and of such hues
As veil the Almighty Spirit, when yet he makes
Spirits perceive his presence.

                         A delight
Comes sudden on my heart, and I am glad
As I myself were there! Nor in this bower,               45
This little lime-tree bower, have I not marked
Much that has soothed me. Pale beneath the blaze
Hung the transparent foliage; and I watched
Some broad and sunny leaf, and loved to see
The shadow of the leaf and stem above                    50
Dappling its sunshine! And that walnut-tree
Was richly tinged, and a deep radiance lay
Full on the ancient ivy, which usurps
Those fronting elms, and now, with blackest mass
Makes their dark branches gleam a lighter hue            55
Through the late twilight: and though now the bat
Wheels silent by, and not a swallow twitters,
Yet still the solitary humble-bee
Sings in the bean-flower! Henceforth I shall know
That Nature ne'er deserts the wise and pure;             60
No plot so narrow, be but Nature there,
No waste so vacant, but may well employ
Each faculty of sense, and keep the heart
Awake to Love and Beauty! and sometimes
'Tis well to be bereft of promised good,                 65
That we may lift the soul, and contemplate
With lively joy the joys we cannot share.

4. The poem is addressed to Charles    5. Lamb was a clerk at the India House,
Lamb, one of the visiting friends.     London.

My gentle-hearted Charles! when the last rook[6]
Beat its straight path along the dusky air
Homewards, I blessed it! deeming its black wing          70
(Now a dim speck, now vanishing in light)
Had crossed the mighty orb's dilated glory,
While thou stood'st gazing; or, when all was still,
Flew creeking o'er thy head, and had a charm
For thee, my gentle-hearted Charles, to whom          75
No sound is dissonant which tells of Life.

1797

THOMAS CAMPION

# Jack and Joan

Jack and Joan they think no ill,
But loving live, and merry still;
Do their week days' work, and pray
Devoutly on the holy day;
Skip and trip it on the green,                         5
And help to choose the summer queen;
Lash out,[1] at a country feast,
Their silver penny with the best.

Well can they judge of nappy[2] ale,
And tell at large a winter tale;                       10
Climb up to the apple loft,
And turn the crabs[3] till they be soft.
Tib is all the father's joy,
And little Tom the mother's boy.
All their pleasure is content;                         15
And care, to pay their yearly rent.

Joan can call by name her cows,
And deck her windows with green boughs;
She can wreaths and tuttyes[4] make,
And trim with plums a bridal cake.                     20
Jack knows what brings gain or loss,
And his long flail can stoutly toss;
Makes the hedge, which others break;[5]
And ever thinks what he doth speak.

Now, you courtly dames and knights,                    25
That study only strange delights,
Though you scorn the homespun gray,
And revel in your rich array;
Though your tongues dissemble deep,
And can your heads from danger keep;                   30
Yet, for all your pomp and train,
Securer lives the silly[6] swain.

1613?

6. Crow.
1. Squander.
2. Heady.
3. Crabapples.

4. Nosegays.
5. The nobility often broke the hedges
while hunting.
6. Simple.

MATTHEW PRIOR

# An Epitaph

Epigraph:  Stet quicunque volet potens
Aulae culmine lubrice etc.
Senec.[1]

Interred beneath this marble stone,
Lies sauntering Jack and idle Joan.
While rolling threescore years and one[2]
Did round this globe their courses run;
If human things went ill or well,              5
If changing empires rose or fell,
The morning passed, the evening came,
And found this couple still the same.
They walked and eat;[3] good folks—what then?
Why then they walked and eat again.              10
They soundly slept the night away;
They did just nothing all the day;
And having buried children four,
Would not take pains to try for more.
Nor sister either had, nor brother:              15
They seemed just tallied[4] for each other.

Their moral[5] and economy[6]
Most perfectly they made agree:
Each virtue kept its proper bound,
Nor trespassed on the other's ground.              20
Nor fame nor censure they regarded;
They neither punished nor rewarded.
He cared not what the footmen did;
Her maids she neither praised, nor chid;[7]
So every servant took his course,              25
And bad at first, they all grew worse.
Slothful disorder filled his stable,
And sluttish plenty decked her table.
Their beer was strong; their wine was port;
Their meal was large; their grace was short.        30
They gave the poor the remnant-meat,
Just when it grew not fit to eat.

They paid the church and parish rate,[8]
And took, but read not the receipt;
For which they claimed their Sunday's due,       35
Of slumbering in an upper pew.

1. A frequently translated passage from Seneca's *Thyestes*:

> Climb at Court for me that will.
> Tottering Favor's slippery hill.
> All I seek is to lie still.
> Settled in some secret nest
> In calm leisure let me rest;
> And far off the public stage
> Pass away my silent age.
> (trans. Andrew Marvell)

2. According to the Bible, man's normal life span is 70, threescore and ten.
3. Ate (a common and proper 18th-century form).
4. Fitted.
5. Morality.
6. Household practice.
7. Chided.
8. Assessments for the clergy and the poor.

No man's defects sought they to know;
So never made themselves a foe.
No man's good deeds did they commend;
So never raised themselves a friend.                          40
Nor cherished they relations poor,
That might decrease their present store;
Nor barn nor house did they repair,
That might oblige their future heir.

They neither added[9] nor confounded,[1]                     45
They neither wanted[2] nor abounded.
Each Christmas they accompts[3] did clear,
And wound their bottom[4] round the year.
Nor tear nor smile did they employ
At news of public grief or joy.                               50
When bells were rung, and bonfires[5] made,
If asked they ne'er denied their aid:
Their jug was to the ringers carried,
Whoever either died or married.
Their billet at the fire was found,                           55
Whoever was deposed, or crowned.

Nor good, nor bad, nor fools, nor wise;
They would not learn, nor could advise:[6]
Without love, hatred, joy, or fear,
They led a kind of—as it were:
Nor wished, nor cared, nor laughed, nor cried:
And so they lived; and so they died.

                                                          1718

THOMAS GRAY

## Elegy Written in a Country Churchyard

The curfew[1] tolls the knell of parting day,
    The lowing herd wind slowly o'er the lea,
The plowman homeward plods his weary way,
    And leaves the world to darkness and to me.

Now fades the glimmering landscape on the sight,            5
    And all the air a solemn stillness holds,
Save where the beetle wheels his droning flight,
    And drowsy tinklings lull the distant folds;

Save that from yonder ivy-mantled tower
    The moping owl does to the moon complain               10
Of such, as wand'ring near her secret bower,
    Molest her ancient solitary reign.

9. Hoarded.
1. Wasted.
2. Were in need.
3. Accounts.
4. Thread: they tied up loose ends.
5. Church-bells were rung for funerals
and weddings; bonfires were lighted when
a new ruler was crowned.
6. Think.
1. As evening approached, a bell signified that fires were to be extinguished.

Beneath those rugged elms, that yew tree's shade,
    Where heaves the turf in many a mold'ring heap,
Each in his narrow cell forever laid,              15
    The rude[2] forefathers of the hamlet sleep.

The breezy call of incense-breathing morn,
    The swallow twittering from the straw-built shed,
The cock's shrill clarion, or the echoing horn,[3]
    No more shall rouse them from their lowly bed.    20

For them no more the blazing hearth shall burn,
    Or busy housewife ply her evening care;
No children run to lisp their sire's return,
    Or climb his knees the envied kiss to share.

Oft did the harvest to their sickle yield,          25
    Their furrow oft the stubborn glebe[4] has broke;
How jocund did they drive their team afield!
    How bowed the woods beneath their sturdy stroke!

Let not Ambition mock their useful toil,
    Their homely joys, and destiny obscure;    30
Nor Grandeur hear with a disdainful smile
    The short and simple annals of the poor.

The boast of heraldry,[5] the pomp of power,
    And all that beauty, all that wealth e'er gave,
Awaits alike the inevitable hour.          35
    The paths of glory lead but to the grave.

Nor you, ye proud, impute to these the fault,
    If Memory o'er their tomb no trophies[6] raise,
Where through the long-drawn aisle and fretted[7] vault
    The pealing anthem swells the note of praise.    40

Can storied[8] urn or animated[9] bust
    Back to its mansion call the fleeting breath?
Can Honor's voice provoke[1] the silent dust,
    Or Flattery soothe the dull cold ear of Death?

Perhaps in this neglected spot is laid          45
    Some heart once pregnant with celestial fire;
Hands that the rod of empire might have swayed,
    Or waked to ecstasy the living lyre.

But Knowledge to their eyes her ample page
    Rich with the spoils of time did ne'er unroll;    50
Chill Penury repressed their noble rage,
    And froze the genial current of the soul.

2. Rustic.
3. Hunting horn.
4. Soil.
5. Noble ancestry.
6. Memorials of accomplishments.

7. Ornamented.
8. With descriptive epitaphs.
9. Lifelike.
1. Enliven.

Full many a gem of purest ray serene,
   The dark unfathomed caves of ocean bear:
Full many a flower is born to blush unseen,      55
   And waste its sweetness on the desert air.

Some village Hampden,[2] that with dauntless breast
   The little tyrant of his fields withstood;
Some mute inglorious Milton here may rest,
   Some Cromwell guiltless of his country's blood.     60

Th' applause of listening senates to command,
   The threats of pain and ruin to despise,
To scatter plenty o'er a smiling land,
   And read their history in a nation's eyes

Their lot forbade: nor circumscribed alone     65
   Their growing virtues, but their crimes confined;
Forbade to wade through slaughter to a throne,
   And shut the gates of mercy on mankind,

The struggling pangs of conscious truth to hide,
   To quench the blushes of ingenuous shame,     70
Or heap the shrine of Luxury and Pride
   With incense kindled at the Muse's flame.

Far from the madding[3] crowd's ignoble strife,
   Their sober wishes never learned to stray;
Along the cool sequestered vale of life     75
   They kept the noiseless tenor[4] of their way.

Yet ev'n these bones from insult to protect
   Some frail memorial still erected nigh,
With uncouth rhymes and shapeless sculpture decked,
   Implores the passing tribute of a sigh.     80

Their name, their years, spelt by th' unlettered Muse,
   The place of fame and elegy supply:
And many a holy text around she strews,
   That teach the rustic moralist to die.

For who to dumb Forgetfulness a prey,     85
   This pleasing anxious being e'er resigned,
Left the warm precincts of the cheerful day,
   Nor cast one longing lingering look behind?

On some fond breast the parting soul relies,
   Some pious drops the closing eye requires;     90
Ev'n from the tomb the voice of Nature cries,
   Ev'n in our ashes live their wonted fires.

2. An opponent of Charles I.    4. Course.
3. Acting as if mad.

For thee, who mindful of the unhonored dead
  Dost in these lines their artless tale relate;
If chance, by lonely contemplation led,          95
  Some kindred spirit shall inquire thy fate,

Haply some hoary-headed swain may say,
  "Oft have we seen him at the peep of dawn
Brushing with hasty steps the dews away
  To meet the sun upon the upland lawn.      100

"There at the foot of yonder nodding beech
  That wreathes its old fantastic roots so high,
His listless length at noontide would he stretch.
  And pore upon the brook that babbles by.

"Hard by yon wood, now smiling as in scorn,     105
  Mutt'ring his wayward fancies he would rove,
Now drooping, woeful wan, like one forlorn,
  Or crazed with care, or crossed in hopeless love.

"One morn I missed him on the customed hill,
  Along the heath and near his favorite tree;    110
Another came; nor yet beside the rill,
  Nor up the lawn, nor at the wood was he;

"The next with dirges due in sad array
  Slow through the churchway path we saw him borne.
Approach and read (for thou canst read) the lay,   115
  Graved on the stone beneath yon aged thorn."

### The Epitaph

*Here rests his head upon the lap of Earth*
  *A youth to Fortune and to Fame unknown,*
*Fair Science*[5] *frowned not on his humble birth,*
  *And Melancholy marked him for her own.*    120

*Large was his bounty, and his soul sincere,*
  *Heaven did a recompense as largely send:*
*He gave to Misery all he had, a tear,*
  *He gained from Heaven ('twas all he wished) a friend.*

*No farther seek his merits to disclose,*    125
  *Or draw his frailties from their dread abode*
*(There they alike in trembling hope repose),*
  *The bosom of his Father and his God.*

1751

5. Learning.

HOWARD NEMEROV

# Life Cycle of Common Man

Roughly figured, this man of moderate habits,
This average consumer of the middle class,
Consumed in the course of his average life span
Just under half a million cigarettes,
Four thousand fifths of gin and about                    5
A quarter as much vermouth; he drank
Maybe a hundred thousand cups of coffee,
And counting his parents' share it cost
Something like half a million dollars
To put him through life. How many beasts          10
Died to provide him with meat, belt and shoes
Cannot be certainly said.
                                        But anyhow,
It is in this way that a man travels through time,
Leaving behind him a lengthening trail                  15
Of empty bottles and bones, of broken shoes,
Frayed collars and worn out or outgrown
Diapers and dinnerjackets, silk ties and slickers.

Given the energy and security thus achieved,
He did . . . ? What? The usual things, of course,     20
The eating, dreaming, drinking and begetting,
And he worked for the money which was to pay
For the eating, et cetera, which were necessary
If he were to go on working for the money, et cetera,
But chiefly he talked. As the bottles and bones     25
Accumulated behind him, the words proceeded
Steadily from the front of his face as he
Advanced into the silence and made it verbal.
Who can tally the tale of his words? A lifetime
Would barely suffice for their repetition;              30
If you merely printed all his commas the result
Would be a very large volume, and the number of times
He said "thank you" or "very little sugar, please,"
Would stagger the imagination. There were also
Witticisms, platitudes, and statements beginning     35
"It seems to me" or "As I always say."

Consider the courage in all that, and behold the man
Walking into deep silence, with the ectoplastic
Cartoon's balloon of speech proceeding
Steadily out of the front of his face, the words       40
Borne along on the breath which is his spirit
Telling the numberless tale of his untold Word[1]
Which makes the world his apple, and forces him to eat.

                                                    1960

---

1. *Logos,* the principle of creation and order.

W. H. AUDEN

# The Unknown Citizen

*(To JS/o7/M/378*
*This Marble Monument*
*Is Erected by the State)*[1]

He was found by the Bureau of Statistics to be
One against whom there was no official complaint,
And all the reports on his conduct agree
That, in the modern sense of an old-fashioned word, he was a saint,
For in everything he did he served the Greater Community.    5
Except for the War till the day he retired
He worked in a factory and never got fired,
But satisfied his employers, Fudge Motors Inc.
Yet he wasn't a scab or odd in his views,
For his Union reports that he paid his dues,    10
(Our report on his Union shows it was sound)
And our Social Psychology workers found
That he was popular with his mates and liked a drink.
The Press are convinced that he bought a paper every day
And that his reactions to advertisements were normal in every way.    15
Policies taken out in his name prove that he was fully insured,
And his Health-card shows he was once in hospital but left it cured.
Both Producers Research and High-Grade Living declare
He was fully sensible to the advantages of the Installment Plan
And had everything necessary to the Modern Man,    20
A phonograph, a radio, a car and a frigidaire.
Our researchers into Public Opinion are content
That he held the proper opinions for the time of year;
When there was peace, he was for peace; when there was war, he
    went.
He was married and added five children to the population,    25
Which our Eugenist says was the right number for a parent of his
    generation,
And our teachers report that he never interfered with their education.
Was he free? Was he happy? The question is absurd:
Had anything been wrong, we should certainly have heard.

1940

MATTHEW ARNOLD

# Lines Written in Kensington Gardens

In this lone, open glade I lie,
Screened by deep boughs on either hand;
And at its end, to stay the eye,
Those black-crowned, red-boled[2] pine-trees stand!

---

1. The title and subtitle parallel the inscription on the Tomb of the Unknown Soldier.

2. Red-trunked.

Birds here make song, each bird has his,                5
Across the girdling city's hum.
How green under the boughs it is!
How thick the tremulous sheep-cries come!

Sometimes a child will cross the glade
To take his nurse his broken toy;                       10
Sometimes a thrush flit overhead
Deep in her unknown day's employ.

Here at my feet what wonders pass,
What endless, active life is here!
What blowing daisies, fragrant grass!                   15
An air-stirred forest, fresh and clear.

Scarce fresher is the mountain-sod
Where the tired angler lies, stretched out,
And, eased of basket and of rod,
Counts his day's spoil, the spotted trout.              20

In the huge world, which roars hard by,
Be others happy if they can!
But in my helpless cradle I
Was breathed on by the rural Pan.[3]

I, on men's impious uproar hurled,                      25
Think often, as I hear them rave,
That peace has left the upper world
And now keeps only in the grave.

Yet here is peace for ever new!
When I who watch them am away,                          30
Still all things in this glade go through
The changes of their quiet day.

Then to their happy rest they pass!
The flowers upclose, the birds are fed,
The night comes down upon the grass,                    35
The child sleeps warmly in his bed.

Calm soul of all things! make it mine
To feel, amid the city's jar,
That there abides a peace of thine,
Man did not make, and cannot mar.                       40

The will to neither strive nor cry,
The power to feel with others give!
Calm, calm me more! nor let me die
Before I have begun to live.

                                                   1852

3. God of shepherds and huntsmen.

WILLIAM BLAKE

# Song of Innocence[1]

Piping down the valleys wild,
Piping songs of pleasant glee,
On a cloud I saw a child,
And he laughing said to me:

"Pipe a song about a Lamb!"                    5
So I piped with merry cheer.
"Piper, pipe that song again";
So I piped: he wept to hear.

"Drop thy pipe, thy happy pipe;
Sing thy songs of happy cheer!"              10
So I sung the same again,
While he wept with joy to hear.

"Piper, sit thee down and write
In a book that all may read."
So he vanished from my sight;               15
And I plucked a hollow reed,

And I made a rural pen,
And I stained the water clear,
And I wrote my happy songs
Every child may joy to hear.                  20

1789

ALEXANDER POPE

# Ode on Solitude

Happy the man, whose wish and care
   A few paternal acres bound,
Content to breathe his native air,
                  In his own ground.

Whose herds with milk, whose fields with bread,      5
   Whose flocks supply him with attire,
Whose trees in summer yield him shade,
                  In winter fire.

Blest, who can unconcern'dly find
   Hours, days, and years slide soft away,          10
In health of body, peace of mind,
                  Quiet by day,

Sound sleep by night; study and ease
   Together mixed; sweet recreation,
And innocence, which most does please             15
                  With meditation.

1. The introductory poem in Blake's volume, *Songs of Innocence.*

Thus let me live, unseen, unknown;
Thus unlamented let me die;
Steal from the world, and not a stone
                    Tell where I lie.                    20

ca. 1700

CHRISTOPHER MARLOWE

## The Passionate Shepherd to His Love

Come live with me and be my love,
And we will all the pleasures prove[1]
That valleys, groves, hills, and fields,
Woods, or steepy mountain yields.

And we will sit upon the rocks,                    5
Seeing the shepherds feed their flocks,
By shallow rivers to whose falls
Melodious birds sing madrigals.

And I will make thee beds of roses
And a thousand fragrant posies,                    10
A cap of flowers, and a kirtle[2]
Embroidered all with leaves of myrtle;

A gown made of the finest wool
Which from our pretty lambs we pull;
Fair lined slippers for the cold,                    15
With buckles of the purest gold;

A belt of straw and ivy buds,
With coral clasps and amber studs:
And if these pleasures may thee move,
Come live with me, and be my love.                    20

The shepherd swains[3] shall dance and sing
For thy delight each May morning:
If these delights thy mind may move,
Then live with me and be my love.

                                                   1600

SIR  WALTER  RALEGH

## The Nymph's Reply to the Shepherd

If all the world and love were young,
And truth in every shepherd's tongue,
These pretty pleasures might me move
To live with thee and be thy love.

Time drives the flocks from field to fold,                    5
When rivers rage, and rocks grow cold,

1. Try.                                    3. Youths.
2. Gown.

And Philomel[1] becometh dumb;
The rest complain of cares to come.

The flowers do fade, and wanton fields
To wayward winter reckoning yields:                    10
A honey tongue, a heart of gall,
Is fancy's spring, but sorrow's fall.

Thy gowns, thy shoes, they beds of roses,
Thy cap, thy kirtle, and thy posies
Soon break, soon wither, soon forgotten;               15
In folly ripe, in reason rotten.

Thy belt of straw and ivy buds,
Thy coral clasps and amber studs,
All these in me no means can move
To come to thee and be thy love.                       20

But could youth last, and love still breed,
Had joys no date,[2] nor age no need,
Then these delights my mind might move
To live with thee and be thy love.

                                                   1600

JOHN DONNE

## The Bait

Come live with me, and be my love,
And we will some new pleasures prove,
Of golden sands, and crystal brooks:
With silken lines, and silver hooks.

There will the river whispering run                     5
Warmed by thy eyes, more than the sun.
And there th' enamored fish will stay,
Begging themselves they may betray.

When thou wilt swim in that live bath,
Each fish, which every channel hath,                   10
Will amorously to thee swim,
Gladder to catch thee, than thou him.

If thou to be so seen be'st loath
By sun, or moon, thou dark'nest both,
And if myself have leave to see,                       15
I need not their light, having thee.

Let others freeze with angling reeds,[1]
And cut their legs with shells and weeds,
Or treacherously poor fish beset
With strangling snare, or windowy net.                 20

1. The nightingale.                     1. Rods.
2. End.

Let coarse bold hands, from slimy nest
The bedded fish in banks out-wrest;
Or curious traitors, sleave-silk[2] flies,
Bewitch poor fishes' wand'ring eyes.

For thee, thou need'st no such deceit,                    25
For thou thyself art thine own bait;
That fish that is not catched thereby,
Alas, is wiser far than I.

                                                    1612

C. DAY LEWIS

## Song

Come, live with me and be my love,
And we will all the pleasures prove
Of peace and plenty, bed and board,
That chance employment may afford.

I'll handle dainties on the docks                          5
And thou shalt read of summer frocks:
At evening by the sour canals
We'll hope to hear some madrigals.

Care on thy maiden brow shall put
A wreath of wrinkles, and thy foot                        10
Be shod with pain: not silken dress
But toil shall tire thy loveliness.

Hunger shall make thy modest zone
And cheat fond death of all but bone—
If these delights thy mind may move,                      15
Then live with me and be my love.

                                                    1935

LOUIS SIMPSON

## The Green Shepherd

Here sit a shepherd and a shepherdess,
He playing on his melancholy flute;
The sea wind ruffles up her simple dress
And shows the delicacy of her foot.

And there you see Constantinople's wall                    5
With arrows and Greek fire, molten lead;
Down from a turret seven virgins fall,
Hands folded, each one praying on her head.

The shepherd yawns and puts his flute away.
It's time, she murmurs, we were going back.               10

2. Untwisted silk.

He offers certain reasons she should stay—
But neither sees the dragon on their track.

A dragon like a car in a garage
Is in the wood, his long tail sticking out.
Here rides St. George[1] swinging his sword and targe,[2]     15
And sticks the grinning dragon in the snout.

Puffing a smoke ring, like the cigarette
Over Times Square,[3] Sir Dragon snorts his last.
St. George takes off his armor in a sweat.
The Middle Ages have been safely passed.     20

What is the sail that crosses the still bay,
Unnoticed by the shepherds? It could be
A caravel that's sailing to Cathay,[4]
Westward from Palos[5] on the unknown sea.

But the green shepherd travels in her eye     25
And whispers nothings in his lady's ear,
And sings a little song, that roses die,
*Carpe diem,*[6] which she seems pleased to hear.

The vessel they ignored still sails away
So bravely on the water, Westward Ho!     30
And murdering, in a religious way,
Brings Jesus to the Gulf of Mexico.

Now Portugal is fading, and the state
Of Castile rising purple on Peru;
Now England, now America grows great—     35
With which these lovers have nothing to do.

What do they care if time, uncompassed, drift
To China, and the crew is a baboon?
But let him whisper always, and her lift
The oceans in her eyelids to the moon.     40

The dragon rises crackling in the air,
And who is god but Dagon?[7] Wings careen,
Rejoicing, on the Russian hemisphere.
Meanwhile, the shepherd dotes upon her skin.

Old Aristotle, having seen this pass,     45
From where he studied in the giant's cave,
Went in and shut his book and locked the brass
And lay down with a shudder in his grave.

1. The patron saint of England and legendary slayer of the dragon.
2. Shield.
3. A cigarette billboard which emitted steam to simulate smoke.
4. China.
5. Columbus sailed from the Spanish port of Palos on his first voyage; Cortez returned there after his conquest of Mexico.
6. "Live for the day": a traditional theme in love poetry.
7. The god of the Philistines, half man, half fish. See *Judges* 16.

The groaning pole had gone more than a mile;
These shepherds did not feel it where they loved,                 50
For time was sympathetic all the while
And on the magic mountain nothing moved.

1959


GARY SNYDER

## Not Leaving the House

When Kai is born
I quit going out

Hang around the kitchen—make cornbread
Let nobody in.
Mail is flat.                                                     5
      Masa lies on her side, Kai sighs,
      Non washes and sweeps
We sit and watch
      Masa nurse, and drink green tea.

Navajo turquoise beads over the bed                              10
A peacock tail feather at the head
A badger pelt from Nagano-ken
For a mattress; under the sheet;
A pot of yogurt setting
Under the blankets, at his feet.                                 15

Masa, Kai,
And Non, our friend
In the green garden light reflected in
Not leaving the house.
From dawn til late at night                                      20
      making a new world of ourselves
      around this life.

1970


FULKE GREVILLE, LORD BROOKE

## The Golden Age Was When the World Was Young

The Golden Age was when the world was young,
Nature so rich, as earth did need no sowing,
Malice not known, the serpents had not stung,
Wit was but sweet affection's overflowing.

Desire was free, and Beauty's first-begotten;                    5
Beauty then neither net,[1] nor made by art,
Words out of thoughts brought forth, and not forgotten,
The laws were inward that did rule the heart.

---

1. Snare.

The Brazen Age[2] is now when earth is worn,
Beauty grown sick, Nature corrupt and nought,                    10
Pleasure untimely dead as soon as born,
Both words and kindness[3] strangers to our thought:

If now this changing world do change her head,[4]
Caelica,[5] what have her new lords for to boast?
The old lord knows Desire is poorly fed,                         15
And sorrows[6] not a wavering province lost,
Since in the gilt age Saturn ruled alone,
    And in this painted, planets every one.
ca. 1585

JOHN MILTON

## At a Solemn Music

Blest[1] pair of Sirens, pledges of Heaven's joy,
Sphere-born harmonious sisters, Voice and Verse,
Wed your divine sounds, and mixed power employ
Dead things with inbreathed sense able to pierce,
And to our high-raised fantasy[2] present                        5
That undisturbed song of pure consent,[3]
Aye sung before the sapphire-colored throne
To him that sits thereon
With saintly shout and solemn jubilee,
Where the bright seraphim in burning row                         10
Their loud uplifted angel-trumpets blow,
And the cherubic host in thousand choirs
Touch their immortal harps of golden wires,
With those just spirits that wear victorious palms,[4]
Hymns devout and holy psalms                                     15
Singing everlastingly;
That we on earth with undiscording voice
May rightly answer that melodious noise;
As once we did, till disproportioned sin
Jarred against nature's chime, and with harsh din                20
Broke the fair music that all creatures made
To their great Lord, whose love their motion swayed
In perfect diapason,[5] whilst they stood
In first obedience, and their state of good.
O may we soon again renew that song,                             25
And keep in tune with Heaven, till God ere long
To his celestial consort us unite.
To live with him, and sing in endless morn of light.
ca. 1632

2. The age of war and violence, usually considered to follow the Golden and Silver Ages.
3. Natural affection.
4. Ruler.
5. The sequence of which this poem is a part is addressed to the lady Caelica.
6. Mourns.

1. Unlike traditional sirens who used sweet song to entice men to destruction.
2. Imagination.
3. Harmony.
4. Indicating victory over sin.
5. Concord. When in tune with the universe, they are "swayed" by the "music of the spheres," the heavenly harmony to which the planets "danced."

ANDREW MARVELL

# The Mower, Against Gardens

Luxurious[1] man, to bring his vice in use,
    Did after him the world seduce,
And from the fields the flowers and plants allure,
    When nature was most plain and pure.
He first enclosed within the garden's square          5
    A dead and standing pool of air,
And a more luscious earth for them did knead,
    Which stupefied them while it fed.
The pink[2] grew then as double as his mind;
    The nutriment did change the kind.                10
With strange perfumes he did the roses taint;
    And flowers themselves were taught to paint.[3]
The tulip, white, did for complexion seek,
    And learned to interline its cheek;
Its onion root[4] they then so high did hold          15
    That one was for a meadow sold.[5]
Another world was searched, through oceans new,
    To find the Marvel of Peru.[6]
And yet these rarities might be allowed
    To man, that sov'reign thing and proud,           20
Had he not dealt[7] between the bark and tree,
    Forbidden mixtures there to see.
No plant now knew the stock from which it came;
    He grafts upon the wild the tame,
That the uncertain and adult'rate fruit               25
    Might put the palate in dispute.
His green seraglio has its eunuchs too,
    Lest any tyrant him outdo;
And in the cherry he does nature vex,
    To procreate without a sex.                       30
'Tis all enforced;[8] the fountain and the grot,
    While the sweet fields do lie forgot,
Where willing nature does to all dispense
    A wild and fragrant innocence;
And fauns and fairies do the meadows till            35
    More by their presence than their skill.
Their statues, polished by some ancient hand,
    May to adorn the gardens stand;
But, howsoe'er the figures do excel,
    The gods themselves with us do dwell.            40

                                            1681

1. Self-indulgent.
2. A *Dianthus* flower; figuratively, the embodiment of perfection.
3. Use artificial coloring.
4. Bulb.
5. In the 17th century tulips were held in extremely high regard, so much so that some countries were said to have tulip-omania.
6. The "four-o'clock" plant.
7. Artificially placed.
8. Imposed.

JONI MITCHELL

# Woodstock[9]

I came upon a child of God
He was walking along the road
And I asked him, where are you going
And this he told me
I'm going on down to Yasgur's farm                                    5
I'm going to join in a rock'n'roll band
I'm going to camp out on the land
And try an' get my soul free
    We are stardust
    We are golden                                    10
    And we've got to get ourselves
    Back to the garden

Then can I walk beside you
I have come here to lose the smog
And I feel tobe a cog in something turning                            15
Well maybe it is just the time of year
Or maybe it's the time of man
I don't know who I am
But life is for learning
    We are stardust
    We are golden                                    20
    And we've got to get ourselves
    Back to the garden

By the time we got to Woodstock
We were half a million strong                                         25
And everywhere there was song and celebration
And I dreamed I saw the bombers
Riding shotgun in the sky
And they were turning into butterflies
Above our nation                                                      30
    We are stardust
    We are golden
    And we've got to get ourselves
    Back to the garden

1969

PERCY BYSSHE SHELLEY

# The World's Great Age Begins Anew[1]

The world's great age begins anew,
   The golden years return,
The earth doth like a snake[2] renew

9. Written after the rock festival there in 1969, celebrating not only the festival but what came to be called the "Woodstock Nation."
1. A chorus from *Hellas*, a "lyrical drama" celebrating the newly proclaimed independence of Greece and describing more generally a universal passion for liberty.
2. Which sheds its skin after hibernation.

Her winter weeds[3] outworn:
Heaven smiles, and faiths and empires gleam,                     5
Like wrecks of a dissolving dream.

A brighter Hellas rears its mountains
    From waves serener far;
A new Peneus[4] rolls his fountains
    Against the morning star.                                    10
Where fairer Tempes[5] bloom, there sleep
Young Cyclads[6] on a sunnier deep.

A loftier Argo[7] cleaves the main,
    Fraught with a later prize;
Another Orpheus[8] sings again,                                  15
    And loves, and weeps, and dies.
A new Ulysses leaves once more
Calypso[9] for his native shore.

Oh, write no more tale of Troy,
    If earth Death's scroll must be!                             20
Nor mix with Laian rage[1] the joy
    Which dawns upon the free:
Although a subtler Sphinx renew
Riddles of death Thebes never knew.

Another Athens shall arise,                                      25
    And to remoter time
Bequeath, like sunset to the skies,
    The splendor of its prime;
And leave, if nought so bright may live,
All earth can take or Heaven can give.                           30

Saturn and Love their long repose
    Shall burst, more bright and good
Than all who fell, than One who rose,
    Than many unsubdued:[2]
Not gold, not blood, their altar dowers,                         35
But votive tears and symbol flowers.

Oh, cease! must hate and death return?
    Cease! must men kill and die?
Cease! drain not to its dregs the urn
    Of bitter prophecy.                                          40

3. Clothes.
4. A river in Thessaly, legendary for its beauty.
5. Tempe was the valley of the Peneus, near Mt. Olympus, and a classical synonym for valleys of serene beauty.
6. Islands in the Archipelago.
7. Jason's ship in which he sailed in search of the Golden Fleece.
8. In Greek legend, an extraordinary poet and musician whose music gained the release of his wife from the realm of the dead—on the condition that he not look at her until they reached earth. At the last moment he broke his pledge and she vanished.

9. An island queen with whom Ulysses spent seven years after the Trojan War before returning home.
1. In a rage Oedipus killed Laius, king of Thebes; he then solved the riddle of the Sphinx and became himself king, marrying Queen Jocasta. Later, Laius and Jocasta turned out to be his own parents.
2. In the envisioned "great age," Saturn and Love are the restored deities. Shelley identified "those who fell" as "the Gods of Greece, Asia, and Egypt"; the "One who rose" as Christ; and the "many unsubdued" as "the monstrous objects of the idolatry of China, India, the Antarctic islands, and the native tribes of America."

The world is weary of the past,
Oh, might it die or rest at last!

1822

ROBERT FROST

## Nothing Gold Can Stay

Nature's first green is gold,
Her hardest hue to hold.
Her early leaf's a flower;
But only so an hour.
Then leaf subsides to leaf.                    5
So Eden sank to grief,
So dawn goes down to day.
Nothing gold can stay.

1923

WILLIAM CONGREVE

## [The Present Time]¹

Should hope and fear thy heart alternate tear,        55
Or love, or hate, or rage, or anxious care,
Whatever passions may thy mind infest,
(Where is that mind which passions ne'er molest?)
Amidst the pangs of such intestine strife,
Still think the present day the last of life;         60
Defer not till tomorrow to be wise,
Tomorrow's sun to thee may never rise.
Or should tomorrow chance to cheer thy sight
With her enlivening and unlooked-for light,
How grateful will appear her dawning rays,            65
As favors unexpected doubly please.
Who thus can think and who such thoughts pursues,
Content may keep his life, or calmly lose;
All proofs of this thou mayest thyself receive,
When leisure from affairs will give thee leave.       70
Come, see thy friend, retired without regret,
Forgetting care, or striving to forget;
In easy contemplation soothing time
With morals much, and now and then with rhyme;
Not so robust in body as in mind,                     75
And always undejected, though declined;
Not wondering at the world's new wicked ways,
Compared with those of our forefathers' days;
For virtue now is neither more or less,
And vice is only varied in the dress.                 80
Believe it, men have ever been the same,
And all the golden age is but a dream.

1729

1. Excerpted from *An Epistle to Viscount Cobham*. Verse epistles were fairly common in the 18th century, taking their cue from the Roman poet Horace.

HENRY VAUGHAN

## The Retreat

Happy those early days! when I
Shined in my angel infancy.
Before I understood this place
Appointed for my second race,
Or taught my soul to fancy aught                          5
But a white, celestial thought;
When yet I had not walked above
A mile or two from my first love,
And looking back, at that short space,
Could see a glimpse of His bright face;                   10
When on some gilded cloud or flower
My gazing soul would dwell an hour,
And in those weaker glories spy
Some shadows of eternity;
Before I taught my tongue to wound                        15
My conscience with a sinful sound,
Or had the black art to dispense
A several[1] sin to every sense,
But felt through all this fleshly dress
Bright shoots of everlastingness.                         20
    O, how I long to travel back,
And tread again that ancient track!
That I might once more reach that plain
Where first I left my glorious train,
From whence th' enlightened spirit sees                   25
That shady city of palm trees.
But, ah! my soul with too much stay
Is drunk, and staggers in the way.
Some men a forward motion love;
But I by backward steps would move,                       30
And when this dust falls to the urn,
In that state I came, return.

1650

ALAN DUGAN

## Winter for an Untenable Situation

Outside it is cold. Inside,
although the fire has gone out
and all the furniture is burnt,
it is much warmer. Oh let
the white refrigerator car                                5
of day go by in glacial thunder:
when it gets dark, and when
the branches of the tree outside
look wet because it is so dark,
oh we will burn the house itself                          10

1. Separate.

for warmth, the wet tree too,
you will burn me, I will burn you,
and when the last brick of the fireplace
has been cracked for its nut of warmth
and the last bone cracked for its coal                         15
and the andirons themselves sucked cold,
we will move on!, remembering
the burning house, the burning tree,
the burning you, the burning me,
the ashes, the brick-dust, the bitter iron,                    20
and the time when we were warm,
and say, "Those were the good old days."

1963

EDWIN ARLINGTON ROBINSON

## Mr. Flood's Party

Old Eben Flood, climbing alone one night
Over the hill between the town below
And the forsaken upland hermitage
That held as much as he should ever know
On earth again of home, paused warily.                         5
The road was his and not a native near;
And Eben, having leisure, said aloud,
For no man else in Tilbury Town to hear:

"Well, Mr. Flood, we have the harvest moon
Again, and we may not have many more;                          10
The bird is on the wing, the poet says,[1]
And you and I have said it here before.
Drink to the bird." He raised up to the light
The jug that he had gone so far to fill,
And answered huskily: "Well, Mr. Flood,                        15
Since you propose it, I believe I will."

Alone, as if enduring to the end
A valiant armor of scarred hopes outworn,
He stood there in the middle of the road
Like Roland's ghost winding a silent horn.[2]                  20
Below him, in the town among the trees,
Where friends of other days had honored him,
A phantom salutation of the dead
Rang thinly till old Eben's eyes were dim.

Then, as a mother lays her sleeping child                      25
Down tenderly, fearing it may awake,
He set the jug down slowly at his feet
With trembling care, knowing that most things break;
And only when assured that on firm earth
It stood, as the uncertain lives of men                        30

1. Edward Fitzgerald, in "The Rubáiyat of Omar Khayyám," so describes the "Bird of Time."     2. In French legend, Roland's powerful ivory horn was used to warn his allies of impending attack.

Assuredly did not, he paced away,
And with his hand extended paused again:

"Well, Mr. Flood, we have not met like this
In a long time; and many a change has come
To both of us, I fear, since last it was                        35
We had a drop together. Welcome home!"
Convivially returning with himself,
Again he raised the jug up to the light;
And with an acquiescent quaver said:
"Well, Mr. Flood, if you insist, I might.                        40

"Only a very little, Mr. Flood—
For auld lang syne. No more, sir; that will do."
So, for the time, apparently it did,
And Eben evidently thought so too;
For soon amid the silver loneliness                             45
Of night he lifted up his voice and sang,
Secure, with only two moons listening,
Until the whole harmonious landscape rang—

"For auld lang syne." The weary throat gave out,
The last word wavered, and the song was done.                   50
He raised again the jug regretfully
And shook his head, and was again alone.
There was not much that was ahead of him,
And there was nothing in the town below—
Where strangers would have shut the many doors                  55
That many friends had opened long ago.

                                                       1921

ALFRED, LORD TENNYSON

# Tears, Idle Tears[1]

Tears, idle tears, I know not what they mean,
Tears from the depth of some divine despair
Rise in the heart, and gather to the eyes,
In looking on the happy autumn-fields,
And thinking of the days that are no more.                       5

Fresh as the first beam glittering on a sail,
That brings our friends up from the underworld,
Sad as the last which reddens over one
That sinks with all we love below the verge;
So sad, so fresh, the days that are no more.                    10

Ah, sad and strange as in dark summer dawns
The earliest pipe of half-awakened birds
To dying ears, when unto dying eyes
The casement slowly grows a glimmering square;
So sad, so strange, the days that are no more.                  15

1. A song from *The Princess,* a long narrative poem about what the mid-nineteenth
century called the "new woman."

Dear as remembered kisses after death,
And sweet as those by hopeless fancy feigned
On lips that are for others; deep as love,
Deep as first love, and wild with all regret;
O Death in Life, the days that are no more! 20

1847

DYLAN THOMAS

## Fern Hill

Now as I was young and easy under the apple boughs
About the lilting house and happy as the grass was green,
    The night above the dingle starry,
      Time let me hail and climb
    Golden in the heydays of his eyes, 5
And honored among wagons I was prince of the apple towns
And once below a time I lordly had the trees and leaves
    Trail with daisies and barley
    Down the rivers of the windfall light.

And as I was green and carefree, famous among the barns 10
About the happy yard and singing as the farm was home,
    In the sun that is young once only,
      Time let me play and be
    Golden in the mercy of his means,
And green and golden I was huntsman and herdsman, the calves 15
Sang to my horn, the foxes on the hills barked clear and cold,
    And the sabbath rang slowly
    In the pebbles of the holy streams.

All the sun long it was running, it was lovely, the hay
Fields high as the house, the tunes from the chimneys, it was air 20
    And playing, lovely and watery
    And fire green as grass.
    And nightly under the simple stars
As I rode to sleep the owls were bearing the farm away,
All the moon long I heard, blessed among stables, the nightjars[1] 25
    Flying with the ricks,[2] and the horses
    Flashing into the dark.

And then to awake, and the farm, like a wanderer white
With the dew, come back, the cock on his shoulder: it was all
    Shining, it was Adam and maiden, 30
    The sky gathered again
    And the sun grew round that very day.
So it must have been after the birth of the simple light
In the first, spinning place, the spellbound horses walking warm
    Out of the whinnying green stable 35
    On to the fields of praise.

1. Birds.      2. Haystacks.

92    *Louis MacNeice*

And honored among foxes and pheasants by the gay house
Under the new made clouds and happy as the heart was long,
    In the sun born over and over,
        I ran my heedless ways,                                    40
    My wishes raced through the house-high hay
And nothing I cared, at my sky-blue trades, that time allows
In all his tuneful turning so few and such morning songs
    Before the children green and golden
        Follow him out of grace,                                   45

Nothing I cared, in the lamb white days, that time would take me
Up to the swallow-thronged loft by the shadow of my hand,
    In the moon that is always rising,
        Nor that riding to sleep
    I should hear him fly with the high fields                     50
And wake to the farm forever fled from the childless land.
Oh as I was young and easy in the mercy of his means,
        Time held me green and dying
    Though I sang in my chains like the sea.

                                                                   1946


D. H. LAWRENCE

## Piano

Softly, in the dusk, a woman is singing to me;
Taking me back down the vista of years, till I see
A child sitting under the piano, in the boom of the tingling strings
And pressing the small, poised feet of a mother who smiles as she sings.

In spite of myself, the insidious mastery of song                 5
Betrays me back, till the heart of me weeps to belong
To the old Sunday evenings at home, with winter outside
And hymns in the cozy parlor, the tinkling piano our guide.

So now it is vain for the singer to burst into clamor
With the great black piano appassionato. The glamour              10
Of childish days is upon me, my manhood is cast
Down in the flood of remembrance, I weep like a child for the past.

                                                                   1918


LOUIS MACNEICE

## Death of an Actress

I see from the paper that Florrie Forde[1] is dead—
Collapsed after singing to wounded soldiers,
At the age of sixty-five. The American notice
Says no doubt all that need be said

---

1. A music hall artiste who specialized in nostalgia and patriotic songs. She made famous such songs as "Pack Up Your Troubles" and "Anybody Here Seen Kelly" and remained popular for more than 40 years until her death in 1940.

About this one-time chorus girl; whose rôle                5
For more than forty stifling years was giving
Sexual, sentimental, or comic entertainment,
A gaudy posy for the popular soul.

Plush and cigars: she waddled into the lights,
Old and huge and painted, in velvet anad tiara,          10
Her voice gone but around her head an aura
Of all her vanilla-sweet forgotten vaudeville nights.

With an elephantine shimmy and a sugared wink
She threw a trellis of Dorothy Perkins roses
Around an audience come from slum and suburb            15
And weary of the tea-leaves in the sink;

Who found her songs a rainbow leading west
To the home they never had, to the chocolate Sunday
Of boy and girl, to cowslip time, to the never-
Ending weekend Islands of the Blest.                    20

In the Isle of Man before the war before
The present one she made a ragtime favorite
Of "Tipperary," which became the swan-song
Of troop-ships on a darkened shore;

And during Munich sang her ancient quiz                 25
Of *Where's Bill Bailey?* and the chorus answered,
Muddling through and glad to have no answer:
Where's Bill Bailey? How do *we* know where he is!

Now on a late and bandaged April day
In a military hospital Miss Florrie                      30
Forde has made her positively last appearance
And taken her bow and gone correctly away.

Correctly. For she stood
For an older England, for children toddling
Hand in hand while the day was bright. Let the wren and robin    35
Gently with leaves cover the Babes in the Wood.

1940

W. B. YEATS

# After Long Silence

Speech after long silence; it is right,
All other lovers being estranged or dead,
Unfriendly lamplight hid under its shade,
The curtains drawn upon unfriendly night,
That we descant and yet again descant                   5
Upon the supreme theme of Art and Song:
Bodily decrepitude is wisdom; young
We loved each other and were ignorant.

1932

ANDREW MARVELL

# Bermudas

Where the remote Bermudas ride,
In th' ocean's bosom unespied,
From a small boat that rowed along,
The listening winds received this song:

"What should we do but sing His praise,                         5
That led us through the watery maze
Unto an isle so long unknown,
And yet far kinder than our own?
Where He the huge sea monsters wracks,[1]
That lift the deep upon their backs;                          10
He lands us on a grassy stage,
Safe from the storms, and prelate's rage.[2]
He gave us this eternal spring
Which here enamels everything,
And sends the fowls to us in care,                            15
On daily visits through the air;
He hangs in shades the orange bright,
Like golden lamps in a green night,
And does in the pomegranates close
Jewels more rich than Ormus[3] shows;                         20
He makes the figs our mouths to meet,
And throws the melons at our feet;
But apples[4] plants of such a price,
No tree could ever bear them twice;
With cedars, chosen by His hand,                              25
From Lebanon, He stores the land,
And makes the hollow seas, that roar,
Proclaim the ambergris[5] on shore;
He cast (of which we rather boast)
The Gospel's pearl upon our coast,                            30
And in these rocks for us did frame
A temple, where to sound His name.
O! let our voice His praise exalt,
Till it arrive at heaven's vault,
Which, thence (perhaps) rebounding, may                       35
Echo beyond the Mexique Bay."[6]

Thus sung they in the English boat,
An holy and a cheerful note;
And all the way, to guide their chime,
With falling oars they kept the time.                         40

1681

1. Destroys.
2. Bishop's rage. Marvell supported the Puritans in the English civil wars.
3. An island off Iran.
4. Pineapples.

5. A waxy substance secreted by the sperm whale and gathered from beaches to use in perfume.
6. Gulf of Mexico.

CLAUDE MCKAY

## The Tropics in New York

Bananas ripe and green, and ginger-root,
  Cocoa in pods and alligator pears,
And tangerines and mangoes and grape fruit,
  Fit for the highest prize at parish fairs,

Set in the window, bringing memories               5
  Of fruit-trees laden by low-singing rills,
And dewy dawns, and mystical blue skies
  In benediction over nun-like hills.

My eyes grew dim, and I could no more gaze;
  A wave of longing through my body swept,       10
And, hungry for the old, familiar ways,
  I turned aside and bowed my head and wept.

                                                              1922

NICHOLAS BRETON

## Rare News

News from the heavens! All wars are at an end,
Twixt higher powers a happy peace concluded;
Fortune and Faith are sworn each other's friend,
And Love's desire shall never be deluded.

Time hath set down the compass of his course,      5
Nature her work and Excellence her art,
Care his content and Cruelty his curse,
Labor his desire and Honor his desert.

Words shall be deeds, and men shall be divine,
Women all saints or angels in degrees;            10
Clouds shall away, the sun shall ever shine,
Heavens shall have power to hinder none of these.
  These are the articles of the conclusion,
  Which, when they fall,[1] then look for a confusion.

                                                              1591

GEORGE BERKELEY

## On the Prospect of Planting Arts and Learning in America

The Muse, disgusted at an age and clime
  Barren of every glorious theme,
In distant lands now waits a better time,
  Producing subjects worthy fame:

---

1. Occur.

In happy climes where from the genial sun                    5
    And virgin earth such scenes ensue,
The force of art by nature seems outdone,
    And fancied beauties by the true:

In happy climes, the seat of innocence,
    Where nature guides and virtue rules,                    10
Where men shall not impose, for truth and sense,
    The pedantry of courts and schools:

There shall be sung another golden age,
    The rise of empire and of arts,
The good and great inspiring epic rage,                      15
    The wisest heads and noblest hearts.

Not such as Europe breeds in her decay;
    Such as she bred when fresh and young,
When heavenly flame did animate her clay,
    By future poets shall be sung.                           20

Westward the course of empire takes its way;
    The first four acts already past,
A fifth shall close the drama with the day;
    Time's noblest offspring is the last.[2]

1752

LOUIS SIMPSON

# In California

Here I am, troubling the dream coast
With my New York face,
Bearing among the realtors
And tennis-players my dark preoccupation.

There once was an epical clatter—                            5
Voices and banjos, Tennessee, Ohio,
Rising like incense in the sight of heaven.
Today, there is an angel in the gate.

Lie back, Walt Whitman,[1]
There, on the fabulous raft with the King and the Duke![2]  10
For the white row of the Marina
Faces the Rock.[3] Turn round the wagons here.

Lie back! We cannot bear
The stars any more, those infinite spaces.
Let the realtors divide the mountain,                        15
For they have already subdivided the valley.

2. The last stanza is the motto of the city of Berkeley, California.
1. Whitman's poetry often (as in "Facing West from California's Shores") celebrated the American dream.
2. Characters in *Huckleberry Finn* who capitalized on the ignorance and kindness of the people they met.
3. A nickname for the federal prison formerly located on Alcatraz Island in San Francisco Bay.

Rectangular city blocks astonished
Herodotus in Babylon,[4]
Cortez in Tenochtitlan,[5]
And here's the same old city-planner, death.                    20

We cannot turn or stay.
For though we sleep, and let the reins fall slack,
The great cloud-wagons move
Outward still, dreaming of a Pacific.

1963

EMILY DICKINSON

## After Great Pain

After great pain, a formal feeling comes—
The Nerves sit ceremonious, like Tombs—
The stiff Heart questions was it He, that bore,
And Yesterday, or Centuries before?

The Feet, mechanical, go round—                                5
Of Ground, or Air, or Ought—
A Wooden way
Regardless grown,
A Quartz contentment, like a stone—

This is the Hour of Lead—                                     10
Remembered, if outlived,
As Freezing Persons recollect the Snow—
First—Chill—then Stupor—then the letting go—
ca. 1862

WILLIAM CARLOS WILLIAMS

## The Red Wheelbarrow

so much depends
upon

a red wheel
barrow

glazed with rain                                              5
water

beside the white
chickens.

1923

4. Herodotus, often called the "father of history," marveled at Babylonian accomplishments.

5. The Aztec capital, taken by Cortez in 1519 after he was cordially received into the city by Montezuma.

EZRA POUND

# In a Station of the Metro[6]

The apparition of these faces in the crowd;
Petals on a wet, black bough.

p. 1913

JULIA FIELDS

# Madness One Monday Evening

Late that mad Monday evening
I made mermaids come from the sea
As the block sky sat
Upon the waves
And night came                                        5
Creeping up to me

(I tell you I made mermaids
Come from the sea)

The green waves lulled and rolled
As I sat by the locust tree                            10
And the bright glare of the neon world
Sent gas-words bursting free—
Their spewed splendor fell on the billows
And gaudy it grew to me
As I sat up upon the shore                             15
And made mermaids come from the sea.

1964

RICHARD WILBUR

# The Beautiful Changes

One wading a Fall meadow finds on all sides
The Queen Anne's Lace[1] lying like lilies
On water; it glides
So from the walker, it turns
Dry grass to a lake, as the slightest shade of you     5
Valleys my mind in fabulous blue Lucernes.[2]

The beautiful changes as a forest is changed
By a chameleon's tuning his skin to it;
As a mantis, arranged
On a green leaf, grows                                 10
Into it, makes the leaf leafier, and proves
Any greenness is deeper than anyone knows.

6. The Paris subway.
1. A delicate-looking plant, with finely divided leaves and flat clusters of small white flowers, sometimes called "wild carrot."

2. Alfalfa, a plant resembling clover, with small purple flowers. Lake Lucerne is famed for deep blue color and its picturesque Swiss setting amid limestone mountains.

Your hands hold roses always in a way that says
They are not only yours; the beautiful changes
In such kind ways,                                          15
Wishing ever to sunder
Things and things' selves for a second finding, to lose
For a moment all that it touches back to wonder.

1947

SAMUEL TAYLOR COLERIDGE

## Kubla Khan: or, a Vision in a Dream[1]

In Xanadu did Kubla Khan
  A stately pleasure-dome decree:
Where Alph, the sacred river, ran
Through caverns measureless to man
  Down to a sunless sea.                                    5
So twice five miles of fertile ground
With walls and towers were girdled round:
And here were gardens bright with sinuous rills
Where blossomed many an incense-bearing tree;
And here were forests ancient as the hills,              10
Enfolding sunny spots of greenery.
But oh! that deep romantic chasm which slanted
Down the green hill athwart a cedarn cover![2]
A savage place! as holy and enchanted
As e'er beneath a waning moon was haunted               15
By woman wailing for her demon-lover![3]
And from this chasm, with ceaseless turmoil seething,
As if this earth in fast thick pants were breathing,
A mighty fountain momently was forced,
Amid whose swift half-intermitted burst                 20
Huge fragments vaulted like rebounding hail,
Or chaffy grain beneath the thresher's flail:
And 'mid these dancing rocks at once and ever
It flung up momently the sacred river.
Five miles meandering with a mazy motion               25
Through wood and dale the sacred river ran,
Then reached the caverns measureless to man,
And sank in tumult to a lifeless ocean:
And 'mid this tumult Kubla heard from far
Ancestral voices prophesying war!                       30

  The shadow of the dome of pleasure
  Floated midway on the waves;
  Where was heard the mingled measure
  From the fountain and the caves.
It was a miracle of rare device,                        35
A sunny pleasure-dome with caves of ice!

1. Coleridge said he wrote this fragment immediately after waking from an opium dream and that after he was interrupted by a caller he was unable to finish the poem.
2. From side to side of a cover of cedar trees.

3. In a famous and often imitated German ballad, the lady Lenore is carried off on horseback by the specter of her lover and married to him at his grave.

A damsel with a dulcimer[4]
In a vision once I saw:
It was an Abyssinian maid,
And on her dulcimer she played,                    40
Singing of Mount Abora.
Could I revive within me
Her symphony and song,
To such a deep delight 'twould win me,
That with music loud and long,                     45
I would build that dome in air,
That sunny dome! those caves of ice!
And all who heard should see them there,
And all should cry, Beware! Beware!
His flashing eyes, his floating hair!              50
Weave a circle round him thrice,
And close your eyes with holy dread,
For he on honey-dew hath fed,
And drunk the milk of Paradise.

1798

ALEXANDER POPE

# [The Hunt][1]

Ye vig'rous swains![2] while youth ferments your blood,     93
And purer spirits swell the sprightly flood,
Now range the hills, the gameful woods beset,
Wind the shrill horn, or spread the waving net.
When milder autumn summer's heat succeeds,
And in the new-shorn field the partridge feeds,
Before his lord the ready spaniel bounds,
Panting with hope, he tries the furrowed grounds;          100
But when the tainted gales the game betray,
Couched close he lies, and meditates the prey;
Secure they trust th' unfaithful field, beset,
'Till hov'ring o'er 'em sweeps the swelling net.
Thus (if small things we may with great compare)[3]       105
When Albion[4] sends her eager sons to war,
Some thoughtless town, with ease and plenty blest,
Near, and more near, the closing lines invest;
Sudden they seize th' amazed, defenseless prize,
And high in air Britannia's standard flies.                110
See! from the brake the whirring pheasant springs,
And mounts exulting on triumphant wings:
Short is his joy; he feels the fiery wound,
Flutters in blood, and panting beats the ground.
Ah! what avail his glossy, varying dyes,                   115
His purple crest, and scarlet-circled eyes,
The vivid green his shining plumes unfold,

4. A stringed instrument, prototype of the piano.
1. From *Windsor Forest*, Pope's didactic descriptive poem about the Peace of Utrecht and the uses of nature.
2. Youths.

3. In *Paradise Lost*, II, 921–22, Milton must "compare great things with small" to suggest the noise Satan hears as he is about to journey toward Hell.
4. England.

His painted wings, and breast that flames with gold?
    Nor yet, when moist Arcturus[5] clouds the sky,
The woods and fields their pleasing toils deny.               120
To plains with well-breathed beagles we repair,
And trace the mazes of the circling hare.
(Beasts, urged by us, their fellow-beasts pursue,
And learn of man each other to undo.)
With slaught'ring guns th' unwearied fowler roves,           125
When frosts have whitened all the naked groves;
Where doves in flocks the leafless trees o'ershade,
And lonely woodcocks haunt the wat'ry glade.
He lifts the tube, and levels with his eye;
Strait a short thunder breaks the frozen sky.                130
Oft, as in airy rings they skim the heath,
The clam'rous lapwings feel the leaden death:
Oft, as the mounting larks their notes prepare,
They fall, and leave their little lives in air.

                                                      1713

RICHARD WILBUR

## She

What was her beauty in our first estate
When Adam's will was whole,[1] and the least thing
Appeared the gift and creature of his king,
How should we guess? Resemblance had to wait

For separation, and in such a place                           5
She so partook of water, light, and trees
As not to look like any one of these.
He woke and gazed into her naked face.

But then she changed, and coming down amid
The flocks of Abel and the fields of Cain,                    10
Clothed in their wish, her Eden graces hid,
A shape of plenty with a mop of grain,

She broke upon the world, in time took on
The look of every labor and its fruits.
Columnar in a robe of pleated lawn                            15
She cupped her patient hand for attributes,

Was radiant captive of the farthest tower
And shed her honor on the fields of war,
Walked in her garden at the evening hour,
Her shadow like a dark ogival[2] door,                        20

Breasted the seas for all the westward ships
And, come to virgin country, changed again—

5. A large star thought to bring rain    2. In the form of a pointed (Gothic)
when it rises in September.               arch.
1. Before the Fall.

A moonlike being truest in eclipse,
And subject goddess of the dreams of men.

Tree, temple, valley, prow, gazelle, machine,                    25
More named and nameless than the morning star,
Lovely in every shape, in all unseen,
We dare not wish to find you as you are,

Whose apparition, biding time until
Desire decay and bring the latter age,                           30
Shall flourish in the ruins of our will
And deck[3] the broken stones like saxifrage.[4]

1961

THEODORE ROETHKE

# I Knew a Woman

I knew a woman, lovely in her bones,
When small birds sighed, she would sigh back at them;
Ah, when she moved, she moved more ways than one:
The shapes a bright container can contain!
Of her choice virtues only gods should speak,                    5
Or English poets who grew up on Greek
(I'd have them sing in chorus, cheek to cheek).

How well her wishes went! She stroked my chin,
She taught me Turn, and Counter-turn, and Stand;[1]
She taught me Touch, that undulant white skin;                   10
I nibbled meekly from her proffered hand;
She was the sickle; I, poor I, the rake,
Coming behind her for her pretty sake
(But what prodigious mowing we did make).

Love likes a gander, and adores a goose:                         15
Her full lips pursed, the errant note to seize;
She played it quick, she played it light and loose;
My eyes, they dazzled at her flowing knees;
Her several parts could keep a pure repose,
Or one hip quiver with a mobile nose                             20
(She moved in circles, and those circles moved).

Let seed be grass, and grass turn into hay:
I'm martyr to a motion not my own;
What's freedom for? To know eternity.
I swear she cast a shadow white as stone.                        25
But who would count eternity in days?
These old bones live to learn her wanton ways:
(I measure time by how a body sways).

1958

3. Adorn.
4. A tufted plant with bright flowers,     1. Literary terms for the parts of a
often rooted in the clefts of rocks.       Pindaric ode.

EDMUND SPENSER

## Was It a Dream

Was it a dream, or did I see it plain?
A goodly table of pure ivory,
All spread with junkets,[1] fit to entertain
The greatest prince with pompous[2] royalty:
'Mongst which, there in a silver dish did lie          5
Two golden apples of unvalued price;
Far passing those which Hercules[3] came by,
Or those which Atalanta[4] did entice.
Exceeding sweet, yet void of sinful vice;
That many sought, yet none could ever taste;          10
Sweet fruit of pleasure, brought from Paradise
By Love himself, and in his garden placed.
    Her breast that table was, so richly spread;
    My thoughts the guests, which would thereon have fed.

1595

JOHN DONNE

## Batter My Heart

Batter my heart, three-personed God; for You
As yet but knock, breathe, shine, and seek to mend;
That I may rise and stand, o'erthrow me, and bend
Your force, to break, blow, burn, and make me new.
I, like an usurped town, to another due,          5
Labor to admit You, but Oh, to no end!
Reason, Your viceroy[1] in me, me should defend,
But is captived, and proves weak or untrue.
Yet dearly I love You, and would be loved fain.[2]
But am betrothed unto Your enemy:          10
Divorce me, untie, or break that knot again,
Take me to You, imprison me, for I,
Except You enthrall me, never shall be free,
Nor ever chaste, except You ravish me.

1633

AMIRI BARAKA (LEROI JONES)

## The World Is Full of Remarkable Things

*for little Bumi*

Quick Night
easy warmth

1. Sweetmeats.
2. Splendid.
3. Hercules' twelfth labor was to gain possession of the golden apples of the Hesperides.
4. In Greek myth, Atalanta agreed to marry anyone who could defeat her in a race; Milanion won by dropping, during the race, three golden apples which Atalanta paused to retrieve.
1. One who rules as the representative of a higher power.
2. Gladly.

The girlmother lies next to me
breathing
coughing                                        5
sighing
at my absence. Bird Plane
Flying near Mecca
Sun sight warm air
through                                         10
my air foils. Womanchild
turns
lays her head
on my
stomach. Night aches                            15
acts
Niggers rage

down the street. (Air
Pocket, sinks
us. She lady                                    20
angel brings
her self
to touch me
grains & grass & long
silences, the dark                              25
ness my natural
element, in
warm black skin
I love &
understand                                      30
things. Sails
cries these
moans, pushed
from her by my
weight, her legs                                35
spreading wrapping
secure the spirit
in her.
            We begin our
ritual breathing                               40
flex the soul clean
out, her eyes slide
into dreams

                                        1966

X. J. KENNEDY

# Nude Descending a Staircase[1]

Toe upon toe, a snowing flesh,
A gold of lemon, root and rind,
She sifts in sunlight down the stairs
With nothing on. Nor on her mind.

1. A celebrated cubist-futurist painting by Marcel Duchamp (1913).

We spy beneath the banister                          5
A constant thresh of thigh on thigh—
Her lips imprint the swinging air
That parts to let her parts go by.

One-woman waterfall, she wears
Her slow descent like a long cape         10
And pausing, on the final stair
Collects her motions into shape.

1961

ROBERT HERRICK

## Upon Julia's Clothes

Whenas in silks my Julia goes
Then, then, methinks, how sweetly flows
That liquefaction of her clothes.

Next, when I cast mine eyes, and see
That brave[1] vibration, each way free,            5
O, how that glittering taketh me!

1648

BARRY SPACKS

## My Clothes

Poor spineless things, the clothes I've shed
in hopes of the essential bed
of love. Like chastened dogs they wait
to be forgiven, stroked, pulled straight.
I lift them to the light, all holes                        5
and patches, all the outworn roles,
the Dandy's musty ornaments,
the Lover's, and the Malcontent's.
The day seeks like a wind its form;
my clothes have kept me from the storm.       10
From age to age though I emerge
from cloying silks or common serge
my mere limbs stutter in the sun;
outside the cave, I come undone.
O, voices in your nakedness,                              15
great dreamers in your skins or less,
make golden ages fill my mind
where ease leaves agony behind
and passion, all her raiment gone,
is beautiful with nothing on.                              20

p. 1967

1. Handsome, showy.

JONATHAN SWIFT

## A Beautiful Young Nymph Going to Bed

Corinna, pride of Drury-Lane,[1]
For whom no shepherd sighs in vain;
Never did Covent Garden[2] boast
So bright a battered, strolling toast;[3]
No drunken rake to pick her up,                                    5
No cellar where on tick[4] to sup;
Returning at the midnight hour;
Four stories climbing to her bow'r;
Then, seated on a three-legged chair,
Takes off her artificial hair:                                     10
Now, picking out a crystal eye,
She wipes it clean, and lays it by.
Her eyebrows from a mouse's hide,
Stuck on with art on either side,
Pulls off with care, and first displays 'em,                       15
Then in a play-book smoothly lays 'em.
Now dextrously her plumpers[5] draws,
That serve to fill her hollow jaws.
Untwists a wire; and from her gums
A set of teeth completely comes.                                   20
Pulls out the rags contrived to prop
Her flabby dugs and down they drop.
Proceeding on, the lovely goddess
Unlaces next her steel-ribbed bodice;
Which by the operator's skill,                                     25
Press down the lumps, the hollows fill,
Up goes her hand, and off she slips
The bolsters that supply her hips.
With gentlest touch, she next explores
Her shankers,[6] issues, running sores,                            30
Effects of many a sad disaster;
And then to each applies a plaster.
But must, before she goes to bed,
Rub off the daubs of white and red;
And smooth the furrows in her front,                               35
With greasy paper stuck upon't.
She takes a bolus[7] e'er she sleeps;
And then between two blankets creeps.
With pains of love tormented lies;
Or if she chance to close her eyes,                                40
Of Bridewell and the Compter[8] dreams,
And feels the lash, and faintly screams;
Or, by a faithless bully drawn,
At some hedge-tavern lies in pawn;
Or to Jamaica seems transported,                                   45

1. The London theatre district, inhabited by many prostitutes.
2. A rival area.
3. A celebrated lady, one who is toasted.
4. Credit.
5. Small balls or discs held in the mouth to fill out hollow cheeks.
6. Cankers.
7. Large pill.
8. Prisons; Bridewell held mostly vagrants and prostitutes.

Alone, and by no planter courted;[9]
Or, near Fleet-Ditch's oozy brinks,[1]
Surrounded with a hundred stinks,
Belated, seems on watch to lie,
And snap some cully[2] passing by;
Or, struck with fear, her fancy runs
On watchmen, constables and duns,
From whom she meets with frequent rubs;
But, never from religious clubs;
Whose favor she is sure to find,                          55
Because she pays them all in kind.
   Corinna wakes. A dreadful sight!
Behold the ruins of the night!
A wicked rat her plaster stole,
Half eat, and dragged it to his hole.                     60
The crystal eye, alas, was missed;
And Puss had on her plumpers pissed.
A pigeon picked her issue-peas;[3]
And Shock her tresses filled with fleas.
   The nymph though in this mangled plight,   65
Must ev'ry morn her limbs unite.
But how shall I describe her arts
To recollect the scattered parts?
Or show the anguish, toil, and pain,
Of gath'ring up herself again?                            70
The bashful muse will never bear
In such a scene to interfere.
Corinna in the morning dizened,
Who sees, will spew; who smells, be poisoned.

                                           1734

EZRA POUND

# The River-Merchant's Wife: A Letter

## (*after Rihaku*[1])

While my hair was still cut straight across my forehead
I played about the front gate, pulling flowers.
You came by on bamboo stilts, playing horse,
You walked about my seat, playing with blue plums.
And we went on living in the village of Chokan:        5
Two small people, without dislike or suspicion.

At fourteen I married My Lord you.
I never laughed, being bashful.
Lowering my head, I looked at the wall.
Called to, a thousand times, I never looked back.        10

At fifteen I stopped scowling,
I desired my dust to be mingled with yours

9. Felons were sometimes transported to America rather than being hanged; they were then indentured for a number of years unless someone bought their freedom.
1. Most of London's sewage went to Fleet Ditch before being dumped into the Thames.

2. Dupe.
3. Peas or other small round objects placed in incisions to drain sores by counter-irritation.
1. The Japanese name for Li Po, an eighth-century Chinese poet.

For ever and for ever and for ever.
Why should I climb the look out?

At sixteen you departed,                                        15
You went into far Ku-to-yen, by the river of swirling eddies,
And you have been gone five months.
The monkeys make sorrowful noise overhead.

You dragged your feet when you went out.
By the gate now, the moss is grown, the different mosses,        20
Too deep to clear them away!
The leaves fall early this autumn, in wind.
The paired butterflies are already yellow with August
Over the grass in the West garden;
They hurt me. I grow older.                                     25
If you are coming down through the narrows of the river Kiang,
Please let me know beforehand,
And I will come out to meet you
        As far as Cho-fu-Sa.

                                                         1915


JOHN CROWE RANSOM

# The Equilibrists

Full of her long white arms and milky skin
He had a thousand times remembered sin.
Alone in the press of people traveled he,
Minding her jacinth,[1] and myrrh,[2] and ivory.

Mouth he remembered: the quaint orifice                          5
From which came heat that flamed upon the kiss,
Till cold words came down spiral from the head.
Grey doves from the officious tower illsped.

Body: it was a white field ready for love,
On her body's field, with the gaunt tower above,                10
The lilies grew, beseeching him to take,
If he would pluck and wear them, bruise and break.

Eyes talking: Never mind the cruel words,
Embrace my flowers, but not embrace the swords.
But what they said, the doves came straightway flying           15
And unsaid: Honor, Honor, they came crying.

Importunate her doves. Too pure, too wise,
Clambering on his shoulder, saying, Arise,
Leave me now, and never let us meet,
Eternal distance now command thy feet.                          20

---

1. An ancient blue gem.          2. An ingredient in perfume and in-
                                 cense.

Predicament indeed, which thus discovers
Honor among thieves, Honor between lovers.
O such a little word is Honor, they feel!
But the grey word is between them cold as steel.

At length I saw these lovers fully were come                    25
Into their torture of equilibrium;
Dreadfully had forsworn each other, and yet
They were bound each to each, and they did not forget.

And rigid as two painful stars, and twirled
About the clustered night their prison world,                   30
They burned with fierce love always to come near,
But Honor beat them back and kept them clear.

Ah, the strict lovers, they are ruined now!
I cried in anger. But with puddled brow
Devising for those gibbeted[3] and brave                        35
Came I descanting: Man, what would you have?

For spin your period out, and draw your breath,
A kinder saeculum[4] begins with Death.
Would you ascend to Heaven and bodiless dwell?
Or take your bodies honorless to Hell?                          40

In Heaven you have heard no marriage is,
No white flesh tinder to your lecheries,
Your male and female tissue sweetly shaped
Sublimed away, and furious blood escaped.

Great lovers lie in Hell, the stubborn ones                     45
Infatuate of the flesh upon the bones;
Stuprate,[5] they rend each other when they kiss,
The pieces kiss again, no end to this.

But still I watched them spinning, orbited nice.
Their flames were not more radiant than their ice.              50
I dug in the quiet earth and wrought the tomb
And made these lines to memorize their doom:

EPITAPH

*Equilibrists lie here; stranger, tread light;*
*Close, but untouching in each other's sight;*
*Mouldered the lips and ashy the tall skull.*                   55
*Let them lie perilous and beautiful.*

1927

3. Hanged and publicly displayed.     5. Having violent sexual intercourse.
4. Generation; era.

HOWARD NEMEROV

# The Goose Fish

On the long shore, lit by the moon
To show them properly alone,
Two lovers suddenly embraced
So that their shadows were as one.
The ordinary night was graced                              5
For them by the swift tide of blood
That silently they took at flood,
And for a little time they prized
    Themselves emparadised.

Then, as if shaken by stage-fright                         10
Beneath the hard moon's bony light,
They stood together on the sand
Embarrassed in each other's sight
But still conspiring hand in hand,
Until they saw, there underfoot,                           15
As though the world had found them out,
The goose fish turning up, though dead,
    His hugely grinning head.

There in the china light he lay,
Most ancient and corrupt and gray                          20
They hesitated at his smile,
Wondering what it seemed to say
To lovers who a little while
Before had thought to understand,
By violence upon the sand,                                 25
The only way that could be known
    To make a world their own.

It was a wide and moony grin
Together peaceful and obscene;
They knew not what he would express,                       30
So finished a comedian
He might mean failure or success,
But took it for an emblem of
Their sudden, new and guilty love
To be observed by, when they kissed,                       35
    That rigid optimist.

So he became their patriarch,
Dreadfully mild in the half-dark.
His throat that the sand seemed to choke,
His picket teeth, these left their mark                    40
But never did explain the joke
That so amused him, lying there
While the moon went down to disappear
Along the still and tilted track
    That bears the zodiac.                                 45

1955

LOUISE BOGAN

# The Crossed Apple

I've come to give you fruit from out my orchard,
Of wide report.
I have trees there that bear me many apples
Of every sort:

Clear, streakéd; red and russet; green and golden;        5
Sour and sweet.
This apple's from a tree yet unbeholden,
Where two kinds meet,—

So that this side is red without a dapple,
And this side's hue                                        10
Is clear and snowy. It's a lovely apple.
It is for you.

Within are five black pips as big as peas,
As you will find,
Potent to breed you five great apple trees               15
Of varying kind:

To breed you wood for fire, leaves for shade,
Apples for sauce.
Oh, this is a good apple for a maid,
It is a cross,                                             20

Fine on the finer, so the flesh is tight,
And grained like silk.
Sweet Burning gave the red side, and the white
Is Meadow Milk.

Eat it; and you will taste more than the fruit:          25
The blossom, too,
The sun, the air, the darkness at the root,
The rain, the dew,

The earth we came to, and the time we flee,
The fire and the breast.                                  30
I claim the white part, maiden, that's for me.
You take the rest.

                                                    1929

KARL SHAPIRO

# Auto Wreck

Its quick soft silver bell beating, beating,
And down the dark one ruby flare
Pulsing out red light like an artery,
The ambulance at top speed floating down
Past beacons and illuminated clocks                       5

Wings in a heavy curve, dips down,
And brakes speed, entering the crowd.
The doors leap open, emptying light;
Stretchers are laid out, the mangled lifted
And stowed into the little hospital.                          10
Then the bell, breaking the hush, tolls once,
And the ambulance with its terrible cargo
Rocking, slightly rocking, moves away,
As the doors, an afterthought, are closed.

We are deranged, walking among the cops          15
Who sweep glass and are large and composed.
One is still making notes under the light.
One with a bucket douches ponds of blood
Into the street and gutter.
One hangs lanterns on the wrecks that cling,     20
Empty husks of locusts, to iron poles.

Our throats were tight as tourniquets,
Our feet were bound with splints, but now,
Like convalescents intimate and gauche,
We speak through sickly smiles and warn          25
With the stubborn saw of common sense,
The grim joke and the banal resolution.
The traffic moves around with care,
But we remain, touching a wound
That opens to our richest horror.                30
Already old, the question Who shall die?
Becomes unspoken Who is innocent?

For death in war is done by hands;
Suicide has cause and stillbirth, logic;
And cancer, simple as a flower, blooms.          35
But this invites the occult mind,
Cancels our physics with a sneer,
And spatters all we knew of denouement
Across the expedient and wicked stones.

1942

ROBERT FRANCIS

# The Base Stealer

Poised between going on and back, pulled
Both ways taut like a tightrope-walker,
Fingertips pointing the opposites,
Now bouncing tiptoe like a dropped ball
Or a kid skipping rope, come on, come on,         5
Running a scattering of steps sidewise,
How he teeters, skitters, tingles, teases,
Taunts them, hovers like an ecstatic bird,
He's only flirting, crowd him, crowd him,
Delicate, delicate, delicate, delicate—now!      10

1960

THEODORE ROETHKE

## My Papa's Waltz

The whiskey on your breath
Could make a small boy dizzy;
But I hung on like death:
Such waltzing was not easy.

We romped until the pans                    5
Slid from the kitchen shelf;
My mother's countenance
Could not unfrown itself.

The hand that held my wrist
Was battered on one knuckle;                 10
At every step you missed
My right ear scraped a buckle.

You beat time on my head
With a palm caked hard by dirt,
Then waltzed me off to bed                   15
Still clinging to your shirt.

                                        1948

RICHARD EBERHART

## The Groundhog

In June, amid the golden fields,
I saw a groundhog lying dead.
Dead lay he; my senses shook,
And mind outshot our naked frailty.
There lowly in the vigorous summer          5
His form began its senseless change,
And made my senses waver dim
Seeing nature ferocious in him.
Inspecting close his maggots' might
And seething cauldron of his being,         10
Half with loathing, half with a strange love,
I poked him with an angry stick.
The fever rose, became a flame
And Vigour circumscribed the skies,
Immense energy in the sun,                   15
And through my frame a sunless trembling.
My stick had done nor good nor harm.
Then stood I silent in the day
Watching the object, as before;
And kept my reverence for knowledge          20
Trying for control, to be still,
To quell the passion of the blood;
Until I had bent down on my knees
Praying for joy in the sight of decay.
And so I left; and I returned                25
In Autumn strict of eye, to see

The sap gone out of the groundhog,
But the bony sodden hulk remained.
But the year had lost its meaning,
And in intellectual chains                                30
I lost both love and loathing,
Mured up[1] in the wall of wisdom.
Another summer took the fields again
Massive and burning, full of life,
But when I chanced upon the spot                          35
There was only a little hair left,
And bones bleaching in the sunlight
Beautiful as architecture;
I watched them like a geometer,[2]
And cut a walking stick from a birch.                     40
It has been three years, now.
There is no sign of the groundhog.
I stood there in the whirling summer,
My hand capped a withered heart,
And thought of China and of Greece,                       45
Of Alexander in his tent;
Of Montaigne in his tower,
Of Saint Theresa[3] in her wild lament.

                                                    1936

LOUISE BOGAN

# The Dragonfly

You are made of almost nothing
But of enough
To be great eyes
And diaphanous double vans;[1]
To be ceaseless movement,                                  5
Unending hunger
Grappling love.

Link between water and air,
Earth repels you.
Light touches you only to shift into iridescence          10
Upon your body and wings.

Twice-born, predator,
You split into the heat.
Swift beyond calculation or capture
You dart into the shadow                                   15
Which consumes you.

You rocket into the day.
But at last, when the wind flattens the grasses,
For you, the design and purpose stop.

1. Confined.
2. Geometrician, one skilled in measuring properties and arrangement.
3. Alexander the Great, ancient king of Macedonia and conqueror of the East; Michel de Montaigne, the Renaissance French essayist who used a tower near his house for a study; and St. Theresa of Spain, famous for intense trances and visions.
    1. Delicate and translucent double wings.

And you fall                                                    20
With the other husks of summer.

                                                             1968

EMILY DICKINSON

## The Spider Holds a Silver Ball

The Spider holds a Silver Ball
In unperceived Hands—
And dancing softly to Himself
His Yarn of Pearl—unwinds—

He plies from Nought to Nought—                                 5
In unsubstantial Trade—
Supplants our Tapestries with His—
In half the period—

An Hour to rear supreme
His Continents of Light—                                       10
Then dangle from the Housewife's Broom—
His Boundaries—forgot—

ca. 1862

WALT WHITMAN

## A Noiseless Patient Spider

A noiseless patient spider,
I marked where on a little promontory it stood isolated,
Marked how to explore the vacant vast surrounding,
It launched forth filament, filament, filament, out of itself,
Ever unreeling them, ever tirelessly speeding them.             5

And you O my soul where you stand,
Surrounded, detached, in measureless oceans of space,
Ceaselessly musing, venturing, throwing, seeking the spheres
        to connect them,
Till the bridge you will need be formed, till the ductile anchor hold,
Till the gossamer thread you fling catch somewhere, O my soul.  10

                                                             1881

ROBERT LOWELL

## Mr. Edwards and the Spider[1]

I saw the spiders marching through the air,
    Swimming from tree to tree that mildewed day
        In latter August when the hay

1. The speaker of the poem is Jonathan Edwards, from East Windsor, Conn. (line 28), the early 19th-century Puritan preacher famous for his powerful rhetoric, sensuous imagery, and vivid portraits of Hell. He is best known for his sermon "Sinners in the Hands of an Angry God" (line 10), but while only a boy of 11 he wrote a meticulous account of the habits of the flying spider. His sermons often compare man to a spider— in his cleverness and ultimate self-destruction.

Came creaking to the barn. But where
　　The wind is westerly,                                          5
Where gnarled November makes the spiders fly
Into the apparitions of the sky,
They purpose nothing but their ease and die
Urgently beating east to sunrise and the sea;

What are we in the hands of the great God?                      10
It was in vain you set up thorn and briar
　　In battle array against the fire
　　And treason crackling in your blood;
　　　For the wild thorns grow tame
And will do nothing to oppose the flame;                        15
Your lacerations tell the losing game
You play against a sickness past your cure.
How will the hands be strong? How will the heart endure?

A very little thing, a little worm,
Or hourglass-blazoned spider, it is said,                        20
　　Can kill a tiger. Will the dead
　　Hold up his mirror and affirm
　　　To the four winds the smell
And flash of his authority? It's well
If God who holds you to the pit of hell,                         25
　　Much as one holds a spider, will destroy,
Baffle and dissipate your soul. As a small boy

On Windsor Marsh, I saw the spider die
When thrown into the bowels of fierce fire:
　　There's no long struggle, no desire                           30
　　To get up on its feet and fly—
　　　It stretches out its feet
And dies. This is the sinner's last retreat;
Yes, and no strength exerted on the heat
Then sinews the abolished will, when sick                        35
And full of burning, it will whistle on a brick.

But who can plumb the sinking of that soul?
Josiah Hawley,[2] picture yourself cast
　　Into a brick-kiln where the blast
　　Fans your quick vitals to a coal—                             40
　　　If measured by a glass,
How long would it seem burning! Let there pass
A minute, ten, ten trillion; but the blaze
Is infinite, eternal: this is death,
To die and know it. This is the Black Widow, death.             45

1946

2. Either Edwards' uncle, Joseph Hawley, Sr., who jeopardized his soul by committing suicide, or Major Joseph Hawley, Jr., Edwards' cousin, who was the leader of public proceedings which led to Edwards' dismissal from his pulpit. The images that follow (and much of the earlier phrasing) is from Edwards' sermon "The Future Punishment of the Wicked Unavoidable and Intolerable."

EDWARD TAYLOR

## Upon a Spider Catching a Fly

Thou sorrow, venom elf:
  Is this thy play,
To spin a web out of thyself
  To catch a fly?
    For why?          5

I saw a pettish[1] wasp
  Fall foul therein,
Whom yet thy whorl-pins[2] did not clasp
  Lest he should fling
    His sting.          10

But as afraid, remote
  Didst stand hereat
And with thy little fingers stroke
  And gently tap
    His back.          15

Thus gently him didst treat
  Lest he should pet,[3]
And in a froppish,[4] waspish heat
  Should greatly fret
    Thy net.          20

Whereas the silly fly,
  Caught by its leg
Thou by the throat tookst hastily
  And hind the head
    Bite dead.          25

This goes to pot,[5] that not
  Nature doth call.
Strive not above what strength hath got
  Lest in the brawl
    Thou fall.          30

This fray seems thus to us.
  Hell's spider gets
His entrails spun to whip-cords[6] thus,
  And wove to nets
    And sets.          35

To tangle Adam's race
  In's stratagems
To their destructions, spoiled, made base
  By venom things,
    Damned sins.         40

1. Ill-tempered.
2. Literally, flywheels (on a spinning wheel); here, legs.
3. Anger.
4. Peevish.
5. Deteriorates.
6. Catgut.

But mighty, gracious Lord
    Communicate
Thy grace to break the cord, afford
    Us glory's gate
        And state.                                      45

We'll nightingale sing like
    When perched on high
In glory's cage, thy glory, bright,
    And thankfully,
        For joy.                                        50

ca. 1700

ROBERT FROST

## Range-Finding

The battle rent a cobweb diamond-strung
And cut a flower beside a groundbird's nest
Before it stained a single human breast.
The stricken flower bent double and so hung.
And still the bird revisited her young.                 5
A butterfly its fall had dispossessed,
A moment sought in air his flower of rest,
Then lightly stooped to it and fluttering clung.
On the bare upland pasture there had spread
O'ernight 'twixt mullein[1] stalks a wheel of thread    10
And straining cables wet with silver dew.
A sudden passing bullet shook it dry.
The indwelling spider ran to greet the fly,
But finding nothing, sullenly withdrew.

                                                        1916

ROBERT FROST

## Design

I found a dimpled spider, fat and white,
On a white heal-all,[2] holding up a moth
Like a white piece of rigid satin cloth—
Assorted characters of death and blight
Mixed ready to begin the morning right,                 5
Like the ingredients of a witches' broth—
A snow-drop spider, a flower like a froth,
And dead wings carried like a paper kite.

What had that flower to do with being white,
The wayside blue and innocent heal-all?                 10
What brought the kindred spider to that height,
Then steered the white moth thither in the night?
What but design of darkness to appall?—
If design govern in a thing so small.

                                                        1936

1. Weed.
2. A plant, also called the "all-heal" and "self-heal," with tightly clustered violet-blue flowers.

STEPHEN SPENDER

## An Elementary School Classroom in a Slum

Far far from gusty waves these children's faces.
Like rootless weeds, the hair torn round their pallor.
The tall girl with her weighed-down head. The paper-
seeming boy, with rat's eyes. The stunted, unlucky heir
Of twisted bones, reciting a father's gnarled disease,      5
His lesson from his desk. At back of the dim class
One unnoted, sweet and young. His eyes live in a dream
Of squirrel's game, in tree room, other than this.
On sour cream walls, donations. Shakespeare's head,
Cloudless at dawn, civilized dome riding all cities.        10
Belled, flowery, Tyrolese valley.[1] Open-handed map
Awarding the world its world. And yet, for these
Children, these windows, not this world, are world,
Where all their future's painted with a fog,
A narrow street sealed in with a lead sky,                  15
Far far from rivers, capes, and stars of words.

Surely, Shakespeare is wicked, the map a bad example
With ships and sun and love tempting them to steal—
For lives that slyly turn in their cramped holes
From fog to endless night? On their slag heap, these children   20
Wear skins peeped through by bones and spectacles of steel
With mended glass, like bottle bits on stones.
All of their time and space are foggy slum.
So blot their maps with slums as big as doom.

Unless, governor, teacher, inspector, visitor,             25
This map becomes their window and these windows
That shut upon their lives like catacombs,
Break O break open till they break the town
And show the children to green fields, and make their world
Run azure on gold sands, and let their tongues             30
Run naked into books, the white and green leaves open
History theirs whose language is the sun.

1939

CZESLAW MILOSZ

## A Poor Christian Looks at the Ghetto[2]

Bees build around red liver,
Ants build around black bone.
It has begun: the tearing, the trampling on silks,
It has begun: the breaking of glass, wood, copper, nickel, silver, foam
Of gypsum, iron sheets, violin strings, trumpets, leaves, balls, crystals.   5
Poof! Phosphorescent fire from yellow walls
Engulfs animal and human hair.

1. A rich and beautiful section of Austria with many scenes like those in typical
paintings of hamlets and picturesque coun-
trysides.

2. Translated from the Polish by the
author.

Bees build around the honeycomb of lungs,
Ants build around white bone.
Torn is paper, rubber, linen, leather, flax,                                    10
Fiber, fabrics, cellulose, snakeskin, wire.
The roof and the wall collapse in flame and heat seizes the foundations.
Now there is only the earth, sandy, trodden down,
With one leafless tree.

Slowly, boring a tunnel, a guardian mole makes his way,                15
With a small red lamp fastened to his forehead.
He touches burned bodies, counts them, pushes on,
He distinguishes human ashes by their luminous vapor,
The ashes of each man by a different part of the spectrum.
Bees build around a red trace.                                                 20
Ants build around the place left by my body.

I am afraid, so afraid of the guardian mole.
He has swollen eyelids, like a Patriarch
Who has sat much in the light of candles
Reading the great book of the species.                                         25
What will I tell him, I, a Jew of the New Testament,
Waiting two thousand years for the second coming of Jesus?
My broken body will deliver me to his sight
And he will count me among the helpers of death:
The uncircumcised.                                                             30

                                                                    1943


JOHN LENNON AND PAUL MC CARTNEY

## A Day in the Life

I read the news today oh boy
About a lucky man who made the grade
And though the news was rather sad
Well I just had to laugh
I saw the photograph.                                                          5
He blew his mind out in a car
He didn't notice that the light had changed
A crowd of people stood and stared
They'd seen his face before
Nobody was really sure                                                         10
If he was from the House of Lords.
I saw a film today oh boy
The English Army had just won the war
A crowd of people turned away                                                  15
But I just had to look
Having read the book.
I'd love to turn you on

Woke up, fell out of bed,
Dragged a comb across my head                                                  20
Found my way downstairs and drank a cup,
And looking up I noticed I was late.

Found my coat and grabbed my hat
Made the bus in seconds flat
Found my way upstairs and had a smoke,                               25
Somebody spoke and I went into a dream.
I read the news today oh boy
Four thousand holes in Blackburn, Lancashire,
And though the holes were rather small
They had to count them all                                          30
Now they know how many holes it takes to fill the Albert Hall.[1]
I'd love to turn you on

1967

WILLIAM BLAKE

## The Garden of Love

I went to the Garden of Love,
And saw what I never had seen:
A Chapel was built in the midst,
Where I used to play on the green.

And the gates of this Chapel were shut,                             5
And "Thou shalt not" writ over the door;
So I turned to the Garden of Love,
That so many sweet flowers bore,

And I saw it was filled with graves,
And tomb-stones where flowers should be;                            10
And Priests in black gowns were walking their rounds,
And binding with briars my joys and desires.

1794

LANGSTON HUGHES

## Harlem

What happens to a dream deferred?

Does it dry up
like a raisin in the sun?
Or fester like a sore—
And then run?                                                       5
Does it stink like rotten meat?
Or crust and sugar over—
like a syrupy sweet?

Maybe it just sags
like a heavy load.                                                  10

*Or does it explode?*

1951

1. The Royal Albert Hall, a large oval amphitheater in London, has nightly concerts
that have included, for example, the Beatles.

JOHN ASHBERY

# These Lacustrine Cities

These lacustrine cities grew out of loathing
Into something forgetful, although angry with history.
They are the product of an idea: that man is horrible, for instance,
Though this is only one example.

They emerged until a tower                                              5
Controlled the sky, and with artifice dipped back
Into the past for swans and tapering branches,
Burning, until all that hate was transformed into useless love.
Then you are left with an idea of yourself
And the feeling of ascending emptiness of the afternoon               10
Which must be charged to the embarrassment of others
Who fly by you like beacons.

The night is a sentinel.
Much of your time has been occupied by creative games
Until now, but we have all-inclusive plans for you.                    15
We had thought, for instance, of sending you to the middle of the
     desert,

To a violent sea, or of having the closeness of the others be air
To you, pressing you back into a startled dream
As sea-breezes greet a child's face.
But the past is already here, and you are nursing some private project.  20

The worst is not over, yet I know
You will be happy here. Because of the logic
Of your situation, which is something no climate can outsmart.
Tender and insouciant by turns, you see.

You have built a mountain of something,                                25
Thoughtfully pouring all your energy into this single monument,
Whose wind is desire starching a petal,
Whose disappointment broke into a rainbow of tears.

                                                              1965

WILLIAM COWPER

# [City Corruption]¹

The town has tinged the country. And the stain        553
Appears a spot upon a vestal's² robe,
The worse for what it soils. The fashion runs
Down into scenes still rural, but alas!
Scenes rarely graced with rural manners now.
Time was when in the pastoral retreat
Th' unguarded door was safe. Men did not watch
T' invade another's right, or guard their own.         560
Then sleep was undisturbed by fear, unscarred

1. From Book IV of *The Task*, a long poem    2. Virgin's.
contrasting the country and the city.

By drunken howlings; and the chilling tale
Of midnight murther³ was a wonder heard
With doubtful credit, told to frighten babes.
But farewell now to unsuspicious nights,                      565
And slumbers unalarmed. Now, 'ere you sleep,
See that your polished arms be primed with care,
And drop the night-bolt. Ruffians are abroad,
And the first larum⁴ of the cock's shrill throat
May prove a trumpet, summoning your ear                        570
To horrid sounds of hostile feet within.
Ev'n daylight has its dangers. And the walk
Through pathless wastes and woods, unconscious once
Of other tenants than melodious birds
Or harmless flocks, is hazardous and bold.                     575
Lamented change! to which full many a cause
Invet'rate, hopeless of a cure, conspires.
The course of human things from good to ill,
From ill to worse, is fatal, never fails.
Increase of pow'r begets increase of wealth,                   580
Wealth luxury, and luxury excess;
Excess, the scrofulous and itchy plague
That seizes first the opulent, descends
To the next rank contagious, and in time
Taints downward all the graduated scale                        585
Of order, from the chariot to the plough.
The rich, and they that have an arm to check
The license of the lowest in degree,
Desert their office; and themselves intent
On pleasure, haunt the capital, and thus,                      590
To all the violence of lawless hands
Resign the scenes their presence might protect.
Authority herself not seldom sleeps,
Though resident, and witness of the wrong.
The plump convivial parson often bears                         595
The magisterial sword in vain, and lays
His rev'rence and his worship both to rest
On the same cushion of habitual sloth.
Perhaps timidity restrains his arm,
When he should strike he trembles, and sets free,              600
Himself enslaved by terror of the band,
Th' audacious convict, whom he dares not bind.
Perhaps, though by profession ghostly pure,
He too may have his vice, and sometimes prove
Less dainty than becomes⁵ his grave outside,                   605
In lucrative concerns. Examine well
His milk-white hand. The palm is hardly clean—
But here and there an ugly smutch appears.
Foh! 'twas a bribe that left it. He has touched
Corruption. Whoso seeks an audit here                          610
Propitious, pays his tribute, game or fish,
Wild-fowl or ven'son, and his errand speeds.
    But faster far and more than all the rest,
A noble cause, which none who bears a spark

3. Murder.                          5. Is fitting for.
4. Alarm.

Of public virtue, ever wished removed,                          615
Works the deplored and mischievous effect.
'Tis universal soldiership[6] has stabbed
The heart of merit in the meaner class.
Arms through the vanity and brainless rage
Of those that bear them in whatever cause,                      620
Seem most at variance with all moral good,
And incompatible with serious thought.
The clown,[7] the child of nature, without guile,
Blest with an infant's ignorance of all
But his own simple pleasures, now and then                      625
A wrestling-match, a foot-race, or a fair,
Is ballotted,[8] and trembles at the news:
Sheepish he doffs his hat, and mumbling swears
A Bible-oath to be whate'er they please,
To do he knows not what. The task performed,                    630
That instant he becomes the sergeant's care,
His pupil, and his torment, and his jest.
His awkward gait, his introverted toes,
Bent knees, round shoulders, and dejected looks,
Procure him many a curse. By slow degrees,                      635
Unapt to learn, and formed of stubborn stuff,
He yet by slow degrees puts off himself,
Grows conscious of a change, and likes it well.
He stands erect, his slouch becomes a walk,
He steps right onward, martial in his air,                      640
His form and movement; is as smart above
As meal and larded locks can make him; wears
His hat or his plumed helmet with a grace,
And his three years of heroship expired,
Returns indignant to the slighted plough.                       645
He hates the field in which no fife or drum
Attends him, drives his cattle to a march,
And sighs for the smart comrades he has left.
'Twere well if his exterior change were all—
But with his clumsy port[9] the wretch has lost                 650
His ignorance and harmless manners too.
To swear, to game, to drink; to show at home
By lewdness, idleness, and sabbath-breach,
The great proficiency he made abroad,
T' astonish and to grieve his gazing friends,                   655
To break some maiden's and his mother's heart,
To be a pest where he was useful once,
Are his sole aim, and all his glory now.
      Man in society is like a flow'r
Blown[1] in its native bed. 'Tis there alone                    660
His faculties expanded in full bloom
Shine out, there only reach their proper use.
But man associated and leagued with man
By regal warrant, or self-joined by bond
For interest-sake, or swarming into clans                       665

6. Because of the Seven Years' War the         7. Peasant.
size of the regular English army and the       8. Conscripted by lottery.
militia were greatly increased in 1757 by      9. Bearing, style.
conscripting   men   for   three-year   terms  1. Destroyed.
(line 644).

Beneath one head for purposes of war,
Like flow'rs selected from the rest, and bound
And bundled close to fill some crowded vase,
Fades rapidly, and by compression marred,
Contracts defilement not to be endured.                  670
Hence chartered boroughs are such public plagues,
And burghers, men immaculate perhaps
In all their private functions, once combined,
Become a loathsome body, only fit
For dissolution, hurtful to the main.                    675
Hence merchants, unimpeachable of sin
Against the charities of domestic life,
Incorporated, seem at once to lose
Their nature, and disclaiming all regard
For mercy and the common rights of man,                  680
Build factories with blood, conducting trade
At the sword's point, and dyeing the white robe
Of innocent commercial justice red.[2]

1785

SAMUEL JOHNSON

## *from* London

Could'st thou resign the park and play[1] content,       210
For the fair banks of Severn or of Trent;[2]
There might'st thou find some elegant retreat,
Some hireling senator's deserted seat;
And stretch thy prospects o'er the smiling land,
For less than rent the dungeons of the Strand;[3]        215
There prune thy walks, support thy drooping flow'rs,
Direct thy rivulets, and twine thy bow'rs;
And, while thy grounds a cheap repast afford,
Despise the dainties of a venal lord:
There ev'ry bush with nature's music rings,              220
There ev'ry breeze bears health upon its wings;
On all thy hours security shall smile,
And bless thine evening walk and morning toil.
    Prepare for death, if here at night you roam,
And sign your will before you sup from home.             225
Some fiery fop, with new commission[4] vain,
Who sleeps on brambles[5] till he kills his man;
Some frolic drunkard, reeling from a feast,
Provokes a broil,[6] and stabs you for a jest.
Yet ev'n these heroes, mischievously gay,                230
Lords of the street, and terrors of the way;

2. An attack upon the East India Company. In a 1784 letter Cowper calls the officials of the company "tyrants" and says that "forgetting the terms of their institution [they] have possessed themselves of an immense territory, which they have ruled with a rod of iron . . . making the happiness of 30 millions of mankind a consideration subordinate to that of their own emolument. . . ."
1. Promenading in the park and attending plays were popular and fashionable amusements, often attacked by 18th-century satirists.
2. In the country.
3. Cramped apartments on the busy street paralleling the River Thames near the center of the city.
4. Eighteenth-century London was plagued by clubs and gangs of men (often nobly born) who taunted each other to violence just for sport.
5. Thorns.
6. Quarrel.

Flushed as they are with folly, youth and wine,
Their prudent insults to the poor confine;
Afar they mark the flambeau's bright approach,[7]
And shun the shining train, and golden coach.                    235
    In vain, these dangers past, your doors you close,
And hope[8] the balmy blessings of repose:
Cruel with guilt, and daring with despair,
The midnight murd'rer bursts the faithless bar;
Invades the sacred hour of silent rest,                          240
And leaves, unseen, a dagger in your breast.
    Scarce can our fields, such crowds at Tyburn[9] die,
With hemp the gallows and the fleet supply.
Propose your schemes, ye Senatorian band,
Whose Ways and Means[1] support the sinking land;                245
Lest ropes be wanting in the tempting spring,
To rig another convoy for the k——g.[2]
    A single jail, in Alfred's golden reign,[3]
Could half the nation's criminals contain;
Fair Justice then, without constraint adored,                    250
Held high the steady scale, but dropped the sword;
No spies were paid, no special juries known,
Blest age! but ah! how diff'rent from our own!

                                                                 1738

ALEXANDER POPE

# *from 1738*[1]

*Virtue* may choose the high or low degree,                      137
'Tis just alike to Virtue, and to me;
Dwell in a monk, or light upon a king,
She's still the same, beloved, contented thing.                  140
*Vice* is undone, if she forgets her birth,
And stoops from angels to the dregs of earth:
But 'tis the *Fall* degrades her to a whore;
Let *Greatness* own her, and she's mean[2] no more:
Her birth, her beauty, crowds and courts confess,                145
Chaste matrons praise her, and grave bishops bless;
In golden chains the willing world she draws,
And hers the gospel is, and hers the laws:
Mounts the tribunal, lifts her scarlet head,
And sees pale Virtue carted[3] in her stead.                     150
Lo! at the wheels of her triumphal car,[4]
Old England's Genius,[5] rough with many a scar,
Dragged in the dust! his arms hang idly round,

7. See a torch indicating the approach of a well-attended group or a luxurious vehicle.
8. Wish for.
9. Until 1783, the place of public execution.
1. "A cant term in the House of Commons for methods of raising money." (Johnson's note)
2. King. It was common practice to omit letters (but usually not enough of them to obscure meaning) when attacking

an office or person who might have legal redress.
3. Alfred the Great ruled the West Saxons, 871–899, and his reign had been glorified since the 12th century.
1. One of Pope's major satires on contemporary corruption.
2. Low in social status.
3. Prostitutes were drawn through the streets in carts as punishment.
4. Chariot.
5. Distinctive characteristic.

His flag inverted trails along the ground!
Our youth, all liv'ried o'er with[6] foreign gold,      155
Before her dance; behind her, crawl the old!
See thronging millions to the pagod[7] run,
And offer country, parent, wife, or son!
Hear her black trumpet through the land proclaim,
That "Not to be corrupted is the Shame."      160
In soldier, churchman, patriot, man in pow'r,
'Tis av'rice all, ambition is no more!
See, all our nobles begging to be slaves!
See, all our fools aspiring to be knaves!
The wit of cheats, the courage of a whore,      165
Are what ten thousand envy and adore.
All, all look up, with reverential awe,
At crimes that 'scape, or triumph o'er the law:
While truth, worth, wisdom, daily they decry—
"Nothing is sacred now but villainy."      170
   Yet may this verse (if such a verse remain)
Show, there was one who held it in disdain.

1738

WILLIAM BLAKE

# London

I wander through each chartered street,
Near where the chartered Thames does flow,
And mark in every face I meet
Marks of weakness, marks of woe.

In every cry of every man,      5
In every Infant's cry of fear,
In every voice, in every ban,
The mind-forged manacles I hear.

How the Chimney-sweeper's cry
Every black'ning Church appalls;      10
And the hapless Soldier's sigh
Runs in blood down Palace walls.

But most through midnight streets I hear
How the youthful Harlot's curse
Blasts the new-born Infant's tear,      15
And blights with plagues the Marriage hearse.

1794

WILLIAM WORDSWORTH

# London, 1802

Milton! thou should'st be living at this hour:
England hath need of thee: she is a fen[1]

6. Clothed as if in the service of.          1. Marsh.
7. Idol.

Of stagnant waters: altar, sword, and pen,
Fireside, the heroic wealth of hall and bower,
Have forfeited their ancient English dower[2]          5
Of inward happiness. We are selfish men;
Oh! raise us up, return to us again;
And give us manners, virtue, freedom, power.
Thy soul was like a star, and dwelt apart:
Thou hadst a voice whose sound was like the sea:      10
Pure as the naked heavens, majestic, free,
So didst thou travel on life's common way,
In cheerful godliness; and yet thy heart
The lowliest duties on herself did lay.

1802

PERCY BYSSHE SHELLEY

# England in 1819

An old, mad, blind, despised, and dying king[1]—
Princes, the dregs of their dull race, who flow
Through public scorn—mud from a muddy spring;
Rulers who neither see, nor feel, nor know,
But leechlike to their fainting country cling,        5
Till they drop, blind in blood, without a blow;
A people starved and stabbed in the untilled field—
An army, which liberticide and prey
Makes as a two-edged sword to all who wield;
Golden and sanguine[2] laws which tempt and slay;    10
Religion Christless, Godless—a book sealed;
A Senate—Time's worst statute[3] unrepealed—
Are graves, from which a glorious Phantom[4] may
Burst, to illumine our tempestuous day.

1819

EARLE BIRNEY

# Irapuato[1]

For reasons any
            brigadier
                    could tell
this is a favorite nook for
                    massacre                           5

Toltex by Mixtex Mixtex by Aztex
Aztex by Spanishtex Spanishtex by
Mexitex by Mexitex by Mexitex by Texaco

---

2. Inheritance.
1. George III, senile for many years, had ruled England since 1760. He died the year after the poem was written.
2. Motivated by greed, resulting in bloodshed.

3. A law discriminating against Catholics.
4. Revolution.
1. A city in central Mexico, northwest of Mexico City.

So any farmer can see how the strawberries
are the biggest and reddest                                     10
   in the whole damn continent

but why
      when arranged under
             the market flies

do they look like small clotting hearts?                        15

                                1962

CLAUDE MC KAY

## America

Although she feeds me bread of bitterness,
And sinks into my throat her tiger's tooth,
Stealing my breath of life, I will confess
I love this cultured hell that tests my youth!
Her vigor flows like tides into my blood,                       5
Giving me strength erect against her hate.
Her bigness sweeps my being like a flood.
Yet as a rebel fronts a king in state,
I stand within her walls with not a shred
Of terror, malice, not a word of jeer.                          10
Darkly I gaze into the days ahead,
And see her might and granite wonders there,
Beneath the touch of Time's unerring hand,
Like priceless treasures sinking in the sand.

                                1922

ROBERT FROST

## U. S. 1946 King's X[1]

Having invented a new Holocaust,
And been the first with it to win a war,
How they make haste to cry with fingers crossed,
King's X—no fairs to use it any more!

                              p. 1946

PETE SEEGER

## The Big Muddy

It was back in nineteen forty-two,
I was part of a good platoon;
We were on maneuvers in a-Loozianna,
One night by the light of the moon;
The captain told us to ford a river,                            5

---

1. Shortly after exploding the two atomic bombs that ended World War II, the United States proposed to share nuclear information with other countries in exchange for an agreement that the information would be used only for peaceful purposes. In children's games, time out is sometimes signaled by crossing fingers and saying "King's X."

And that's how it all begun.
We were knee deep in the Big Muddy
But the big fool said to move on.

The sergeant said, "Sir, are you sure,
This is the best way back to the base?"          10
"Sergeant, go on; I once forded this river
Just a mile above this place;
It'll be a little soggy but just keep slogging,
We'll soon be on dry ground."
We were waist deep in the Big Muddy          15
And the big fool said to push on.

The sergeant said, "With all this equipment
No man'll be able to swim";
"Sergeant, don't be a nervous nellie,"[1]
The Captain said to him;          20
"All we need is a little determination;
Men, follow me, I'll lead on."
We were neck deep in the Big Muddy
And the big fool said to push on.

All of a sudden, the moon clouded over,          25
We heard a gurgling cry;
A few seconds later, the captain's helmet
Was all that floated by;
The sergeant said, "Turn around men,
I'm in charge from now on."          30
And we just made it out of the Big Muddy
With the captain dead and gone.

We stripped and dived and found his body
Stuck in the old quicksand;
I guess he didn't know that the water was deeper          35
Than the place he'd once before been;
Another stream had joined the Big Muddy
Just a half mile from where we'd gone.
We'd been lucky to escape from the Big Muddy
When the damn fool said to push on.          40

Well, maybe you'd rather not draw any moral,
I'll leave that to yourself;
Maybe you're still walking and you're still talking
And you'd like to keep your health;
But every time I read the papers          45
That old feeling comes on:
Waist deep in the Big Muddy
And the big fool says to push on.

Waist deep in the Big Muddy
And the Big Fool says to push on;          50
Waist deep in the Big Muddy
And the Big Fool says to push on;

1. A term denoting timidity, often applied in the 1960s to one who opposed aggressive military policy.

Waist deep! Neck deep! Soon even a tall
Man'll be over his head!
Waist deep in the Big Muddy                    55
And the Big Fool says to push on!

1967

CLAUDE MCKAY

## The White House[1]

Your door is shut against my tightened face,
And I am sharp as steel with discontent;
But I possess the courage and the grace
To bear my anger proudly and unbent.
The pavement slabs burn loose beneath my feet,    5
And passion rends my vitals as I pass,
A chafing savage, down the decent street,
Where boldly shines your shuttered door of glass.
Oh, I must search for wisdom every hour,
Deep in my wrathful bosom sore and raw,           10
And find in it the superhuman power
To hold me to the letter of your law!
Oh, I must keep my heart inviolate
Against the poison of your deadly hate.

1937

MARI EVANS

## When in Rome

Marrie dear
the box is full . . .
take
whatever you like
to eat . . .                                       5

　　(an egg
　　or soup
　　. . . there ain't no meat.)

there's endive there
and                                                10
cottage cheese . . .

　　(whew! if I had some
　　black-eyed peas . . .)

there's sardines
on the shelves                                     15

1. For many years this poem was anthologized as "White Houses" because the first anthologist to include the poem, Alain Locke, had changed the title against the author's wishes. In his autobiography, *A Long Way from Home* (1937), McKay wrote: "My title . . . had no reference to the official residence of the President of the United States. . . . The title 'White Houses' changed the whole symbolic intent and meaning of the poem, making it appear as if the burning ambition of the black malcontent was to enter white houses in general."

and such . . .
but
don't
get my anchovies . . .

they cost                                          20
too much!

  (me get the
  anchovies indeed!
  what she think, she got—
  a bird to feed?)                                 25

there's plenty in there
to fill you up . . .

  (yes'm. just the
  sight's
  enough!                                          30

Hope I lives till I get
home
I'm tired of eatin'
what they eats in Rome . . .)

                                        p. 1963

RAY DUREM

# Award

*A Gold Watch to the FBI*
*Man who has followed*
*me for 25 years.*

Well, old spy
looks like I
led you down some pretty blind alleys,
took you on several trips to Mexico,
fishing in the high Sierras,                       5
jazz at the Philharmonic.[1]
You've watched me all your life,
I've clothed your wife,
put your two sons through college.
what good has it done?                             10
the sun keeps rising every morning.
ever see me buy an Assistant President?
or close a school?
or lend money to Trujillo?[2]
ever catch me rigging airplane prices?            15
I bought some after-hours whiskey in L. A.
but the Chief got his pay.
I ain't killed no Koreans
or fourteen-year-old boys in Mississippi.
neither did I bomb Guatemala,                     20

1. A popular annual series of concerts at Philharmonic Hall, Los Angeles, since the mid 1940s.

2. Dictator of the Dominican Republic, whose support by the U. S. was often under attack.

or lend guns to shoot Algerians.
I admit I took a Negro child
to a white rest room in Texas,
but she was my daughter, only three,
who had to pee.                                                    25

                                                              p. 1964

KENNETH KOCH

## You Were Wearing

You were wearing your Edgar Allan Poe printed cotton blouse.
In each divided up square of the blouse was a picture of Edgar Allan
   Poe.
Your hair was blonde and you were cute. You asked me, "Do most boys
   think that most girls are bad?"
I smelled the mould of your seaside resort hotel bedroom on your hair
   held in place by a John Greenleaf Whittier clip.
"No," I said, "it's girls who think that boys are bad." Then we read
   *Snowbound* together                                           5
And ran around in an attic, so that a little of the blue enamel was
   scraped off my George Washington, Father of His Country, shoes.

Mother was walking in the living room, her Strauss Waltzes comb in
   her hair.
We waited for a time and then joined her, only to be served tea in cups
   painted with pictures of Herman Melville
As well as with illustrations from his book *Moby Dick* and from his
   novella, *Benito Cereno.*
Father came in wearing his Dick Tracy necktie: "How about a drink,
   everyone?"                                                     10
I said, "Let's go outside a while." Then we went onto the porch and sat
   on the Abraham Lincoln swing.
You sat on the eyes, mouth, and beard part, and I sat on the knees.
In the yard across the street we saw a snowman holding a garbage can
   lid smashed into a likeness of the mad English king, George the
   Third.

                                                              1962

T. S. ELIOT

## The Love Song of J. Alfred Prufrock

> *S'io credesse che mia risposta fosse*
> *A persona che mai tornasse al mondo,*
> *Questa fiamma staria senza piu scosse.*
> *Ma perciocche giammai di questo fondo*
> *Non torno vivo alcun, s'i'odo il vero,*
> *Senza tema d'infamia ti rispondo.*[1]

Let us go then, you and I,
When the evening is spread out against the sky

1. Dante's *Inferno*, XXVII, 61–66. In the Eighth Chasm, Dante and Vergil meet Count
Guido de Montefeltrano, one of the False Counselors. The spirits there are in the form of
flames, and Guido speaks from the trembling tip of the flame, responding to Dante's request that he tell his life story: "If I thought that my answer were to someone who would
ever go back to earth, this flame would be still, without any more movement. But because
no one has ever gone back alive from this chasm (if what I hear is true) I answer you
without fear of infamy."

Like a patient etherized upon a table;
Let us go, through certain half-deserted streets,
The muttering retreats                                                          5
Of restless nights in one-night cheap hotels
And sawdust restaurants with oyster-shells:
Streets that follow like a tedious argument
Of insidious intent
To lead you to an overwhelming question . . .                                  10
Oh, do not ask, "What is it?"
Let us go and make our visit.

　　In the room the women come and go
Talking of Michelangelo.

　　The yellow fog that rubs its back upon the window-panes,                      15
The yellow smoke that rubs its muzzle on the window-panes
Licked its tongue into the corners of the evening,
Lingered upon the pools that stand in drains,
Let fall upon its back the soot that falls from chimneys,
Slipped by the terrace, made a sudden leap,                                     20
And seeing that it was a soft October night,
Curled once about the house, and fell asleep.

　　And indeed there will be time[2]
For the yellow smoke that slides along the street,
Rubbing its back upon the window-panes;                                         25
There will be time, there will be time
To prepare a face to meet the faces that you meet;
There will be time to murder and create,
And time for all the works and days[3] of hands
That lift and drop a question on your plate;                                    30
Time for you and time for me,
And time yet for a hundred indecisions,
And for a hundred visions and revisions,
Before the taking of a toast and tea.

　　In the room the women come and go                                            35
Talking of Michelangelo.

　　And indeed there will be time
To wonder, "Do I dare?" and, "Do I dare?"
Time to turn back and descend the stair,
With a bald spot in the middle of my hair—                                      40
(They will say: "How his hair is growing thin!")
My morning coat, my collar mounting firmly to the chin,
My necktie rich and modest, but asserted by a simple pin—
(They will say: "But how his arms and legs are thin!")
Do I dare                                                                       45
Disturb the universe?

　　2. See *Ecclesiastes* 3:1ff.: "To everything there is a season, and a time to every purpose under the heaven: A time to be born, and a time to die; a time to plant, and a time to pluck up that which is planted; A time to kill, and a time to heal. . . ." Also see Marvell's "To His Coy Mistress": "Had we but world enough and time. . . ."
　　3. Hesiod's ancient Greek didactic poem *Works and Days* prescribed in practical detail how to conduct one's life.

In a minute there is time
For decisions and revisions which a minute will reverse.

For I have known them all already, known them all:—
Have known the evenings, mornings, afternoons,                        50
I have measured out my life with coffee spoons;
I know the voices dying with a dying fall
Beneath the music from a farther room.
   So how should I presume?

And I have known the eyes already, known them all—                   55
The eyes that fix you in a formulated phrase,
And when I am formulated, sprawling on a pin,
When I am pinned and wriggling on the wall,
Then how should I begin
To spit out all the butt-ends of my days and ways?                   60
   And how should I presume?

And I have known the arms already, known them all—
Arms that are braceleted and white and bare
(But in the lamplight, downed with light brown hair!)
Is it perfume from a dress                                           65
That makes me so digress?
Arms that lie along a table, or wrap about a shawl.
   And should I then presume?
   And how should I begin?

          .   .   .   .   .

Shall I say, I have gone at dusk through narrow streets              70
And watched the smoke that rises from the pipes
Of lonely men in shirt-sleeves, leaning out of windows? . . .

I should have been a pair of ragged claws
Scuttling across the floors of silent seas.

          .   .   .   .   .

And the afternoon, the evening, sleeps so peacefully!               75
Smoothed by long fingers,
Asleep . . . tired . . . or it malingers,
Stretched on the floor, here beside you and me.
Should I, after tea and cakes and ices,
Have the strength to force the moment to its crisis?                8c
But though I have wept and fasted, wept and prayed,
Though I have seen my head (grown slightly bald) brought in upon
      a platter,[4]
I am no prophet—and here's no great matter;
I have seen the moment of my greatness flicker,
And I have seen the eternal Footman hold my coat, and snicker,      85
And in short, I was afraid.

And would it have been worth it, after all,
After the cups, the marmalade, the tea,
Among the porcelain, among some talk of you and me,
Would it have been worth while,                                      90

4. See *Matthew* 14:1–12 and *Mark* 6:17–29: John the Baptist was decapitated, upon
Salome's request and at Herod's command, and his head delivered on a platter.

To have bitten off the matter with a smile,
To have squeezed the universe into a ball[5]
To roll it toward some overwhelming question,
To say: "I am Lazarus,[6] come from the dead,
Come back to tell you all, I shall tell you all"— 95
If one, settling a pillow by her head,
    Should say:"That is not what I meant at all.
    That is not it, at all."

    And would it have been worth it, after all,
Would it have been worth while, 100
After the sunsets and the dooryards and the sprinkled streets,
After the novels, after the teacups, after the skirts that trail along the
    floor—
And this, and so much more?—
It is impossible to say just what I mean!
But as if a magic lantern[7] threw the nerves in patterns on a screen: 105
Would it have been worth while
If one, settling a pillow or throwing off a shawl,
And turning toward the window, should say:
    "That is not it at all,
    That is not what I meant, at all." 110
    . . . . .

No! I am not Prince Hamlet, nor was meant to be;
Am an attendant lord,[8] one that will do
To swell a progress,[9] start a scene or two,
Advise the prince; no doubt, an easy tool,
Deferential, glad to be of use, 115
Politic, cautious, and meticulous;
Full of high sentence, but a bit obtuse;
At times, indeed, almost ridiculous—
Almost, at times, the Fool.

    I grow old . . . I grow old . . . 120
I shall wear the bottoms of my trousers rolled.

    Shall I part my hair behind? Do I dare to eat a peach?
I shall wear white flannel trousers, and walk upon the beach.
I have heard the mermaids singing, each to each.

    I do not think that they will sing to me. 125

    I have seen them riding seaward on the waves
Combing the white hair of the waves blown back
When the wind blows the water white and black.

    We have lingered in the chambers of the sea
By sea-girls wreathed with seaweed red and brown 130
Till human voices wake us, and we drown.

**1917**

5. See Marvell's "To His Coy Mistress," lines 41–42: "Let us roll all our strength and all / our sweetness up into one ball. . . ."
6. One Lazarus was raised from the dead by Jesus (see *John* 1:1 to 2:2), and another (in the parable of the rich man Dives) is discussed in terms of returning from the dead to warn the living (*Luke* 16:19–31).
7. A nonelectric projector used as early as the 17th century.
8. Like Polonius in *Hamlet*, who is full of maxims ("high sentence," line 117).
9. Procession of state.

W. D. SNODGRASS

# The Campus on the Hill

Up the reputable walks of old established trees
They stalk, children of the *nouveaux riches;* chimes
Of the tall Clock Tower drench their heads in blessing:
"I don't wanna play at your house;
I don't like you any more."                                          5
My house stands opposite, on the other hill,
Among meadows, with the orchard fences down and falling;
Deer come almost to the door.
You cannot see it, even in this clearest morning.
White birds hang in the air between                                  10
Over the garbage landfill and those homes thereto adjacent,
Hovering slowly, turning, settling down
Like the flakes sifting imperceptibly onto the little town
In a waterball of glass.
And yet, this morning, beyond this quiet scene,                      15
The floating birds, the backyards of the poor,
Beyond the shopping plaza, the dead canal, the hillside lying tilted in
    the air,
Tomorrow has broken out today:
Riot in Algeria, in Cyprus, in Alabama;
Aged in wrong, the empires are declining,                            20
And China gathers, soundlessly, like evidence.
What shall I say to the young on such a morning?—
Mind is the one salvation?—also grammar?—
No; my little ones lean not toward revolt. They
Are the Whites, the vaguely furiously driven, who resist            25
Their souls with such passivity
As would make Quakers swear. All day, dear Lord, all day
They wear their godhead lightly.
They look out from their hill and say,
To themselves, "We have nowhere to go but down;                      30
The great destination is to stay."
Surely the nations will be reasonable;
They look at the world—don't they?—the world's way?
The clock just now has nothing more to say.

                                                                    1959

PERCY BYSSHE SHELLEY

# Political Greatness

Nor happiness, nor majesty, nor fame,
Nor peace, nor strength, nor skill in arms or arts,
Shepherd those herds whom tyranny makes tame;
Verse echoes not one beating of their hearts,
History is but the shadow of their shame;                            5
Art veils her glass, or from the pageant starts
As to oblivion their blind millions fleet,
Staining that Heaven with obscene imagery
Of their own likeness. What are numbers knit
By force or custom? Man who man would be,                            10

Must rule the empire of himself; in it
Must be supreme, establishing his throne
On vanquished will, quelling the anarchy
Of hopes and fears, being himself alone.

1821

ANDREI VOZNESENSKY

# Antiworlds[1]

The clerk Bukashkin is our neighbor:
His face is grey as blotting-paper.

But like balloons of blue or red,
Bright Antiworlds
    float over his head!   5
On them reposes, prestidigitous,
Ruling the cosmos, a demon-magician,
Anti-Bukashkin the Academician,
Lapped in the arms of Lollobrigidas.

But Anti-Bukashkin's dreams are the color  10
Of blotting-paper, and couldn't be duller.

Long live Antiworlds! They rebut
With dreams the rat-race and the rut.
For some to be clever, some must be boring.
No deserts? No oases, then.    15

There are no women—
     just anti-men.
In the forests, anti-machines are roaring.
There's the dirt of the earth, as well as the salt.
If the earth broke down, the sun would halt.  20

Ah, my critics; how I love them.
Upon the neck of the keenest of them,
Fragrant and bald as fresh-baked bread,
There shines a perfect anti-head . . .

. . . I sleep with windows open wide;  25
Somewhere a falling star invites,
And skyscrapers
    like stalactites,
Hang from the planet's underside.
There, upside down     30
    below me far,
Stuck like a fork into the earth,
Or perching like a carefree moth,
My little Antiworld,
    there you are!   35

---

1. Voznesensky uses, often playfully, the vocabulary and ideas of modern science. According to the concept of antimatter, particles of equal mass but with opposite magnetic value exist for all atoms. Translated from the Russian by Richard Wilbur.

In the middle of the night, why is it
That Antiworlds are moved to visit?

Why do they sit together, gawking
At the television, and never talking?

Between them not one word has passed.          40
Their first strange meeting is their last.

Neither can manage the least *bon ton.*
Oh, how they'll blush for it, later on!

Their ears are burning like a pair
Of crimson butterflies, hovering there . . .          45

. . . A distinguished lecturer lately told me,
"Antiworlds are a total loss."

Still, my apartment-cell won't hold me;
I thrash in my sleep, I turn and toss.

And, radio-like, my cat lies curled          50
With his green eye tuned in to the world.

                                               1962

ANONYMOUS

# The Lady Fortune

The lady Fortune is bothe freend and fo.
Of poure she maketh riche, of riche poure also;
She turneth wo[1] al into wele,[2] and wele al into wo.
Ne truste no man to this wele, the wheel it turneth so.

ca. 1325

AMY LOWELL

# Patterns

I walk down the garden-paths,
And all the daffodils
Are blowing, and the bright blue squills.[1]
I walk down the patterned garden-paths
In my stiff, brocaded gown.          5
With my powdered hair and jeweled fan,
I too am a rare
Pattern. As I wander down
The garden-paths.

My dress is richly figured,          10
And the train
Makes a pink and silver stain

---

1. Woe.
2. Weal: well-being, prosperity.

1. Bell-shaped flowers.

On the gravel, and the thrift
Of the borders.
Just a plate of current fashion,                                    15
Tripping by in high-heeled, ribboned shoes.
Not a softness anywhere about me,
Only whalebone and brocade.
And I sink on a seat in the shade
Of a lime tree. For my passion                                     20
Wars against the stiff brocade.
The daffodils and squills
Flutter in the breeze
As they please.
And I weep;                                                        25
For the lime-tree is in blossom
And one small flower has dropped upon my bosom.

And the plashing of waterdrops
In the marble fountain
Comes down the garden-paths.                                        30
The dripping never stops.
Underneath my stiffened gown
Is the softness of a woman bathing in a marble basin,
A basin in the midst of hedges grown
So thick, she cannot see her lover hiding,                          35
But she guesses he is near,
And the sliding of the water
Seems the stroking of a dear
Hand upon her.
What is Summer in a fine brocaded gown!                             40
I should like to see it lying in a heap upon the ground.
All the pink and silver crumpled up on the ground.

I would be the pink and silver as I ran along the paths,
And he would stumble after,
Bewildered by my laughter.                                          45
I should see the sun flashing from his sword-hilt and the buckles on his
      shoes.
I would choose
To lead him in a maze along the patterned paths,
A bright and laughing maze for my heavy-booted lover.
Till he caught me in the shade,                                     50
And the buttons of his waistcoat bruised my body as he clasped me,
Aching, melting, unafraid.
With the shadows of the leaves and the sundrops
And the plopping of the waterdrops,
All about us in the open afternoon—                                 55
I am very like to swoon
With the weight of this brocade,
For the sun sifts through the shade.

Underneath the fallen blossom
In my bosom,                                                        60
Is a letter I have hid.
It was brought to me this morning by a rider from the Duke.

"Madam, we regret to inform you that Lord Hartwell
Died in action Thursday se'nnight."[2]
As I read it in the white, morning sunlight,                              65
The letters squirmed like snakes.
"Any answer, Madam?" said my footman.[3]
"No," I told him.
"See that the messenger takes some refreshment.
No, no answer."                                                          70
And I walked into the garden,
Up and down the patterned paths,
In my stiff, correct brocade.
The blue and yellow flowers stood up proudly in the sun,
Each one.                                                                75
I stood upright too,
Held rigid to the pattern
By the stiffness of my gown.
Up and down I walked,
Up and down.                                                             80

In a month he would have been my husband.
In a month, here, underneath this lime,
We would have broke the pattern;
He for me, and I for him,
He as Colonel, I as Lady,                                                85
On this shady seat.
He had a whim
That sunlight carried blessing.
And I answered, "It shall be as you have said."
Now he is dead.                                                          90

In Summer and in Winter I shall walk
Up and down
The patterned garden-paths
In my stiff, brocaded gown.
The squills and daffodils                                                95
Will give place to pillared roses, and to asters, and to snow.
I shall go
Up and down,
In my gown.
Gorgeously arrayed,                                                     100
Boned and stayed.
And the softness of my body will be guarded from embrace
By each button, hook, and lace.
For the man who should loose me is dead,
Fighting with the Duke in Flanders,                                     105
In a pattern called a war.
Christ! What are patterns for?

                                                                        1916

2. A week ago Thursday.          3. Servant.

PAUL SIMON

## Patterns

The night set softly
With the hush of falling leaves
Casting shivering shadows
On the houses through the trees
And light from a street lamp                              5
Paints a pattern on my wall
Like the pieces of a puzzle
Or a child's uneven scrawl.

Up a narrow flight of stairs
In a narrow little room                                   10
As I lie upon my bed
In the early evening gloom.
Impaled on my wall
My eyes can dimly see
The pattern of my life                                    15
And the puzzle that is me.

From the moment of my birth
To the instant of my death
There are patterns I must follow
Just as I must breathe each breath.                       20
Like a rat in a maze
The path before me lies
And the pattern never alters
Until the rat dies.

And the pattern still remains                             25
On the wall where darkness fell
And it's fitting that it should
For in darkness I must dwell.
Like the color of my skin
Or the day that I grow old                                30
My life is made of patterns
That can scarcely be controlled.

                                                     1965

RICHARD WILBUR

## Advice to a Prophet

When you come, as you soon must, to the streets of our city,
Mad-eyed from stating the obvious,
Not proclaiming our fall but begging us
In God's name to have self-pity,

Spare us all word of the weapons, their force and range,     5
The long numbers that rocket the mind;
Our slow, unreckoning hearts will be left behind,
Unable to fear what is too strange.

Nor shall you scare us with talk of the death of the race.
How should we dream of this place without us?—                    10
The sun mere fire, the leaves untroubled about us,
A stone look on the stone's face?

Speak of the world's own change. Though we cannot conceive
Of an undreamt thing, we know to our cost
How the dreamt cloud crumbles, the vines are blackened by frost,   15
How the view alters. We could believe,

If you told us so, that the white-tailed deer will slip
Into perfect shade, grown perfectly shy,
The lark avoid the reaches of our eye,
The jack-pine lose its knuckled grip                               20

On the cold ledge, and every torrent burn
As Xanthus[1] once, its gliding trout
Stunned in a twinkling. What should we be without
The dolphin's arc, the dove's return,

These things in which we have seen ourselves and spoken?           25
Ask us, prophet, how we shall call
Our natures forth when that live tongue is all
Dispelled, that glass obscured or broken

In which we have said the rose of our love and the clean
Horse of our courage, in which beheld                              30
The singing locust of the soul unshelled,
And all we mean or wish to mean.

Ask us, ask us whether with the worldless rose
Our hearts shall fail us; come demanding
Whether there shall be lofty or long standing                      35
When the bronze annals of the oak-tree close.

                                                             1961

ARTHUR HUGH CLOUGH

# The Latest Decalogue

Thou shalt have one God only; who
Would be at the expense of two?
No graven images may be
Worshipped, except the currency.
Swear not at all; for, for thy curse                               5
Thine enemy is none the worse.
At church on Sunday to attend
Will serve to keep the world thy friend.
Honor thy parents; that is, all

1. A river in Homer's *Iliad*, Book XXI, set afire by the gods to rescue Achilles from
its swirling eddies:
>                  Now glow the waves, the fishes pant for breath,
>                  The eels lie twisting in the pangs of death:
>                  Now flounce aloft, now dive the scaly fry,
>                  Or gasping, turn their bellies to the sky.
>                         (translation by Alexander Pope, 1720)

From whom advancement may befall.                    10
Thou shalt not kill; but need'st not strive
Officiously to keep alive.
Do not adultery commit;
Advantage rarely comes of it.
Thou shalt not steal; an empty feat,                 15
When it's so lucrative to cheat.
Bear not false witness; let the lie
Have time on its own wings to fly.
Thou shalt not covet; but tradition
Approves all forms of competition.                   20

1862

DUDLEY RANDALL

# Booker T. and W. E. B.[1]

"It seems to me," said Booker T.,
"It shows a mighty lot of cheek
To study chemistry and Greek
When Mister Charlie needs a hand
To hoe the cotton on his land,                        5
And when Miss Ann looks for a cook,
Why stick your nose inside a book?"

"I don't agree," said W.E.B.
"If I should have the drive to seek
Knowledge of chemistry or Greek,                     10
I'll do it. Charles and Miss can look
Another place for hand or cook.
Some men rejoice in skill of hand,
And some in cultivating land,
But there are others who maintain                    15
The right to cultivate the brain."

"It seems to me," said Booker T.,
"That all you folks have missed the boat
Who shout about the right to vote,
And spend vain days and sleepless nights             20
In uproar over civil rights.
Just keep your mouths shut, do not grouse,
But work, and save, and buy a house."

"I don't agree," said W.E.B.,
"For what can property avail                          25
If dignity and justice fail?
Unless you help to make the laws,
They'll steal your house with trumped-up clause.
A rope's as tight, a fire as hot,
No matter how much cash you've got.                   30

1. Booker T. Washington (1856–1915), founder of Tuskegee Institute, who was willing to sacrifice the vote for economic power, and Dr. W[illiam] E[dward] B[urghardt] DuBois (1868–1963), sociologist, editor of *Crisis*, and a founder of the NAACP (1910).

Speak soft, and try your little plan,
But as for me, I'll be a man."

"It seems to me," said Booker T.—

"I don't agree,"
Said W.E.B.                                    35
                                               1966

ROBERT FROST

## A Semi-Revolution

I advocate a semi-revolution.
The trouble with a total revolution
(Ask any reputable Rosicrucian[2])
Is that it brings the same class up on top.
Executives of skillful execution                5
Will therefore plan to go halfway and stop.
Yes, revolutions are the only salves,
But they're one thing that should be done by halves.

                                               1942

EZRA POUND

## Commission[1]

Go, my songs, to the lonely and the unsatisfied,
Go also to the nerve-racked, go to the enslaved-by-convention,
Bear to them my contempt for their oppressors.
Go as a great wave of cool water,
Bear my contempt of oppressors.                 5

Speak against unconscious oppression,
Speak against the tyranny of the unimaginative,
Speak against bonds.
Go to the bourgeoise who is dying of her ennuis,
Go to the women in suburbs.                     10
Go to the hideously wedded,
Go to them whose failure is concealed,
Go to the unluckily mated,
Go to the bought wife,
Go to the woman entailed.[2]                    15

Go to those who have delicate lust,
Go to those whose delicate desires are thwarted,
Go like a blight upon the dullness of the world;
Go with your edge against this,
Strengthen the subtle cords,                    20
Bring confidence upon the algae and the tentacles of the soul.

2. A member of a secret religious society devoted to mysticism and astrology.
1. Poems or books of poems are sometimes sent into the world with an "envoi" or commission ("Go, little book . . .").

2. Involuntarily committed. Property limited to a specific line of heirs is said to be entailed; the term is not usually applied to people.

Go in a friendly manner,
Go with an open speech.
Be eager to find new evils and new good,
Be against all forms of oppression.                                    25
Go to those who are thickened with middle age,
To those who have lost their interest.

Go to the adolescent who are smothered in family—
Oh how hideous it is
To see three generations of one house gathered together!    30
It is like an old tree with shoots,
And with some branches rotted and falling.

Go out and defy opinion,
Go against this vegetable bondage of the blood.
Be against all sorts of mortmain.[3]                                   35

p. 1913

3. Impersonal ownership.

# II

THOMAS HARDY

## Channel Firing[1]

That night your great guns, unawares,
Shook all our coffins as we lay,
And broke the chancel window squares,[2]
We thought it was the Judgment-day[3]

And sat upright. While drearisome                    5
Arose the howl of wakened hounds:
The mouse let fall the altar-crumb,[4]
The worms drew back into the mounds,

The glebe cow[5] drooled. Till God called, "No;
It's gunnery practice out at sea                     10
Just as before you went below;
The world is as it used to be:

"All nations striving strong to make
Red war yet redder. Mad as hatters
They do no more for Christés sake                    15
Than you who are helpless in such matters.

"That this is not the judgment-hour
For some of them's a blessed thing,
For if it were they'd have to scour
Hell's floor for so much threatening . . .           20

"Ha, ha. It will be warmer when
I blow the trumpet (if indeed
I ever do; for you are men,
And rest eternal sorely need)."

So down we lay again. "I wonder,                     25
Will the world ever saner be,"
Said one, "than when He sent us under
In our indifferent century!"

And many a skeleton shook his head.
"Instead of preaching forty year,"                   30
My neighbor Parson Thirdly said,
"I wish I had stuck to pipes and beer."

1. Naval practice on the English Channel preceded the outbreak of World War I in the summer of 1914.
2. The windows near the altar in a church.
3. When, according to tradition, the dead will be awakened.
4. Breadcrumbs from the sacrament.
5. Parish cow pastured on the meadow next to the churchyard.

Again the guns disturbed the hour,
Roaring their readiness to avenge.
As far inland as Stourton Tower,                                    35
And Camelot, and starlit Stonehenge.[6]

April, 1914

EMILY DICKINSON

# I Heard a Fly Buzz

I heard a Fly buzz—when I died—
The Stillness in the Room
Was like the Stillness in the Air—
Between the Heaves of Storm—

The Eyes around—had wrung them dry—                               5
And Breaths were gathering firm
For that last Onset—when the King
Be witnessed—in the Room—

I willed my Keepsakes—Signed away
What portion of me be                                            10
Assignable—and then it was
There interposed a Fly—

With Blue—uncertain stumbling Buzz—
Between the light—and me—
And then the Windows failed—and then                             15
I could not see to see—

ca. 1862

ROBERT BROWNING

# Soliloquy of the Spanish Cloister[1]

Gr-r-r—there go, my heart's abhorrence!
  Water your damned flower-pots, do!
If hate killed men, Brother Lawrence,
  God's blood, would not mine kill you!
What? your myrtle-bush wants trimming?                           5
  Oh, that rose has prior claims—
Needs its leaden vase filled brimming?
  Hell dry you up with its flames!

At the meal we sit together:
  *Salve tibi!*[2] I must hear                                   10
Wise talk of the kind of weather,
  Sort of season, time of year:
*Not a plenteous cork-crop: scarcely*

---

6. Stourton Tower, built in the 18th century to commemorate King Alfred's ninth-century victory over the Danes, in Stourhead Park, Wiltshire. Camelot is the legendary site of King Arthur's court, said to have been in Cornwall or Somerset. Stonehenge, a circular formation of upright stones dating from about 1800 B.C., is on Salisbury Plain, Wiltshire; it is thought to have been a ceremonial site for political and religious occasions or an early scientific experiment in astronomy.
  1. Monastery.
  2. Hail to thee. Italics usually indicate the words of Brother Lawrence.

Dare we hope oak-galls,[3] I doubt:
What's the Latin name for "parsley"?     15
What's the Greek name for Swine's Snout?

Whew! We'll have our platter burnished,
   Laid with care on our own shelf!
With a fire-new spoon we're furnished,
   And a goblet for ourself,     20
Rinsed like something sacrificial
   Ere 'tis fit to touch our chaps[4]—
Marked with L. for our initial!
   (He-he! There his lily snaps!)

*Saint*, forsooth! While brown Dolores     25
   Squats outside the Convent bank
With Sanchicha, telling stories,
   Steeping tresses in the tank,
Blue-black, lustrous, thick like horsehairs,
   —Can't I see his dead eye glow,     30
Bright as 'twere a Barbary corsair's?[5]
   (That is, if he'd let it show!)

When he finishes refection,[6]
   Knife and fork he never lays
Cross-wise, to my recollection,     35
   As do I, in Jesu's praise.
I the Trinity illustrate,
   Drinking watered orange-pulp—
In three sips the Arian[7] frustrate;
   While he drains his at one gulp.     40

Oh, those melons? If he's able
   We're to have a feast! so nice!
One goes to the Abbot's table,
   All of us get each a slice.
How go on your flowers? None double?     45
   Not one fruit-sort can you spy?
Strange!—And I, too, at such trouble,
   Keep them close-nipped on the sly!

There's a great text in Galatians,[8]
   Once you trip on it, entails     50
Twenty-nine distinct damnations,
   One sure, if another fails:
If I trip him just a-dying,
   Sure of heaven as sure can be,
Spin him round and send him flying     55
   Off to hell, a Manichee?[9]

3. Abnormal growth on oak trees, used for tanning.
4. Jaws.
5. African pirate's.
6. A meal.
7. A heretical sect which denied the Trinity.
8. "Cursed is every one that continueth not in all things which are written in the book of law to do them," *Galatians* 3:10. *Galatians* 5:15–23 provides a long list of possible offenses, but they do not add up to 29.
9. A heretic. According to the Manichean heresy, the world was divided into the forces of good and evil, equally powerful.

Or, my scrofulous French novel
    On grey paper with blunt type!
Simply glance at it, you grovel
    Hand and foot in Belial's gripe:[1]                 60
If I double down its pages
    At the woeful sixteenth print,
When he gathers his greengages,
    Ope a sieve and slip it in't?

Or, there's Satan!—one might venture                    65
    Pledge one's soul to him, yet leave
Such a flaw in the indenture
    As he'd miss till, past retrieve,
Blasted lay that rose-acacia
    We're so proud of! *Hy, Zy, Hine* . . .[2]          70
'St, there's Vespers! *Plena gratiâ*
    *Ave, Virgo.*[3] Gr-r-r—you swine!

                                                        1842

JOHN DONNE

# Song

Go, and catch a falling star,
    Get with child a mandrake root,[1]
Tell me, where all past years are,
    Or who cleft the devil's foot,
Teach me to hear mermaids singing                        5
Or to keep off envy's stinging,
            And find
            What wind
Serves to advance an honest mind.

If thou beest born to strange sights,[2]                10
    Things invisible to see,
Ride ten thousand days and nights,
    Till age snow white hairs on thee;
Thou, when thou return'st, wilt tell me
All strange wonders that befell thee,                   15
            And swear,
            No where
Lives a woman true, and fair.

If thou find'st one, let me know:
    Such a pilgrimage were sweet.                       20
Yet do not, I would not go,
    Though at next door we might meet:
Though she were true when you met her,
And last till you write your letter,

1. In the clutches of Satan.
2. Possibly the beginning of an incantation or curse.
3. The opening words of the *Ave Maria*, here reversed: "Full of grace, Hail, Virgin."

1. The forked mandrake root is said to be shaped like the lower half of a human torso.
2. I.e., if you have supernatural powers.

> Yet she                                        25
> Will be
> False, ere I come, to two, or three.

                                                1633

SIR PHILIP SIDNEY

# In Martial Sports

In martial sports I had my cunning[1] tried,
 And yet to break more staves did me address,[2]
 While, with the people's shouts, I must confess,
Youth, luck, and praise even filled my veins with pride.
When Cupid, having me his slave descried                    5
 In Mars's livery,[3] prancing in the press,[4]
 "What now, Sir Fool!" said he (I would no less).
"Look here, I say!" I looked, and Stella spied,
 Who, hard by, made a window send forth light.
My heart then quaked, then dazzled were mine eyes:          10
One hand forgot to rule,[5] th'other to fight,
 Nor trumpet's sound I heard, nor friendly cries;
 My foe came on, and beat the air for me,[6]
 Till that her blush taught me my shame to see.

1582

GEORGE HERBERT

# The Collar

I struck the board[1] and cried, "No more;
 I will abroad!
What? shall I ever sigh and pine?
My lines[2] and life are free, free as the road,
 Loose as the wind, as large as store.[3]                   5
 Shall I be still in suit?[4]
Have I no harvest but a thorn
To let me blood, and not restore
What I have lost with cordial[5] fruit?
 Sure there was wine                                        10
Before my sighs did dry it; there was corn
Before my tears did drown it.
Is the year only lost to me?
Have I no bays[6] to crown it,
No flowers, no garlands gay? All blasted?                   15
 All wasted?
Not so, my heart; but there is fruit,
 And thou hast hands.
Recover all thy sigh-blown age
On double pleasures: leave thy cold dispute                 20
Of what is fit, and not. Forsake thy cage,

1. Skill.
2. I.e., he addressed himself to further combat.
3. Clad in armor.
4. Crowd of contenders.
5. Rein the horse.
6. I.e., the opponent's blows struck only air because the speaker was elsewhere.

1. Table.
2. Lot.
3. A storehouse; i.e., in abundance.
4. In service to another.
5. Reviving, restorative.
6. Wreaths of triumph.

Thy rope of sands,[7]
Which petty thoughts have made, and made to thee
Good cable, to enforce and draw,
And be thy law,                                    25
While thou didst wink[8] and wouldst not see.
Away! take heed;
I will abroad.
Call in thy death's-head[9] there; tie up thy fears.
He that forbears                                   30
To suit and serve his need,
Deserves his load."
But as I raved and grew more fierce and wild
At every word,
Methought I heard one calling, *Child!*            35
And I replied, *My Lord*.

1633

A. R. AMMONS

# Needs

I want something suited to my special needs
I want chrome hubcaps, pin-on attachments
and year round use year after year
I want a workhorse with smooth uniform cut,
dozer blade and snow blade & deluxe steering       5
wheel
I want something to mow, throw snow, tow
and sow with
I want precision reel blades
I want a console styled dashboard                  10
I want an easy spintype recoil starter
I want combination bevel and spur gears, 14
gauge stamped steel housing and
washable foam element air cleaner
I want a pivoting front axle and extrawide         15
turf tires
I want an inch of foam rubber inside a vinyl
covering
and especially if it's not too much, if I
can deserve it, even if I can't pay for it         20
I want to mow while riding.

1970

BEN JONSON

# In the Person of Woman Kind

## *A Song Apologetic*

Men if you love us, play no more
The fools or tyrants with your friends,

---

7. Moral restrictions.
8. I.e., close your eyes to the weaknesses of such restrictions.

9. *Memento mori*, a skull intended to remind men of their mortality.

To make us still sing o'er and o'er,
  Our own false praises, for your ends:
    We have both wits,[1] and fancies[2] too,                                5
    And if we must, let's sing of you.

Nor do we doubt, but that we can,
  If we would search with care and pain,
Find some one good, in some one man;
    So going thorow[3] all your strain:[4]                                  10
    We shall, at last, of parcels[5] make
    One good enough for a song's sake.

And as a cunning painter takes
  In any curious piece you see
More pleasure while the thing he makes                                      15
Then when 'tis made, why so will we.
    And having pleased our art, we'll try
    To make a new, and hang that by.

                                                                        1640

SONIA SANCHEZ

## 221–1424

### (*San/francisco/suicide/number*)

hello.
      are u the
suicide man? well
i'm callen to say
that i'm fixen to                                                            5
hang it up.
            what's that man?
i mean i'm gonna do
myself in—i'm
checken out.                                                                10
            what's that man?
yeh. that's right. i feel the
need to do away with myself.
why?
      ohhhh man. cuz                                                        15
i'm blk. liven in a
wite/psychotic/neurotic
schizophrenic/society where
all honkies have been plannen
my death since . . .                                                        20
            what's that
u say? when did i first
feel that honkies?
            yeh. honkies.
yeh. i'll spell it for u.      HONKIES . . .                                25
were tryen to kill me?

1. Intellects.                    4. Kind; i.e., all men.
2. Imaginations.                  5. Particles; i.e., make one good man
3. Through.                       from the good particles of all men.

                              well. man. it ain't
exactly my discovery.
                              but it's been happenen
for bout 400 yrs.                                              30
                    what's that?
can i au-then-ti-cate that?
                              how u
spell that man?    oh yeh?
now what that mean? oh yeh?                                    35
well that ain't one of my words.
but mannnn.
                    don't u read the fucken papers?
don't u live?
                    what's that? u say it's                   40
all improven for us negroes.
                              what kind
of fool are u? what u? some kind of
wite/liberal/pacificist/jew?
                              all u                            45
honkies are alike.
                    shit man u
ain't got no kind of understanding. hey.
                              what's that
funny sound like u belch/en or somethin?                      50
oh u record/en the conversation.
                              i'm on a
sort of candid telephone.
                              what's that u say?
i sound better?    yeh.                                       55
                    matter of fact
i do.
     feel like go/en out and
do/en in a couple honkies.
yeh. honkies. hey. u still there?                             60
yeh. well i'm gonna split.
hey. u know what?
                    u don't sound so gooood.
yehhhh if i wuz u
                    i'd hang it up mannnNN.                    65
                    bye now!

                                                           1970

GEORGE GORDON, LORD BYRON

## On This Day I Complete My Thirty- Sixth Year

*Missolonghi,[1] January 22, 1824*

'Tis time this heart should be unmoved,
    Since others it hath ceased to move:

---

1. A town in Greece where Byron had gone to assist the Greeks in their war for independence from Turkey. He had organized an expedition, subsidized it, and tried to
train the troops himself. He died there less than three months later.

Yet, though I cannot be beloved,
 Still let me love!

My days are in the yellow leaf;                                    5
 The flowers and fruits of love are gone;
The worm, the canker,[2] and the grief
 Are mine alone!

The fire that on my bosom preys
 Is lone as some volcanic isle;                                   10
No torch is kindled at its blaze—
 A funeral pile.

The hope, the fear, the jealous care,
 The exalted portion of the pain
And power of love, I cannot share,                               15
 But wear the chain.

But 'tis not *thus*—and 'tis not *here*—
 Such thoughts should shake my soul, nor *now*,
Where glory decks the hero's bier,
 Or binds his brow.                                              20

The sword, the banner, and the field,
 Glory and Greece, around me see!
The Spartan, borne upon his shield,
 Was not more free.

Awake! (not Greece—she *is* awake!)                             25
 Awake, my spirit! Think through *whom*
Thy life-blood tracks its parent lake,
 And then strike home!

Tread those reviving passions down,
 Unworthy manhood!—unto thee                                    30
Indifferent should the smile or frown
 Of beauty be.

If thou regrett'st thy youth, *why live?*
 The land of honorable death
Is here:—up to the field, and give                              35
 Away thy breath!

Seek out—less often sought than found—
 A soldier's grave, for thee the best;
Then look around, and choose thy ground,
 And take thy rest.                                             40

                                                1824

2. Infection.

DIANE WAKOSKI

# A Poet Recognizing the Echo of the Voice

## I. Isolation of Beautiful Women

"How were you able to get ten of the world's
most beautiful women to marry you?"
"I just asked them. You know, men all over
the world dream about Lana Turner, desire
her want to be with her. But very very
few ever ask her to marry them."

paraphrase of an interview with Artie Shaw

We are burning
in our heads
at night,
bonfires of our own bodies.
Persia reduces our heads                                    5
to star sapphires and lapis lazuli.[1]
Silver threads itself
into the lines of our throats
and glitters every time we speak.
Old alchemical riddles[2]                                   10
are solved in the dreams of men
who marry other women and think of us.
Anyone who sees us
will hold our small hands,
like mirrors in which they see themselves,       15
and try to initial our arms
with desperation.
Everyone wants to come close to
the cinnamon of our ears.
Every man wants to explore our bodies            20
and fill up our minds.
Riding their motorcycles along collapsing grey highways,
they sequester their ambivalent hunting clothes
between our legs,
reminding themselves of their value                 25
by quoting mining stock prices, and ours.
But men do not marry us,
do not ask us to share their lives,
do not survive the bonfires
hot enough to melt steel.                                    30
To alchemize rubies.

We live the loneliness
that men run after,
and we,
the precious rocks of the earth                        35
are made harder,
more fiery
more beautiful,
more complex,

1. Blue gems.
2. Problems. Alchemy was devoted to        finding an elixir which would turn baser
metals to gold (line 31).

by all the pressing,                                          40
the burying,
the plundering;

even your desertions,
your betrayals,
your failure to understand and love us,                       45
your unwillingness to face the world
as staunchly as we do;
these things
which ravage us,
cannot destroy our lives,                                     50
though they often take our bodies.
We are the earth.
We wake up
finding ourselves
glinting in the dark                                          55
after thousands of years
of pressing.

### II. Movement to Establish My Identity

> I know what wages beauty gives,
> How hard a life her servant lives . . .
>             "To A Young Beauty," w. b. YEATS

A woman wakes up
finds herself
glinting in the dark;                                         60
the earth holds her
as a precious rock
in a mine

her breath is a jumble
of sediments,                                                 65
of mixed strata,
of the valuable,
beautiful,
of bulk.

All men are miners;                                           70
willing to work hard
and cover themselves with pit dirt;
to dig out;
to weigh;
to possess.                                                   75

Mine is a place.
Mine is a designation.
A man says, "it is mine,"
but he hacks,
chops apart the mine                                          80
to discover,
to plunder,
what's in it/ Plunder,

that is the word.
Plunder.                                                                    85

A woman wakes up
finds herself
scarred
but still glinting
in the dark.                                                                90

### III. Beauty

only God, my dear,
Could love you for yourself alone
And not your yellow hair.
"For Anne Gregory," w. b. yeats

and if I cut off my long hair,
if I stopped speaking,
if I stopped dreaming for other people about parts of the car,
stopped handing them tall creamy flowered silks
and loosing the magnificent hawks to fly in their direction,     95
stopped exciting them with the possibilities
of a thousand crystals under the fingernail
to look at while writing a letter,
if I stopped crying for the salvation of the tea ceremony,
stopped rushing in excitedly with a spikey bird-of-paradise,[3]   100
and never let them see how accurate my pistol shooting is,
who would I be?

Where is the real me
I want them all to love?

We are all the textures we wear.                                    105

We frighten men with our steel;
we fascinate them with our silk;
we seduce them with our cinnamon;
we rule them with our sensuous voices;
we confuse them with our submissions.                               110
Is there anywhere
a man
who
will not punish us
for our beauty?                                                     115

He is the one
we all search for,
chanting names for exotic oceans of the moon.

He is the one
we all anticipate,                                                  120
pretending these small pedestrians

3. A bright, spectacular plant.

jaywalking into our lives
are he.
He is the one
we all anticipate;                                        125
beauty looks for its match,
confuses the issue
with a mystery that does not exist:
the rock
that cannot burn.                                         130

We are burning
in our heads at night
the incense of our histories, finding
you have used our skulls
for ashtrays.                                             135
                                                        1970

CAROLYN  KIZER

## A Widow in Wintertime

Last night a baby gargled in the throes
Of a fatal spasm. My children are all grown
Past infant strangles; so, reassured, I knew
Some other baby perished in the snow.
But no. The cat was making love again.                    5

Later, I went down and let her in.
She hung her tail, flagging from her sins.
Though she'd eaten, I forked out another dinner,
Being myself hungry all ways, and thin
From metaphysic famines she knows nothing of,            10

The feckless beast! Even so, resemblances
Were on my mind: female and feline, though
She preens herself from satisfaction, and does
Not mind lying even in snow. She is
Lofty and bedraggled, without need to choose.            15

As an ex-animal, I look fondly on
Her excesses and simplicities, and would not return
To them; taking no marks for what I have become,
Merely that my nine lives peal in my ears again
And again, ring in these austerities,                    20

These arbitrary disciplines of mine,
Most of them trivial: like covering
The children on my way to bed, and trying
To live well enough alone, and not to dream
Of grappling in the snow, claws plunged in fur,          25

Or waken in a caterwaul of dying.
                                                        1961

LOUIS MACNEICE

## Sunday Morning

Down the road someone is practicing scales,
The notes like little fishes vanish with a wink of tails,
Man's heart expands to tinker with his car
For this is Sunday morning, Fate's great bazaar;
Regard these means as ends, concentrate on this Now,    5
And you may grow to music or drive beyond Hindhead[1] anyhow,
Take corners on two wheels until you go so fast
That you can clutch a fringe or two of the windy past,
That you can abstract this day and make it to the week of time
A small eternity, a sonnet self-contained in rhyme.    10
But listen, up the road, something gulps, the church spire
Opens its eight bells out, skulls' mouths which will not tire
To tell how there is no music or movement which secures
Escape from the weekday time. Which deadens and endures.

1935

WALLACE STEVENS

## Sunday Morning

I

Complacencies of the peignoir, and late
Coffee and oranges in a sunny chair,
And the green freedom of a cockatoo
Upon a rug mingle to dissipate
The holy hush of ancient sacrifice.    5
She dreams a little, and she feels the dark
Encroachment of that old catastrophe,[2]
As a calm darkens among water-lights.
The pungent oranges and bright, green wings
Seem things in some procession of the dead,    10
Winding across wide water, without sound.
The day is like wide water, without sound,
Stilled for the passing of her dreaming feet
Over the seas, to silent Palestine,
Dominion of the blood and sepulchre.    15

II

Why should she give her bounty to the dead?
What is divinity if it can come
Only in silent shadows and in dreams?
Shall she not find in comforts of the sun,
In pungent fruit and bright, green wings, or else    20
In any balm or beauty of the earth,
Things to be cherished like the thought of heaven?
Divinity must live within herself:
Passions of rain, or moods in falling snow;
Grievings in loneliness, or unsubdued    25

1. In Surrey; the direction of a typical    2. The Crucifixion.
Sunday outing from London.

Elations when the forest blooms; gusty
Emotions on wet roads on autumn nights;
All pleasures and all pains, remembering
The bough of summer and the winter branch.
These are the measures destined for her soul.                    30

### III

Jove[3] in the clouds had his inhuman birth.
No mother suckled him, no sweet land gave
Large-mannered motions to his mythy mind
He moved among us, as a muttering king,
Magnificent, would move among his hinds,[4]              35
Until our blood, commingling, virginal,
With heaven, brought such requital to desire
The very hinds discerned it, in a star.[5]
Shall our blood fail? Or shall it come to be
The blood of paradise? And shall the earth          40
Seem all of paradise that we shall know?
The sky will be much friendlier then than now,
A part of labor and a part of pain,
And next in glory to enduring love,
Not this dividing and indifferent blue.              45

### IV

She says, "I am content when wakened birds,
Before they fly, test the reality
Of misty fields, by their sweet questionings;
But when the birds are gone, and their warm fields
Return no more, where, then, is paradise?"          50
There is not any haunt of prophecy,
Nor any old chimera of the grave,
Neither the golden underground, nor isle
Melodious, where spirits gat[6] them home,
Nor visionary south, nor cloudy palm          55
Remote on heaven's hill, that has endured
As April's green endures, or will endure
Like her remembrance of awakened birds,
Or her desire for June and evening, tipped
By the consummation of the swallow's wings.          60

### V

She says, "But in contentment I still feel
The need of some imperishable bliss."
Death is the mother of beauty; hence from her,
Alone, shall come fulfillment to our dreams
And our desires. Although she strews the leaves          65
Of sure obliteration on our paths,
The path sick sorrow took, the many paths
Where triumph rang its brassy phrase, or love
Whispered a little out of tenderness,
She makes the willow shiver in the sun          70
For maidens who were wont to sit and gaze

---

3. Jupiter, the chief Roman god.          5. The star of Bethlehem.
4. Lowliest rural subjects.          6. Got.

Upon the grass, relinquished to their feet.
She causes boys to pile new plums and pears
On disregarded plate.[7] The maidens taste
And stray impassioned in the littering leaves.                   75

### VI

Is there no change of death in paradise?
Does ripe fruit never fall? Or do the boughs
Hang always heavy in that perfect sky,
Unchanging, yet so like our perishing earth,
With rivers like our own that seek for seas                      80
They never find, the same receding shores
That never touch with inarticulate pang?
Why set the pear upon those river-banks
Or spice the shores with odors of the plum?
Alas, that they should wear our colors there,                    85
The silken weavings of our afternoons,
And pick the strings of our insipid lutes!
Death is the mother of beauty, mystical,
Within whose burning bosom we devise
Our earthly mothers waiting, sleeplessly.                        90

### VII

Supple and turbulent, a ring of men
Shall chant in orgy[8] on a summer morn
Their boisterous devotion to the sun,
Not as a god, but as a god might be,
Naked among them, like a savage source.                          95
Their chant shall be a chant of paradise,
Out of their blood, returning to the sky;
And in their chant shall enter, voice by voice,
The windy lake wherein their lord delights,
The trees, like serafin,[9] and echoing hills,                   100
That choir among themselves long afterward.
They shall know well the heavenly fellowship
Of men that perish and of summer morn.
And whence they came and whither they shall go
The dew upon their feet shall manifest.                          105

### VIII

She hears, upon that water without sound,
A voice that cries, "The tomb in Palestine
Is not the porch of spirits lingering.
It is the grave of Jesus, where he lay."
We live in an old chaos of the sun,                              110
Or old dependency of day and night,
Or island solitude, unsponsored, free,
Of that wide water, inescapable.
Deer walk upon our mountains, and the quail

7. "Plate is used in the sense of so-called family plate. Disregarded refers to the disuse into which things fall that have been possessed for a long time. I mean, therefore, that death releases and renews. What the old have come to disregard, the young inherit and make use of" (*Letters of Wallace Stevens* [1966], pp. 183–184).
8. Ceremonial revelry.
9. Seraphim, the highest of the nine orders of angels.

Whistle about us their spontaneous cries;                    115
Sweet berries ripen in the wilderness;
And, in the isolation of the sky,
At evening, casual flocks of pigeons make
Ambiguous undulations as they sink,
Downward to darkness, on extended wings.          120

1915

WILLIAM SHAKESPEARE

## Hark, Hark! the Lark[1]

Hark, hark! the lark at heaven's gate sings,
   And Phoebus[2] 'gins arise,
His steeds to water at those springs
   On chaliced[3] flowers that lies;
And winking Mary-buds[4] begin                           5
   To ope their golden eyes:
With every thing that pretty is,
   My lady sweet, arise!
     Arise, arise!

ca. 1610

JOHN DONNE

## The Sun Rising

Busy old fool, unruly sun,
   Why dost thou thus,
Through windows, and through curtains, call on us?
Must to thy motions lovers' seasons run?
     Saucy pedantic wretch, go chide          5
     Late schoolboys, and sour prentices,[1]
Go tell court-huntsmen that the king will ride,
Call country ants[2] to harvest offices;
Love, all alike, no season knows, nor clime,
Nor hours, days, months, which are the rags of time.     10

Thy beams, so reverend and strong
   Why shouldst thou think?
I could eclipse and cloud them with a wink,
But that I would not lose her sight so long:
     If her eyes have not blinded thine,          15
     Look, and tomorrow late, tell me
Whether both the Indias[3] of spice and mine
Be where thou left'st them, or lie here with me.
Ask for those kings whom thou saw'st yesterday,
And thou shalt hear, all here in one bed lay.             20

She is all states, and all princes I,
   Nothing else is.

1. From *Cymbeline*, Act II, sc. iii.     1. Apprentices.
2. Apollo, the sun god.     2. Farmworkers.
3. Cup-shaped.     3. The East and West Indies, commer-
4. Buds of marigolds.     cial sources of spices and gold.

Princes do but play us; compared to this,
All honor's mimic,[4] all wealth alchemy.[5]
    Thou, sun, art half as happy as we,           25
    In that the world's contracted thus;
Thine age asks[6] ease, and since thy duties be
To warm the world, that's done in warming us.
Shine here to us, and thou art every where;
This bed thy center[7] is, these walls thy sphere.     30

1633

JOHN DONNE

# The Good-Morrow

I wonder, by my troth, what thou and I
    Did, till we loved? were we not weaned till then?
But sucked on country pleasures, childishly?
    Or snorted[1] we in the Seven Sleepers' den?[2]
'Twas so; but[3] this, all pleasures fancies be.     5
If ever any beauty[4] I did see,
Which I desired, and got,[5] 'twas but a dream of thee.

And now good-morrow to our waking souls,
    Which watch not one another out of fear;
For love, all love of other sights controls,     10
    And makes one little room an everywhere.
Let sea-discoverers to new worlds have gone,
Let maps to other,[6] worlds on worlds have shown,
Let us possess one world, each hath one, and is one.

My face in thine eye, thine in mine appears,[7]     15
    And true plain hearts do in the faces rest;
Where can we find two better hemispheres,
    Without sharp north, without declining west?
Whatever dies was not mixed equally,[8]
If our two loves be one, or, thou and I     20
Love so alike that none do slacken, none can die.

1633

WILLIAM EMPSON

# Aubade[1]

Hours before dawn we were woken by the quake.
My house was on a cliff. The thing could take
Bookloads off shelves, break bottles in a row.
Then the long pause and then the bigger shake.
It seemed the best thing to be up and go.     5

4. Hypocritical.
5. Imposture, like the "scientific" procedures for turning base metals into gold.
6. Requires.
7. Of orbit.
1. Snored.
2. According to tradition, seven Christian youths escaped Roman persecution by sleeping in a cave for 187 years.
3. Except for.

4. Beautiful woman.
5. Sexually possessed.
6. Other people.
7. I.e., each is reflected in the other's eyes.
8. Perfectly mixed elements, according to scholastic philosophy, were stable and immortal.
1. A morning song in which lovers welcome the new day.

And far too large for my feet to step by.
I hoped that various buildings were brought low.
The heart of standing is you cannot fly.

It seemed quite safe till she got up and dressed.
The guarded tourist makes the guide the test.                10
Then I said The Garden? Laughing she said No.
Taxi for her and for me healthy rest.
It seemed the best thing to be up and go.

The language problem but you have to try.
Some solid ground for lying could she show?                 15
The heart of standing is you cannot fly.

None of these deaths were her point at all.
The thing was that being woken he would bawl
And finding her not in earshot he would know.
I tried saying Half an Hour to pay this call.               20
It seemed the best thing to be up and go.

I slept, and blank as that I would yet lie.
Till you have seen what a threat holds below
The heart of standing is you cannot fly.

Tell me again about Europe and her pains,                   25
Who's tortured by the drought, who by the rains.
Glut me with floods where only the swine can row
Who cuts his throat and let him count his gains.
It seemed the best thing to be up and go.

A bedshift flight to a Far Eastern sky.                      30
Only the same war² on a stronger toe.
The heart of standing is you cannot fly.

Tell me more quickly what I lost by this,
Or tell me with less drama what they miss
Who call no die³ a god for a good throw,                     35
Who say after two aliens had one kiss
It seemed the best thing to be up and go.

But as to risings, I can tell you why.
It is on contradiction that they grow.
It seemed the best thing to be up and go.                    40
Up was the heartening and the strong reply.
The heart of standing is we cannot fly.

1940

LOUIS MAC NEICE

# Aubade

Having bitten on life like a sharp apple
Or, playing it like a fish, been happy,

2. *"The same war* in Tokyo then was the     3. Singular of dice.
Manchurian Incident." (Empson's note)

Having felt with fingers that the sky is blue,
What have we after that to look forward to?

Not the twilight of the gods but a precise dawn          5
Of sallow and grey bricks, and newsboys crying war.

                                                        1935

RICHARD WILBUR

## Love Calls Us to the Things of This World[1]

The eyes open to a cry of pulleys,[2]
And spirited from sleep, the astounded soul
Hangs for a moment bodiless and simple
As false dawn.
                    Outside the open window                 5
The morning air is all awash with angels.

    Some are in bed-sheets, some are in blouses,
Some are in smocks: but truly there they are.
Now they are rising together in calm swells
Of halcyon[3] feeling, filling whatever they wear        10
With the deep joy of their impersonal breathing;
    Now they are flying in place,[4] conveying
The terrible speed of their omnipresence, moving
And staying like white water; and now of a sudden
They swoon down into so rapt a quiet                     15
That nobody seems to be there.
                                The soul shrinks

    From all that it is about to remember,
From the punctual rape of every blesséd day,
And cries,                                               20
            "Oh, let there be nothing on earth but laundry,
Nothing but rosy hands in the rising steam
And clear dances done in the sight of heaven."

    Yet, as the sun acknowledges
With a warm look the world's hunks and colors,           25
The soul descends once more in bitter love
To accept the waking body, saying now
In a changed voice as the man yawns and rises,

    "Bring them down from their ruddy gallows;
Let there be clean linen for the backs of thieves;       30
Let lovers go fresh and sweet to be undone,
And the heaviest nuns walk in a pure floating
Of dark habits,
                keeping their difficult balance."

                                                        1956

1. A recurrent theme in St. Augustine's    then sent outdoors to dry.
*Confessions.*                              3. Serene.
    2. Laundry pulleys, designed so that    4. Like planes in a formation.
clothes can be hung on the line inside and

JONATHAN SWIFT

## A Description of the Morning

Now hardly[1] here and there a hackney-coach[2]
Appearing, showed the ruddy morn's approach.
Now Betty[3] from her master's bed had flown,
And softly stole to discompose her own.
The slip shod 'prentice from his master's door          5
Had pared the dirt, and sprinkled round the floor.
Now Moll had whirled her mop with dext'rous airs,
Prepared to scrub the entry and the stairs.
The youth with broomy stumps began to trace[4]
The kennel-edge[5] where wheels had worn the place.      10
The small-coal man[6] was heard with cadence deep,
Till drowned in shriller notes of chimney-sweep:
Duns[7] at his lordship's gate began to meet;
And brick-dust Moll had screamed through half the street.[8]
The turnkey now his flock returning sees,                15
Duly let out a-nights to steal for fees.[9]
The watchful bailiffs[1] take their silent stands,
And schoolboys lag with satchels in their hands.

p. 1709

BOB DYLAN

## Mister Tambourine Man

### Chorus

Hey, Mister Tambourine Man, play a song for me,
I'm not sleepy and there ain't no place I'm going to.
Hey, Mister Tambourine Man, play a song for me,
In the jingle, jangle morning I'll come followin' you.

### I

Though I know that evenin's empire has returned into sand     5
Vanished from my hand,
Left me blindly here to stand
But still no sleepin'.
My weariness amazes me,
I'm branded on my feet,                                        10
I have no one to meet,
And the ancient empty street's
Too dead for dreamin'.
*Chorus*

1. Scarcely; i.e., they are just beginning to appear.
2. Hired coach.
3. A stock name for a servant girl. Moll (lines 7, 14) is a frequent lower-class nickname.
4. "To find old Nails." (Swift's note)
5. Edge of the gutter which ran down the middle of the street.
6. A seller of coal and charcoal.
7. Bill collectors.
8. Selling powdered brick which was used to clean knives.
9. Jailers collected fees from prisoners for their keep and often let them out at night so they could steal to pay expenses.
1. Looking for those on their "wanted" lists.

II

Take me on a trip upon your magic swirlin' ship,
My senses have been stripped,                                      15
My hands can't feel to grip,
My toes too numb to step,
Wait only for my boot heels to be wanderin'.
I'm ready to go anywhere,
I'm ready for to fade                                              20
Into my own parade.
Cast your dancin' spell my way,
I promise to go under it.
*Chorus*


III

Though you might hear laughin', spinnin', swingin' madly through the
      sun,
It's not aimed at anyone,                                          25
It's just escapin' on the run,
And but for the sky there are no fences facin'.
And if you hear vague traces
Of skippin' reels of rhyme
To your tambourine in time,                                        30
It's just a ragged clown behind,
I wouldn't pay it any mind,
It's just a shadow
You're seein' that he's chasin'.
*Chorus*


IV

Take me disappearin' through the smoke rings of my mind            35
Down the foggy ruins of time,
Far past the frozen leaves,
The haunted, frightened trees
Out to the windy beach
Far from the twisted reach of crazy sorrow.                        40
Yes, to dance beneath the diamond sky
With one hand wavin' free,
Silhouetted by the sea,
Circled by the circus sands,
With memory and fate                                               45
Driven deep beneath the waves.
Let me forget about today until tomorrow.
*Chorus*

                                                             1964


RICHARD WILBUR

## After the Last Bulletins

After the last bulletins the windows darken
And the whole city founders readily and deep,
Sliding on all its pillows
To the thronged Atlantis[1] of personal sleep,

---

1. A large mythic island supposed to have once existed in the Atlantic, later submerged
by an earthquake.

And the wind rises. The wind rises and bowls       5
The day's litter of news in the alleys. Trash
Tears itself on the railings,
Soars and falls with a soft crash,

Tumbles and soars again. Unruly flights
Scamper the park, and taking a statue for dead      10
Strike at the positive eyes,
Batter and flap the stolid head

And scratch the noble name. In empty lots
Our journals spiral in a fierce noyade[2]
Of all we thought to think,                15
Or caught in corners cramp and wad

And twist our words. And some from gutters flail
Their tatters at the tired patrolman's feet,
Like all that fisted snow
That cried beside his long retreat            20

Damn you! damn you! to the emperor's horse's heels.
Oh none too soon through the air white and dry
Will the clear announcer's voice
Beat like a dove, and you and I

From the heart's anarch and responsible town      25
Return by subway-mouth to life again,
Bearing the morning papers,
And cross the park where saintlike men,

White and absorbed, with stick and bag remove
The litter of the night, and footsteps rouse       30
With confident morning sound
The songbirds in the public boughs.

                                       1956

MATTHEW ARNOLD

# Dover Beach[1]

The sea is calm tonight.
The tide is full, the moon lies fair
Upon the straits; on the French coast the light
Gleams and is gone; the cliffs of England stand,
Glimmering and vast, out in the tranquil bay.       5
Come to the window, sweet is the night-air!
Only, from the long line of spray
Where the sea meets the moon-blanched land,
Listen! you hear the grating roar
Of pebbles which the waves draw back, and fling,     10
At their return, up the high strand,
Begin, and cease, and then again begin,

2. Execution by drowning.             Channel. The lights on the French coast
1. At the narrowest point on the English     (lines 3–4) would be about 20 miles away.

With tremulous cadence slow, and bring
The eternal note of sadness in.

Sophocles long ago                                          15
Heard it on the Aegean, and it brought
Into his mind the turbid ebb and flow
Of human misery;[2] we
Find also in the sound a thought,
Hearing it by this distant northern sea.                    20

The Sea of Faith
Was once, too, at the full, and round earth's shore
Lay like the folds of a bright girdle furled.
But now I only hear
Its melancholy, long, withdrawing roar,                     25
Retreating, to the breath
Of the night-wind, down the vast edges drear
And naked shingles[3] of the world.

Ah, love, let us be true
To one another! for the world, which seems                  30
To lie before us like a land of dreams,
So various, so beautiful, so new,
Hath really neither joy, nor love, nor light,
Nor certitude, nor peace, nor help for pain;
And we are here as on a darkling plain                      35
Swept with confused alarms of struggle and flight,
Where ignorant armies clash by night.

ca. 1851

ANDREW   MARVELL

# The Garden

How vainly men themselves amaze[1]
To win the palm, the oak, or bays,[2]
And their incessant labors see
Crowned from some single herb, or tree,
Whose short and narrow-vergéd[3] shade                      5
Does prudently their toils upbraid;
While all flowers and all trees do close[4]
To weave the garlands of repose!

Fair Quiet, have I found thee here,
And Innocence, thy sister dear?                             10
Mistaken long, I sought you then
In busy companies of men.
Your sacred plants,[5] if here below,
Only among the plants will grow;

2. In *Antigone*, lines 583–91, the chorus compares the fate of the house of Oedipus to the waves of the sea.
3. Pebble-strewn beaches.
1. Become frenzied.

2. Awards for athletic, civic, and literary achievements.
3. Narrowly cropped.
4. Unite.
5. Cuttings.

Society is all but rude[6]                                              15
To[7] this delicious solitude.

No white nor red was ever seen
So am'rous as this lovely green.
Fond lovers, cruel as their flame,
Cut in these trees their mistress' name:                               20
Little, alas, they know, or heed
How far these beauties hers exceed!
Fair trees, wheresoe'er your barks I wound,
No name shall but your own be found.

When we have run our passion's heat,                                   25
Love hither makes his best retreat.
The gods, that mortal beauty chase,
Still in a tree did end their race:
Apollo hunted Daphne so,
Only that she might laurel grow;                                       30
And Pan did after Syrinx speed,
Not as a nymph, but for a reed.[8]

What wondrous life is this I lead!
Ripe apples drop about my head;
The luscious clusters of the vine                                      35
Upon my mouth do crush their wine;
The nectarine and curious[9] peach
Into my hands themselves do reach;
Stumbling on melons, as I pass,
Insnared with flowers, I fall on grass.                                40

Meanwhile the mind, from pleasure less,
Withdraws into its happiness;[1]
The mind, that ocean where each kind
Does straight its own resemblance find;[2]
Yet it creates, transcending these,                                    45
Far other worlds and other seas,
Annihilating[3] all that's made
To a green thought in a green shade.

Here at the fountain's sliding foot,
Or at some fruit tree's mossy root,                                    50
Casting the body's vest[4] aside,
My soul into the boughs does glide:
There, like a bird, it sits and sings,
Then whets[5] and combs its silver wings,
And, till prepared for longer flight,                                  55
Waves in its plumes the various[6] light.

---

6. Barbarous.
7. Compared to.
8. In Ovid's *Metamorphoses*, Daphne, pursued by Apollo, is turned into a laurel, and Syrinx, pursued by Pan, into a reed which Pan makes into a flute.
9. Exquisite.
1. I.e., the mind withdraws from lesser sense pleasure into contemplation.
2. All land creatures were supposed to have corresponding sea-creatures.
3. Reducing to nothing by comparison.
4. Vestment, clothing; the flesh is being considered as simply clothing for the soul.
5. Preens.
6. Many-colored.

Such was that happy garden-state,
While man there walked without a mate:
After a place so pure, and sweet,
What other help could yet be meet![7]                    60
But 'twas beyond a mortal's share
To wander solitary there:
Two paradises 'twere in one
To live in paradise alone.

How well the skillful gardener drew                      65
Of flowers and herbs this dial[8] new,
Where, from above, the milder sun
Does through a fragrant zodiac run;
And as it works, th' industrious bee
Computes its time as well as we!                         70
How could such sweet and wholesome hours
Be reckoned but with herbs and flowers?

1681

BEN JONSON

# Still to Be Neat[1]

Still[2] to be neat, still to be dressed,
As you were going to a feast;
Still to be powdered, still perfumed;
Lady, it is to be presumed,
Though art's hid causes are not found,                   5
All is not sweet, all is not sound.

Give me a look, give me a face
That makes simplicity a grace;
Robes loosely flowing, hair as free;
Such sweet neglect more taketh me                        10
Than all th' adulteries of art.
They strike mine eyes, but not my heart.

1609

ROBERT HERRICK

# Delight in Disorder

A sweet disorder in the dress
Kindles in clothes a wantonness.
A lawn[1] about the shoulders thrown
Into a fine distractiön;
An erring lace, which here and there                     5
Enthralls the crimson stomacher,[2]
A cuff neglectful, and thereby
Ribbands[3] to flow confusedly;

7. Appropriate.
8. A garden planted in the shape of a sundial, complete with zodiac.
1. A song from Jonson's play, *The Silent Woman*.

2. Continually.
1. Scarf of fine linen.
2. Ornamental covering for the breasts.
3. Ribbons.

A winning wave, deserving note,
In the tempestuous petticoat;         10
A careless shoestring, in whose tie
I see a wild civility;
Do more bewitch me than when art
Is too precise[4] in every part.

                  1648

GERARD MANLEY HOPKINS

# Pied Beauty[1]

Glory be to God for dappled things—
  For skies of couple-color as a brinded[2] cow;
    For rose-moles all in stipple[3] upon trout that swim;
Fresh-firecoal chestnut-falls;[4] finches' wings;
  Landscape plotted and pieced—fold, fallow, and plow;     5
    And all trades, their gear and tackle and trim.
All things counter, original, spare, strange;
  Whatever is fickle, freckled (who knows how?)
    With swift, slow; sweet, sour; adazzle, dim;
He fathers-forth whose beauty is past change:        10
              Praise him.

1877

W. H. AUDEN

# Hammerfest[1]

For over forty years I'd paid it atlas homage,[2]
  The northernmost township on earth, producing
The best deep-frozen fish sticks you can buy: for three days,
  I pottered round, a monolingual[3] pilgrim,
And drank the beer of the world's most northern brewery.    5
  Though miles beyond the Moral Circle,[4] I saw
No orgies, no great worms, nor dreamed of any during
  Three sunny nights: louts, though—German this time[5]—
Had left their usual mark. How much reverence could I,
  Can anyone past fifty, afford to lose?        10

Was it as worldly as it looked? I might have thought so
  But for my ears: something odd was happening
Soundwise. A word, a laugh, a footstep, a truck's outcry,
  Each utterance rang singular, staccato,
To be cut off before it could be contradicted        15
  Or confused by others: a listening terrain

4. In the 16th and 17th centuries Puritans were often called Precisians because of their fastidiousness.
1. Particolored beauty: having patches or sections of more than one color.
2. Streaked or spotted.
3. Rose-colored dots or flecks.
4. Fallen chestnuts as red as burning coals.
1. A small town in Norway, "the north- ernmost township on earth" (line 2).
2. Admired it on maps.
3. Speaking only one language.
4. "A jocular term, used by southern Norwegians for the Arctic circle." (Auden's note)
5. "In 1945 the retreating *Wehrmacht* burnt down every single house." (Auden's note)

Seized on them all and never gave one back in echo,
  As if to land as desolate, as far up,
Whatever noise our species cared to make still mattered.
  Here was a place we had yet to disappoint.                      20

The only communities it had to judge us by
  Were cenobite,[6] mosses and lichen, sworn to
Station and reticence: its rocks knew almost nothing,
  Nothing about the glum Reptilian Empire
Or the epic journey of the Horse, had heard no tales             25
  Of that preglacial Actium[7] when the huge
Archaic shrubs went down before the scented flowers,
  And earth was won for color. For all it knew,
Religion had begun with the Salvation Army,
  Warfare with motorized resentful conscripts.                   30

Ground so bare might take a century to realize
  How we behave to regions or to beings
Who have anything we're after: to have disgusted
  Millions of acres of good-natured topsoil
Is an achievement of a sort, to fail to notice                  35
  How garden plants and farmyard beasts look at us,
Or refuse to look, to picture all of them as dear
  Faithful old retainers, another, but why
Bring that up now? My intrusion had not profaned it:
  If innocence is holy, it was holy.                             40

                                                              1965


MATTHEW PRIOR

# To a Child of Quality Five Years Old,
# the Author Supposed Forty[1]

Lords, knights, and squires, the numerous band
  That wear the fair Miss Mary's fetters,
Were summoned, by her high command,
  To show their passions by their letters.

My pen amongst the rest I took,                                  5
  Lest those bright eyes that cannot read
Should dart their kindling fires, and look
  The power they have to be obeyed.

Nor quality nor[2] reputation
  Forbid me yet my flame to tell;                               10
Dear five years old befriends my passion,
  And I may write till she can spell.

---

6. Monastic.
7. The historical Actium was the site of Augustus's famous naval victory over Antony, 31 B.C.
1. Addressed to Lady Mary Villiers, daughter of Edward Villiers, the first Earl of Jersey. Prior was actually about 30 or 35 when the poem was written. "Quality" (see line 9) connotes aristocratic social degree.
2. Neither . . . nor (a common 18th-century construction).

For while she makes her silk-worms beds
  With all the tender things I swear,
Whilst all the house my passion reads,                          15
  In papers round her baby's[3] hair,

She may receive and own[4] my flame,
  For though the strictest prudes should know it,
She'll pass for a most virtuous dame,
  And I for an unhappy poet.                                    20

Then too, alas! when she shall tear
  The lines some younger rival sends,
She'll give me leave to write, I fear,
  And we shall still continue friends.

For, as our different ages move,                                25
  'Tis so ordained, would fate but mend it!
That I shall be past making love
  When she begins to comprehend it.

ca. 1700

YVOR WINTERS

# At the San Francisco Airport

*To my daughter, 1954*

This is the terminal: the light
Gives perfect vision, false and hard;
The metal glitters, deep and bright.
Great planes are waiting in the yard—
They are already in the night.                                  5

And you are here beside me, small,
Contained and fragile, and intent
On things that I but half recall—
Yet going whither you are bent.
I am the past, and that is all.                                 10

But you and I in part are one:
The frightened brain, the nervous will,
The knowledge of what must be done,
The passion to acquire the skill
To face that which you dare not shun.                           15

The rain of matter upon sense
Destroys me momently. The score:
There comes what will come. The expense
Is what one thought, and something more—
One's being and intelligence.                                   20

3. Doll's.                    4. Acknowledge.

This is the terminal, the break.
Beyond this point, on lines of air,
You take the way that you must take;
And I remain in light and stare—
In light, and nothing else, awake.                    25

1954

HELEN CHASIN

## The Word *Plum*

The word *plum* is delicious

pout and push, luxury of
self-love, and savoring murmur

full in the mouth and falling
like fruit                                              5

taut skin
pierced, bitten, provoked into
juice, and tart flesh

question
and reply, lip and tongue                              10
of pleasure.

                                                      1968

ROBERT FROST

## Fragmentary Blue

Why make so much of fragmentary blue
In here and there a bird, or butterfly,
Or flower, or wearing-stone, or open eye,
When heaven presents in sheets the solid hue?

Since earth is earth, perhaps, not heaven (as yet)—    5
Though some savants make earth include the sky;
And blue so far above us comes so high,
It only gives our wish for blue a whet.

                                                      1923

J. V. CUNNINGHAM

## Meditation on Statistical Method

Plato,[1] despair!
We prove by norms
How numbers bear
Empiric[2] forms,

How random wrong                                        5
Will average right

1. Whose philosophy assumed that all    Ideal world.
physical things pre-existed as forms in an    2. Empirical: observable.

If time be long
And error slight;

But in our hearts
Hyperbole                                           10
Curves and departs
To infinity.

Error is boundless.
Nor hope nor doubt,
Though both be groundless,                          15
Will average out.

1947

WILLIAM SHAKESPEARE

## That Time of Year

That time of year thou mayst in me behold
When yellow leaves, or none, or few, do hang
Upon those boughs which shake against the cold,
Bare ruined choirs, where late the sweet birds sang.
In me thou see'st the twilight of such day            5
As after sunset fadeth in the west;
Which by and by[1] black night doth take away,
Death's second self,[2] that seals up all in rest.
In me thou see'st the glowing of such fire,
That on the ashes of his youth doth lie,              10
As the deathbed whereon it must expire,
Consumed with that which it was nourished by.
This thou perceiv'st, which makes thy love more strong,
To love that well which thou must leave ere long.

1609

WILLIAM SHAKESPEARE

## When I Do Count the Clock

When I do count the clock that tells the time,
And see the brave[1] day sunk in hideous night;
When I behold the violet past prime,
And sable curls, all silvered o'er with white;
When lofty trees I see barren of leaves,               5
Which erst[2] from heat did canopy the herd,
And summer's green all girded up in sheaves
Borne on the bier with white and bristly beard;
Then of thy beauty do I question make,
That thou among the wastes of time must go,            10
Since sweets and beauties do themselves forsake
And die as fast as they see others grow;
And nothing 'gainst Time's scythe can make defense
Save breed,[3] to brave[4] him when he takes thee hence.

1609

1. Shortly.                          2. Once, formerly.
2. Sleep.                            3. Children.
1. Splendid, glorious.               4. Defy.

EDWARD TAYLOR

# Housewifery

Make me, O Lord, Thy spinning-wheel complete.[1]
Thy holy Word my distaff make for me;
Make mine affections Thy swift flyers neat;
And make my soul Thy holy spool to be;
My conversation make to be Thy reel,                    5
And reel the yarn thereon spun of Thy wheel.

Make me Thy loom then; knit therein this twine;
And make Thy Holy Spirit, Lord, wind quills;
Then weave the web Thyself. The yarn is fine.
Thine ordinances make my fulling mills.                  10
Then dye the same in heavenly colors choice,
All pinked[2] with varnished[3] flowers of paradise.

Then clothe therewith mine understanding, will,
Affections,[4] judgment, conscience, memory,
My words and actions, that their shine may fill          15
My ways with glory and Thee glorify.
Then mine apparel shall display before Ye
That I am clothed in holy robes for glory.

ca. 1700

JEAN TOOMER

# Song of the Son[1]

Pour O pour that parting soul in song,
O pour it in the sawdust glow of night,
Into the velvet pine-smoke air tonight,
And let the valley carry it along.
And let the valley carry it along.                       5

O land and soil, red soil and sweet-gum tree,
So scant of grass, so profligate of pines,
Now just before an epoch's sun declines
Thy son, in time, I have returned to thee,
Thy son, I have in time returned to thee.                10

In time, for though the sun is setting on
A song-lit race of slaves, it has not set;
Though late, O soil, it is not too late yet
To catch thy plaintive soul, leaving, soon gone,
Leaving, to catch thy plaintive soul soon gone.          15

1. Stanzas 1 and 2 specify parts of the spinning wheel and loom: the distaff (line 2) holds the fibers, flyers (line 3) twist the fibers, the spool (line 4) receives the spun thread, and the reel (line 5) stores the thread; quills (line 8) are bobbins holding the thread in the shuttle of the loom, and in the fulling mills (line 10) the cloth is cleaned and thickened.
2. Decorated.
3. Shining.
4. Emotions.
1. From the novel *Cane*.

O Negro slaves, dark purple ripened plums,
Squeezed, and bursting in the pine-wood air,
Passing, before they strip the old tree bare
One plum was saved for me, one seed becomes

An everlasting song, a singing tree,                    20
Caroling softly souls of slavery,
What they were, and what they are to me,
Caroling softly souls of slavery.

                                                        1923

JOHN LENNON AND PAUL MCCARTNEY

## Lucy in the Sky with Diamonds

Picture yourself in a boat on a river,
With tangerine trees and marmalade skies
Somebody calls you, you answer quite slowly,
A girl with kaleidoscope eyes.
Cellophane flowers of yellow and green,                 5
Towering over your head.
Look for the girl with the sun in her eyes,
And she's gone.
Lucy in the sky with diamonds.

Follow her down to a bridge by a fountain               10
Where rocking horse people eat marshmallow pies,
Everyone smiles as you drift past the flowers,
That grow so incredibly high.
Newspaper taxis appear on the shore,
Waiting to take you away.                               15
Climb in the back with your head in the clouds.
And you're gone.
Lucy in the sky with diamonds.

Picture yourself on a train in a station,
With plasticine[2] porters with looking glass ties,    20
Suddenly someone is there at the turnstile,
The girl with the kaleidoscope eyes.

                                                        1967

SIR PHILIP SIDNEY

## A Strife Is Grown

A strife is grown between Virtue and Love,
While each pretends[1] that Stella must be his:
Her eyes, her lips, her all, saith Love, do this,
Since they do wear his[2] badge, most firmly prove.
But Virtue thus that title doth disprove:              5
That Stella (O dear name!) that Stella is
That virtuous soul, sure heir of heav'nly bliss,

2. Made of a plastic substitute for the      1. Claims.
wax or clay ordinarily used in modeling.     2. Love's.

Not this fair outside which our hearts doth move.
And therefore, though her beauty and her grace
Be Love's indeed, in Stella's self he may                    10
By no pretense claim any manner place.
Well, Love, since this demur[3] our suit doth stay,
Let Virtue have that Stella's self; yet thus,
That Virtue but that body grant to us.

1582

EDMUND SPENSER

## Ye Tradeful Merchants

Ye tradeful merchants, that with weary toil
Do seek most precious things to make your gain;
And both the Indias[1] of their treasure spoil;
What needeth you to seek so far in vain?
For lo, my love doth in herself contain                       5
All this world's riches that may far be found:
If sapphires, lo, her eyes be sapphires plain;
If rubies, lo, her lips be rubies sound;
If pearls, her teeth be pearls, both pure and round;
If ivory, her forehead ivory ween;[2]                         10
If gold, her locks are finest gold on ground;
If silver, her fair hands are silver sheen;[3]
But that which fairest is, but few behold,
Her mind, adorned with virtues manifold.

1595

JOHN DONNE

## A Valediction: Forbidding Mourning

As virtuous men pass mildly away,
    And whisper to their souls to go,
Whilst some of their sad friends do say,
    "The breath goes now," and some say, "No,"

So let us melt, and make no noise,                            5
    No tear-floods, nor sigh-tempests move;
'Twere profanation of our joys
    To tell the laity our love.

Moving of the earth[1] brings harms and fears,
    Men reckon what it did and meant;                         10
But trepidation of the spheres,[2]
    Though greater far, is innocent.

---

3. Objection.
1. The East and West Indies, sources of
spices and precious metals.
2. Seems to be ivory.
3. Shining silver.
1. Earthquakes.

2. The Renaissance hypothesis that the
celestial spheres trembled and thus caused
unexpected variations in their orbits. Such
movements are "innocent" because earth-
lings do not observe or fret about them.

Dull sublunary[3] lovers' love
    (Whose soul is sense) cannot admit
Absence, because it doth remove                    15
    Those things which elemented[4] it.

But we, by a love so much refined
    That our selves know not what it is,
Inter-assured of the mind,
    Care less, eyes, lips, and hands to miss.      20

Our two souls therefore, which are one,
    Though I must go, endure not yet
A breach, but an expansion,
    Like gold to airy thinness beat.

If they be two, they are two so                    25
    As stiff twin compasses are two:
Thy soul, the fixed foot, makes no show
    To move, but doth, if the other do;

And though it in the center sit,
    Yet when the other far doth roam,              30
It leans, and hearkens after it,
    And grows erect, as that comes home.

Such wilt thou be to me, who must,
    Like the other foot, obliquely run;
Thy firmness makes my circle[5] just,             35
    And makes me end where I begun.

1611(?)


BEN JONSON

## The Hourglass

Do but consider this small dust,
    Here running in the glass,
        By atoms[1] moved;
Could you believe that this,
    The body ever was                              5
        Of one that loved?
And in his mistress' flame, playing like a fly,[2]
    Turned to cinders by her eye?
Yes; and in death, as life, unblest,
    To have't expressed,
Even ashes of lovers find no rest.

1640

3. Below the moon; i.e., changeable. According to the traditional cosmology which Donne invokes here, the moon was considered the dividing line between the immutable celestial world and the earthly mortal one.
4. Comprised.
5. A traditional symbol of perfection.

1. Hypothetical bodies, thought to be incapable of further division and thus among the ultimate particles of matter (OED).
2. Any two-winged insect (including the moth and butterfly), a symbol of transitory life, especially in its self-destructive attraction to flame.

JOHN DONNE

# The Canonization

For God's sake hold your tongue and let me love!
  Or chide my palsy or my gout,
My five grey hairs or ruined fortune flout;
With wealth your state, your mind with arts improve,
    Take you a course, get you a place,       5
    Observe his Honor or his Grace,
Or the king's real or his stampéd face[1]
    Contemplate; what you will, approve,
      So you will let me love.

Alas, alas, who's injured by my love?      10
  What merchant's ships have my sighs drowned?
Who says my tears have overflowed his ground?
When did my colds a forward spring remove?
    When did the heats which my veins fill
    Add one man to the plaguy bill?[2]      15
Soldiers find wars, and lawyers find out still
    Litigious men which quarrels move,
      Though she and I do love.

Call us what you will, we are made such by love.
  Call her one, me another fly,      20
We're tapers[3] too, and at our own cost die;
And we in us find th' eagle and the dove.[4]
    The phoenix riddle[5] hath more wit[6]
    By us; we two, being one, are it.
So to one neutral thing both sexes fit,      25
    We die and rise the same, and prove
      Mysterious by this love.

We can die by it, if not live by love;
  And if unfit for tombs and hearse
Our legend be, it will be fit for verse;      30
And if no piece of chronicle we prove,[7]
    We'll build in sonnets[8] pretty rooms
    (As well a well-wrought urn becomes[9]
The greatest ashes, as half-acre tombs),
    And by these hymns all shall approve      35
      Us canonized for love.

---

1. On coins.
2. List of plague victims.
3. Which consume themselves. To "die" is Renaissance slang for consummating the sexual act, which was popularly believed to shorten life by one day. "fly": a traditional symbol of transitory life.
4. Traditional symbols of strength and purity.
5. According to tradition, only one phoenix existed at a time, dying in a funeral pyre of its own making and being reborn from its own ashes. The bird's existence was thus a riddle akin to a religious mystery (line 27), and a symbol sometimes fused with Christian representations of immortality.
6. Meaning.
7. I.e., if we don't turn out to be an authenticated piece of historical narrative.
8. Love poems. In Italian, *stanza* means rooms.
9. Befits.

And thus invoke us: "You whom reverent love
   Made one another's hermitage,
You to whom love was peace, that now is rage,
Who did the whole world's soul extract, and drove[1]      40
   Into the glasses of your eyes
   (So made such mirrors and such spies
That they did all to you epitomize)
   Countries, towns, courts; beg from above
     A pattern of your love!"        45

                           1633

SIR PHILIP SIDNEY

# With How Sad Steps, O Moon

With how sad steps, O Moon, thou climb'st the skies!
How silently, and with how wan a face!
What! may it be that even in heavenly place
That busy archer[2] his sharp arrows tries?
Sure, if that long-with-love-acquainted eyes      5
Can judge of love, thou feel'st a lover's case;
I read it in thy looks; thy languished grace[3]
To me, that feel the like, thy state descries.
Then, even of fellowship, O Moon, tell me,
Is constant love deemed there but want of wit?[4]      10
Are beauties[5] there as proud as here they be?
Do they above, love to be loved, and yet
Those lovers scorn whom that love doth possess?
Do they call virtue there ungratefulness?[6]

1582

DONALD JUSTICE

# Here in Katmandu[1]

We have climbed the mountain,
There's nothing more to do.
It is terrible to come down
To the valley
Where, amidst many flowers,      5
One thinks of snow,

As, formerly, amidst snow,
Climbing the mountain,
One thought of flowers,
Tremulous, ruddy with dew,      10
In the valley.
One caught their scent coming down.

1. Compressed.
2. Cupid.
3. Manner.
4. Lack of imagination.
5. Beautiful women.

6. "Do they call ungratefulness there a virtue." (Charles Lamb)
1. The capital city of Nepal, about 100 miles west of Mt. Everest.

It is difficult to adjust, once down,
To the absence of snow.
Clear days, from the valley,                            15
One looks up at the mountain.
What else is there to do?
Prayerwheels, flowers!

Let the flowers
Fade, the prayerwheels run down.                        20
What have these to do
With us who have stood atop the snow
Atop the mountain,
Flags seen from the valley?

It might be possible to live in the valley,             25
To bury oneself among flowers,
If one could forget the mountain,
How, setting out before dawn,
Blinded with snow,
One knew what to do.                                    30

Meanwhile it is not easy here in Katmandu,
Especially when to the valley
That wind which means snow
Elsewhere, but here means flowers,
Comes down,                                             35
As soon it must, from the mountain.

1960

WALLACE STEVENS

# Disillusionment of Ten O'clock

The houses are haunted
By white night-gowns
None are green,
Or purple with green rings,
Or green with yellow rings,                             5
Or yellow with blue rings.
None of them are strange,
With socks of lace
And beaded ceintures.[1]
People are not going                                    10
To dream of baboons and periwinkles.[2]
Only, here and there, an old sailor,
Drunk and asleep in his boots,
Catches tigers
In red weather.                                         15

1923

1. Cinctures: belts, girdles.          2. Sea snails.

ALGERNON CHARLES SWINBURNE

# When the Hounds of Spring[1]

When the hounds of spring are on winter's traces,
　The mother of months[2] in meadow or plain
Fills the shadows and windy places
　With lisp of leaves and ripple of rain;
And the brown bright nightingale amorous　　　　　5
Is half assuaged for Itylus,[3]
For the Thracian ships and the foreign faces,
　The tongueless vigil and all the pain.

Come with bows bent and with emptying of quivers,[4]
　Maiden most perfect, lady of light,　　　　　　10
With a noise of winds and many rivers,
　With a clamor of waters, and with might;
Bind on thy sandals, O thou most fleet,
Over the splendor and speed of thy feet;
For the faint east quickens, the wan west shivers,　　15
　Round the feet of the day and the feet of the night.

Where shall we find her, how shall we sing to her,
　Fold our hands round her knees, and cling?
O that man's heart were as fire and could spring to her,
　Fire, or the strength of the streams that spring!　　20
For the stars and the winds are unto her
As raiment, as songs of the harp player;
For the risen stars and the fallen cling to her,
　And the southwest wind and the west wind sing.

For winter's rains and ruins are over,　　　　　　25
　And all the season of snows and sins;
The days dividing lover and lover,
　The light that loses, the night that wins;
And time remembered is grief forgotten,
And frosts are slain and flowers begotten,　　　　30
And in green underwood and cover
　Blossom by blossom the spring begins.

The full streams feed on flower of rushes,
　Ripe grasses trammel a traveling foot,
The faint fresh flame of the young year flushes　　35
　From leaf to flower and flower to fruit;
And fruit and leaf are as gold and fire,
And the oat[5] is heard above the lyre,

1. The opening chorus from *Atalanta in Calydon*, Swinburne's verse drama about the Greek legend of Atalanta.
2. The chorus is addressed to Artemis (Roman name Diana); as moon goddess she is the "mother of months."
3. After being raped by her brother-in-law (Tereus, king of Thrace) and having her tongue cut out, Philomela was changed into a nightingale. Her sister Procne, Tereus' wife, then cut up her own son, Itylus, and served the flesh to her husband.
4. Artemis was also goddess of hunting and protectress of women.
5. A musical pipe made of oaten straw.

And the hooféd heel of a satyr[6] crushes
The chestnut husk at the chestnut root.                    40

And Pan by noon and Bacchus by night,
Fleeter of foot than the fleet-foot kid,
Follows with dancing and fills with delight
The Maenad and the Bassarid;
And soft as lips that laugh and hide,                      45
The laughing leaves of the trees divide,
And screen from seeing and leave in sight
The god pursuing, the maiden hid.

The ivy falls with the Bacchanal's hair
Over her eyebrows hiding her eyes;                         50
The wild vine slipping down leaves bare
Her bright breast shortening into sighs;
The wild vine slips with the weight of its leaves,
But the berried ivy catches and cleaves
To the limbs that glitter, the feet that scare            55
The wolf that follows, the fawn that flies.

                                                          1865

JOHN  DRYDEN

# Mac Flecknoe

*Or, A Satire upon the True-Blue-Protestant Poet, T. S.[1]*

All human things are subject to decay,
And, when fate summons, monarchs must obey.
This Flecknoe found, who, like Augustus,[2] young
Was called to empire, and had governed long;
In prose and verse, was owned, without dispute,           5
Through all the realms of Nonsense, absolute.
This aged prince, now flourishing in peace,
And blessed with issue of a large increase,
Worn out with business, did at length debate
To settle the succession of the State;                    10
And, pond'ring which of all his sons was fit
To reign, and wage immortal war with wit,[3]
Cried: " 'Tis resolved; for nature pleads that he
Should only rule, who most resembles me.

6. Half men, half goats who were attendants of Dionysus (or Bacchus [line 41]), god of wine. The chief satyr was Pan (line 41). The festivals honoring Dionysus (Dionysia or Bacchanalia) often developed into wild orgies. The Maenad and the Bassarid (line 44) were groups of Dionysian devotees who participated in the festival.
1. Thomas Shadwell, a competent but pretentious dramatist who considered himself an heir to Ben Jonson (lines 80, 175ff.). According to Dryden, he is instead Mac (son of) Flecknoe: his work belongs in a tradition of Nonsense and Dullness of the sort written by Richard Flecknoe, an Irish Catholic priest and poor contemporary poet. Throughout, the poem pretends to uphold this tradition and "honors" its practitioners: older playwrights like Thomas Dekker (line 87), Thomas Heywood, James Shirley (lines 29, 102) and translators like John Ogilby (lines 102, 174). In opposition are such figures as Jonson, the playwrights John Fletcher (line 79), Sir George Etherege (line 151) and of course Dryden himself.
2. Octavius Caesar (63 B.C.–14 A.D.), who ruled Rome by age 32 and remained emperor for 45 years.
3. A conveniently ambiguous term, meaning imagination, intelligence, discretion, and verbal ingenuity.

Sh——[4] alone my perfect image bears, [15]
Mature in Dullness from his tender years:
Sh—— alone, of all my sons, is he
Who stands confirmed in full stupidity.
The rest to some faint meaning make pretense,
But Sh—— never deviates into sense. [20]
Some beams of wit on other souls may fall,
Strike through, and make a lucid interval;
But Sh——'s genuine night admits no ray,
His rising fogs prevail upon the day.
Besides, his goodly fabric fills the eye,[5] [25]
And seems designed for thoughtless majesty;
Thoughtless as monarch oaks that shade the plain,
And, spread in solemn state, supinely reign.
Heywood and Shirley were but types[6] of thee,
Thou last great prophet of tautology.[7] [30]
Even I, a dunce of more renown than they,
Was sent before but to prepare thy way;[8]
And coarsely clad in Norwich drugget[9] came
To teach the nations in thy greater name.
My warbling lute, the lute I whilom[1] strung [35]
When to King John of Portugal[2] I sung,
Was but the prelude to that glorious day,
When thou on silver Thames didst cut thy way,
With well-timed oars before the royal barge,
Swelled with the pride of thy celestial charge; [40]
And big with hymn, commander of a host,
The like was ne'er in Epsom blankets tossed.[3]
Methinks I see the new Arion[4] sail,
The lute still trembling underneath thy nail.
At thy well-sharpened thumb from shore to shore [45]
The treble squeaks for fear, the basses roar:
Echoes from Pissing Alley Sh—— call,
And Sh—— they resound from A—— Hall.[5]
About thy boat the little fishes throng,
As at the morning toast[6] that floats along. [50]
Sometimes, as prince of thy harmonious band,
Thou wield'st thy papers in thy threshing hand.
St. André's feet ne'er kept more equal time,
Not ev'n the feet of thy own *Psyche's* rhyme;[7]

4. Omitting letters from a satiric victim's name was common practice, ostensibly to protect the author from libel proceedings, but sometimes to produce comic effects (see, e.g., lines 47, 103).
5. Shadwell was fat.
6. In 17th-century theology, Old Testament figures who were said to prefigure Christ were called "types" of him.
7. Redundancy.
8. As John the Baptist, clad in coarse clothes, prepared the way for Christ. See *Mark* 1 or *Matthew* 3.
9. Coarse wool.
1. Formerly. The word was already archaic by Dryden's time.
2. Whom Flecknoe claimed as a patron.
3. Once a primitive means of inducing labor, blanket-tossing had become a staple in slapstick comedy. Shadwell uses it in

*The Virtuoso.* From here on several of Shadwell's works and characters are mentioned or glanced at: *Epsom Wells here, Psyche* (lines 54, 90, 125, 180) *The Miser* (line 91), *The Humorists* (line 92), *The Hypocrite* (line 92), and *The Virtuoso* again (line 149). Raymond (line 93) is a character in *The Humorists,* Bruce (line 93) and Sir Formal (line 168) in *The Virtuoso,* and Nicander (line 179) in *Psyche.*
4. The original Arion, an ancient Greek poet, was cast into the sea but saved by dolphins when his singing charmed them.
5. Aston Hall: apparently Dryden's invention. Two different London alleys were actually called Pissing Alley.
6. Sewage.
7. St. André, a French dancing master who choreographed Shadwell's opera *Psyche.*

Though they in number as in sense excel:                       55
So just, so like tautology, they fell,
That, pale with envy, Singleton[8] forswore
The lute and sword, which he in triumph bore,
And vowed he ne'er would act Villerius[9] more."
Here stopped the good old sire, and wept for joy         60
In silent raptures of the hopeful boy.
All arguments, but most his plays, persuade,
That for anointed Dullness he was made.
    Close to the walls which fair Augusta[1] bind,
(The fair Augusta much to fears inclined)              65
An ancient fabric,[2] raised t'inform the sight,
There stood of yore, and Barbican it hight:[3]
A watchtower once; but now, so fate ordains,
Of all the pile an empty name remains.
From its old ruins brothel-houses rise,               70
Scenes of lewd loves, and of polluted joys,
Where their vast courts the mother-strumpets keep,
And, undisturbed by watch, in silence sleep.
Near these a nursery[4] erects its head,
Where queens are formed, and future heroes bred;       75
Where unfledged actors learn to laugh and cry,
Where infant punks[5] their tender voices try,
And little Maximins[6] the gods defy.
Great Fletcher never treads in buskins here,
Nor greater Jonson dares in socks appear;             80
But gentle Simkin[7] just reception finds
Amidst this monument of vanished minds:
Pure clinches,[8] the suburbian Muse affords,
And Panton,[9] waging harmless war with words.
Here Flecknoe, as a place to fame well known,          85
Ambitiously designed his Sh——'s throne.
For ancient Dekker prophesied long since,
That in this pile should reign a mighty prince,
Born for a scourge of wit, and flail of sense;
To whom true Dullness should some *Psyches* owe,       90
But worlds of *Misers* from his pen should flow;
*Humorists* and *Hypocrites* it should produce,
Whole Raymond families, and tribes of Bruce.
    Now Empress Fame had published the renown
Of Sh——'s coronation through the town.            95
Roused by report of Fame, the nations meet,
From near Bunhill, and distant Watling Street.[1]
No Persian carpets spread th' imperial way,
But scattered limbs of mangled poets lay:

8. John Singleton, a theater musician.
9. A role in Sir William Davenant's *The Siege of Rhodes* (1656), the first English opera.
1. London. Walls enclosed the City proper.
2. Structure.
3. I.e., it was called Barbican.
4. A school for young actors.
5. Prostitutes.
6. Maximin was the ranting hero of Dryden's own *Tyrannic Love*, an early play

he had come to dislike.
7. A simpleton type-character.
8. Puns.
9. Edward Panton, a minor contemporary writer.
1. Watling Street begins near Bunhill but becomes the Great Northern Road to the North of England and in Dryden's day was called Watling Street for its whole length. The location of the throne is in a generally run-down area.

From dusty shops neglected authors come,                          100
Martyrs of pies, and relics of the bum.[2]
Much Heywood, Shirley, Ogilby there lay,
But loads of Sh—— almost choked the way.
Bilked stationers[3] for yeomen stood prepared,
And Herringman[4] was captain of the guard.                        105
The hoary prince in majesty appeared,
High on a throne of his own labors reared.
At his right hand our young Ascanius[5] sat,
Rome's other hope, and pillar of the state.
His brows thick fogs, instead of glories, grace,                   110
And lambent Dullness played around his face.
As Hannibal did to the altars come,
Sworn by his sire a mortal foe to Rome;[6]
So Sh—— swore, nor should his vow be vain,
That he till death true Dullness would maintain;                   115
And, in his father's right, and realm's defense,
Ne'er to have peace with wit, nor truce with sense.
The king himself the sacred unction made,
As king by office, and as priest by trade.
In his sinister hand, instead of ball,[7]                          120
He placed a mighty mug of potent ale;
*Love's Kingdom*[8] to his right he did convey,
At once his scepter, and his rule of sway;
Whose righteous lore the prince had practiced young,
And from whose loins recorded *Psyche* sprung.                     125
His temples, last, with poppies[9] were o'erspread,
That nodding seemed to consecrate his head.
Just at that point of time, if fame not lie,
On his left hand twelve reverend owls[1] did fly.
So Romulus, 'tis sung, by Tiber's brook,                           130
Presage of sway from twice six vultures took.
Th' admiring throng loud acclamations make,
And omens of his future empire take.
The sire then shook the honors of his head,
And from his brows damps of oblivion shed                          135
Full on the filial Dullness: long he stood,
Repelling from his breast the raging god;
At length burst out in this prophetic mood:
   "Heavens bless my son, from Ireland let him reign
To far Barbadoes on the western main;[2]                           140
Of his dominion may no end be known,
And greater than his father's be his throne;
Beyond *Love's Kingdom* let him stretch his pen!"
He paused, and all the people cried, "Amen."

2. The sheets from unsold books were used in various places, including bakeries and privies.
3. Booksellers, who were the honor guard (yeomen).
4. Henry Herringman, who had published both Shadwell's and Dryden's works.
5. Son of Aeneas.
6. According to Livy, Hannibal took such an oath at the age of nine. In 216 B.C. he nearly conquered Rome, but he was later beaten badly.
7. The "golden orb" (a globe surmounted by a cross) which the monarch holds in his left hand during coronation; he holds the scepter in his right hand.
8. A play by Flecknoe.
9. Shadwell was an opium addict.
1. Formerly, a standard symbol of stupidity. The flight of 12 vultures confirmed to Romulus the site of the future Rome.
2. A vast unpopulated area, mostly ocean.

Then thus continued he: "My son, advance                    145
Still in new impudence, new ignorance.
Success let others teach, learn thou from me
Pangs without birth, and fruitless industry.
Let *Virtuosos* in five years be writ;
Yet not one thought accuse thy toil of wit.                  150
Let gentle George[3] in triumph tread the stage,
Make Dorimant betray, and Loveit rage;
Let Cully, Cockwood, Fopling charm the pit,
And in their folly show the writer's wit.
Yet still thy fools shall stand in thy defense,              155
And justify their author's want of sense.
Let 'em be all by thy own model made
Of Dullness, and desire no foreign aid:
That they to future ages may be known,
Not copies drawn, but issue of thy own.                      160
Nay, let thy men of wit too be the same,
All full of thee, and differing but in name;
But let no alien S—dl—y[4] interpose
To lard with wit thy hungry *Epsom* prose.
And when false flowers of rhetoric thou wouldst cull,        165
Trust nature, do not labor to be dull;
But write thy best, and top; and, in each line,
Sir Formal's oratory will be thine:
Sir Formal, though unsought, attends thy quill,
And does thy northern dedications[5] fill.                   170
Nor let false friends seduce thy mind to fame,
By arrogating Jonson's hostile name.
Let father Flecknoe fire thy mind with praise,
And uncle Ogilby thy envy raise.
Thou art my blood, where Jonson has no part:                 175
What share have we in nature, or in art?
Where did his wit on learning fix a brand,
And rail at arts he did not understand?
Where made he love in Prince Nicander's vein,
Or swept the dust in *Psyche's* humble strain?               180
Where sold he bargains,[6] (whip-stitch, kiss my arse,)
Promised a play and dwindled to a farce?
When did his Muse from Fletcher scenes purloin,
As thou whole Eth'rege dost transfuse to thine?
But so transfused, as oil on water's flow,                   185
His always floats above, thine sinks below.
This is thy province, this thy wondrous way,
New humors[7] to invent for each new play:
This is that boasted bias of thy mind,
By which one way, to Dullness, 'tis inclined;               190
Which makes thy writings lean on one side still,
And, in all changes, that way bends thy will.

3. Etherege. Lines 152–53 name five
characters in his plays.
4. Sir Charles Sedley, wit and gentleman-
poet, who was rumored to have helped
Shadwell write *Epsom Wells.*
5. Shadwell often dedicated his works
to the Duke of Newcastle.
6. Coarse rejoinders. The quoted examples echo a character in Shadwell's *The
Virtuoso.*
7. Jonson's plays were often called
humors comedies because they featured
type-characters dominated by a particular
whim or caprice. The types were by Shadwell's day well defined, and to claim "new"
ones would be pretentious.

Nor let thy mountain-belly make pretense
Of likeness; thine's a tympany[8] of sense.
A tun[9] of man in thy large bulk is writ,                          195
But sure thou'rt but a kilderkin[1] of wit.
Like mine, thy gentle numbers feebly creep;
Thy tragic Muse gives smiles, thy comic sleep.
With whate'er gall thou set'st thyself to write,
Thy inoffensive satires never bite.                                 200
In thy felonious heart, though venom lies,
It does but touch thy Irish pen, and dies.
Thy genius calls thee not to purchase fame
In keen iambics,[2] but mild anagram.
Leave writing plays, and choose for thy command                     205
Some peaceful province in acrostic land.
There thou may'st wings display and altars raise,[3]
And torture one poor word ten thousand ways.
Or, if thou wouldst thy diff'rent talents suit,
Set thy own songs, and sing them to thy lute."                      210
    He said: but his last words were scarcely heard,
For Bruce and Longvil[4] had a trap prepared,
And down they sent the yet declaiming bard.
Sinking he left his drugget robe behind,
Borne upwards by a subterranean wind.                               215
The mantle fell to the young prophet's part,[5]
With double portion of his father's art.

                                                        1682

ANONYMOUS

# Frankie and Johnny

Frankie and Johnny were lovers,
    Lordy, how they could love,
Swore to be true to each other,
    True as the stars up above,
        He was her man, but he done her wrong.                      5

Frankie went down to the corner,
    To buy her a bucket of beer,
Frankie says "Mister Bartender,
    Has my lovin' Johnny been here?
        He is my man, but he's doing me wrong."                     10

"I don't want to cause you no trouble
    Don't want to tell you no lie,
I saw your Johnny half-an-hour ago
    Making love to Nelly Bly.
        He is your man, but he's doing you wrong."                  15

8. A swelling or puffing up.
9. Large wine cask.
1. Quarter-tun.
2. Sharp satires.
3. Earlier in the 17th century it had been fashionable to write such shaped poems.
4. Characters in *The Virtuoso* who set up such a trap for Sir Formal Trifle.
5. *II Kings* 2 recounts the descent of the prophet's mantle from Elijah to Elisha.

Frankie went down to the hotel
  Looked over the transom so high,
There she saw her lovin' Johnny
  Making love to Nelly Bly.
     He was her man; he was doing her wrong.    20

Frankie threw back her kimono,
  Pulled out her big forty-four;
Rooty-toot-toot: three times she shot
  Right through that hotel door,
     She shot her man, who was doing her wrong.    25

"Roll me over gently,
  Roll me over slow,
Roll me over on my right side,
  'Cause these bullets hurt me so,
     I was your man, but I done you wrong."    30

Bring all your rubber-tired hearses
  Bring all your rubber-tired hacks,
They're carrying poor Johnny to the burying ground
  And they ain't gonna bring him back,
     He was her man, but he done her wrong.    35

Frankie says to the sheriff,
  "What are they going to do?"
The sheriff he said to Frankie,
  "It's the 'lectric chair for you.
     He was your man, and he done you wrong."    40

"Put me in that dungeon,
  Put me in that cell,
Put me where the northeast wind
  Blows from the southeast corner of hell,
     I shot my man, 'cause he done me wrong."    45

                    (19th century)

ANONYMOUS

# Lord Randal

"O where hae ye been, Lord Randal, my son?
O where hae ye been, my handsome young man?"
"I hae been to the wild wood; mother, make my bed soon,
For I'm weary wi' hunting, and fain wald[1] lie down."

"Where gat ye your dinner, Lord Randal, my son?    5
Where gat ye your dinner, my handsome young man?"
"I dined wi' my true-love; mother, make my bed soon,
For I'm weary wi' hunting, and fain wald lie down."

"What gat ye to your dinner, Lord Randal, my son?
What gat ye to your dinner, my handsome young man?"    10

1. Would like to.

"I gat eels boiled in broo; mother, make my bed soon,
For I'm weary wi' hunting, and fain wald lie down."

"What became of your bloodhounds, Lord Randal, my son?
What became of your bloodhounds, my handsome young man?"
"O they swelled and they died; mother, make my bed soon,    15
For I'm weary wi' hunting, and fain wald lie down."

"O I fear ye are poisoned, Lord Randal, my son!
O I fear ye are poisoned, my handsome young man!"
"O yes! I am poisoned; mother, make my bed soon,
For I'm sick at the heart, and I fain wald lie down."    20

(date of composition uncertain)

ANONYMOUS

# Lord Randal

"O where ha' you been, Lord Randal, my son?
And where ha' you been, my handsome young man?"
"I ha' been at the greenwood; mother, mak my bed soon,
For I'm wearied wi' huntin', and fain wad[1] lie down."

"And wha met ye there, Lord Randal, my son?    5
And wha met you there, my handsome young man?"
"O I met wi' my true-love; mother, mak my bed soon,
For I'm wearied wi' huntin', and fain wad lie down."

"And what did she give you, Lord Randal, my son?
And what did she give you, my handsome young man?"    10
"Eels fried in a pan; mother, mak my bed soon,
For I'm wearied wi' huntin', and fain wad lie down."

"And wha gat your leavin's, Lord Randal, my son?
And wha gat your leavin's, my handsome young man?"
"My hawks and my hounds; mother, mak my bed soon,    15
For I'm wearied wi' huntin', and fain wad lie down."

"And what becam of them, Lord Randal, my son?
And what becam of them, my handsome young man?"
"They stretched their legs out and died; mother, mak my bed soon,
For I'm wearied wi' huntin', and fain wad lie down."    20

"O I fear you are poisoned, Lord Randal, my son!
I fear you are poisoned, my handsome young man!"
"O yes, I am poisoned; mother, mak my bed soon,
For I'm sick at the heart, and I fain wad lie down."

"What d' ye leave to your mother, Lord Randal, my son?    25
What d' ye leave to your mother, my handsome young man?"
"Four and twenty milk kye;[2] mother, mak my bed soon,
For I'm sick at the heart, and I fain wad lie down."

1. Would like to.    2. Cows.

"What d' ye leave to your sister, Lord Randal, my son?
What d' ye leave to your sister, my handsome young man?"    30
"My gold and my silver; mother, mak my bed soon,
For I'm sick at the heart, and I fain wad lie down."

"What d' ye leave to your brother, Lord Randal, my son?
What d' ye leave to your brother, my handsome young man?"
"My houses and my lands; mother, mak my bed soon,    35
For I'm sick at the heart, and I fain wad lie down."

"What d' ye leave to your true-love, Lord Randal, my son?
What d' ye leave to your true-love, my handsome young man?"
"I leave her hell and fire; mother, mak my bed soon,
For I'm sick at the heart, and I fain wad lie down."    40

(date of composition uncertain)

ANONYMOUS

# Sir Patrick Spens

The king sits in Dumferling toune,[1]
    Drinking the blude-reid[2] wine:
"O whar will I get guid sailor,
    To sail this ship of mine?"

Up and spake an eldern knicht,    5
    Sat at the king's richt knee:
"Sir Patrick Spens is the best sailor
    That sails upon the sea."

The king has written a braid[3] letter
    And signed it wi' his hand,    10
And sent it to Sir Patrick Spens,
    Was walking on the sand.

The first line that Sir Patrick read,
    A loud lauch[4] lauched he;
The next line that Sir Patrick read,    15
    The tear blinded his ee.[5]

"O wha is this has done this deed,
    This il deed done to me,
To send me out this time o' the year,
    To sail upon the sea?    20

"Make haste, make haste, my merry men all,
    Our guid ship sails the morn."
"O say na sae,[6] my master dear,
    For I fear a deadly storm.

"Late, late yestre'en I saw the new moon    25
    Wi' the auld moon in her arm,

1. Town.
2. Blood-red.
3. Broad: explicit.

4. Laugh.
5. Eye.
6. Not so.

And I fear, I fear, my dear mastér,
   That we will come to harm."

O our Scots nobles were richt laith[7]
   To weet their cork-heeled shoon,[8]
But lang owre a'[9] the play were played
   Their hats they swam aboon.[1]

O lang, lang, may their ladies sit,
   Wi' their fans into their hand,
Or ere they see Sir Patrick Spens
   Come sailing to the land.

O lang, lang, may the ladies stand
   Wi' their gold kems[2] in their hair,
Waiting for their ain[3] dear lords,
   For they'll see them na mair.

Half o'er, half o'er to Aberdour
   It's fifty fadom deep,
And there lies guid Sir Patrick Spens
   Wi' the Scots lords at his feet.

(probably 13th century)

ANONYMOUS

# The Dying Cowboy[1]

As I rode out by Tom Sherman's bar-room,
As I rode out so early one day,
'Twas there I espied a handsome young cowboy,
All dressed in white linen, all clothed for the grave.

"I see by your outfit that you are a cowboy,"
These words he did say as I boldly stepped by.
"Come sit down beside me and hear my sad story,
For I'm shot in the breast and I know I must die.

"Then beat your drums slowly and play your fife lowly,
And play the dead march as you carry me along,
And take me to the graveyard and throw the sod o'er me,
For I'm a young cowboy and I know I've done wrong.

"'Twas once in the saddle I used to go dashing,
'Twas once in the saddle I used to go gay,
But I first took to drinking and then to card-playing,
Got shot in the body and I'm dying today.

"Let sixteen gamblers come handle my coffin,
Let sixteen young cowboys come sing me a song,

30

35

40

5

10

15

7. Right loath: very reluctant.
8. To wet their cork-heeled shoes. Cork was expensive, and therefore such shoes were a mark of wealth and status.
9. Before all.

1. Their hats swam above them.
2. Combs.
3. Own.
1. Also known as "The Streets of Laredo."

Take me to the green valley and lay the sod o'er me,
For I'm a poor cowboy and I know I've done wrong.                    20

"Go bring me back a cup of cool water
To cool my parched lips," this cowboy then said.
Before I returned, his soul had departed
And gone to his Maker—the cowboy lay dead.

We swung our ropes slowly and rattled spurs lowly,                   25
And gave a wild whoop as we carried him on,
For we all loved our comrade, so brave, young and handsome,
We all loved our comrade, although he'd done wrong.

(probably late 19th century)

ALFRED, LORD TENNYSON

# Morte d'Arthur[1]

So all day long the noise of battle rolled
Among the mountains by the winter sea,
Until King Arthur's table, man by man,
Had fallen in Lyonnesse[2] about their lord,
King Arthur; then, because his wound was deep,               5
The bold Sir Bedivere uplifted him,
Sir Bedivere, the last of all his knights,
And bore him to a chapel nigh the field,
A broken chancel with a broken cross,
That stood on a dark strait of barren land.                  10
On one side lay the ocean, and on one
Lay a great water, and the moon was full.
   Then spake King Arthur to Sir Bedivere:
"The sequel[3] of today unsolders all
The goodliest fellowship of famous knights                   15
Whereof this world holds record. Such a sleep
They sleep—the men I loved. I think that we
Shall never more, at any future time,
Delight our souls with talk of knightly deeds,
Walking about the gardens and the halls                      20
Of Camelot, as in the days that were.
I perish by this people which I made—
Though Merlin sware that I should come again
To rule once more—but let what will be be,
I am so deeply smitten through the helm                      25
That without help I cannot last till morn.
Thou therefore take my brand[4] Excalibur,
Which was my pride; for thou rememberest how
In those old days, one summer noon, an arm
Rose up from out the bosom of the lake,                      30
Clothed in white samite,[5] mystic, wonderful,
Holding the sword—and how I rowed across

1. Tennyson once intended to write an epic poem on the Arthurian legend, but this narrative of Arthur's death is all that he completed. He later published it in two forms: separately with a brief dramatic framework which introduces a narrator to tell the story, and then, in expanded form, as a part of *Idylls of the King*.
2. According to legend, an island country off the coast of Cornwall.
3. Result.
4. Sword.
5. A heavy silk fabric, often interwoven with silver or gold.

And took it, and have worn it, like a king;
And, wheresoever I am sung or told
In aftertime, this also shall be known.                          35
But now delay not; take Excalibur,
And fling him far into the middle mere;[6]
Watch what thou seest, and lightly[7] bring me word."
   To him replied the bold Sir Bedivere:
"It is not meet, Sir King, to leave thee thus,                   40
Aidless, alone, and smitten through the helm.
A little thing may harm a wounded man.
Yet I thy hest will all perform at full,
Watch what I see, and lightly bring thee word."
   So saying, from the ruined shrine he stepped          45
And in the moon athwart the place of tombs,
Where lay the mighty bones of ancient men,
Old knights, and over them the sea-wind sang
Shrill, chill, with flakes of foam. He, stepping down
By zigzag paths and juts of pointed rock,                        50
Came on the shining levels of the lake.
   There drew he forth the brand Excalibur,
And o'er him, drawing it, the winter moon,
Brightening the skirts of a long cloud, ran forth
And sparkled keen with frost against the hilt;                   55
For all the haft twinkled with diamond sparks,
Myriads of topaz-lights, and jacinth-work
Of subtlest jewelry. He gazed so long
That both his eyes were dazzled, as he stood,
This way and that dividing the swift mind,                       60
In act to throw; but at the last it seemed
Better to leave Excalibur concealed
There in the many-knotted water-flags,
That whistled stiff and dry about the marge.[8]
So strode he back slow to the wounded king.                      65
   Then spake King Arthur to Sir Bedivere:
"Hast thou performed my mission which I gave?
What is it thou hast seen, or what hast heard?"
   And answer made the bold Sir Bedivere:
"I heard the ripple washing in the reeds,                        70
And the wild water lapping on the crag."
   To whom replied King Arthur, faint and pale:
"Thou hast betrayed thy nature and thy name,
Not rendering true answer, as beseemed
Thy fealty,[9] nor like a noble knight;                          75
For surer sign had followed, either hand,
Or voice, or else a motion of the mere.
This is a shameful thing for men to lie.
Yet now, I charge thee, quickly go again
As thou art lief[1] and dear, and do the thing                   80
I bade thee, watch, and lightly bring me word."
   Then went Sir Bedivere the second time
Across the ridge, and paced beside the mere,
Counting the dewy pebbles, fixed in thought;

6. Middle of the lake.        9. Obligation of loyalty.
7. Quickly.             1. Beloved.
8. Margin: edge.

But when he saw the wonder of the hilt,                          85
How curiously[2] and strangely chased,[3] he smote
His palms together, and he cried aloud:
"And if indeed I cast the brand away,
Surely a precious thing, one worthy note,
Should thus be lost forever from the earth,                      90
Which might have pleased the eyes of many men.
What good should follow this, if this were done?
What harm, undone? deep harm to disobey,
Seeing obedience is the bond of rule.
Were it well to obey then, if a king demand                      95
An act unprofitable, against himself?
The king is sick, and knows not what he does.
What record, or what relic of my lord
Should be to aftertime, but empty breath
And rumors of a doubt? but were this kept,                       100
Stored in some treasure-house of mighty kings,
Someone might show it at a joust of arms,
Saying, 'King Arthur's sword, Excalibur,
Wrought by the lonely maiden of the lake.
Nine years she wrought it, sitting in the deeps                  105
Upon the hidden bases of the hills.'
So might some old man speak in the aftertime
To all the people, winning reverence;
But now much honor and much fame were lost."
    So spake he, clouded with his own conceit,[4]                110
And hid Excalibur the second time,
And so strode back slow to the wounded king.
    Then spoke King Arthur, breathing heavily:
"What is it thou hast seen, or what hast heard?"
    And answer made the bold Sir Bedivere:                      115
"I heard the water lapping on the crag,
And the long ripple washing in the reeds."
    To whom replied King Arthur, much in wrath:
"Ah, miserable and unkind, untrue,
Unknightly, traitor-hearted! Woe is me!                          120
Authority forgets a dying king,
Laid widowed of the power in his eye
That bowed the will. I see thee what thou art,
For thou, the latest-left of all my knights,
In whom should meet[5] the offices of all,                      125
Thou wouldst betray me for the precious hilt;
Either from lust of gold, or like a girl
Valuing the giddy pleasure of the eyes.
Yet, for a man may fail in duty twice,
And the third time may prosper, get thee hence;                 130
But, if thou spare to fling Excalibur,
I will arise and slay thee with my hands."
    Then quickly rose Sir Bedivere, and ran,
And, leaping down the ridges lightly, plunged
Among the bulrush-beds, and clutched the sword,                 135
And strongly wheeled and threw it. The great brand
Made lightnings in the splendor of the moon,

2. Artfully.                    4. Fanciful notion.
3. Engraved or embossed.        5. Unite.

And flashing round and round, and whirled in an arch,
Shot like a streamer of the northern morn,[6]
Seen where the moving isles[7] of winter shock          140
By night, with noises of the northern sea.
So flashed and fell the brand Excalibur;
But ere he dipped the surface, rose an arm
Clothed in white samite, mystic, wonderful,
And caught him by the hilt, and brandished him          145
Three times, and drew him under in the mere.
And lightly went the other to the king.
    Then spoke King Arthur, drawing thicker breath:
"Now see I by thine eyes that this is done.
Speak out; what is it thou hast heard, or seen?"          150
    And answer made the bold Sir Bedivere:
"Sir King, I closed mine eyelids, lest the gems
Should blind my purpose, for I never saw,
Nor shall see, here or elsewhere, till I die,
Not though I live three lives of mortal men,          155
So great a miracle as yonder hilt.
Then with both hands I flung him, wheeling him;
But when I looked again, behold an arm,
Clothed in white samite, mystic, wonderful,
That caught him by the hilt, and brandished him          160
Three times, and drew him under in the mere."
    And answer made King Arthur, breathing hard:
"My end draws nigh; 'tis time that I were gone.
Make broad thy shoulders to receive my weight,
And bear me to the margin; yet I fear          165
My wound hath taken cold, and I shall die."
    So saying, from the pavement he half rose,
Slowly, with pain, reclining on his arm,
And looking wistfully with wide blue eyes
As in a picture. Him Sir Bedivere          170
Remorsefully regarded through his tears,
And would have spoken, but he found not words,
Then took with care, and kneeling on one knee,
O'er both his shoulders drew the languid hands,
And rising bore him through the place of tombs.          175
    But, as he walked, King Arthur panted hard,
Like one that feels a nightmare on his bed
When all the house is mute. So sighed the king,
Muttering and murmuring at his ear, "Quick, quick!
I fear it is too late, and I shall die."          180
But the other swiftly strode from ridge to ridge,
Clothed with his breath, and looking, as he walked,
Larger than human on the frozen hills.
He heard the deep behind him, and a cry
Before. His own thought drove him like a goad.          185
Dry clashed his harness in the icy caves
And barren chasms, and all to left and right
The bare black cliff clanged round him, as he based
His feet on juts of slippery crag that rang
Sharp-smitten with the dint of arméd heels—          190

6. The Northern Lights.          7. Icebergs.

And on a sudden, lo! the level lake,
And the long glories of the winter moon.
   Then saw they how there hove a dusky barge,
Dark as a funeral scarf from stem to stern,
Beneath them; and descending they were ware                195
That all the decks were dense with stately forms
Black-stoled, black-hooded, like a dream—by these
Three queens with crowns of gold—and from them rose
A cry that shivered to the tingling stars,
And, as it were one voice, an agony                         200
Of lamentation, like a wind that shrills
All night in a waste land, where no one comes,
Or hath come, since the making of the world.
   Then murmured Arthur, "Place me in the barge,"
And to the barge they came. There those three queens        205
Put forth their hands, and took the king, and wept.
But she that rose the tallest of them all
And fairest laid his head upon her lap,
And loosed the shattered casque,[8] and chafed his hands,
And called him by his name, complaining loud,               210
And dropping bitter tears against his brow
Striped with dark blood; for all his face was white
And colorless, and like the withered moon
Smote by the fresh beam of the springing east;
And all his greaves and cuisses[9] dashed with drops        215
Of onset,[1] and the light and lustrous curls—
That made his forehead like a rising sun
High from the dais-throne—were parched with dust;
Or, clotted into points and hanging loose,
Mixed with the knightly growth that fringed his lips.       220
So like a shattered column lay the king;
Not like that Arthur who, with lance in rest,
From spur to plume a star of tournament,
Shot through the lists at Camelot, and charged
Before the eyes of ladies and of kings.                     225
   Then loudly cried the bold Sir Bedivere:
"Ah! my Lord Arthur, whither shall I go?
Where shall I hide my forehead and my eyes?
For now I see the true old times are dead,
When every morning brought a noble chance,                  230
And every chance brought out a noble knight.
Such times have been not since the light that led
The holy Elders with the gift of myrrh.[2]
But now the whole ROUND TABLE is dissolved
Which was an image of the mighty world;                     235
And I, the last, go forth companionless,
And the days darken round me, and the years,
Among new men, strange faces, other minds."
   And slowly answered Arthur from the barge:
"The old order changeth, yielding place to new,            240
And God fulfills himself in many ways,
Lest one good custom should corrupt the world.

8. Helmet.
9. Armor to protect the shins and thighs.
1. Blood from the battle.

2. The star that guided the Magi to Bethlehem.

Comfort thyself: what comfort is in me?
I have lived my life, and that which I have done
May He within Himself make pure! but thou,                    245
If thou shouldst never see my face again,
Pray for my soul. More things are wrought by prayer
Than this world dreams of. Wherefore, let thy voice
Rise like a fountain for me night and day.
For what are men better than sheep or goats              250
That nourish a blind life within the brain,
If, knowing God, they lift not hands of prayer
Both for themselves and those who call them friend?
For so the whole round earth is every way
Bound by gold chains about the feet of God.               255
But now farewell. I am going a long way
With these thou seest—if indeed I go—
For all my mind is clouded with a doubt—
To the island-valley of Avilion;[3]
Where falls not hail, or rain, or any snow,               260
Nor ever wind blows loudly, but it lies
Deep-meadowed, happy, fair with orchard lawns
And bowery hollows crowned with summer sea,
Where I will heal me of my grievous wound."
    So said he, and the barge with oar and sail          265
Moved from the brink, like some full-breasted swan
That, fluting a wild carol ere her death,
Ruffles her pure cold plume, and takes the flood
With swarthy webs. Long stood Sir Bedivere
Revolving many memories, till the hull                     270
Looked one black dot against the verge of dawn,
And on the mere the wailing died away.

1833–34

ROBERT BROWNING

# My Last Duchess

### *Ferrara*[1]

That's my last Duchess painted on the wall,
Looking as if she were alive. I call
That piece a wonder, now: Frà Pandolf's hands[2]
Worked busily a day, and there she stands.
Will't please you sit and look at her? I said          5
"Frà Pandolf" by design, for never read
Strangers like you that pictured countenance,
The depth and passion of its earnest glance,
But to myself they turned (since none puts by
The curtain I have drawn for you, but I)                10
And seemed as they would ask me, if they durst,
How such a glance came there; so, not the first

3. Avalon, where, according to Celtic mythology, heroes dwell after death.
1. Alfonso II, Duke of Ferrara in Italy in the mid-16th century, is the presumed speaker of the poem, which is loosely based on historical events. The Duke's first wife —whom he had married when she was 14 —died under suspicious circumstances at 17, and he then negotiated through an agent (to whom the poem is spoken) for the hand of the niece of the Count of Tyrol in Austria.
2. Frà Pandolf is, like Claus (line 56), fictitious.

Are you to turn and ask thus. Sir, 'twas not
Her husband's presence only, called that spot
Of joy into the Duchess' cheek: perhaps                          15
Frà Pandolf chanced to say "Her mantle laps
Over my lady's wrist too much," or "Paint
Must never hope to reproduce the faint
Half-flush that dies along her throat": such stuff
Was courtesy, she thought, and cause enough             20
For calling up that spot of joy. She had
A heart—how shall I say?—too soon made glad,
Too easily impressed; she liked whate'er
She looked on, and her looks went everywhere.
Sir, 'twas all one! My favor at her breast,                       25
The dropping of the daylight in the West,
The bough of cherries some officious fool
Broke in the orchard for her, the white mule
She rode with round the terrace—all and each
Would draw from her alike the approving speech,     30
Or blush, at least. She thanked men,—good! but thanked
Somehow—I know not how—as if she ranked
My gift of a nine-hundred-years-old name
With anybody's gift. Who'd stoop to blame
This sort of trifling? Even had you skill                          35
In speech—which I have not—to make your will
Quite clear to such an one, and say, "Just this
Or that in you disgust me; here you miss,
Or there exceed the mark"—and if she let
Herself be lessoned so, nor plainly set                           40
Her wits to yours, forsooth, and made excuse,
—E'en then would be some stooping; and I choose
Never to stoop. Oh sir, she smiled, no doubt,
Whene'er I passed her; but who passed without
Much the same smile? This grew; I gave commands    45
Then all smiles stopped together. There she stands
As if alive. Will't please you rise? We'll meet
The company below, then. I repeat,
The Count your master's known munificence
Is ample warrant that no just pretense                           50
Of mine for dowry will be disallowed;
Though his fair daughter's self, as I avowed
At starting, is my object. Nay, we'll go
Together down, sir. Notice Neptune, though,
Taming a sea-horse, thought a rarity,                             55
Which Claus of Innsbruck cast in bronze for me!

                                                                    1842

DANTE GABRIEL ROSSETTI

# The Blessed Damozel

The blessed damozel[1] leaned out
    From the gold bar of Heaven;

---

1. A "poetic" version of damsel, an unmarried woman.

Her eyes were deeper than the depth
  Of waters stilled at even;
She had three lilies in her hand,          5
  And the stars in her hair were seven.

Her robe, ungirt from clasp to hem,
  No wrought flowers did adorn,
But a white rose of Mary's gift,
  For service meetly worn;                10
Her hair that lay along her back
  Was yellow like ripe corn.²

Herseemed³ she scarce had been a day
  One of God's choristers;
The wonder was not yet quite gone         15
  From that still look of hers;
Albeit, to them she left, her day
  Had counted as ten years.

(To one it is ten years of years.
  . . . Yet now, and in this place,       20
Surely she leaned o'er me—her hair
  Fell all about my face. . . .
Nothing: the autumn-fall of leaves.
  The whole year sets apace.)

It was the rampart⁴ of God's house        25
  That she was standing on;
By God built over the sheer depth
  The which is Space begun;
So high, that looking downward thence
  She scarce could see the sun.           30

It lies in Heaven, across the flood
  Of ether, as a bridge.
Beneath the tides of day and night
  With flame and darkness ridge
The void, as low as where this earth      35
  Spins like a fretful midge.⁵

Around her, lovers, newly met
  'Mid deathless love's acclaims,
Spoke evermore among themselves
  Their heart-remembered names;           40
And the souls mounting up to God
  Went by her like thin flames.

And still she bowed herself and stooped
  Out of the circling charm;
Until her bosom must have made            45
  The bar she leaned on warm,
And the lilies lay as if asleep
  Along her bended arm.

2. Grain.                    4. Outer fortification.
3. It seemed to her.         5. Insect.

From the fixed place of Heaven she saw
    Time like a pulse shake fierce         50
Through all the worlds. Her gaze still strove
    Within the gulf to pierce
Its path: and now she spoke as when
    The stars sang in their spheres.

The sun was gone now; the curled moon       55
    Was like a little feather
Fluttering far down the gulf; and now
    She spoke through the still weather.
Her voice was like the voice the stars
    Had when they sang together.         60

(Ah, sweet! Even now, in that bird's song,
    Strove not her accents there,
Fain to be hearkened?[6] When those bells
    Possessed the midday air,
Strove not her steps to reach my side       65
    Down all the echoing stair?)

"I wish that he were come to me,
    For he will come," she said.
"Have I not prayed in Heaven?—on earth,
    Lord, Lord, has he not prayed?         70
Are not two prayers a perfect strength?
    And shall I feel afraid?

"When round his head the aureole[7] clings,
    And he is clothed in white,
I'll take his hand and go with him        75
    To the deep wells of light;
As unto a stream we will step down,
    And bathe there in God's sight.

"We two will stand beside that shrine,
    Occult,[8] withheld, untrod,        80
Whose lamps are stirred continually
    With prayer sent up to God;
And see our old prayers, granted, melt
    Each like a little cloud.

"We two will lie i' the shadow of        85
    That living mystic tree[9]
Within whose secret growth the Dove
    Is sometimes felt to be,
While every leaf that His plumes touch
    Saith His Name audibly.         90

"And I myself will teach to him,
    I myself, lying so,
The songs I sing here; which his voice

6. Eager to be heard.
7. Halo.
8. Concealed.

9. The tree of life, described in *Revelation* 22:2, which bears 12 kinds of fruit in the New Jerusalem.

Shall pause in, hushed and slow,
And find some knowledge at each pause,                    95
    Or some new thing to know."

(Alas! We two, we two, thou say'st!
    Yea, one wast thou with me
That once of old. But shall God lift
    To endless unity                                     100
The soul whose likeness with thy soul
    Was but its love for thee?)

"We two," she said, "will seek the groves
    Where the lady Mary is,
With her five handmaidens, whose names                   105
    Are five sweet symphonies,
Cecily, Gertrude, Magdalen,
    Margaret, and Rosalys.

"Circlewise sit they, with bound locks
    And foreheads garlanded;                             110
Into the fine cloth white like flame
    Weaving the golden thread,
To fashion the birth-robes for them
    Who are just born, being dead.

"He shall fear, haply, and be dumb;                      115
    Then will I lay my cheek
To his, and tell about our love,
    Not once abashed or weak;
And the dear Mother will approve
    My pride, and let me speak.                          120

"Herself shall bring us, hand in hand,
    To Him round whom all souls
Kneel, the clear-ranged unnumbered heads
    Bowed with their aureoles;
And angels meeting us shall sing                          125
    To their citherns and citoles.[1]

"There will I ask of Christ the Lord
    Thus much for him and me—
Only to live as once on earth
    With Love—only to be,                                130
As then awhile, forever now,
    Together, I and he."

She gazed and listened and then said,
    Less sad of speech than mild—
"All this is when he comes." She ceased.                 135
    The light thrilled toward her, filled
With angels in strong, level flight.
    Her eyes prayed, and she smiled.

---

1. Antique stringed instruments.

(I saw her smile.) But soon their path
    Was vague in distant spheres;        140
And then she cast her arms along
    The golden barriers,
And laid her face between her hands,
    And wept. (I heard her tears.)

1850

X. J. KENNEDY

## First Confession

Blood thudded in my ears. I scuffed,
    Steps stubborn, to the telltale booth
Beyond whose curtained portal coughed
    The robed repositor of truth.

The slat shot back. The universe        5
    Bowed down his cratered dome to hear
Enumerated my each curse,
    The sip snitched from my old man's beer,

My sloth pride envy lechery,
    The dime held back from Peter's Pence[1]    10
With which I'd bribed my girl to pee
    That I might spy her instruments.

Hovering scale-pans when I'd done
    Settled their balance slow as silt
While in the restless dark I burned    15
    Bright as a brimstone in my guilt

Until as one feeds birds he doled[2]
    Seven Our Fathers and a Hail
Which I to double-scrub my soul
    Intoned twice at the altar rail    20

Where Sunday in seraphic[3] light
    I knelt, as full of grace as most,
And stuck my tongue out at the priest:
    A fresh roost for the Holy Ghost.

1961

JOHN DONNE

## The Relic

When my grave is broke up again
Some second guest to entertain[1]
(For graves have learned that woman-head,[2]
To be to more than one a bed)

---

1. Hearth money: annual contributions by Roman Catholic households for the support of the Holy See (Rome).
2. Set penance at.

3. Angelic.
1. In Donne's time, burial grounds were often re-used.
2. Womanly characteristic.

And he that digs it spies                                      5
A bracelet of bright hair about the bone,
        Will he not let us alone,
And think that there a loving couple lies,
Who thought that this device might be some way
To make their souls, at the last busy day,[3]          10
Meet at this grave, and make a little stay?[4]
        If this fall in a time, or land,
        Where mis-devotion[5] doth command,
        Then he that digs us up will bring
        Us to the Bishop and the King              15
        To make us relics; then
Thou shalt be a Mary Magdalen,[6] and I
        A something else[7] thereby;
All women shall adore us, and some men;
And, since at such time miracles are sought,      20
I would that age were by this paper taught
What miracles we harmless lovers wrought.

        First, we loved well and faithfully,
        Yet knew not what we loved, nor why;
        Difference of sex no more we knew,          25
        Than our guardian angels do;
        Coming and going, we
Perchance might kiss,[8] but not between those meals;
        Our hands ne'er touched the seals
Which nature, injured by late law,[9] sets free.      30
        These miracles we did; but now, alas,
        All measure, and all language, I should pass,
        Should I tell what a miracle she was.

                                              1633

PHILIP LARKIN

# Church Going

Once I am sure there's nothing going on
I step inside, letting the door thud shut.
Another church: matting, seats, and stone,
And little books; sprawlings of flowers, cut
For Sunday, brownish now; some brass and stuff      5
Up at the holy end; the small neat organ;
And a tense, musty, unignorable silence,
Brewed God knows how long. Hatless, I take off
My cycle-clips in awkward reverence,

3. Judgment Day. A risen body which had lost any parts was supposed to gather them before appearing at the Heavenly bar of justice.
4. Short visit.
5. Catholicism, which may, under specified conditions, canonize as saints dead persons who lived exceptional lives. Two miracles (line 20) must be certified before canonization can take place, and things belonging to such saints were then declared relics (line 16). Many scholars believe that the poem was addressed to a Catholic woman friend and that the jocular allusion gently teases their differences of belief. Donne was an Anglican priest.
6. The harlot, forgiven by Jesus, who later came to his tomb. See *Luke* 7:37–50 and *Matthew* 27:56.
7. Perhaps John the Beloved, one of Jesus' disciples.
8. Ceremonially, on meeting and parting.
9. Imposed on nature after the Fall.

Move forward, run my hand around the font.[1]    10
From where I stand, the roof looks almost new—
Cleaned, or restored? Someone would know: I don't.
Mounting the lectern, I peruse a few
Hectoring[2] large-scale verses, and pronounce
"Here endeth" much more loudly than I'd meant.    15
The echoes snigger briefly. Back at the door
I sign the book, donate an Irish sixpence,
Reflect the place was not worth stopping for.

Yet stop I did: in fact I often do,
And always end much at a loss like this,    20
Wondering what to look for; wondering, too,
When churches fall completely out of use
What we shall turn them into, if we shall keep
A few cathedrals chronically on show,
Their parchment, plate and pyx[3] in locked cases,    25
And let the rest rent-free to rain and sheep.
Shall we avoid them as unlucky places?

Or, after dark, will dubious women come
To make their children touch a particular stone;
Pick simples[4] for a cancer; or on some    30
Advised night see walking a dead one?
Power of some sort or other will go on
In games, in riddles, seemingly at random;
But superstition, like belief, must die,
And what remains when disbelief has gone?    35
Grass, weedy pavement, brambles, buttress, sky,

A shape less recognizable each week,
A purpose more obscure. I wonder who
Will be the last, the very last, to seek
This place for what it was; one of the crew    40
That tap and jot and know what rood-lofts[5] were?
Some ruin-bibber,[6] randy for antique,
Or Christmas-addict, counting on a whiff
Of gown-and-bands and organ-pipes and myrrh?
Or will he be my representative,    45

Bored, uninformed, knowing the ghostly silt
Dispersed, yet tending to this cross of ground
Through suburb scrub because it held unspilt
So long and equably what since is found
Only in separation—marriage, and birth,    50
And death, and thoughts of these—for whom was built
This special shell? For, though I've no idea
What this accoutered frowsty barn is worth,
It pleases me to stand in silence here;

1. A bowl for baptismal water, mounted on a stone pedestal.
2. Intimidating.
3. A container for the Eucharist.
4. Medicinal herbs.
5. Galleries atop the screens (on which crosses are mounted) which divide the naves or main bodies of churches from the choirs or chancels.
6. Literally, ruin-drinker: someone extremely attracted to antiquarian objects.

A serious house on serious earth it is,                         55
In whose blent air all our compulsions meet,
Are recognized, and robed as destinies.
And that much never can be obsolete,
Since someone will forever be surprising
A hunger in himself to be more serious,                         60
And gravitating with it to this ground,
Which, he once heard, was proper to grow wise in,
If only that so many dead lie round.

                                                          1955


ROBERT FROST

## Stopping by Woods on a Snowy Evening

Whose woods these are I think I know.
His house is in the village, though;
He will not see me stopping here
To watch his woods fill up with snow.

My little horse must think it queer                              5
To stop without a farmhouse near
Between the woods and frozen lake
The darkest evening of the year.

He gives his harness bells a shake
To ask if there is some mistake.                                10
The only other sound's the sweep
Of easy wind and downy flake.

The woods are lovely, dark, and deep,
But I have promises to keep,
And miles to go before I sleep,                                 15
And miles to go before I sleep.

                                                          1923


M. CARL HOLMAN

## Three Brown Girls Singing

In the ribs of an ugly school building
Three rapt faces
Fuse one pure sound in a shaft of April light:
Three girls, choir robes over their arms, in a stairwell singing
Compose the irrelevancies of a halting typewriter,             5
Chalk dust and orange peel,
A French class drilling,
Into a shimmering column of flawed perfection;
Lasting as long
As their fresh, self-wondering voices climb to security;       10
Outlasting
The childbed death of one,
The alto's divorce,
The disease-raddled face of the third
Whose honey brown skin                                          15

Glows now in a nimbus[1] of dust motes,
But will be as estranged
As that faceless and voiceless typist
Who, unknown and unknowing, enters the limpid column,
Joins chalk, French verbs, the acrid perfume of oranges,                    20
To mark the periphery
Of what shall be saved from calendars and decay.

p. 1963

EDWIN ARLINGTON ROBINSON

## Richard Cory

Whenever Richard Cory went down town,
We people on the pavement looked at him:
He was a gentleman from sole to crown,
Clean favored, and imperially slim.

And he was always quietly arrayed,                                          5
And he was always human when he talked;
But still he fluttered pulses when he said,
"Good-morning," and he glittered when he walked.

And he was rich—yes, richer than a king—
And admirably schooled in every grace:                                      10
In fine, we thought that he was everything
To make us wish that we were in his place.

So on we worked, and waited for the light,
And went without the meat, and cursed the bread;
And Richard Cory, one calm summer night,                                    15
Went home and put a bullet through his head.

1897

EDWIN ARLINGTON ROBINSON

## Miniver Cheevy

Miniver Cheevy, child of scorn,
  Grew lean while he assailed the seasons;
He wept that he was ever born,
  And he had reasons.

Miniver loved the days of old                                               5
  When swords were bright and steeds were prancing;
The vision of a warrior bold
  Would set him dancing.

Miniver sighed for what was not,
  And dreamed, and rested from his labors;                                  10
He dreamed of Thebes and Camelot,
  And Priam's neighbors.[2]

1. Halo.
2. Thebes was a site in ancient Greek civilization and legend; Camelot, the leg-endary site of King Arthur's court; Priam, ancient king of Troy and father of Hector.

Miniver mourned the ripe renown
   That made so many a name so fragrant;
He mourned Romance, now on the town,                    15
   And Art, a vagrant.

Miniver loved the Medici,[3]
   Albeit he had never seen one;
He would have sinned incessantly
   Could he have been one.                          20

Miniver cursed the commonplace
   And eyed a khaki suit with loathing;
He missed the mediæval grace
   Of iron clothing.

Miniver scorned the gold he sought,                      25
   But sore annoyed was he without it;
Miniver thought, and thought, and thought,
   And thought about it.

Miniver Cheevy, born too late,
   Scratched his head and kept on thinking;          30
Miniver coughed, and called it fate,
   And kept on drinking.

                      1910

JOHN DRYDEN

# [Portrait of "Og"][1]

Now stop your noses, readers, all and some,
For here's a tun[2] of midnight-work to come,
Og from a treason-tavern rolling home.
Round as a globe, and liquored ev'ry chink,            460
Goodly and great he sails behind his link,[3]
With all this bulk there's nothing lost in Og,
For ev'ry inch that is not fool is rogue:
A monstrous mass of foul corrupted matter,
As all the devils had spewed to make the batter.       465
When wine has given him courage to blaspheme,
He curses God, but God before cursed him;
And if man could have reason, none has more,
That made his paunch so rich, and him so poor.
With wealth he was not trusted, for Heav'n knew         470
What 'twas of old to pamper up a Jew;[4]
To what would he on quail and pheasant swell,
That ev'n on tripe and carrion could rebel?

3. The Renaissance family of bankers
and merchants who ruled Florence for two
centuries. Great patrons of the arts and
responsible for much significant architecture, sculpture, and painting, they were
also known as one of the most ruthless ruling groups in history.
   1. From Part II of *Absalom and Achito-
phel*, an allegory of an attempt to overthrow Charles II. "Og" is a satiric portrait
of Thomas Shadwell, a contemporary dramatist and the "hero" of *Mac Flecknoe*.
   2. Large wine-cask. Shadwell was fat.
   3. Torch-carrier. Citizens who traveled
the streets at night used such linkboys for
protection.
   4. Englishmen, in Dryden's allegory
which compares King Charles to King David
(line 488) in ancient Israel. The would-be
usurper, Charles's illegitimate son, the
Duke of Monmouth, is Absalom (line 507).

But though Heav'n made him poor (with rev'rence speaking)
He never was a poet of God's making.                                    475
The midwife laid her hand on his thick skull
With this prophetic blessing: *Be thou dull;*
Drink, swear, and roar, forbear no lewd delight
Fit for thy bulk, do anything but write:
Thou art of lasting make, like thoughtless men,                          480
A strong nativity—but for the pen;
Eat opium, mingle arsenic in thy drink,
Still thou mayst live, avoiding pen and ink.
I see, I see, 'tis counsel given in vain,
For treason botched in rhyme will be thy bane;                           485
Rhyme is the rock on which thou art to wreck,
'Tis fatal to thy fame and to thy neck:
Why should thy meter good King David blast?
A psalm of his will surely be thy last.
Dar'st thou presume in verse to meet thy foes,                           490
Thou whom the penny pamphlet foiled in prose?
Doeg,[5] whom God for mankind's mirth has made,
O'ertops thy talent in thy very trade;
Doeg to thee, thy paintings are so coarse,
A poet is, though he's the poet's horse.                                 495
A double noose thou on thy neck dost pull,
For writing treason, and for writing dull;
To die for faction is a common evil,
But to be hanged for nonsense is the devil.
Hadst thou the glories of thy king expressed,                            500
Thy praises had been satire at the best;
But thou in clumsy verse, unlicked, unpointed,
Hast shamefully defied the Lord's anointed:
I will not rake the dunghill of thy crimes,
For who would read thy life that reads thy rhymes?                       505
But of King David's foes, be this the doom,
May all be like the young man Absalom;
And for my foes, may this their blessing be,
To talk like Doeg, and to write like thee.

1682

JOHN WILMOT, EARL OF ROCHESTER

## The Maimed Debauchee

As some brave admiral, in former war
    Deprived of force, but pressed with courage still,
Two rival fleets appearing from afar,
    Crawls to the top of an adjacent hill;

From whence (with thoughts full of concern) he views          5
    The wise, and daring, conduct of the fight:
And each bold action to his mind renews,
    His present glory, and his past delight.

5. Elkanah Settle, another minor contemporary dramatist.

From his fierce eyes flashes of rage he throws,
   As from black clouds when lightning breaks away,        10
Transported, thinks himself amidst his foes,
   And absent, yet enjoys the bloody day.

So when my days of impotence approach,
   And I'm by love and wine's unlucky chance,
Forced from the pleasing billows of debauch        15
   On the dull shore of lazy temperance,

My pains at last some respite shall afford,
   While I behold the battles you maintain:
When fleets of glasses sail around the board,
   From whose broad-sides volleys of wit shall rain.        20

Nor shall the sight of honorable scars,
   Which my too forward valor did procure,
Frighten new-listed soldiers from the wars:
   Past joys have more than paid what I endure.

Should some brave[1] youths (worth being drunk) prove nice,[2]    25
   And from their fair inviters meanly shrink,
'Twould please the ghost of my departed vice,
   If, at my counsel, they repent and drink.

Or should some cold-complexioned sot forbid,
   With his dull morals, our night's brisk alarms;        30
I'll fire his blood by telling what I did,
   When I was strong, and able to bear arms.

I'll tell of whores attacked, their lords at home,
   Bawds' quarters beaten up, and fortress won;
Windows demolished, watches overcome,        35
   And handsome[3] ills by my contrivance done.

Nor shall our love-fits, Cloris,[4] be forgot,
   When each the well-looked link-boy[5] strove t'enjoy
And the best kiss was the deciding lot,
   Whether the boy used you, or I the boy.        40

With tales like these I will such heat inspire
   As to important mischief shall incline;
I'll make him long some ancient church to fire,
   And fear no lewdness they're called to by wine.

Thus statesman-like I'll saucily impose,        45
   And, safe from danger, valiantly advise:
Sheltered in impotence, urge you to blows,
   And, being good for nothing else, be wise.

ca. 1675

1. Splendid, fine.
2. Reluctant.
3. Numerous.
4. One of the standard names used by 17th-century poets for women they addressed or celebrated.
5. Attractive torch-carrier.

EZRA POUND

# The Garden

*En robe de parade.*—Samain[1]

Like a skein of loose silk blown against a wall
She walks by the railing of a path in Kensington Gardens,[2]
And she is dying piece-meal
    of a sort of emotional anæmia.

And round about there is a rabble                                    5
Of the filthy, sturdy, unkillable infants of the very poor.
They shall inherit the earth.

In her is the end of breeding.
Her boredom is exquisite and excessive.
She would like some one to speak to her,                             10
And is almost afraid that I
    will commit that indiscretion.

1916

TED HUGHES

# Secretary

If I should touch her she would shriek and weeping
Crawl off to nurse the terrible wound: all
Day like a starling under the bellies of bulls
She hurries among men, ducking, peeping,

Off in a whirl at the first move of a horn.                          5
At dusk she scuttles down the gauntlet of lust
Like a clockwork mouse. Safe home at last
She mends her socks with holes, shirts that are torn

For father and brother, and a delicate supper cooks:
Goes to bed early, shuts out with the light                          10
Her thirty years, and lies with buttocks tight,
Hiding her lovely eyes until day break.

1957

1. Albert Samain, late 19th-century French poet. The phrase is from the first line of the prefatory poem in his first book of poems, *Au Jardin de l'Infante:* "Mon âme est une infante en robe de parade" ("My soul is an Infanta in ceremonial dress"). An "Infanta" is a daughter of the Spanish royal family which, long inbred, had for many years been afflicted with a real blood disease, hemophilia.
2. A fashionable park near the center of London.

JOHN BETJEMAN

# In Westminster Abbey[1]

Let me take this other glove off
  As the *vox humana*[2] swells,
And the beauteous fields of Eden
  Bask beneath the Abbey bells.
Here, where England's statesmen lie,                5
Listen to a lady's cry.

Gracious Lord, oh bomb the Germans.
  Spare their women for Thy Sake,
And if that is not too easy
  We will pardon Thy Mistake.                   10
But, gracious Lord, whate'er shall be,
Don't let anyone bomb me.

Keep our Empire undismembered
  Guide our Forces by Thy Hand,
Gallant blacks from far Jamaica,                    15
  Honduras and Togoland;
Protect them Lord in all their fights,
And, even more, protect the whites.

Think of what our Nation stands for,
  Books from Boots[3] and country lanes,       20
Free speech, free passes, class distinction,
  Democracy and proper drains.
Lord, put beneath Thy special care
One-eighty-nine Cadogan Square.[4]

Although dear Lord I am a sinner,                   25
  I have done no major crime;
Now I'll come to Evening Service
  Whensoever I have the time.
So, Lord, reserve for me a crown,
And do not let my shares go down.                   30

I will labor for Thy Kingdom,
  Help our lads to win the war,
Send white feathers to the cowards[5]
  Join the Women's Army Corps,[6]
Then wash the Steps around Thy Throne               35
In the Eternal Safety Zone.

1. The famous Gothic church in London in which English monarchs are crowned and famous Englishmen are buried (see lines 5, 39–40).
2. Organ tones which resemble the human voice.
3. A chain of London pharmacies.
4. Presumably where the speaker lives, in a fairly fashionable area.

5. White feathers were sometimes given, or sent, to men not in uniform, to suggest that they were cowards and should join the armed forces.
6. The speaker uses the old World War I name (Women's Army Auxiliary Corps) of the Auxiliary Territorial Service, an organization which performed domestic (and some foreign) defense duties.

Now I feel a little better,
What a treat to hear Thy Word
Where the bones of leading statesmen,
Have so often been interred.                    40
And now, dear Lord, I cannot wait
Because I have a luncheon date.

1940

SAMUEL ALLEN

## To Satch[1]

Sometimes I feel like I will *never* stop
Just go on forever
Till one fine mornin'
I'm gonna reach up and grab me a handfulla stars
Throw out my long lean leg                        5
And whip three hot strikes burnin' down the heavens
And look over at God and say
*How about that!*

p. 1963

ANNE SEXTON

## Her Kind

I have gone out, a possessed witch,
haunting the black air, braver at night;
dreaming evil, I have done my hitch
over the plain houses, light by light:
lonely thing, twelve-fingered, out of mind.          5
A woman like that is not a woman, quite.
I have been her kind.

I have found the warm caves in the woods,
filled them with skillets, carvings, shelves,
closets, silks, innumerable goods;                   10
fixed the suppers for the worms and the elves:
whining, rearranging the disaligned.
A woman like that is misunderstood.
I have been her kind.

I have ridden in your cart, driver,                  15
waved my nude arms at villages going by,
learning the last bright routes, survivor
where your flames still bite my thigh
and my ribs crack where your wheels wind.

---

1. Leroy ("Satchell") Paige, legendary pitcher in the Negro American League for
many years. No one knows exactly how old he was when he finally was allowed to pitch
in the Major Leagues after World War II, but he dates back to the era of Babe Ruth
and Lou Gehrig (he pitched effectively against them in exhibition games); he is generally
agreed to have been past 40, the oldest "rookie" in the history of Organized Baseball.
He continued to pitch effectively for several years and made a one-game "comeback" in
1965, pitching 3 scoreless innings at about 60 years of age. His witty proverbs and
formulas for staying young are nearly as legendary as his pitching.

A woman like that is not ashamed to die.                    20
I have been her kind.

                                                          1960

LEONARD COHEN

## Suzanne

Suzanne take you down
To her place by the river,
You can hear the boats go by
You can spend the night beside her,
And you know that she's half crazy,                         5
And that's why you want to be there;
And she feeds you tea and oranges—
That come all the way from China;
And just when you mean to tell her
That you have no love to give her                          10
She gets you on her wave length
And lets the river answer
That you've always been her lover,

And you want to travel with her,
And you want to travel blind,                              15
And you know that you can trust her,
For you've touched her perfect body
With your mind.

And Jesus was a sailor
When He walked upon the water,                             20
And He spent a long time watching
From a lonely wooden tower,
And when He knew for certain
Only drowning men could see Him
He said, "All men shall be brothers, then,                 25
Until the sea shall free them,"
But He Himself was broken
Long before the sky would open,
Forsaken, almost human,
He sank beneath your wisdom                                30
Like a stone.

And you want to travel with Him,
And you want to travel blind,
And you think you maybe trust Him,
For He's touched your perfect body,                        35
With His mind.

Suzanne take your hand
And leads you to the river;
She's wearing rags and feathers
From Salvation Army counters.                              40
And the sun pours down like honey
On our lady of the harbor;

And she shows you where to look
Amid the garbage and the flowers.
There are heroes in the seaweed,                          45
There are children in the morning,
They are leaning out for love,
And they will lean that way forever,
While Suzanne holds the mirror.

And you want to travel with her,                          50
And you want to travel blind,
And you think maybe you'll trust her,
For you've touched her perfect body,
With your mind.

                                                        1967

JONATHAN SWIFT

## On Stella's Birthday, 1719

Stella this day is thirty-four,[1]
(We shan't dispute a year or more)
However Stella, be not troubled,
Although thy size and years are doubled,
Since first I saw thee at sixteen                          5
The brightest virgin on the green,
So little is thy form declined
Made up so largely in thy mind.
Oh, would it please the gods to split
Thy beauty, size, and years, and wit,                     10
No age could furnish out a pair
Of nymphs so graceful, wise and fair
With half the luster of your eyes,
With half your wit, your years and size:
And then before it grew too late,                         15
How should I beg of gentle Fate,
(That either nymph might have her swain,[2])
To split my worship too in twain.

1719

JULIAN BOND

## The Bishop of Atlanta: Ray Charles

The Bishop seduces the world with his voice
Sweat strangles mute eyes
As insinuations gush out through a hydrant of sorrow
Dreams, a world never seen
Moulded on Africa's anvil, tempered down home            5
Documented in cries and wails
Screaming to be ignored, crooning to be heard
Throbbing from the gutter
On Saturday night

1. Stella is Swift's pet name for Hester
Johnson, a close friend for many years. She
was actually 38.
2. Servant, admirer, lover.

Silver offering only                                                    10
The Right Reverend's back in town
Don't it make you feel all right?

p. 1963

EMILY DICKINSON

## A Narrow Fellow in the Grass

A narrow Fellow in the Grass
Occasionally rides—
You may have met Him—did you not
His notice sudden is—

The Grass divides as with a Comb—                                        5
A spotted shaft is seen—
And then it closes at your feet
And opens further on—

He likes a Boggy Acre
A Floor too cool for Corn—                                              10
Yet when a Boy, and Barefoot—
I more than once at Noon

Have passed, I thought, a Whip lash
Unbraiding in the Sun
When stooping to secure it                                              15
It wrinkled, and was gone—

Several of Nature's People
I know, and they know me—
I feel for them a transport
Of cordiality—                                                          20

But never met this Fellow
Attended, or alone
Without a tighter breathing
And Zero at the Bone—

1866

DIANE WAKOSKI

## The Buddha Inherits 6 Cars on His Birthday

### I. *The Red Car*

I believe it was out of the red one that George Washington stepped,
or someone who looked like G. W.
The corridor was made of fibrous blood
and his feet sank in darkly
as teeth into a pear. Going past the service desk                        5
he was paged by a man who had sitting in front of him a
tall jelly glass holding his false teeth. The gums,
false pink.

G. W. was in no mood for dalliance.
"Send all the seamstresses up at once," he said,                    10
and when they got there he undressed them all,
picked the most voluptuous one
and gave her some cloth to
sew.

II. *The Blue Car*
It smelled like new rubber inside.                                  15
The man who drove it had no imagination.
"Will I turn into a machine," he thought,
but no
in a few days they found
a desert rat driving that new blue Ford.                            20
And it seemed peculiar
but it's easier not to question things
these days.

III. *The Green Car*
Emily and James stepped out of their green car.
It was made of old metal melted down.                               25
In your Lee corduroy dungarees and sweatshirt you
look so handsome.
I'm not particular
as long as you have money and style.
This money is easy to spend,                                        30
but if you tried to stuff dollars bills inside me you'd find
a yawning gap, hole
at the bottom where everything falls out
Oh pity
there is such an empty space                                        35
Oh pity
that the lives of some of us are
so vain.

IV. *The Yellow Car*
A very small man met a very large woman.
They were both in the teen-age section of the library.             40
They discovered they both liked the Mona Lisa. They
discovered they both listened to the 1812 Overture.
When true love comes,
               hallelujah
                         you know it!                               45

V. *The Two-Tone Car*
There are fish that change color for camouflage, but it is a fact that
blind ones never do. Experimentation follows it up. Scientists painted
a tank black at one end and white at the other. It was observed that a
certain fish would become grey as he got just in the middle at the
dividing line. This was the only time he showed up as a different color  50
from his surroundings, either black or white. Apparently, he could not
make an instantaneous change. At the dividing line he always turned
grey.

VI. *Old Cars*

In my car of crocodile teeth, in my
car of old candle wax, in                                                    55
my car of tiger paws padding the waspy dust, in my car of
cat's teeth crushing the brittle insect wings, in my
car of leather straps, in my car of folded paper, silvery and pink,
in my car of Alpine tents, in my car of bits & braces,
in my car of fishing line, in my car at the bottom of a                      60
violin, in my car as small as a flea hopping on the dog,
in my own car I want to drive
everywhere
every place there is to go.

1970

WILLIAM BLAKE

# And Did Those Feet[1]

And did those feet in ancient time
  Walk upon England's mountains green?
And was the holy Lamb of God
  On England's pleasant pastures seen?

And did the Countenance Divine                                               5
  Shine forth upon our clouded hills?
And was Jerusalem builded here
  Among these dark Satanic Mills?[2]

Bring me my Bow of burning gold!
  Bring me my Arrows of desire!                                              10
Bring me my Spear! O clouds, unfold!
  Bring me my Chariot of fire!

I will not cease from Mental Fight,
  Nor shall my Sword sleep in my hand,
Till we have built Jerusalem[3]                                              15
  In England's green and pleasant Land.

ca. 1805

1. The prefatory poem to *Milton*, a long poem which asks for an art based on prophetic inspiration and which attacks traditional art and poetry built on Greek and Roman models. This prose passage introduces the poem:

The stolen and perverted writings of Homer and Ovid, of Plato and Cicero, which all men ought to contemn, are set up by artifice against the sublime of the Bible; but when the New Age is at leisure to pronounce, all will be set right, and those grand works of the more ancient and consciously and professedly inspired men will hold their proper rank, and the daughters of memory shall become the daughters of inspiration. Shakespeare and Milton were both curbed by the general malady and infection from the silly Greek and Latin slaves of the sword.
Rouse up, O young men of the New Age! Set your foreheads against the ig-norant hirelings! For we have hirelings in the camp, the court and the university, who would, if they could, forever depress mental and prolong corporeal war. Painters, on you I call! Sculptors! Architects! Suffer not the fashionable fools to depress your powers by the prices they pretend to give for contemptible works or the expensive advertising boasts that they make of such works; believe Christ and his apostles that there is a class of men whose whole delight is in destroying. We do not want either Greek or Roman models if we are but just and true to our own imaginations, those worlds of eternity in which we shall live forever, in Jesus our Lord.
2. In Blake's symbolic system, the unproductive, solipsistic activities of Urizen, an oppressive giver of abstract laws.
3. The New Jerusalem, described in *Revelation* 21.

WALT WHITMAN

# When Lilacs Last in the Dooryard Bloomed[1]

### 1

When lilacs last in the dooryard bloomed,
And the great star early drooped in the western sky in the night,
I mourned, and yet shall mourn with ever-returning spring.

Ever-returning spring, trinity sure to me you bring,
Lilac blooming perennial and drooping star in the west,                  5
And thought of him I love.

### 2

O powerful western fallen star!
O shades of night—O moody, tearful night!
O great star disappeared—O the black murk that hides the star!
O cruel hands that hold me powerless—O helpless soul of me!          10
O harsh surrounding cloud that will not free my soul.

### 3

In the dooryard fronting an old farm-house near the white-washed
    palings,
Stands the lilac-bush tall-growing with heart-shaped leaves of rich
    green,
With many a pointed blossom rising delicate, with the perfume strong
    I love,
With every leaf a miracle—and from this bush in the dooryard,          15
With delicate-colored blossoms and heart-shaped leaves of rich green,
A sprig with its flower I break.

### 4

In the swamp in secluded recesses,
A shy and hidden bird is warbling a song.

Solitary the thrush,                                                                      20
The hermit withdrawn to himself, avoiding the settlements,
Sings by himself a song.

Song of the bleeding throat,
Death's outlet song of life (for well dear brother I know,
If thou wast not granted to sing thou would'st surely die).              25

### 5

Over the breast of the spring, the land, amid cities,
Amid lanes and through old woods, where lately the violets peeped
    from the ground, spotting the gray debris,
Amid the grass in the fields each side of the lanes, passing the endless
    grass,
Passing the yellow-speared wheat, every grain from its shroud in the
    dark-brown fields uprisen,
Passing the apple-tree blows of white and pink in the orchards,          30
Carrying a corpse to where it shall rest in the grave,
Night and day journeys a coffin.

1. The "occasion" of the poem is the assassination of Abraham Lincoln.

6

Coffin that passes through lanes and streets,[2]
Through day and night with the great cloud darkening the land,
With the pomp of the inlooped flags with the cities draped in black,    35
With the show of the States themselves as of crepe-veiled women
    standing,
With processions long and winding and the flambeaus of the night,
With the countless torches lit, with the silent sea of faces and the un-
    bared heads,
With the waiting depot, the arriving coffin, and the somber faces,
With dirges through the night, with the thousand voices rising strong
    and solemn,    40
With all the mournful voices of the dirges poured around the coffin,
The dim-lit churches and the shuddering organs—where amid these
    you journey,
With the tolling tolling bells' perpetual clang,
Here, coffin that slowly passes,
I give you my sprig of lilac.    45

7

( Nor for you, for one alone,
Blossoms and branches green to coffins all I bring,
For fresh as the morning, thus would I chant a song for you O sane
    and sacred death.

All over bouquets of roses,
O death, I cover you over with roses and early lilies,    50
But mostly and now the lilac that blooms the first,
Copious I break, I break the sprigs from the bushes,
With loaded arms I come, pouring for you,
For you and the coffins all of you O death.)

8

O western orb sailing the heaven,    55
Now I know what you must have meant as a month since I walked,
As I walked in silence the transparent shadowy night,
As I saw you had something to tell as you bent to me night after night,
As you drooped from the sky low down as if to my side (while the
    other stars all looked on),
As we wandered together the solemn night (for something I know
    not what kept me from sleep),    60
As the night advanced, and I saw on the rim of the west how full you
    were of woe,
As I stood on the rising ground in the breeze in the cool transparent
    night,
As I watched where you passed and was lost in the netherward black
    of the night,
As my soul in its trouble dissatisfied sank, as where you sad orb,
Concluded, dropped in the night, and was gone.    65

9

Sing on there in the swamp,
O singer bashful and tender, I hear your notes, I hear your call,

2. The funeral cortege stopped at many towns between Washington and Springfield,
Illinois, where Lincoln was buried.

I hear, I come presently, I understand you,
But a moment I linger, for the lustrous star has detained me,
The star my departing comrade holds and detains me.                    70

### 10
O how shall I warble myself for the dead one there I loved?
And how shall I deck my song for the large sweet soul that has gone?
And what shall my perfume be for the grave of him I love?
Sea-winds blown from east and west,
Blown from the Eastern sea and blown from the Western sea, till there
    on the prairies meeting,                                           75
These and with these and the breath of my chant,
I'll perfume the grave of him I love.

### 11
O what shall I hang on the chamber walls?
And what shall the pictures be that I hang on the walls,
To adorn the burial-house of him I love?                               80

Pictures of growing spring and farms and homes,
With the Fourth-month eve at sundown, and the gray smoke lucid and
    bright,
With floods of the yellow gold of the gorgeous, indolent, sinking sun,
    burning, expanding the air,
With the fresh sweet herbage under foot, and the pale green leaves of
    the trees prolific,
In the distance the flowing glaze, the breast of the river, with a wind-
    dapple here and there,                                             85
With ranging hills on the banks, with many a line against the sky, and
    shadows,
And the city at hand with dwellings so dense, and stacks of chimneys,
And all the scenes of life and the workshops, and the workmen home-
    ward returning.

### 12
Lo, body and soul—this land,
My own Manhattan with spires, and the sparkling and hurrying tides,
    and the ships,
The varied and ample land, the South and the North in the light,      90
    Ohio's shores and flashing Missouri,
And ever the far-spreading prairies covered with grass and corn.

Lo, the most excellent sun so calm and haughty,
The violet and purple morn with just-felt breezes,
The gentle soft-born measureless light,                                95
The miracle spreading bathing all, the fulfilled noon,
The coming eve delicious, the welcome night and the stars,
Over my cities shining all, enveloping man and land.

### 13
Sing on, sing on you gray-brown bird,
Sing from the swamps, the recesses, pour your chant from the bushes, 100
Limitless out of the dusk, out of the cedars and pines.

Sing on dearest brother, warble your reedy song,
Loud human song, with voice of uttermost woe.

O liquid and free and tender!
O wild and loose to my soul—O wondrous singer!                    105
You only I hear—yet the star holds me (but will soon depart),
Yet the lilac with mastering odor holds me.


### 14

Now while I sat in the day and looked forth,
In the close of the day with its light and the fields of spring, and the
    farmers preparing their crops,
In the large unconscious scenery of my land with its lakes and forests, 110
In the heavenly aerial beauty (after the perturbed winds and the
    storms),
Under the arching heavens of the afternoon swift passing, and the
    voices of children and women.
The many-moving sea-tides, and I saw the ships how they sailed,
And the summer approaching with richness, and the fields all busy
    with labor,
And the infinite separate houses, how they all went on, each with its
    meals and minutia of daily usages,                         115
And the streets how their throbbings throbbed, and the cities pent—lo,
    then and there,
Falling upon them all and among them all, enveloping me with the rest,
Appeared the cloud, appeared the long black trail,
And I knew death, its thought, and the sacred knowledge of death.

Then with the knowledge of death as walking one side of me,         120
And the thought of death close-walking the other side of me,
And I in the middle as with companions, and as holding the hands of
    companions,
I fled forth to the hiding receiving night that talks not,
Down to the shores of the water, the path by the swamp in the dim-
    ness,
To the solemn shadowy cedars and ghostly pines so still.           125

And the singer so shy to the rest received me,
The gray-brown bird I know received us comrades three,
And he sang the carol of death, and a verse for him I love.

From deep secluded recesses,
From the fragrant cedars and the ghostly pines so still,           130
Came the carol of the bird.

And the charm of the carol rapt me,
As I held as if by their hands my comrades in the night,
And the voice of my spirit tallied the song of the bird.

*Come lovely and soothing death,*                                  135
*Undulate round the world, serenely arriving, arriving,*
*In the day, in the night, to all, to each,*
*Sooner or later delicate death.*

*Praised be the fathomless universe,*
*For life and joy, and for objects and knowledge curious,*         140
*And for love, sweet love—but praise! praise! praise!*
*For the sure-enwinding arms of cool-enfolding death.*

*Dark mother always gliding near with soft feet,*
*Have none chanted for thee a chant of fullest welcome?*
*Then I chant it for thee, I glorify thee above all,*                    145
*I bring thee a song that when thou must indeed come, come unfalter-*
    *ingly.*

*Approach strong deliveress,*
*When it is so, when thou hast taken them I joyously sing the dead,*
*Lost in the loving floating ocean of thee,*
*Laved in the flood of thy bliss O death.*                              150

*From me to thee glad serenades,*
*Dances for thee I propose saluting thee, adornments and feastings for*
    *thee,*
*And the sights of the open landscape and the high-spread sky are*
    *fitting,*
*And life and the fields, and the huge and thoughtful night.*

*The night in silence under many a star,*                              155
*The ocean shore and the husky whispering wave whose voice I know,*
*And the soul turning to thee O vast and well-veiled death,*
*And the body gratefully nestling close to thee.*

*Over the tree-tops I float thee a song,*
*Over the rising and sinking waves, over the myriad fields and the*
    *prairies wide,*                                                    160
*Over the dense-packed cities all and the teeming wharves and ways,*
*I float this carol with joy, with joy to thee O death.*

### 15

To the tally of my soul,
Loud and strong kept up the gray-brown bird,
With pure deliberate notes spreading filling the night.                165

Loud in the pines and cedars dim,
Clear in the freshness moist and the swamp-perfume,
And I with my comrades there in the night.

While my sight that was bound in my eyes unclosed,
As to long panoramas of visions.                                       170

And I saw askant[3] the armies,
I saw as in noiseless dreams hundreds of battle-flags,
Borne through the smoke of the battles and pierced with missiles I saw
    them,
And carried hither and yon through the smoke, and torn and bloody,
And at last but a few shreds left on the staffs (and all in silence),  175
And the staffs all splintered and broken.

I saw battle-corpses, myriads of them,
And the white skeletons of young men, I saw them,
I saw the debris and debris of all the slain soldiers of the war,

---

3. Askance: sideways.

But I saw they were not as was thought,                                    180
They themselves were fully at rest, they suffered not,
The living remained and suffered, the mother suffered,
And the wife and the child and the musing comrade suffered,
And the armies that remained suffered.

### 16

Passing the visions, passing the night,                                    185
Passing, unloosing the hold of my comrades' hands,
Passing the song of the hermit bird and the tallying song of my soul,
Victorious song, death's outlet song, yet varying ever-altering song,
As low and wailing, yet clear the notes, rising and falling, flooding the
     night,
Sadly sinking and fainting, as warning and warning, and yet again
     bursting with joy,                                                    190
Covering the earth and filling the spread of the heaven,
As that powerful psalm in the night I heard from recesses,
Passing, I leave thee lilac with heart-shaped leaves,
I leave thee there in the door-yard, blooming, returning with spring.

I cease from my song for thee,                                             195
 From my gaze on thee in the west, fronting the west, communing with
     thee,
O comrade lustrous with silver face in the night.

Yet each to keep and all, retrievements out of the night,
The song, the wondrous chant of the gray-brown bird,
And the tallying chant, the echo aroused in my soul,                       200
With the lustrous and drooping star with the countenance full of woe,
With the holders holding my hand nearing the call of the bird,
Comrades mine and I in the midst, and their memory ever to keep, for
     the dead I loved so well,
For the sweetest, wisest soul of all my days and lands—and this for his
     dear sake,
Lilac and star and bird twined with the chant of my soul,                  205
There in the fragrant pines and the cedars dusk and dim.
1865–66

BEN JONSON

# Inviting a Friend to Supper[1]

   Tonight, grave sir, both my poor house and I
   Do equally desire your company;
   Not that we think us worthy such a guest,
   But that your worth will dignify our feast,
   With those that come, whose grace may make that seem        5
   Something, which else could hope for no esteem.
   It is the fair acceptance, sir, creates
   The entertainment perfect, not the cates.[2]
   Yet shall you have, to rectify[3] your palate,
   An olive, capers, or some better salad                      10

1. A 17th-century version of Horace,        2. Delicacies.
*Epistles* I, v.                            3. Restore to healthy condition.

Ushering the mutton; with a short-legged hen,
If we can get her, full of eggs; and then,
Lemons, and wine for sauce: to these, a cony[4]
Is not to be despaired of for our money;
And though fowl now be scarce, yet there are clerks,                    15
The sky not falling,[5] think we may have larks.
I'll tell you of more, and lie, so you will come:
Of partridge, pheasant, woodcock, of which some
May yet be there; and godwit if we can:
Gnat, rail, and ruff,[6] too. Howsoe'er,[7] my man[8]                    20
Shall read a piece of Vergil, Tacitus,
Livy, or of some better book to us,
Of which we'll speak our minds, amidst our meat;
And I'll profess no verses to repeat:[9]
To this, if aught appear, which I not know of,                          25
That will the pastry, not my paper, show of.
Digestive cheese, and fruit there sure will be;
But that which most doth take my muse and me,
Is a pure cup of rich Canary wine,
Which is the Mermaid's[1] now, but shall be mine:                       30
Of which had Horace, or Anacreon tasted,
Their lives, as do their lines, till now had lasted.
Tobacco, nectar, or the Thespian[2] spring,
Are all but Luther's beer, to[3] this I sing.
Of this we will sup free, but moderately,                               35
And we will have no Pooly or Parrot[4] by;
Nor shall our cups make any guilty men,
But at our parting, we will be as when
We innocently met. No simple word
That shall be uttered at our mirthful board                            40
Shall make us sad next morning, or affright
The liberty that we'll enjoy tonight.

1616

JOHN DONNE

## Hymn to God My God, in My Sickness

Since I am coming to that holy room
    Where, with Thy choir of saints forevermore,
I shall be made Thy Music, as I come
    I tune the instrument here at the door,
    And what I must do then, think here before.                         5

Whilst my physicians by their love are grown
    Cosmographers, and I their map,[1] who lie

4. Rabbit.
5. If the sky doesn't fall.
6. Fowl. "Gnat" was a nickname for the Lesser Tern.
7. In any case.
8. Servant.
9. I.e., I'll pretend I won't recite poems.
1. I.e., it now belongs to the Mermaid Tavern.

2. Associated with the Muses.
3. Inferior brew compared to.
4. Known government informers.
1. Because the various parts of the world and orders of being were thought to correspond closely and reflect one another, man was often called a "microcosm," or little world.

Flat on this bed, that by them may be shown
   That this is my South-west discovery[2]
   *Per fretum febris,*[3] by these straits to die,          10

I joy, that in these straits, I see my West;[4]
   For, though their current yield return to none,
What shall my West hurt me? As West and East
   In all flat maps (and I am one) are one,
   So death doth touch the resurrection.          15

Is the Pacific Sea my home? Or are
   The Eastern riches? Is *Jerusalem?*
*Anyan,*[5] and *Magellan,* and *Gibraltar,*
   All straits, and none but straits, are ways to them,
   Whether where *Japhet* dwelt, or *Cham,* or *Shem.*[6]    20

We think that *Paradise* and *Calvary,*
   *Christ's* Cross, and *Adam's* tree, stood in one place;
Look, Lord, and find both *Adams* met in me;
   As the first *Adam's* sweat surrounds my face,
   May the last *Adam's* blood my soul embrace.      25

So in His purple wrapped, receive me, Lord,
   By these His thorns give me His other crown;
And, as to others' souls I preached Thy word,
   Be this my text, my sermon to mine own,
   Therefore that He may raise, the Lord throws down.   30

1635

GERARD MANLEY HOPKINS

# The Windhover[1]

### To Christ Our Lord

I caught this morning morning's minion,[2] king-
     dom of daylight's dauphin,[3] dapple-dawn-drawn Falcon, in his
     riding
  Of the rolling level underneath him steady air, and striding
High there, how he rung upon the rein of a wimpling[4] wing
In his ecstasy! then off, off forth on swing,          5
     As a skate's heel sweeps smooth on a bow-bend: the hurl and
     gliding
  Rebuffed the big wind. My heart in hiding
Stirred for a bird,—the achieve of, the mastery of the thing!

2. Magellan, in 1520, discovered the South American straits which are named for him; they are southwest of England.
3. Through the straits of fever.
4. West, because the sun sets there, often connotes death, and the East life or rebirth (line 13).
5. Bering.
6. Noah's sons who, after the Flood, settled Europe, Africa, and Asia, respectively.
1. A small hawk, the kestrel, which habitually hovers in the air, headed into the wind.
2. Favorite, beloved.
3. Heir to regal splendor.
4. Rippling.

Brute beauty and valor and act, oh, air, pride, plume, here
     Buckle![5] AND the fire that breaks from thee then, a billion    10
Times told lovelier, more dangerous, O my chevalier![6]

     No wonder of it: sheér plód makes plow down sillion[7]
Shine, and blue-bleak embers, ah my dear,
     Fall, gall themselves, and gash gold-vermilion.
1877


GALWAY KINNELL

# To Christ our Lord

The legs of the elk punctured the snow's crust
And wolves floated lightfooted on the land
Hunting Christmas elk living and frozen;
Inside snow melted in a basin, and a woman basted
A bird spread over coals by its wings and head.    5

Snow had sealed the windows; candles lit
The Christmas meal. The Christmas grace chilled
The cooked bird, being long-winded and the room cold.
During the words a boy thought, it is fitting
To eat this creature killed on the wing?    10

He had killed it himself, climbing out
Alone on snowshoes in the Christmas dawn,
The fallen snow swirling and the snowfall gone,
Heard its throat scream as the rifle shouted,
Watched it drop, and fished from the snow the dead.    15

He had not wanted to shoot. The sound
Of wings beating into the hushed air
Had stirred his love, and his fingers
Froze in his gloves, and he wondered,
Famishing, could he fire? Then he fired.    20

Now the grace praised his wicked act. At its end
The bird on the plate
Stared at his stricken appetite.
There had been nothing to do but surrender,
To kill and to eat; he ate as he had killed, with wonder.    25

At night on snowshoes on the drifting field
He wondered again, for whom had love stirred?
The stars glittered on the snow and nothing answered.
Then the Swan spread her wings, cross of the cold north,
The pattern and mirror of the acts of earth.    30
    1960

5. Several meanings may apply: to join closely, to prepare for battle, to grapple with, to collapse.
6. Horseman, knight.

7. The narrow strip of land between furrows in an open field divided for separate cultivation.

ROBERT SOUTHWELL

# The Burning Babe

As I in hoary winter's night stood shivering in the snow,
Surprised I was with sudden heat, which made my heart to glow;
And lifting up a fearful eye to view what fire was near,
A pretty Babe all burning bright, did in the air appear,
Who, scorchéd with excessive heat, such floods of tears did shed,    5
As though His floods should quench His flames which with His tears
    were fed.
"Alas!" quoth He, "but newly born, in fiery heats I fry,
Yet none approach to warm their hearts or feel my fire but I!
My faultless breast the furnace is, the fuel wounding thorns,
Love is the fire, and sighs the smoke, the ashes shame and scorns;    10
The fuel Justice layeth on, and Mercy blows the coals,
The metal in this furnace wrought are men's defiléd souls,
For which, as now on fire I am to work them to their good,
So will I melt into a bath to wash them in My blood."
With this He vanished out of sight, and swiftly shrunk away,    15
And straight I calléd unto mind that it was Christmas-day.
ca. 1595

T. S. ELIOT

# Journey of the Magi[1]

"A cold coming we had of it,
Just the worst time of the year
For a journey, and such a long journey:
The ways deep and the weather sharp,
The very dead of winter."[2]    5
And the camels galled, sore-footed, refractory,
Lying down in the melting snow.
There were times we regretted
The summer palaces on slopes, the terraces,
And the silken girls bringing sherbet.    10
Then the camel men cursing and grumbling
And running away, and wanting their liquor and women,
And the night-fires going out, and the lack of shelters,
And the cities hostile and the towns unfriendly
And the villages dirty and charging high prices:    15
A hard time we had of it.
At the end we preferred to travel all night,
Sleeping in snatches,
With the voices singing in our ears, saying
That this was all folly.    20

    Then at dawn we came down to a temperate valley,
Wet, below the snow line, smelling of vegetation;
With a running stream and a water-mill beating the darkness,

---

1. The wise men who followed the star    2. An adaptation of a passage from a
of Bethlehem. See *Matthew* 2:1–12.    1622 sermon by Lancelot Andrewes.

And three trees on the low sky,[3]
And an old white horse galloped away in the meadow.                    25
Then we came to a tavern with vine-leaves over the lintel,
Six hands at an open door dicing for pieces of silver,
And feet kicking the empty wine-skins.
But there was no information, and so we continued
And arrived at evening, not a moment too soon                          30
Finding the place; it was (you may say) satisfactory.

    All this was a long time ago, I remember,
And I would do it again, but set down
This set down
This: were we led all that way for                                     35
Birth or Death? There was a Birth, certainly,
We had evidence and no doubt. I had seen birth and death,
But had thought they were different; this Birth was
Hard and bitter agony for us, like Death, our death.
We returned to our places, these Kingdoms,[4]                          40
But no longer at ease here, in the old dispensation,
With an alien people clutching their gods.
I should be glad of another death.

                                                     1927

JOHN PEALE BISHOP

# Twelfth Night[1]

All night I thought on those wise men who took
A midnight leave of towers and came peering
Pyramidally down to the dark guards
And stared apart, each with a mad, hid look
Twitching his mummied beard                                            5
                        while the night swords
Conferred and chains fell and the unwieldy bar
Slid and swung back
                 then wandered out to name
The living demon of an unnamed star.[2]                                10

All night I followed them and came at last
On a low hutch propped in an alleyway
And stretched aside
                while one by one they passed
Those stilted mages[3] mitered in stiff blue                           15
Under the sagging beams and through the stalls.

Following, through stench and misty fug[4] I saw
And nothing were clearer in the scrupulous day

3. Suggestive of the three crosses of the Crucifixion (*Luke* 23:32–33). The Magi see several objects which suggest later events in Christ's life: pieces of silver (see *Matthew* 26:14–16), the dicing (see *Matthew* 27:35), the white horse (see *Revelation* 6:2 and 19:11–16), and the empty wine-skins (see *Matthew* 9:14–17, possibly relevant also to lines 41–42).
4. The Bible only identifies the wise men as "from the East," and subsequent tradition has made them kings. In Persia, Magi were members of an ancient priestly caste.
1. According to post-Biblical tradition, the wise men reached Bethlehem twelve days after the birth of Christ.
2. The star of Bethlehem. See *Matthew* 2:1–12.
3. Magicians.
4. Close, stuffy atmosphere.

The rigid drooping of their ancient palls[5]
Burnish with light, where on a toss of straw                        20
Swaddled in rags, to their abashment, lay
Not the pedantic god whose name thy knew
But a small child petulant with cries.
With courtesies unperturbed and slow
They laid their gifts down, unburnt scents and gold:               25
But gray evasions shamed their skeptic eyes
And the starved hands were suddenly boned with cold
As plucking their gorgeous skirts they shook to go.

1923

W. B. YEATS

## The Magi[1]

Now as at all times I can see in the mind's eye,
In their stiff, painted clothes, the pale unsatisfied ones
Appear and disappear in the blue depth of the sky
With all their ancient faces like rain-beaten stones,
And all their helms of silver hovering side by side,                5
And all their eyes still fixed, hoping to find once more,
Being by Calvary's turbulence[2] unsatisfied,
The uncontrollable mystery on the bestial floor.

1914

e. e. cummings

## the season 'tis, my lovely lambs

the season 'tis, my lovely lambs,

of Sumner Volstead Christ and Co.[1]
the epoch of Mann's righteousness
the age of dollars and no sense.
Which being quite beyond dispute                                    5

as prove from Troy (N. Y.) to Cairo
(Egypt) the luminous dithyrambs[2]
of large immaculate unmute
antibolshevistic gents
(each manufacturing word by word                                    10
his own unrivalled brand of pyro
-technic blurb anent[3] the (hic)
hero dead that gladly (sic)

5. Robes.
1. The three wise men who visited the Christ child at Bethlehem (see *Matthew* 2:1–12). Here they seem to be identified with the Magi of Persia, an ancient priestly class associated with magic and sorcery.
2. The Crucifixion. See *Luke* 23:33–45.
1. The Volstead Act (1919) gave the federal government power to enforce Prohibition. "Sumner": possibly Charles Sumner, a late 19th-century U. S. senator who was considered the leading representative of the Puritan spirit in American politics, but more probably William Sumner, a late 19th and early 20th-century laissez-faire theorist who opposed laws regulating monopolies. The Mann Act (1910) made taking a woman across a state line "for immoral purposes" a federal offense.
2. Vehement expressions on neon signs.
3. In reference to (a somewhat affected term common in early businessese). "Hic" (line 12), Latin for "here," and "sic" (line 13), Latin for "thus," sometimes appear in similar incongruent contexts, ostensibly as shortcuts to saying "here is an example" or "it is correct as it stands," but often to show off. There are, of course, also puns on both terms.

in far lands perished of unheard
of maladies including flu)                                                    15

my little darlings, let us now
passionately remember how—
braving the worst, of peril heedless,
each braver than the other, each
(a typewriter within his reach)                                               20
upon his fearless derrière
sturdily seated—Colonel Needless
To Name and General You know who
a string of pretty medals drew

(while messrs jack james john and jim                                         25
in token of their country's love
received my dears the order of
The Artificial Arm and Limb)

—or, since bloodshed and kindred questions
inhibit unprepared digestions,                                                30
come: let us mildly contemplate
beginning with his wellfilled pants
earth's biggest grafter, nothing less;
the Honorable Mr. (guess)
who, breathing on the ear of fate,                                            35
landed a seat in the legislat-
ure whereas tommy so and so
(an erring child of circumstance
whom the bulls[4] nabbed at 33rd)

pulled six months for selling snow[5]                                         40

                                                                              1926

HOWARD NEMEROV

# Boom!

## Sees Boom in Religion, Too

Atlantic City, June 23, 1957 (AP).—President Eisenhower's pastor said
tonight that Americans are living in a period of "unprecedented religious
activity" caused partially by paid vacations, the eight-hour day and modern
conveniences.
    "These fruits of material progress," said the Rev. Edward L. R. Elson
of the National Presbyterian Church, Washington, "have provided the
leisure, the energy, and the means for a level of human and spiritual
values never before reached."

Here at the Vespasian-Carlton,[1] it's just one
religious activity after another; the sky
is constantly being crossed by cruciform[2]
airplanes, in which nobody disbelieves
for a second and the tide, the tide                                           5

4. Police.
5. Cocaine, but also a reminder of the
Season.
1. Vespasian was emperor of Rome 70–

79, shortly after the reign of Nero. In
French, *vespasienne* means public toilet.
2. Cross-shaped.

of spiritual progress and prosperity
miraculously keeps rising, to a level
never before attained. The churches are full,
the beaches are full, and the filling-stations
are full, God's great ocean is full                                    10
of paid vacationers praying an eight-hour day
to the human and spiritual values, the fruits,
the leisure, the energy, and the means, Lord,
the means for the level, the unprecedented level,
and the modern conveniences, which also are full.                      15
Never before, O Lord, have the prayers and praises
from belfry and phonebooth, from ballpark and barbecue
the sacrifices, so endlessly ascended.

It was not thus when Job in Palestine
sat in the dust and cried, cried bitterly;[3]                          20
when Damien kissed the lepers on their wounds
it was not thus;[4] it was not thus
when Francis worked a fourteen-hour day
strictly for the birds;[5] when Dante took
a week's vacation without pay and it rained                            25
part of the time,[6] O Lord, it was not thus.

But now the gears mesh and the tires burn
and the ice chatters in the shaker and the priest
in the pulpit and Thy Name, O Lord,
is kept before the public, while the fruits                            30
ripen and religion booms and the level rises
and every modern convenience runneth over,
that it may never be with us as it hath been
with Athens and Karnak and Nagasaki,[7]
nor Thy sun for one instant refrain from shining                       35
on the rainbow Buick by the breezeway
or the Chris Craft with the uplift life raft;
that we may continue to be the just folks we are,
plain people with ordinary superliners and
disposable diaperliners, people of the stop'n'shop                     40
'n'pray as you go, of hotel, motel, boatel,
the humble pilgrims of no deposit no return
and please adjust thy clothing, who will give to Thee,
if Thee will keep us going, our annual
Miss Universe, for Thy Name's Sake, Amen.                              45

1960

3. According to the *Book of Job,* he was afflicted with the loss of prosperity, children, and health as a test of his faith. His name means, in Hebrew, "he cries"; see especially *Job* 2:7–13.

4. "Father Damien" (Joseph Damien de Veuster, 1840–1889), a Roman Catholic missionary from Belgium, was known for his work among lepers in Hawaii; he ultimately contracted leprosy himself and died there.

5. St. Francis of Assisi, 13th-century founder of the Franciscan order, was noted for his love of all living things, and one of the most famous stories about him tells of his preaching to the birds. "Strictly for the birds": a mid-20th-century expression for worthless or unfashionable activity.

6. Dante's journey through Hell, Purgatory, and Paradise (in *The Divine Comedy*) takes a week, beginning on Good Friday, 1300. It rains in the third chasm of Hell.

7. Athens, the cultural center of ancient civilization; Karnak, a village on the Nile, built on the site of ancient Thebes; Nagasaki, a large Japanese port city, virtually destroyed by a U.S. atomic bomb in 1945.

JOHN MILTON

# [Before the Fall][1]

She as a veil down to the slender waist                                304
Her unadorned golden tresses wore
Dishevelled, but in wanton[2] ringlets waved
As the vine curls her tendrils, which implied
Subjection,[3] but required with gentle sway,
And by her yielded, by him best received,
Yielded with coy[4] submission, modest pride,                          310
And sweet reluctant amorous delay.
Nor those mysterious parts were then concealed,
Then was not guilty shame, dishonest shame
Of nature's works, honor dishonorable,
Sin-bred, how have ye troubled all mankind                             315
With shows instead, mere shows of seeming pure,
And banished from man's life his happiest life,
Simplicity and spotless innocence.
So passed they naked on, nor shunned the sight
Of God or angel, for they thought no ill.                              320
So hand in hand they passed, the loveliest pair
That ever since in love's embraces met,
Adam the goodliest man of men since born
His sons, the fairest of her daughters Eve.
Under a tuft of shade that on a green                                  325
Stood whispering soft, by a fresh fountain side
They sat them down, and after no more toil
Of their sweet gardening labor than sufficed
To recommend cool zephyr, and made ease
More easy, wholesome thirst and appetite                               330
More grateful, to their supper fruits they fell,
Nectarine[5] fruits which the compliant boughs
Yielded them, sidelong as they sat recline
On the soft downy bank damasked[6] with flowers:
The savory pulp they chew, and in the rind                             335
Still as they thirsted scoop the brimming stream;
Nor gentle purpose,[7] nor endearing smiles
Wanted,[8] nor youthful dalliance as beseems
Fair couple, linked in happy nuptial league,
Alone as they. About them frisking played                             340
All beasts of the earth, since wild, and of all chase[9]
In wood or wilderness, forest or den;
Sporting the lion ramped, and in his paw
Dandled the kid; bears, tigers, ounces,[1] pards,
Gamboled before them, the unwieldy elephant                           345
To make them mirth used all his might, and wreathed
His lithe proboscis; close the serpent sly

1. From *Paradise Lost*, Book IV. For the
Biblical description of Eden, see *Genesis*
2:8–25.
2. Luxuriant.
3. The idea derives from *Genesis* 3:16
and *I Corinthians* 11:9–10.
4. Shy.
5. Sweet as nectar, the traditional drink
of the gods.
6. Variegated.
7. Conversation. "Nor . . . nor": neither
. . . nor (a common 17th-century construction).
8. Were lacking.
9. Tracts of land.
1. Lynxes. "pards": leopards.

Insinuating, wove with Gordian[2] twine
His braided train, and of his fatal guile
Gave proof unheeded; others on the grass                    350
Couched, and now filled with pasture gazing sat,
Or bedward ruminating: for the sun
Declined was hasting now with prone career
To the Ocean Isles,[3] and in the ascending scale
Of heaven the stars that usher evening rose.                355

1667

CHRISTINA ROSSETTI

# Eve

"While I sit at the door,
Sick to gaze within,
Mine eye weepeth sore
For sorrow and sin:
As a tree my sin stands                                     5
To darken all lands;
Death is the fruit it bore.

"How have Eden bowers grown
Without Adam to bend them!
How have Eden flowers blown,                                10
Squandering their sweet breath,
Without me to tend them!
The Tree of Life was ours,
Tree twelvefold-fruited,[1]
Most lofty tree that flowers,                               15
Most deeply rooted:
I chose the Tree of Death.[2]

"Hadst thou but said me nay,
    Adam, my brother,
I might have pined away—                                    20
    I, but none other:
God might have let thee stay
Safe in our garden,
By putting me away
Beyond all pardon.                                          25

"I, Eve, sad mother
Of all who must live,
I, not another,
Plucked bitterest fruit to give
My friend, husband, lover.                                  30
O wanton eyes run over!

---

2. Like the Gordian knot, a legendary intricate knot, finally cut by Alexander the Great.
3. The Azores; i.e., westward.
1. The tree of life is so described in *Revelation* 22:2, 14, but the account there is of the New Jerusalem, not of Eden.

2. The *Genesis* account distinguishes between the tree of life and the tree of the knowledge of good and evil; the latter is forbidden, and eating of it brings labor, sickness, and death into the world. See *Genesis* 2:9, 3:1–24.

Who but I should grieve?—
Cain hath slain his brother:[3]
Of all who must die mother,
Miserable Eve!"                                              35

Thus she sat weeping,
Thus Eve our mother,
Where one lay sleeping
Slain by his brother.
Greatest and least                                          40
Each piteous beast
To hear her voice
Forgot his joys
And set aside his feast.

The mouse paused in his walk                                45
And dropped his wheaten stalk:
Grave cattle wagged their heads
In rumination;
The eagle gave a cry
From his cloud station:                                     50
Larks on thyme beds
Forbore to mount or sing;
Bees drooped upon the wing;
The raven perched on high
Forgot his ration;                                          55
The conies[4] in their rock,
A feeble nation,
Quaked sympathetical;
The mocking-bird left off to mock;
Huge camels knelt as if                                     60
In deprecation;
The kind hart's tears were falling;
Chattered the wistful stork;
Dove-voices with a dying fall
Cooed desolation                                            65
Answering grief by grief.

Only the serpent in the dust,
Wriggling and crawling,
Grinned an evil grin, and thrust
His tongue out with its fork.                               70

1865

RALPH HODGSON

# Eve

Eve, with her basket, was
Deep in the bells[1] and grass,
Wading in bells and grass

---

3. Abel (see *Genesis* 4:1–15).                in *Proverbs* 30:26.
4. A common term for rabbits, but here       1. Bluebells.
probably the small pachyderms mentioned

Up to her knees,
Picking a dish of sweet                    5
Berries and plums to eat,
Down in the bells and grass
Under the trees.

Mute as a mouse in a
Corner the cobra lay,                      10
Curled round a bough of the
Cinnamon tall. . . .
Now to get even and
Humble proud heaven[2] and—
Now was the moment or                      15
Never at all.

"Eva!" Each syllable
Light as a flower fell,
"Eva!" he whispered the
Wondering maid.                            20
Soft as a bubble sung
Out of a linnet's lung,
Soft and most silverly
"Eva!" he said.

Picture that orchard sprite,               25
Eve, with her body white,
Supple and smooth to her
Slim finger tips,
Wondering, listening,
Listening, wondering,                      30
Eve with a berry
Half-way to her lips.

Oh, had our simple Eve
Seen through the make-believe!
Had she but known the                      35
Pretender he was!
Out of the boughs he came,
Whispering still her name,
Tumbling in twenty rings
Into the grass.                            40

Here was the strangest pair
In the world anywhere,
Eve in the bells and grass
Kneeling, and he
Telling his story low. . . .               45
Singing birds saw them go
Down the dark path to
The Blasphemous Tree.[3]

2. The tradition of the angels' rebellion and expulsion from heaven is largely post-Biblical, based on deduction drawn from several Biblical passages, such as *Isaiah* 14:12, *Luke* 10:18, and *Matthew* 25:41.

3. The tree of knowledge. The tradition that the Fall was sexual dates back at least to the third century, but neither Jews nor Christians have accepted it as orthodox interpretation.

Oh, what a clatter when
Titmouse and Jenny Wren                           50
Saw him successful and
Taking his leave!
How the birds rated him!
How they all hated him!
How they all pitied                               55
Poor motherless Eve!

Picture her crying
Outside in the lane,
Eve, with no dish of sweet
Berries and plums to eat,                          60
Haunting the gate of the
Orchard in vain. . . .
Picture the lewd delight
Under the hill to night—
"Eva!" the toast goes round,                       65
"Eva!" again.

1917

VASSAR MILLER

# Adam's Footprint

Once as a child I loved to hop
On round plump bugs and make them stop
Before they crossed a certain crack.
My bantam brawn could turn them back,
My crooked step wrenched straight to kill          5
Live pods that then screwed tight and still.

Small sinner, stripping boughs of pears,
Shinnied past sweet and wholesome airs,
How could a tree be so unclean?
Nobody knows but Augustine.[1]                     10
He nuzzled pears for dam-sin's dugs[2]—
And I scrunched roly-poly bugs.

No wolf's imprint or tiger's trace
Does Christ hunt down to catch with grace
In nets of love the devious preys                  15
Whose feet go softly all their days:
The foot of Adam leaves the mark
Of some child scrabbling in the dark.

1956

1. In his *Confessions*, Book II, St. Augustine agonizes over his theft, from a nearby tree, of pears he did not really want and meditates on the human tendency to want what is forbidden.
2. I.e., as if they were the breasts of mother-sin (with, of course, more than one pun on "dam").

ROBERT FROST

## Never Again Would Birds' Song Be the Same

He would declare and could himself believe
That the birds there in all the garden round
From having heard the daylong voice of Eve
Had added to their own an oversound,
Her tone of meaning but without the words.                5
Admittedly an eloquence so soft
Could only have had an influence on birds
When call or laughter carried it aloft.
Be that as may be, she was in their song.
Moreover her voice upon their voices crossed            10
Had now persisted in the woods so long
That probably it never would be lost.
Never again would birds' song be the same.
And to do that to birds was why she came.

1942

W. S. MERWIN

## Noah's Raven[3]

Why should I have returned?
My knowledge would not fit into theirs.
I found untouched the desert of the unknown,
Big enough for my feet. It is my home.
It is always beyond them. The future                     5
Splits the present with the echo of my voice.
Hoarse with fulfillment, I never made promises.

1963

DENISE LEVERTOV

## The Ache of Marriage

The ache of marriage:

thigh and tongue, beloved,
are heavy with it,
it throbs in the teeth

We look for communion                                    5
and are turned away, beloved,
each and each

It is leviathan[1] and we
in its belly

---

3. According to *Genesis* 8:7, Noah sent a raven out a window of the ark when the Flood waters were partially abated, and the raven flew "to and fro" until the waters were dried up from the earth. A dove, by contrast (see *Genesis* 8:8–9), returned immediately because she "found no rest for the sole of her foot."

1. A sea monster (see *Job* 41:1), often identified with the "great fish" which swallowed Jonah and kept him in its belly for three days (see *Jonah* 1:17).

looking for joy, some joy 10
not to be known outside it

two by two in the ark² of
the ache of it.

1964

EDGAR ALLAN POE

## To Helen¹

Helen, thy beauty is to me
Like those Nicéan² barks of yore,
That gently, o'er a perfumed sea,
The weary, way-worn wanderer bore
To his own native shore. 5

On desperate seas long wont to roam,
Thy hyacinth hair, thy classic face,
Thy Naiad airs³ have brought me home
To the glory that was Greece
And the grandeur that was Rome. 10

Lo! in yon brilliant window-niche
How statue-like I see thee stand,
The agate lamp within thy hand!
Ah, Psyche,⁴ from the regions which
Are Holy Land!⁵ 15

1831

WALTER SAVAGE LANDOR

## Past Ruined Ilion Helen Lives

Past ruined Ilion¹ Helen lives,
Alcestis rises from the shades;²
Verse calls them forth; 'tis verse that gives
Immortal youth to mortal maids.

2. According to *Genesis* 7:9, all beasts and creatures "went in two and two . . . into the ark, male and female," and their isolation lasted until the Flood ended civilization. Another kind of ark, a chest containing the Ten Commandments and later called the Ark of the Covenant of God, was carried everywhere on their wanderings by the ancient Hebrews as a symbol of God's presence (see, e.g., *I Kings* 8:1–11 and *II Samuel* 6); it was later built into the eastern wall of synagogues to symbolize the Holy of Holies of the Temple.
1. Helen of Troy, the traditional type of beauty. Hers was "the face that launched a thousand ships," and her elopement caused the siege and destruction of Troy described in Homer's *Iliad* and the first books of Vergil's *Aeneid*. After the war she returned to her husband.
2. The reference is uncertain: possibly, the island of Nysa (which Milton's *Para-*

*dise Lost* calls the "Nyseian Isle," IV, 275) in the river Triton in North Africa, where Bacchus was safely protected from Rhea; or pertaining to the ancient city of Nicaea, a Byzantine seaport.
3. Graceful manners of a water nymph.
4. A beautiful maiden who, according to Apuleius's *Golden Ass*, was beloved by Cupid but deprived of him when she lit a lamp, disobeying his order that she never seek to know who he was. The word *psyche* in Greek means "soul."
5. In an 1836 review essay, Poe facetiously quotes a medieval monk who said that "Helen represents the Human Soul—Troy is Hell."
1. Ilium, another name for Troy.
2. According to Greek legend, Alcestis volunteered to die instead of her condemned husband, but Hercules brought her back from Hades ("the shades").

Soon shall Oblivion's deepening veil     5
Hide all the peopled hills you see,
The gay, the proud, while lovers hail
In distant ages you and me.

The tear for fading beauty check,
  For passing glory cease to sigh;     10
One form shall rise above the wreck,
  One name, Ianthe,[3] shall not die.

1831

CHRISTOPHER MARLOWE

# Was This the Face that Launched a Thousand Ships[1]

Was this the face that launched a thousand ships,
And burnt the topless towers of Ilium?[2]
Sweet Helen, make me immortal with a kiss!
Her lips suck forth my soul;[3] see where it flies.
Come, Helen, come, give me my soul again.     5
Here will I dwell, for heaven is in these lips,
And all is dross that is not Helena.
I will be Paris, and for love of thee
Instead of Troy shall Wittenberg[4] be sacked,
And I will combat with weak Menelaus,[5]     10
And wear thy colors on my pluméd crest.
Yea, I will wound Achilles in the heel,
And then return to Helen for a kiss.
O, thou art fairer than the evening's air,
Clad in the beauty of a thousand stars.     15
Brighter art thou than flaming Jupiter,
When he appeared to hapless Semele;[6]
More lovely than the monarch of the sky,
In wanton Arethusa's azured arms,[7]
And none but thou shalt be my paramour.     20

ca. 1588–92

---

3. Landor often wrote poems to or about "Ianthe," a real or imaginary beautiful friend.

1. From Marlowe's play, *Dr. Faustus.* The title character overwhelmingly desires power through knowledge and sells his soul to the devil to gain it. In the last act, he conjures up Helen from the dead and speaks these lines.

2. Another name for Troy.

3. In Greek, the word for soul and breath were the same (*psuche* or *psyche*), and according to some philosophers the soul was present in breath.

4. The setting for Marlowe's play.

5. Helen's husband. Paris, Helen's abductor, later fought with Menelaus in single combat during the Trojan War and was badly beaten (*Iliad,* III). He later killed Achilles (line 12), however, when the gods directed his arrow so that it struck Achilles' only vulnerable part.

6. Jupiter (Zeus, Jove) was the father of Semele's child, Dionysus, but when she asked that he appear before her as the god of thunder, the lightning killed her.

7. In Greek mythology, Arethusa was a wood-nymph bathing in a river when Alpheus, the god of the stream, began to pursue her. Diana helped her escape underground, and she later re-emerged as a fountain, but even so Alpheus finally caught her and his waters were mingled with hers. See Ovid's *Metamorphoses,* Book V. "Wanton": merciless, luxuriant.

H. D. (HILDA DOOLITTLE)

## Helen

All Greece[1] hates
the still eyes in the white face,
the luster as of olives
where she stands,
and the white hands.                                    5

All Greece reviles
the wan face when she smiles,
hating it deeper still
when it grows wan and white,
remembering past enchantments            10
and past ills.

Greece sees unmoved
God's daughter, born of love,[2]
the beauty of cool feet
and slenderest of knees,                            15
could love indeed the maid,
only if she were laid,
white ash amid funereal cypresses.

                                                              1924

PAUL VALÉRY

## Helen, the Sad Queen[1]

Azure, 'tis I, come from Elysian shores,[2]
To hear the waves break on sonorous steps,
And see again the sunrise full of ships,
Rising from darkness upon golden oars.

My solitary arms call on the kings                    5
Whose salty beards amused my silver hands.
I wept; they sang of triumphs in far lands,
And gulfs fled backwards upon watery wings.

I hear the trumpet and martial horn
That wield the rhythm of the beating blade,      10
The song of rowers binding the tumult.

And the gods! exalting on the prow with scorn
Their ancient smile that the slow waves insult,
Hold out their sculptured arms to my sad shade.

                                                              1920

1. Helen's husband, Menelaus, was King
of Sparta; the Greeks attacked Troy to get
her back from Paris, son of the Trojan
king.
2. Helen was the daughter of Zeus, king
of the gods, and Leda.
    1. Translated from the French by Janet
Lewis.
    2. Where, according to Greek mythol-
ogy, the blessed abide.

PAUL VALÉRY

## Hélène

Azur! c'est moi . . . Je viens des grottes de la mort
Entendre l'onde se rompre aux degrés sonores,
Et je revois les galères dans les aurores
Ressusciter de l'ombre au fil des rames d'or.

Mes solitaires mains appellent les monarques        5
Dont la barbe de sel amusait mes doigts purs;
Je pleurais. Ils chantaient leurs triomphes obscurs
Et les golfes enfouis aux poupes de leurs barques,

J'entends les conques profondes et les clairons
Militaires rythmer le vol des avirons;        10
Le chant clair des rameurs enchaîne le tumulte,

Et les Dieux, à la proue héroïque exaltés
Dans leur sourire antique et que l'écume insulte
Tendent vers moi leurs bras indulgents et sculptés.

                                                1920

W. B. YEATS

## When Helen Lived

We have cried in our despair
That men desert,
For some trivial affair
Or noisy, insolent sport,
Beauty that we have won        5
From bitterest hours;
Yet we, had we walked within
Those topless towers[1]
Where Helen walked with her boy,[2]
Had given but as the rest        10
Of the men and women of Troy,
A word and a jest.

                                                1914

ALFRED, LORD TENNYSON

## Ulysses[1]

It little profits that an idle king,
By this still hearth, among these barren crags,

1. See Marlowe's "Is This the Face that Launched a Thousand Ships," line 2.
2. Paris, Helen's young lover with whom she had run away to Troy, proved a coward in direct combat against her husband, Menelaus; according to *The Iliad*, Book III, after the disastrous fight Helen made love to him "on the well-known bed," but his countrymen scorned him.

1. After the end of the Trojan War, Ulysses (or Odysseus), King of Ithaca and one of the Greek heroes of the war, returned to his island home (line 34). Homer's account of the situation is in the *Odyssey*, Book XI, but Dante's account of Ulysses in *The Inferno*, XXVI, is the more immediate background of the poem.

Matched with an agéd wife,[2] I mete and dole
Unequal laws unto a savage race,
That hoard, and sleep, and feed, and know not me.                    5

I cannot rest from travel; I will drink
Life to the lees.[3] All times I have enjoyed
Greatly, have suffered greatly, both with those
That loved me, and alone; on shore, and when
Through scudding drifts the rainy Hyades[4]                          10
Vexed the dim sea. I am become a name;
For always roaming with a hungry heart
Much have I seen and known—cities of men
And manners, climates, councils, governments,
Myself not least, but honored of them all—                           15
And drunk delight of battle with my peers,
Far on the ringing plains of windy Troy.
I am a part of all that I have met;
Yet all experience is an arch wherethrough
Gleams that untraveled world, whose margin fades                     20
For ever and for ever when I move.
How dull it is to pause, to make an end,
To rust unburnished, not to shine in use!
As though to breathe were life. Life piled on life
Were all too little, and of one to me                                25
Little remains; but every hour is saved
From that eternal silence, something more,
A bringer of new things; and vile it were
For some three suns to store and hoard myself,
And this gray spirit yearning in desire                              30
To follow knowledge like a sinking star,
Beyond the utmost bound of human thought.

This is my son, mine own Telemachus,
To whom I leave the scepter and the isle—
Well-loved of me, discerning to fulfill                              35
This labor by slow prudence to make mild
A rugged people, and through soft degrees
Subdue them to the useful and the good.
Most blameless is he, centered in the sphere
Of common duties, decent not to fail                                 40
In offices of tenderness, and pay
Meet adoration to my household gods,
When I am gone. He works his work, I mine.

There lies the port; the vessel puffs her sail:
There gloom the dark, broad seas. My mariners,                       45
Souls that have toiled, and wrought, and thought with me—
That ever with a frolic welcome took
The thunder and the sunshine, and opposed
Free hearts, free foreheads—you and I are old;
Old age hath yet his honor and his toil.                             50

2. Penelope.
3. All the way down to the bottom of the cup.
4. A group of stars which were supposed to predict rain when they rose at the same time as the sun.

Death closes all; but something ere the end,
Some work of noble note, may yet be done,
Not unbecoming men that strove with Gods.
The lights begin to twinkle from the rocks;
The long day wanes; the slow moon climbs; the deep          55
Moans round with many voices. Come, my friends.
'Tis not too late to seek a newer world.
Push off, and sitting well in order smite
The sounding furrows; for my purpose holds
To sail beyond the sunset, and the baths                    60
Of all the western stars, until I die.
It may be that the gulfs will wash us down;[5]
It may be we shall touch the Happy Isles,[6]
And see the great Achilles, whom we knew.
Though much is taken, much abides; and though               65
We are not now that strength which in old days
Moved earth and heaven, that which we are, we are:
One equal temper of heroic hearts,
Made weak by time and fate, but strong in will
To strive, to seek, to find, and not to yield.             70

1833

EDMUND SPENSER

## Penelope, for Her Ulysses' Sake

Penelope,[1] for her Ulysses' sake,
Devised a web her wooers to deceive;
In which the work that she all day did make,
The same at night she did again unreave:
Such subtle craft my damsel[2] doth conceive,               5
Th' importune suit of my desire to shun:
For all that I in many days do weave,
In one short hour I find by her undone.
So, when I think to end that I begun,
I must begin and never bring to end:                        10
For with one look she spills[3] that long I spun;
And with one word my whole year's work doth rend.
Such labor like the spider's web I find,
Whose fruitless work is broken with least wind.

1595

5. Beyond the Gulf of Gibraltar was
supposed to be a chasm that led to Hades.
6. Elysium, the Islands of the Blessed,
where heroes like Achilles (line 64) abide
after death.
1. Famous for her long-suffering faith-
fulness to her husband, Ulysses, during the
Trojan War. She ingeniously devised a
series of tricks to deceive the men who
pursued her during Ulysses' 20-year absence. The "never-ending, still beginning"
web was a shroud she was weaving for her
father-in-law; she promised her suitors she
would make a choice when she finished,
but each night she unraveled what she had
done during the day. See Homer's *Odyssey*,
II, XIX, and XXIV.
2. Spenser's sonnet is part of a sequence
recounting a courtship.
3. Destroys.

PETER VIERECK

# Kilroy[1]

Also Ulysses once—that other war.[2]
    (Is it because we find his scrawl
    Today on every privy door
    That we forget his ancient role?)
Also was there—he did it for the wages—        5
When a Cathay-drunk Genoese set sail.[3]
*Whenever "longen folk to goon on pilgrimages,"*[4]
*Kilroy is there;*
        *he tells The Miller's Tale.*

At times he seems a paranoiac king        10
Who stamps his crest on walls and says "My Own!"
But in the end he fades like a lost tune,
Tossed here and there, whom all the breezes sing.
"Kilroy was here"; these words sound wanly gay,
    Haughty yet tired with long marching.        15
He is Orestes[5]—guilty of what crime?—
    For whom the Furies still are searching;
    When they arrive, they find their prey
(Leaving his name to mock them) went away.
Sometimes he does not flee from them in time:        20
*"Kilroy was—"*
        (*with his blood a dying man*
        *Wrote half the phrase out in Bataan.*[6])

Kilroy, beware. "HOME" is the final trap
That lurks for you in many a wily shape:        25
In pipe-and-slippers plus a Loyal Hound
    Or fooling around, just fooling around.
Kind to the old (their warm Penelope[7])
But fierce to boys,
        thus "home" becomes that sea,        30
Horribly disguised, where you were always drowned—
    (How could suburban Crete[8] condone
The yarns you would have V-mailed[9] from the sun?)—
And folksy fishes sip Icarian tea.[1]

---

1. A fictitious character in World War II who symbolized American daring and ingenuity; the phrase "Kilroy was here" was carved and scribbled everywhere, all over the world.
2. The Trojan War, in which Ulysses became a hero and a mythic symbol of the bold voyager who thrived on action and adventure.
3. When Columbus set sail from Genoa, he intended to find a new trade route to China (Cathay).
4. An early line in the "General Prologue" to Chaucer's *Canterbury Tales*, explaining the rationale for the journey on which the *Tales* are built. "The Miller's Tale" (line 9) is the bawdiest of the tales, and one of the most spirited.
5. The son of Agamemnon and Clytemnestra in Greek myth. After his mother killed his father, he avenged the death by killing her, and the Furies (line 17) pursued him from country to country.
6. The site, in the Philippine Islands, of two major battle campaigns in World War II.
7. Wife of Ulysses.
8. According to Pindar, the Cretans were incredible liars.
9. V-Mail was an overseas military mail system used in World War II. Letters were microfilmed, for compact transportation, and then re-enlarged before delivery.
1. Icarus, the son of Daedalus, flew with his father from Crete (line 32), but he strayed too near the sun, the wax which attached his wings melted, and he fell into the sea, which then became known as the Icarian Sea. "Icarian" once meant venturesome.

*One stab of hopeless wings imprinted your*                    35
    *Exultant Kilroy-signature*
*Upon sheer sky for all the world to stare:*
    *"I was there! I was there! I was there!"*

God is like Kilroy. He, too, sees it all;
That's how He knows of every sparrow's fall;[2]              40
That's why we prayed each time the tightropes cracked
On which our loveliest clowns contrived their act.
The G. I. Faustus[3] who was
           everywhere
Strolled home again. "What was it like outside?"            45
Asked Can't, with his good neighbors Ought and But
And pale Perhaps and grave-eyed Better Not;
For "Kilroy" means: the world is very wide.
      He was there, he was there, he was there!

*And in the suburbs Can't sat down and cried.*              50

                              1948

PAUL GOODMAN

# Wonders of *The Iliad*

Here are a dozen wonders of *The Iliad*:
Apollo squatting shoots his silver bow against the ships.
The soldiery attack across the prairie like chattering cranes.
Queen Helen comes forth on the wall to watch and says, "*There* is my
    husband—if he ever was; but where are Castor and Pollux? where
    are they?"
The goddess drags the unwilling queen to bed with Alexander.[1]        5
Little Astyanax screams at Hector's helmet, and his father picks him
    up.
Glaucus and Diomed pause in the fight, and exchange armor.
At last the others in dark pomp depart; and left alone, Achilles calls
    out to his lover.[2]
He brawls with the Scamander River swirling about his knees.
His horse speaks to him.                                                 10
Knight Hector's body is dragged by the pitiless wheels.
His body is kept uncorrupted by the gods.
And Achilles honors the white hairs of Priam.
—These abide in my imagination, behind my eyes, most of my life;
    and to the extent that men are like them, I regard men as human.

                              p. 1953

---

2. According to *Matthew* 10:29, even a sparrow "shall not fall on the ground" without God's knowledge of it.

3. The 16th-century astrologer and magician who became a symbol of man's desire to know everything regardless of the cost.

1. Paris.

2. Patroclus.

ROBERT LOWELL

# Falling Asleep over *The Aeneid*

An old man in Concord forgets to go to morning service. He
falls asleep, while reading Vergil, and dreams that he is Aeneas
at the funeral of Pallas, an Italian prince.[1]

The sun is blue and scarlet on my page,
And *yuck-a, yuck-a, yuck-a, yuck-a,* rage
The yellowhammers[2] mating. Yellow fire
Blankets the captives dancing on their pyre,
And the scorched lictor[3] screams and drops his rod.          5
Trojans are singing to their drunken God,
Ares.[4] Their helmets catch on fire. Their files
Clank by the body of my comrade—miles
Of filings! Now the scythe-wheeled chariot rolls
Before their lances long as vaulting poles,          10
And I stand up and heil the thousand men,
Who carry Pallas to the bird-priest.[5] Then
The bird-priest groans, and as his birds foretold,
I greet the body, lip to lip. I hold
The sword that Dido used.[6] It tries to speak,          15
A bird with Dido's sworded breast. Its beak
Clangs and ejaculates the Punic[7] word
I hear the bird-priest chirping like a bird.
I groan a little. "Who am I, and why?"
It asks, a boy's face, though its arrow-eye          20
Is working from its socket. "Brother, try,
O Child of Aphrodite,[8] try to die:
To die is life." His harlots hang his bed
With feathers of his long-tailed birds. His head
Is yawning like a person. The plumes blow;          25
The beard and eyebrows ruffle. Face of snow,[9]
You are the flower that country girls have caught,
A wild bee-pillaged honey-suckle brought
To the returning bridegroom—the design
Has not yet left it, and the petals shine;          30
The earth, its mother, has, at last, no help:
It is itself. The broken-winded yelp
Of my Phoenician hounds, that fills the brush
With snapping twigs and flying, cannot flush
The ghost of Pallas. But I take his pall,[1]          35
Stiff with its gold and purple, and recall

1. Pallas, the son of Evander the Ar-
cadian, an ally of Aeneas. Pallas's death
is recounted in Book X, and his body is
ceremoniously sent home by Aeneas in
Book XI.
2. Golden-winged woodpeckers, a New
England bird.
3. A Roman officer who executed judgment upon offenders.
4. The god of war, also called Mars
(see line 51). At the time of Pallas's death
the forces of Aeneas seem to be faring
badly.
5. An augur, a Roman priest who foretold events by observing actions of birds.

6. Book IV of *The Aeneid* recounts
Aeneas's affair with Dido, queen of
Carthage. When Aeneas leaves her, she
builds her own funeral pyre and stabs
herself with Aeneas's sword.
7. Carthaginian.
8. Aeneas is the son of the goddess
Aphrodite (Venus) and the mortal An-
chises (see line 52).
9. Vergil describes Pallas's face as "pale
as snow" (Copley translation). Lowell's
details and phrasing in most of the reverie
are extremely close to the opening lines of
Book XI of *The Aeneid*.
1. Cover for the coffin.

How Dido hugged it to her, while she toiled,
Laughing—her golden threads, a serpent coiled
In cypress. Now I lay it like a sheet;
It clinks and settles down upon his feet,                    40
The careless yellow hair that seemed to burn
Beforehand. Left foot, right foot—as they turn,
More pyres are rising: armored horses, bronze,
And gagged Italians, who must file by ones
Across the bitter river, when my thumb                      45
Tightens into their wind-pipes. The beaks drum;
Their headman's cow-horned death's-head bites its tongue,
And stiffens, as it eyes the hero slung
Inside his feathered hammock on the crossed
Staves of the eagles that we winged. Our cost               50
Is nothing to the lovers, whoring Mars[2]
And Venus, father's lover. Now his car's
Plumage is ready, and my marshals fetch
His squire, Acoetes,[3] white with age, to hitch
Aethon, the hero's charger, and its ears                    55
Prick, and it steps and steps, and stately tears
Lather its teeth; and then the harlots bring
The hero's charms and baton—but the King,
Vain-glorious Turnus, carried off the rest.[4]
"I was myself, but Ares thought it best                      60
The way it happened." At the end of time,
He sets his spear, as my descendants climb
The knees of Father Time, his beard of scalps,
His scythe, the arc of steel that crowns the Alps.
The elephants of Carthage[5] hold those snows,              65
Turms of Numidian horse[6] unsling their bows,
The flaming turkey-feathered arrows swarm
Beyond the Alps. "Pallas," I raise my arm
And shout, "Brother, eternal health. Farewell
Forever." Church is over, and its bell                       70
Frightens the yellowhammers, as I wake
And watch the whitecaps wrinkle up the lake.
Mother's great-aunt, who died when I was eight,
Stands by our parlor saber. "Boy, it's late.
Vergil must keep the Sabbath." Eighty years!                 75
It all comes back. My Uncle Charles appears.
Blue-capped and bird-like. Phillips Brooks[7] and Grant
Are frowning at his coffin, and my aunt,
Hearing his colored volunteers parade
Through Concord, laughs, and tells her English maid          80
To clip his yellow nostril hairs, and fold
His colors on him. . . . It is I, I hold
His sword to keep from falling, for the dust
On the stuffed birds is breathless, for the bust

2. Paramour of several goddesses, including Aphrodite.
3. Who guarded Pallas's body.
4. As spoils. Turnus killed Pallas, and Aeneas will in turn kill him to conclude *The Aeneid*.
5. Proverbially strong. Hannibal used them to cross the Alps in his famous roundabout attack on Rome.
6. Troops of horsemen. Numidia was in Africa, near Carthage.
7. 19th-century Episcopal bishop and hymn-writer.

Of young Augustus[8] weighs on Vergil's shelf:                    85
It scowls into my glasses at itself.

1950

JONATHAN SWIFT

## Baucis and Philemon

*Imitated from the Eighth Book of Ovid*

In ancient times, as story tells,
The saints would often leave their cells,[1]
And stroll about, but hide their quality,
To try good people's hospitality.

It happened on a winter-night,                                   5
(As authors of the legend write)
Two brother-hermits, saints by trade,
Taking their tour in masquerade,
Disguised in tattered habits, went
To a small village down in Kent;                                 10
Where, in the strollers' canting strain,
They begged from door to door in vain;
Tried ev'ry tone might pity win,
But not a soul would let them in.

Our wand'ring saints in woeful state,                            15
Treated at this ungodly rate,
Having through all the village passed,
To a small cottage came at last;
Where dwelt a good old honest ye'man,
Called in the neighborhood, Philemon.                            20
Who kindly did the saints invite
In his poor hut to pass the night:
And then the hospitable sire
Bid Goody[2] Baucis mend the fire;
While he from out the chimney took                               25
A flitch of bacon off the hook;
And freely from the fattest side,
Cut out large slices to be fried:
Then stepped aside to fetch 'em drink,
Filled a large jug up to the brink;                              30
And saw it fairly twice go round;
Yet (what was wonderful) they found
'Twas still replenished to the top,
As if they ne'er had touched a drop.
The good old couple were amazed,                                 35
And often on each other gazed:
For both were frighted to the heart,

8. Who became emperor of Rome at age 32.
1. In Ovid's story the visitors are gods, not saints; Swift's version throughout adapts details to English and Christian frames of reference. Judeo-Christian tradition tells a similar story of hospitality to divine guests and punishment of the unrighteous; see *Genesis* 18.
2. Short for Goodwife, an old term of civility for a married woman of humble station.

And just began to cry—What *art!*
Then softly turned aside to view,
Whether the lights were burning blue[3]                    40
The gentle pilgrims soon aware on't,
Told 'em their calling, and their errant:[4]
Good folks, you need not be afraid,
We are but saints, the hermits said;
No hurt shall come to you or yours;                        45
But, for that pack of churlish boors,
Not fit to live on Christian ground.
They and their houses shall be drowned:
While you shall see your cottage rise,
And grow a church[5] before your eyes.                     50

    They scarce had spoke; when fair and soft,
The roof began to mount aloft;
Aloft rose ev'ry beam and rafter;
The heavy wall climbed slowly after.

    The chimney widened and grew higher,     55
Became a steeple with a spire.

    The kettle to the top was hoist,
And there stood fastened to a joist;
But with the up-side down, to show
Its inclination for below.                                 60
In vain; for some superior force,
Applied at bottom, stops its course;
Doomed ever in suspense to dwell;
'Tis now no kettle, but a bell.

    A wooden jack, which had almost         65
Lost, by disuse, the art to roast,
A sudden alteration feels,
Increased by new intestine wheels:
And what exalts the wonder more,
The number made the motion flower,                         70
The flyer, which, though 't had leaden feet,
Turned round so quick, you scarce could see't;
Now slackened by some secret pow'r,
Can hardly move an inch an hour.
The jack and chimney, near allied,                         75
Had never left each other's side;
The chimney to a steeple grown,
The jack would not be left alone;
But, up against the steeple reared,
Became a clock, and still adhered:                         80
And still its love to household cares,
By a shrill voice at noon declares,
Warning the cook-maid not to burn
That roast meat, which it cannot turn.

3. A sign of witchcraft.       5. In Ovid, a temple.
4. Errand.

The groaning chair was seen to crawl,                    85
Like an huge snail half up the wall;
There stuck aloft in public view;
And with small change, a pulpit grew.

The porringers,[6] that in a row
Hung high, and made a glitt'ring show,                   90
To a less noble substance changed,
Were now but leathern buckets, ranged.

The ballads pasted on the wall,
Of *Joan* of *France,* and *English Moll,*
Fair *Rosamond,* and *Robin Hood,*                       95
The *Little Children in the Wood;*[7]
Now seemed to look abundance better,
Improved in picture, size, and letter;
And high, in order placed describe
The heraldry of ev'ry tribe.                             100

A bedstead of the antique mode,
Compact of timber many a load;
Such as our grandsires wont to use,
Was metamorphosed into pews;
Which still their ancient nature keep,                   105
By lodging folks disposed to sleep.

The cottage, by such feats as these,
Grown to a church by just degrees;
The hermits then desire their host
To ask for what he fancied most.                         110
Philemon, having paused a while,
Returned them thanks in homely style;
Then said; my house is grown so fine,
Methinks I still would call it mine:
I'm old, and fain would live at ease.                    115
Make me the parson, if you please.

He spoke, and presently he feels
His grazier's coat fall down his heels:
He sees, yet hardly can believe,
About each arm a pudding sleeve:                         120
His waistcoat to a cassock grew,
And both assumed a sable hue;
But being old, continued just
As thread-bare, and as full of dust.[8]
His talk was now of tithes and dues:                     125
Could smoke his pipe, and read the news,
Knew how to preach old sermons next,
Vamped[9] in the preface, and the text;

6. Porridge-dishes or basins.
7. Folk ballads of the sort poor people in the 18th century might display on their walls. Moll, e.g., is Moll Cutpurse (Mary Frith), a famous 17th-century thief.
8. English clergymen, especially country parsons, were notoriously poorly paid in the 18th century, except for a privileged minority. Swift was Dean of St. Patrick's, Dublin. The following lines pursue other standard jokes about the clergy.
9. Patched.

At Christ'nings well could act his part,
And had the service all by heart:                    130
Wished women might have children fast,
And thought whose sow had farrowed last:
Against Dissenters would repine,
And stood up firm for Right Divine:
Found his head filled with many a system,            135
But classic authors—he ne'er missed 'em.

Thus having furbished up a parson,
Dame Baucis next they played their farce on:
Instead of home-spun coifs[1] were seen
Good pinners edged with colbertine.                  140
Her petticoat, transformed apace,
Became black satin flounced with lace.
Plain *Goody* would no longer down;
'Twas *Madam,* in her grogram[2] gown.
Philemon was in great surprise,                      145
And hardly could believe his eyes:
Amazed to see her look so prim:
And she admired as much at him.

Thus happy in their change of life,
Were several years the man and wife:                 150
When on a day, which proved their last,
Discoursing o'er old stories past;
They went by chance, amidst their talk,
To the churchyard, to fetch a walk:
When Baucis hastily cried out,                       155
My dear, I see your forehead sprout!
Sprout, quoth the man, what's this you tell us?
I hope you don't believe me jealous:[3]
But yet, methinks, I feel it true;
And really yours is budding too—                     160
Nay—now I cannot stir my foot;
It feels as if 'twere taking root.

Description would but tire my muse:
In short, they both were turned to yews.

Old Goodman Dobson, of the green,                    165
Remembers he the trees hath seen;
He'll talk of them from noon to night,
And goes with folks to show the sight;
On Sundays, after evening prayer,
He gathers all the parish there;                     170
Points out the place of either yew:
Here Baucis, there Philemon grew;
'Till once, a parson of our town,
To mend his barn, cut Baucis down;

1. Close-fitting caps, which were re-
placed by caps with two long flaps ("pinners," line 140), worn in the 18th century
by women of rank. "colbertine": open lace.

2. Silk or a silk mixture.
3. Cuckolds, according to tradition,
sprouted horns on their foreheads.

At which, 'tis hard to be believed,                     175
How much the other tree was grieved:
Grew scrubby, died a-top, was stunted:
So, the next parson stubbed and burnt it.

1709

MATTHEW ARNOLD

# Philomela[1]

Hark! ah, the nightingale—
The tawny-throated!
Hark, from that moonlit cedar what a burst!
What triumph! hark!—what pain!

O wanderer from a Grecian shore,                         5
Still, after many years, in distant lands,
Still nourishing in thy bewildered brain
That wild, unquenched, deep-sunken, old-world pain—
Say, will it never heal?
And can this fragrant lawn                               10
With its cool trees, and night,
And the sweet, tranquil Thames,
And moonshine, and the dew,
To thy racked heart and brain
Afford no balm?                                          15

Dost thou tonight behold,
Here, through the moonlight on this English grass,
The unfriendly palace in the Thracian wild?
Dost thou again peruse
With hot cheeks and seared eyes                          20
The too clear web,[2] and thy dumb sister's shame?
Dost thou once more assay
Thy flight, and feel come over thee,
Poor fugitive, the feathery change
Once more, and once more seem to make resound            25
With love and hate, triumph and agony,
Lone Daulis, and the high Cephissian vale?[3]
Listen, Eugenia[4]—
How thick the bursts come crowding through the leaves!
Again—thou hearest?                                      30
Eternal passion!
Eternal pain!

1848

1. According to Greek legend, Philomela turned into a nightingale at Daulis (line 27) after a bizarre series of events and revenges. Philomela's husband, King Tereus of Thrace, raped her sister, Procne, and cut out her tongue (see line 21) to prevent disclosure. But Procne wove a tapestry revealing the story and then killed Tereus' son in revenge and fed him the flesh. The gods turned Philomela into a nightingale and Procne into a swallow so that they could escape Tereus' wrath. In some versions, the roles of the sisters are reversed; see, e.g., Swinburne's "When the Hounds of Spring."
2. The tapestry.
3. The home of Tereus.
4. An imaginary listener.

T. S. ELIOT

# Sweeney Among the Nightingales

ὤμοι, πέπληγμαι καιρίαν πληγὴν ἔσω.[1]

Apeneck Sweeney[2] spreads his knees
Letting his arms hang down to laugh,
The zebra stripes along his jaw
Swelling to maculate[3] giraffe.

The circles of the stormy moon                                    5
Slide westward toward the River Plate,[4]
Death and the Raven[5] drift above
And Sweeney guards the hornéd gate.[6]

Gloomy Orion and the Dog[7]
Are veiled; and hushed the shrunken seas;              10
The person in the Spanish cape
Tries to sit on Sweeney's knees

Slips and pulls the table cloth
Overturns a coffee-cup,
Reorganized upon the floor                                       15
She yawns and draws a stocking up;

The silent man in mocha brown
Sprawls at the window-sill and gapes;
The waiter brings in oranges
Bananas figs and hothouse grapes;                           20

The silent vertebrate in brown
Contracts and concentrates, withdraws;
Rachel *née* Rabinovitch
Tears at the grapes with murderous paws;

She and the lady in the cape                                       25
Are suspect, thought to be in league;
Therefore the man with heavy eyes
Declines the gambit, shows fatigue,

Leaves the room and reappears
Outside the window, leaning in,                                  30
Branches of wistaria
Circumscribe a golden grin;

1. The cry of Agamemnon as he is stabbed by his wife Clytemnestra inside the palace: "Oh, I have been struck a mortal blow—within," Aeschylus, *Agamemnon*, line 1343. Agamemnon, the king of Mycenae in Greek legend, had just returned from the Trojan War, where he had been a leader and hero.
2. Eliot's respresentation, in several different poems, of modern vulgarity.
3. Spotted.

4. The Rio de la Plata, an estuary between Uruguay and Argentina.
5. The constellation Corvus of the Southern Hemisphere.
6. The gate, according to Greek legend, through which true dreams come; false dreams come through the gates of ivory.
7. Sirius, the dog-star, and the constellation Orion, named (because of its appearance) for the giant hunter of Greek myth.

The host with someone indistinct
Converses at the door apart,
The nightingales are singing near                    35
The Convent of the Sacred Heart,

And sang within the bloody wood
When Agamemnon cried aloud,
And let their liquid siftings fall
To stain the stiff dishonored shroud.                40

                                                     1920

BARNABY BARNES

## Jove for Europa's Love Took Shape of Bull[1]

Jove for Europa's love took shape of bull,
And for Calisto played Diana's part,
And in a golden shower he filled full
The lap of Danae, with celestial art.[2]
Would I were changed but to my mistress' gloves,     5
That those white lovely fingers I might hide;
That I might kiss those hands which mine heart loves!
Or else that chain of pearl (her neck's vain pride)
Made proud with her neck's veins, that I might fold
About that lovely neck, and her paps tickle!         10
Or her to compass, like a belt of gold!
Or that sweet wine, which down her throat doth trickle,
To kiss her lips and lie next at her heart,
Run through her veins, and pass by pleasure's part!

                                                     1593

THOMAS LODGE

## I Would in Rich and Golden-Colored Rain

I would in rich and golden-colored rain[1]
With tempting showers in pleasant sort descend
Into fair Phillis' lap, my lovely friend,
When sleep her sense with slumber doth restrain.
I would be changéd to a milk-white bull,             5
When midst the gladsome fields she should appear,
By pleasant fineness to surprise my dear
Whilst from their stalks she pleasant flowers did pull.
I were content to weary out my pain
To be Narcissus,[2] so she were a spring,            10
To drown in her those woes my heart do wring.

1. This poem has often been attacked for
its attempt to use too many mythological
references too fast and for its gross application of the shape-shifting idea.
2. In his various seductions Jove (Jupiter, Zeus) assumed various forms: to seduce Europa he became a white bull and
carried her off. Calisto he seduced in his
own form, but she was later turned into a
she-bear and ultimately into a constellation
(Diana was goddess of the hunt). Danae

was locked up in a tower to prevent her
from marrying, but Jove transformed himself into a shower of gold to gain access
to her.
1. See Note 2 to "Jove for Europa's
Love," above.
2. A beautiful youth who admired his
own reflection in a fountain, mistook it for
the presiding nymph of the place, and
leaped into the water.

And more I wish transforméd to remain,
That whilst I thus in pleasure's lap did lie,
I might refresh desire, which else would die.

1593

ROBERT GRAVES

## Apollo[1] of the Physiologists

Despite this learned cult's official
And seemingly sincere denial
That they either reject or postulate
God, or God's scientific surrogate,
Prints of a deity occur *passim*                                5
Throughout their extant literature: they make him
A dumb, dead-pan Apollo with a profile
Drawn in Victorian-Hellenistic style—
The pallid, bald, partitioned head suggesting
Wholly abstract cerebral functioning,                           10
Or nude and at full length, this deity
Displays digestive, venous, respiratory
And nervous systems painted in bold color
On his immaculate exterior.
Sometimes, *in verso*,[2] a bald, naked Muse,                   15
His consort, flaunts her arteries and sinews,
While, upside-down, crouched in her chaste abdomen,
Adored by men and wondered at by women,
Hangs a Victorian-Hellenistic foetus—
Fruit of her academic god's afflatus.                           20

1945

e. e. cummings

## chanson innocente

in Just-
spring      when the world is mud-
luscious the little
lame balloonman

whistles      far      and wee                                  5

and eddieandbill come
running from marbles and
piracies and it's
spring

when the world is puddle-wonderful                              10

the queer
old balloonman whistles

---

1. In Greek and Roman mythology, god
of music, poetry, and the healing arts. He
is represented as the perfection of youthful
manhood.
2. On the left-hand page.

far      and      wee
and bettyandisbel come dancing

from hop-scotch and jump-rope and                     15

it's
spring
and
     the

          goat-footed                                 20

balloonMan         whistles
far
and
wee[3]

                                              1923

ISHMAEL REED

# I Am a Cowboy in the Boat of Ra

"The devil must be forced to reveal any such physical evil (potions, charms, fetishes, etc.) still outside the body and these must be burned."—RITUALE ROMANUM, *published 1947, endorsed by the coat of arms and introduction letter from Francis Cardinal Spellman*

I am a cowboy in the boat of Ra,[1]
sidewinders in the saloons of fools
bit my forehead    like        O
the untrustworthiness of Egyptologists
Who do not know their trips. Who was that                    5
dog-faced man? they asked, the day I rode
from town.

School marms with halitosis cannot see
the Nefertiti[2] fake chipped on the run by slick
germans, the hawk behind Sonny Rollins' head or               10
the ritual beard of his axe,[3] a longhorn winding
its bells thru the Field of Reeds.

I am a cowboy in the boat of Ra. I bedded
down with Isis,[4] Lady of the Boogaloo, dove
down deep in her horny, stuck up her Wells-Far-ago            15

3. Pan, whose Greek name means "everything," is traditionally represented with a syrinx (or the pipes of Pan). The upper half of his body is human, the lower half goat, and as the father of Silenus he is associated with the spring rites of Dionysus.
1. The chief of the ancient Egyptian gods, the creator and protector of men and the vanquisher of evil. He was one of the many forms of the sun-god, and all the pharaohs are supposed to descend from him. Throughout, the poem draws heavily upon Egyptian mythology as well as upon American cowboy lore.

2. 14th-century B.C. Egyptian queen. The most famous bust of her (of painted limestone) was discovered and taken to Berlin in 1933. Elsewhere, Reed says that German scholars are responsible for the notion that her dynasty was white.
3. Musical instrument. Sonny Rollins was considered one of the most innovative young jazz musicians of the late 1950s and early 1960s, a modernizer of the tenor sax tradition established by Coleman Hawkins.
4. The principal goddess of ancient Egypt; cows were sacred to her.

in daring midday get away. "Start grabbing the
blue," i said from top of my double crown.

I am a cowboy in the boat of Ra. Ezzard Charles[5]
of the Chisholm Trail. Took up the bass but they
blew off my thumb. Alchemist in ringmanship but a                    20
sucker for the right cross.

I am a cowboy in the boat of Ra. Vamoosed from
the temple i bide my time. The price on the wanted
poster was a-going down, outlaw alias copped my stance
and moody greenhorns were making me dance; while my mouth's    25
shooting iron got its chambers jammed.

I am a cowboy in the boat of Ra. Boning-up in
the ol West i bide my time. You should see
me pick off these tin cans whippersnappers. I
write the motown long plays for the comeback of            30
Osiris.[6] Make them up when stars stare at sleeping
steer out here near the campfire. Women arrive
on the backs of goats and throw themselves on
my Bowie.[7]

I am a cowboy in the boat of Ra. Lord of the lash,    35
the Loup Garou[8] Kid. Half breed son of Pisces and
Aquarius. I hold the souls of men in my pot. I do
the dirty boogie with scorpions. I make the bulls
keep still and was the first swinger to grape the taste.

I am a cowboy in his boat. Pope Joan[9] of the          40
Ptah Ra.[1] C/mere a minute willya doll?
Be a good girl and
Bring me my Buffalo horn of black powder
Bring me my headdress of black feathers
Bring me my bones of Ju-Ju snake                          45
Go get my eyelids of red paint.
Hand me my shadow
I'm going into town after Set[2]

I am a cowboy in the boat of Ra
look out Set      here i come Set                          50
to get Set        to sunset Set

5. World heavyweight boxing champion, 1949–51.

6. Husband of Isis and one of the major gods of Egyptian mythology. He is the constant foe of his brother Set (line 48), a pervasive fertility symbol, and he often represents the setting sun. He was also, according to legend, the mortal king who changed Egypt from a primitive society to a civilized one, teaching his people to grow corn and make wine from the grape. He died violently, tricked by Set, but later rose from the dead.

7. Heavy-sheathed hunting knife, more than a foot long, named after James Bowie, who died at the Alamo.

8. The leader of the giants in Rabelais' *Gargantua and Pantagruel*, and a character in Reed's novel, *Yellow Back Radio Broke-down*. "Loup-garou" in French means werewolf, and in voodoo it refers to a priest who has run amuck or gone mad.

9. A mythical female pope, supposed to have succeeded Leo IV to the papacy in 855.

1. The chief god of Memphis, the capital of ancient Egypt.

2. Brother of Osiris, usually portrayed as the principle of evil itself, but sometimes as the protector of the sun-god's boat. As ugly as his brother is beautiful, he is associated with the opposite of Osiris' qualities and dominions; he is, e.g., connected with deserts, as Osiris is with fertile land.

to unseat Set      to Set down Set
                   usurper of the Royal couch
                   imposter RAdio of Moses' bush[3]
                   party pooper O hater of dance          55
                   vampire outlaw of the milky way

                                                          1969

DAVID DIOP

# Africa[1]

Africa my Africa
Africa of proud warriors in ancestral savannahs[2]
Africa of whom my grandmother sings
On the banks of the distant river
I have never known you                                   5
But your blood flows in my veins[3]
Your beautiful black blood that irrigates the fields
The blood of your sweat
The sweat of your work
The work of your slavery                                 10
The slavery of your children
Africa tell me Africa
Is this you this back that is bent
This back that breaks under the weight of humiliation
This back trembling with red scars                       15
And saying yes to the whip under the midday sun
But a grave voice answers me
Impetuous son that tree young and strong
That tree there
In splendid loneliness amidst white and faded flowers    20
That is Africa your Africa
That grows again patiently obstinately
And its fruit gradually acquire
The bitter taste of liberty.

                                                          1956

LANGSTON HUGHES

# The Negro Speaks of Rivers

I've known rivers:
I've known rivers ancient as the world and older than the flow of human
     blood in human veins.

My soul has grown deep like the rivers.

I bathed in the Euphrates when dawns were young.
I built my hut near the Congo and it lulled me to sleep.          5

3. Which, according to *Exodus* 3:2, burned but was not consumed and from which Moses heard the voice of God telling him to lead the Israelites out of Egypt.
1. Translated from the French by Gerard Moore and Ulli Beier.

2. Flat, treeless grasslands.
3. Diop was born in France of a Senegalese father and a Cameroonian mother; during his childhood he traveled back and forth to West Africa.

I looked upon the Nile and raised the pyramids above it.
I heard the singing of the Mississippi when Abe Lincoln went down
  to New Orleans, and I've seen its muddy bosom turn all golden in
  the sunset.

I've known rivers:
Ancient, dusky rivers.

My soul has grown deep like the rivers.                                  10

1926

MARGARET DANNER

## The Dance of the Abakweta[1]

Imagine what Mrs. Haessler would say
if she could see the African youth dance
their well-versed initiation. At first glance
as they bend to an invisible barre[2]
you would know that she had designed their costumes.          5

For though they were made of pale beige bamboo straw
their lines were the classic tutu.[3] Nothing varied.
Each was cut short to the thigh and carried
high to a degree of right angles. Nor was there a flaw
in their leotards. Made of leopard skin or the hide          10

of a goat, or the Gauguin-colored Okapi's striped coat
they were cut in her reverenced "tradition."
She would have approved their costumes and positions.
And since neither Iceland nor Africa is too remote
for her vision she would have wanted to form               15

a "traditional" ballet. Swan Lake, Scheherazade or
(after seeing their incredible leaps)
Les Orientales. Imagine the exotic sweep
of such a ballet, and from the way the music pours
over these dancers (this tinkling of bells, talking          20

of drums, and twanging of tan, sandalwood harps)
from this incomparable music, Mrs. Haessler of Vassar can
glimpse strains of Tchaikovsky, Chopin
to accompany her undeviatingly sharp
"traditional" ballet. I am certain that if she could         25
tutor these potential protegés, as
quick as Aladdin rubbing his lamp, she would.

1968

1. An initiation dance of the Bantus in which young men entering adulthood dance from village to village for three months.
2. A wooden bar fastened to the walls of a dance studio, used by dancers for support in classroom exercises.
3. Short ballet skirt of gathered sheer fabric.

JOHN PEALE BISHOP

## Speaking of Poetry

The ceremony must be found
that will wed Desdemona to the huge Moor.[1]

It is not enough—
to win the approval of the Senator
or to outwit his disapproval; honest Iago[2]                              5
can manage that: it is not enough. For then,
though she may pant again in his black arms
(his weight resilient as a Barbary stallion's)
she will be found
when the ambassadors of the Venetian state arrive          10
again smothered. These things have not been changed,
not in three hundred years.

(Tupping is still tupping
though that particular word is obsolete.[3]
Naturally, the ritual would not be in Latin.)                      15

For though Othello had his blood from kings
his ancestry was barbarous, his ways African,
his speech uncouth. It must be remembered
that though he valued an embroidery—
three mulberries proper on a silk like silver—                  20
it was not for the subtlety of the stitches,
but for the magic in it. Whereas, Desdemona
once contrived to imitate in needlework
her father's shield, and plucked it out
three times, to begin again, each time                              25
with diminished colors. This is a small point
but indicative.

Desdemona was small and fair,
delicate as a grasshopper
at the tag-end of summer: a Venetian                               30
to her noble finger tips.

O, it is not enough
that they should meet, naked, at dead of night
in a small inn on a dark canal. Procurers
less expert than Iago can arrange as much.                       35

The ceremony must be found

Traditional, with all its symbols
ancient as the metaphors in dreams;

---

1. Othello. In Shakespeare's play Desdemona is, of course, married to Othello, but
the ceremony was performed secretly and
her father and the other Venetian senators
are outraged nearly to the point of killing
Othello. As a military leader, he is their
hero, but he is not their idea of an appropriate husband for a Venetian aristocrat.
2. Othello often addresses the play's villain as "Honest Iago."
3. When he announces the elopement to
Desdemona's father, Iago says that "an old
black ram is tupping your white ewe" (Act
I, sc. i, 88–89).

strange, with never before heard music; continuous
until the torches deaden at the bedroom door.                    40
1925

KENNETH HANSON

## The Distance Anywhere

My neighbor, a lady from Fu-kien[1]
has rearranged her yard completely.
She has cut down the willow tree,
burning it, piecemeal, against a city
ordinance, and has put in its place                    5
her garden of strange herbs.

I confess I resent the diligence
her side of the fence—the stink
of that oriental spinach she hangs
on the clothesline to dry, and the squawk                    10
of the chicken I suspect she keeps,
against a city ordinance, shut up
in the white garage, eventual soup.

But when, across the rows of what-
ever she grows, she brings her                    15
fabulous speech to bear, birds
in the trees, the very butterflies
unbend, acknowledging, to syllables
of that exacter scale, she'd make
the neighborhood, the unaccustomed                    20
air, for all the world to see,
sight, sound and smell, Fu-kien,
beyond our ordinances, clear.

1954

KENNETH PATCHEN

## Gautama in the Deer Park at Benares[2]

In a hut of mud and fire
Sits this single man—"Not to want
Money, to want a life in the world,
To want no trinkets on my name"—
And he was rich; his life lives where                    5
Death cannot go; his honor stares
At the sun.

The fawn sleeps. The little winds
Ruffle the earth's green hair. It is
Wonderful to live. My sword rusts                    10
In the pleasant rain. I shall not think

1. Province in southeastern China.
2. Where Gautama first preached after
he reached the state of perfect illumination
(nirvana) and thereby became a Buddha
("the enlightened").

Anymore. I touch the face of my friend;
He shows his dirty teeth as he scratches
At a flea—and we grin. It is warm
And the rice stirs usefully in our bellies.                    15

The fawn raises its head—the sun floods
Its soft eye with the kingdoms of life—
I think we should all go to sleep now,
And not care anymore.

1943

RALPH WALDO EMERSON

## Brahma[1]

If the red slayer[2] think he slays,
    Or if the slain think he is slain,
They know not well the subtle ways
    I keep, and pass, and turn again.

Far or forgot to me is near;                                    5
    Shadow and sunlight are the same;
The vanished gods to me appear;
    And one to me are shame and fame.

They reckon ill who leave me out;
    When me they fly, I am the wings;                           10
I am the doubter and the doubt,
    And I the hymn the Brahmin sings.

The strong gods[3] pine for my abode,
    And pine in vain the sacred Seven;[4]
But thou, meek lover of the good!                               15
    Find me, and turn thy back on heaven.

1856

JAMES WRIGHT

## As I Step Over a Puddle at the End of Winter, I Think of an Ancient Chinese Governor

And how can I, born in evil days
and fresh from failure, ask a kindness
of Fate?        —Written A.D. 819

Po Chu-i, balding old politician,
  What's the use?
I think of you,
Uneasily entering the gorges of the Yang-Tze,
When you were being towed up the rapids               5

1. Both the supreme god of the Hindus and the absolute, unchanging, and impersonal reality which contrasts with the changing and illusory world of experience.
2. Siva the destroyer, with Brahma and Vishnu one of the persons of the Hindu Trimurti (trinity). He represents the destructive principle in life, but also the restorative principle.
3. Devas, similar to angels.
4. The highest Hindu saints.

Toward some political job or other
In the city of Chungshou.
You made it, I guess,
By dark.

But it is 1960, it is almost spring again,                    10
And the tall rocks of Minneapolis
Build me my own black twilight
Of bamboo ropes and waters.
Where is Yuan Chen, the friend you loved?
Where is the sea, that once solved the whole loneliness        15
Of the Midwest? Where is Minneapolis? I can see nothing
But the great terrible oak tree darkening with winter.
Did you find the city of isolated men beyond mountains?
Or have you been holding the end of a frayed rope
For a thousand years?                                          20

1963

TU FU

## Night in the House by the River[1]

It is late in the year;
Yin and Yang[2] struggle
In the brief sunlight.
On the desert mountains
Frost and snow                                                 5
Gleam in the freezing night.
Past midnight,
Drums and bugles ring out,
Violent, cutting the heart.
Over the Triple Gorge the Milky Way                            10
Pulsates between the stars.
The bitter cries of thousands of households
Can be heard above the noise of battle.
Everywhere the workers sing wild songs.
The great heroes and generals of old time                      15
Are yellow dust forever now.
Such are the affairs of men.
Poetry and letters
Persist in silence and solitude.

ca. 750

W. B. YEATS

## Easter 1916[1]

I have met them at close of day
Coming with vivid faces

1. Translated from the Chinese by Kenneth Rexroth.
2. The passive and active cosmic principles, always complementary, in Chinese dualistic philosophy.
1. The famous Easter uprising began on Easter Monday when an Irish republic was proclaimed by nationalist leaders, but English military forces responded quickly; by April 29, some 300 people were dead and the Nationalists surrendered. Early in May, 15 leaders (including the four mentioned in lines 75–76) were executed, and more than 2,000 were held prisoners.

From counter or desk among grey
Eighteenth-century houses.
I have passed with a nod of the head                    5
Or polite meaningless words,
Or have lingered awhile and said
Polite meaningless words,
And thought before I had done
Of a mocking tale or a gibe                              10
To please a companion
Around the fire at the club,
Being certain that they and I
But lived where motley[2] is worn:
All changed, changed utterly:                            15
A terrible beauty is born.

That woman's[3] days were spent
In ignorant good-will,
Her nights in argument
Until her voice grew shrill.                              20
What voice more sweet than hers
When, young and beautiful,
She rode to harriers?[4]
This man[5] had kept a school
And rode our wingéd horse;[6]                            25
This other[7] his helper and friend
Was coming into his force;
He might have won fame in the end,
So sensitive his nature seemed,
So daring and sweet his thought.                         30
This other man[8] I had dreamed
A drunken, vainglorious lout.
He had done most bitter wrong
To some who are near my heart,
Yet I number him in the song;                            35
He, too, has resigned his part
In the casual comedy;
He, too, has been changed in his turn,
Transformed utterly:
A terrible beauty is born.                               40

Hearts with one purpose alone
Through summer and winter seem
Enchanted to a stone
To trouble the living stream.
The horse that comes from the road,                      45

2. The particolored clothing of a professional fool or jester, at court or in a play.
3. Countess Constance Georgina Markiewicz, a beautiful and well-born young woman from County Sligo who became a vigorous and bitter nationalist. At first condemned to death, she later had her sentence commuted to life imprisonment, and she gained amnesty in 1917.
4. Hounds.
5. Patrick Pearse, who led the assault on the Dublin Post Office from which the proclamation of a republic was issued. A schoolmaster by profession, he had vigorously supported the restoration of the Gaelic language in Ireland and was an active political writer and poet.
6. Pegasus, the traditional symbol of poetic inspiration.
7. Thomas MacDonagh, also a writer and teacher.
8. Major John MacBride, who had married Yeats's beloved Maud Gonne in 1903 but separated from her two years later.

The rider, the birds that range
From cloud to tumbling cloud,
Minute by minute they change;
A shadow of cloud on the stream
Changes minute by minute;                                    50
A horse-hoof slides on the brim,
And a horse plashes within it;
The long-legged moor-hens dive,
And hens to moor-cocks call;
Minute by minute they live:                                  55
The stone's in the midst of all.

Too long a sacrifice
Can make a stone of the heart.
O when may it suffice?
That is Heaven's part, our part                              60
To murmur name upon name,
As a mother names her child
When sleep at last has come
On limbs that had run wild.
What is it but nightfall?                                    65
No, no, not night but death;
Was it needless death after all?
For England may keep faith[9]
For all that is done and said.
We know their dream; enough
To know they dreamed and are dead;                           70
And what if excess of love
Bewildered them till they died?
I write it out in a verse—
MacDonagh and MacBride                                       75
And Connolly[10] and Pearse
Now and in time to be,
Wherever green is worn,
Are changed, changed utterly:
A terrible beauty is born.                                   80

1916

W. B. YEATS

## The Second Coming[1]

Turning and turning in the widening gyre[2]
The falcon cannot hear the falconer;
Things fall apart; the center cannot hold;
Mere anarchy is loosed upon the world,
The blood-dimmed tide is loosed, and everywhere        5

9. Before the uprising the English had promised eventual home rule to Ireland.
10. James Connolly, the leader of the Easter uprising.
1. The Second Coming of Christ, according to *Matthew* 24:29–44, will come after a time of "tribulation." Disillusioned by Ireland's continued civil strife, Yeats saw his time as the end of another historical cycle. In *A Vision* (1937) Yeats describes his view of history as dependent on cycles of about 2000 years: the birth of Christ had ended the cycle of Greco-Roman civilization, and now the Christian cycle seemed near an end, to be followed by an antithetical cycle, ominous in its portents.
2. Literally, the widening spiral of a falcon's flight. "Gyre" is Yeats's term for a cycle of history, which he diagramed in terms of a series of interpenetrating cones.

The ceremony of innocence is drowned;
The best lack all conviction, while the worst
Are full of passionate intensity.

Surely some revelation is at hand;
Surely the Second Coming is at hand.                                    10
The Second Coming! Hardly are those words out
When a vast image out of *Spiritus Mundi*[3]
Troubles my sight: somewhere in sands of the desert
A shape with lion body and the head of a man,
A gaze blank and pitiless as the sun,                                   15
Is moving its slow thighs, while all about it
Reel shadows of the indignant desert birds.[4]
The darkness drops again; but now I know
That twenty centuries of stony sleep
Were vexed to nightmare by a rocking cradle,                            20
And what rough beast, its hour come round at last,
Slouches towards Bethlehem to be born?

p. 1920

W. B. YEATS

# Leda and the Swan[1]

A sudden blow: the great wings beating still
Above the staggering girl, her thighs caressed
By the dark webs, her nape caught in his bill,
He holds her helpless breast upon his breast.

How can those terrified vague fingers push                              5
The feathered glory from her loosening thighs?
And how can body, laid in that white rush,
But feel the strange heart beating where it lies?

A shudder in the loins engenders there
The broken wall, the burning roof and tower                             10
And Agamemnon dead.
                        Being so caught up,
So mastered by the brute blood of the air,
Did she put on his knowledge with his power
Before the indifferent beak could let her drop?

1923

3. Or *Anima Mundi*, the spirit or soul of the world, a consciousness in which the individual participates. Yeats considered this universal consciousness or memory a fund from which poets drew their images and symbols. In *Per Amica Silentia Lunae* he wrote: "Before the mind's eye, whether in sleep or waking, came images that one was to discover presently in some book one had never read, and after looking in vain for explanation . . . , I came to believe in a great memory passing on from generation to generation."
4. Yeats later writes of the "brazen winged beast . . . described in my poem *The Second Coming*" as "associated with laughing, ecstatic destruction." "Our civili-

zation was about to reverse itself, or some new civilization about to be born from all that our age had rejected . . . ; because we had worshipped a single god it would worship many."
1. According to Greek myth, Zeus took the form of a swan to seduce Leda, who became the mother of Helen of Troy and also of Clytemnestra, Agamemnon's wife and murderer. Helen's abduction from her husband, Menelaus, brother of Agamemnon, began the Trojan War (line 10). Yeats described the visit of Zeus to Leda as an annunciation like that to Mary (see *Luke* 1:26–38): "I imagine the annunciation that founded Greece as made to Leda. . . ." (*A Vision*).

W. B. YEATS

# Sailing to Byzantium[1]

### I

That[2] is no country for old men. The young
In one another's arms, birds in the trees
—Those dying generations—at their song,
The salmon-falls, the mackerel-crowded seas
Fish, flesh, or fowl, commend all summer long 5
Whatever is begotten, born, and dies.
Caught in that sensual music all neglect
Monuments of unaging intellect.

### II

An aged man is but a paltry thing,
A tattered coat upon a stick, unless 10
Soul clap its hands and sing, and louder sing
For every tatter in its mortal dress,
Nor is there singing school but studying
Monuments of its own magnificence;
And therefore I have sailed the seas and come 15
To the holy city of Byzantium.

### III

O sages standing in God's holy fire
As in the gold mosaic of a wall,
Come from the holy fire, perne in a gyre,[3]
And be the singing-masters of my soul. 20
Consume my heart away; sick with desire
And fastened to a dying animal
It knows not what it is; and gather me
Into the artifice of eternity.

### IV

Once out of nature I shall never take 25
My bodily form from any natural thing,

1. The ancient name of Istanbul, the capital and holy city of Eastern Christendom from the late fourth century until 1453. It was famous for its stylized and formal mosaics, its symbolic, nonnaturalistic art, and its highly developed intellectual life. Yeats repeatedly uses it to symbolize a world of artifice and timelessness, free from the decay and death of the natural and sensual world. In *A Vision*, Yeats wrote: "I think if I could be given a month of Antiquity and leave to spend it where I chose, I would spend it in Byzantium a little before Justinian opened St. Sophia and closed the Academy of Plato [about 535 A.D.]. I think I could find in some little wineshop some philosophical worker in mosaic who could answer all my questions, the supernatural descending nearer to him than to Plotinus even, for the pride of his delicate skill would make what was an instrument of power to princes and clerics, a murderous madness in the mob, show as a lovely flexible presence like that of a perfect human body. I think that in early Byzantium, maybe never before or since in recorded history, religious, aesthetic and practical life were one, that architect and artificers . . . spoke to the multitude and the few alike. The painter, the mosaic worker, the worker in gold and silver, the illuminator of sacred books, were almost impersonal, almost perhaps without the consciousness of individual design, absorbed in their subject-matter and that the vision of the whole people. They could . . . weave all into a vast design, the work of many that seemed the work of one, that made building, picture, metal-work or rail and lamp, seem but a single image. . . ."

2. Ireland, as an instance of the natural, temporal world.

3. I.e., whirl in a coiling motion, so that his soul may merge with its motion as the timeless world invades the cycles of history and nature. The gyre in "The Second Coming" moves in the opposite direction, up and out centripetally, so that "things fall apart." "Perne" is Yeats's coinage (from the noun "pirn"): to spin around in the kind of spiral pattern that thread makes as it comes off a bobbin or spool.

But such a form as Grecian goldsmiths make
Of hammered gold and gold enameling
To keep a drowsy Emperor awake;[4]
Or set upon a golden bough[5] to sing                    30
To lords and ladies of Byzantium
Of what is past, or passing, or to come.

                                                            1927

W. B. YEATS

# Two Songs from a Play[1]

### I

I saw a staring virgin stand
Where holy Dionysus[2] died,
And tear the heart out of his side,
And lay the heart upon her hand
And bear that beating heart away;                        5
And then did all the Muses sing
Of Magnus Annus[3] at the spring,
As though God's death were but a play.

Another Troy must rise and set,
Another lineage feed the crow,                          10
Another Argo's[4] painted prow
Drive to a flashier bauble yet.
The Roman Empire stood appalled:
It dropped the reigns of peace and war
When that fierce virgin and her Star                    15
Out of the fabulous darkness called.

### II

In pity for man's darkening thought
He walked that room[5] and issued thence
In Galilean turbulence;
The Babylonian starlight brought                        20
A fabulous, formless darkness in;
Odor of blood when Christ was slain
Made all Platonic tolerance vain
And vain all Doric discipline.

---

4. "I have read somewhere that in the Emperor's palace at Byzantium was a tree made of gold and silver, and artificial birds that sang." (Yeats's note)
5. In Book VI of *The Aeneid*, the sybil tells Aeneas that he must pluck a golden bough from a nearby tree in order to descend to Hades. There is only one such branch there, and when it is plucked an identical one takes its place.
1. "These songs are sung by the Chorus in a play [Yeats's *The Resurrection*] that has for its theme Christ's first appearance to the Apostles after the Resurrection, a play intended for performance in a drawing-room or studio." (Yeats's note) The first song opens the play, the second ends it.
2. Who, according to Greek tradition,
rose each year in the spring. The "staring virgin" is Athene (Minerva), the classical goddess of wisdom, parallel to "that fierce virgin" (Mary) in line 15. In the play, his followers pass in the street outside, celebrating his rebirth, while in the room are taking place events in the Christian cycle which is to destroy the Greco-Roman one.
3. The Great Year, a complete turning of the Great Wheel, a period of 26,000 years which encompasses 12 cycles in Yeats's system.
4. Argo was Jason's ship in which he sailed in search of the Golden Fleece.
5. Which is the play's setting. Near the end, Christ appears in the room, and his body is touched by a Greek who had earlier been skeptical of his risen reality.

Everything that man esteems                                    25
Endures a moment or a day.
Love's pleasure drives his love away,
The painter's brush consumes his dreams;
The herald's cry, the soldier's tread
Exhaust his glory and his might:                               30
Whatever flames upon the night
Man's own resinous heart has fed.

1927

W. B. YEATS

# Among School Children

I

I walk through the long schoolroom questioning;
A kind old nun in a white hood replies;
The children learn to cipher and to sing,
To study reading-books and history,
To cut and sew, be neat in everything                          5
In the best modern way—the children's eyes
In momentary wonder stare upon
A sixty-year-old smiling public man.[1]

II

I dream of a Ledaean body,[2] bent
Above a sinking fire, a tale that she                          10
Told of a harsh reproof, or trivial event
That changed some childish day to tragedy—
Told, and it seemed that our two natures blent
Into a sphere from youthful sympathy,
Or else, to alter Plato's parable,                             15
Into the yolk and white of the one shell.[3]

III

And thinking of that fit of grief or rage
I look upon one child or t'other there
And wonder if she stood so at that age—
For even daughters of the swan can share                       20
Something of every paddler's heritage—
And had that color upon cheek or hair,
And thereupon my heart is driven wild:
She stands before me as a living child.

1. At 60 (in 1925) Yeats had been a senator of the Irish Free State.
2. Like that of Helen of Troy, daughter of Leda. The memory dream is of Maud Gonne (see also lines 29–30), with whom Yeats had long been hopelessly in love.
3. In Plato's *Symposium*, the origin of human love is explained by parable: Human beings were once spheres, but Zeus was fearful of their power and cut them in half; now each half longs to be re-united with its missing half. Helen and Pollux were hatched from one of two eggs born to Leda after her union with Zeus in the form of a swan; the other contained Castor and Clytemnestra. According to Yeats in *A Vision*, "from one of [Leda's] eggs came Love and from the other War."

IV

Her present image floats into the mind—                                                25
Did Quattrocento finger[4] fashion it
Hollow of cheek as though it drank the wind
And took a mess of shadows for its meat?
And I though never of Ledaean kind
Had pretty plumage once—enough of that,                                        30
Better to smile on all that smile, and show
There is a comfortable kind of old scarecrow.

V

What youthful mother, a shape upon her lap
Honey of generation[5] had betrayed,
And that must sleep, shriek, struggle to escape                                35
As recollection or the drug decide,
Would think her son, did she but see that shape
With sixty or more winters on its head,
A compensation for the pang of his birth,
Or the uncertainty of his setting forth?                                              40

VI

Plato thought nature but a spume that plays
Upon a ghostly paradigm of things;[6]
Solider Aristotle played the taws
Upon the bottom of a king of kings;[7]
World-famous golden-thighed Pythagoras[8]                                45
Fingered upon a fiddle-stick or strings
What a star sang and careless Muses heard:
Old clothes upon old sticks to scare a bird.

VII

Both nuns and mothers worship images,
But those the candles light are not as those                                       50
That animate a mother's reveries,
But keep a marble or a bronze repose.
And yet they too break hearts—O Presences
That passion, piety or affection knows,
And that all heavenly glory symbolize—                                             55
O self-born mockers of man's enterprise;

4. Fifteenth-century artists, who fall within the 15th Phase of the Christian cycle. Yeats especially admired Botticelli, and in *A Vision* praises his "deliberate strangeness everywhere [which] gives one an emotion of mystery which is new to painting." Botticelli is grouped with those who make "intellect and emotion, *primary* curiosity and the *antithetical* dream . . . for the moment one."
5. "I have taken the 'honey of generation' from Porphyry's essay on 'The Cave of the Nymphs' [*Odyssey*, Book XIII], but find no warrant in Porphyry for considering it the 'drug' that destroys the 'recollection' of prenatal freedom. He blamed a cup of oblivion given in the zodiacal sign of Cancer." (Yeats's note) Porphyry, a third-century Greek scholar and neoplatonic philosopher, says "honey of generation" means the "pleasure arising from copulation" which draws souls "downward" to generation.
6. Plato considered the world of nature an imperfect and illusory copy of the ideal world.
7. Aristotle, the teacher of Alexander the Great, disciplined him with a strap ("taw," line 43). His philosophy, insisting on the interdependence of form and matter, took the world of nature far more seriously than did Plato's.
8. Sixth-century B.C. Greek mathematician and philosopher, whose elaborate philosophical system included the doctrine of the harmony of the spheres. He was highly revered, and one legend describes his godlike golden thighs.

VIII

Labor is blossoming or dancing where
The body is not bruised to pleasure soul,
Nor beauty born out of its own despair,
Nor blear-eyed wisdom out of midnight oil.                    60
O chestnut-tree, great-rooted blossomer,
Are you the leaf, the blossom or the bole?[9]
O body swayed to music, O brightening glance,
How can we know the dancer from the dance?

1927

W. B. YEATS

# Byzantium[1]

The unpurged images of day recede;
The Emperor's drunken soldiery are abed;
Night resonance recedes, night-walkers' song
After great cathedral gong;
A starlit or a moonlit dome[2] disdains                        5
All that man is,
All mere complexities,
The fury and the mire of human veins.

Before me floats an image, man or shade,
Shade more than man, more image than a shade;                 10
For Hades' bobbin bound in mummy-cloth
May unwind the winding path;[3]
A mouth that has no moisture and no breath
Breathless mouths may summon;
I hail the superhuman;                                         15
I call it death-in-life and life-in-death.

Miracle, bird or golden handiwork,
More miracle than bird or handiwork,
Planted on the star-lit golden bough,
Can like the cocks of Hades crow,[4]                          20
Or, by the moon embittered, scorn aloud
In glory of changeless metal

9. Trunk.
1. In his diary for April 30, 1930, Yeats sketched the following "Subject for a Poem": "Describe Byzantium as it is in the system towards the end of the first Christian millennium. A walking mummy. Flames at the street corners where the soul is purified, birds of hammered gold singing in the golden trees, in the harbor [dolphins], offering their backs to the wailing dead that they may carry them to paradise."
2. In *A Vision*, Yeats described the 28 phases of the moon in psychological terms related to his system. In Phase 1, only stars are visible ("starlit") and "body is completely absorbed in its supernatural environment." In its opposite, Phase 15, when the moon it full ("moonlit"), the mind is "completely absorbed in being."
3. A volume in which "Byzantium" appeared, *The Winding Stair and Other Poems*, contains many similar images; of this volume Yeats wrote: "In this book and elsewhere I have used towers, and one tower in particular, as symbols and have compared their winding stairs to the philosophical gyres, but it is hardly necessary to interpret what comes from the main track of thought and expression. Shelley uses towers constantly as symbols, and there are gyres in Swedenborg, and in Thomas Aquinas and certain classical authors."
4. As the bird of dawn, the cock had from antiquity been a symbol of rebirth and resurrection.

Common bird or petal
And all complexities of mire or blood.

At midnight on the Emperor's pavement flit          25
Flames that no fagot[5] feeds, nor steel has lit,
Nor storm disturbs, flames begotten of flame,
Where blood-begotten spirits come
And all complexities of fury leave,
Dying into a dance,                                 30
An agony of trance,
An agony of flame that cannot singe a sleeve.

Astraddle on the dolphin's mire and blood,[6]
Spirit after spirit! The smithies break the flood,
The golden smithies of the Emperor!                35
Marbles of the dancing floor
Break bitter furies of complexity,
Those images that yet
Fresh images beget,
That dolphin-torn, that gong-tormented sea.        40

1932

W. B. YEATS

# Crazy Jane Talks with the Bishop[1]

I met the Bishop on the road
And much said he and I.
"Those breasts are flat and fallen now,
Those veins must soon be dry;
Live in a heavenly mansion,                         5
Not in some foul sty."

"Fair and foul are near of kin,
And fair needs foul," I cried.
"My friends are gone, but that's a truth
Nor grave nor bed denied,                           10
Learned in bodily lowliness
And in the heart's pride.

"A woman can be proud and stiff
When on love intent;
But Love has pitched his mansion in                 15
The place of excrement;
For nothing can be sole or whole
That has not been rent."

1933

5. Bundle of sticks.
6. In ancient art, dolphins symbolize the soul moving from one state to another, and sometimes they provide a vehicle for the dead. Palaemon, for example, in Greek tradition is often mounted on a dolphin.
1. Crazy Jane appears in a series of poems written in the early 1930s, usually juxtaposed with a rational figure who sees things in terms of antitheses while she sees them as paradoxes. Yeats said that she was "more or less founded upon an old woman who lives in a little cottage near Gort. She loves her flower-garden . . . and [has] an amazing power of audacious speech. She is the local satirist and a really terrible one."

W. B. YEATS

# The Circus Animals' Desertion[1]

### I

I sought a theme and sought for it in vain,
I sought it daily for six weeks or so.
Maybe at last, being but a broken man,
I must be satisfied with my heart, although
Winter and summer till old age began                    5
My circus animals were all on show,
Those stilted boys, that burnished chariot,
Lion and woman and the Lord knows what.

### II

What can I but enumerate old themes?
First that sea-rider Oisin[2] led by the nose            10
Through three enchanted islands, allegorical dreams,
Vain gaiety, vain battle, vain repose,
Themes of the embittered heart, or so it seems,
That might adorn old songs or courtly shows;
But what cared I that set him on to ride,               15
I, starved for the bosom of his faery bride?

And then a counter-truth filled out its play,
*The Countess Cathleen*[3] was the name I gave it;
She, pity-crazed, had given her soul away,
But masterful Heaven had intervened to save it.        20
I thought my dear[4] must her own soul destroy,
So did fanaticism and hate enslave it,
And this brought forth a dream and soon enough
This dream itself had all my thought and love.

And when the Fool and Blind Man stole the bread        25
Cuchulain fought the ungovernable sea;[5]
Heart-mysteries there, and yet when all is said
It was the dream itself enchanted me:
Character isolated by a deed
To engross the present and dominate memory.            30
Players and painted stage took all my love,
And not those things that they were emblems of.

### III

Those masterful images because complete
Grew in pure mind, but out of what began?
A mound of refuse or the sweepings of a street,        35
Old kettles, old bottles, and a broken can,

1. The "animals" are early themes and images in Yeats's poetry, and he here reviews some of them.
2. The subject of an 1889 long poem. Oisin was a legendary figure, beguiled to faery land for 150 years, who returned to find his friends dead in his native Ireland.
3. An 1892 play, in which the countess sells her soul to the devil to get food for hungry people but nevertheless gains Heaven.
4. Maud Gonne.
5. In a 1904 play, *On Baile's Strand*.

Old iron, old bones, old rags, that raving slut
Who keeps the till. Now that my ladder's gone,
I must lie down where all the ladders start,
In the foul rag-and-bone shop of the heart.                    40

                                                          1939

ANONYMOUS

## Thomas Rymer

True Thomas lay o'er yond grassy bank,
    And he beheld a lady gay,
A lady that was brisk and bold,
    Come riding o'er the ferny brae.[1]

Her skirt was of the grass-green silk,                          5
    Her mantel of the velvet fine,
At ilka tett[2] of her horse's mane
    Hung fifty silver bells and nine.

True Thomas he took off his hat,
    And bowed him low down till his knee:                       10
"All hail, thou mighty Queen of Heaven!
    For your peer on earth I never did see."

"O no, O no, True Thomas," she says,
    "That name does not belong to me;
I am but the queen of fair Elfland,                             15
    And I'm come here for to visit thee.

"But ye maun[3] go wi' me now, Thomas,
    True Thomas, ye maun go wi' me,
For ye maun serve me seven years,
    Through weel or wae[4] as may chance to be."                20

She turned about her milk-white steed,
    And took True Thomas up behind,
And aye whene'er her bridle rang,
    The steed flew swifter than the wind.

For forty days and forty nights                                 25
    He wade through red blude to the knee,
And he saw neither sun nor moon,
    But heard the roaring of the sea.

O they rade on, and farther on,
    Until they came to a garden green:                          30
"Light down, light down, ye lady free,[5]
    Some of that fruit let me pull to thee."

1. Hillside.                    4. Weal or woe: good or bad fortune.
2. Every lock.                  5. Noble lady.
3. Must.

"O no, O no, True Thomas," she says,
  "That fruit maun not be touched by thee,
For a' the plagues that are in hell                                35
  Light on the fruit of this country.

"But I have a loaf here in my lap,
  Likewise a bottle of claret wine,
And now ere we go farther on,
  We'll rest a while, and ye may dine."                            40

When he had eaten and drunk his fill,
  "Lay down your head upon my knee,"
The lady said, "ere we climb yon hill,
  And I will show you ferlies⁶ three.

"O see not ye yon narrow road,                                     45
  So thick beset wi' thorns and briars?
That is the path of righteousness,
  Though after it but few enquires.

"And see not ye that braid,⁷ braid road,
  That lies across yon lilly leven?⁸                               50
That is the path of wickedness,
  Though some call it the road to heaven.

"And see not ye that bonny road,
  Which winds about the ferny brae?
That is the road to fair Elfland,                                  55
  Where you and I this night maun gae.⁹

"But Thomas, ye maun hold your tongue,
  Whatever you may hear or see,
For gin¹ ae² word you should chance to speak,
  You will ne'er get back to your ain³ country."                   60

He has gotten a coat of the even⁴ cloth,
  And a pair of shoes of velvet green,
And till seven years were past and gone
  True Thomas on earth was never seen.
                                              (date uncertain)

SIR THOMAS WYATT

## To His Lute

My lute, awake! Perform the last
Labor that thou and I shall waste,
And end that I have now begun;
For when this song is sung and past,
My lute, be still, for I have done.                                5

---

6. Marvels.                    1. If.
7. Broad.                      2. One.
8. Lovely glade.               3. Own.
9. Go.                         4. Smooth.

As to be heard where ear is none,
As lead to grave[1] in marble stone,
My song may pierce her heart as soon.
Should we then sigh, or sing, or moan?
No, no, my lute, for I have done.                    10

The rocks do not so cruelly
Repulse the waves continually
As she my suit and affection;
So that I am past remedy,
Whereby my lute and I have done.                      15

Proud of the spoil that thou hast got
Of simple hearts, thorough[2] love's shot;
By whom, unkind, thou hast them won,
Think not he hath his bow forgot,
Although my lute and I have done.                      20

Vengeance shall fall on thy disdain
That makest but game on earnest pain;
Think not alone under the sun
Unquit[3] to cause thy lovers plain,
Although my lute and I have done.                      25

Perchance thee lie withered and old
The winter nights that are so cold,
Plaining in vain unto the moon.
Thy wishes then dare not be told.
Care then who list,[4] for I have done.                 30

And then may chance thee to repent
The time that thou hast lost and spent
To cause thy lovers sigh and swoon.
Then shalt thou know beauty but lent,
And wish and want as I have done.                      35

Now cease, my lute. This is the last
Labor that thou and I shall waste,
And ended is that we begun.
Now is this song both sung and past.
My lute, be still, for I have done.                    40

ca. 1535

ALEXANDER POPE

## *from* Epistle to a Lady

Men, some to bus'ness, some to pleasure take;         215
But ev'ry woman is at heart a rake;
Men, some to quiet, some to public strife;
But ev'ry lady would be queen for life.

---

1. Engrave: carve; i.e., it is as likely as that lead can carve marble.
2. Through.
3. Unrevenged.
4. Likes.

Yet mark the fate of a whole sex of queens!
Pow'r all their end, but beauty all the means.                220
In youth they conquer with so wild a rage
As leaves them scarce a subject in their age:
For foreign glory, foreign joy, they roam;
No thought of peace or happiness at home.
But wisdom's triumph is well-timed retreat,                  225
As hard a science to the fair as great!
Beauties, like tyrants, old and friendless grown,
Yet hate repose, and dread to be alone,
Worn out in public, weary ev'ry eye,
Nor leave one sigh behind them when they die.                230
    Pleasures the sex, as children birds, pursue,
Still out of reach, yet never out of view;
Sure, if they catch, to spoil the toy at most,
To covet flying, and regret when lost;
At last, to follies youth could scarce defend,               235
It grows their age's prudence to pretend;
Ashamed to own they gave delight before,
Reduced to feign it, when they give no more:
As hags hold sabbaths,[5] less for joy than spite,
So these their merry, miserable night;                       240
Still round and round the ghosts of beauty glide,
And haunt the places where their honor died.
    See how the world its veterans rewards!
A youth of frolics, an old age of cards;
Fair to no purpose, artful to no end,                        245
Young without lovers, old without a friend;
A fop their passion, but their prize a sot,
Alive, ridiculous, and dead, forgot!

1735

SAMUEL BUTLER

# [Sir Hudibras][1]

When civil fury first grew high,
And men fell out, they knew not why;
When hard words, jealousies,[2] and fears
Set folks together by the ears.
And made them fight, like mad or drunk,                       5
For Dame Religion as for punk,[3]
Whose honesty they all durst swear for,
Though not a man of them knew wherefore;
When gospel trumpeter, surrounded
With long-eared rout, to battle sounded;                      10
And pulpit, drum ecclesiastic,
Was beat with fist instead of a stick;

---

5. Witches' sabbaths, late night meetings of witches and demons, characterized by wild feasting and dancing.
    1. From *Hudibras*, Butler's long burlesque poem about England's Civil War. Sir Hudibras, humpbacked and potbellied, is a humorless Presbyterian justice who sets out to reform his country and countrymen. This passage describes his learning and intellectual talents.
    2. Suspicions.
    3. A prostitute.

Then did Sir Knight abandon dwelling,
And out he rode a-colonelling.

. . . . .

He was in logic a great critic,                              65
Profoundly skilled in analytic;
He could distinguish and divide
A hair 'twixt south and southwest side;
On either which he would dispute,
Confute, change hands, and still confute.        70
He'd undertake to prove by force
Of argument, a man's no horse.
He'd prove a buzzard is no fowl,
And that a lord may be an owl,
A calf an alderman, a goose a justice,          75
And rooks⁴ committee-men and trustees.
He'd run in debt by disputation,
And pay with ratiocination.
All this by syllogism, true
In mood and figure, he would do.                80
    For rhetoric, he could not ope
His mouth but out there flew a trope;⁵
And when he happened to break off
I' th' middle of his speech, or cough,
H' had hard words ready to show why,           85
And tell what rules he did it by.
Else, when with greatest art he spoke,
You'd think he talked like other folk;
For all a rhetorician's rules
Teach nothing but to name his tools.           90

. . . . .

    In mathematics he was greater               119
Than Tycho Brahe or Erra Pater;⁶
For he by geometric scale
Could take the size of pots of ale;
Resolve by sines and tangents straight
If bread or butter wanted weight,⁷
And wisely tell what hour o' th' day          125
The clock does strike, by algebra.
    Besides, he was a shrewd philosopher,
And had read every text and gloss over;
Whate'er the crabbed'st author hath,
He understood b' implicit faith;              130
Whatever skeptic could inquire for,
For every *why* he had a *wherefore;*
Knew more than forty of them do,
As far as words and terms could go;
All which he understood by rote,              135
And, as occasion served, would quote,

4. Crows. "Rooks" was slang for cheats; "buzzard": worthless person; "owl": a stupid person who appears wise; "calf": dolt; "goose": simpleton.
5. Figure of speech.
6. Brahe was the Danish astronomer who sought a middle way between the Ptolemaic and Copernican systems; Erra Pater, the suppositious author of a 16th-century almanac which was arranged so that it could be used in any year.
7. Lacked weight; i.e., whether they weighed what their seller claimed.

No matter whether right or wrong;
They might be either said or sung.
His notions fitted things so well,
That which was which he could not tell,                    140
But oftentimes mistook the one
For th' other, as great clerks have done.
He could reduce all things to acts,
And knew their natures by abstracts;
Where entity and quiddity,                                 145
The ghosts of defunct bodies, fly;
Where Truth in person does appear,
Like words congealed in northern air.
He knew what's what, and that's as high
As metaphysic wit can fly.                                 150

1663

GEORGE GORDON, LORD BYRON

*from* Don Juan[1]

"Difficile est proprie communia dicere."[2]
—Horace

"Dost thou think, because thou art virtuous, there shall be no more cakes and ale?
Yes, by Saint Anne, and ginger shall be hot i' the mouth, too!"—Shakespeare, *Twelfth
Night, or What You Will.*

*Fragment*

I would to heaven that I were so much clay,
    As I am blood, bone, marrow, passion, feeling—
Because at least the past were passed away—
    And for the future—(but I write this reeling,
Having got drunk exceedingly today,
    So that I seem to stand upon the ceiling)
I say—the future is a serious matter—
And so—for God's sake—hock[3] and soda-water!

*from Canto I*

1

I want a hero: an uncommon want,
    When every year and month sends forth a new one,
Till, after cloying the gazettes with cant,[4]
    The age discovers he is not the true one;
Of such as these I should not care to vaunt.              5
    I'll therefore take our ancient friend Don Juan—
We all have seen him, in the pantomine,[5]
Sent to the devil somewhat ere his time.

1. The first stanza printed here is a manuscript fragment; the others are from Canto I.
2. Horace, *Ars Poetica,* line 128. Byron translated the line this way: " 'Tis no slight task to write on common things." More literally, "It is difficult to treat the universal in an original way." The context suggests that by "universal" Horace means the materials of epic.
3. *Hochheimer:* white German wine.
4. The fashionable language of the moment.
5. The legend of Don Juan, a 14th-century rake, was a frequent subject of plays, opera, and pantomime.

### 5

Brave men were living before Agamemnon[6]                    33
And since, exceeding valorous and sage,
A good deal like him too, though quite the same none;
But then they shone not on the poet's page,
And so have been forgotten—I condemn none,
But can't find any in the present age
Fit for my poem (that is, for my new one);
So, as I said, I'll take my friend Don Juan.              40

### 6

Most epic poets plunge *"in medias res"*[7]
(Horace makes this the heroic turnpike road),
And then your hero tells, whene'er you please,
What went before—by way of episode,
While seated after dinner at his ease,                     45
Beside his mistress in some soft abode,
Palace, or garden, paradise, or cavern,
Which serves the happy couple for a tavern.

### 7

That is the usual method, but not mine—
My way is to begin with the beginning;                     50
The regularity of my design
Forbids all wandering as the worst of sinning,
And therefore I shall open with a line
(Although it cost me half an hour in spinning)
Narrating somewhat of Don Juan's father,                   55
And also of his mother, if you'd rather.

                                                         1819

EDMUND SPENSER

## [The Bower of Bliss][1]

There the most daintie Paradise on ground,                 514
  It selfe doth offer to his sober eye,
In which all pleasures plenteously abound,
  And none does others happinesse envye:
The painted[2] flowers, the trees upshooting hye,
The dales for shade, the hilles for breathing space,
The trembling groves, the Christall[3] running by;         520
And that, which all faire workes doth most aggrace,[4]
The art, which all that wrought, appearéd in no place.

One would have thought, (so cunningly, the rude,
  And scornéd parts were mingled with the fine,)
That nature had for wantonesse ensude[5]                   525

6. Who commanded the Greek forces in the Trojan War. Line 33 is directly translated from one of Horace's odes.
7. Into the middle of the subject.
1. From Book II, Canto xii, of *The Faerie Queene*, Spenser's allegorical epic about religion, morality, and politics. Sir Guyon, exemplifying Temperance, is the hero of Book II, and in this famous episode has entered the Bower, where the witch Acrasia sets all kinds of sensual pleasures before him. Spenser took many of the details from Tasso's *Gerusalem Liberata*. He deliberately uses archaic words and expressions, and the text here is left unmodernized.
2. Variegated.
3. Clear stream.
4. Add grace to.
5. Imitated.

Art, and that Art at nature did repine;
So striving each th'other to undermine,
Each did the others worke more beautifie;
So diff'ring both in willes, agreed in fine:[6]
So all agreed through sweete diversitie,                    530
This Gardin to adorne with all varietie.

And in the midst of all, a fountaine stood,
Of richest substaunce, that on earth might bee,
So pure and shiny, that the silver flood
Through every channell running one might see;              535
Most goodly it with curious imageree
Was over-wrought, and shapes of naked boyes,
Of which some seemd with lively jollitee,
To fly about, playing their wanton toyes,[7]
Whilest others did them selves embay[8] in liquid joyes.    540

And over all, of purest gold was spred,
A trayle of yvie in his native hew:
For the rich mettall was so colouréd,
That wight,[9] who did not well avis'd it vew,
Would surely deeme it to be yvie trew:                     545
Low his lascivious armes adown did creepe,
That themselves dipping in the silver dew,
Their fleecy flowres they tenderly did steepe,
Which drops of Christall seemd for wantones to weepe.[1]

Infinit streames continually did well                      550
Out of this fountaine, sweet and faire to see,
The which into an ample laver[2] fell,
And shortly grew to so great quantitie,
That like a little lake it seemd to bee;
Whose depth exceeded not three cubits hight,[3]            555
That through the waves one might the bottom see,
All pav'd beneath with Jaspar shining bright,
That seemd the fountaine in that sea did sayle upright.

And all the margent round about was set,
With shady Laurell trees, thence to defend[4]              560
The sunny beames, which on the billowes bet,[5]
And those which therein bathéd, mote[6] offend.
As *Guyon* hapned by the same to wend,
Two naked Damzelles he therein espyde,
Which therein bathing, seeméd to contend,                  565
And wrestle wantonly, ne car'd to hyde,
Their dainty parts from vew of any, which them eyde.

Sometimes the one would lift the other quight
Above the waters, and then downe againe

6. At last, finally.
7. Sports.
8. Bathe.
9. Person; i.e., anyone who didn't look
carefully.
1. I.e., the flowers seemed to weep

"Christall" drops.
2. The basin of the fountain.
3. About five feet.
4. Fend off.
5. Beat.
6. Might.

Her plong, as over maisteréd by might,                          570
Where both awhile would coveréd remaine,
And each the other from to rise restraine;
The whiles their snowy limbes, as through a vele,
So through the Christall waves appearéd plaine:
Then suddeinly both would themselves unhele,[7]            575
And th'amarous sweet spoiles to greedy eyes revele.

As that faire Starre, the messenger of morne,
His deawy face out of the sea doth reare:
Or as the *Cyprian* goddesse,[8] newly borne
Of th'Oceans fruitfull froth, did first appeare:              580
Such seemed they, and so their yellow heare
Christalline humour[9] droppéd downe apace.
Whom such when *Guyon* saw, he drew him neare,
And somewhat gan relent his earnest pace,
His stubborne brest gan secret pleasaunce to embrace.    585

The wanton Maidens him espying, stood
Gazing a while at his unwonted guise;[1]
Then th'one her selfe low duckéd in the flood,
Abasht, that her a straunger did avise:[2]
But th'other rather higher did arise,                            590
And her two lilly paps aloft displayd,
And all, that might his melting hart entise
To her delights, she unto him bewrayd:[3]
The rest hid underneath, him more desirous made.

With that, the other likewise up arose,                        595
And her faire lockes, which formerly were bownd
Up in one knot, she low adowne did lose:[4]
Which flowing long and thick, her cloth'd arownd,
And th'yvorie in golden mantle gownd:
So that faire spectacle from him was reft,[5]               600
Yet that, which reft it, no lesse faire was fownd:
So hid in lockes and waves from lookers theft,
Nought but her lovely face she for his looking left.

Withall she laughéd, and she blusht withall,
That blushing to her laughter gave more grace,          605
And laughter to her blushing, as did fall:
Now when they spide the knight to slacke his pace,
Them to behold, and in his sparkling face
The secret signes of kindled lust appeare,
Their wanton meriments they did encreace,                610
And to him beckned, to approch more neare,
And shewd him many sights, that courage cold could reare.[6]

1590

---

7. Uncover.
8. Venus, the Roman goddess of beauty and sensual love, at first worshiped primarily on the islands of Cyprus and Cythera. She was sometimes said to have sprung from sea foam.
9. Moisture.

1. Unfamiliar style.
2. Look at.
3. Revealed.
4. Loosen.
5. Withheld.
6. I.e., that could arouse even cold dispositions.

PERCY BYSSHE SHELLEY

# Ode to the West Wind

### I

O wild West Wind, thou breath of Autumn's being,
Thou, from whose unseen presence the leaves dead
Are driven, like ghosts from an enchanter fleeing,

Yellow, and black, and pale, and hectic red,
Pestilence-stricken multitudes: O thou,                              5
Who chariotest to their dark wintry bed

The wingéd seeds, where they lie cold and low,
Each like a corpse within its grave, until
Thine azure sister of the Spring shall blow

Her clarion[1] o'er the dreaming earth, and fill                     10
(Driving sweet buds like flocks to feed in air)
With living hues and odors plain and hill:

Wild Spirit, which art moving everywhere;
Destroyer and preserver; hear, oh, hear!

### II

Thou on whose stream, mid the steep sky's commotion,                15
Loose clouds like earth's decaying leaves are shed,
Shook from the tangled boughs of Heaven and Ocean,

Angels[2] of rain and lightning: there are spread
On the blue surface of thine aëry surge,
Like the bright hair uplifted from the head                         20

Of some fierce Maenad,[3] even from the dim verge
Of the horizon to the zenith's height,
The locks of the approaching storm. Thou dirge

Of the dying year, to which this closing night
Will be the dome of a vast sepulcher,                               25
Vaulted with all thy congregated might

Of vapors, from whose solid atmosphere
Black rain, and fire, and hail will burst: oh, hear!

### III

Thou who didst waken from his summer dreams
The blue Mediterranean, where he lay,                               30
Lulled by the coil of his crystálline streams,

1. Trumpet-call.
2. Messengers.
3. A frenzied female votary of Dionysus, the Greek god of vegetation and fertility who was supposed to die in the fall and rise again each spring.

Beside a pumice isle in Baiae's bay,[4]
And saw in sleep old palaces and towers
Quivering within the wave's intenser day,

All overgrown with azure moss and flowers        35
So sweet, the sense faints picturing them! Thou
For whose path the Atlantic's level powers

Cleave themselves into chasms, while far below
The sea-blooms and the oozy woods which wear
The sapless foliage of the ocean, know        40

Thy voice, and suddenly grow gray with fear,
And tremble and despoil themselves:[5] oh, hear!

IV

If I were a dead leaf thou mightest bear;
If I were a swift cloud to fly with thee;
A wave to pant beneath thy power, and share        45

The impulse of thy strength, only less free
Than thou, O uncontrollable! If even
I were as in my boyhood, and could be

The comrade by thy wanderings over Heaven,
As then, when to outstrip thy skyey speed        50
Scarce seemed a vision; I would ne'er have striven

As thus with thee in prayer in my sore need.
Oh, lift me as a wave, a leaf, a cloud!
I fall upon the thorns of life! I bleed!

A heavy weight of hours has chained and bowed        55
One too like thee: tameless, and swift, and proud.

V

Make me thy lyre,[6] even as the forest is:
What if my leaves are falling like its own!
The tumult of thy mighty harmonies

Will take from both a deep, autumnal tone,        60
Sweet though in sadness. Be thou, Spirit fierce,
My spirit! Be thou me, impetuous one!

Drive my dead thoughts over the universe
Like withered leaves to quicken a new birth!
And, by the incantation of this verse,        65

Scatter, as from an unextinguished hearth
Ashes and sparks, my words among mankind!
Be through my lips to unawakened earth

4. Where Roman emperors had erected villas, west of Naples. "pumice": made of porous lava turned to stone.
5. "The vegetation at the bottom of the sea . . . sympathizes with that of the land in the change of seasons." (Shelley's note)
6. Aeolian lyre, a wind harp.

The trumpet of a prophecy! O Wind,
If Winter comes, can Spring be far behind?                    70

                                                        1820

WILLIAM  WORDSWORTH

# Lines Composed a Few Miles above Tintern Abbey on Revisiting the Banks of the Wye During a Tour, July 13, 1798[1]

Five years have passed; five summers, with the length
Of five long winters! and again I hear
These waters, rolling from their mountain-springs
With a soft inland murmur. Once again
Do I behold these steep and lofty cliffs,                    5
That on a wild secluded scene impress
Thoughts of more deep seclusion; and connect
The landscape with the quiet of the sky.
The day is come when I again repose
Here, under this dark sycamore, and view                     10
These plots of cottage-ground, these orchard tufts,
Which at this season, with their unripe fruits,
Are clad in one green hue, and lose themselves
'Mid groves and copses.[2] Once again I see
These hedge-rows, hardly hedge-rows, little lines            15
Of sportive wood run wild: these pastoral farms,
Green to the very door; and wreaths of smoke
Sent up, in silence, from among the trees!
With some uncertain notice, as might seem
Of vagrant dwellers in the houseless woods,                  20
Or of some hermit's cave, where by his fire
The hermit sits alone.
                        These beauteous forms,
Through a long absence, have not been to me
As is a landscape to a blind man's eye;
But oft, in lonely rooms, and 'mid the din                   25
Of towns and cities, I have owed to them,
In hours of weariness, sensations sweet,
Felt in the blood, and felt along the heart;
And passing even into my purer mind,
With tranquil restoration—feelings too                       30
Of unremembered pleasure: such, perhaps,
As have no slight or trivial influence
On that best portion of a good man's life,
His little, nameless, unremembered acts
Of kindness and of love. Nor less, I trust,                  35
To them I may have owed another gift,
Of aspect more sublime; that blesséd mood,
In which the burthen[3] of the mystery,

---

1. Wordsworth had first visited the Wye
valley and the ruins of the medieval abbey
there in 1793, while on a solitary walking
tour. He was 23 then, 28 when he wrote
this poem.
2. Thickets.
3. Burden.

In which the heavy and the weary weight
Of all this unintelligible world,                                    40
Is lightened—that serene and bless&eacute;d mood,
In which the affections gently lead us on—
Until, the breath of this corporeal frame
And even the motion of our human blood
Almost suspended, we are laid asleep                                 45
In body, and become a living soul;
While with an eye made quiet by the power
Of harmony, and the deep power of joy,
We see into the life of things.
                                         If this
Be but a vain belief, yet, oh! how oft—                              50
In darkness and amid the many shapes
Of joyless daylight; when the fretful stir
Unprofitable, and the fever of the world,
Have hung upon the beatings of my heart—
How oft, in spirit, have I turned to thee,                           55
O sylvan Wye! thou wanderer through the woods,
How often has my spirit turned to thee!

    And now, with gleams of half-extinguished thought,
With many recognitions dim and faint,
And somewhat of a sad perplexity,                                    60
The picture of the mind revives again;
While here I stand, not only with the sense
Of present pleasure, but with pleasing thoughts
That in this moment there is life and food
For future years. And so I dare to hope,                             65
Though changed, no doubt, from what I was when first
I came among these hills; when like a roe
I bounded o'er the mountains, by the sides
Of the deep rivers, and the lonely streams,
Wherever nature led: more like a man                                 70
Flying from something that he dreads than one
Who sought the thing he loved. For nature then
(The coarser[4] pleasures of my boyish days,
And their glad animal movements all gone by)
To me was all in all—I cannot paint                                  75
What then I was. The sounding cataract
Haunted me like a passion; the tall rock,
The mountain, and the deep and gloomy wood,
Their colors and their forms, were then to me
An appetite; a feeling and a love,                                   80
That had no need of a remoter charm,
By thought supplied, nor any interest
Unborrowed from the eye. That time is past,
And all its aching joys are now no more,
And all its dizzy raptures. Not for this                             85
Faint I,[5] nor mourn nor murmur; other gifts
Have followed; for such loss, I would believe,

4. Physical.                              5. Am I discouraged.

Abundant recompense. For I have learned
To look on nature, not as in the hour
Of thoughtless youth; but hearing oftentimes                    90
The still, sad music of humanity,
Nor harsh nor grating, though of ample power
To chasten and subdue. And I have felt
A presence that disturbs me with the joy
Of elevated thoughts; a sense sublime                           95
Of something far more deeply interfused,
Whose dwelling is the light of setting suns,
And the round ocean and the living air,
And the blue sky, and in the mind of man:
A motion and a spirit, that impels                             100
All thinking things, all objects of all thought,
And rolls through all things. Therefore am I still
A lover of the meadows and the woods
And mountains; and of all that we behold
From this green earth; of all the mighty world                 105
Of eye, and ear—both what they half create,
And what perceive; well pleased to recognize
In nature and the language of the sense
The anchor of my purest thoughts, the nurse,
The guide, the guardian of my heart, and soul                  110
Of all my moral being.
                        Nor perchance,
If I were not thus taught, should I the more
Suffer my genial spirits[6] to decay:
For thou art with me here upon the banks
Of this fair river; thou my dearest Friend,[7]                 115
My dear, dear Friend; and in thy voice I catch
The language of my former heart, and read
My former pleasures in the shooting lights
Of thy wild eyes. Oh! yet a little while
May I behold in thee what I was once,                          120
My dear, dear Sister! and this prayer I make,
Knowing that Nature never did betray
The heart that loved her; 'tis her privilege,
Through all the years of this our life, to lead
From joy to joy: for she can so inform                         125
The mind that is within us, so impress
With quietness and beauty, and so feed
With lofty thoughts, that neither evil tongues,
Rash judgments, nor the sneers of selfish men,
Nor greetings where no kindness is, nor all                    130
The dreary intercourse of daily life,
Shall e'er prevail against us, or disturb
Our cheerful faith that all which we behold
Is full of blessings. Therefore let the moon
Shine on thee in thy solitary walk;                            135
And let the misty mountain-winds be free
To blow against thee: and, in after years,

6. Natural disposition; i.e., the spirits     7. His sister Dorothy.
that are part of his individual genius.

When these wild ecstasies shall be matured
Into a sober pleasure; when thy mind
Shall be a mansion for all lovely forms,                    140
Thy memory be as a dwelling-place
For all sweet sounds and harmonies; oh! then,
If solitude, or fear, or pain, or grief,
Should be thy portion, with what healing thoughts
Of tender joy wilt thou remember me,                       145
And these my exhortations! Nor, perchance—
If I should be where I no more can hear
Thy voice, nor catch from thy wild eyes these gleams
Of past existence—wilt thou then forget
That on the banks of this delightful stream                150
We stood together; and that I, so long
A worshiper of Nature, hither came
Unwearied in that service; rather say
With warmer love—oh! with far deeper zeal
Of holier love. Nor wilt thou then forget,                 155
That after many wanderings, many years
Of absence, these steep woods and lofty cliffs,
And this green pastoral landscape, were to me
More dear, both for themselves and for thy sake!

                                                           1798

MARIANNE MOORE

# The Hero

Where there is personal liking we go.
  Where the ground is sour; where there are
  weeds of beanstalk height,
  snakes' hypodermic teeth, or
  the wind brings the "scarebabe voice"                      5
  from the neglected yew set with
  the semi-precious cat's eyes of the owl—
awake, asleep, "raised ears extended to fine points," and so
on—love won't grow.

We do not like some things, and the hero                    10
  doesn't; deviating head-stones
  and uncertainty;
  going where one does not wish
  to go; suffering and not
  saying so; standing and listening where something          15
  is hiding. The hero shrinks
as what it is flies out on muffled wings, with twin yellow
eyes—to and fro—

with quavering water-whistle note, low,
  high, in basso-falsetto chirps                             20
  until the skin creeps.
  Jacob when a-dying, asked
  Joseph: Who are these? and blessed

both sons, the younger most, vexing Joseph.[1] And
    Joseph was vexing to some.[2]          25
Cincinnatus[3] was: Regulus:[4] and some of our fellow
    men have been, though

devout, like Pilgrim[5] having to go slow
    to find his roll; tired but hopeful—
    hope not being hope          30
    until all ground for hope has
    vanished; and lenient, looking
    upon a fellow creature's error with the
    feelings of a mother—a
woman or a cat. The decorous frock-coated Negro    35
    by the grotto

answers the fearless sightseeing hobo
    who asks the man she's with, what's this,
    what's that, where's Martha
    buried, "Gen-ral Washington          40
    there; his lady, here"; speaking
    as if in a play—not seeing her; with a
    sense of human dignity
and reverence for mystery, standing like the shadow
    of the willow.          45

Moses would not be grandson to Pharaoh.
    It is not what I eat that is
    my natural meat,
    the hero says. He's not out
    seeing a sight but the rock          50
    crystal thing to see—the startling El Greco
    brimming with inner light—that
covets nothing that it has let go. This then you may know
    as the hero.

          1935

WALT WHITMAN

# Facing West from California's Shores

Facing west, from California's shores,
Inquiring, tireless, seeking what is yet unfound,
I, a child, very old, over waves, towards the house of maternity,[1] the
    land of migrations, look afar,

1. According to *Genesis* 48:1–14, Jacob gave Joseph's younger son the primary blessing. When he was young, Jacob had tricked his father (Isaac) into blessing him above his elder brother; see *Genesis* 27.
2. Potiphar's wife, for example; see *Genesis* 39.
3. A legendary Roman hero of the 5th century B.C. who left his plow to become dictator for 16 days.
4. Third-century B.C. Roman consul who defeated the Carthaginians and led the African campaign.
5. Christian, the hero of *Pilgrim's Progress*, carelessly leaves his "roll" (parchment scroll) behind in a fit of discouragement on the Hill Difficulty. The roll, given to him by Evangelist at his first setting out, is inscribed, "Fly from the wrath to come," and Christian considers it "the assurance of his life, and acceptance at the desired haven."
1. Asia, as the supposed birthplace of the human race.

Look off the shores of my Western sea, the circle almost circled:
For starting westward from Hindustan, from the vales of Kashmere,    5
From Asia, from the north, from the God, the sage, and the hero,
From the south, from the flowery peninsulas and the spice islands,
Long having wandered since, round the earth having wandered,
Now I face home again, very pleased and joyous;
(But where is what I started for, so long ago?                       10
And why is it yet unfound?)

1860

ALLEN GINSBERG

## A Supermarket in California

What thoughts I have of you tonight, Walt Whitman,[1] for I walked down the sidestreets under the trees with a headache self-conscious looking at the full moon.

In my hungry fatigue, and shopping for images, I went into the neon fruit supermarket, dreaming of your enumerations![2]

What peaches and what penumbras! Whole families shopping at night! Aisles full of husbands! Wives in the avocados, babies in the tomatoes!—and you, Garcia Lorca,[3] what were you doing down by the watermelons?

I saw you, Walt Whitman, childless, lonely old grubber, poking among the meats in the refrigerator and eyeing the grocery boys.

I heard you asking questions of each: Who killed the pork chops?    5
What price bananas? Are you my Angel?

I wandered in and out of the brilliant stacks of cans following you, and followed in my imagination by the store detective.

We strode down the open corridors together in our solitary fancy tasting artichokes, possessing every frozen delicacy, and never passing the cashier.

Where are we going, Walt Whitman? The doors close in an hour. Which way does your beard point tonight?

(I touch your book and dream of our odyssey in the supermarket and feel absurd.)

Will we walk all night through solitary streets? The trees add     10
shade to shade, lights out in the houses, we'll both be lonely.

Will we stroll dreaming of the lost America of love past blue automobiles in driveways, home to our silent cottage?

Ah, dear father, graybeard, lonely old courage-teacher, what America did you have when Charon quit poling his ferry and you got out on a smoking bank and stood watching the boat disappear on the black waters of Lethe?[4]

Berkeley 1955

1. Whitman's free verse, strong individualism, and passionate concern with America as an idea have led many modern poets to consider him the father of a new poetry.
2. Whitman's highly rhetorical poetry often contains long lists or parallel constructions piled up for cumulative effect.
3. Early 20th-century Spanish poet and playwright, author of *Blood Wedding*. Murdered in 1936, at the beginning of the Spanish Civil War, his works were banned by the Franco government.
4. The River of Forgetfulness in Hades. Charon is the boatman who, according to classical myth, ferries souls to Hades.

WILLIAM ERNEST HENLEY

# Rondel

Beside the idle summer sea
And in the vacant summer days,
Light Love came fluting down the ways
Where you were loitering with me.

Who has not welcomed, even as we                    5
That jocund minstrel and his lays
Beside the idle summer sea,
And in the vacant summer days?

We listened, we were fancy-free;
And lo! in terror and amaze,                         10
We stood alone—alone at gaze
With an implacable memory,
Beside the idle summer sea.

1888

SIR PHILIP SIDNEY

# Farewell, O Sun

Farewell, O sun, Arcadia's[1] clearest light;
Farewell, O pearl, the poor man's plenteous treasure;
Farewell, O golden staff,[2] the weak man's might;
Farewell, O joy, the joyful's only pleasure;
Wisdom, farewell, the skill-less man's direction;    5
Farewell, with thee farewell all our affection.

For what place now is left for our affection,
Now that of purest lamp[3] is quenched the light
Which to our darkened minds was best direction?
Now that the mine is lost[4] of all our treasure;    10
Now death hath swallowed up our worldly pleasure,
We orphans made, void of all public might!

Orphans, indeed, deprived of father's might,
For he our father was in all affection,
In our well-doing placing all his pleasure,          15
Still studying how to us to be a light.
As well he was in peace a safest treasure,
In war his wit and word was our direction.

Whence, whence, alas, shall we seek our direction,
When that we fear our hateful neighbor's might,      20
Who long have gaped to get Arcadians' treasure?
Shall we now find a guide of such affection,

1. A place of idyllic happiness. The    2. Support of life.
poem is from Sidney's long pastoral ro-  3. The sun.
mance, *Arcadia*.                        4. Emptied.

Who for our sakes will think all travail[5] light,
And make his pain to keep us safe his pleasure?

No, no; forever gone is all our pleasure,                           25
For ever wandering from all good direction,
For ever blinded of our clearest light,
For ever laméd of our surest might,
For ever banished from well-placed affection,
For ever robbed of all our royal treasure.                          30

Let tears for him therefore be all our treasure,
And in our wailful naming him our pleasure;
Let hating of our selves be our affection,
And unto death bend still our thought's direction.
Let us against our selves employ our might,                         35
And putting out our eyes seek we our light.

Farewell our light, farewell our spoiled treasure,
Farewell our might, farewell our daunted pleasure,
Farewell direction, farewell all affection.

                                                                    1590

WILLIAM EMPSON

# Missing Dates

Slowly the poison the whole blood stream fills.
It is not the effort nor the failure tires.
The waste remains, the waste remains and kills.

It is not your system or clear sight that mills
Down small to the consequence a life requires;                      5
Slowly the poison the whole blood stream fills.

They bled an old dog dry yet the exchange rills
Of young dog blood gave but a month's desires[1]
The waste remains, the waste remains and kills.

It is the Chinese tombs and the slag hills                          10
Usurp the soil, and not the soil retires.
Slowly the poison the whole blood stream fills.

Not to have fire is to be a skin that shrills.
The complete fire is death. From partial fires
The waste remains, the waste remains and kills.                     15

It is the poems you have lost, the ills
From missing dates, at which the heart expires.
Slowly the poison the whole blood stream fills.
The waste remains, the waste remains and kills.

                                                                    1940

5. Labor.
1. "It is true about the old dog, at least I saw it reported somewhere, but the legend that a fifth or some such part of the soil of China is given up to ancestral tombs [lines 10–11] is (by the way) not true." (Empson's note)

EDWIN MORGAN

## Opening the Cage: *14 variations on 14 words*

I have nothing to say and I am saying it and that is poetry. John Cage[2]

I have to say poetry and is that nothing and am I saying it
I am and I have poetry to say and is that nothing saying it
I am nothing and I have poetry to say and that is saying it
I that am saying poetry have nothing and it is I and to say
And I say that I am to have poetry and saying it is nothing          5
I am poetry and nothing and saying it is to say that I have
To have nothing is poetry and I am saying that and I say it
Poetry is saying I have nothing and I am to say that and it
Saying nothing I am poetry and I have to say that and it is
It is and I am and I have poetry saying say that to nothing          10
It is saying poetry to nothing and I say I have and am that
Poetry is saying I have it and I am nothing and to say that
And that nothing is poetry I am saying and I have to say it
Saying poetry is nothing and to that I say I am and have it

1968

EDMUND SPENSER

## Happy Ye Leaves

Happy ye leaves[1] whenas those lily hands,
Which hold my life in their dead-doing[2] might,
Shall handle you and hold in love's soft bands,
Like captives trembling at the victor's sight.
And happy lines on which, with starry light,          5
Those lamping eyes will deign sometimes to look,
And read the sorrows of my dying sprite,[3]
Written with tears in heart's close[4] bleeding book.
And happy rhymes bathed in the sacred brook
Of Helicon,[5] whence she derivéd is;          10
When ye behold that angel's blessed look,
My soul's long-lackéd food, my heaven's bliss.
Leaves, lines and rhymes, seek her to please alone,
Whom if ye please, I care for other none!

1595

2. Twentieth-century American composer, noted for his startling experiments in sound and silence.
1. Of the book of poems celebrating the woman these "lines" (line 5) go on to describe.
2. Death-dealing.

3. Spirit.
4. Secretly.
5. A mountain sacred to the muses. Classical writers described a fountain or spring on the mountain as a source of poetic inspiration; medieval writers often called the spring itself Helicon.

FRANCESCO PETRARCA (PETRARCH)

## Amor Che Nel Penser Mio Vive e Regna[6]

Amor che nel penser mio vive e regna
e 'l suo seggio maggior nel mio cor tene,
talor armato ne la fronte vene,
ivi si loca, et ivi pon sua insegna.

Quella ch'amare e sofferir ne 'nsegna                    5
e vol che 'l gran desio, l'accesa spene,
ragion, vergogna e reverenza affrene,
di nostro ardir fra se stessa si sdegna.

Onde Amor paventoso fugge al core,
lasciando ogni sua impresa, e piange, e trema;          10
ivi s'asconde, e non appar più fore.

Che poss'io far, temendo il mio signore,
se non star seco infin a l'ora estrema?
ché bel fin fa chi ben amando more.

ca. 1335

SIR THOMAS WYATT

## The Long Love that in My Thought Doth Harbor[1]

The long love that in my thought doth harbor,
And in mine heart doth keep his residence,
Into my face presseth with bold pretense
And there encampeth, spreading his banner.

She that me learneth[2] to love and suffer              5
And wills that my trust and lust's negligence
Be reined by reason, shame, and reverence
With his hardiness takes displeasure.

Wherewithal unto the heart's forest he fleeth,
Leaving his enterprise with pain and cry,               10
And there him hideth, and not appeareth.

What may I do, when my master feareth,
But in the field with him to live and die?
For good is the life ending faithfully.

1557

---

6. A literal translation:

Love, who lives and reigns in my mind and maintains his throne in my heart, sometimes issues forth armed onto my forehead, where he makes camp and plants his flag.

She who teaches Love and me to love and suffer and who insists that reason, modesty, and reverence curb high desire and fiery hope is deeply offended by our zeal.

Therefore, Love retreats frightened into my heart, abandoning his whole undertaking, and weeps, and trembles; he hides himself there, and does not venture out again.

What can I do, since my lord Love is afraid, except stay with him to the moment of my death? Because whoever dies loving well makes a good end.

1. Like Surrey's "Love, that Doth Reign," a translation of Petrarch's "Amor Che Nel Penser."

2. Teaches me.

HENRY HOWARD, EARL OF SURREY

# Love, that Doth Reign and Live Within My Thought[1]

Love, that doth reign and live within my thought,
And built his seat within my captive breast,
Clad in the arms wherein with me he fought,
Oft in my face he doth his banner rest.
But she that taught me love and suffer pain,                    5
My doubtful hope and eke[2] my hot desire
With shamefast[3] look to shadow and refrain,
Her smiling grace converteth straight to ire.
And coward Love, then, to the heart apace
Taketh his flight, where he doth lurk and plain,[4]            10
His purpose lost, and dare not show his face.
For my lord's guilt thus faultless bide I pain,
Yet from my lord shall not my foot remove:
Sweet is the death that taketh end by love.

1557

SIR PHILIP SIDNEY

# When Nature Made Her Chief Work, Stella's Eyes[1]

When Nature made her chief work, Stella's eyes,[2]
In color black[3] why wrapped she beams so bright?
Would she in beamy black, like painter wise,
Frame daintiest luster mixed of shades and light?
Or did she else that sober hue devise,                          5
In object best to knit and strength our sight,
Lest if no veil those brave gleams did disguise,
They sunlike should more dazzle than delight?
Or would she her miraculous power show,
That, whereas black seems Beauty's contrary,                   10
She even in black doth make all beauties flow?
Both so and thus: she, minding[4] Love should be
Placed ever there, gave him this mourning weed
To honor all their deaths who for her bleed.

1582

HENRY CONSTABLE

# My Lady's Presence Makes the Roses Red

My lady's presence makes the roses red
Because to see her lips they blush for shame.

1. Like Wyatt's "The Long Love that in My Thought Doth Harbor," a translation of Petrarch's "Amor Che Nel Penser."
2. Also.
3. Shamefaced: modest.
4. Complain: lament.
1. From Sidney's sonnet sequence, *Astrophel and Stella*, usually credited with having started the vogue of sonnet sequences in Elizabethan England.
2. Following Petrarch's lead, Sidney and other English sonneteers developed a series of exaggerated conventions to describe the physical features of the women they celebrated. The excessive brightness of the eyes—almost always compared favorably with the sun's brightness—was an expected feature.
3. Black was frequently used in the Renaissance to mean absence of light, and ugly or foul (see line 10).
4. Remembering that.

The lily's leaves, for envy, pale became,
And her white hands in them this envy bred.
The marigold the leaves abroad doth spread          5
Because the sun's and her power is the same.
The violet of purple color came,
Dyed in the blood she made my heart to shed.
In brief, all flowers from her their virtue take;
From her sweet breath their sweet smells do proceed;     10
The living heat which her eyebeams doth make
Warmeth the ground and quickeneth the seed.
The rain wherewith she watereth the flowers
Falls from mine eyes, which she dissolves in showers.

1594

WILLIAM SHAKESPEARE

## My Mistress' Eyes Are Nothing like the Sun[1]

My mistress' eyes are nothing like the sun;
Coral is far more red than her lips' red;
If snow be white, why then her breasts are dun;[2]
If hairs be wires, black wires grow on her head.[3]
I have seen roses damasked[4] red and white,          5
But no such roses see I in her cheeks;
And in some perfumes is there more delight
Than in the breath that from my mistress reeks.
I love to hear her speak, yet well I know
That music hath a far more pleasing sound;          10
I grant I never saw a goddess go;[5]
My mistress, when she walks, treads on the ground.
And yet, by heaven, I think my love as rare
As any she belied with false compare.

1609

HENRY CONSTABLE

## Miracle of the World

Miracle of the world, I never will deny
That former poets praise the beauty of their days,
But all those beauties were but figures[1] of thy praise,
And all those poets did of thee but prophesy.
Thy coming to the world hath taught us to descry          5
What Petrarch's Laura[2] meant, for truth the lip bewrays.[3]
Lo, why th' Italians, yet which never saw thy rays,
To find out Petrarch's sense such forgéd glosses try:
The beauties, which he in a veil enclosed, beheld

1. See Sidney's "When Nature Made
Her Chief Work, Stella's Eyes," and notes.
2. Mouse-colored.
3. Women in traditional sonnets have
hair of gold. Many poets who use the
Petrarchan conventions also wrote poems
which teased or deflated the conventions.
4. Variegated.

5. Walk.
1. Prefigurations, like people in the Old
Testament who, according to Christian
typology, prefigured Christ.
2. The woman celebrated in Petrarch's
14th-century sonnets. Constable's sequence
of sonnets is addressed to "Diana."
3. Reveals.

But revelations were within his secret heart,[4]     10
By which in parables thy coming he foretold.
His songs were hymns of thee, which only now before
Thy image should be sung; for thou that goddess art
Which only we without idolatry adore.

1594

SAMUEL DANIEL

## Let Others Sing of Knights and Paladins

Let others sing of knights and paladins
In agéd accents of untimely[5] words,
Paint shadows in imaginary lines
Which well the reach of their high wits records;
But I must sing of thee, and those fair eyes.     5
Authentic shall my verse in time to come,
When yet th' unborn shall say, "Lo where she lies,
Whose beauty made him speak that else was dumb."
These are the arks, the trophies I erect,
That fortify thy name against old age;     10
And these thy sacred virtues must protect
Against the dark and time's consuming rage.
Though th' error of my youth they shall discover,
Suffice, they show I lived and was thy lover.

1592

WILLIAM SHAKESPEARE

## Let Me Not to the Marriage of True Minds

Let me not to the marriage of true minds
Admit impediments.[1] Love is not love
Which alters when it alteration finds,
Or bends with the remover to remove:
Oh, no! it is an ever-fixéd mark,     5
That looks on tempests and is never shaken;
It is the star to every wandering bark,
Whose worth's unknown, although his height be taken.[2]
Love's not Time's fool, though rosy lips and cheeks
Within his bending sickle's compass come;     10
Love alters not with his brief hours and weeks,
But bears it out even to the edge of doom.[3]
If this be error and upon me proved,
I never writ, nor no man ever loved.

1609

4. I.e., once the beauties are actually seen (in Diana), Petrarch's mysterious descriptions turn out to be private revelations of the future.
5. Outdated.
1. The Marriage Service contained this address to the observers: "If any of you know cause or just impediments why these persons should not be joined together . . . ."
2. I.e., measuring the altitude of stars (for purposes of navigation) is not a measurement of value.
3. End of the world.

WILLIAM SHAKESPEARE

## When, in Disgrace with Fortune and Men's Eyes

When, in disgrace[1] with fortune and men's eyes,
I all alone beweep my outcast state,
And trouble deaf heaven with my bootless[2] cries,
And look upon myself and curse my fate,
Wishing me like to one more rich in hope,                    5
Featured like him, like him with friends possessed,
Desiring this man's art, and that man's scope,
With what I most enjoy contented least;
Yet in these thoughts myself almost despising,
Haply[3] I think on thee, and then my state,               10
Like to the lark at break of day arising
From sullen[4] earth, sings hymns at heaven's gate;
For thy sweet love remembered such wealth brings
That then I scorn to change my state with kings.

1609

WILLIAM SHAKESPEARE

## Poor Soul, the Center of My Sinful Earth

Poor soul, the center of my sinful earth,
Thrall to[1] these rebel pow'rs that thee array![2]
Why dost thou pine within and suffer dearth,
Painting thy outward walls so costly gay?
Why so large cost, having so short a lease,                  5
Dost thou upon thy fading mansion spend?
Shall worms, inheritors of this excess,
Eat up thy charge? Is this thy body's end?
Then, soul, live thou upon thy servant's loss,
And let that pine to aggravate[3] thy store;               10
Buy terms divine in selling hours of dross:
Within be fed, without be rich no more.
So shalt thou feed on death, that feeds on men,
And death once dead, there's no more dying then.

1609

THOMAS LODGE

## Devoid of Reason

Devoid of reason, thrall to foolish ire,
I walk and chase a savage fairy still,
Now near the flood, straight on the mounting hill,
Now midst the woods of youth, and vain desire.
For leash I bear a cord of careful grief;                   5
For brach[1] I lead an overforward mind;

1. Disfavor.
2. Futile.
3. By chance.
4. Mournful.
1. The original text is faulty here, and "Thrall to" is an emendation. Other possi-

bilities include "Pressed by," "Rebuke," "Lord of," and "Starved by."
2. Deck out; or, possibly, afflict.
3. Increase.
1. A hound which hunts by scent.

My hounds are thoughts, and rage despairing blind,
Pain, cruelty, and care without relief.
But they, perceiving that my swift pursuit
My flying fairy cannot overtake,                           10
With open mouths their prey on me do make,
Like hungry hounds that lately lost their suit,
And full of fury on their master feed,
To hasten on my hapless death with speed.

1593

EDMUND SPENSER

## Like as a Huntsman after Weary Chase

Like as a huntsman after weary chase,
Seeing the game from him escaped away,
Sits down to rest him in some shady place,
With panting hounds beguiléd of their prey:
So, after long pursuit and vain assay,[1]                   5
When I all weary had the chase forsook,
The gentle deer returned the self-same way,
Thinking to quench her thirst at the next brook:
There she, beholding me with milder look,
Sought not to fly, but fearless still did bide;             10
Till I in hand her yet half trembling took,
And with her own good-will[2] her firmly tied.
Strange thing, meseemed,[3] to see a beast so wild,
So goodly[4] won with her own will beguiled.

1595

SIR PHILIP SIDNEY

## What, Have I Thus Betrayed My Liberty?

What, have I thus betrayed my liberty?
Can those black beams such burning marks[1] engrave
In my free side? or am I born a slave,
Whose neck becomes[2] such yoke of tyranny?
Or want[3] I sense to feel my misery?                       5
Or sprite,[4] disdain of such disdain to have?
Who for long faith, though daily help I crave,
May get no alms but scorn of beggary.[5]
Virtue, awake! Beauty but beauty is.
I may, I must, I can, I will, I do                          10
Leave following that which it is gain to miss.
Let her go! Soft, but here she comes! Go to,
Unkind, I love you not! O me, that eye
Doth make my heart give to my tongue the lie!

1582

---

1. Attempt.                          2. Befits.
2. Acquiescence.                     3. Lack.
3. It seemed to me.                  4. Spirit.
4. Easily.                           5. I.e., contempt for my beggarly condi-
1. Slaves had formerly been branded.  tion.

ELIZABETH BARRETT BROWNING

## How Do I Love Thee?

How do I love thee? Let me count the ways.
I love thee to the depth and breadth and height
My soul can reach, when feeling out of sight
For the ends of Being and ideal Grace.
I love thee to the level of every day's                    5
Most quiet need, by sun and candlelight.
I love thee freely, as men strive for Right;
I love thee purely, as they turn from Praise;
I love thee with the passion put to use
In my old griefs, and with my childhood's faith.          10
I love thee with a love I seemed to lose
With my lost saints—I love thee with the breath,
Smiles, tears of all my life!—and, if God choose,
I shall but love thee better after death.

1850

JOHN MILTON

## When I Consider How My Light Is Spent

When I consider how my light is spent
Ere half my days,[1] in this dark world and wide,
And that one talent which is death to hide[2]
Lodged with me useless, though my soul more bent
To serve therewith my Maker, and present               5
My true account, lest He returning chide.
"Doth God exact day-labor, light denied?"
I fondly[3] ask. But Patience, to prevent
That murmur, soon replies, "God doth not need
Either man's work or his own gifts; who best          10
Bear His mild yoke, they serve Him best. His state
Is kingly. Thousands at His bidding speed
And post o'er land and ocean without rest;
They also serve who only stand and wait."
ca. 1652

JOHN MILTON

## On the Late Massacre in Piedmont[1]

Avenge, O Lord, thy slaughtered saints, whose bones
Lie scattered on the Alpine mountains cold;
Ev'n them who kept thy truth so pure of old,
When all our fathers worshiped stocks and stones,

1. Milton was in his early forties when
he became totally blind.
2. In Jesus' parable of the talents, the
servant who buries his talent loses what
he has and is cast into "outer darkness";
see *Matthew* 25:14–30.
3. Foolishly.
1. On Easter Sunday, 1655, the Duke of
Savoy's forces massacred 1700 members of
the Waldensian sect in the Piedmont in
northwestern Italy. The sect, founded in
1170, existed at first within the Roman
Catholic Church, but its vigorous con-
demnation of church rites and policies
(especially of the use of icons—see line 4)
led to a total break. Until the year of the
massacre the group had been allowed freedom of worship.

Forget not: in thy book record their groans                    5
Who were thy sheep, and in their ancient fold
Slain by the bloody Piedmontese, that rolled
Mother with infant down the rocks. Their moans
The vales redoubled to the hills, and they
To Heav'n. Their martyred blood and ashes sow                 10
O'er all th' Italian fields, where still doth sway
The triple Tyrant:[2] that from these may grow
A hundredfold who, having learnt thy way,
Early may fly the Babylonian woe.[3]

1655

PERCY BYSSHE SHELLEY

## Ozymandias[1]

I met a traveler from an antique land
Who said: Two vast and trunkless legs of stone
Stand in the desert. . . . Near them, on the sand,
Half sunk, a shattered visage lies, whose frown,
And wrinkled lip, and sneer of cold command,                   5
Tell that its sculptor well those passions read
Which yet survive, stamped on these lifeless things,
The hand that mocked them, and the heart that fed:
And on the pedestal these words appear:
"My name is Ozymandias, King of Kings:                         10
Look on my works, ye Mighty, and despair!"
Nothing beside remains. Round the decay
Of that colossal wreck, boundless and bare
The lone and level sands stretch far away.

1818

DON FRANCISCO A. QUEVEDO

## I Saw the Ramparts of My Native Land[2]

I saw the ramparts of my native land,
One time so strong, now dropping in decay,
Their strength destroyed by this new age's way,
That has worn out and rotted what was grand.
I went into the fields: there I could see                      5
The sun drink up the waters newly thawed,
And on the hills the moaning cattle pawed;
Their miseries robbed the day of light for me.

I went into my house: I saw how spotted,
Decaying things made that old home their prize.                10

---

2. The Pope's tiara has three crowns.
3. Protestants in Milton's day associated Catholicism with Babylonian decadence, called the church "the whore of Babylon," and read the prophecy of *Revelation* 17 and 18 as an allegory of its coming destruction.
1. The Greek name for Rameses II, 13th-century B.C. pharaoh of Egypt. According to a first—century B.C. Greek historian, Diodorus Siculus, the largest statue in Egypt was inscribed: "I am Ozymandias, king of kings; if anyone wishes to know what I am and where I lie, let him surpass me in some of my exploits."
2. Translated from the Spanish by John Masefield.

My withered walking-staff had come to bend;
I felt the age had won; my sword was rotted,
And there was nothing on which to set my eyes
That was not a reminder of the end.

ca. 1635

# e. e. cummings

## a salesman

a salesman is an it that stinks Excuse

Me whether it's president of the you were say
or a jennelman name misder finger isn't
important whether it's millions of other punks
or just a handful absolutely doesn't                                    5
matter and whether it's in lonjewray

or shrouds is immaterial it stinks

a salesman is an it that stinks to please

but whether to please itself or someone else
makes no more difference than if it sells                              10
hate condoms education snakeoil vac
uumcleaners terror strawberries democ
ra (caveat emptor[1]) cy superfluous hair

or Think We've Met subhuman rights Before

1944

HELENE JOHNSON

## Sonnet to a Negro in Harlem

You are disdainful and magnificent—
Your perfect body and your pompous gait,
Your dark eyes flashing solemnly with hate,
Small wonder that you are incompetent
To imitate those whom you so despise—                                  5
Your shoulders towering high above the throng,
Your head thrown back in rich, barbaric song,
Palm trees and mangoes stretched before your eyes.
Let others toil and sweat for labor's sake
And wring from grasping hands their meed[2] of gold.                   10
Why urge ahead your supercilious feet?
Scorn will efface each footprint that you make.
I love your laughter arrogant and bold.
You are too splendid for this city street.

p. 1927

1. Literally, "let the buyer beware":
the principle that the seller is not responsi-
ble for a product unless he provides a       formal guarantee.
2. Reward.

GWENDOLYN BROOKS

## First Fight. Then Fiddle.

First fight. Then fiddle. Ply the slipping string
With feathery sorcery; muzzle the note
With hurting love; the music that they wrote
Bewitch, bewilder. Qualify to sing
Threadwise. Devise no salt, no hempen thing                    5
For the dear instrument to bear. Devote
The bow to silks and honey. Be remote
A while from malice and from murdering.
But first to arms, to armor. Carry hate
In front of you and harmony behind.                            10
Be deaf to music and to beauty blind.
Win war. Rise bloody, maybe not too late
For having first to civilize a space
Wherein to play your violin with grace.

1949

JOHN KEATS

## On First Looking into Chapman's Homer[1]

Much have I traveled in the realms of gold,
And many goodly states and kingdoms seen;
Round many western islands have I been
Which bards in fealty[2] to Apollo hold.
Oft of one wide expanse had I been told                        5
That deep-browed Homer ruled as his demesne;[3]
Yet did I never breathe its pure serene[4]
Till I heard Chapman speak out loud and bold:
Then felt I like some watcher of the skies
When a new planet swims into his ken;[5]                        10
Or like stout Cortez[6] when with eagle eyes
He stared at the Pacific—and all his men
Looked at each other with a wild surmise—
Silent, upon a peak in Darien.

1816

GEORGE STARBUCK

## On First Looking in on Blodgett's *Keats's "Chapman's Homer"* (*Sum.* ½C. M9–11)

Mellifluous as bees, these brittle men
droning of Honeyed Homer give me hives.
I scratch, yawn like a bear, my arm arrives

1. Chapman's were among the most famous Renaissance translations; his *Iliad* was completed in 1611, *The Odyssey* in 1616. Keats wrote the sonnet after being led to Chapman by his former teacher and reading *The Iliad* all night long.
2. Literally, the loyalty owed by a vassal to his feudal lord. Apollo was the Greek and Roman god of poetry and music.
3. Estate, feudal possession.
4. Atmosphere.
5. Range of vision.
6. Actually, Balboa; he first viewed the Pacific from Darien, in Panama.

at yours—oh, Honey, and we're back again,
me the Balboa, you the Darien,                                        5
lording the loud Pacific sands, our lives
as hazarded as when a petrel dives
to yank the dull sea's coverlet, or when,
breaking from me across the sand that's rink
and record of our weekend boning up                                  10
on *The Romantic Agony*,[7] you sink
John Keats a good surf-fisher's cast out—plump
in the sun's wake—and the parched pages drink
that great whales' blanket party hump and hump.

                                                                     1960

HELEN CHASIN

## Joy Sonnet in a Random Universe

Sometimes I'm happy: la la la la la la la
la la la la la la la la la la la la la la la la la
la la la la. Tum tum ti tum. La la la la la la
la la la la la la la la la la la la la la la la la.
Hey nonny nonny. La la la la la la la la la      5
la la la la la la la la la la la. Vo do di o do.
Poo poo pi doo. La la la la la la la la la la
la la la la la la la la la la la la la la la la la
la la. Whack a doo. La la la la la la. Sh-
boom, sh-boom. La la la la la la la la la la      10
la la la la la la la la la la la la la la la la la
la la. Dum di dum. La la la la la la la la la
la la la la la la la la la. Tra la la. Tra la la
la la la la la la la la la la. Yeah yeah yeah.

                                                                     1968

DANTE GABRIEL ROSSETTI

## A Sonnet Is a Moment's Monument

A Sonnet is a moment's monument—
    Memorial from the Soul's eternity
    To one dead deathless hour. Look that it be,
Whether for lustral[1] rite or dire portent,
Of its own arduous fullness reverent.                                5
    Carve it in ivory or in ebony,
    As Day or Night may rule; and let Time see
Its flowering crest impearled and orient.[2]

A Sonnet is a coin: its face reveals
    The soul—its converse, to what Power 'tis due—                   10
Whether for tribute to the august appeals
    Of Life or dower in Love's high retinue,

---

7. The title, conveniently enough, of a     1. Purificatory.
scholarly book about several writers, in-    2. Sparkling.
cluding Keats.

It serve; or, 'mid the dark wharf's cavernous breath,
In Charon's[3] palm it pay the toll to Death.

1881

JOHN KEATS

# On the Sonnet

If by dull rhymes our English must be chained,
And like Andromeda,[1] the sonnet sweet
Fettered, in spite of painéd loveliness,
Let us find, if we must be constrained,
Sandals more interwoven and complete        5
To fit the naked foot of Poesy:[2]
Let us inspect the lyre, and weigh the stress
Of every chord,[3] and see what may be gained
By ear industrious, and attention meet;
Misers of sound and syllable, no less        10
Than Midas[4] of his coinage, let us be
Jealous[5] of dead leaves in the bay-wreath crown;[6]
So, if we may not let the Muse be free,
She will be bound with garlands of her own.

1819

WILLIAM WORDSWORTH

# Nuns Fret Not

Nuns fret not at their convent's narrow room;
And hermits are contented with their cells;
And students with their pensive citadels;
Maids at the wheel, the weaver at his loom,
Sit blithe and happy; bees that soar for bloom,        5
High as the highest Peak of Furness-fells,[1]
Will murmur by the hour in foxglove bells:[2]
In truth the prison, unto which we doom
Ourselves, no prison is: and hence for me,
In sundry moods, 'twas pastime to be bound        10
Within the sonnet's scanty plot of ground;
Pleased if some souls (for such there needs must be)
Who have felt the weight of too much liberty,
Should find brief solace there, as I have found.

1807

3. The boatman who, in classical myth, rowed souls of the dead across the River Styx. Ancient Greeks put a small coin in the hand of the dead to pay his fee.
1. Who, according to Greek myth, was chained to a rock so that she would be devoured by a sea monster. She was rescued by Perseus, who married her. When she died she was placed among the stars.
2. In a letter which contained this sonnet, Keats expressed impatience with the traditional Petrarchan and Shakespearean sonnet forms: "I have been endeavoring to discover a better sonnet stanza than we have."

3. Lyre-string.
4. The legendary king of Phrygia who asked, and got, the power to turn all he touched to gold.
5. Suspiciously watchful.
6. The bay tree was sacred to Apollo, god of poetry, and bay wreaths came to symbolize true poetic achievement. The withering of the bay tree is sometimes considered an omen of death.
1. Mountains in England's Lake District, where Wordsworth lived.
2. Flowers from which digitalis (a heart medicine) began to be made in 1799.

LOUISE BOGAN

## Single Sonnet

Now, you great stanza, you heroic mould,
Bend to my will, for I must give you love:
The weight in the heart that breathes, but cannot move,
Which to endure flesh only makes so bold.

Take up, take up, as it were lead or gold                    5
The burden; test the dreadful mass thereof.
No stone, slate, metal under or above
Earth, is so ponderous, so dull, so cold.

Too long as ocean bed bears up the ocean,
As earth's core bears the earth, have I borne this;          10
Too long have lovers, bending for their kiss,
Felt bitter force cohering without motion.

Staunch meter, great song, it is yours, at length,
To prove how stronger you are than my strength.

1937

WILLIAM BLAKE

## The Lamb

Little Lamb, who made thee?
Dost thou know who made thee?
Gave thee life, and bid thee feed
By the stream and o'er the mead;
Gave thee clothing of delight,                               5
Softest clothing woolly bright;
Gave thee such a tender voice,
Making all the vales rejoice?
Little Lamb, who made thee?
Dost thou know who made thee?                                10

Little Lamb, I'll tell thee!
Little Lamb, I'll tell thee:
He is callèd by thy name,
For he calls himself a Lamb,
He is meek and he is mild;                                   15
He became a little child.
I a child and thou a lamb,
We are callèd by his name.
Little Lamb, God bless thee!
Little Lamb, God bless thee!                                 20

1789

WILLIAM BLAKE

## The Tiger

Tiger, Tiger, burning bright
In the forests of the night,
What immortal hand or eye
Could frame thy fearful symmetry?

In what distant deeps or skies       5
Burnt the fire of thine eyes?
On what wings dare he aspire?
What the hand dare seize the fire?

And what shoulder and what art,
Could twist the sinews of thy heart?       10
And when thy heart began to beat,
What dread hand, and what dread feet?

What the hammer? What the chain?
In what furnace was thy brain?
What the anvil? What dread grasp       15
Dare its deadly terrors clasp?

When the stars threw down their spears
And watered heaven with their tears,
Did he smile his work to see?
Did he who made the Lamb make thee?       20

Tiger, Tiger, burning bright
In the forests of the night,
What immortal hand or eye
Dare frame thy fearful symmetry?

1794

ANDREW MARVELL

## An Horatian Ode upon Cromwell's Return from Ireland[1]

The forward[2] youth that would appear[3]
Must now forsake his Muses dear,
    Nor in the shadows sing
    His numbers[4] languishing.

'Tis time to leave the books in dust       5
And oil th' unuséd armor's rust,
    Removing from the wall
    The corslet[5] of the hall.

1. In 1650, having just conquered Ireland, Cromwell returned to England to prepare a campaign against the Scots. Charles I, the deposed king, had been executed a year and a half before.
2. Ambitious.
3. Win recognition.
4. Verses.
5. Suit of armor.

So restless Cromwell could not cease
In the inglorious arts of peace,                                10
   But through adventurous war
   Urgéd his active star;

And, like the three-forked lightning, first
Breaking the clouds where it was nursed,
   Did thorough[6] his own side                      15
   His fiery way divide.[7]

For 'tis all one to courage high,
The emulous[8] or enemy;
   And with such, to inclose[9]
   Is more than to oppose.                           20

Then burning through the air he went,
And palaces and temples rent;
   And Caesar's head at last
   Did through his laurels blast.[1]

'Tis madness to resist or blame                                 25
The force of angry Heaven's flame;[2]
   And, if we would speak true,
   Much to the man is due;

Who, from his private gardens, where
He livéd reservéd and austere                                   30
   (As if his highest plot
   To plant the bergamot),[3]

Could by industrious valor climb
To ruin the great work of Time,
   And cast the kingdoms old                          35
   Into another mold.

Though Justice against Fate complain,
And plead the ancient rights in vain;
   But those do hold or break,
   As men are strong or weak.                         40

Nature, that hateth emptiness,
Allows of penetration[4] less,
   And therefore must make room
   Where greater spirits come.

What field of all the civil wars,                               45
Where his were not the deepest scars?

6. Through.
7. Cromwell began as a Presbyterian, the majority group in the anti-Royalist forces, but became a leader among the Independents, a smaller group.
8. Envious.
9. Restrain. Some scholars regard the difficulty of this stanza as deliberate and prudent.

1. Laurel was used for crowns because, according to tradition, it was lightning-proof. "Caesar": Charles I.
2. In classical times, lightning was sometimes regarded as the jealousy of the gods, sometimes as divine judgment.
3. A kind of pear.
4. The occupation of the same space by two bodies at the same time (OED).

And Hampton shows what part
He had of wiser art;[5]

Where, twining subtle fears with hope,
He wove a net of such a scope,                                    50
   That Charles himself might chase
   To Carisbrooke's narrow case.

That thence the royal actor borne
The tragic scaffold might adorn;
   While round, the arméd bands                          55
   Did clap their bloody hands.

He nothing common did or mean
Upon that memorable scene;
   But with his keener eye
   The axe's edge did try;[6]                              60

Nor called the gods with vulgar spite
To vindicate his helpless right,
   But bowed his comely head
   Down, as upon a bed.

This was that memorable hour                                      65
Which first assured the forcéd power.
   So when they did design
   The Capitol's first line,[7]

A bleeding head, where they begun,
Did fright the architects to run;                                 70
   And yet in that the State
   Foresaw its happy fate.

And now the Irish are ashamed
To see themselves in one year tamed;
   So much one man can do,                                75
   That does both act and know.

They can affirm his praises best,
And have, though overcome, confessed
   How good he is, how just,
   And fit for highest trust;                              80

Nor yet grown stiffer with command,
But still in the Republic's hand—
   How fit he is to sway
   That can so well obey.

5. Charles, first confined at Hampton Court, briefly escaped to Carisbrooke Castle (line 52) on the Isle of Wight. At the time many thought Cromwell had contrived to let him escape in order to provide an excuse for execution.
6. In Latin, the same word (*acies*) means both eye-beam and sword-edge.

7. The foundations of Rome. According to tradition, workmen found a human head (*caput*) while digging the foundations of the temple of Jupiter there, interpreted the find as an omen that Rome would be head of an empire, and named the site Capitoline Hill.

He to the Commons' feet presents                                    85
A kingdom[8] for his first year's rents;
And, what he may, forbears[9]
His fame, to make it theirs;

And has his sword and spoils ungirt,
To lay them at the public's skirt:                                  90
So when the falcon high
Falls heavy from the sky,

She, having killed, no more does search
But on the next green bough to perch;
Where, when he first does lure,                                     95
The falconer has her sure.

What may not then our Isle presume
While victory his crest does plume!
What may not others fear
If thus he crown each year!                                         100

A Caesar he ere long to Gaul,
To Italy an Hannibal,
And to all states not free
Shall climacteric[1] be.

The Pict[2] no shelter now shall find                               105
Within his parti-colored mind;[3]
But from this valor sad[4]
Shrink underneath the plaid;

Happy, if in the tufted brake[5]
The English hunter him mistake;[6]                                  110
Nor lay his hounds in near
The Caledonian deer.[7]

But thou, the wars' and Fortune's son,
March indefatigably on;
And for the last effect                                             115
Still keep thy sword erect;

Besides the force it has to fright[8]
The spirits of the shady night,
The same arts that did gain
A power must it maintain.                                           120

**1681**

---

8. Ireland.
9. Deflects.
1. A crucial period of change.
2. Scot. The Romans called the Scots *Picti* ("painted men") because they went to battle with painted bodies (see line 106).
3. The Scots felt divided loyalties: the Stuart line of kings came to power from Scotland, but most Scots were Presbyterians.
4. Steadfast.
5. Thicket.
6. Overlook.
7. The Scots.
8. The hilt of the sword, as a sign of the cross.

JOHN MILTON

# *from* Paradise Lost[1]

I

Of man's first disobedience, and the fruit[2]
Of that forbidden tree whose mortal taste
Brought death into the world, and all our woe,
With loss of Eden, till one greater Man
Restore us, and regain the blissful seat,                    5
Sing, Heav'nly Muse,[3] that, on the secret top
Of Oreb, or Sinai, didst inspire
That shepherd who first taught the chosen seed
In the beginning how the Heav'ns and Earth
Rose out of Chaos: or, if Sion hill                          10
Delight thee more, and Siloa's brook that flowed
Fast[4] by the oracle of God, I thence
Invoke thy aid to my adventurous song,
That with no middle flight intends to soar
Above th' Aonian mount,[5] while it pursues                  15
Things unattempted yet in prose or rhyme.
And chiefly thou, O Spirit,[6] that dost prefer
Before all temples th' upright heart and pure,
Instruct me, for thou know'st; thou from the first
Wast present, and, with mighty wings outspread,             20
Dovelike sat'st brooding on the vast abyss,
And mad'st it pregnant: what in me is dark
Illumine; what is low, raise and support;
That, to the height of this great argument,[7]
I may assert Eternal Providence,                            25
And justify the ways of God to men.
    Say first (for Heav'n hides nothing from thy view,
Nor the deep tract of Hell), say first what cause
Moved our grand parents, in that happy state,
Favored of Heav'n so highly, to fall off                    30
From their Creator, and transgress his will
For[8] one restraint, lords of the world besides?
Who first seduced them to that foul revolt?
Th' infernal serpent; he it was, whose guile,

---

1. The opening lines of Books I and II and a short passage from Book III. The first passage states the poem's subject, and the second describes Satan's beginning address to the council of fallen angels meeting to discuss strategy; in the third, God is looking down from Heaven at his new human creation and watching Satan approach the Earth.
2. The apple, but also the consequences.
3. Addressing one of the muses and asking for aid is a convention for the opening lines of an epic; Milton complicates the standard procedure here by describing sources and circumstances of Judeo-Christian revelation rather than specifically invoking one of the nine classical muses. Sinai is the spur of Mount Oreb, where Moses ("That shepherd," line 8, who was traditionally regarded as author of the first five books of the Bible) received the Law; Sion hill and Siloa (lines 10–11), near Jerusalem, correspond to the traditional mountain (Helicon) and springs of classical tradition. Later, in Book VII, Milton calls upon Urania, the muse of astronomy, but he does not mention by name the muse of epic poetry, Calliope.
4. Close.
5. Mt. Helicon, home of the classical muses.
6. The divine voice that inspired the Hebrew prophets. *Genesis* 1:2 says that "the Spirit of God moved upon the face of the waters" as part of the process of the original creation; Milton follows tradition in making the inspirational and communicative function of God present in creation itself. The passage echoes and merges many Biblical references to divine creation and revelation.
7. Subject.
8. Because of. "besides": in all other respects.

Stirred up with envy and revenge, deceived                    35
The mother of mankind, what time⁹ his pride
Had cast him out from Heav'n, with all his host
Of rebel angels, by whose aid, aspiring
To set himself in glory above his peers,
He trusted to have equaled the Most High,                     40
If he opposed; and with ambitious aim
Against the throne and monarchy of God,
Raised impious war in Heav'n and battle proud,
With vain attempt. Him the Almighty Power
Hurled headlong flaming from th' ethereal sky,                45
With hideous ruin and combustion down
To bottomless perdition, there to dwell
In adamantine chains and penal fire,
Who durst defy th' Omnipotent to arms.¹

❖ ❖ ❖

II
High on a throne of royal state, which far
Outshone the wealth of Ormus and of Ind,²
Or where the gorgeous East with richest hand
Show'rs on her kings barbaric pearl and gold,
Satan exalted sat, by merit raised                            5
To that bad eminence; and, from despair
Thus high uplifted beyond hope, aspires
Beyond thus high, insatiate to pursue
Vain war with Heav'n, and by success³ untaught,
His proud imaginations thus displayed:                        10
    "Powers and Dominions, Deities of Heav'n,
For since no deep within her gulf can hold
Immortal vigor, though oppressed and fall'n,
I give not Heav'n for lost. From this descent
Celestial virtues rising will appear                          15
More glorious and more dread than from no fall,
And trust themselves to fear no second fate.
Me though just right and the fixed laws of Heav'n
Did first create your leader, next, free choice,
With what besides, in council or in fight,                    20
Hath been achieved of merit, yet this loss,
Thus far at least recovered, hath much more
Established in a safe unenvied throne
Yielded with full consent. The happier state
In Heav'n, which follows dignity, might draw                  25
Envy from each inferior; but who here
Will envy whom the highest place exposes
Foremost to stand against the Thunderer's aim
Your bulwark, and condemns to greatest share
Of endless pain? Where there is then no good                  30
For which to strive, no strife can grow up there
From faction; for none sure will claim in hell
Precédence, none, whose portion is so small

9. When.
1. After invoking the muse and giving a
brief summary of the poem's subject, an
epic regularly begins *in medias res* (in the
midst of things).
2. Hormuz, an island in the Persian
Gulf, famous for pearls, and India.
3. Outcome, either good or bad.

Of present pain, that with ambitious mind
Will covet more. With this advantage then                    35
To union, and firm faith, and firm accord,
More than can be in Heav'n, we now return
To claim our just inheritance of old,
Surer to prosper than prosperity
Could have assured us; and by what best way,                 40
Whether of open war or covert guile,
We now debate; who can advise, may speak."

❖   ❖   ❖

### III

❖   ❖   ❖

Now had th' Almighty Father from above,                      56
From the pure empyrean where he sits
High throned above all height, bent down his eye,
His own works and their works at once to view:
About him all the sanctities of Heav'n[4]                    60
Stood thick as stars, and from his sight received
Beatitude past utterance; on his right
The radiant image of his glory sat,
His only Son. On earth he first beheld
Our two first parents, yet the only two                      65
Of mankind, in the happy garden placed,
Reaping immortal fruits of joy and love,
Uninterrupted joy, unrivaled love,
In blissful solitude. He then surveyed
Hell and the gulf between, and Satan there                   70
Coasting the wall of Heav'n on this side Night
In the dun air sublime,[5] and ready now
To stoop[6] with wearied wings and willing feet
On the bare outside of this world, that seemed
Firm land embosomed without firmament,                       75
Uncertain which, in ocean or in air.

1667

ALEXANDER POPE

## *from* The Dunciad[1]

High on a gorgeous seat, that far outshone
Henley's gilt tub, or Fleckno's Irish throne,[2]
Or that where on her Curlls[3] the public pours,
All-bounteous, fragrant grains and golden show'rs,

4. The hierarchies of angels.
5. Aloft in the twilight atmosphere.
6. Swoop down, like a bird of prey.
1. Pope's mock-heroic poem about the decay of modern literature, learning, and morality. The selection is from Book II, in which the goddess Dulness declares "high heroic games" (line 18) to celebrate the coronation of Colley Cibber as king of Dulness. The games parallel, in debased fashion, the heroic games described in *The Aeneid*, Book VI, and the opening lines here echo *Paradise Lost*, Book II.
2. "Orator" Henley, a spell-binding speaker who made ostentatious public declamations, usually nonsensical. "tub": a nickname, because of its appearance, for the pulpit of the Dissenters. Fleckno is the dying King of Nonsense portrayed in Dryden's *Mac Flecknoe*.
3. Edmund Curll, an unscrupulous contemporary publisher and bookseller, often reprinted books published by others, taking advantage of lax copyright regulations. He also kept a stable of hack writers to turn out material on topics of ephemeral interest, and reportedly sometimes hired thugs to steal manuscripts (see lines 113–16). He was once pilloried, and the public —as was their custom—pelted him with used malt grains and eggs (golden show'rs, line 4).

Great Cibber[4] sate: The proud Parnassian[5] sneer,                5
The conscious simper, and the jealous leer,
Mix on his look: All eyes direct their rays
On him, and crowds turn coxcombs[6] as they gaze.
His peers shine round him with reflected grace,
New edge their Dulness, and new bronze their face.            10
So from the sun's broad beam, in shallow urns
Heav'ns twinkling sparks draw light, and point their horns.
    Not with more glee, by hands Pontific crowned,
With scarlet hats wide-waving circlet round,
Rome in her capitol saw Querno sit,                          15
Throned on sev'n hills, the Antichrist of wit.[7]
    And now the Queen, to glad her sons, proclaims
By herald hawkers,[8] high heroic games.
They summon all her race: an endless band
Pours forth, and leaves unpeopled half the land.             20
A motley mixture! in long wigs, in bags,
In silks, in crapes, in garters,[9] and in rags,
From drawing rooms, from colleges, from garrets,
On horse, on foot, in hacks,[1] and gilded chariots:
All who true Dunces in her cause appeared,                   25
And all who knew those Dunces to reward.
    Amid that area wide they took their stand,
Where the tall maypole once o'er-looked the Strand;[2]
But now (so Anne and Piety ordain)
A church collects the saints of Drury-Lane.[3]               30
    With authors, stationers[4] obeyed the call,
(The field of glory is a field for all.)
Glory, and gain, th'industrious tribe provoke;
And gentle Dulness ever loves a joke.
A poet's form she placed before their eyes,                  35
And bade the nimblest racer seize the prize;
No meager, muse-rid mope, adust[5] and thin,
In a dun[6] nightgown of his own loose skin;
But such a bulk as no twelve bards could raise,
Twelve starv'ling bards of these degen'rate days.            40
All as a partridge plump, full-fed, and fair,
She formed this image of well-bodied air;
With pert flat[7] eyes she windowed well its head;
A brain of feathers, and a heart of lead;
And empty words she gave, and sounding strain,               45
But senseless, lifeless! idol void and vain!

4. Colley Cibber, a comic actor, theatre manager, and mediocre playwright, was appointed Poet Laureate by George II in 1730, and his obligatory odes on the occasions of the king's birthday and New Year's Day produced considerable mirth.
5. Mount Parnassus was sacred to Apollo and the muses.
6. Fops.
7. "Camillo Querno was of Apulia, who hearing the great encouragement which Leo X gave to poets, traveled to Rome with a harp in his hand, and sung to it twenty thousand verses of a poem called *Alexias*. He was introduced as a buffoon to Leo, and promoted to the honor of the Laurel, a jest which the court of Rome and the Pope himself entered into so far as to cause him to ride on an elephant to the Capitol, and to hold a solemn festival on his coronation; at which it is recorded the poet himself was so transported as to weep for joy. He was ever after a constant frequenter of the Pope's table, drank abundantly, and poured forth verses without number." (Pope's note)
8. Peddlers.
9. The Order of the Garter was the highest order of knighthood.
1. Hired carriages.
2. A busy street near the River Thames.
3. Prostitutes.
4. Booksellers.
5. Gloomy and parched-looking.
6. Mouse-colored.
7. Dull.

Never was dashed out, at one lucky hit,
A fool, so just a copy of a wit;
So like, that critics said, and courtiers swore,
A wit it was, and called the phantom More.[8]    50
    All gaze with ardor: some a poet's name,
Others a sword-knot[9] and laced suit inflame.
But lofty Lintot[1] in the circle rose:
"This prize is mine; who tempt it are my foes;
With me began this genius, and shall end."    55
He spoke: and who with Lintot shall contend?
    Fear held them mute. Alone, untaught to fear,
Stood dauntless Curll: "Behold that rival here!
The race by vigor, not by vaunts is won;
So take the hindmost, Hell."—He said, and run.    60
Swift as a bard the bailiff leaves behind,
He left huge Lintot, and outstripped the wind.
As when a dab-chick[2] waddles through the copse[3]
On feet and wings, and flies, and wades, and hops;
So lab'ring on, with shoulders, hands, and head,    65
Wide as a windmill all his figure spread,
With arms expanded Bernard rows his state,
And left-legged Jacob[4] seems to emulate:
Full in the middle way there stood a lake,
Which Curll's Corinna[5] chanced that morn to make:    70
(Such was her wont, at early dawn to drop
Her evening cates[6] before his neighbor's shop,)
Here fortuned Curll to slide; loud shout the band,
And Bernard! Bernard! rings through all the Strand.
Obscene with filth the miscreant lies bewrayed,    75
Fall'n in the plash his wickedness had laid:
Then first (if poets aught of truth declare)
The caitiff vaticide[7] conceived a pray'r.
    Hear Jove! whose name my bards and I adore,
As much at least as any god's, or more;    80
And him and his, if more devotion warms,
Down with the Bible, up with the Pope's Arms.[8]
    A place there is, betwixt earth, air, and seas,
Where, from ambrosia,[9] Jove retires for ease.
There in his seat two spacious vents appear,    85
On this he sits, to that he leans his ear.
And hears the various vows of fond[1] mankind;
Some beg an eastern, some a western wind:
All vain petitions, mounting to the sky,
With reams abundant this abode supply;    90
Amused he reads, and then returns the bills
Signed with that ichor[2] which from Gods distils.

8. James Moore Smythe, who once used some lines of Pope in his own poem.
9. A decorative ribbon for a sword.
1. Bernard Lintot, a bookseller, who was very tall (see lines 62, 65–67).
2. A bird which sometimes looks very awkward in its half-running, half-flying motion described in line 64. The long simile here "imitates" epic simile.
3. Thicket.
4. Jacob Tonson, a bookseller known for his physical clumsiness.

5. Elizabeth Thomas, who gained possession of some of Pope's private letters and allowed Curll to print them.
6. Delicacies, choice foods.
7. Villainous poet-killer.
8. Shops were designated by symbols: the Bible was Curll's shop sign; the Pope's Arms, Lintot's.
9. The food and drink of the gods; i.e., Jove retires after dinner.
1. Foolish.
2. The body fluid of the classical gods.

In office here fair Cloacina[3] stands,
And ministers to Jove with purest hands.
Forth from the heap she picked her vot'ry's[4] pray'r,                95
And placed it next him, a distinction rare!
Oft had the Goddess heard her servant's call,
From her black grottos[5] near the Temple-wall,
List'ning delighted to the jest unclean
Of linkboys vile, and watermen[6] obscene;                100
Where as he fished her nether realms[7] for wit,
She oft had favored him, and favors yet.
Renewed by ordure's sympathetic force,[8]
As oiled with magic juices for the course,
Vig'rous he rises; from th' effluvia strong                105
Imbibes new life, and scours[9] and stinks along;
Re-passes Lintot, vindicates[1] the race,
Nor heeds the brown dishonors of his face.
    And now the victor stretched his eager hand
Where the tall Nothing stood, or seemed to stand;                110
A shapeless shade, it melted from his sight,
Like forms in clouds, or visions of the night.
To seize his papers, Curll, was next thy care;
His papers light, fly diverse, tossed in air;
Songs, sonnets, epigrams the winds uplift,                115
And whisk 'em back to Evans, Young, and Swift.[2]
Th'embroidered suit at least he deemed his prey;
That suit an unpaid taylor snatched away.
No rag, no scrap, of all the beau, or wit,
That once so fluttered, and that once so writ.                120

1743

JONATHAN  SWIFT

# A Satirical Elegy

### On the Death of a Late Famous General[1]

His Grace? impossible? what dead?
Of old age too, and in his bed?
And could that Mighty Warrior fall?
And so inglorious, after all!
Well, since he's gone, no matter how,                5
The last loud trump[2] must wake him now;
And, trust me, as the noise grows stronger,
He'd wish to sleep a little longer.

3. "The Roman Goddess of the common sewers." (Pope's note)
4. Devotee's.
5. Coal wharves in a London district known as the Temple.
6. Linkboys were torch bearers; watermen, hired boatmen on the Thames.
7. Sewers (to find abandoned manuscripts ["wit"]).
8. I.e., stimulated by the occult influence of a corresponding substance.
9. Hurries.
1. Claims victory in.
2. "Some of those persons whose writings, epigrams, or jests he [James Moore Smythe, the "tall Nothing"] had owned." (Pope's note) Abel Evans, a minor contemporary poet; Edward Young, a poet and satirist; Jonathan Swift, author of *Gulliver's Travels* and a close friend of Pope's. All were clergymen.
1. John Churchill, the first Duke of Marlborough, whose brilliant military exploits had made him an English hero. His later pettiness and civilian politics tarnished, in the eyes of some, his earlier glory, but the poem exaggerates his loss of reputation.
2. On Judgment Day, when the dead are supposed to be awakened.

And could he be indeed so old
As by the newspapers we're told?[3]    10
Threescore, I think, is pretty high;
'Twas time in conscience he should die.
This world he cumbered long enough;
He burnt his candle to the snuff;
And that's the reason, some folks think,    15
He left behind *so great a stink.*

Behold his funeral appears,
Nor widow's sighs, nor orphan's tears,
Wont at such times each heart to pierce,
Attend the progress of his hearse.    20
But what of that, his friends may say,
He had those honors in his day;
True to his profit and his pride,
He made them weep before he died.

Come hither, all ye empty things,    25
Ye bubbles[4] raised by breath of Kings,
Who float upon the tide of state,
Come hither, and behold your fate.
Let pride be taught by this rebuke,
How very mean a thing's a Duke;    30
From all his ill-got honors flung,
Turned to that dirt from whence he sprung.

1722

JOHN MILTON

# Lycidas[1]

In this monody the author bewails a learned friend, unfortunately drowned in his passage from Chester on the Irish Seas, 1637.[2] And by occasion foretells the ruin of our corrupted clergy then in their height.

Yet once more, O ye laurels, and once more
Ye myrtles brown, with ivy never sere,[3]
I come to pluck your berries harsh and crude,[4]
And with forced fingers rude,
Shatter your leaves before the mellowing year.    5
Bitter constraint, and sad occasion dear,[5]
Compels me to disturb your season due:
For Lycidas is dead, dead ere his prime,
Young Lycidas, and hath not left his peer.
Who would not sing for Lycidas? He knew    10
Himself to sing, and build the lofty rhyme.

3. Marlborough died at age 72.
4. Insubstantial things. Marlborough was made a Duke in 1689, two days before William became king, in a deal made during the succession crisis.
1. The name of a shepherd in Vergil's *Eclogue* III. Milton's elegy works from the convention of treating the dead man as if he were a shepherd and also transforms other details to a pastoral setting and situation.

2. Edward King, a student with Milton at Cambridge, and at the time of his death a young clergyman. "monody": a song sung by a single voice.
3. Withered. The laurel, myrtle, and ivy were all materials used to construct traditional evergreen garlands signifying poetic accomplishment. "brown": dusky, dark.
4. Unripe.
5. Dire.

He must not float upon his wat'ry bier
Unwept, and welter[6] to the parching wind,
Without the meed[7] of some melodious tear.
Begin then, sisters of the sacred well,[8]                                    15
That from beneath the seat of Jove doth spring,
Begin, and somewhat loudly sweep the string.
Hence with denial vain and coy excuse;
So may some gentle muse[9]
With lucky words favor my destined urn,                                       20
And as he passes turn,
And bid fair peace be to my sable shroud.
For we were nursed upon the self-same hill,
Fed the same flock, by fountain, shade, and rill.
Together both, ere the high lawns[1] appeared                                 25
Under the opening eyelids of the morn,
We drove afield, and both together heard
What time the gray-fly winds[2] her sultry horn,
Batt'ning[3] our flocks with the fresh dews of night,
Oft till the star that rose, at ev'ning, bright,                              30
Towards Heav'n's descent had sloped his westering wheel.
Meanwhile the rural ditties were not mute,
Tempered to the oaten flute;[4]
Rough satyrs danced, and fauns with clov'n heel,
From the glad sound would not be absent long,                                 35
And old Damaetas[5] loved to hear our song.
But O the heavy change, now thou art gone,
Now thou art gone, and never must return!
Thee, shepherd, thee the woods and desert caves,
With wild thyme and the gadding[6] vine o'ergrown,                            40
And all their echoes mourn.
The willows and the hazel copses[7] green
Shall now no more be seen,
Fanning their joyous leaves to thy soft lays.
As killing as the canker[8] to the rose,                                      45
Or taint-worm to the weanling herds that graze,
Or frost to flowers, that their gay wardrobe wear,
When first the white-thorn blows:[9]
Such, Lycidas, thy loss to shepherd's ear.
Where were ye, nymphs,[1] when the remorseless deep                           50
Closed o'er the head of your loved Lycidas?
For neither were ye playing on the steep,
Where your old Bards, the famous Druids, lie,
Nor on the shaggy top of Mona high,
Nor yet where Deva spreads her wizard stream:[2]                              55
Ay me, I fondly[3] dream!

6. Tumble about.
7. Tribute.
8. The muses, who lived on Mt. Helicon.
At the foot of the mountain were two
fountains, or wells, where the muses danced
around Jove's altar.
9. Poet.
1. Grasslands: pastures.
2. Blows; i.e., the insect hum of midday.
3. Fattening.
4. Shepherds' pipes.
5. A traditional pastoral name, possibly
referring here to a Cambridge tutor.

6. Wandering.
7. Thickets.
8. Cankerworm.
9. Blossoms.
1. Nature deities.
2. The River Dee, reputed to have prophetic powers. "Mona": the Isle of An-
glesey. The steep (line 52) may be a burial
ground, in northern Wales, for Druids,
ancient priests and magicians; all three lo-
cations are near the place where King
drowned.
3. Foolishly.

Had ye been there—for what could that have done?
What could the Muse[4] herself that Orpheus bore,
The Muse herself, for her enchanting[5] son
Whom universal nature did lament,                                    60
When by the rout that made the hideous roar,
His gory visage down the stream was sent,
Down the swift Hebrus to the Lesbian shore?
    Alas! What boots[6] it with uncessant care
To tend the homely slighted shepherd's trade,                       65
And strictly meditate the thankless Muse?
Were it not better done, as others use,[7]
To sport with Amaryllis in the shade,
Or with the tangles of Neaera's hair?
Fame is the spur that the clear spirit doth raise                   70
(That last infirmity of noble mind)
To scorn delights, and live laborious days;
But the fair guerdon[8] when we hope to find,
And think to burst out into sudden blaze,
Comes the blind Fury[9] with th' abhorréd shears,                   75
And slits the thin-spun life. "But not the praise,"
Phoebus[1] replied, and touched my trembling ears:
"Fame is no plant that grows on mortal soil,
Nor in the glistering foil[2]
Set off to th' world, nor in broad rumor lies,                      80
But lives and spreads aloft by those pure eyes
And perfect witness of all-judging Jove;
As he pronounces lastly on each deed,
Of so much fame in Heav'n expect thy meed."
    O fountain Arethuse,[3] and thou honored flood,                 85
Smooth-sliding Mincius, crowned with vocal reeds,
That strain I heard was of a higher mood.
But now my oat[4] proceeds,
And listens to the herald of the sea,[5]
That came in Neptune's plea.                                        90
He asked the waves and asked the felon-winds,
What hard mishap hath doomed this gentle swain,[6]
And questioned every gust of rugged wings
That blows from off each beakéd promontory.
They knew not of his story,                                         95
And sage Hippotades[7] their answer brings:
That not a blast was from his dungeon strayed;

4. Calliope, the muse of epic poetry, whose son Orpheus was torn limb from limb by frenzied orgiasts. His head, thrown into the Hebrus (lines 62–63), floated into the sea and finally to Lesbos, where it was buried.
5. Orpheus was reputed to be able to charm even inanimate things with his music; he once persuaded Pluto to release his dead wife, Eurydice, from the infernal regions.
6. Profits.
7. Customarily do. Amaryllis (line 68) and Neaera (line 69) are stock names of women celebrated in pastoral love poetry.
8. Reward.
9. Atropos, the Fate who cuts the threads of human life after they are spun

and measured by her two sisters.
1. Apollo, god of poetic inspiration. In Roman tradition, touching the ears of one's hearers meant asking them to remember what they heard.
2. Flashy setting, used to make inferior gems glitter.
3. A Sicilian fountain, associated with the pastoral poetry of Theocritus. The River Mincius (line 86) is associated with Vergil's pastorals.
4. Oaten pipe: pastoral song.
5. Triton, who maintains the innocence of Neptune, the Roman god of the sea, in the death of Lycidas.
6. Youth, shepherd, poet.
7. Aeolus, god of the winds and son of Hippotas.

The air was calm, and on the level brine,
Sleek Panopë[8] with all her sisters played.
It was that fatal and perfidious bark                            100
Built in th' eclipse, and rigged with curses dark,
That sunk so low that sacred head of thine.
Next Camus,[9] reverend sire, went footing slow,
His mantle hairy, and his bonnet sedge,
Inwrought with figures dim, and on the edge          105
Like to that sanguine flower inscribed with woe.[1]
"Ah! who hath reft," quoth he, "my dearest pledge?"
Last came, and last did go,
The pilot of the Galilean Lake;[2]
Two massy keys he bore of metals twain               110
(The golden opes, the iron shuts amain).
He shook his mitered locks, and stern bespake:
"How well could I have spared for thee, young swain,
Enow[3] of such as for their bellies' sake
Creep and intrude, and climb into the fold![4]        115
Of other care they little reck'ning make,
Than how to scramble at the shearers' feast,
And shove away the worthy bidden guest.
Blind mouths! that scarce themselves know how to hold
A sheep-hook,[5] or have learned aught else the least   120
That to the faithful herdman's art belongs!
What recks it[6] them? What need they? They are sped,[7]
And when they list,[8] their lean and flashy songs
Grate on their scrannel[9] pipes of wretched straw.
The hungry sheep look up and are not fed,             125
But swoln with wind, and the rank mist they draw,
Rot inwardly, and foul contagion spread,
Besides what the grim wolf with privy paw[1]
Daily devours apace, and nothing said;
But that two-handed engine[2] at the door             130
Stands ready to smite once, and smite no more."
    Return, Alpheus,[3] the dread voice is past,
That shrunk thy streams; return, Sicilian Muse,
And call the vales, and bid them hither cast
Their bells and flowrets of a thousand hues.          135
Ye valleys low, where the mild whispers use,[4]

---

8. According to Vergil, the greatest of the Nereids (sea nymphs).
9. God of the River Cam, which flows through Cambridge.
1. The hyacinth, which was supposed to bear marks that meant "alas" because the flower was created by Phoebus from the blood of a youth he had killed accidentally.
2. St. Peter, a fisherman before he became a disciple. According to *Matthew* 16:19, Christ promised him "the keys of the kingdom of heaven"; he was traditionally regarded as the first head of the church, hence the bishop's miter in line 112.
3. The old plural of "enough."
4. According to *John* 10:1, "He that entereth not by the door into the sheepfold, but climbeth up some other way . . . is a thief and a robber."
5. A bishop's staff was shaped like a

sheephook to suggest his role as "pastor" (shepherd) of the flock of saints.
6. Does it matter to.
7. Have attained their purpose—but also, destroyed.
8. Desire.
9. Feeble.
1. The Roman Catholic Church.
2. Not identified. Guesses include the two-handed sword of the archangel Michael, the two houses of Parliament, and St. Peter's keys.
3. A river god who, according to Ovid, fell in love with Arethusa. She fled in the form of an underground stream and became a fountain in Sicily, but Alpheus dived under the sea and at last his waters mingled with hers. See above, line 85. "Sicilian Muse": the muse of Theocritus.
4. Frequent.

Of shades and wanton winds and gushing brooks,
On whose fresh lap the swart star[5] sparely looks,
Throw hither all your quaint enameled eyes,
That on the green turf suck the honeyed showers,                    140
And purple all the ground with vernal flowers.
Bring the rathe[6] primrose that forsaken dies,
The tufted crow-toe, and pale jessamine,
The white pink, and the pansy freaked[7] with jet,
The glowing violet,                                                 145
The musk-rose, and the well-attired woodbine,
With cowslips wan that hang the pensive head,
And every flower that sad embroidery wears.
Bid amaranthus[8] all his beauty shed,
And daffodillies fill their cups with tears,                        150
To strew the laureate hearse[9] where Lycid lies.
For so to interpose a little ease,
Let our frail thoughts dally with false surmise.
Ay me! Whilst thee the shores and sounding seas
Wash far away, where'er thy bones are hurled,                       155
Whether beyond the stormy Hebrides,[1]
Where thou perhaps under the whelming tide
Visit'st the bottom of the monstrous world;[2]
Or whether thou to our moist vows denied,
Sleep'st by the fable of Bellerus old,[3]                           160
Where the great vision of the guarded mount
Looks toward Namancos and Bayona's hold;
Look homeward, Angel, now, and melt with ruth.[4]
And, O ye dolphins,[5] waft the hapless youth.
    Weep no more, woeful shepherds, weep no more,                   165
For Lycidas your sorrow is not dead,
Sunk though he be beneath the wat'ry floor,
So sinks the day-star[6] in the ocean bed,
And yet anon repairs his drooping head,
And tricks[7] his beams, and with new-spangled ore                 170
Flames in the forehead of the morning sky:
So Lycidas sunk low, but mounted high,
Through the dear might of him that walked the waves,[8]
Where, other groves and other streams along,
With nectar pure his oozy locks he laves,                           175
And hears the unexpressive nuptial song,[9]
In the blest kingdoms meek of joy and love.
There entertain him all the saints above,
In solemn troops and sweet societies
That sing, and singing in their glory move,                         180

5. Sirius, the Dog Star, which supposedly withers plants in late summer.
6. Early.
7. Flecked.
8. A legendary flower that cannot fade.
9. Bier.
1. Islands off Scotland, the northern edge of the sea where King drowned.
2. World where monsters live.
3. A legendary giant, supposedly buried at Land's End in Cornwall. At the tip of Land's End is St. Michael's Mount (line 161), from which the archangel is pictured looking south across the Atlantic toward Spanish (Catholic) strongholds ("Namancos and Bayona," line 162).
4. Pity.
5. According to Roman legend, dolphins brought the body of a drowned youth, Melicertes, to land, where a temple was erected to him as the protector of sailors.
6. The sun.
7. Dresses.
8. Christ. See *Matthew* 14:25–26.
9. Sung at the "marriage of the Lamb," according to *Revelation* 19. "unexpressive": inexpressible.

And wipe the tears forever from his eyes.
Now, Lycidas, the shepherds weep no more;
Henceforth thou art the genius[1] of the shore,
In thy large recompense, and shalt be good
To all that wander in that perilous flood.                          185
    Thus sang the uncouth swain[2] to th' oaks and rills,
While the still morn went out with sandals gray;
He touched the tender stops of various quills,[3]
With eager thought warbling his Doric[4] lay.
And now the sun had stretched out all the hills,             190
And now was dropped into the western bay.
At last he rose, and twitched his mantle blue:
Tomorrow to fresh woods, and pastures new.

                                                                              1637

NICHOLAS BRETON

## The Plowman's Song

In the merry month of May,
In a morn by break of day,
Forth I walked by the wood side,
Whereas May was in his pride.
There I spied, all alone,                                                  5
Phyllida and Corydon.[1]
Much ado there was, God wot,[2]
He would love and she would not.
She said, never man was true;
He said, none was false to you.                                       10
He said, he had loved her long;
She said, love should have no wrong.
Corydon would kiss her then;
She said, maids must kiss no men
Till they did for good and all.                                        15
Then she made the shepherd call
All the heavens to witness truth,
Never loved a truer youth.
Thus, with many a pretty oath,
Yea and nay, and faith and troth,                             20
Such as silly[3] shepherds use
When they will not love abuse,
Love, which had been long deluded,
Was with kisses sweet concluded:
And Phyllida with garlands gay                                 25
Was made the Lady of the May.

                                                                              1591

1. Protecting deity.
2. Unlettered shepherd: i.e., Milton.
3. Reeds in the shepherd's pipes.
4. The Greek dialect of Theocritus, Bion, and Moschus, the first writers of pastoral.

1. Traditional pastoral names for a shepherdess and shepherd.
2. Knows.
3. Simple, unsophisticated, innocent.

ROBERT LOWELL

# Skunk Hour

## (*For Elizabeth Bishop*)

Nautilus Island's hermit
heiress still lives through winter in her Spartan cottage;
her sheep still graze above the sea.
Her son's a bishop. Her farmer
is first selectman[1] in our village,                                      5
she's in her dotage.

Thirsting for
the hierarchic privacy
of Queen Victoria's century,
she buys up all                                                            10
the eyesores facing her shore,
and lets them fall.

The season's ill—
we've lost our summer millionaire,
who seemed to leap from an L. L. Bean[2]                                   15
catalogue. His nine-knot yawl
was auctioned off to lobstermen.
A red fox stain covers Blue Hill.

And now our fairy
decorator brightens his shop for fall,                                     20
his fishnet's filled with orange cork,
orange, his cobbler's bench and awl,
there is no money in his work,
he'd rather marry.

One dark night,                                                            25
my Tudor Ford climbed the hill's skull,
I watched for love-cars. Lights turned down,
they lay together, hull to hull,
where the graveyard shelves on the town. . . .
My mind's not right.                                                       30

A car radio bleats,
"Love, O careless Love. . . ."[3] I hear
my ill-spirit sob in each blood cell,
as if my hand were at its throat. . . .
I myself am hell;                                                          35
nobody's here—

only skunks, that search
in the moonlight for a bite to eat.
They march on their soles up Main Street:

1. An elected New England town official.     3. A popular song.
2. Famous old Maine sporting goods firm.

white stripes, moonstruck eyes' red fire                                          40
under the chalk-dry and spar spire
of the Trinitarian Church.

I stand on top
of our back steps and breathe the rich air—
a mother skunk with her column of kittens swills the garbage pail.    45
She jabs her wedge head in a cup
of sour cream, drops her ostrich tail,
and will not scare.

                                                                      1959

ETHERIDGE KNIGHT

## Hard Rock Returns to Prison from the Hospital for the Criminal Insane

Hard Rock was "known not to take no shit
From nobody," and he had the scars to prove it:
Split purple lips, lumped ears, welts above
His yellow eyes, and one long scar that cut
Across his temple and plowed through a thick                          5
Canopy of kinky hair.

The WORD was that Hard Rock wasn't a mean nigger
Anymore, that the doctors had bored a hole in his head,
Cut out part of his brain, and shot electricity
Through the rest. When they brought Hard Rock back,                   10
Handcuffed and chained, he was turned loose,
Like a freshly gelded stallion, to try his new status.
And we all waited and watched, like indians at a corral,
To see if the WORD was true.

As we waited we wrapped ourselves in the cloak                        15
Of his exploits: "Man, the last time, it took eight
Screws[1] to put him in the Hole." "Yeah, remember when he
Smacked the captain with his dinner tray?" "He set
The record for time in the Hole—67 straight days!"
"Ol Hard Rock! man, that's one crazy nigger."                         20
And then the jewel of a myth that Hard Rock had once bit
A screw on the thumb and poisoned him with syphilitic spit.

The testing came, to see if Hard Rock was really tame.
A hillbilly called him a black son of a bitch
And didn't lose his teeth, a screw who knew Hard Rock                 25
From before shook him down and barked in his face.
And Hard Rock did *nothing*. Just grinned and looked silly,
His eyes empty like knot holes in a fence.

And even after we discovered that it took Hard Rock
Exactly 3 minutes to tell you his first name,                         30

---

1. Guards. "Hole": solitary confinement.

We told ourselves that he had just wised up,
Was being cool; but we could not fool ourselves for long,
And we turned away, our eyes on the ground. Crushed.
He had been our Destroyer, the doer of things
We dreamed of doing but could not bring ourselves to do,                   35
The fears of years, like a biting whip,
Had cut grooves too deeply across our backs.

1968

GEORGE HERBERT

## The Windows[1]

Lord, how can man preach Thy eternal word?
        He is a brittle, crazy[2] glass:
Yet in Thy temple Thou dost him afford
        This glorious and transcendent place,
        To be a window, through Thy grace.                                 5

But when Thou dost anneal[3] in glass Thy story,
        Making Thy life to shine within
The holy Preachers; then the light and glory
        More rev'rend grows, and more doth win:
        Which else shows wat'rish, bleak, and thin.                        10

Doctrine and life, colors and light, in one
        When they combine and mingle, bring
A strong regard and awe: but speech alone
        Doth vanish like a flaring[4] thing,
        And in the ear, not conscience, ring.                             15

1633

WALLACE STEVENS

## The World as Meditation

J'ai passé trop de temps à travailler mon violon, à voyager. Mais l'exercice essentiel
du compositeur—la méditation—rien ne l'a jamais suspendu en moi . . . Je vis un
rêve permanent, qui ne s'arrête ni nuit ni jour.
                                                        GEORGES ENESCO[1]

Is it Ulysses that approaches from the east,[2]
The interminable adventurer? The trees are mended.
That winter is washed away. Someone is moving

On the horizon and lifting himself up above it.
A form of fire approaches the cretonnes of Penelope,                       5
Whose mere savage presence awakens the world in which she dwells.

1. One of the lyrics from *The Temple*, a
book of poems meditating on parts of the
church, holy days, and aspects of Christian
faith and practice.
    2. Full of cracks.
    3. Strengthen glass by heating.
    4. Unsteadily burning.
    1. Rumanian violinist, conductor, and
composer (1881–1955): "I have spent too

much time working at my violin and traveling. But the essential exercise of the composer—meditation—nothing has ever kept
me from that. I live a permanent dream
which does not stop, night or day."
    2. During Ulysses' absence to fight the
Trojan War, Penelope remained at home
for twenty years, besieged by suitors.

She has composed, so long, a self with which to welcome him,
Companion to his self for her, which she imagined,
Two in a deep-founded sheltering, friend and dear friend.

The trees had been mended, as an essential exercise                    10
In an inhuman meditation, larger than her own.
No winds like dogs watched over her at night.

She wanted nothing he could not bring her by coming alone.
She wanted no fetchings. His arms would be her necklace
And her belt, the final fortune of their desire.                       15

But was it Ulysses? Or was it only the warmth of the sun
On her pillow? The thought kept beating in her like her heart.
The two kept beating together. It was only day.

It was Ulysses and it was not. Yet they had met,
Friend and dear friend and a planet's encouragement.                   20
The barbarous strength within her would never fail.

She would talk a little to herself as she combed her hair,
Repeating his name with its patient syllables,
Never forgetting him that kept coming constantly so near.

1954

EDMUND  WALLER

# On St. James's Park

### As Lately Improved by His Majesty [1]

Of the first Paradise there's nothing found;
Plants set by Heaven are vanished, and the ground;
Yet the description lasts; who knows the fate
Of lines that shall this paradise relate?
    Instead of rivers rolling by the side                              5
Of Eden's garden, here flows in the tide;[2]
The sea, which always served his empire, now
Pays tribute to our Prince's pleasure too.
Of famous cities we the founders know;
But rivers, old as seas, to which they go,                             10
Are nature's bounty; 'tis of more renown
To make a river, than to build a town.
    For future shade, young trees upon the banks
Of the new stream appear in even ranks;
The voice of Orpheus, or Amphion's hand,[3]                            15
In better order could not make them stand;
May they increase as fast, and spread their boughs,
As the high fame of their great owner grows!

1. Charles II, who became king of England in 1660 when the Monarchy was restored. St. James's Park was adjacent to his palace, Whitehall (line 87).
2. One of the improvements was the introduction of a stream diverted from the tidal River Thames.

3. Musicians of fabulous power, according to Greek legend. The poet Orpheus sang so beautifully that even inanimate objects responded. Amphion built Thebes with his lute, by charming stones into appropriate places in the houses and walls.

May he live long enough to see them all
Dark shadows cast, and as his palace tall!                    20
Methinks I see the love that shall be made,
The lovers walking in that amorous shade;
The gallants dancing by the river's side;
They bathe in summer, and in winter slide.
Methinks I hear the music in the boats,                       25
And the loud echo which returns the notes;
While overhead a flock of new-sprung[4] fowl
Hangs in the air, and does the sun control,
Darkening the sky; they hover o'er, and shroud
The wanton[5] sailors with a feathered cloud.                 30
Beneath, a shoal of silver fishes glides,
And plays about the gilded barges' sides;
The ladies, angling in the crystal lake,
Feast on the waters with the prey they take;
At once victorious with their lines, and eyes,                35
They make the fishes, and the men, their prize.
A thousand Cupids on the billows ride,
And sea-nymphs enter with the swelling tide;
From Thetis[6] sent as spies, to make report,
And tell the wonders of her sovereign's court.                40
All that can, living, feed the greedy eye,
Or dead, the palate, here you may descry;
The choicest things that furnished Noah's ark,
Or Peter's sheet,[7] inhabiting this park;
All with a border of rich fruit-trees crowned,               45
Whose loaded branches hide the lofty mound.
Such various ways the spacious alleys lead,
My doubtful Muse knows not what path to tread.
Yonder, the harvest of cold months laid up,
Gives a fresh coolness to the royal cup;                      50
There ice, like crystal firm, and never lost,
Tempers hot July with December's frost;
Winter's dark prison, whence he cannot fly,
Though the warm spring, his enemy, draws nigh.
Strange! that extremes should thus preserve the snow,         55
High on the Alps, or in deep caves below.
    Here, a well-polished Mall gives us the joy
To see our Prince his matchless force employ;
His manly posture, and his graceful mien,
Vigor and youth, in all his motions seen;                     60
His shape so lovely, and his limbs so strong,
Confirm our hopes we shall obey him long.
No sooner has he touched the flying ball,[8]
But 'tis already more than half the Mall;
And such a fury from his arm has got,                         65
As from a smoking culverin[9] 'twere shot.

---

4. Newly risen from cover.
5. Sportive.
6. In Greek tradition, chief of the Nereids (sea nymphs).
7. According to *Luke* 5:1–11, Christ miraculously filled the nets of Simon the fisherman (later St. Peter) so that his boat nearly sank. "sheet": section of the boat.
8. In the game of pell-mell, a favorite sport of the king. A ball is hit repeatedly with a mallet until it goes through a distant arch; the person having fewest strokes wins.
9. Cannon.

Near this my Muse, what most delights her, sees
A living gallery of aged trees;
Bold sons of earth, that thrust their arms so high,
As if once more they would invade the sky.[1]                    70
In such green palaces the first kings reigned,
Slept in their shades, and angels entertained;
With such old counselors they did advise,
And, by frequenting sacred groves, grew wise.
Free from the impediments of light and noise,                   75
Man, thus retired, his nobler thoughts employs.
Here Charles contrives the ordering of his states,
Here he resolves his neighboring princes' fates;
What nation shall have peace, where war be made,
Determined is in this oraculous shade;                          80
The world, from India to the frozen north,
Concerned in what this solitude brings forth.
His fancy, objects from his view receives;
The prospect, thought and contemplation gives.
That seat of empire here salutes his eye,                       85
To which three kingdoms[2] do themselves apply;
The structure by a prelate[3] raised, Whitehall,
Built with the fortune of Rome's capitol;
Both, disproportioned to the present state
Of their proud founders, were approved by Fate.                 90
From hence he does that antique pile behold,
Where royal heads receive the sacred gold;
It gives them crowns, and does their ashes keep;
There made like gods, like mortals there they sleep;
Making the circle of their reign complete,                      95
Those suns of empire! where they rise, they set.
When others fell, this, standing, did presage
The crown should triumph over popular rage;
Hard by that house, where all our ills were shaped,
The auspicious temple stood, and yet escaped.                   100
So snow on Ætna does unmelted lie,
Whence rolling flames and scattered cinders fly;
The distant country in the ruin shares;
What falls from heaven the burning mountain spares.
Next, that capacious hall he sees, the room                     105
Where the whole nation does for justice come;
Under whose large roof flourishes the gown,
And judges grave, on high tribunals, frown.
Here, like the people's pastor he does go,
His flock subjected to his view below;[4]                       110
On which reflecting in his mighty mind,
No private passion does indulgence find;

1. The Titans, giant children of Heaven and Earth, made war on Heaven, according to early Greek mythology. The following lines draw on the tradition that the Druids of ancient Britain held their rites in sacred oak groves. The emphasis on the ancient significance of trees to kings and counselors probably derives from a famous episode in 1651. Fleeing from the Parliamentary forces after the battle of Worcester, Charles hid in an oak tree, thus surviving to reestablish the Monarchy.
2. England, Ireland, and Scotland.
3. Cardinal Wolsey. Whitehall was built in the 13th century and was the residence of the Archbishop of Canterbury until Henry VIII ousted Wolsey as chief minister, broke with Rome, and confiscated the structure for the Crown.
4. A medal struck for the Coronation of Charles II pictured the king as a shepherd tending his sheep.

The pleasures of his youth[5] suspended are,
And made a sacrifice to public care.
Here, free from court compliances, he walks,                    115
And with himself, his best adviser, talks;
How peaceful olive may his temples shade,
For mending laws, and for restoring trade;
Or, how his brows may be with laurel charged,
For nations conquered, and our bounds enlarged.[6]              120
Of ancient prudence here he ruminates,
Of rising kingdoms, and of falling states;
What ruling arts gave great Augustus[7] fame,
And how Alcides[8] purchased such a name.
His eyes, upon his native palace bent,                          125
Close by, suggest a greater argument.[9]
His thoughts rise higher, when he does reflect
On what the world may from that star expect
Which at his birth appeared, to let us see
Day, for his sake, could with the night agree;[10]             130
A prince, on whom such different lights did smile,
Born the divided world to reconcile!
Whatever Heaven, or high extracted blood
Could promise, or foretell, he will make good;
Reform these nations, and improve them more,                    135
Than this fair park, from what it was before.

                                                              1661

PHILIP FRENEAU

# The Deserted Farm-House

This antique dome[1] the insatiate tooth of time
  Now level with the dust has almost laid;
Yet ere 'tis gone, I seize my humble theme
  From these low ruins, that his years have made.

Behold the unsocial hearth—where once the fires                 5
  Blazed high, and soothed the storm-stayed traveler's woes;
See! the weak roof, that abler props requires,
  Admits the winds, and swift descending snows.

Here, to forget the labors of the day,
  No more the swains[2] at evening hours repair,              10
But wandering flocks assume the well known way
  To shun the rigors of the midnight air.

---

5. Well known amatory adventures, and not so totally suspended, as it turned out.
6. The olive wreath was originally presented to the victor in the Olympic games and the laurel wreath in the Pythian games. Later the wreath took on political significance and was associated with military victories.
7. The first emperor of Rome, whose reign (31 B.C.–14 A.D.) was characterized by stability and literary accomplishment. The comparison to Augustus became commonplace in the early years of Charles II's reign.
8. Hercules, who, according to Greek tradition, won immortality by performing his famous twelve labors.
9. Meaning.
10. When Charles II was born, a bright star was said to have been seen over London at noon.
1. House.
2. Shepherds.

In yonder chamber, half to ruin gone,
    Once stood the ancient housewife's curtained[3] bed—
Timely the prudent matron has withdrawn,           15
    And each domestic comfort with her fled.

The trees, the flowers that her own hands had reared,
    The plants, the vines, that were so verdant seen—
The trees, the flowers, the vines have disappeared,
    And every plant has vanished from the green.      20

So sits in tears on wide Campania's plain
    Rome, once the mistress of a world enslaved;
That triumphed o'er the land, subdued the main,
    And Time himself, in her wild transports, braved.

So sits in tears on Palestina's shore          25
    The Hebrew town,[4] of splendor once divine—
Her kings, her lords, her triumphs are no more;
    Slain are her priests, and ruined every shrine.

Once, in the bounds of this deserted room,
    Perhaps some swain nocturnal courtship made,     30
Perhaps some Sherlock[5] mused amidst the gloom;
    Since Love and Death forever seek the shade.

Perhaps some miser, doomed to discontent,
    Here counted o'er the heaps acquired with pain;
He to the dust—his gold, on traffic sent,        35
    Shall ne'er disgrace these moldering walls again.

Nor shall the glow-worm fopling,[6] sunshine bred,
    Seek, at the evening hour this wonted dome—
Time has reduced the fabric to a shed,
    Scarce fit to be the wandering beggar's home.     40

And none but I its dismal case lament—
    None, none but I o'er its cold relics mourn,
Sent by the muse (the time perhaps misspent)
    To write dull stanzas on this dome forlorn.

ca. 1772

PERCY BYSSHE SHELLEY

# Mont Blanc[1]

### *Lines Written in the Vale of Chamouni*

I

The everlasting universe of things
Flows through the mind, and rolls its rapid waves,

---

3. With a curtain all around it.
4. Jerusalem.
5. Probably Paul Sherlock (1595–1646), a Jesuit controversialist who was reported to have injured his health by flagellation and the wearing of hair shirts.

6. Literally, a little dandy or coxcomb.
1. The highest peak in Europe, inaccessible at the summit. Its snows melt into the River Arve and the Chamonix valley in France, near the borders of Switzerland and Italy.

Now dark—now glittering—now reflecting gloom—
Now lending splendor, where from secret springs
The source of human thought its tribute brings                 5
Of waters—with a sound but half its own,
Such as a feeble brook will oft assume
In the wild woods, among the mountains lone,
Where waterfalls around it leap forever,
Where woods and winds contend, and a vast river              10
Over its rocks ceaselessly bursts and raves.


                              II
Thus thou, Ravine of Arve—dark, deep Ravine—
Thou many-colored, many-voicéd vale,
Over whose pines, and crags, and caverns sail
Fast cloud-shadows and sunbeams: awful scene,                15
Where Power in likeness of the Arve comes down
From the ice-gulfs that gird his secret throne,
Bursting through these dark mountains like the flame
Of lightning through the tempest; thou dost lie,
Thy giant brood of pines around thee clinging,               20
Children of elder time, in whose devotion
The chainless winds still come and ever came
To drink their odors, and their mighty swinging
To hear—an old and solemn harmony;
Thine earthly rainbows stretched across the sweep            25
Of the ethereal waterfall, whose veil
Robes some unsculptured image; the strange sleep
Which when the voices of the desert fail
Wraps all in its own deep eternity;
Thy caverns echoing to the Arve's commotion,                 30
A loud, lone sound no other sound can tame;
Thou art pervaded with that ceaseless motion,
Thou art the path of that unresting sound—
Dizzy Ravine! and when I gaze on thee
I seem as in a trance sublime and strange                    35
To muse on my own separate fantasy,
My own, my human mind, which passively
Now renders and receives fast influencings,
Holding an unremitting interchange
With the clear universe of things around;                    40
One legion of wild thoughts, whose wandering wings
Now float above thy darkness, and now rest
Where that or thou art no unbidden guest,
In the still cave of the witch Poesy,
Seeking among the shadows that pass by                       45
Ghosts of all things that are, some shade of thee,
Some phantom, some faint image; till the breast
From which they fled recalls them, thou art there!


                             III
Some say that gleams of a remoter world
Visit the soul in sleep, that death is slumber,              50
And that its shapes the busy thoughts outnumber
Of those who wake and live. I look on high;
Has some unknown omnipotence unfurled

The veil of life and death? or do I lie
In dream, and does the mightier world of sleep          55
Spread far around and inaccessibly
Its circles? For the very spirit fails,
Driven like a homeless cloud from steep to steep
That vanishes among the viewless[2] gales!
Far, far above, piercing the infinite sky,               60
Mont Blanc appears—still, snowy, and serene—
Its subject mountains their unearthly forms
Pile around it, ice and rock; broad vales between
Of frozen floods, unfathomable deeps,
Blue as the overhanging heaven, that spread            65
And wind among the accumulated steeps;
A desert peopled by the storms alone,
Save when the eagle brings some hunter's bone,
And the wolf tracks her there—how hideously
Its shapes are heaped around! rude, bare, and high,     70
Ghastly, and scarred, and riven. Is this the scene
Where the old Earthquake-demon taught her young
Ruin? Were these their toys? or did a sea
Of fire envelop once this silent snow?[3]
None can reply—all seems eternal now.                   75
The wilderness has a mysterious tongue
Which teaches awful doubt, or faith, so mild,
So solemn, so serene, that man may be,
But for such faith, with nature reconciled;
Thou hast a voice, great Mountain, to repeal            80
Large codes of fraud and woe; not understood
By all, but which the wise, and great, and good
Interpret, or make felt, or deeply feel.

                          IV
The fields, the lakes, the forests, and the streams,
Ocean, and all the living things that dwell             85
Within the daedal[4] earth; lightning, and rain,
Earthquake, and fiery flood, and hurricane,
The torpor of the year when feeble dreams
Visit the hidden buds, or dreamless sleep
Holds every future leaf and flower; the bound           90
With which from that detested trance they leap;
The works and ways of man, their death and birth,
And that of him and all that his may be;
All things that move and breathe with toil and sound
Are born and die; revolve, subside, and swell.          95
Power dwells apart in its tranquillity,
Remote, serene, and inaccessible:
And *this*, the naked countenance of earth,
On which I gaze, even these primeval mountains
Teach the adverting mind. The glaciers creep           100
Like snakes that watch their prey, from their far fountains,
Slow rolling on; there, many a precipice,

2. Invisible.
3. According to scientific theories of the time, the earth was originally round and smooth, and mountains resulted from floods, earthquakes, or fires bursting from the earth's center.
4. Varied.

Frost and the Sun in scorn of mortal power
Have piled: dome, pyramid, and pinnacle,
A city of death, distinct with many a tower          105
And wall impregnable of beaming ice.
Yet not a city, but a flood of ruin
Is there, that from the boundaries of the sky
Rolls its perpetual stream; vast pines are strewing
Its destined path, or in the mangled soil             110
Branchless and shattered stand; the rocks, drawn down
From yon remotest waste, have overthrown
The limits of the dead and living world,
Never to be reclaimed. The dwelling place
Of insects, beasts, and birds, becomes its spoil      115
Their food and their retreat for ever gone,
So much of life and joy is lost. The race
Of man flies far in dread; his work and dwelling
Vanish, like smoke before the tempest's stream,
And their place is not known. Below, vast caves       120
Shine in the rushing torrents' restless gleam,
Which from those secret chasms in tumult welling
Meet in the vale, and one majestic River,
The breath and blood of distant lands, forever
Rolls its loud waters to the ocean waves,             125
Breathes its swift vapors to the circling air.


                          v

Mont Blanc yet gleams on high—the power is there,
The still and solemn power of many sights,
And many sounds, and much of life and death.
In the calm darkness of the moonless nights,          130
In the lone glare of day, the snows descend
Upon that Mountain; none beholds them there,
Nor when the flakes burn in the sinking sun,
Or the star-beams dart through them—Winds contend
Silently there, and heap the snow with breath         135
Rapid and strong, but silently! Its home
The voiceless lightning in these solitudes
Keeps innocently, and like vapor broods
Over the snow. The secret Strength of things
Which governs thought, and to the infinite dome       140
Of Heaven is as a law, inhabits thee!
And what were thou, and earth, and stars, and sea,
If to the human mind's imaginings
Silence and solitude were vacancy?

                                    1817


CHARLES TOMLINSON

# At Barstow[1]

Nervy with neons, the main drag
was all there was. A placeless place.
A faint flavor of Mexico in the tacos

1. The first town west of the desert on the main highway into Southern California.

tasting of gasoline. Trucks refueled
before taking off through space. Someone lived                5
in the houses with their houseyards wired
like tiny Belsens.[2] The Götterdämmerung[3]
would be like this. No funeral pyres, no choirs
of lost trombones. An Untergand[4]
without a clang, without                                      10
a glimmer of gone glory
however dimmed. At the motel desk
was a photograph of Roy Rogers
signed. It was here
he made a stay. He did not                                    15
ride away on Trigger
through the high night, the tilted
Pleiades overhead, the polestar low, no
going off until
the eyes of beer-cans                                         20
had ceased to glint at him
and the desert darknesses
had quenched the neons. He was spent.
He was content. Down he lay.
The passing trucks patrolled his sleep,                       25
the shifted gears contrived
a muffled fugue against the fading of his day
and his dustless, undishonored stetson rode
beside the bed,
glowed in the pulsating, never-final twilight                 30
there, at that execrable conjunction
of gasoline and desert air.

1966

MARTIAL

## You've Told Me, Maro[1]

You've told me, Maro, whilst you live
You'd not a single penny give,
But that whene'er you chanced to die,
You'd leave a handsome legacy;
You must be mad beyond redress,                               5
If my next wish you cannot guess.

ca. 100

MARTIAL

## Fair, Rich, and Young[2]

Fair, rich, and young? How rare is her perfection,
Were it not mingled with one foul infection?
I mean, so proud a heart, so cursed a tongue,
As makes her seem, nor fair, nor rich, nor young.

ca. 80–85

2. Nazi death camps.
3. End of the world.
4. Destruction, ruin.

1. Translated from the Latin by F. Lewis.
2. Translated from the Latin by Sir John Harington.

MARTIAL

## Tomorrow You Will Live[3]

Tomorrow you will live, you always cry;
In what fair country does this morrow lie,
That 'tis so mighty long ere it arrive?
Beyond the Indies does this morrow live?
'Tis so far-fetched, this morrow, that I fear          5
'Twill be both very old and very dear.
"Tomorrow I will live," the fool does say;
Today itself's too late—the wise lived yesterday.

ca. 85–90

MARTIAL

## He, unto Whom Thou Art So Partial[4]

He, unto whom thou art so partial,
Oh, reader! is the well-known Martial,
The Epigrammatist: while living,
Give him the fame thou wouldst be giving;
So shall he hear, and feel, and know it—          5
Post-obits rarely reach a poet.

ca. 80–85

MARTIAL

## Non Amo Te

Non amo te, Sabidi, nec possum dicere quare;
Hoc tantum posso dicere, non amo te.

ca. 80–85

TOM BROWN

## I Do Not Love Thee, Dr. Fell[5]

I do not love thee, Dr. Fell,
The reason why I cannot tell;
But this I know, and know full well,
I do not love thee, Dr. Fell.

ca. 1680

3. Translated from the Latin by Abraham Cowley.
4. Translated from the Latin by George Gordon, Lord Byron.
5. A version of Martial's "Non Amo Te," above. According to tradition, Brown while a student at Oxford got into trouble and was taken to the dean, Dr. John Fell; Brown was expelled, but Dr. Fell decided to waive the expulsion if he could translate the expulsion if he could translate late, extempore, a Martial epigram: this was the result.

PALLADAS ( from the *Greek Anthology* )[6]

# This Life a Theater[7]

This life a theater we well may call,
  Where every actor must perform with art;
Or laugh it through and make a farce of all,
  Or learn to bear with grace his tragic part.

ca. 400

PALLADAS  (from the *Greek Anthology*)

# Naked I Came[8]

Naked I reached the world at birth;
Naked I pass beneath the earth:
Why toil I, then, in vain distress,
Seeing the end is nakedness?

ca. 400

MELEAGER  (from the *Greek Anthology*)

# I'll Twine White Violets[9]

I'll twine white violets and the myrtle green;
Narcissus will I twine and lilies sheen;
I'll twine sweet crocus and the hyacinth blue;
And last I twine the rose, love's token true:
That all may form a wreath of beauty, meet[1]
To deck my Heliodora's tresses sweet.

ca. 90 B.C.

MELEAGER  (from the *Greek Anthology*)

# Her Voice[2]

I swear it, by Love I swear it!

More sweet to me is Hêliodôra's voice
Than the holy harp of Lêto's golden Son.[3]

ca. 90 B.C.

MELEAGER  (from the *Greek Anthology*)

# That Morn which Saw Me Made a Bride[4]

That morn which saw me made a bride,
The evening witnessed that I died.

6. A collection of epigrams compiled from earlier anthologies by a Byzantine scholar, Cephalus, in the 10th century.
7. Translated from the Greek by Robert Bland.
8. Translated from the Greek by A. J. Butler.
9. Translated from the Greek by Goldwin Smith.
1. Appropriate.
2. Translated from the Greek by Dudley Fitts.
3. Apollo, in Greek mythology the god of music and poetry.
4. Translated from the Greek by Robert Herrick.

Those holy lights, wherewith they guide
Unto the bed the bashful bride,
Served but as tapers for to burn,                    5
And light my relics to their urn.
This epitaph which here you see,
Supplied the epithalamy.[5]

ca. 90 B.C.


ANONYMOUS  (from the *Greek Anthology*)

## Brief Autumnal[6]

Green grape, and you refused me.
Ripe grape, and you sent me packing.
Must you deny me a bite of your raisin?


ASCLEPIADES  (from the *Greek Anthology*)

## To His Mistress[7]

You deny me: and to what end?
There are no lovers, dear, in the under world,
No love but here: only the living know
The sweetness of Aphroditê[8]—
                          but below,
But in Acherôn,[9] careful virgin, dust and ashes
Will be our only lying down together.

ca. 290 B.C.


SAMUEL TAYLOR COLERIDGE

## What Is an Epigram?

What is an epigram? a dwarfish whole,
Its body brevity, and wit its soul.

                                    p. 1802


ANONYMOUS translation of a Latin distich

## [Epigrams]

Three things must epigrams, like bees, have all,
A sting, and honey, and a body small.

5. Epithalamium: marriage song.
6. Translated from the Greek by Dudley Fitts.
7. Translated from the Greek by Dudley Fitts.
8. Greek goddess of love.
9. Hades.

WILLIAM WALSH

## An Epigram

An epigram should be—if right—
Short, simple, pointed, keen, and bright,
   A lively little thing!
Like wasp, with taper body—bound
By lines—not many, neat and round,         5
   All ending in a sting.

ca. 1690

ROBERT HAYMAN

## To the Reader

Sermons and epigrams have a like end,
To improve, to reprove, and to amend.
Some pass without this use, 'cause they are witty;
And so do many sermons, more's the pity.

                                  1628

WILLIAM BLAKE

## Her Whole Life Is an Epigram

Her whole life is an epigram: smack, smooth & neatly penned,
Platted quite neat to catch applause, with a sliding noose at the end.
ca. 1793–1811

JOHN SHEFFIELD, DUKE OF BUCKINGHAMSHIRE

## Written over a Gate

Here lives a man, who, by relation,
Depends upon predestination;
For which the learnéd and the wise
His understanding much despise:
But I pronounce with loyal tongue         5
Him in the right, them in the wrong;
For how could such a wretch succeed,
But that, alas, it was decreed?

ca. 1680

BEN JONSON

## Epitaph on Elizabeth, L. H.

Wouldst thou hear what man can say
In a little? Reader, stay.
Underneath this stone doth lie
As much beauty as could die;
Which in life did harbor give         5
To more virtue than doth live.

> If at all she had a fault,
> Leave it buried in this vault.
> One name was Elizabeth;
> Th' other, let it sleep with death:          10
> Fitter, where it died, to tell,
> Than that it lived at all. Farewell.

1616

HIL'AIRE BELLOC

## The Statue

When we are dead, some hunting-boy will pass
And find a stone half-hidden in tall grass
And grey with age: but having seen that stone
(Which was your image), ride more slowly on.

1923

GEORGE GORDON, LORD BYRON

## An Epitaph for Castlereagh[1]

> Posterity will ne'er survey
>   A nobler grave than this;
> Here lie the bones of Castlereagh:
>   Stop, traveler, . . .

1820

WILLIAM STAFFORD

## The Epitaph Ending in And

In the last storm, when hawks
blast upward and a dove is
driven into the grass, its broken wings
a delicate design, the air between
wracked thin where it stretched before,          5
a clear spring bent close too often
(that Earth should ever have such wings
burnt on in blind color!), this will be
good as an epitaph:

Doves did not know where to fly, and          10

1966

ROBERT BURNS

## On James Grieve, Laird of Boghead, Tarbolton[2]

> Here lies Boghead amang the dead,
>   In hopes to get salvation;

1. Robert Stewart Londonderry, known by the courtesy title of Viscount Castlereagh (1769–1822), was secretary of war 1805–09 and foreign secretary 1812–22; he was identified with the English government's repressive policies between 1815 and 1819 and often attacked by liberal Romantics.
2. Burns described Grieve as "A sanctimonious rascal of the first water."

But if such as he, in Heav'n may be,
Then welcome, hail! damnation.

1784

JOHN GAY

## My Own Epitaph

Life is a jest; and all things show it.
I thought so once; but now I know it.

1720

J. V. CUNNINGHAM

## When I Shall Be Without Regret

When I shall be without regret
And shall mortality forget,
When I shall die who lived for this,
I shall not miss the things I miss.
And you who notice where I lie          5
Ask not my name. It is not I.

1947

J. V. CUNNINGHAM

## Here Lies My Wife

Here lies my wife. Eternal peace
Be to us both with her decease.

1959

X. J. KENNEDY

## Epitaph for a Postal Clerk

Here lies wrapped up tight in sod
Henry Harkins c/o God.
On the day of Resurrection
May be opened for inspection.

1961

WILLIAM BROWNE

## On the Death of Marie, Countess of Pembroke

Underneath this sable hearse
Lies the subject of all verse:
Sidney's sister, Pembroke's mother;
Death, ere thou has slain another,
Fair, and learned, and good as she,     5
Time shall throw a dart at thee.

Marble piles let no man raise
To her name for after days;
Some kind woman borne as she,
Reading this, like Niobe[3]
Shall turn marble and become
Both her mourner and her tomb.

1621

RICHARD CRASHAW

## An Epitaph upon a Young Married Couple, Dead and Buried Together

To these, whom death again did wed,
This grave's their second marriage-bed.
For though the hand of fate could force
'Twixt soul and body a divorce,
It could not sunder man and wife          5
'Cause they both livéd but one life.
Peace, good reader. Do not weep.
Peace, the lovers are asleep.
They, sweet turtles,[4] folded lie
In the last knot love could tie.          10
And though they lie as they were dead,
Their pillow stone, their sheets of lead,
(Pillow hard, and sheets not warm)
Love made the bed; they'll take no harm;
Let them sleep, let them sleep on.        15
Till this stormy night be gone,
Till th' eternal morrow dawn;
Then the curtains will be drawn
And they wake into a light,
Whose day shall never die in night.       20

1646

ALEXANDER POPE

## Three Epitaphs on John Hewet and Sarah Drew

I

EPITAPH ON JOHN HEWET AND SARAH DREW
IN THE CHURCHYARD AT STANTON HARCOURT

NEAR THIS PLACE LIE THE BODIES OF
JOHN HEWET AND SARAH DREW,
AN INDUSTRIOUS YOUNG MAN AND
VIRTUOUS MAIDEN OF THIS PARISH;
CONTRACTED IN MARRIAGE

3. In Greek fable, the mother of twelve children, all of whom died. She wept herself to death and was turned into a stone from which water ran.
4. Turtledoves.

WHO BEING WITH MANY OTHERS AT HARVEST
WORK, WERE BOTH IN AN INSTANT KILLED
BY LIGHTNING ON THE LAST DAY OF JULY
1718

Think not by rigorous judgment seized,
  A pair so faithful could expire;
Victims so pure Heav'n saw well pleased
And snatched them in celestial fire.

Live well and fear no sudden fate;                    5
  When God calls virtue to the grave,
Alike 'tis justice, soon or late,
  Mercy alike to kill or save.

Virtue unmoved can hear the call,
And face the flash that melts the ball.              10

II

When Eastern lovers feed the fun'ral fire,
On the same pile the faithful fair expire;
Here pitying Heav'n that virtue mutual found,
And blasted both, that it might neither wound.
Hearts so sincere th' Almighty saw well pleased,      5
Sent his own lightning, and the victims seized.

III

Here lie two poor lovers, who had the mishap
Though very chaste people, to die of a clap.

1718

ALEXANDER POPE

## Epigram from the French

Sir, I admit your gen'ral rule
That every poet is a fool.
But you yourself may serve to show it,
That every fool is not a poet.

1732

THEODORE ROETHKE

## Epigram: Pipling

Behold the critic, pitched like the *castrati*,[5]
Imperious youngling, though approaching forty;
He heaps few honors on a living head;
He loves himself, and the illustrious dead;
He pipes, he squeaks, he quivers through his nose—    5
Some cannot praise him: *I* am one of those.

p. 1955

5. Male singers castrated before puberty so that they could retain their high-pitched voices.

DOROTHY PARKER

# Comment

Oh, life is a glorious cycle of song,
A medley of extemporanea;
And love is a thing that can never go wrong;
And I am Marie of Rumania.

1926

J. V. CUNNINGHAM

# Epitaph for Someone or Other

Naked I came, naked I leave the scene,
And naked was my pastime in between.

1950

MATTHEW PRIOR

# A True Maid

No, no; for my virginity,
   When I lose that, says Rose, I'll die:
Behind the elms, last night, cried Dick,
   Rose, were you not extremely sick?

1718

THEODORE ROETHKE

# Epigram: The Mistake

He left his pants upon a chair:
She was a widow, so she said:
But he was apprehended, bare,
By one who rose up from the dead.

p. 1957

GEORGE GRANVILLE, LORD LANSDOWNE

# Cloe

Bright as the day, and, like the morning, fair,
Such Cloe is—and common as the air.

1732

WALTER DE LA MARE

# Slim Cunning Hands

Slim cunning hands at rest, and cozening eyes—
Under this stone one loved too wildly lies;
How false she was, no granite could declare;
   Nor all earth's flowers, how fair.

1950

ROBERT HERRICK

## Upon Julia's Voice

So smooth, so sweet, so silv'ry is thy voice,
As, could they hear, the damned would make no noise,
But listen to thee (walking in thy chamber)
Melting melodious words, to lutes of amber.[6]

1648

EZRA POUND

## The Bathtub

As a bathtub lined with white porcelain,
When the hot water gives out or goes tepid,
So is the slow cooling of our chivalrous passion,
O my much praised but-not-altogether-satisfactory lady.

p. 1913

WILLIAM BLAKE

## What Is It Men in Women Do Require?

What is it men in women do require?
The lineaments of Gratified Desire.
What is it women do in men require?
The lineaments of Gratified Desire.

ca. 1793–1811

HOWARD NEMEROV

## Epigram: Political Reflexion

loquitur[7] the sparrow in the zoo.

No bars are set too close, no mesh too fine
To keep me from the eagle and the lion,
Whom keepers feed that I may freely dine.
This goes to show that if you have the wit
To be small, common, cute, and live on shit,          5
Though the cage fret kings, you may make free with it.

1958

e. e. cummings

## a politician

a politician is an arse upon
which everyone has sat except a man

1944

6. Made of an alloy of gold and silver.     7. I.e., the sparrow is the speaker.

W. H. AUDEN

## Epitaph on a Tyrant

Perfection, of a kind, was what he was after,
And the poetry he invented was easy to understand;
He knew human folly like the back of his hand,
And was greatly interested in armies and fleets;
When he laughed, respectable senators burst with laughter,    5
And when he cried the little children died in the streets.

p. 1939

ANONYMOUS

## Epigram on the Year 1390–1

The ax was sharpe, the stokke was harde,
In the xiiii yere of Kyng Richarde.

1391

SIR JOHN HARINGTON

## Epigram: Of Treason

Treason doth never prosper, what's the reason?
For if it prosper, none dare call it treason.

1615

WALTER SAVAGE LANDOR

## The Georges

George the First was always reckoned
Vile, but viler George the Second;
And what mortal ever heard
Any good of George the Third?
When from earth the Fourth descended    5
(God be praised!) the Georges ended.

p. 1855

JOHN WILMOT, EARL OF ROCHESTER

## Impromptu on Charles II

God bless our good and gracious king,
   Whose promise none relies on,
Who never said a foolish thing,
   Nor ever did a wise one.

ca. 1670–80

PETER PINDAR

# Epigram

Midas, they say, possessed the art of old
Of turning whatsoe'er he touched to gold;
This modern statesmen can reverse with ease—
Touch *them* with gold, *they'll turn to what you please.*
ca. 1780

TIMOTHY CLINCH

# Politicians, 1972

From platforms old, and promising correction,
They ride electrons, hell-bent for election.
1972

J. V. CUNNINGHAM

# History of Ideas

God is love. Then by conversion
Love is God, and sex conversion.

1947

JOHN DONNE

# Antiquary

If in his study Hammon hath such care
T'hang all old strange things, let his wife beware.

1633

ISAAC BICKERSTAFFE

# An Expostulation

When late I attempted your pity to move,
What made you so deaf to my prayers?
Perhaps it was right to dissemble your love,
But—why did you kick me down stairs?
ca. 1765

WILLIAM WALSH

# Thraso

Thraso picks quarrels when he's drunk at night;
When sober in the morning dares not fight.
Thraso, to shun those ills that may ensue,
Drink not at night, or drink at morning too.
ca. 1690

HENRY ALDRICH

# Why I Drink

If on my theme I rightly think,
There are five reasons why I drink—
Good wine, a friend, because I'm dry,
Or lest I should be by and by,
Or any other reason why.

ca. 1690

MATTHEW PRIOR

# Epigram

Rise not till noon, if life be but a dream,
    As Greek and Roman poets have expressed:
Add good example to so grave a theme,
    For he who sleeps the longest lives the best.

ca. 1710–20

SAMUEL BUTLER

# Inventions

All the inventions that the world contains
Were not by reason first found out, nor brains;
But pass for theirs who had the luck to light
Upon them by mistake or oversight.

ca. 1670

COUNTEE CULLEN

# For a Lady I Know

She even thinks that up in heaven
Her class lies late and snores,
While poor black cherubs rise at seven
To do celestial chores.

1925

J. V. CUNNINGHAM

# All in Due Time

All in due time: love will emerge from hate,
And the due deference of truth from lies.
If not quite all things come to those who wait
They will not need them: in due time one dies.

1950

WALTER SAVAGE LANDOR

## Various the Roads of Life

Various the roads of life; in one
All terminate, one lonely way.
We go; and "Is he gone?"
Is all our best friends say.

1846

STEPHEN CRANE

## A Man Said to the Universe

A man said to the universe:
"Sir, I exist!"
"However," replied the universe,
"The fact has not created in me
A sense of obligation."

1899

EDMUND WALLER

## Long and Short Life

Circles are praised, not that abound
In largeness, but the exactly round:
So life we praise that does excel
Not in much time, but acting well.

1645

ROBERT FROST

## Boeotian

I love to toy with the Platonic notion
That wisdom need not be of Athens Attic,[8]
But well may be Laconic, even Boeotian.
At least I will not have it systematic.

1942

WALLACE STEVENS

## Adult Epigram

The romance of the precise is not the elision
Of the tired romance of imprecision.
It is the ever-never-changing same,
An appearance of Again, the diva-dame.

1947

---

8. Centered in Athens, the Attic culture was regarded as the superior one in Greece. The Laconian or Laconic culture (in the area around Sparta) was less sophisticated, and the Boeotians (from the area around Thebes) were regarded as extreme dullards.

FRANCIS QUARLES

# Be Sad, My Heart

Be sad, my heart, deep dangers wait thy mirth:
Thy soul's waylaid by sea, by hell, by earth:
Hell has her hounds; earth, snares; the sea, a shelf;
But, most of all, my heart, beware thyself.

1635

STEPHEN CRANE

# Tradition

Tradition, thou art for suckling children,
Thou art the enlivening milk for babes;
But no meat for men is in thee.
Then—
But, alas, we all are babes.

1895

FRANCES CORNFORD

# Parting in Wartime

How long ago Hector[9] took off his plume,
Not wanting that his little son should cry,
Then kissed his sad Andromache good-bye—
And now we three in Euston[1] waiting-room.

1948

A. R. AMMONS

# Hippie Hop

I have no program for
saving this world or scuttling
the next: I know no political,
sexual, racial cures: I make
analogies, my bucketful of                        5
flowers: I give flowers to people
of all policies, sexes, and races
including the vicious, the
uncertain, and the white.

1970

SONIA SANCHEZ

# Small Comment

the nature of the beast is the
man or to be more specific

9. The noblest chieftain in ancient Troy.    1. A London railway station.

the nature of the man is his
bestial nature or to
bring it to its elemental terms                5
the nature of nature is
the bestial survival of the
fittest the strongest the richest
or to really examine
the scene we cd say that               10
the nature of any beast is
bestial unnatural and natural
in its struggle for superiority
and survival but to really
be with it we will say that the man       15
is a natural beast bestial in
his lusts natural in his
bestiality and expanding
and growing on the national
scene to be the most               20
bestial and natural of
any beast. you dig?

                                              1969


RYŌTA

# Haiku[2]

Oh, the wide world's ways!
    Cherry blossoms left unwatched
        even for three days!

ca. 1760


ISSA

# Spring Rain

Rain on a spring day:
    to the grove is blown a letter
        someone threw away.

ca. 1800


TANIGUCHI BUSON

# As the Spring Rains Fall

As the spring rains fall,
    soaking in them, on the roof,
        is a child's rag ball.

ca. 1740

---

2. This poem and the following two were translated from the Japanese by Harold G. Henderson.

SAMUEL TAYLOR COLERIDGE

# Metrical Feet

### Lesson for a Boy

Trōchĕe trĭps frŏm lōng tŏ shŏrt;[1]
From long to long in solemn sort
Slōw Spōndēe stālks; strōng fōōt! yet ill able
Ĕvĕr tŏ cōme ŭp wĭth Dāctўl trĭsўllăblĕ.
Ĭāmbĭcs mārch frŏm shŏrt tŏ lōng—                                     5
Wĭth ă lēap ănd ă bōūnd thĕ swĭft Ānăpĕsts thrōng;
One syllable long, with one short at each side,
Ămphĭbrăchўs hāstes wĭth ă stātelў stride—
Fĭrst ănd lāst bēĭng lōng, mĭddlĕ shŏrt, Āmphĭmācer
Strĭkes hĭs thūndĕrĭng hōōfs lĭke ă prōūd hĭgh-brĕd Rācer.           10
If Derwent[2] be innocent, steady, and wise,
And delight in the things of earth, water, and skies;
Tender warmth at his heart, with these meters to show it,
With sound sense in his brains, may make Derwent a poet—
May crown him with fame, and must win him the love               15
Of his father on earth and his Father above.
　　　　　My dear, dear child!
Could you stand upon Skiddaw,[3] you would not from its whole ridge
See a man who so loves you as your fond s. T. COLERIDGE.
1806

CLEMENT MOORE

# A Visit from St. Nicholas

'Twas the night before Christmas, when all through the house
Not a creature was stirring, not even a mouse.
The stockings were hung by the chimney with care,
In hopes that ST. NICHOLAS soon would be there;
The children were nestled all snug in their beds,                 5
While visions of sugar-plums danced in their heads;
And mamma in her 'kerchief, and I in my cap,
Had just settled our brains for a long winter's nap,
When out on the lawn there arose such a clatter,
I sprang from the bed to see what was the matter.                10
Away to the window I flew like a flash,
Tore open the shutters and threw up the sash.
The moon on the breast of the new-fallen snow
Gave the luster of mid-day to objects below,
When, what to my wondering eyes should appear,                   15
But a miniature sleigh, and eight tiny reindeer,
With a little old driver, so lively and quick,
I knew in a moment it must be St. Nick.

1. The long and short marks over syllables are Coleridge's; the kinds of metrical feet named and exemplified here are defined in the glossary.
2. Written originally for Coleridge's son Hartley, the poem was later adapted for his younger son, Derwent.
3. A mountain in the lake country of northern England (where Coleridge lived in his early years), near the town of Derwent.

More rapid than eagles his coursers they came,
And he whistled, and shouted, and called them by name: 20
"Now, *Dasher!* now, *Dancer!* now, *Prancer* and *Vixen!*
On, *Comet!* on, *Cupid!* on, *Donder* and *Blitzen!*
To the top of the porch! to the top of the wall!
Now dash away! dash away! dash away all!"
As dry leaves that before the wild hurricane fly, 25
When they meet with an obstacle, mount to the sky,
So up to the house-top the coursers they flew,
With the sleigh full of toys, and St. Nicholas too.
And then, in a twinkling, I heard on the roof
The prancing and pawing of each little hoof. 30
As I drew in my head, and was turning around,
Down the chimney St. Nicholas came with a bound.
He was dressed all in fur, from his head to his foot,
And his clothes were all tarnished with ashes and soot;
A bundle of toys he had flung on his back, 35
And he looked like a peddler just opening his pack.
His eyes—how they twinkled! his dimples how merry!
His cheeks were like roses, his nose like a cherry!
His droll little mouth was drawn up like a bow,
And the beard of his chin was as white as the snow; 40
The stump of a pipe he held tight in his teeth,
And the smoke it encircled his head like a wreath;
He had a broad face and a little round belly,
That shook, when he laughed, like a bowlful of jelly.
He was chubby and plump, a right jolly old elf, 45
And I laughed when I saw him, in spite of myself;
A wink of his eye and a twist of his head,
Soon gave me to know I had nothing to dread.
He spoke not a word, but went straight to his work,
And filled all the stockings; then turned with a jerk, 50
And laying his finger aside of his nose
And giving a nod, up the chimney he rose.
He sprang to his sleigh, to his team gave a whistle,
And away they all flew like the down of a thistle,
But I heard him exclaim, ere he drove out of sight, 55
"*Happy Christmas to all, and to all a good-night.*"

1822

MATTHEW PRIOR

# The Secretary

*Written at The Hague, in the Year 1696[1]*

While with labor assid'ous due pleasure I mix,
And in one day atone for the business of six,
In a little Dutch-chaise on a Saturday night,
On my left hand my Horace, a nymph on my right.
No memoir[2] to compose, and no post-boy[3] to move, 5
That on Sunday may hinder the softness of love;

1. Prior was then secretary to the English ambassador at The Hague.
2. Memorandum.
3. Letter carrier.

For her, neither visits, nor parties of tea,
Nor the long-winded cant of a dull refugee.
This night and the next shall be hers, shall be mine,
To good or ill fortune the third we resign:                    10
Thus scorning the world, and superior to fate,
I drive on my car in processional state;
So with Phia through Athens Pisistratus rode,
Men thought her Minerva, and him a new God.[4]
But why should I stories of Athens rehearse,                   15
 Where people knew love, and were partial to verse,
Since none can with justice my pleasures oppose,
In Holland half-drownded in int'rest[5] and prose:
By Greece and past ages, what need I be tried,
When the Hague and the present are both on my side,            20
And is it enough, for the joys of the day,
To think what Anacreon,[6] or Sappho would say.
When good Vandergoes, and his provident vrough,[7]
As they gaze on my triumph, do freely allow,
That search all the province, you'll find no man there is      25
So blessed as the *Englishen Heer Secretaris*.

1696

ANONYMOUS

# Limericks

There once was a spinster of Ealing,
Endowed with such delicate feeling,
 That she thought an armchair
 Should not have its legs bare—
So she kept her eyes trained on the ceiling.

❀   ❀

I sat next to the Duchess at tea.
It was just as I thought it would be:
 Her rumblings abdominal
 Were simply phenomenal
And everyone thought it was me.

❀   ❀

A charming young woman named Pat
Would invite one to do this and that.
 When speaking of this
 She meant more than a kiss
So imagine her meaning of that.

4. According to Herodotus, Pisistratus (an Athenian tyrant) was returned to power by a hoax; the beautiful Phia, disguised as the goddess Athene (Minerva), publicly proclaimed her wish that he be restored.

5. Political influence.
6. An ancient Greek poet who, like Sappho (of ancient Lesbos), wrote love lyrics.
7. Wife. "Vandergoes": a common Dutch surname.

There was a young lady of Trent
Who said that she knew what it meant
      When men asked her to dine:
      Private room, lots of wine.
She knew—O she knew!—but she went.

∘ ∘

An ambitious gay boy of Khartoum
Took a Lesbian up to his room.
      But they argued all night
      About who had the right
To do what, and with which, and to whom.

∘ ∘

A staid schizophrenic named Struther,
When told of the death of his brother,
      Said: "Yes, I am sad;
      It makes me feel bad,
But then, I still have each other."

∘ ∘

There once was a pious young priest
Who lived almost wholly on yeast.
      He said, "It's so plain
      We must all rise again
That I'd like to get started at least."

∘ ∘

There once was a bright young physician
Who was known for his vast erudition;
      He felt it a crime
      To waste any time
So he read while engaged in coition.

JONATHAN SWIFT

## Clever Tom Clinch Going to Be Hanged

As clever Tom Clinch, while the rabble was bawling,
Rode stately through Holborn,[1] to die in his calling;
He stopped at the George[2] for a bottle of sack,
And promised to pay for it when he'd come back.
His waistcoat and stockings, and breeches were white,      5
His cap had a new cherry ribbon to tie 't.
The maids to the doors and the balconies ran,
And said, lack-a-day! he's a proper young man.
But, as from the windows the ladies he spied,
Like a beau in the box,[3] he bowed low on each side;      10
And when his last speech the loud hawkers did cry,[4]
He swore from his cart, it was all a damned lie.

1. The road to the gallows at Tyburn from Newgate prison and the Tower of London.
2. A tavern.
3. At a theater.
4. Offer for sale. "Last Speeches" and "Dying Words" of condemned criminals were written in advance by hack writers and sold during public hangings.

The hangman for pardon fell down on his knee;
Tom gave him a kick in the guts for his fee.
Then said, I must speak to the people a little,                    15
But I'll see you all damned before I will *whittle*.[5]
My honest friend Wild,[6] may he long hold his place,
He lengthened my life with a whole year of grace.
Take courage, dear comrades, and be not afraid,
Nor slip this occasion to follow your trade.[7]                    20
My conscience is clear, and my spirits are calm,
And thus I go off without Pray'r-Book or Psalm.
Then follow the practice of clever Tom Clinch,
Who hung like a hero, and never would flinch.

ca. 1722

GEORGE GORDON, LORD BYRON

## The Destruction of Sennacherib[1]

The Assyrian came down like the wolf on the fold,
And his cohorts were gleaming in purple and gold;
And the sheen of their spears was like stars on the sea,
When the blue wave rolls nightly on deep Galilee.

Like the leaves of the forest when Summer is green,            5
That host with their banners at sunset were seen:
Like the leaves of the forest when Autumn hath blown,
That host on the morrow lay withered and strown.

For the Angel of Death spread his wings on the blast,
And breathed in the face of the foe as he passed;             10
And the eyes of the sleepers waxed deadly and chill,
And their hearts but once heaved, and for ever grew still!

And there lay the steed with his nostril all wide,
But through it there rolled not the breath of his pride;
And the foam of his gasping lay white on the turf,           15
And cold as the spray of the rock-beating surf.

And there lay the rider distorted and pale,
With the dew on his brow, and the rust on his mail:
And the tents were all silent, the banners alone,
The lances unlifted, the trumpet unblown.                    20

And the widows of Ashur are loud in their wail,
And the idols are broke in the temple of Baal;[2]
And the might of the Gentile, unsmote by the sword,
Hath melted like snow in the glance of the Lord!

1815

5. Confess at the gallows.
6. Jonathan Wild, who used a minor city position to run a theft ring and control almost totally the London underworld in the early 1720s.
7. Pickpockets especially took advantage of the jostling crowds and careless merriment at executions.
1. King of Assyria who besieged Jerusalem during Hezekiah's reign as king of

Judah. According to *II Kings* 18 and 19, Hezekiah paid ransom but refused to give up faith in his God, who promised that Jerusalem would not be taken. Hezekiah's loyalty was finally rewarded when "the angel of the lord went out, and smote in the camp of the Assyrians an hundred four score and five thousand." (*II Kings* 19:35)
2. God of the Assyrians.

WILLIAM BLAKE

# Ah Sunflower

Ah Sunflower! weary of time,
Who countest the steps of the Sun,
Seeking after that sweet golden clime
Where the traveler's journey is done,

Where the Youth pined away with desire,          5
And the pale Virgin shrouded in snow,
Arise from their graves and aspire,
Where my Sunflower wishes to go.

1794

ALEXANDER POPE

# [Sound and Sense][1]

But most by numbers[2] judge a poet's song,          337
And smooth or rough, with them, is right or wrong;
In the bright muse though thousand charms conspire,[3]
Her voice is all these tuneful fools admire,          340
Who haunt Parnassus[4] but to please their ear,
Not mend their minds; as some to church repair,
Not for the doctrine, but the music there.
These, equal syllables[5] alone require,
Though oft the ear the open vowels tire,          345
While expletives[6] their feeble aid do join,
And ten low words oft creep in one dull line,
While they ring round the same unvaried chimes,
With sure returns of still expected rhymes.
Wheree'er you find "the cooling western breeze,"          350
In the next line, it "whispers through the trees";
If crystal streams "with pleasing murmurs creep,"
The reader's threatened (not in vain) with "sleep."
Then, at the last and only couplet fraught
With some unmeaning thing they call a thought,          355
A needless Alexandrine[7] ends the song,
That, like a wounded snake, drags its slow length along.
Leave such to tune their own dull rhymes, and know
What's roundly smooth, or languishingly slow;
And praise the easy vigor of a line,          360
Where Denham's strength and Waller's[8] sweetness join.
True ease in writing comes from art, not chance,
As those move easiest who have learned to dance.

1. From *An Essay on Criticism*, Pope's poem on the art of poetry and the problems of literary criticism. The passage excerpted here follows a discussion of several common weaknesses of critics: failure to regard an author's intention, for example, or over-emphasis on clever metaphors and ornate style.
2. Meter, rhythm, sound.
3. Unite.
4. A mountain in Greece, traditionally associated with the muses and considered the seat of poetry and music.
5. Regular accents.
6. Filler words, such as "do."
7. A six-foot line, sometimes used in pentameter poems to vary the pace mechanically. Line 357 is an alexandrine.
8. Sir John Denham and Edmund Waller, 17th-century poets credited with perfecting the heroic couplet.

'Tis not enough no harshness gives offense,
The sound must seem an echo to the sense:
Soft is the strain when Zephyr[9] gently blows,
And the smooth stream in smoother numbers flows;
But when loud surges lash the sounding shore,
The hoarse, rough verse should like the torrent roar.
When Ajax[1] strives, some rock's vast weight to throw,          370
The line too labors, and the words move slow;
Not so, when swift Camilla[2] scours the plain,
Flies o'er th' unbending corn, and skims along the main.
Hear how Timotheus'[3] varied lays surprise,
And bid alternate passions fall and rise!                        375
While, at each change, the son of Libyan Jove[4]
Now burns with glory, and then melts with love;
Now his fierce eyes with sparkling fury glow,
Now sighs steal out, and tears begin to flow:
Persians and Greeks like turns of nature[5] found,               380
And the world's victor stood subdued by sound!
The pow'r of music all our hearts allow,
And what Timotheus was, is DRYDEN now.

                                                                 1711


WILLIAM SHAKESPEARE

## Like as the Waves

Like as the waves make towards the pebbled shore,
So do our minutes hasten to their end,
Each changing place with that which goes before,
In sequent[1] toil all forwards do contend.[2]
Nativity,[3] once in the main[4] of light,                       5
Crawls to maturity, wherewith being crowned,
Crooked[5] eclipses 'gainst his glory fight,
And Time that gave doth now his gift confound.[6]
Time doth transfix[7] the flourish set on youth
And delves the parallels[8] in beauty's brow,                    10
Feeds on the rarities of nature's truth,
And nothing stands but for his scythe to mow.
And yet to times in hope[9] my verse shall stand,
Praising thy worth, despite his cruel hand.

                                                                 1609

---

9. The west wind.
1. A Greek hero of the Trojan War, noted for his strength.
2. A woman warrior in *The Aeneid*.
3. The court-musician of Alexander the Great, celebrated in a famous poem by Dryden (see line 383) for the power of his music over Alexander's emotions.
4. In Greek tradition, the chief god of any people was often given the name Zeus (Jove), and the chief god of Libya (the Greek name for all of Africa) was called

Zeus Ammon. Alexander visited his oracle and was proclaimed son of the god.
5. Similar alternations of emotion.
1. Successive.
2. Struggle.
3. New-born life.
4. High seas.
5. Perverse.
6. Bring to nothing.
7. Pierce.
8. Lines, wrinkles.
9. In the future.

EDMUND SPENSER

# One Day I Wrote Her Name upon the Strand

One day I wrote her name upon the strand,
But came the waves and washéd it away.
Again I wrote it with a second hand,
But came the tide, and made my pains his prey.
Vain man, said she, that dost in vain assay          5
A mortal thing so to immortalize,
For I myself shall, like to this, decay,
And eke¹ my name be wipéd out likewise.
Not so, quoth I; let baser things devise²
To die in dust, but you shall live by fame:          10
My verse your virtues rare shall eternize,
And in the heavens write your glorious name.
Where, whenas death shall all the world subdue,
Our love shall live, and later life renew.

1595

ROBERT BURNS

# Afton Water

Flow gently, sweet Afton,¹ among thy green braes,²
Flow gently, I'll sing thee a song in thy praise;
My Mary's asleep by thy murmuring stream,
Flow gently, sweet Afton, disturb not her dream.

Thou stock dove whose echo resounds through the glen,    5
Ye wild whistling blackbirds in yon thorny den,
Thou green-crested lapwing thy screaming forbear,
I charge you disturb not my slumbering fair.

How lofty, sweet Afton, thy neighboring hills,
Far marked with the courses of clear, winding rills;    10
Th re daily I wander as noon rises high,
My flocks and my Mary's sweet cot³ in my eye.

How pleasant thy banks and green valleys below,
Where wild in the woodlands the primroses blow;
There oft as mild evening weeps over the lea,          15
The sweet-scented birk⁴ shades my Mary and me.

Thy crystal stream, Afton, how lovely it glides,
And winds by the cot where my Mary resides;
How wanton thy waters her snowy feet lave,
As gathering sweet flowerets she stems thy clear wave.   20

1. Moreover.                    2. Hillsides.
2. Prepare.                     3. Cottage.
1. A small river in Ayrshire, Scotland.    4. Birch.

Flow gently, sweet Afton, among thy green braes,
Flow gently, sweet river, the theme of my lays;
My Mary's asleep by thy murmuring stream,
Flow gently, sweet Afton, disturb not her dream.

1792

SIR JOHN DENHAM

# [The Thames]¹

My eye, descending from the hill, surveys
Where Thames amongst the wanton² valleys strays.
Thames, the most loved of all the ocean's sons
By his old sire, to his embraces runs,
Hasting to pay his tribute to the sea
Like mortal life to meet eternity.
Though with those streams he no resemblance hold,          165
Whose foam is amber and their gravel gold;
His genuine, and less guilty wealth t'explore,
Search not his bottom, but survey his shore,
O'er which he kindly spreads his spacious wing,
And hatches plenty for th' ensuing spring.                 170
Nor then destroys it with too fond a stay,
Like mothers which their infants overlay;³
Nor with a sudden and impetuous wave,
Like profuse kings, resumes⁴ the wealth he gave.
No unexpected inundations spoil                            175
The mower's hopes nor mock the plowman's toil;
But God-like his unwearied bounty flows,
First loves to do, then loves the good he does.
Nor are his blessings to his banks confined,
But free and common as the sea or wind;                    180
When he to boast, or to disperse his stores,
Full of the tributes of his grateful shores,
Visits the world, and in his flying towers⁵
Brings home to us, and makes both Indies ours;
Finds wealth where 'tis, bestows it where it wants,        185
Cities in deserts, woods in cities plants.
So that to us no thing, no place is strange,
While his fair bosom is the world's exchange.
O could I flow like thee, and make thy stream
My great example, as it is my theme!                       190
Though deep, yet clear, though gentle, yet not dull,
Strong without rage, without o'er-flowing full.

1655

1. From *Cooper's Hill*, a didactic-descriptive poem about a hill near London and about the poetical and religious scenes it had, over the years, surveyed.
2. Luxuriant.
3. Stifle.
4. Takes back.
5. Ships.

JAMES MERRILL

# Watching the Dance

1. BALANCHINE'S[1]

Poor savage, doubting that a river flows
But for the myriad eddies made
By unseen powers twirling on their toes,

Here in this darkness it would seem
You had already died, and were afraid.                    5
Be still. Observe the powers. Infer the stream.

2. DISCOTHÈQUE

Having survived entirely your own youth,
Last of your generation, purple gloom
Investing you, sit, Jonah,[2] beyond speech,

And let towards the brute volume VOOM whale mouth      10
VAM pounding viscera VAM VOOM
A teenage plankton luminously twitch.

                                                       1967


HART CRANE

# *from* The Bridge[1]

The nasal whine of power whips a new universe . . .        63
Where spouting pillars spoor the evening sky,
Under the looming stacks of the gigantic power house
Stars prick the eyes with sharp ammoniac proverbs,
New verities, new inklings in the velvet hummed
Of dynamos, where hearing's leash is strummed . . .
Power's script—wound, bobbin-bound, refined—
Is stropped to the slap of belts on booming spools, spurred   70
Into the bulging bouillon, harnessed jelly of the stars.
Towards what? The forked crash of split thunder parts
Our hearing momentwise; but fast in whirling armatures,
As bright as frogs' eyes, giggling in the girth
Of steely gizzards—axle-bound, confined                    75
In coiled precision, bunched in mutual glee
The bearings glint—O murmurless and shined
In oilrinsed circles of blind ecstasy!

                                                       1930

---

1. George Balanchine, Russian-born (1894) ballet choreographer and teacher.
2. According to *Jonah* 4, Jonah sat in gloom near Nineveh after its residents repented and God decided to spare the city from destruction.

1. From "Cape Hatteras," Section IV of *The Bridge,* Crane's epic about the history of America.

JOHN DRYDEN

# A Song for St. Cecilia's Day[1]

## I

From harmony, from heav'nly harmony
This universal frame began:
When Nature[2] underneath a heap
Of jarring atoms lay,
And could not heave her head,                                      5
The tuneful voice was heard from high:
"Arise, ye more than dead."
Then cold, and hot, and moist, and dry,
In order to their stations leap,
    And Music's pow'r obey.                       10
From harmony, from heav'nly harmony
This universal frame began:
From harmony to harmony
Through all the compass of the notes it ran,
The diapason closing full in man.[3]                              15

## II

What passion cannot Music raise and quell!
    When Jubal[4] struck the chorded shell,
    His list'ning brethren stood around,
    And, wond'ring, on their faces fell
    To worship that celestial sound.                   20
Less than a god they thought there could not dwell
    Within the hollow of that shell
    That spoke so sweetly and so well.
What passion cannot Music raise and quell!

## III

    The TRUMPET's loud clangor                      25
    Excites us to arms
    With shrill notes of anger,
    And mortal alarms.
    The double double double beat
    Of the thundering DRUM                             30
Cries: "Hark! the foes come;
Charge, charge, 'tis too late to retreat."

## IV

The soft complaining FLUTE
In dying notes discovers

1. St. Cecilia, a third-century Roman who became a Christian martyr and the patron saint of music, is said to be the inventor of the organ. In late 17th-century England her festival day (November 22) was elaborately celebrated with concerts, religious services, and the commissioning of original compositions like this ode, which was first set to music by Giovanni Baptiste Draghi and later by Handel.
2. The created world, ordered by the Divine Word, according to *Genesis* 1. According to Epicurean physics, atoms of the four elements (earth, fire, water, air [line 8]) were discordant and at war ("jarring," line 4), and Dryden follows traditional Judeo-Christian thought in describing the elements being put into place ("stations," line 9) by divine power. The tradition that the world moves according to harmonious musical principles—and that an unheard "music of the spheres" represents that harmony—goes back to Pythagoras, a sixth-century B.C. Greek philosopher and mathematician.
3. Total concord, which culminates in man, the highest earthly creation in the Chain of Being.
4. "The father of all such as handle the harp and organ." (*Genesis* 4:21)

The woes of hopeless lovers,      35
Whose dirge is whispered by the warbling LUTE.

### V
Sharp VIOLINS proclaim
Their jealous pangs, and desperation,
Fury, frantic indignation,
Depth of pains, and height of passion,      40
For the fair, disdainful dame.

### VI
But O! what art can teach,
What human voice can reach,
The sacred ORGAN's praise?
Notes inspiring holy love,      45
Notes that wing their heav'nly ways
To mend the choirs above.

### VII
Orpheus[5] could lead the savage race;
And trees unrooted left their place,
Sequacious of[6] the lyre.      50
But bright Cecilia raised the wonder higher:
When to her ORGAN vocal breath was given,
An angel heard, and straight appeared,
Mistaking earth for heaven.

GRAND CHORUS
*As from the power of sacred lays*      55
*   The spheres began to move,*
*And sung the great Creator's praise*
*   To all the blest above;*
*So, when the last and dreadful hour*
*This crumbling pageant[7] shall devour,*      60
*The* TRUMPET *shall be heard on high,*[8]
*The dead shall live, the living die,*
*And Music shall untune the sky.*

1687

A. B. SPELLMAN

# John Coltrane[1]

### *An Impartial Review*

may he have new life like the fall
fallen tree, wet moist rotten enough
to see shoots stalks branches & green
leaves (& may the roots) grow into his side.

5. Whose music was supposed to be so powerful that he could control even inanimate objects.
6. Made slavish by.
7. The world as stage.
8. According to *I Corinthians* 15:52, "the trumpet shall sound and the dead shall be raised incorruptible" on Judgment Day.
1. Controversial jazz musician (1926–67), whose tenor sax style finally came to be recognized as the most innovative in modern jazz.

around the back of the mind, in its closet
is a string, i think, a coil around things.
listen to *summertime*, think of spring, negroes
cats in the closet, anything that makes a rock

of your eye. imagine you steal. you are frightened
you want help. you are sorry you are born with ears    10

p. 1964

THOMAS HARDY

## During Wind and Rain

They sing their dearest songs—
He, she, all of them—yea,
Treble and tenor and bass,
   And one to play;
With the candles mooning each face. . . .    5
   Ah, no; the years O!
How the sick leaves reel down in throngs!

They clear the creeping moss—
Elders and juniors—aye,
Making the pathway neat    10
   And the garden gay;
And they build a shady seat. . . .
   Ah, no; the years, the years;
See, the white stormbirds wing across!

They are blithely breakfasting all—    15
Men and maidens—yea,
Under the summer tree,
   With a glimpse of the bay,
While pet fowl come to the knee. . . .
   Ah, no; the years O!    20
And the rotten rose is ripped from the wall.

They change to a high new house,
He, she, all of them—aye,
Clocks and carpets, and chairs
   On the lawn all day,    25
And brightest things that are theirs. . . .
   Ah, no; the years, the years;
Down their carved names the rain drop ploughs.

1917

JOHN DRYDEN

## To the Memory of Mr. Oldham[1]

Farewell, too little, and too lately known,
Whom I began to think and call my own;

1. John Oldham (1653–83), who like Dryden (see lines 3–6) wrote satiric poetry.

For sure our souls were near allied, and thine
Cast in the same poetic mold with mine.
One common note on either lyre did strike,                    5
And knaves and fools we both abhorred alike.
To the same goal did both our studies drive;
The last set out the soonest did arrive.
Thus Nisus fell upon the slippery place,
While his young friend performed and won the race.[2]        10
O early ripe! to thy abundant store
What could advancing age have added more?
It might (what nature never gives the young)
Have taught the numbers[3] of thy native tongue.
But satire needs not those, and wit will shine               15
Through the harsh cadence of a rugged line.[4]
A noble error, and but seldom made,
When poets are by too much force betrayed.
Thy generous fruits, though gathered ere their prime,
Still showed a quickness; and maturing time                  20
But mellows what we write to the dull sweets of rhyme.
Once more, hail and farewell; farewell, thou young,
But ah too short, Marcellus[5] of our tongue;
Thy brows with ivy, and with laurels bound;
But fate and gloomy night encompass thee around.             25

1684

ALFRED, LORD TENNYSON

# Break, Break, Break

Break, break, break,
   On thy cold gray stones, O Sea!
And I would that my tongue could utter
   The thoughts that arise in me.

O well for the fisherman's boy,                              5
   That he shouts with his sister at play!
O well for the sailor lad,
   That he sings in his boat on the bay!
And the stately ships go on
   To their haven under the hill;                      10
But O for the touch of a vanished hand,
   And the sound of a voice that is still!

Break, break, break,
   At the foot of thy crags, O Sea!
But the tender grace of a day that is dead                   15
   Will never come back to me.

ca. 1834

---

2. In Vergil's *Aeneid* (Book V), Nisus (who is leading the race) falls and then trips the second runner so that his friend Euryalus can win.
3. Rhythms.

4. In Dryden's time, R's were pronounced with a harsh, trilling sound.
5. The nephew of the Roman emperor Augustus; he died at 20, and Vergil celebrated him in *The Aeneid*, Book VI.

BEN JONSON

## Slow, Slow, Fresh Fount[1]

Slow, slow, fresh fount, keep time with my salt tears;
  Yet slower, yet, O faintly gentle springs!
List to the heavy part the music bears,
  Woe weeps out her division,[2] when she sings.
    Droop herbs, and flowers;                              5
    Fall grief in showers;
    Our beauties are not ours:
      O, I could still
(Like melting snow upon some craggy hill)
  Drop, drop, drop, drop,                                   10
Since nature's pride is now a withered daffodil.

                                                    1600


THOMAS NASHE

## Spring, the Sweet Spring

Spring, the sweet spring, is the year's pleasant king,
Then blooms each thing, then maids dance in a ring,
Cold doth not sting, the pretty birds do sing:
  Cuckoo, jug-jug, pu-we, to-witta-woo![3]

The palm and may make country houses gay,                  5
Lambs frisk and play, the shepherds pipe all day,
And we hear aye birds tune this merry lay:
  Cuckoo, jug-jug, pu-we, to-witta-woo!

The fields breathe sweet, the daisies kiss our feet,
Young lovers meet, old wives a-sunning sit,                10
In every street these tunes our ears do greet:
  Cuckoo, jug-jug, pu-we, to-witta-woo!
    Spring, the sweet spring!

                                                    1592


ANONYMOUS

## Sumer Is Icumen In

  Sumer is icumen in,
    Loudé sing cuccu!
  Groweth sed[1] and bloweth med
  And springth the wodé[2] nu.
    Sing cuccu!                                             5

---

1. A song from *Cynthia's Revels*, a satiric comedy. In the play, Echo sings the
song for Narcissus, who had seen his reflection in a fountain, become entranced by
it, and been transformed into a flower
(line 11).
2. Portion. "Division," in musical terminology, also means "variation on a
theme."
3. The calls of the cuckoo, nightingale,
lapwing, and owl, respectively.
1. Seed. "med": meadow.
2. Wood. "nu": now.

Ewé bleteth after lomb,
  Loweth after calvé cu;[3]
Bullock sterteth,[4] bucké verteth;
  Murie[5] sing cuccu!
    Cuccu, cuccu,                                        10
  Wel singes thu, cuccu,
  Ne swik[6] thu naver nu.

*Sing cuccu nu! Sing cuccu!*
*Sing cuccu! Sing cuccu nu!*

ca. 1225

DONALD JUSTICE

# Counting the Mad

This one was put in a jacket,
This one was sent home,
This one was given bread and meat
But would eat none,
And this one cried No No No No                          5
All day long.

This one looked at the window
As though it were a wall,
This one saw things that were not there,
This one things that were,                               10
And this one cried No No No No
All day long.

This one thought himself a bird,
This one a dog,
And this one thought himself a man,                      15
An ordinary man,
And cried and cried No No No No
All day long.

1960

BEN JONSON

# The Faery Beam upon You[1]

The Faery beam upon you,
The stars to-glister on you,
  A moon of light,
  In the noon of night,
Till the fire-drake[2] hath o'ergone you!                5

---

3. Cow.
4. Leaps. "verteth": farts.
5. Merrily.
6. Stop. "thu": thou; "naver": never.

1. A song from *The Gypsies Meta-morphosed*, a masque.
2. Firedragon: will-o'-the-wisp. "o'er-gone": overtaken.

The wheel of fortune guide you,
The boy with the bow[3] beside you;
    Run aye[4] in the way,
    Till the bird of day,
And the luckier lot betide you!                    10

                                                1621


ROBERT HERRICK

## The Night-Piece, to Julia[5]

Her eyes the glow-worm lend thee,
The shooting stars attend thee;
    And the elves also,
    Whose little eyes glow
Like the sparks of fire, befriend thee.            5

No will-o'-th'-wisp mislight thee;
Nor snake, or slow-worm bite thee:
    But on, on thy way,
    Not making a stay,
Since ghost there's none to affright thee.         10

Let not the dark thee cumber;
What though the moon does slumber:
    The stars of the night
    Will lend thee their light,
Like tapers clear without number.                  15

Then, Julia, let me woo thee,
Thus, thus to come unto me:
    And when I shall meet
    Thy silv'ry feet,
My soul I'll pour into thee.                       20

                                                1648


SIR THOMAS WYATT

## The Lover's Lute Cannot Be Blamed

### *Though It Sing of His Lady's Unkindness*

Blame not my lute, for he must sound
Of this or that as liketh[1] me;
For lack of wit the lute is bound
To give such tunes as pleaseth me.
Though my songs be somewhat strange,           5
And speak such words as touch thy change,
        Blame not my lute!

My lute, alas, doth not offend,
Though that perforce he must agree

---

3. Cupid.                          5. See Jonson's "The Faery Beam upon
4. Always.                         You," above.
                                    1. Pleases.

To sound such tunes as I intend,                         10
To sing to them that heareth me.
Then, though my songs be somewhat plain,
And toucheth some that use to feign,
     Blame not my lute!

My lute and strings may not deny                         15
But as I strike they must obey;
Break not them then so wrongfully,
But wreak thyself some other way.
And though the songs which I indite[2]
Do quit thy change with rightful spite,                  20
     Blame not my lute!

Spite asketh spite, and changing change,
And falséd faith must needs be known;
The faults so great, the case so strange,
Of right it must abroad be blown.                        25
Then since that by thine own desert
My songs do tell how true thou art,
     Blame not my lute!

Blame but thyself that hast misdone
And well deservéd to have blame;                         30
Change thou thy way, so evil begun,
And then my lute shall sound that same.
But if till then my fingers play,
By thy desert, their wonted way,
     Blame not my lute!                35

Farewell, unknown, for though thou break
My strings in spite with great disdain,
Yet have I found out for thy sake
Strings for to string my lute again.
And if, perchance, this sely[3] rhyme                    40
Do make thee blush, at any time,
     Blame not my lute!

ca. 1535

GERARD MANLEY HOPKINS

# Spring and Fall:

### *To a Young Child*

Márgarét áre you gríeving
Over Goldengrove unleaving?
Leáves, líke the things of man, you
With your fresh thoughts care for, can you?
Áh! ás the heart grows older                             5
It will come to such sights colder
By and by, nor spare a sigh

2. Compose.                              3. Simple.

Though worlds of wanwood[1] leafmeal lie;
And yet you will weep and know why.
Now no matter, child, the name:                    10
Sórrow's spríngs áre the same.
Nor mouth had, no nor mind, expressed
What heart heard of, ghost[2] guessed:
It ís the blight man was born for,
It is Margaret you mourn for.                       15

1880

LEWIS CARROLL

# Jabberwocky[1]

'Twas brillig, and the slithy toves
    Did gyre and gimble in the wabe;
All mimsy were the borogoves,
    And the mome raths outgrabe.

"Beware the Jabberwock, my son!                     5
    The jaws that bite, the claws that catch!
Beware the Jubjub bird, and shun
    The frumious Bandersnatch!"

He took his vorpal sword in hand:
    Long time the manxome foe he sought—           10
So rested he by the Tumtum tree,
    And stood awhile in thought.

And as in uffish thought he stood,
    The Jabberwock, with eyes of flame,
Came whiffling through the tulgey wood,             15
    And burbled as it came!

One, two! One, two! And through and through
    The vorpal blade went snicker-snack!
He left it dead, and with its head
    He went galumphing back.                        20

"And hast thou slain the Jabberwock?
    Come to my arms, my beamish boy!
O frabjous day! Callooh! Callay!"
    He chortled in his joy.

'Twas brillig, and the slithy toves                 25
    Did gyre and gimble in the wabe;
All mimsy were the borogoves,
    And the mome raths outgrabe.

1871

1. Pale, gloomy woods. "leafmeal": broken up, leaf by leaf (analogous to "piecemeal").
2. Soul.
1. Of the "hard words" in this poem, Carroll wrote: "Humpty-Dumpty's theory, of two meanings packed into one word like a portmanteau, seems to me the right explanation for all. For instance, take the two words 'fuming' and 'furious.' Make up your mind that you will say both words, but leave it unsettled which you will say first. . . . If you have that rarest of gifts, a perfectly balanced mind, you will say 'frumious.'"

ROBERT HERRICK

# This Cross-Tree Here

This   cross-tree   here
Doth   JESUS   bear,
Who sweetened first,
Then Death accursed.
Here all things ready are, make haste, make haste away;
For, long this work will be, & very short this day.
Why then, go on to act: Here's wonders to be done,
Before the last, least sand of Thy ninth hour be run;
Or ere dark clouds do dull, or dead the Midday's sun.[1]
Act when Thou wilt,
Blood will be spilt;
Pure balm, that shall
Bring health to all.
Why   then,   begin
To   pour   first   in
Some drops of wine,
Instead   of   brine,
To search the wound,
So   long   unsound:
And when that's done
Let   oil,   next,   run,
To   cure   the   sore
Sin   made   before.
And O! Dear Christ,
E'en   as   Thou   di'st,
Look down, and see
Us weep for Thee.
And tho (Love knows)
Thy   dreadful   woes
We   cannot   ease;
Yet do Thou please,
Who   mercy   art,
T'accept each heart,
That   gladly   would
Help,   if   it   could.
Mean while let me,
Beneath   this   tree,
This   honor   have,
To make my grave.

1647

---

1. According to *Matthew* 27:45, during the crucifixion "from the sixth hour there was darkness over all the land unto the ninth hour," when Christ died.

**GEORGE HERBERT**

# The Altar

A broken ALTAR, Lord, Thy servant rears,
Made of a HEART, and cemented with tears;
 Whose parts are as Thy hand did frame;
 No workman's tool hath touched the same.
    A    HEART    alone
    Is    such    a    stone
    As    nothing    but
    Thy power doth cut.
    Wherefore each part
    Of my hard HEART
    Meets in this frame,
    To praise Thy name:
That, if I chance to hold my peace,
These stones to praise Thee may not cease.
O, let Thy blessed SACRIFICE be mine,
And    sanctify    this    ALTAR    to    be    Thine.

1633

**GEORGE HERBERT**

# Easter Wings

Lord, who createdst man in wealth and store,[1]
Though foolishly he lost the same,
 Decaying more and more,
  Till he became
   Most poor:
    With thee
    O let me rise
  As larks,[2] harmoniously,
 And sing this day thy victories:
Then shall the fall further the flight in me.

My tender age in sorrow did begin;
And still with sicknesses and shame
 Thou didst so punish sin,
  That I became
   Most thin.
    With thee
    Let me combine,
  And feel this day thy victory;
 For, if I imp[3] my wing on thine,
Affliction shall advance the flight in me.

1633

1. In plenty.
2. Which herald the morning.
3. Engraft. In falconry, to engraft feathers in a damaged wing, so as to restore the powers of flight (OED).

ROBERT HERRICK

## The Pillar of Fame

Fame's pillar here, at last, we set,
Out-during *Marble, Brass,* or *Jet,*[1]
Charmed and enchanted so,
As to withstand the blow
Of        overthrow:
Nor shall the seas,
Or        OUTRAGES
Of storms o'erbear
What we up-rear,
Tho Kingdoms fall,
This    pillar    never    shall
Decline  or  waste  at  all;
But stand for ever by his own
Firm and well fixed foundation.

1648

EDWIN MORGAN

## Pomander[2]

pomander
open pomander
open poem and her
open poem and him
open poem and hymn
hymn and hymen leander
high man pen meander
o pen poem me and her
pen me poem me and him
om mane padme hum
pad me home panda hand
open up o holy panhandler
ample panda pen or bamboo pond
ponder a bonny poem pomander opener
open banned peon penman hum and banter
open hymn and pompom band and panda hamper
o i am a pen open man or happener
i am open manner happener
happy are we open
poem and a pom
poem and a panda
poem and aplomb

1968

1. Black lignite or black marble. "Out-during": out-lasting.   2. A shaped container of aromatic substances, used to ward off infection.

ROBERT HOLLANDER

# You Too? Me Too—Why Not?
## Soda Pop

```
          I am
          look
          ing at
          the Co
          caCola
          bottle
          which is
          green wi
          th ridges
          just  like
       c     c     c
       o     o     o
       l     l     l
       u     u     u
       m     m     m
       n     n     n
       s     s     s
       and on itself it says
```

COCA-COLA
reg.u.s.pat.off.

exactly like an art pop
statue of that kind of
bottle but not so green
that the juice inside
gives other than the co
lor it has when I pour
it out in a clear glass
glass on this table top
(It's making me thirsty
all this winking and
beading of Hippocrene
please let me pause
drinking the fluid in)
ah! it is enticing how
each color is the same
brown in green bottle
brown in uplifted glass
making each utensil on
the table laid a brown
fork in a brown shade
making me long to watch
them harvesting the crop
which makes the deep-aged
rich brown wine of America
that is to say which makes
soda                     pop

p. 1968

LEWIS CARROLL

# Acrostic[3]

Little maidens, when you look
On this little storybook,
Reading with attentive eye
Its enticing history,
Never think that hours of play                              5
Are your only HOLIDAY,
And that in a HOUSE of joy
Lessons serve but to annoy:
If in any HOUSE you find
Children of a gentle mind,                                 10
Each the others pleasing ever—
Each the others vexing never—
Daily work and pastime daily
In their order taking gaily—
Then be very sure that they                                15
Have a life of HOLIDAY.

*Christmas* 1861

SIR JOHN DAVIES

# Of Astraea[1]

Early before the day doth spring,
Let us awake, my muse, and sing;
It is no time to slumber,
So many joys this time doth bring,
As time will fail to number.                               5

But whereto shall we bend our lays?
Even up to Heaven, again to raise
The maid, which thence descended
Hath brought again the golden days,
And all the world amended.[2]                              10

Rudeness itself she doth refine,
Even like an alchemist[3] divine,
Gross times of iron turning
Into the purest form of gold:
Not to corrupt till Heaven wax old,                        15
And be refined with burning.

1599

---

3. Inscribed in a copy of Catherine Sinclair's book, *Holiday House*, presented to three sisters whose first names are spelled out vertically by the first letters of each line.
1. One of Davies' 26 "Hymns of Astraea in Acrostic Verse." Queen Elizabeth was often celebrated as "Astraea," the classical goddess of justice, innocence, and purity.

"Elisabetha Regina": Elizabeth the Queen.
2. When corruption overtook the Golden Age, Astraea was (according to legend) the last immortal to leave the Earth, and she was transformed into the constellation Virgo.
3. Who sought a formula for turning baser metals to gold.

EDWIN MORGAN

## The Computer's First Christmas Card

```
j o l l y m e r r y
h o l l y b e r r y
j o l l y b e r r y
m e r r y h o l l y
h a p p y j o l l y            5
j o l l y j e l l y
j e l l y b e l l y
b e l l y m e r r y
h o l l y h e p p y
j o l l y M o l l y           10
m a r r y J e r r y
m e r r y H a r r y
h o p p y B a r r y
h e p p y J a r r y
b o p p y h e p p y           15
b e r r y j o r r y
j o r r y j o l l y
m o p p y j e l l y
M o l l y m e r r y
J e r r y j o l l y           20
b e l l y b o p p y
j o r r y h o p p y
h o l l y m o p p y
B a r r y m e r r y
J a r r y h a p p y           25
h a p p y b o p p y
b o p p y j o l l y
j o l l y m e r r y
m e r r y m e r r y
m e r r y m e r r y           30
m e r r y C h r i s
a m m e r r y a s a
C h r i s m e r r y
a S M E R R Y C H R
Y S A N T H E M U M           35
```

1968

EDWIN MORGAN

# Message Clear

```
        am              i
                            if
    i am                    he
        he r        o
        h     ur   t                        5
        the re              and
        he      re          and
        he re
      a               n   d
          th   e   r           e            10
    i am     r                   ife
                   i n
               s     ion and
    i                   d     i e
        am  e re    ct                      15
        am  e re    ction
                     o          f
            the                 life
                     o          f
        m   e            n                  20
              sur e
            the            d     i e
      i       s
              s   e t   and
    i am the   sur         d                25
        a   t   res   t
                     o          life
    i am  he r                  e
    i a            ct
    i       r   u       n                   30
    i   m   e e     t
    i             t         i e
    i       s     t   and
    i am th         o     th
    i am   r         a                      35
    i am the  su    n
    i am the  s     on
    i am the  e   rect on       e if
    i am     re        n   t
    i am     s       a       fe             40
    i am     s   e   n   t
    i   he e             d
    i   t e s   t
    i       re          a d
      a   th re          a d                45
      a       s   t on         e
      a   t   re         a d
      a   th r       on         e
    i       resurrect
                        a     life          50
    i am           i n         life
    i am     resurrection
    i am the resurrection and
    i am
    i am the resurrection and the life[1]   55
```

                                    1968

1. *John* 11:25.

**RICHARD KOSTELANETZ**

# Tribute to Henry Ford

### TRIBUTE TO HENRY FORD 1

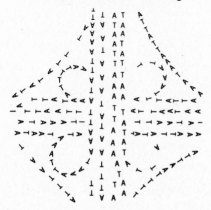

### TRIBUTE TO HENRY FORD 2

### TRIBUTE TO HENRY FORD 3

p. 1969

e. e. cummings

l(a

l(a

le
af
fa

ll                                              5

s)
one
l

iness

1958

# III

ANONYMOUS

## Though Amaryllis Dance in Green[1]

Though Amaryllis dance in green
    Like fairy queen;
    And sing full clear
Corinna can, with smiling cheer;
Yet since their eyes make heart so sore,    5
Heigh ho, heigh ho, 'chill[2] love no more.

My sheep are lost for want of food,
    And I so wood,[3]
    That all the day
I sit and watch a herdmaid gay,    10
Who laughs to see me sigh so sore,
Heigh ho, heigh ho, 'chill love no more.

Her loving looks, her beauty bright
    Is such delight,
    That all in vain    15
I love to like,[4] and lose my gain
For her that thanks me not therefor,
Heigh ho, heigh ho, 'chill love no more.

Ah wanton[5] eyes, my friendly foes,
    And cause of woes,    20
    Your sweet desire
Breeds flames of ice and freeze in fire.
Ye scorn to see me weep so sore,
Heigh ho, heigh ho, 'chill love no more.

Love ye who list,[6] I force him not,    25
    Sith, God it wot,[7]
    The more I wail,
The less my sighs and tears prevail.
What shall I do but say therefore,
Heigh ho, heigh ho, 'chill love no more.    30

1588

1. From a popular song book, *Psalms, Sonnets, and Songs of Sadness and Piety,* by William Byrd. Amaryllis (line 1) and Corinna (line 4) are typical women's names in Elizabethan lyrics.
2. I will (a rural dialect form: [i]ch [w]ill).
3. Frantic, wild, out of my mind.
4. Pretend. "gain": worldly possessions.
5. Playful, merciless.
6. Wish to.
7. Knows. "Sith": since.

SIR PHILIP SIDNEY

## Let Dainty Wits Cry on the Sisters Nine[1]

Let dainty wits cry on the Sisters nine,[2]
That bravely masked,[3] their fancies may be told;
Or Pindar's apes[4] flaunt they in phrases fine,
Enam'ling with pied flowers their thoughts of gold.
Or else let them in statelier glory shine,                               5
Ennobling new-found tropes[5] with problems old;
Or with strange similes enrich each line,
Of herbs or beasts, which Ind or Afric[6] hold.
For me, in sooth, no Muse but one I know;
Phrases and problems[7] from my reach do grow,                           10
And strange things cost too dear for my poor sprites.[8]
How then? Even thus: in Stella's face I read
What Love and Beauty be, then all my deed
But copying is, what in her Nature writes.

1582

CHRISTOPHER MARLOWE

## [The Seduction of Hero][1]

And now she lets him whisper in her ear,
Flatter, entreat, promise, protest, and swear;
Yet ever as he greedily assayed
To touch those dainties, she the harpy played,                          270
And every limb did, as a soldier stout,
Defend the fort and keep the foeman out;
For though the rising ivory mount he scaled,
Which is with azure circling lines empaled,
Much like a globe (a globe may I term this,                             275
By which love sails to regions full of bliss)
Yet there with Sisyphus[2] he toiled in vain,
Till gentle parley did the truce obtain.
Wherein Leander on her quivering breast,
Breathless spoke something, and sighed out the rest;                    280
Which so prevailed, as he with small ado
Enclosed her in his arms and kissed her too.
And every kiss to her was as a charm,

1. From Sidney's sonnet sequence, *Astrophel and Stella*. In this sonnet Sidney reviews several contemporary styles of writing.
2. The muses. "cry": call. The "dainty wits" believe in the poetic frenzy of direct inspiration.
3. Ornately arrayed. "fancies": creatures of imagination. "told": articulated.
4. Imitators of Pindar, fifth-century B.C. Greek poet known for his lofty verse. The French Pléiade (Ronsard, for example) affected such high style.
5. Figures of speech, rhetorical devices (heavily used by self-conscious early Elizabethan poets).
6. India or Africa. The Euphuists elaborated their prose in this formulaic way.

7. Pithy sayings and philosophical questions.
8. Spirits.
1. From Sestiad II of *Hero and Leander*, a long narrative poem begun by Marlowe and later completed by George Chapman. It retells the ancient Greek legend of two lovers: Hero, a priestess of Venus, falls in love with Leander, who each night swims the Hellespont to see her. Leander ultimately drowns on one of these swims, and Hero then drowns herself in the same sea. The excerpt here describes the first seduction; Leander has just arrived at Hero's tower, soaking wet and naked, and Hero hides from him, in her bed.
2. Whose mythological task was to roll a stone uphill forever.

And to Leander as a fresh alarm,[3]
So that the truce was broke, and she, alas,                    285
Poor silly[4] maiden, at his mercy was.
Love is not full of pity, as men say,
But deaf and cruel where he means to prey.
Even as a bird, which in our hands we wring,
Forth plungeth and oft flutters with her wing,                290
She trembling strove; this strife of hers, like that
Which made the world, another world begat
Of unknown joy. Treason was in her thought,
And cunningly to yield herself she sought.
Seeming not won, yet won she was at length;                   295
In such wars women use but half their strength.
Leander now, like Theban Hercules,
Entered the orchard of th' Hesperides,[5]
Whose fruit none rightly can describe but he
That pulls or shakes it from the golden tree.                 300
And now she wished this night were never done,
And sighed to think upon th' approaching sun;
For much it grieved her that the bright daylight
Should know the pleasure of this blessed night,
And them like Mars and Erycine[6] display,                    305
Both in each other's arms chained as they lay.
Again she knew not how to frame her look,
Or speak to him who in a moment took
That which so long, so charily she kept;
And fain by stealth away she would have crept,                310
And to some corner secretly have gone,
Leaving Leander in the bed alone.
But as her naked feet were whipping out,
He on the sudden clinged her so about,
That mermaid-like unto the floor she slid,                    315
One half appeared, the other half was hid.
Thus near the bed she blushing stood upright,
And from her countenance behold ye might
A kind of twilight break, which through the hair,
As from an orient cloud, glimpse here and there;             320
And round about the chamber this false morn
Brought forth the day before the day was born.
So Hero's ruddy cheek Hero betrayed,
And her all naked to his sight displayed;
Whence his admiring eyes more pleasure took                   325
Than Dis[7] on heaps of gold fixing his look.
By this, Apollo's golden harp began
To sound forth music to the ocean;[8]
Which watchful Hesperus no sooner heard,
But he the day-bright-bearing car prepared,                   330
And ran before, as harbinger of light,

3. Call to action.
4. Helpless.
5. Three sisters, who guarded the apples
Hera (Juno) received as a wedding gift.
Hercules' last labor was to gain access to
the apples.
6. Venus, goddess of love. "Mars": god
of war. Vulcan, Venus's husband, once

caught her in bed with Mars and exposed
them to the laughter of other gods.
7. Pluto, god of wealth.
8. Prelude to the sun's rising. Hesperus
(line 329) is here conceived as the morning
star; as god of the sun, Apollo is often portrayed driving a golden chariot ("car,"
line 330).

And with his flaring beams mocked ugly Night
Till she, o'ercome with anguish, shame, and rage,
Danged[9] down to Hell her loathsome carriage.

1598

THOMAS CAMPION

## My Sweetest Lesbia[10]

My sweetest Lesbia, let us live and love,
And though the sager sort our deeds reprove,
Let us not weigh them. Heaven's great lamps do dive
Into their west, and straight again revive,
But soon as once set is our little light,     5
Then must we sleep one ever-during night.

If all would lead their lives in love like me,
Then bloody swords and armor should not be;
No drum nor trumpet peaceful sleeps should move,
Unless alarm came from the camp of love.     10
But fools do live, and waste their little light,
And seek with pain their ever-during night.

When timely death my life and fortune ends,
Let not my hearse be vexed with mourning friends,
But let all lovers, rich in triumph, come     15
And with sweet pastimes grace my happy tomb;
And Lesbia, close up thou my little light,
And crown with love my ever-during night.

1601

EDMUND SPENSER

## Prothalamion[1]

Calme was the day, and through the trembling ayre,
Sweete breathing Zephyrus[2] did softly play
A gentle spirit, that lightly did delay
Hot Titans[3] beames, which then did glyster fayre:
When I whom sullein care,     5
Through discontent of my long fruitlesse stay
In Princes Court, and expectation vayne
Of idle hopes, which still doe fly away,
Like empty shaddowes, did aflict my brayne,
Walkt forth to ease my payne     10
Along the shoare of silver streaming Themmes,
Whose rutty[4] Bancke, the which his River hemmes,
Was paynted all with variable flowers,
And all the meades[5] adornd with daintie gemmes,

9. Dashed.
10. A version of Catullus, V, "Vivamus, mea Lesbia, atque amemus," one of the most frequently translated and imitated poems among English Renaissance poets.
1. A marriage song celebrating the double marriage of Elizabeth and Katherine Somerset, daughters of the Earl of Worces-ter, to Henry Gilford and William Peter. Spenser's diction and spelling, deliberately archaic, are here left unmodernized.
2. The west wind.
3. The sun's.
4. Rooty.
5. Meadows.

Fit to decke maydens bowres, 15
And crowne their Paramours,
Against the Brydale day, which is not long:
    Sweete Themmes runne softly, till I end my Song.

There, in a Meadow, by the Rivers side,
A flocke of Nymphes I chauncéd to espy, 20
All lovely Daughters of the Flood[6] thereby,
With goodly greenish locks[7] all loose untyde,
As[8] each had bene a Bryde,
And each one had a little wicker basket,
Made of fine twigs entrayléd curiously, 25
In which they gathered flowers to fill their flasket:[9]
And with fine Fingers, cropt full feateously[1]
The tender stalkes on hye.
Of every sort, which in that Meadow grew,
They gathered some; the Violet pallid blew, 30
The little Dazie, that at evening closes,
The virgin Lillie, and the Primrose trew,
With store of vermeil[2] Roses,
To decke their Bridegromes posies,
Against the Brydale day, which was not long: 35
    Sweete Themmes runne softly, till I end my Song.

With that, I saw two Swannes[3] of goodly hewe,
Come softly swimming downe along the Lee,[4]
Two fairer Birds I yet never did see:
The snow which doth the top of Pindus[5] strew, 40
Did never whiter shew,
Nor Jove himselfe when he a Swan would be
For love of Leda, whiter did appeare:[6]
Yet Leda was they say as white as he,
Yet not so white as these, nor nothing neare; 45
So purely white they were,
That even the gentle streame, the which them bare,
Seem'd foule to them, and bad his billowes spare
To wet their silken feathers, least they might
Soyle their fayre plumes with water not so fayre, 50
And marre their beauties bright,
That shone as heavens light,
Against their Brydale day, which was not long:
    Sweete Themmes runne softly, till I end my Song.

Eftsoones[7] the Nymphes, which now had Flowers their fill, 55
Ran all in haste, to see that silver brood,
As they came floating on the Christal Flood.
Whom when they sawe, they stood amazéd still,
Their wondring eyes to fill,
Them seem'd they never saw a sight so fayre, 60

6. River Thames.
7. Traditional for water nymphs and mermaids.
8. As if.
9. Shallow flower-basket.
1. Deftly.
2. Vermilion: bright red.
3. The ladies Somerset.

4. The River Lea, which flows into the Thames near Greenwich.
5. The Greek mountain range in which Parnassus, sacred to the Muses, is the highest peak.
6. Jove (Zeus) took the form of a swan to woo Leda, a mortal.
7. Very soon.

Of Fowles so lovely, that they sure did deeme
Them heavenly borne, or to be that same payre
Which through the Skie draw Venus silver Teeme,[8]
For sure they did not seeme
To be begot of any earthly Seede,                                  65
But rather Angels or of Angels breede:
Yet were they bred of Somers-heat they say,
In sweetest Season, when each Flower and weede
The earth did fresh aray,
So fresh they seem'd as day,                                       70
Even as their Brydale day, which was not long:
    Sweete Themmes runne softly, till I end my Song.

Then forth they all out of their baskets drew,
Great store of Flowers, the honour of the field,
That to the sense did fragrant odours yeild,                       75
All which upon those goodly Birds they threw,
And all the Waves did strew,
That like old Peneus[9] Waters they did seeme,
When downe along by pleasant Tempes shore
Scattred with Flowres, through Thessaly they streeme,              80
That they appeare through Lillies plenteous store,
Like a Brydes Chamber flore:
Two of those Nymphes, meane while, two Garlands bound,
Of freshest Flowres which in that Mead they found,
The which presenting all in trim Array,                            85
Their snowie Foreheads therewithall they crownd,
Whil'st one did sing this Lay,
Prepar'd against that Day,
Against their Brydale day, which was not long:
    Sweete Themmes runne softly, till I end my Song.        90

Ye gentle Birdes, the worlds faire ornament,
And heavens glorie, whom this happie hower
Doth leade unto your lovers blisfull bower,
Joy may you have and gentle hearts content
Of your loves couplement:                                          95
And let faire Venus, that is Queene of love,
With her heart-quelling Sonne[1] upon you smile,
Whose smile they say, hath vertue to remove
All Loves dislike, and friendships faultie guile
For ever to assoile.[2]                                            100
Let endlesse Peace your steadfast hearts accord,
And blessed Plentie wait upon your bord,
And let your bed with pleasures chast abound,
That fruitfull issue may to you afford,
Which may your foes confound,                                      105
And make your joyes redound,
Upon your Brydale day, which is not long:
    Sweete Themmes run softly, till I end my Song.

8. Venus, Roman goddess of love, was sometimes portrayed as riding on or drawn by white swans.
9. The chief river of Thessaly, which flows through the Vale of Tempe, near the legendary abode of the gods.
1. Cupid.
2. Absolve.

So ended she; and all the rest around
To her redoubled that her undersong,[3]          110
Which said, their bridale daye should not be long.
And gentle Eccho from the neighbour ground,
Their accents did resound.
So forth those joyous Birdes did passe along,
Adowne the Lee, that to them murmurde low,          115
As he would speake, but that he lackt a tong,
Yet did by signes his glad affection show,
Making his streame run slow.
And all the foule which in his flood did dwell
Gan flock about these twaine, that did excell          120
The rest, so far, as Cynthia doth shend[4]
The lesser starres. So they enrangéd well,
Did on those two attend,
And their best service lend,
Against their wedding day, which was not long:          125
     Sweete Themmes run softly, till I end my Song.

At length they all to mery London came,
To mery London, my most kyndly Nurse,
That to me gave this Lifes first native sourse:
Though from another place I take my name,          130
An house of auncient fame.[5]
There when they came, whereas those bricky towres,[6]
The which on Themmes brode agéd backe doe ryde,
Where now the studious Lawyers have their bowers
There whylome wont the Templer Knights to byde,          135
Till they decayd through pride:
Next whereunto there standes a stately place,[7]
Where oft I gaynéd giftes and goodly grace
Of that great Lord, which therein wont to dwell,
Whose want too well now feeles my freendles case:          140
But Ah here fits not well
Olde woes but joyes to tell
Against the bridale daye, which is not long:
     Sweete Themmes runne softly, till I end my Song.

Yet therein now doth lodge a noble Peer,          145
Great Englands glory and the Worlds wide wonder,
Whose dreadfull name, late through all Spaine did thunder,
And Hercules two pillors[8] standing neere,
Did make to quake and feare:
Faire branch of Honor, flower of Chevalrie,          150
That fillest England with thy triumphes fame,
Joy have thou of thy noble victorie,
And endlesse happinesse of thine owne name
That promiseth the same:

3. Re-echoed her refrain.
4. Surpass. "Cynthia," as a surname of Diana, was a name for the moon, and also one of the names often used by poets for Queen Elizabeth.
5. The Spencers of Althorpe, near Northampton, relatives of the author.
6. The Temple, once the residence of the Knights Templar, later the residence of law students (line 134).
7. The house, until 1590, of Spenser's patron, the Earl of Leicester; but at the time of the poem, Essex House, occupied by the Earl of Essex (line 145), who sacked the city of Cadiz in August, 1596.
8. The straits of Gibraltar.

That through thy prowesse and victorious armes,                    155
Thy country may be freed from forraine harmes:
And great Elisaes[9] glorious name may ring
Through al the world, fil'd with thy wide Alarmes,
Which some brave muse may sing
To ages following,                                                 160
Upon the Brydale day, which is not long:
    Sweete Themmes runne softly, till I end my Song.

From those high Towers, this noble Lord issuing,
Like Radiant Hesper[1] when his golden hayre
In th'Ocean billowes he hath Bathéd fayre,                         165
Descended to the Rivers open vewing,
With a great traine ensuing.
Above the rest were goodly to bee seene
Two gentle Knights of lovely face and feature
Beseeming well the bower of anie Queene,                           170
With gifts of wit and ornaments of nature,
Fit for so goodly stature:
That like the twins of Jove[2] they seem'd in sight,
Which decke the Bauldricke of the Heavens bright.
They two forth pacing to the Rivers side,                          175
Received those two faire Brides, their Loves delight,
Which at th'appointed tyde,
Each one did make his Bryde,
Against their Brydale day, which is not long:
    Sweete Themmes runne softly, till I end my Song.               180

                                                                   1596

ELIZABETH

# When I Was Fair and Young[1]

When I was fair and young, and favor graced me,
    Of many was I sought, their mistress for to be;
But I did scorn them all, and answered them therefore,
    "Go, go, go, seek some otherwhere,
        Importune me no more!"                                     5

How many weeping eyes I made to pine with woe,
    How many sighing hearts, I have no skill to show;
Yet I the prouder grew, and answered them therefore,
    "Go, go, go, seek some otherwhere,
        Importune me no more!"                                     10

Then spake fair Venus' son, that proud victorious boy,[2]
    And said: "Fine dame, since that you be so coy,
I will so pluck your plumes that you shall say no more,
    'Go, go, go, seek some otherwhere,
        Importune me no more!' "                                   15

9. Elizabeth's.
1. Hesperus, the evening star.
2. Castor and Pollux, born of Jove to
Leda (see lines 42–43), who as the constellation Gemini form part of the zodiac
("the Bauldricke of the Heavens," line

174).
1. The attribution of this poem to the
Queen is by no means certain; but she was
highly—and perhaps excessively—praised
by her subjects for her poetic talents.
2. Cupid.

When he had spake these words, such change grew in my breast
   That neither night nor day since that, I could take any rest.
Then lo! I did repent that I had said before,
   "Go, go, go, seek some otherwhere,
     Importune me no more!"            20

ca. 1585?

WILLIAM SHAKESPEARE

## Two Loves I Have

Two loves I have of comfort and despair,
Which like two spirits do suggest me still:[1]
The better angel is a man right fair,
The worser spirit a woman, colored ill.[2]
To win me soon to hell, my female evil       5
Tempteth my better angel from my side,
And would corrupt my saint to be a devil,
Wooing his purity with her foul pride.
And whether that my angel be turned fiend
Suspect I may, but not directly tell;       10
But being both from[3] me, both to each[4] friend,
I guess one angel in another's hell:
Yet this shall I ne'er know, but live in doubt,
Till my bad angel fire[5] my good one out.

p. 1599

THOMAS CAMPION

## There Is a Garden in Her Face

There is a garden in her face,
Where roses and white lilies grow,
A heavenly paradise is that place,
Wherein all pleasant fruits do flow.
There cherries grow, which none may buy     5
Till "Cherry ripe!"[1] themselves do cry.

Those cherries fairly do enclose
Of orient pearl a double row,
Which when her lovely laughter shows,
They look like rosebuds filled with snow.     10
Yet them nor peer nor prince can buy,
Till "Cherry ripe!" themselves do cry.

Her eyes like angels watch them still;
Her brows like bended bows do stand,
Threatening with piercing frowns to kill     15
All that attempt with eye or hand
Those sacred cherries to come nigh,
Till "Cherry ripe!" themselves do cry.

ca. 1617

---

1. Tempt me constantly.          4. Each other.
2. Dark.                   5. Drive out with fire.
3. Away from.         1. A cry of London street vendors.

THOMAS CAMPION

# I Care Not for These Ladies

I care not for these ladies,
That must be wooed and prayed;
Give me kind Amaryllis,
The wanton country maid.
Nature art disdaineth;                                    5
Her beauty is her own.
    Her when we court and kiss,
    She cries, "Forsooth, let go!"
    But when we come where comfort is,
    She never will say no.                                10

If I love Amaryllis,
She gives me fruit and flowers:
But if we love these ladies,
We must give golden showers.
Give them gold that sell love;                           15
Give me the nut-brown lass
    Who, when we court and kiss,
    She cries, "Forsooth, let go!"
    But when we come where comfort is,
    She never will say no.                                20

These ladies must have pillows
And beds by strangers wrought;
Give me a bower of willows,
Of moss and leaves unbought,
And fresh Amaryllis,                                     25
With milk and honey fed,
    Who, when we court and kiss,
    She cries, "Forsooth, let go!"
    But when we come where comfort is,
    She never will say no.                                30

1601

ANONYMOUS

# Crabbed Age and Youth

Crabbed age and youth cannot live together:
Youth is full of pleasance,[1] age is full of care;
Youth like summer morn, age like winter weather;
Youth like summer brave,[2] age like winter bare.
Youth is full of sport, age's breath is short;           5
    Youth is nimble, age is lame;
Youth is hot and bold, age is weak and cold;
    Youth is wild, and age is tame.
Age, I do abhor thee; youth, I do adore thee;
    Oh! my love, my love is young:                        10

1. Delight.                            2. Showy, full of splendor.

Age, I do defy thee: Oh! sweet shepherd, hie thee,
For methinks thou stay'st too long.

p. 1599

GEORGE PEELE

# A Farewell to Arms[1]

His golden locks time hath to silver turned;
  Oh, time too swift, oh, swiftness never ceasing!
His youth 'gainst time and age hath ever spurned,[2]
  But spurned in vain; youth waneth by increasing.
Beauty, strength, youth, are flowers but fading seen;      5
Duty, faith, love, are roots, and ever green.

His helmet now shall make a hive for bees,
  And lover's sonnets turned to holy psalms,
A man-at-arms must now serve on his knees,
  And feed on prayers, which are age his[3] alms;          10
But though from court to cottage he depart,
His saint is sure of his unspotted heart.

And when he saddest sits in homely cell,
  He'll teach his swains this carol for a song:
Blest be the hearts that wish my sovereign well,          15
  Cursed be the souls that think her any wrong!
Goddess, allow this aged man his right,
To be your beadsman[4] now, that was your knight.

1590

ANONYMOUS

# The Silver Swan

The silver swan, who living had no note,
When death approached, unlocked her silent throat;
Leaning her breast against the reedy shore,
Thus sung her first and last, and sung no more:
"Farewell, all joys; Oh death, come close mine eyes;      5
More geese than swans now live, more fools than wise."

1612

WILLIAM SHAKESPEARE

# Spring[1]

When daisies pied and violets blue
  And ladysmocks all silver-white
And cuckoobuds of yellow hue

1. From *Polyhymnia,* a verse description of a 1590 jousting tournament on Queen Elizabeth's birthday. Sir Henry Lee, who had for years been the Queen's champion in such contests, that year (at age 60) retired in favor of a younger man.
2. Kicked.

3. Age's (a common Elizabethan possessive form).
4. One who prays for the soul of another (OED).
1. Like "Winter" (below), a song from *Love's Labors Lost,* Act V, sc. ii.

Do paint the meadows with delight,
The cuckoo then, on every tree,                              5
Mocks married men;[2] for thus sings he,
      Cuckoo;
Cuckoo, cuckoo: Oh word of fear,
Unpleasing to a married ear!

When shepherds pipe on oaten straws,                         10
      And merry larks are plowmen's clocks,
When turtles tread,[3] and rooks, and daws,
      And maidens bleach their summer smocks,
The cuckoo then, on every tree,
Mocks married men; for thus sings he,                        15
      Cuckoo;
Cuckoo, cuckoo: Oh word of fear,
Unpleasing to a married ear!

                                                      ca. 1595

WILLIAM SHAKESPEARE

## Winter

When icicles hang by the wall
      And Dick the shepherd blows[1] his nail,
And Tom bears logs into the hall,
      And milk comes frozen home in pail.
When blood is nipped and ways be foul,                       5
Then nightly sings the staring owl,
      Tu-who;
Tu-whit, tu-who: a merry note,
While greasy Joan doth keel[2] the pot.

When all aloud the wind doth blow,                           10
      And coughing drowns the parson's saw,[3]
And birds sit brooding in the snow,
      And Marian's nose looks red and raw,
When roasted crabs[4] hiss in the bowl,
Then nightly sings the staring owl,                          15
      Tu-who;
Tu-whit, tu-who: a merry note
While greasy Joan doth keel the pot.

                                                      ca. 1595

SIR PHILIP SIDNEY

## Come Sleep, O Sleep[1]

Come Sleep, O Sleep, the certain knot of peace,
The baiting-place[2] of wit, the balm of woe,
The poor man's wealth, the prisoner's release,

2. By the resemblance of its call to the word "cuckold."
3. Copulate. "turtles": turtledoves.
1. Breathes on for warmth. "nail": fingernail; i.e., hands.
2. Cool: stir to keep it from boiling over.

3. Maxim, proverb.
4. Crabapples.
1. A sonnet addressed to sleep was a conventional part of the Elizabethan sonnet sequences.
2. A refreshment stop for travelers and horses.

Th'indifferent[3] judge between the high and low;
With shield of proof[4] shield me from out the prease[5]          5
Of those fierce darts Despair at me doth throw;
O make in me those civil wars to cease:
I will good tribute pay, if thou do so.
Take thou of me smooth pillows, sweetest bed,
A chamber deaf to noise and blind to light,          10
A rosy garland and a weary head;
And if these things, as being thine by right,
Move not thy heavy grace, thou shalt in me,
Livelier[6] than elsewhere, Stella's image see.

1582

SAMUEL DANIEL

## Care-Charmer Sleep

Care-charmer Sleep, son of the sable Night,
Brother to Death, in silent darkness born:
Relieve my languish and restore the light;
With dark forgetting of my cares, return.
And let the day be time enough to mourn          5
The shipwreck of my ill-adventured youth;
Let waking eyes suffice to wail their scorn
Without the torment of the Night's untruth.
Cease, dreams, th' imagery of our day desires,
To model forth the passions of the morrow;          10
Never let rising sun approve you[1] liars,
To add more grief to aggravate my sorrow.
Still let me sleep, embracing clouds in vain,
And never wake to feel the day's disdain.

1592

BARTHOLOMEW GRIFFIN

## Care-Charmer Sleep

Care-charmer Sleep, sweet ease in restless misery,
The captive's liberty, and his freedom's song,
Balm of the bruised heart, man's chief felicity,
Brother of quiet Death, when life is too, too long!
A comedy it is, and now an history—          5
What is not sleep unto the feeble mind!
It easeth him that toils and him that's sorry,
It makes the deaf to hear, to see the blind.
Ungentle Sleep, thou helpest all but me,
For when I sleep my soul is vexéd most.          10
It is Fidessa[2] that doth master thee;
If she approach, alas, thy power is lost.
But here she is. See, how he runs amain!
I fear at night he will not come again.

1596

3. Impartial.
4. Proven strength.
5. Press: throng.
6. More lifelike.

1. Prove you to be.
2. The heroine of Griffin's sonnet sequence, of which this poem is a part.

CHRISTOPHER MARLOWE

# [The Overreacher]¹

In thee, thou valiant man of Persia,                                      166
I see the folly of thy emperor.
Art thou but captain of a thousand horse,
That, by characters graven in thy brows,
And by thy martial face and stout aspect,                                 170
Deserv'st to have the leading of an host?
Forsake thy king, and do but join with me,
And we will triumph over all the world.
I hold the Fates bound fast in iron chains,
And with my hand turn Fortune's wheel about;                              175
And sooner shall the sun fall from his sphere
Than Tamburlaine be slain or overcome.
Draw forth thy sword, thou mighty man-at-arms,
Intending but to raze my charmèd skin,
And Jove himself will stretch his hand from heaven                        180
To ward the blow, and shield me safe from harm.
See how he rains down heaps of gold in showers,
As if he meant to give my soldiers pay;
And, as a sure and grounded argument
That I shall be the monarch of the East,                                  185
He sends this Soldan's daughter rich and brave,
To be my queen and portly emperess.²
If thou wilt stay with me, renownèd man,
And lead thy thousand horse with my conduct,
Besides thy share of this Egyptian prize,                                 190
Those thousand horse shall sweat with martial spoil
Of conquered kingdoms and of cities sacked.
Both we will walk upon the lofty cliffs;
And Christian merchants, that with Russian stems³
Plough up huge furrows in the Caspian Sea,                                195
Shall vail⁴ to us as lords of all the lake.
Both we will reign as consuls of the earth,
And mighty kings shall be our senators.
Jove sometime maskèd in a shepherd's weed;
And by those steps that he hath scaled the heavens                        200
May we become immortal like the gods.
Join with me now in this my mean⁵ estate
(I call it mean because, being yet obscure,
The nations far-removèd admire me not)
And when my name and honor shall be spread                                205
As far as Boreas claps his brazen wings,
Or fair Boötes sends his cheerful light,

---

1. From *Tamburlaine* (Part I), Marlowe's play about Tamburlaine's rise to power from low beginnings as a shepherd boy. Tamburlaine is usually considered the epitome of the "overreacher," one whose ambition is boundless and who will not rest until he has extended himself too far. In this speech from Act I, sc. ii, the hero addresses a military leader of the enemy.

2. The beautiful daughter of the Soldan of Egypt has, moments before, been led in captive, bearing with her the considerable wealth she carried when intercepted. "brave": well-dressed; "portly": stately.
3. Prows of ships.
4. Lower their sails in salute. "lake": ocean.
5. Low.

Then shalt thou be competitor with me,
And sit with Tamburlaine in all his majesty.

ca. 1590

GILES FLETCHER

## In Time the Strong

In time the strong and stately turrets fall,
In time the rose and silver lilies die,
In time the monarchs captive are and thrall,
In time the sea and rivers are made dry;
The hardest flint in time doth melt asunder;          5
Still-living fame in time doth fade away;
The mountains proud we see in time come under;
And earth, for age, we see in time decay.
The sun in time forgets for to retire
From out the east where he was wont to rise;          10
The basest thoughts we see in time aspire,
And greedy minds in time do wealth despise.
Thus all, sweet fair, in time must have an end,
Except thy beauty, virtues, and thy friend.

1593

FULKE GREVILLE, LORD BROOKE

## The World, that All Contains, Is Ever Moving

The world, that all contains, is ever moving,
The stars within their spheres for ever turned;
Nature (the queen of change) to change is loving,
And form to matter new is still adjourned.[1]

Fortune, our fancy-god,[2] to vary liketh;          5
Place is not bound to things within it placed;
The present time upon time passéd striketh;
With Phoebus'[3] wandering course the earth is graced.

The air still moves, and by its moving cleareth;
The fire up ascends, and planets[4] feedeth;          10
The water passeth on, and all lets weareth;[5]
The earth stands still, yet change of changes breedeth.

Her plants, which summer ripes, in winter fade;
Each creature in unconstant mother[6] lieth;
Man made of earth, and for whom earth is made,          15
Still dying lives, and living ever dieth.
    Only like fate sweet Myra never varies,
    Yet in her eyes the doom of all change carries.

ca. 1585

1. Transferred.
2. Imaginary god.
3. The sun's.
4. Stars, which supposedly feed on fire,
the purest of the four elements.
5. Erodes all obstructions.
6. The earth.

JOSEPH HALL

# Satire III[1]

With some pot-fury,[2] ravished from their wit,
They sit and muse on some no-vulgar writ.[3]
As frozen dunghills in a winter's morn,
That void of vapor seeméd all beforn,[4]
Soon as the sun sends out his piercing beams                5
Exhale out filthy smoke and stinking steams,
So doth the base and the fore-barren brain
Soon as the raging wine begins to reign.
One higher pitched doth set his soaring thought
On crownéd kings that Fortune hath low brought,[5]          10
Or some uprearéd, high-aspiring swain,
As it might be the Turkish Tamburlaine.[6]
Then weeneth he[7] his base drink-drownéd sprite
Rapt to the threefold loft of heaven's height,
When he conceives upon his feignéd stage                    15
The stalking steps of his great personage,
Graced with huff-cap[8] terms and thundering threats,
That his poor hearers' hair quite upright sets.
Such soon as some brave-minded hungry youth
Sees fitly frame to his wide-strainéd mouth                 20
He vaunts his voice upon an hired stage,
With high-set steps and princely carriage;
Now swooping in side-robes of royalty
That erst did scrub in lousy brokery.[9]
There if he can with terms Italianate,                      25
Big-sounding sentences, and words of state,
Fair patch me up his pure iambic verse,
He ravishes the gazing scaffolders.[1]
Then certes was the famous Corduban[2]
Never but half so high tragedian.                           30
Now, lest such frightful shows of Fortune's fall
And bloody tyrant's rage should chance[3] appall
The dead-struck audience, 'midst the silent rout
Comes leaping in a self-misforméd lout,
And laughs, and grins, and frames his mimic face,           35
And jostles straight into the prince's place.
Then doth the theater echo all aloud
With gladsome noise of that applauding crowd.
A goodly hotchpotch! when vile russetings[4]
Are matched with monarchs and with mighty kings.            40
A goodly grace to sober tragic Muse
When each base clown his clumsy fist doth bruise,[5]

1. From Book I of Hall's satires, originally called *Virgidemiarum* ("a harvest of
switches").
2. Brew-inspired frenzy.
3. Writing that is not in the vernacular;
i.e., some Latin treatise.
4. Before.
5. A popular work of the early Elizabethan period, *The Mirror for Magistrates*,
told cautionary tales of how the mighty fell.
6. *Tamburlaine*, Marlowe's play in two
parts, described the rise to power of a
Scythian (not Turkish) shepherd youth
("swain," line 11).
7. He believes. "sprite": spirit.
8. Blustering.
9. Second-hand clothing.
1. Spectators.
2. Seneca, the greatest Roman tragedian,
born at Cordova. "certes": certainly.
3. By chance: accidentally.
4. Peasants, who wore coarse woolen
("russet") clothes.
5. Bruise his hands from banging on
benches to applaud. "clown": rustic, farm
hand.

And show his teeth in double rotten row,
For laughter at his self-resembled show.
Meanwhile our poets in high parliament                    45
Sit watching every word and gesturement,
Like curious censors of some doughty gear,
Whispering their verdict in their fellow's ear.
Woe to the word whose margent[6] in their scroll
Is noted with a black condemning coal!                    50
But if each period[7] might the synod please,
Ho!—Bring the ivy boughs and bands of bays.[8]
Now when they part and leave the naked stage
'Gins the bare hearer, in a guilty rage,
To curse and ban, and blame his lickerous[9] eye          55
That thus hath lavished his late halfpenny.[10]
Shame that the Muses should be bought and sold
For every peasant's brass, on each scaffold!

1597

ROBERT HERRICK

## To the Virgins, to Make Much of Time

Gather ye rosebuds while ye may,
    Old time is still a-flying;
And this same flower that smiles today
    Tomorow will be dying.

The glorious lamp of heaven, the sun,                     5
    The higher he's a-getting,
The sooner will his race be run,
    And nearer he's to setting.

That age is best which is the first,
    When youth and blood are warmer;                      10
But being spent, the worse, and worst
    Times still succeed the former.

Then be not coy, but use your time,
    And, while ye may, go marry;
For, having lost but once your prime,                     15
    You may forever tarry.

1648

EDMUND WALLER

## Song

Go, lovely rose!
Tell her that wastes her time and me
    That now she knows,
When I resemble[1] her to thee,
How sweet and fair she seems to be.                       5

---

6. Margin.                        9. Greedy.
7. Sentence.                      10. The admission fee for the pit.
8. Symbols of literary attainment.    1. Compare.

Tell her that's young,
And shuns to have her graces spied,
That hadst thou sprung
In deserts, where no men abide,
Thou must have uncommended died.                    10

Small is the worth
Of beauty from the light retired;
Bid her come forth,
Suffer herself to be desired,
And not blush so to be admired.                     15

Then die! that she
The common fate of all things rare
May read in thee;
How small a part of time they share
That are so wondrous sweet and fair!                20

1645

JOHN DONNE

# The Flea

Mark but this flea, and mark in this[1]
How little that which thou deny'st me is;
It sucked me first, and now sucks thee,
And in this flea our two bloods mingled be;
Thou know'st that this cannot be said                5
A sin, nor shame, nor loss of maidenhead,
    Yet this enjoys before it woo,
    And pampered[2] swells with one blood made of two,
    And this, alas, is more than we would do.[3]

Oh stay, three lives in one flea spare,               10
Where we almost, yea more than, married are.
This flea is you and I, and this
Our marriage bed, and marriage temple is;
Though parents grudge, and you, we're met
And cloistered in these living walls of jet.          15
    Though use[4] make you apt to kill me,
    Let not to that, self-murder added be,
    And sacrilege, three sins in killing three.

Cruel and sudden, hast thou since
Purpled thy nail in blood of innocence?               20
Wherein could this flea guilty be,
Except in that drop which it sucked from thee?
Yet thou triumph'st, and say'st that thou
Find'st not thyself, nor me, the weaker now;

1. Medieval preachers and rhetoricians asked their hearers to "mark" (look at) an object which illustrated a moral or philosophical lesson they wished to emphasize.
2. Fed luxuriously.
3. According to contemporary medical theory, conception involved the literal mingling of the lovers' blood.
4. Habit.

'Tis true; then learn how false, fears be;                    25
Just so much honor, when thou yield'st to me,
Will waste, as this flea's death took life from thee.

1633

ROBERT HERRICK

## Corinna's Going A-Maying

Get up, get up, for shame! the blooming morn
Upon her wings presents the god unshorn.[1]
    See how Aurora[2] throws her fair
    Fresh-quilted[3] colors through the air:
    Get up, sweet slug-a-bed, and see                    5
    The dew bespangling herb and tree.
Each flower has wept, and bowéd toward the east,
Above an hour since; yet you not dressed,
    Nay, not so much as out of bed?
    When all the birds have matins[4] said,            10
    And sung their thankful hymns, 'tis sin,
    Nay, profanation to keep in,
Whenas a thousand virgins on this day
Spring, sooner than the lark, to fetch in May.[5]

Rise, and put on your foliage, and be seen            15
To come forth, like the springtime, fresh and green,
    And sweet as Flora.[6] Take no care
    For jewels for your gown, or hair;
    Fear not; the leaves will strew
    Gems in abundance upon you;                        20
Besides, the childhood of the day has kept,
Against[7] you come, some orient[8] pearls unwept;
    Come, and receive them while the light
    Hangs on the dew-locks of the night,
    And Titan[9] on the eastern hill                    25
    Retires himself, or else stands still,
Till you come forth. Wash, dress, be brief in praying:
Few beads[1] are best when once we go a-Maying.

Come, my Corinna, come; and, coming, mark
How each field turns[2] a street, each street a park    30
    Made green and trimmed with trees; see how
    Devotion gives each house a bough
    Or branch: each porch, each door, ere this,
    An ark, a tabernacle is,
Made up of whitethorn neatly interwove,                35
As if here were those cooler shades of love.

---

1. Apollo, the sun god, whose golden hair represents the sun's rays.
2. Goddess of the dawn.
3. Mingled.
4. Morning prayers.
5. The traditional celebration of May Day morning included the gathering of white hawthorn blossoms and boughs to decorate houses and streets.
6. Goddess of flowers.
7. Until.
8. Shining.
9. The sun.
1. Prayers.
2. Turns into.

Can such delights be in the street,
And open fields, and we not see 't?
Come, we'll abroad; and let's obey
The proclamation made for May,                          40
And sin no more, as we have done, by staying.
But, my Corinna, come, let's go a-Maying.

There's not a budding boy or girl this day
But is got up, and gone to bring in May;
   A deal of youth, ere this, is come                   45
   Back, and with whitethorn laden home.
Some have dispatched their cakes and cream
   Before that we have left to dream;
And some have wept, and wooed, and plighted troth,
And chose their priest, ere we can cast off sloth.      50
   Many a green-gown³ has been given,
   Many a kiss, both odd and even,
   Many a glance, too, has been sent
   From out the eye, love's firmament;
Many a jest told of the keys betraying                  55
This night, and locks picked; yet we're not a-Maying.

Come, let us go while we are in our prime,
And take the harmless folly of the time.
   We shall grow old apace, and die
   Before we know our liberty.                          60
   Our life is short, and our days run
   As fast away as does the sun;
And as a vapor, or a drop of rain,
Once lost, can ne'er be found again:
   So when or you or⁴ I are made                        65
   A fable, song, or fleeting shade,
   All love, all liking, all delight
   Lies drowned with us in endless night.
Then while time serves, and we are but decaying,
Come, my Corinna, come, let's go a-Maying.              70

1648

WILLIAM SHAKESPEARE

## O Mistress Mine¹

O mistress mine, where are you roaming?
O stay and hear; your true love's coming,
   That can sing both high and low.
Trip no further, pretty sweeting;
Journeys end in lovers meeting,                         5
   Every wise man's son doth know.

What is love? 'tis not hereafter;
Present mirth hath present laughter;
   What's to come is still unsure:

---

3. Grass-stained gown.              1. A song from *Twelfth Night*, Act II,
4. Either . . . or.                 sc. iii.

In delay there lies no plenty;                          10
Then come kiss me, sweet and twenty,
Youth's a stuff will not endure.

                                                    1602

BEN JONSON

## Come, My Celia[1]

Come, my Celia, let us prove,[2]
While we can, the sports of love;
Time will not be ours forever:
He at length our good will sever.
Spend not, then, his gifts in vain;                     5
Suns that set may rise again,
But if once we lose this light,
'Tis with us perpetual night.
Why should we defer our joys?
Fame and rumor are but toys.                            10
Cannot we delude the eyes
Of a few poor household spies?
Or his easier ears beguile,
Thus removéd by our wile?
'Tis no sin love's fruits to steal,                     15
But the sweet thefts to reveal;
To be taken, to be seen,
These have crimes accounted been.

                                                    1606

ALFRED, LORD TENNYSON

## Now Sleeps the Crimson Petal[1]

Now sleeps the crimson petal, now the white;
Nor waves the cypress in the palace walk;
Nor winks the gold fin in the porphyry font;[2]
The firefly wakens; waken thou with me.

Now droops the milk-white peacock like a ghost,         5
And like a ghost she glimmers on to me.

Now lies the Earth all Danaë[3] to the stars,
And all thy heart lies open unto me.

Now slides the silent meteor on, and leaves
A shining furrow, as thy thoughts in me.                10

Now folds the lily all her sweetness up,
And slips into the bosom of the lake;

1. A song from *Volpone,* sung by the play's villain and would-be seducer. Part of the poem paraphrases Catullus, V, as does Campion's "My Sweetest Lesbia."
2. Try.
1. A song from *The Princess,* in the form of a ghazal.
2. Stone fishbowl. "porphyry": a red stone containing fine white crystals.
3. A princess, confined in a tower, seduced by Zeus after he became a shower of gold in order to gain access to her.

So fold thyself, my dearest, thou, and slip
Into my bosom and be lost in me.

1847

X. J. KENNEDY

# In a Prominent Bar in Secaucus One Day

*To the tune of "The Old Orange Flute" or
the tune of "Sweet Betsy from Pike"*

In a prominent bar in Secaucus[1] one day
Rose a lady in skunk with a topheavy sway,
Raised a knobby red finger—all turned from their beer—
While with eyes bright as snowcrust she sang high and clear:

"Now who of you'd think from an eyeload of me                5
That I once was a lady as proud as could be?
Oh I'd never sit down by a tumbledown drunk
If it wasn't, my dears, for the high cost of junk.

"All the gents used to swear that the white of my calf
Beat the down of a swan by a length and a half.                10
In the kerchief of linen I caught to my nose
Ah, there never fell snot, but a little gold rose.

"I had seven gold teeth and a toothpick of gold,
My Virginia cheroot was a leaf of it rolled
And I'd light it each time with a thousand in cash—           15
Why the bums used to fight if I flicked them an ash.

"Once the toast of the Biltmore,[2] the belle of the Taft,
I would drink bottle beer at the Drake, never draft,
And dine at the Astor on Salisbury steak
With a clean tablecloth for each bite I did take.              20

"In a car like the Roxy[3] I'd roll to the track,
A steel-guitar trio, a bar in the back,
And the wheels made no noise, they turned over so fast,
Still it took you ten minutes to see me go past.

"When the horses bowed down to me that I might choose,         25
I bet on them all, for I hated to lose.
Now I'm saddled each night for my butter and eggs
And the broken threads race down the backs of my legs.

"Let you hold in mind, girls, that your beauty must pass
Like a lovely white clover that rusts with its grass.          30
Keep your bottoms off barstools and marry you young
Or be left—an old barrel with many a bung.

"For when time takes you out for a spin in his car
You'll be hard-pressed to stop him from going too far

1. A small, smoggy town on the Hackensack River in New Jersey, a few miles west of Manhattan.
2. Like the Taft, Drake, and Astor, a once fashionable New York hotel.
3. A luxurious old New York theater and movie house, the site of many "World Premieres" in the heyday of Hollywood.

And be left by the roadside, for all your good deeds,     35
Two toadstools for tits and a face full of weeds."

All the house raised a cheer, but the man at the bar
Made a phonecall and up pulled a red patrol car
And she blew us a kiss as they copped her away
From that prominent bar in Secaucus, N.J.     40

1961

ANDREW MARVELL

# To His Coy Mistress

Had we but world enough, and time,
This coyness,[1] lady, were no crime.
We would sit down, and think which way
To walk, and pass our long love's day.
Thou by the Indian Ganges' side     5
Shouldst rubies[2] find: I by the tide
Of Humber[3] would complain. I would
Love you ten years before the Flood,
And you should if you please refuse
Till the conversion of the Jews.[4]     10
My vegetable love[5] should grow
Vaster than empires, and more slow;
An hundred years should go to praise
Thine eyes, and on thy forehead gaze;
Two hundred to adore each breast,     15
But thirty thousand to the rest.
An age at least to every part,
And the last age should show your heart.
For, lady, you deserve this state;[6]
Nor would I love at lower rate.     20
    But at my back I always hear
Time's wingèd chariot hurrying near;
And yonder all before us lie
Deserts of vast eternity.
Thy beauty shall no more be found,     25
Nor, in thy marble vault, shall sound
My echoing song; then worms shall try
That long preserved virginity,
And your quaint honor turn to dust,
And into ashes all my lust:     30
The grave's a fine and private place,
But none, I think, do there embrace.
    Now therefore, while the youthful hue
Sits on thy skin like morning dew,[7]

1. Hesitancy, modesty (not necessarily suggesting calculation).
2. Talismans which are supposed to preserve virginity.
3. A small river which flows through Marvell's home town, Hull. "complain": write love complaints, conventional songs lamenting the cruelty of love.
4. Which, according to popular Christian belief, will occur just before the end of the world.
5. Which is capable only of passive growth, not of consciousness. The "Vegetable Soul" is lower than the other two divisions of the Soul, "Animal" and "Rational."
6. Dignity.
7. The text reads "glew." "Lew" (warmth) has also been suggested as an emendation.

And while thy willing soul transpires[8]                   35
At every pore with instant fires,
Now let us sport us while we may,
And now, like am'rous birds of prey,
Rather at once our time devour
Than languish in his slow-chapped[9] pow'r.              40
Let us roll all our strength and all
Our sweetness up into one ball,
And tear our pleasures with rough strife
Thorough[1] the iron gates of life.
Thus, though we cannot make our sun               45
Stand still,[2] yet we will make him run.[3]

                                                        1681

# e. e. cummings

## (ponder,darling,these busted statues

(ponder,darling,these busted statues
of yon motheaten forum be aware
notice what hath remained
—the stone cringes
clinging to the stone,how obsolete          5

lips utter their extant smile . . . .
remark

a few deleted of texture
or meaning monuments and dolls

resist Them Greediest Paws of careful        10
time[1] all of which is extremely
unimportant)whereas Life

matters if or

when the your- and my-
idle vertical worthless                          15
self unite in a peculiarly
momentary

partnership(to instigate
constructive
              Horizontal                          20
business . . . . even so,let us make haste
—consider well this ruined aqueduct

lady,
which used to lead something into somewhere)

                                                        1926

8. Breathes forth.
9. Slow-jawed. Chronos (Time), ruler
of the world in early Greek myth, devoured
all of his children except Zeus, who was
hidden. Later, Zeus seized power (see
line 46 and note).
1. Through.

2. To lengthen his night of love with
Alcmene, Zeus made the sun stand still.
  3. Each sex act was believed to shorten
life by one day.
1. See "To His Coy Mistress," above,
especially lines 39–40.

WILLIAM HABINGTON

## To Roses in the Bosom of Castara

Ye blushing virgins happy are
In the chaste nunn'ry of her breasts,
For he'd profane so chaste a fair,[1]
Whoe'er should call them Cupid's nests.

Transplanted thus, how bright ye grow,          5
How rich a perfume do ye yield.
In some close garden, cowslips so
Are sweeter than i' th' open field.

In those white cloisters live secure
From the rude blasts of wanton breath,          10
Each hour more innocent and pure,
Till you shall wither into death.

Then that which living gave you room,
Your glorious sepulcher shall be;
There wants[2] no marble for a tomb,            15
Whose breast hath marble been to me.

1634


GEORGE HERBERT

## Virtue

Sweet day, so cool, so calm, so bright,
    The bridal of the earth and sky;
The dew shall weep thy fall tonight,
    For thou must die.

Sweet rose, whose hue, angry and brave,         5
    Bids the rash gazer wipe his eye;
Thy root is ever in its grave,
    And thou must die.

Sweet spring, full of sweet days and roses,
    A box where sweets[1] compacted lie;        10
My music shows ye have your closes,[2]
    And all must die.

Only a sweet and virtuous soul,
    Like seasoned timber, never gives;
But though the whole world turn to coal,[3]     15
    Then chiefly[4] lives.

1633

1. Beautiful woman.
2. Lacks.
1. Perfumes.
2. "Close": the conclusion of a musical

phrase, theme, or movement (OED).
3. Become cinders (on Judgment Day; see *II Peter* 3:10).
4. Then most of all.

FRANCIS QUARLES

# Hos Ego Versiculos[1]

Like to the damask rose you see,
Or like the blossom on the tree,
Or like the dainty flower of May,
Or like the morning to the day,
Or like the sun, or like the shade,                5
Or like the gourd which Jonas had;[2]
 Even such is man whose thread is spun,[3]
 Drawn out and cut, and so is done.

The rose withers, the blossom blasteth,
The flower fades, the morning hasteth:             10
The sun sets, the shadow flies,
The gourd consumes, and man he dies.

Like to the blaze of fond[4] delight;
Or like a morning clear and bright;
Or like a frost, or like a shower;                 15
Or like the pride of Babel's Tower;[5]
Or like the hour that guides[6] the time;
Or like to beauty in her prime;
 Even such is man, whose glory lends
 His life a blaze or two, and ends.            20

Delights vanish; the morn o'ercasteth,
The frost breaks, the shower hasteth;
The Tower falls, the hour spends;
The beauty fades, and man's life ends.

1629

ROBERT BURNS

# A Red, Red Rose

O, my luve's like a red, red rose
That's newly sprung in June.
O, my luve is like the melodie
That's sweetly played in tune.

---

1. Part of a phrase from Vergil: "Hos ego versiculos feci, tulit alter honores": "I wrote these little lines; another wears the honors." Many verses in the early to mid-17th century were written according to this formula ("Like to the . . .") and they were variously ascribed in collections of poetry.
2. According to *Jonah* 4:5–7, God sent a large gourd to shade Jonah and "deliver him from his grief" after the city of Nineveh repented and was spared from divine wrath; the next day "God prepared a worm . . . , and it smote the gourd that it withered."

3. In Greek mythology, one of the Fates (Clotho) draws the thread of life from her distaff, Lachesis spins out the events between life and death, and Atropos cuts the thread.
4. Foolish.
5. According to *Genesis* 11, men after the flood built the Tower of Babel thinking its top could "reach unto heaven" and "make us a name," but God punished their pride by scattering them over the earth and confounding language so that they could no longer understand one another.
6. Controls fleetingly.

As fair art thou, my bonnie lass,                    5
So deep in luve am I;
And I will luve thee still, my dear,
Till a' the seas gang[7] dry.

Till a' the seas gang dry, my dear,
And the rocks melt wi' the sun;                      10
And I will luve thee still, my dear,
While the sands o' life shall run.

And fare thee weel, my only luve,
And fare thee weel a while!
And I will come again, my luve,                      15
Though it were ten thousand mile.

1796

WILLIAM ERNEST HENLEY

## I Send You Roses

I send you roses—red, like love,
    And white, like death, sweet friend:
Born in your bosom to rejoice,
    Languish, and droop, and end.

If the white roses tell of death,                    5
    Let the red roses mend
The talk with true stories of love
    Unchanging till the end.

Red and white roses, love and death—
    What else is left to send?                       10
For what is life but love, the means,
    And death, true Wife, the end?

1901

W. B. YEATS

## The Rose of the World

Who dreamed that beauty passes like a dream?
For these red lips, with all their mournful pride,
Mournful that no new wonder may betide,
Troy passed away in one high funeral gleam,[1]
And Usna's children[2] died.                          5

We and the laboring world are passing by:
Amid men's souls, that waver and give place
Like the pale waters in their wintry race,

---

7. Go.
1. The Trojan War was fought over Helen, the wife of King Menelaus; she eloped with Paris, and the Greeks besieged Troy to get her back.
2. In Irish legend, beheaded by Conchubar, in jealousy over the love of Deirdre.

Under the passing stars, foam of the sky,
Lives on this lonely face.                                    10

Bow down, archangels, in your dim abode:
Before you were, or any hearts to beat,
Weary and kind one lingered by His seat;
He made the world to be a grassy road
Before her wandering feet.                                    15

1893

BROTHER ANTONINUS

## The Dark Roots of the Rose

The dark roots of the rose cry in my heart.
They pierce through rock-ribs of my stony flesh,
Invest the element, the loam of life.
They twist and mesh.

The red blood of the rose beats on, beats on,       5
Of passion poured, of fiery love composed,
Virtue redeemed, the singular crest of life,
And pride deposed.

Love cries regenerate and lust moans consumed,
Shaken in terror on that rage of breath.            10
Untrammeled still the red rose burns on
And knows no death.

Petal by crimson petal, leaf by leaf,
Unfolds the luminous core, the bright abyss,
Proffers at last the exquisite delight              15
Of the long kiss.

Until shall pass away the wasted means
Leaving in essence what time held congealed:
The Sign of God evoked from the splendid flesh
Of the Rose[1] revealed.                            20

1967

ROBERT FROST

## The Rose Family[2]

The rose is a rose,
And was always a rose.
But the theory now goes
That the apple's a rose,
And the pear is, and so's       5
The plum, I suppose.
The dear only knows
What will next prove a rose.

1. The "Rose of Sharon" mentioned in *Song of Songs* 2:1 has traditionally been interpreted as Christ, and the rose has also become a symbol of the Virgin Mary.
2. A response to Gertrude Stein's famous line, "A rose is a rose is a rose."

You, of course, are a rose—
But were always a rose.                                                10

1928

**ROBERT HERRICK**

## The Funeral Rites of the Rose

The Rose was sick, and smiling died;
And (being to be sanctified)
About the bed, there sighing stood
The sweet, and flowery sisterhood.
Some hung the head, while some did bring        5
(To wash her) water from the spring.
Some laid her forth, while others wept,
But all a solemn fast there kept.
The holy sisters some among
The sacred dirge and trental[1] sung.           10
But ah! what sweets smelt everywhere,
As[2] Heaven had spent all perfumes there.
At last, when prayers for the dead,
And rites were all accomplishéd;
They, weeping, spread a lawny loom,[3]           15
And closed her up, as in a tomb.

1648

**WILLIAM BLAKE**

## The Sick Rose[1]

O rose, thou art sick.
The invisible worm
That flies in the night
In the howling storm

Has found out thy bed                            5
Of crimson joy,
And his dark secret love
Does thy life destroy.

1794

**e. e. cummings**

## the rose is dying

the rose
is dying the
lips of an old man murder

the petals
hush                                             5

1. Literally, a set of thirty requiem masses.
2. As if. "spent": used up.
3. Linen-like cloth.

1. In Renaissance emblem books, the scarab beetle, worm, and rose are closely associated: The beetle feeds on dung, and the smell of the rose is fatal to it.

mysteriously
invisible mourners move
with prose faces and sobbing, garments
The symbol of the rose

motionless                                          10
with grieving feet and
wings
mounts

against the margins of steep song
a stallion sweetness     ,the                       15

lips of an old man murder

the petals.

1923

DONALD JUSTICE

## Southern Gothic

*(for W.E.B. & P.R.)*

Something of how the homing bee at dusk
Seems to inquire, perplexed, how there can be
No flowers here, not even withered stalks of flowers,
Conjures a garden where no garden is
And trellises too frail almost to bear            5
The memory of a rose, much less a rose.
Great oaks, more monumentally great oaks now
Than ever when the living rose was new,
Cast shade that is the more completely shade
Upon a house of broken windows merely            10
And empty nests up under broken eaves.
No damask any more prevents the moon,
But it unravels, peeling from a wall,
Red roses within roses within roses.

1960

WILLIAM CARLOS WILLIAMS

## Poem

The rose fades
and is renewed again
by its seed, naturally
but where

save in the poem                                  5
shall it go
to suffer no diminution
of its splendor

1962

WALLACE STEVENS

# Martial Cadenza

### I

Only this evening I saw again low in the sky
The evening star, at the beginning of winter, the star
That in spring will crown every western horizon,
Again . . . as if it came back, as if life came back,
Not in a later son, a different daughter, another place,    5
But as if evening found us young, still young,
Still walking in a present of our own.

### II

It was like sudden time in a world without time,
This world, this place, the street in which I was,
Without time: as that which is not has no time,    10
Is not, or is of what there was, is full
Of the silence before the armies, armies without
Either trumpets or drums, the commanders mute, the arms
On the ground, fixed fast in a profound defeat.

### III

What had this star to do with the world it lit,    15
With the blank skies over England, over France
And above the German camps? It looked apart.
Yet it is this that shall maintain—Itself
Is time, apart from any past, apart
From any future, the ever-living and being,    20
The ever-breathing and moving, the constant fire,

### IV

The present close, the present realized,
Not the symbol but that for which the symbol stands,
The vivid thing in the air that never changes,
Though the air change. Only this evening I saw it again,    25
At the beginning of winter, and I walked and talked
Again, and lived and was again, and breathed again
And moved again and flashed again, time flashed again.

1942

RICHARD WILBUR

# All These Birds

Agreed that all these birds,
Hawk or heavenly lark or heard-of nightingale,
Perform upon the kitestrings of our sight
In a false distance, that the day and night
Are full of wingéd words    5
                gone rather stale,

That nothing is so worn
As Philomel's[1] bosom-thorn,

That it is, in fact, the male
Nightingale which sings, and that all these creatures wear          10
Invisible armor such as Hébert beheld
His water-ousel through, as, wrapped or shelled
In a clear bellying veil
                    or bubble of air,
It bucked the flood to feed          15
At the stream-bottom.[2] Agreed

That the sky is a vast claire[3]
In which the gull, despite appearances, is not
Less claustral[4] than the oyster in its beak
And dives like nothing human; that we seek          20
Vainly to know the heron
                    (but can plot
What angle of the light
Provokes its northern flight.)

Let them be polyglot[5]          25
And wordless then, those boughs that spoke with Solomon
In Hebrew canticles, and made him wise;·
And let a clear and bitter wind arise
To storm into the hotbeds
                    of the sun,          30
And there, beyond a doubt,
Batter the Phoenix[6] out.

Let us, with glass or gun,
Watch (from our clever blinds) the monsters of the sky
Dwindle to habit, habitat, and song,          35
And tell the imagination it is wrong
Till, lest it be undone,
                    it spin a lie
So fresh, so pure, so rare
As to possess the air.          40

Why should it be more shy
Than chimney-nesting storks, or sparrows on a wall?
Oh, let it climb wherever it can cling
Like some great trumpet-vine, a natural thing
To which all birds that fly          45
                    come natural.
Come, stranger, sister, dove:
Put on the reins of love.

                                        1956

---

1. The nightingale's.
2. Water-ousels dive into streams and
remain for long periods, seeming to "fly"
underwater.
3. Oyster pond, usually built for ob-
servation purposes.

4. Secluded.
5. Many-languaged.
6. Legendary one-of-a-kind bird that
dies in flames and then rises from its own
ashes.

WILLIAM SHAKESPEARE

# All the World's a Stage[1]

All the world's a stage,                                    139
And all the men and women merely players.
They have their exits and their entrances,
And one man in his time plays many parts,
His acts being seven ages. At first, the infant,
Mewling and puking in the nurse's arms.
Then the whining schoolboy, with his satchel          145
And shining morning face, creeping like snail
Unwillingly to school. And then the lover,
Sighing like furnace, with a woeful ballad[2]
Made to his mistress' eyebrow. Then a soldier,
Full of strange oaths and bearded like the pard,[3]    150
Jealous in honor,[4] sudden and quick in quarrel,
Seeking the bubble reputation
Even in the cannon's mouth. And then the justice,
In fair round belly with good capon lined,[5]
With eyes severe and beard of formal cut,              155
Full of wise saws[6] and modern instances;
And so he plays his part. The sixth age shifts
Into the lean and slippered pantaloon,[7]
With spectacles on nose and pouch on side;
His youthful hose, well saved, a world too wide        160
For his shrunk shank, and his big manly voice,
Turning again toward childish treble, pipes
And whistles in his sound. Last scene of all,
That ends this strange eventful history,
Is second childishness and mere oblivion,              165
Sans teeth, sans eyes, sans taste, sans everything.

ca. 1599

EDMUND SPENSER

# Of This World's Theater in Which We Stay

Of this world's theater in which we stay,
My love, like the spectator, idly sits;
Beholding me, that all the pageants[1] play,
Disguising diversly my troubled wits.
Sometimes I joy when glad occasion fits,                5
And mask in mirth like to a comedy:
Soon after, when my joy to sorrow flits,
I wail and make my woes a tragedy.
Yet she, beholding me with constant eye,

1. A speech by Jaques in *As You Like It*, Act II, sc. vii. The metaphor of the world as stage (and the stage as a little world) dates from classical antiquity, and the motto of the newly opened Globe Theater (where *As You Like It* was played) was "Totus mundus agit histrionem": "All the world plays the actor."
2. Verse, song.
3. Leopard.
4. Zealous in pursuing fame; sensitive about his good name.
5. Well fed with presents (from those who seek his favorable judgment).
6. Sayings: maxims.
7. A ridiculous old man in Italian comedy.
1. Roles.

Delights not in my mirth, nor rues[2] my smart:                    10
But when I laugh, she mocks; and when I cry
She laughs and hardens evermore her heart.
What then can move her? If nor mirth nor moan,
She is no woman, but a senseless stone.

1595

FRANCIS QUARLES

## My Soul, Sit Thou a Patient Looker-on[3]

My soul, sit thou a patient looker-on;
Judge not the play before the play is done.
Her plot has many changes: every day
Speaks a new scene. The last act crowns the play.

1635

JOHN DONNE

## This Is My Play's Last Scene

This is my play's last scene, here heavens appoint
My pilgrimage's last mile; and my race,
Idly yet quickly run, hath this last pace,
My span's[1] last inch, my minute's last point;
And gluttonous death will instantly unjoint               5
My body and soul, and I shall sleep a space;
But my ever-waking part shall see that face
Whose fear[2] already shakes my every joint.
Then, as my soul to heaven, her first seat, takes flight,
And earth-born body in the earth shall dwell,             10
So, fall my sins, that all may have their right,
To where they're bred, and would press me, to hell.
Impute me righteous, thus purged of evil,
For thus I leave the world, the flesh, the devil.[3]

1633

SIR WALTER RALEGH

## What Is Our Life? A Play of Passion

What is our life? A play of passion;
Our mirth, the music of division;[1]
Our mothers' wombs the tiring-houses[2] be
Where we are dressed for this short comedy.
Heaven the judicious sharp spectator is,                  5
That sits and marks still[3] who doth act amiss;
Our graves that hide us from the searching sun
Are like drawn curtains when the play is done.

2. Pities.
3. The concluding epigram to Quarles'
*Emblem XV*, depicting and then meditating
upon a scene presided over by Satan, who
has usurped God's throne.
1. Literally, a "span" is the distance
from the tip of the thumb to the tip of the
little finger; traditionally, a representation
of the shortness of human life.
2. The fear of whom.
3. The traditional Three Temptations.
1. A rapid melodic passage, or a variation on a musical theme.
2. Dressing rooms.
3. Observes constantly.

Thus march we, playing, to our latest rest,
Only we die in earnest—that's no jest.                    10

1612

ALGERNON CHARLES SWINBURNE

## Stage Love

When the game began between them for a jest,
He played king and she played queen to match the best;
Laughter soft as tears, and tears that turned to laughter,
These were things she sought for years and sorrowed after.

Pleasure with dry lips, and pain that walks by night;      5
All the sting and all the stain of long delight;
These were things she knew not of, that knew not of her,
When she played at half a love with half a lover.

Time was chorus, gave them cues to laugh or cry;
They would kill, befool, amuse him, let him die;           10
Set him webs to weave today and break tomorrow,
Till he died for good in play, and rose in sorrow.

What the years mean; how time dies and is not slain;
How love grows and laughs and cries and wanes again;
These were things she came to know, and take their measure,  15
When the play was played out so for one man's pleasure.

1866

W.  B.  YEATS

## Lapis Lazuli[1]

*(for Harry Clifton)*

I have heard that hysterical women say
They are sick of the palette and fiddle-bow,
Of poets that are always gay,
For everybody knows or else should know
That if nothing drastic is done                            5
Aeroplane and Zeppelin will come out,
Pitch like King Billy[2] bomb-balls in
Until the town lie beaten flat.

All perform their tragic play,
There struts Hamlet, there is Lear,                        10
That's Ophelia, that Cordelia;
Yet they, should the last scene be there,
The great stage curtain about to drop,
If worthy their prominent part in the play,

1. A deep blue semiprecious stone, often meticulously carved (see lines 37–49).
2. Kaiser Wilhelm, Emperor of Germany in World War I. "King Billy" was originally a nickname for William III (William of Orange), King of England 1689– 1702, who subdued Ireland and destroyed much of the city of Limerick by bombardment. He was often nicknamed and attacked in ballads and lampoons; another of his names was "Wee Willie Winkie."

Do not break up their lines to weep.                    15
They know that Hamlet and Lear are gay;
Gaiety transfiguring all that dread.
All men have aimed at, found and lost;
Black out; Heaven blazing into the head:
Tragedy wrought to its uttermost.                       20
Though Hamlet rambles and Lear rages,
And all the drop-scenes drop at once
Upon a hundred thousand stages,
It cannot grow by an inch or an ounce.

On their own feet they come, or on shipboard,           25
Camel-back, horse-back, ass-back, mule-back,
Old civilizations put to the sword.
Then they and their wisdom went to rack:
No handiwork of Callimachus,[3]
Who handled marble as if it were bronze,                30
Made draperies that seemed to rise
When sea-wind swept the corner, stands;
His long lamp-chimney shaped like the stem
Of a slender palm, stood but a day;
All things fall and are built again,                    35
And those that build them again are gay.

Two Chinamen, behind them a third,
Are carved in lapis lazuli,[4]
Over them flies a long-legged bird,
A symbol of longevity;                                  40
The third, doubtless a serving-man,
Carries a musical instrument.

Every discoloration of the stone,
Every accidental crack or dent,
Seems a water-course or an avalanche,                   45
Or lofty slope where it still snows
Though doubtless plum or cherry-branch
Sweetens the little half-way house
Those Chinamen climb towards, and I
Delight to imagine them seated there;                   50
There, on the mountain and the sky,
On all the tragic scene they stare.
One asks for mournful melodies;
Accomplished fingers begin to play.
Their eyes mid many wrinkles, their eyes,               55
Their ancient, glittering eyes, are gay.

1938

3. Fifth-century B.C. Greek sculptor. Of him Yeats wrote the following in *A Vision:* "With Callimachus pure Ionic revives again . . . ; upon the only example of his work known to us, a marble chair, a Persian is represented, and may one not discover a Persian symbol in that bronze lamp, shaped like a palm . . . ? But he was an archaistic workman, and those who set him to work brought back public life to an older form."
4. ". . . someone has sent me a present of a great piece [of lapis lazuli] carved by some Chinese sculptor into the semblance of a mountain with temple, trees, paths and an ascetic and pupil about to climb the mountain. Ascetic, pupil, hard stone, eternal theme of the sensual east. The heroic cry in the midst of despair. But no, I am wrong, the east has its solutions always and therefore knows nothing of tragedy. It is we, not the east, that must raise the heroic cry." (Yeats to Dorothy Wellesley, July 6, 1935, in *Letters on Poetry* [London: Oxford University Press, 1940]).

GEOFFREY CHAUCER

## Whan that Aprill with His Shoures Soote[1]

Whan that Aprill with his shoures soote[2]
The droghte[3] of March hath perced to the roote,
And bathed every veyne[4] in swich licour,
Of which vertu[5] engendred is the flour;
Whan Zephyrus[6] eek with his sweete breeth                    5
Inspired hath in every holt and heeth[7]
The tendre croppes, and the yonge sonne[8]
Hath in the Ram his halfe cours yronne,
And smale foweles[9] maken melodye
That slepen[1] al the nyght with open yë—                      10
So priketh hem[2] Nature in hir corages—
Thanne longen[3] folk to goon on pilgrimages,
And palmeres[4] for to seken straunge strondes
To ferne halwes, kowthe[5] in sondry londes;
And specially from every shires[6] ende                        15
Of Engelond to Caunterbury they wende,[7]
The holy blisful martir for to seke
That hem hath holpen[8] whan that they were seeke.

ca. 1386

DYLAN THOMAS

## The Force that Through the Green Fuse Drives the Flower

The force that through the green fuse drives the flower
Drives my green age; that blasts the roots of trees
Is my destroyer.
And I am dumb to tell the crooked rose
My youth is bent by the same wintry fever.                     5

The force that drives the water through the rocks
Drives my red blood; that dries the mouthing streams
Turns mine to wax.
And I am dumb to mouth unto my veins
How at the mountain spring the same mouth sucks.               10

---

1. The opening lines of the "General Prologue" to *The Canterbury Tales,* a series of stories told by pilgrims going to Canterbury.
2. Sweet showers.
3. Drought. "perced": pierced.
4. Vein: vessel of sap. "swich licour": such liquid.
5. By the power ("vertu") of which. "flour": flower.
6. The west wind, traditionally the spring wind which renews life. "eek": also.
7. Woods and field.
8. Sun: "young" because it has run only halfway (line 8) through its course in Aries (the Ram), the first sign of the zodiac in the solar year. "croppes": shoots, sprouts.
9. Fowls: birds.
1. Sleep. "yë": eye.
2. Them. "hir corages": their hearts.
3. Long: desire. "goon": go.
4. Pilgrims who range widely to far-off shrines ("ferne halwes") on the foreign shores of the Holy Land ("straunge strondes").
5. Known.
6. Shire's: county's.
7. Go. At Canterbury was the shrine of St. Thomas à Becket ("the holy blisful martir"), murdered in Canterbury Cathedral in 1170.
8. Helped. "seeke": sick.

The hand that whirls the water in the pool
Stirs the quicksand; that ropes the blowing wind
Hauls my shroud sail.
And I am dumb to tell the hanging man
How of my clay is made the hangman's lime.                    15

The lips of time leech to the fountain head;
Love drips and gathers, but the fallen blood
Shall calm her sores.
And I am dumb to tell a weather's wind
How time has ticked a heaven round the stars.               20

And I am dumb to tell the lover's tomb
How at my sheet goes the same crooked worm.

1934

HENRY HOWARD, EARL OF SURREY

# The Soote Season

The soote[1] season, that bud and bloom forth brings,
With green hath clad the hill and eke[2] the vale;
The nightingale with feathers new she sings;
The turtle[3] to her make hath told her tale.
Summer is come, for every spray[4] now springs;                5
The hart hath hung his old head on the pale;
The buck in brake his winter coat he flings;
The fishes float with new repairéd scale;
The adder all her slough away she slings;
The swift swallow pursueth the flies small;                   10
The busy bee her honey now she mings;[5]
Winter is worn, that was the flower's bale.[6]
   And thus I see among these pleasant things
   Each care decays, and yet my sorrow springs.

1557

GEORGE HERBERT

# The Flower

How fresh, O Lord, how sweet and clean
Are thy returns! Ev'n as the flowers in spring,
   To which, besides their own demean,[1]
The late-past frosts tributes of pleasure bring.
     Grief melts away                                 5
     Like snow in May,
  As if there were no such cold thing.

Who would have thought my shriveled heart
Could have recovered greenness? It was gone
   Quite under ground, as flowers depart                  10

1. Sweet.
2. Also.
3. Turtledove. "make": mate.
4. Sprout, shoot.

5. Remembers.
6. Enemy, instrument of death.
1. Demesne: estate.

To see their mother-root when they have blown;[2]
Where they together
All the hard weather,
Dead to the world, keep house unknown.

These are thy wonders, Lord of power,                15
Killing and quickning, bringing down to hell
And up to heaven in an hour,
Making a chiming of a passing-bell.[3]
We say amiss,
This or that is:                20
Thy word is all, if we could spell.

O that I once past changing were,
Fast in thy Paradise, where no flower can wither!
Many a spring I shoot up fair,
Off'ring[4] at heav'n, growing and groaning thither;                25
Nor doth my flower
Want a spring-shower,
My sins and I joining together.

But while I grow in a straight line,
Still upwards bent, as if heav'n were mine own,                30
Thy anger comes, and I decline.
What frost to that? What pole is not the zone
Where all things burn,
When thou dost turn,
And the least frown of thine is shown?                35

And now in age I bud again,
After so many deaths I live and write;
I once more smell the dew and rain,
And relish versing. O my only light,
It cannot be                40
That I am he
On whom thy tempests fell all night.

These are thy wonders, Lord of love,
To make us see we are but flowers that glide;
Which when we once can find and prove,                45
Thou hast a garden for us where to bide.
Who would be more,
Swelling through store,[5]
Forfeit their Paradise by their pride.

1633

ANDREW MARVELL

# On a Drop of Dew

See how the orient[1] dew,
Shed from the bosom of the morn

2. Bloomed.
3. Which tolls for death.
4. Aiming.

5. Possessions.
1. Shining.

Into the blowing roses,
Yet careless of its mansion new
For[2] the clear region where 'twas born                         5
    Round in itself incloses,
    And in its little globe's extent
Frames as it can its native element;
    How it the purple flow'r does slight,
    Scarce touching where it lies,                              10
But gazing back upon the skies,
    Shines with a mournful light
        Like its own tear,
Because so long divided from the sphere.[3]
    Restless it rolls and unsecure,                            15
    Trembling lest it grow impure,

Till the warm sun pity its pain,
And to the skies exhale it back again.
    So the soul, that drop, that ray
Of the clear fountain of eternal day,                          20
Could it within the human flower be seen,
    Rememb'ring still its former height,
    Shuns the sweet leaves and blossoms green;
    And, recollecting its own light,
Does, in its pure and circling thoughts, express              25
The greater Heaven in an Heaven less.
    In how coy[4] a figure wound,
    Every way it turns away;
    So the world excluding round,
    Yet receiving in the day:                                  30
    Dark beneath, but bright above,
    Here disdaining, there in love.

How loose and easy hence to go,
How girt and ready to ascend;
    Moving but on a point below,                               35
    It all about does upwards bend.
Such did the manna's sacred dew distill,
White and entire, though congealed and chill;[5]
Congealed on earth, but does, dissolving, run
Into the glories of th' almighty sun.                          40

1681

HENRY KING

# Sic Vita[1]

Like to the falling of a star,
Or as the flights of eagles are,
Or like the fresh spring's gaudy hue,
Or silver drops of morning dew,
Or like a wind that chafes the flood,                          5

2. By reason of.
3. Of heaven.
4. Reserved, withdrawn, modest.
5. In the wilderness, the Israelites fed
upon manna from heaven (distilled from
the dew; see *Exodus* 16:10–21); manna
became a traditional symbol for divine
grace.
1. Thus is life.

Or bubbles which on water stood:
Even such is man, whose borrowed light
Is straight called in, and paid tonight.

The wind blows out, the bubble dies;
The spring entombed in autumn lies;                    10
The dew dries up, the star is shot;
The flight is past, and man forgot.

                                                      1657

JOSEPH ADDISON

## The Spacious Firmament on High[2]

The spacious firmament on high,
With all the blue ethereal sky,
And spangled heav'ns, a shining frame,
Their great Original proclaim:
Th' unwearied sun, from day to day,                    5
Does his Creator's power display,
And publishes to ev'ry land
The work of an Almighty Hand.

Soon as the ev'ning shades prevail,
The moon takes up the wondrous tale,                   10
And nightly to the list'ning earth
Repeats the story of her birth:
Whilst all the stars that round her burn,
And all the planets, in their turn,
Confirm the tidings as they roll,                      15
And spread the truth from pole to pole.

What though, in solemn silence, all
Move round the dark terrestrial ball?
What though nor real voice nor sound
Amid their radiant orbs be found?                      20
In reason's ear they all rejoice,
And utter forth a glorious voice,
Forever singing, as they shine,
"The Hand that made us is divine."

                                                      p. 1712

BEN JONSON

## To Penshurst[1]

Thou art not, Penshurst, built to envious show,
Of touch[2] or marble; nor canst boast a row

2. In an essay accompanying this poem on its first publication in *The Spectator*, Addison cites *Psalm* 19 ("The heavens declare the glory of God; and the firmament showeth his handiwork") and writes: "The Supreme Being has made the best arguments for his own existence, in the formation of the heaven and the earth, and these are arguments which a man of sense cannot forbear attending to, who is out of the noise and hurry of human affairs."

1. The country seat (in Kent) of the Sidney family, owned by Sir Robert, brother of the poet, Sir Philip. Jonson's celebration of the estate is one of the earliest "house" poems and a prominent example of topographical or didactic-descriptive poetry.

2. Touchstone: basanite, a smooth dark stone similar to black marble.

Of polished pillars, or a roof of gold;
Thou hast no lantern[3] whereof tales are told,
Or stair, or courts; but stand'st an ancient pile,                          5
And, these grudged at,[4] art reverenced the while.
Thou joy'st in better marks, of soil, of air,
Of wood, of water; therein thou art fair.
Thou hast thy walks for health, as well as sport;
Thy mount, to which the dryads[5] do resort,                               10
Where Pan and Bacchus[6] their high feasts have made,
Beneath the broad beech and the chestnut shade,
That taller tree, which of a nut was set
At his great birth[7] where all the Muses met.
There in the writhéd bark are cut the names                                15
Of many a sylvan, taken with his flames;[8]
And thence the ruddy satyrs oft provoke
The lighter fauns to reach thy Lady's Oak.[9]
Thy copse too, named of Gamage,[1] thou hast there,
That never fails to serve thee seasoned deer                               20
When thou wouldst feast, or exercise, thy friends.
The lower land, that to the river bends,
Thy sheep, thy bullocks, kine, and calves do feed;
The middle grounds thy mares and horses breed.
Each bank doth yield thee conies;[2] and the tops,                         25
Fertile of wood, Ashore and Sidney's copse,[3]
To crown thy open table, doth provide
The purpled pheasant with the speckled side;
The painted partridge lies in every field,
And for thy mess is willing to be killed.                                  30
And if the high-swollen Medway[4] fail thy dish,
Thou hast thy ponds that pay thee tribute fish,
Fat agéd carps that run into thy net,
And pikes, now weary their own kind to eat,
As loath the second draught[5] or cast to stay,                            35
Officiously[6] at first themselves betray;
Bright eels that emulate them, and leap on land
Before the fisher, or into his hand.
Then hath thy orchard fruit, thy garden flowers,
Fresh as the air, and new as are the hours.                                40
The early cherry, with the later plum,
Fig, grape, and quince, each in his time doth come;
The blushing apricot and woolly peach
Hang on thy walls, that every child may reach.
And though thy walls be of the country stone,                              45
They're reared with no man's ruin, no man's groan;
There's none that dwell about them wish them down,
But all come in, the farmer and the clown,[7]

3. A glassed or open tower or dome atop the roof.
4. I.e., although these (more pretentious structures) are envied. "the while": anyway.
5. Wood nymphs.
6. Ancient gods of nature and wine, both associated with spectacular feasting and celebration.
7. Sir Philip Sidney's, on November 30, 1554; the tree stood for nearly 150 years.
8. Inspired by Sidney's love poetry. "sylvan": forest dweller, rustic.

9. Where, according to legend, a former lady of the house (Lady Leicester) began labor pains. "satyrs": half-men, half-goats who participated in the rites of Bacchus.
1. The maiden name of the owner's wife. "copse": thicket.
2. Rabbits.
3. Two spinneys, or little woods.
4. A river bordering the estate.
5. Of a net. "stay": await.
6. Obligingly.
7. Rustic, peasant.

And no one empty-handed, to salute
Thy lord and lady, though they have no suit.[8]      50
Some bring a capon, some a rural cake,
Some nuts, some apples; some that think they make
The better cheeses bring 'em, or else send
By their ripe daughters, whom they would commend
This way to husbands, and whose baskets bear      55
An emblem of themselves in plum or pear.
But what can this (more than express their love)
Add to thy free[9] provisions, far above
The need of such? whose liberal board doth flow
With all that hospitality doth know;      60
Where comes no guest but is allowed to eat,
Without his fear, and of thy lord's own meat;
Where the same beer and bread, and selfsame wine,
That is his lordship's shall be also mine.
And I not fain[1] to sit (as some this day      65
At great men's tables), and yet dine away.[2]
Here no man tells[3] my cups; nor, standing by,
A waiter doth my gluttony envý,
But gives me what I call, and lets me eat;
He knows below he shall find plenty of meat.      70
Thy tables hoard not up for the next day;
Nor, when I take my lodging, need I pray
For fire, or lights, or livery;[4] all is there,
As if thou then wert mine, or I reigned here:
There's nothing I can wish, for which I stay.      75
That found King James when, hunting late this way
With his brave son, the prince,[5] they saw thy fires
Shine bright on every hearth, as the desires
Of thy Penates[6] had been set on flame
To entertain them; or the country came      80
With all their zeal to warm their welcome here.
What (great I will not say, but) sudden cheer
Didst thou then make 'em! and what praise was heaped
On thy good lady then! who therein reaped
The just reward of her high housewifery;[7]      85
To have her linen, plate, and all things nigh,
When she was far; and not a room but dressed
As if it had expected such a guest!
These, Penshurst, are thy praise, and yet not all.
Thy lady's noble, fruitful, chaste withal.      90
His children thy great lord may call his own,
A fortune in this age but rarely known.
They are, and have been, taught religion; thence
Their gentler spirits have sucked innocence.
Each morn and even they are taught to pray,      95
With the whole household, and may, every day,
Read in their virtuous parents' noble parts
The mysteries of manners, arms, and arts.

---

8. Request for favors.
9. Generous.
1. Obliged.
2. Possibly, "elsewhere," because they do not get enough to eat; or "away" in the sense of far from the party of honor.

3. Counts.
4. Provisions (or, possibly, servants).
5. Prince Henry, who died in 1612.
6. Roman household gods who cared for the family's welfare.
7. Domestic economy.

Now, Penshurst, they that will proportion[8] thee
With other edifices, when they see                                 100
Those proud, ambitious heaps, and nothing else,
May say, their lords have built, but thy lord dwells.

1616

WILLIAM SHAKESPEARE

# [Order and Degree][1]

The heavens themselves, the planets, and this center[2]           85
Observe degree, priority, and place,
Insisture,[3] course, proportion, season, form,
Office, and custom, in all line of order.
And therefore is the glorious planet Sol[4]
In noble eminence enthroned and sphered                           90
Amidst the other,[5] whose med'cinable eye
Corrects the influence[6] of evil planets,
And posts, like the commandment of a king,
Sans check to good and bad. But when the planets
In evil mixture to disorder wander,                               95
What plagues, and what portents, what mutiny,
What raging of the sea, shaking of earth,
Commotion in the winds, frights, changes, horrors,
Divert and crack, rend and deracinate,
The unity and married calm of states                             100
Quite from their fixure[7]? O, when degree is shaked,
Which is the ladder of all high designs,
The enterprise is sick. How could communities,
Degrees in schools, and brotherhoods in cities,
Peaceful commerce from dividable shores,                          105
The primogenity[8] and due of birth,
Prerogative of age, crowns, scepters, laurels,
But by degree, stand in authentic place?
Take but degree away, untune that string,
And hark what discord follows. Each thing meets                   110
In mere oppugnancy.[9] The bounded waters
Should lift their bosoms higher than the shores
And make a sop[1] of all this solid globe;
Strength should be lord of imbecility,[2]
And the rude son should strike his father dead;                  115
Force should be right, or rather, right and wrong,
Between whose endless jar[3] justice resides,
Should lose their names, and so should justice too;
Then everything include itself in power,
Power into will, will into appetite,                              120
And appetite, an universal wolf,
So doubly seconded with will and power,
Must make perforce an universal prey,

8. Compare.
1. A speech by Ulysses to other Greek
leaders in *Troilus and Cressida*, Act I,
sc. iii.
2. Earth.
3. Regularity.
4. The sun.
5. Others.

6. Astrological effect.
7. Fixed place, stability.
8. Rights of the first-born son.
9. Total war.
1. Sponge.
2. Weakness.
3. Conflict.

And last eat up himself. Great Agamemnon,[4]
This chaos, when degree is suffocate,                                    125
Follows the choking.
And this neglection of degree it is
That by a pace goes backward with a purpose
It hath to climb. The general's disdained
By him one step below, he by the next,                                   130
That next by him beneath; so every step,
Exampled by the first pace[5] that is sick
Of his superior, grows to an envious fever
Of pale and bloodless emulation.

                                                          ca. 1601

SIR JOHN DAVIES

## *from* Orchestra: or, A Poem on Dancing[1]

And merry Bacchus[2] practiced dancing too,                              589
And to the Lydian numbers[3] rounds did make;
The like he did in the eastern India do,
And taught them all, when Phoebus[4] did awake,
And when at night he did his coach forsake,
To honor heaven and heaven's great rolling eye
With turning dances and with melody.                                     595

Thus they who first did found a commonweal,
And they who first religion did ordain,
By dancing first the people's hearts did steal;[5]
Of whom we now a thousand tales do feign.
Yet do we now their perfect rules retain,                                600
And use them still in such devices new
As in the world, long since their withering, grew.

For after towns and kingdoms founded were,
Between great states arose well-ordered war,
Wherein most perfect measure doth appear;                                605
Whether their well-set ranks respected are
In quadrant forms or semicircular,
Or else the march, when all the troops advance
And to the drum in gallant order dance.

And after wars, when white-winged victory                                610
Is with a glorious triumph beautified,
And every one doth *Io, Io!*[6] cry,
While all in gold the conqueror doth ride,
The solemn pomp that fills the city wide

4. One of the leaders addressed by Ulysses.
5. Step of another rebel.
1. Part of a long speech by Antinous to Penelope, giving philosophical and historical reasons why she should "dance" with him while her husband (Ulysses) is away at war.
2. Roman god of wine, whose festivals featured—among other things—vigorous dancing.
3. Rhythms. Once a prosperous city in Asia Minor, Lydia later became famous for luxury and dissipation.
4. Apollo in his form as the sun god, often portrayed driving a golden chariot ("coach," line 593) across the sky.
5. This and what follows in the next four stanzas draws on the traditional praise of music as cosmic harmonizer. Throughout the poem, Davies alludes to the traditional idea that the order of the universe depends upon musical principles.
6. A Greek and Latin exclamation of joy.

Observes such rank and measure everywhere                     615
As if they all together dancing were.

The like just order mourners do observe,
But with unlike affection and attire,
When some great man that nobly did deserve,
And whom his friends impatiently desire,                      620
Is brought with honor to his latest fire.
The dead corpse too in that sad dance is moved,
As if both dead and living dancing loved.

A diverse cause, but like solemnity,
Unto the temple leads the bashful bride,                      625
Which blusheth like the Indian ivory
Which is with dip of Tyrian purple dyed;
A golden troop doth pass on every side
Of flourishing young men and virgins gay,
Which keep fair measure all the flowery way.                  630

And not alone the general multitude,
But those choice Nestors,[7] which in council grave
Of cities and of kingdoms do conclude,
Most comely order in their sessions have;
Wherefore the wise Thessalians ever gave                      635
The name of leader of their country's dance
To him that had their country's governance.[8]

And those great masters of the liberal arts
In all their several schools do dancing teach;
For humble grammar first doth set the parts                   640
Of congruent and well-according speech,
Which rhetoric, whose state the clouds doth reach,
And heavenly poetry do forward lead,
And divers measures diversely do tread.

For Rhetoric, clothing speech in rich array,                  645
In looser numbers teacheth her to range
With twenty tropes,[9] and turnings every way,
And various figures, and licentious change;
But poetry, with rule and order strange,
So curiously doth move each single pace,                      650
As all is marred if she one foot misplace.

These arts of speech the guides and marshals are,
But logic leadeth reason in a dance,
Reason, the cynosure[1] and bright lodestar
In this world's sea, to avoid the rocks of chance;            655
For with close following and continuance
One reason doth another so ensue
As, in conclusion, still the dance is true.

---

7. Nestor was the oldest and most experienced among the Greeks in the Trojan
War.
   8. The term is "coryphaeus."

9. Figures of speech.
   1. Literally, the constellation Ursa
Minor, the "Lesser Bear," which contains
in its tail the polestar.

So music to her own sweet tunes doth trip,
With tricks of 3, 5, 8, 15, and more;                                           660
So doth the art of numbering seem to skip
From even to odd, in her proportioned score;
So do those skills, whose quick eyes do explore
The just dimension both of earth and heaven,
In all their rules observe a measure even.                                      665

Lo! this is Dancing's true nobility,
Dancing, the child of Music and of Love;
Dancing itself, both love and harmony,
Where all agree and all in order move;
Dancing, the art that all arts do approve;                                      670
The fair character of the world's consent,
The heaven's true figure, and th' earth's ornament.

                                                                                1596


THEODORE ROETHKE

# Four for Sir John Davies[1]

I   *The Dance*

Is that dance slowing in the mind of man
That made him think the universe could hum?
The great wheel turns its axle when it can;
I need a place to sing, and dancing-room,
And I have made a promise to my ears                                            5
I'll sing and whistle romping with the bears.

For they are all my friends: I saw one slide
Down a steep hillside on a cake of ice,—
Or was that in a book? I think with pride:
A caged bear rarely does the same thing twice                                   10
In the same way: O watch his body sway!—
This animal remembering to be gay.

I tried to fling my shadow at the moon,
The while my blood leaped with a wordless song.
Though dancing needs a master, I had none                                       15
To teach my toes to listen to my tongue.
But what I learned there, dancing all alone,
Was not the joyless motion of a stone.

I take this cadence from a man named Yeats;
I take it, and I give it back again:                                            20
For other tunes and other wanton beats
Have tossed my heart and fiddled through my brain.
Yes, I was dancing-mad, and how
That came to be the bears and Yeats would know.

1. See the poem by Davies, above.

II    *The Partner*

Between such animal and human heat                                    25
I find myself perplexed. What is desire?—
The impulse to make someone else complete?
That woman would set sodden straw on fire.
Was I the servant of a sovereign wish,
Or ladle rattling in an empty dish?                                   30

We played a measure with commingled feet:
The lively dead had taught us to be fond.
Who can embrace the body of his fate?
Light altered light along the living ground.
She kissed me close, and then did something else.                     35
My marrow beat as wildly as my pulse.

I'd say it to my horse: we live beyond
Our outer skin. Who's whistling up my sleeve?
I see a heron prancing in his pond;
I know a dance the elephants believe.                                 40
The living all assemble! What's the cue?—
Do what the clumsy partner wants to do!

Things loll and loiter. Who condones the lost?
This joy outleaps the dog. Who cares? Who cares?
I gave her kisses back, and woke a ghost.                             45
O what lewd music crept into our ears!
The body and the soul know how to play
In that dark world where gods have lost their way.

III    *The Wraith*

Incomprehensible gaiety and dread
Attended what we did. Behind, before,                                 50
Lay all the lonely pastures of the dead;
The spirit and the flesh cried out for more.
We two, together, on a darkening day
Took arms against our own obscurity.

Did each become the other in that play?                               55
She laughed me out, and then she laughed me in;
In the deep middle of ourselves we lay;
When glory failed, we danced upon a pin.
The valley rocked beneath the granite hill;
Our souls looked forth, and the great day stood still.                60

There was a body, and it cast a spell,—
God pity those but wanton to the knees,—
The flesh can make the spirit visible;
We woke to find the moonlight on our toes.
In the rich weather of a dappled wood                                 65
We played with dark and light as children should.

What shape leaped forward at the sensual cry?—
Sea-beast or bird flung toward the ravaged shore?
Did space shake off an angel with a sigh?
We rose to meet the moon, and saw no more.                            70

It was and was not she, a shape alone,
Impaled on light, and whirling slowly down.

IV   *The Vigil*

Dante attained the purgatorial hill,
Trembled at hidden virtue without flaw,
Shook with a mighty power beyond his will,—        75
Did Beatrice deny what Dante saw?
All lovers live by longing, and endure:
Summon a vision and declare it pure.

Though everything's astonishment at last,
Who leaps to heaven at a single bound?        80
The links were soft between us; still, we kissed;
We undid chaos to a curious sound:
The waves broke easy, cried to me in white;
Her look was morning in the dying light.

The visible obscures. But who knows when?        85
Things have their thought: they are the shards of me;
I thought that once, and thought comes round again;
Rapt, we leaned forth with what we could not see.
We danced to shining; mocked before the black
And shapeless night that made no answer back.        90

The world is for the living. Who are they?
We dared the dark to reach the white and warm.
She was the wind when wind was in my way;
Alive at noon, I perished in her form.
Who rise from flesh to spirit know the fall:        95
The word outleaps the world, and light is all.

1953

EDMUND WALLER

# The Dancer

Behold the brand[1] of beauty tossed!
See how the motion does dilate the flame!
Delighted love his spoils does boast,
And triumph in this game.
Fire, to no place confined,        5
Is both our wonder and our fear;
Moving the mind,
As lightning hurled through the air.

High heaven the glory does increase
Of all her shining lamps, this artful way;        10
The sun in figures, such as these,
Joys with the moon to play;
To the sweet strains they advance,
Which do result from their own spheres,[2]

1. Torch.
2. According to the Pythagorean tradition, the planets produce, by their harmonious movement, the "music of the spheres," and their "cosmic dance" then seems to move to the music.

As this nymph's dance                                    15
Moves with the numbers[3] which she hears.

1645

ALEXANDER WHITAKER

## Leaving the Dance

The dinosaurus courteously
Went to join prehistory.
He mildly told our hosts that he
Had quite enjoyed their company,
And going out, as some might do,                         5
He may have bent a shrub or two,
But nothing more—with elegance
He tipped his hat and left the dance.

I rather think such form is best;
Without disturbing any guest                             10
He simply left, and all the rest
Continued dancing undistressed.
(Though some, I've noticed, quite deplore
The way we scar the ballroom floor
Or swing upon the chandelier—                            15
They quietly sneak out the rear.)

The violinists in the wings,
Who all night long have strummed such things
As made us move like gorgeous kings,
Now scrape their bows on loosened strings.               20
Our hosts yawn in the smoke-filled air,
And the drummer has removed his snare.
It's time to go—with elegance
Let's get our things and leave the dance.

p. 1971

WALLACE STEVENS

## The Idea of Order at Key West

She sang beyond the genius of the sea.
The water never formed to mind or voice,
Like a body wholly body, fluttering
Its empty sleeves; and yet its mimic motion
Made constant cry, caused constantly a cry,             5
That was not ours although we understood,
Inhuman, of the veritable ocean.

The sea was not a mask. No more was she.
The song and water were not medleyed sound
Even if what she sang was what she heard,               10
Since what she sang was uttered word by word.
It may be that in all her phrases stirred

3. Rhythms.

The grinding water and the gasping wind;
But it was she and not the sea we heard.

For she was the maker of the song she sang.                    15
The ever-hooded, tragic-gestured sea
Was merely a place by which she walked to sing.
Whose spirit is this? we said, because we knew
It was the spirit that we sought and knew
That we should ask this often as she sang.                     20

If it was only the dark voice of the sea
That rose, or even colored by many waves;
If it was only the outer voice of sky
And cloud, of the sunken coral water-walled,
However clear, it would have been deep air,                    25
The heaving speech of air, a summer sound
Repeated in a summer without end
And sound alone. But it was more than that,
More even than her voice, and ours, among
The meaningless plungings of water and the wind,               30
Theatrical distances, bronze shadows heaped
On high horizons, mountainous atmospheres
Of sky and sea.
             It was her voice that made
The sky acutest at its vanishing.
She measured to the hour its solitude.                         35
She was the single artificer of the world
In which she sang. And when she sang, the sea,
Whatever self it had, became the self
That was her song, for she was the maker. Then we,
As we beheld her striding there alone,                         40
Knew that there never was a world for her
Except the one she sang and, singing, made.

Ramon Fernandez,[1] tell me, if you know,
Why, when the singing ended and we turned
Toward the town, tell why the glassy lights,                   45
The lights in the fishing boats at anchor there,
As the night descended, tilting in the air,
Mastered the night and portioned out the sea,
Fixing emblazoned zones and fiery poles,
Arranging, deepening, enchanting night.                        50

Oh! Blessed rage for order, pale Ramon,
The maker's rage to order words of the sea,
Words of the fragrant portals, dimly-starred,
And of ourselves and of our origins,
In ghostlier demarcations, keener sounds.                      55

                                                              1935

1. French classicist and critic, 1894–
1944, who emphasized the ordering role of
a writer's consciousness upon the materials
he used. Stevens denied that he had Fernandez in mind, saying that he combined
a Spanish first name and surname at random: "I knew of Ramon Fernandez, the
critic, and had read some of his criticisms,
but I did not have him in mind." (*Letters*
[New York: Knopf, 1960], p. 798) Later,
Stevens wrote to another correspondent
that he did not have the critic "consciously"
in mind. (*Letters*, p. 823)

LANGSTON HUGHES

# Pennsylvania Station[2]

The Pennsylvania Station in New York
Is like some vast basilica of old
That towers above the terrors of the dark
As bulwark and protection to the soul.
Now people who are hurrying alone                          5
And those who come in crowds from far away
Pass through this great concourse of steel and stone
To trains, or else from trains out into day.
And as in great basilicas of old
The search was ever for a dream of God,                    10
So here the search is still within each soul
Some seed to find that sprouts a holy tree
To glorify the earth—and you—and me.

                                                p. 1962

HOWARD NEMEROV

# The Town Dump

"The art of our necessities is strange,
That can make vile things precious."[1]

A mile out in the marshes, under a sky
Which seems to be always going away
In a hurry, on that Venetian land threaded
With hidden canals, you will find the city
Which seconds ours (so cemeteries, too,                    5
Reflect a town from hillsides out of town),
Where Being most Becomingly[2] ends up
Becoming some more. From cardboard tenements,
Windowed with cellophane, or simply tenting
In paper bags, the angry mackerel eyes                     10
Glare at you out of stove-in, sunken heads
Far from the sea; the lobster, also, lifts
An empty claw in his most minatory
Of gestures; oyster, crab, and mussel shells
Lie here in heaps, savage as money hurled                  15
Away at the gate of hell. If you want results,
These are results.
                    Objects of value or virtue,
However, are also to be picked up here,
Though rarely, lying with bones and rotten meat,
Eggshells and mouldy bread, banana peels                   20
No one will skid on, apple cores that caused
Neither the fall of man nor a theory

2. Until it was razed in the 1960s to make way for the new Madison Square Garden, Pennsylvania Station was one of the most imposing buildings in New York, two blocks long and with stately Romanesque columns. It was the usual terminal for Negroes migrating from the rural South.

1. *King Lear*, Act III, sc. ii, lines 70–71.
2. "Being" and "Becoming" have been, since Heraclitus, the standard antinomies in Western philosophy, standing for (respectively) the eternal and that which changes.

Of gravitation.[3] People do throw out
The family pearls by accident, sometimes,
Not often; I've known dealers in antiques                    25
To prowl this place by night, with flashlights, on
The off-chance of somebody's having left
Derelict chairs which will turn out to be
By Hepplewhite,[4] a perfect set of six
Going to show, I guess, that in any sty                      30
Someone's heaven may open and shower down
Riches responsive to the right dream; though
It is a small chance, certainly, that sends
The ghostly dealer, heavy with fly-netting
Over his head, across these hills in darkness,               35
Stumbling in cut-glass goblets, lacquered cups,
And other products of his dreamy midden[5]
Penciled with light and guarded by the flies.

For there are flies, of course. A dynamo
Composed, by thousands, of our ancient black                 40
Retainers, hums here day and night, steady
As someone telling[6] beads, the hum becoming
A high whine at any disturbance; then,
Settled again, they shine under the sun
Like oil-drops, or are invisible as night,                   45
By night.
            All this continually smoulders,
Crackles, and smokes with mostly invisible fires
Which, working deep, rarely flash out and flare,
And never finish. Nothing finishes;
The flies, feeling the heat, keep on the move.               50

Among the flies, the purefying fires,
The hunters by night, acquainted with the art
Of our necessities, and the new deposits
That each day wastes with treasure, you may say
There should be ratios. You may sum up                       55
The results if you want results. But I will add
That wild birds, drawn to the carrion and flies,
Assemble in some numbers here, their wings
Shining with light, their flight enviably free,
Their music marvelous, though sad, and strange.              60

                                                        1958

THOMAS HARDY

# Hap[1]

If but some vengeful god would call to me
From up the sky, and laugh: "Thou suffering thing,

---

3. According to legend, Sir Isaac Newton's discovery of the principle of gravitation followed his being hit on the head by a falling apple.

4. A late 18th-century cabinet maker and furniture designer, famed for his simplification of neoclassic lines. No pieces known to have been actually made by Hepplewhite survive.

5. Refuse heap. (The term is usually used to describe those primitive refuse heaps which have been untouched for centuries and in which archeologists dig for shards and artifacts of older cultures.)

6. Counting.

1. Chance.

Know that thy sorrow is my ecstasy,
That thy love's loss is my hate's profiting!"

Then would I bear it, clench myself, and die,                    5
Steeled by the sense of ire unmerited;
Half-eased in that a Powerfuller than I
Had willed and meted me the tears I shed.

But not so. How arrives it[2] joy lies slain,
And why unblooms the best hope ever sown?                    10
—Crass Casualty[3] obstructs the sun and rain,
And dicing Time for gladness casts a moan. . . .
These purblind Doomsters[4] had as readily strown
Blisses about my pilgrimage as pain.

1866

JULIAN BOND

# Rotation

Like plump green floor plans
the pool tables squat
Among fawning mahogany Buddhas with felt heads.
Like clubwomen blessed with adultery
The balls dart to kiss                    5
and tumble erring members into silent oblivion.
Right-angled over the verdant barbered turf
Sharks point long fingers at the multi-colored worlds
and play at percussion
Sounding cheap plastic clicks                    10
in an 8-ball universe built for ivory.

p. 1964

TURNER CASSITY

# Calvin in the Casino[1]

*(He apostrophizes a roulette ball)*

Sphere of pure chance, free agent of no cause,
Your progress is a motion without laws.

Let every casuist henceforth rejoice
To cite your amoralities of choice,

By whose autonomy one apprehends                    5
The limits where predestination ends;

Where the Eternal Will divides its see[2]
In latitudes of probability,

2. How does it happen that.
3. Chance.
4. Those who decide one's fate.
1. John Calvin (1509–1564), a French

theologian best known for his doctrine of
predestination.
2. Area of jurisdiction (usually used to
describe the power of bishops).

And the divine election is obscured
Through being momently and long endured.     10

It is obscured and is rejustified,
That stands fulfilled in being here denied,

Lest its caprice should lead the mind to curse
A biased and encircling universe,

Or its vagaries urge us to reject     15
That one same Will which chooses the elect.

1966

A. R. AMMONS

# Cascadilla Falls

I went down by Cascadilla
Falls this
evening, the
stream below the falls,
and picked up a     5
handsized stone
kidney-shaped, testicular, and

thought all its motions into it,
the 800 mph earth spin,
the 190-million-mile yearly     10
displacement around the sun,
the overriding
grand
haul

of the galaxy with the 30,000     15
mph of where
the sun's going:
thought all the interweaving
motions
into myself: dropped     20

the stone to dead rest:
the stream from other motions
broke
rushing over it:
shelterless,     25
I turned

to the sky and stood still:
oh
I do
not know where I am going     30
that I can live my life
by this single creek.

1970

WALLACE STEVENS

# Anecdote of the Jar

I placed a jar in Tennessee,
And round it was, upon a hill.
It made the slovenly wilderness
Surround that hill.

The wilderness rose up to it,                5
And sprawled around, no longer wild.
The jar was round upon the ground
And tall and of a port in air.

It took dominion everywhere.
The jar was gray and bare.                    10
It did not give of bird or bush,
Like nothing else in Tennessee.

                                        1923


ARTHUR GUITERMAN

# On the Vanity of Earthly Greatness

The tusks that clashed in mighty brawls
Of mastodons, are billiard balls.

The sword of Charlemagne the Just
Is ferric oxide known as rust.

The grizzly bear whose potent hug           5
Was feared by all, is now a rug.

Great Caesar's bust in on the shelf,
And I don't feel so well myself!

                                        1930


RICHARD ARMOUR

# Hiding Place

A speaker at a meeting of the New York State Frozen Food Locker Association
declared that the best hiding place in event of an atomic explosion is a frozen-
food locker, where "radiation will not penetrate."[1]          NEWS ITEM.

          Move over, ham
            And quartered cow,
          My Geiger[2] says
            The time is now.

1. Before home freezers became popular,        2. Geiger counter: used to detect radia-
many Americans rented lockers in specially     tion.
equipped commercial buildings.

Yes, now I lay me                                                    5
    Down to sleep,
And if I die,
    At least I'll keep.

                                                                  1954


SYLVIA PLATH

# The Hanging Man

By the roots of my hair some god got hold of me.
I sizzled in his blue volts like a desert prophet.

The nights snapped out of sight like a lizard's eyelid:
A world of bald white days in a shadeless socket.

A vulturous boredom pinned me in this tree.                          5
If he were I, he would do what I did.

                                                                  1966


THOM GUNN

# On the Move

### "Man, you gotta Go."

The blue jay scuffling in the bushes follows
Some hidden purpose, and the gust of birds
That spurts across the field, the wheeling swallows,
Have nested in the trees and undergrowth.
Seeking their instinct, or their poise, or both,                     5
One moves with an uncertain violence
Under the dust thrown by a baffled sense
Or the dull thunder of approximate words.

On motorcycles, up the road, they come:
Small, black, as flies hanging in heat, the Boys,                   10
Until the distance throws them forth, their hum
Bulges to thunder held by calf and thigh.
In goggles, donned impersonality,
In gleaming jackets trophied with the dust,
They strap in doubt—by hiding it, robust—                           15
And almost hear a meaning in their noise.

Exact conclusion of their hardiness
Has no shape yet, but from known whereabouts
They ride, direction where the tires press.
They scare a flight of birds across the field:                      20
Much that is natural, to the will must yield.
Men manufacture both machine and soul,
And use what they imperfectly control
To dare a future from the taken routes.

It is a part solution, after all.                              25
One is not necessarily discord
On earth; or damned because, half animal,
One lacks direct instinct, because one wakes
Afloat on movement that divides and breaks.
One joins the movement in a valueless world,      30
Choosing it, till, both hurler and the hurled,
One moves as well, always toward, toward.

A minute holds them, who have come to go:
The self-defined, astride the created will
They burst away; the towns they travel through    35
Are home for neither bird nor holiness,
For birds and saints complete their purposes.
At worst, one is in motion; and at best,
Reaching no absolute, in which to rest,
One is always nearer by not keeping still.         40
*California*, 1957


MARK STRAND

## Keeping Things Whole

In a field
I am the absence
of field.
This is
always the case.                                     5
Wherever I am
I am what is missing.

When I walk
I part the air
and always                                          10
the air moves in
to fill the spaces
where my body's been.

We all have reasons
for moving.                                         15
I move
to keep things whole.

                                        1968


WILLIAM CARLOS WILLIAMS

## Poem

The plastic surgeon who has
concerned himself
with the repair of the mole

on my ear could not be
more pointedly                                                    5
employed

let all men confess it
Gauguin or Van Gogh[1]
were intimates

who fell out finally                                             10
and parted going
to the ends of the earth

to be apart, wild men
one of them cut
his ear off with a pair of shears                               15

which made him none the less
a surpassing genius
this happened

yesterday forgive him
he was mad                                                       20
and who among us has retained

his sanity or balance
in the course the
events have taken since those days

1962

JOHN BERRYMAN

## 1 September 1939[2]

The first, scattering rain on the Polish cities.
That afternoon a man squat' on the shore
Tearing a square of shining cellophane.
Some easily, some in evident torment tore,
Some for a time resisted, and then burst.                        5
All this depended on fidelity . .
One was blown out and borne off by the waters,
The man was tortured by the sound of rain.

Children were sent from London in the morning
But not the sound of children reached his ear.                  10
He found a mangled feather by the lake,
Lost in the destructive sand this year
Like feathery independence, hope. His shadow
Lay on the sand before him, under the lake

1. Paul Gauguin (1848–1903) and Vincent Van Gogh (1853–1890) spent time together at Arles in 1888, and after a quarrel Van Gogh cut off a piece of his right ear. Van Gogh recorded the event in his famous "Self-Portrait," and he was soon after hospitalized for madness.
2. The following group of poems (to p. 454) is not annotated; see the Note on Arrangement in the Foreword.

As under the ruined library our learning.                    15
The children play in the waves until they break.

The Bear crept under the Eagle's wing and lay
Snarling; the other animals showed fear,
Europe darkened its cities. The man wept,
Considering the light which had been there,              20
The feathered gull against the twilight flying.
As the little waves ate away the shore
The cellophane, dismembered, blew away.
The animals ran, the Eagle soared and dropt.

1939


THOMAS HARDY

# The Darkling Thrush

I leant upon a coppice gate
    When Frost was specter gray,
And Winter's dregs made desolate
    The weakening eye of day.
The tangled bine-stems scored the sky              5
    Like strings of broken lyres,
And all mankind that haunted nigh
    Had sought their household fires.

The land's sharp features seemed to be
    The Century's corpse outleant,              10
His crypt the cloudy canopy,
    The wind his death-lament.
The ancient pulse of germ and birth
    Was shrunken hard and dry,
And every spirit upon earth              15
    Seemed fervorless as I.

At once a voice arose among
    The bleak twigs overhead
In a full-hearted evensong
    Of joy illimited;              20
An aged thrush, frail, gaunt, and small,
    In blast-beruffled plume,
Had chosen thus to fling his soul
    Upon the growing gloom.

So little cause for carolings              25
    Of such ecstatic sound
Was written on terrestrial things
    Afar or nigh around,
That I could think there trembled through
    His happy good-night air              30
Some blessed Hope, whereof he knew
    And I was unaware.

December 31, 1900

JOHN MILTON

## On the New Forcers of Conscience
## under the Long Parliament

Because you have thrown off your prelate lord,
And with stiff vows renounced his liturgy
To seize the widowed whore Plurality
From them whose sin ye envied, not abhorred,
Dare ye for this adjure the civil sword                      5
To force our consciences that Christ set free,
And ride us with a classic hierarchy
Taught ye by mere A. S. and Rutherford?
Men whose life, learning, faith, and pure intent
Would have been held in high esteem with Paul               10
Must now be named and printed heretics
By shallow Edwards and Scotch what-d'ye-call:
But we do hope to find out all your tricks,
Your plots and packing worse than those of Trent,
That so the Parliament                                      15
May with their wholesome and preventive shears
Clip your phylacteries, though balk your ears,
And succor our just fears
When they shall read this clearly on your charge:
*New presbyter* is but *old priest* writ large.             20

ca. 1646

ANONYMOUS "NURSERY RHYMES"

## Humpty Dumpty

Humpty Dumpty sat on a wall,
Humpty Dumpty had a great fall.
    All the king's horses,
    And all the king's men,
Couldn't put Humpty together again.                          5

## Wee Willie Winkie

Wee Willie Winkie runs through the town,
Upstairs and downstairs in his night-gown,
Rapping at the window, crying through the lock,
Are the children all in bed, for now it's eight o'clock?

## Georgie Porgie

Georgie Porgie, pudding and pie,
Kissed the girls and made them cry;
When the boys came out to play,
Georgie Porgie ran away.

## London Bridge

London Bridge
Is Broken down,
Dance over my Lady Lee,
London Bridge
Is Broken down,                                    5
With a gay Lady.

How shall we build
It up again,
Dance over my Lady Lee.
How shall we build                                 10
It up again,
With a gay Lady.

Build it up with
Gravel, and Stone,
Dance over my Lady Lee.                            15
Build it up with
Gravel, and Stone,
With a gay Lady.

Gravel, and Stone
Will wash away,                                    20
Dance over my Lady Lee.
Gravel, and Stone,
Will wash away,
With a gay Lady.

Build it up with                                   25
Iron, and Steel,
Dance over my Lady Lee.
Build it up with
Iron, and Steel,
With a gay Lady.                                   30

Iron, and Steel,
Will bend, and Bow,
Dance over my Lady Lee.
Iron, and Steel,
Will bend, and Bow,                                35
With a gay Lady.

Build it up with
Silver, and Gold,
Dance over my Lady Lee.
Build it up with                                   40
Silver, and Gold,
With a gay Lady.

Silver, and Gold,
Will be stoln away,
Dance over my Lady Lee.                            45

Silver, and Gold,
Will be stoln away,
With a gay Lady.

Then we'll set
A Man to Watch,                          50
Dance over my Lady Lee.
Then we'll set
A Man to Watch
With a gay Lady.

SAMUEL JOHNSON

### On Colley Cibber

Augustus still survives in Maro's strain,
And Spenser's verse prolongs Eliza's reign;
Great George's acts let tuneful Cibber sing;
For Nature formed the poet for the king.

ca. 1741

e. e. cummings

### poem, or beauty hurts mr. vinal

take it from me kiddo
believe me
my country, 'tis of

you, land of the Cluett
Shirt Boston Garter and Spearmint          5
Girl With The Wrigley Eyes (of you
land of the Arrow Ide
and Earl &
Wilson
Collars) of you i                          10
sing:land of Abraham Lincoln and Lydia E. Pinkham,
land above all of Just Add Hot Water And Serve—
from every B. V. D.

let freedom ring

amen. i do however protest, anent the un       15
-spontaneous and otherwise scented merde which
greets one (Everywhere Why) as divine poesy per
that and this radically defunct periodical. i would
suggest that certain ideas gestures
rhymes, like Gillette Razor Blades          20
having been used and reused
to the mystical moment of dullness emphatically are
Not To Be Resharpened.  (Case in point

if we are to believe these gently O sweetly
melancholy trillers amid the thrillers      25

these crepuscular violinists among my and your
skyscrapers—Helen & Cleopatra were Just Too Lovely,
The Snail's On The Thorn enter Morn and God's
In His andsoforth

do you get me?  ) according                                    30
to such supposedly indigenous
throstles Art is O World O Life
a formula: example, Turn Your Shirttails Into
Drawers and If It Isn't An Eastman It Isn't A
Kodak therefore my friends let                                 35
us now sing each and all fortissimo A-
mer
i

ca, I
love,                                                          40
You. And there're a
hun-dred-mil-lion-oth-ers, like
all of you successfully if
delicately gelded(or spaded)
gentlemen(and ladies)—pretty                                   45

littleliverpill-
hearted-Nujolneeding-There's-A-Reason
americans(who tensetendoned and with
upward vacant eyes, painfully
perpetually crouched, quivering, upon the                      50
sternly allotted sandpile
—how silently
emit a tiny violetflavoured nuisance: Odor?

ono.
comes out like a ribbon lies flat on the brush                 55

                                                             1926

AMIRI BARAKA (LE ROI JONES)

# In Memory of Radio

Who has ever stopped to think of the divinity of Lamont Cranston?
(Only Jack Kerouac, that I know of: & me.
The rest of you probably had on WCBS and Kate Smith,
Or something equally unattractive.)

What can I say?                                                5
It is better to have loved and lost
Than to put linoleum in your living rooms?

Am I a sage or something?
Mandrake's hypnotic gesture of the week?
(Remember, I do not have the healing powers of Oral Roberts . . .    10
I cannot, like F. J. Sheen, tell you how to get saved & *rich!*
I cannot even order you to gaschamber satori like Hitler or Goody Knight

& Love is an evil word.
Turn it backwards/see, what I mean?
An evol word. & besides                                    15
Who understands it?
I certainly wouldn't like to go out on that kind of limb.

Saturday mornings we listened to *Red Lantern* & his undersea folk.
At 11, *Let's Pretend*/& we did/& I, the poet, still do, Thank God!

What was it he used to say (after the transformation, when he was safe  20
& invisible & the unbelievers couldn't throw stones?) "Heh, heh, heh,
Who knows what evil lurks in the hearts of men? The Shadow knows."

O, yes he does
O, yes he does.
An evil word it is,                                        25
This Love.

                                                           1961

KENNETH FEARING

# Dirge

1-2-3 was the number he played but today the number came 3-2-1;
Bought his Carbide at 30, and it went to 29; had the favorite at Bowie
        but the track was slow—

O executive type, would you like to drive a floating-power, knee-action,
        silk-upholstered six? Wed a Hollywood star? Shoot the course in
        58? Draw to the ace, king, jack?
O fellow with a will who won't take no, watch out for three cigarettes
        on the same, single match; O democratic voter born in August
        under Mars, beware of liquidated rails—

Denouement to denouement, he took a personal pride in the certain,
        certain way he lived his own, private life,                    5
But nevertheless, they shut off his gas; nevertheless, the bank foreclosed;
        nevertheless, the landlord called; nevertheless, the radio broke,

And twelve o'clock arrived just once too often,
Just the same he wore one gray tweed suit, bought one straw hat, drank
        one straight Scotch, walked one short step, took one long look,
        drew one deep breath,
Just one too many,

And wow he died as wow he lived,                                       10
Going whop to the office and blooie home to sleep and biff got married
        and bam had children and oof got fired,
Zowie did he live and zowie did he die,

With who the hell are you at the corner of his casket, and where the
        hell're we going on the right-hand silver knob, and who the hell
        cares walking second from the end with an American Beauty
        wreath from why the hell not,

Very much missed by the circulation staff of the New York Evening
Post; deeply, deeply mourned by the B.M.T.

Wham, Mr. Roosevelt; pow, Sears Roebuck; awk, big dipper; bop,
summer rain;                                                                    15
Bong, Mr., bong, Mr., bong, Mr., bong.

1935

ALLEN GINSBERG

# Howl (Part I)

*(for Carl Solomon)*

I saw the best minds of my generation destroyed by madness, starving
hysterical naked,
dragging themselves through the negro streets at dawn looking for an
angry fix,
angelheaded hipsters burning for the ancient heavenly connection to
the starry dynamo in the machinery of night,
who poverty and tatters and hollow-eyed and high sat up smoking in
the supernatural darkness of cold-water flats floating across the
tops of cities contemplating jazz,
who bared their brains to Heaven under the El and saw Mohammedan
angels staggering on tenement roofs illuminated,                                5
who passed through universities with radiant cool eyes hallucinating
Arkansas and Blake-light tragedy among the scholars of war,
who were expelled from the academies for crazy & publishing obscene
odes on the windows of the skull,
who cowered in unshaven rooms in underwear, burning their money in
wastebaskets and listening to the Terror through the wall,
who got busted in their pubic beards returning through Laredo with
a belt of marijuana for New York,
who ate fire in paint hotels or drank turpentine in Paradise Alley, death,
or purgatoried their torsos night after night                                   10
with dreams, with drugs, with waking nightmares, alcohol and cock
and endless balls,
incomparable blind streets of shuddering cloud and lightning in the
mind leaping toward poles of Canada & Paterson, illuminating
all the motionless world of Time between,
Peyote solidities of halls, backyard green tree cemetery dawns, wine
drunkenness over the rooftops, storefront boroughs of teahead
joyride neon blinking traffic light, sun and moon and tree
vibrations in the roaring winter dusks of Brooklyn, ashcan
rantings and kind king light of mind,
who chained themselves to subways for the endless ride from Battery
to holy Bronx on benzedrine until the noise of wheels and
children brought them down shuddering mouth-wracked and
battered bleak of brain all drained of brilliance in the drear
light of Zoo,
who sank all night in submarine light of Bickford's floated out and sat
through the stale beer afternoon in desolate Fugazzi's, listening
to the crack of doom on the hydrogen jukebox,                                   15

who talked continuously seventy hours from park to pad to bar to
Bellevue to museum to the Brooklyn Bridge,
a lost battalion of platonic conversationalists jumping down the stoops
off fire escapes off windowsills off Empire State out of the moon,
yacketayakking screaming vomiting whispering facts and memories
and anecdotes and eyeball kicks and shocks of hospitals and
jails and wars,
whole intellects disgorged in total recall for seven days and nights with
brilliant eyes, meat for the Synagogue cast on the pavement,
who vanished into nowhere Zen New Jersey leaving a trail of ambiguous
picture postcards of Atlantic City Hall,                                   20
suffering Eastern sweats and Tangerian bone-grindings and migraines
of China under junk-withdrawal in Newark's bleak furnished
room,
who wandered around and around at midnight in the railroad yard
wondering where to go, and went, leaving no broken hearts,
who lit cigarettes in boxcars boxcars boxcars racketing through snow
toward lonesome farms in grandfather night,
who studied Plotinus Poe St. John of the Cross telepathy and bop
kaballa because the cosmos instinctively vibrated at their feet
in Kansas,
who loned it through the streets of Idaho seeking visionary indian
angels who were visionary indian angels,                                   25
who thought they were only mad when Baltimore gleamed in supernatural ecstasy,
who jumped in limousines with the Chinaman of Oklahoma on the
impulse of winter midnight streetlight smalltown rain,
who lounged hungry and lonesome through Houston seeking jazz or sex
or soup, and followed the brilliant Spaniard to converse about
America and Eternity, a hopeless task, and so took ship to Africa,
who disappeared into the volcanoes of Mexico leaving behind nothing
but the shadow of dungarees and the lava and ash of poetry
scattered in fireplace Chicago,
who reappeared on the West Coast investigating the F.B.I. in beards
and shorts with big pacifist eyes sexy in their dark skin passing
out incomprehensible leaflets,                                             30
who burned cigarette holes in their arms protesting the narcotic
tobacco haze of Capitalism,
who distributed Supercommunist pamphlets in Union Square weeping
and undressing while the sirens of Los Alamos wailed them
down, and wailed down Wall, and the Staten Island Ferry also
wailed,
who broke down crying in white gymnasiums naked and trembling
before the machinery of other skeletons,
who bit detectives in the neck and shrieked with delight in policecars
for committing no crime but their own wild cooking pederasty
and intoxication,
who howled on their knees in the subway and were dragged off the
roof waving genitals and manuscripts,                                      35
who let themselves be fucked in the ass by saintly motorcyclists, and
screamed with joy,
who blew and were blown by those human seraphim, the sailors,
caresses of Atlantic and Caribbean love,

who balled in the morning in the evenings in rosegardens and the grass
of public parks and cemeteries scattering their semen freely to
whomever come who may,
who hiccupped endlessly trying to giggle but wound up with a sob
behind a partition in a Turkish Bath when the blonde & naked
angel came to pierce them with a sword,
who lost their loveboys to the three old shrews of fate the one eyed
shrew of the heterosexual dollar the one eyed shrew that winks
out of the womb and the one eyed shrew that does nothing but
sit on her ass and snip the intellectual golden threads of the
craftsman's loom,                                                    40
who copulated ecstatic and insatiate with a bottle of beer a sweetheart
a package of cigarettes a candle and fell off the bed, and continued along the floor and down the hall and ended fainting on
the wall with a vision of ultimate cunt and come eluding the
last gyzym of consciousness,
who sweetened the snatches of a million girls trembling in the sunset,
and were red eyed in the morning but prepared to sweeten the
snatch of the sunrise, flashing buttocks under barns and naked
in the lake,
who went out whoring through Colorado in myriad stolen night-cars,
N.C., secret hero of these poems, cocksman and Adonis of
Denver—joy to the memory of his innumerable lays of girls in
empty lots & diner backyards, moviehouses' rickety rows, on
mountaintops in caves or with gaunt waitresses in familiar
roadside lonely petticoat upliftings & especially secret gas-station
solipsisms of johns, & hometown alleys too,
who faded out in vast sordid movies, were shifted in dreams, woke on a
sudden Manhattan, and picked themselves up out of basements
hungover with heartless Tokay and horrors of Third Avenue
iron dreams & stumbled to unemployment offices,
who walked all night with their shoes full of blood on the snowbank
docks waiting for a door in the East River to open to a room
full of steamheat and opium,                                         45
who created great suicidal dramas on the apartment cliff-banks of the
Hudson under the wartime blue floodlight of the moon & their
heads shall be crowned with laurel in oblivion,
who ate the lamb stew of the imagination or digested the crab at the
muddy bottom of the rivers of Bowery,
who wept at the romance of the streets with their pushcarts full of
onions and bad music,
who sat in boxes breathing in the darkness under the bridge, and rose
up to build harpsichords in their lofts,
who coughed on the sixth floor of Harlem crowned with flame under
the tubercular sky surrounded by orange crates of theology,        50
who scribbled all night rocking and rolling over lofty incantations which
in the yellow morning were stanzas of gibberish,
who cooked rotten animals lung heart feet tail borsht & tortillas dreaming of the pure vegetable kingdom,
who plunged themselves under meat trucks looking for an egg,
who threw their watches off the roof to cast their ballot for Eternity
outside of Time, & alarm clocks fell on their heads every day
for the next decade,
who cut their wrists three times successively unsuccessfully, gave up

and were forced to open antique stores where they thought they
were growing old and cried,                                           55
who were burned alive in their innocent flannel suits on Madison
Avenue amid blasts of leaden verse & the tanked-up clatter of
the iron regiments of fashion & the nitroglycerine shrieks of the
fairies of advertising & the mustard gas of sinister intelligent
editors, or were run down by the drunken taxicabs of Absolute
Reality,
who jumped off the Brooklyn Bridge this actually happened and walked
away unknown and forgotten into the ghostly daze of China-
town soup alleyways & firetrucks, not even one free beer,
who sang out of their windows in despair, fell out of the subway window, jumped in the filthy Passaic, leaped on negroes, cried all
over the street, danced on broken wineglasses barefoot smashed
phonograph records of nostalgic European 1930's German jazz
finished the whiskey and threw up groaning into the bloody
toilet, moans in their ears and the blast of colossal steamwhistles,
who barreled down the highways of the past journeying to each other's
hotrod-Golgotha jail-solitude watch or Birmingham jazz in-
carnation,
who drove crosscountry seventytwo hours to find out if I had a vision
or you had a vision or he had a vision to find out Eternity,        60
who journeyed to Denver, who died in Denver, who came back to
Denver & waited in vain, who watched over Denver & brooded
& loned in Denver and finally went away to find out the Time, &
now Denver is lonesome for her heroes,
who fell on their knees in hopeless cathedrals praying for each other's
salvation and light and breasts, until the soul illuminated its
hair for a second,
who crashed through their minds in jail waiting for impossible criminals with golden heads and the charm of reality in their hearts
who sang sweet blues to Alcatraz,
who retired to Mexico to cultivate a habit, or Rocky Mount to tender
Buddha or Tangiers to boys or Southern Pacific to the black
locomotive or Harvard to Narcissus to Woodlawn to the daisy-
chain or grave,
who demanded sanity trials accusing the radio of hypnotism & were
left with their insanity & their hands & a hung jury,               65
who threw potato salad at CCNY lecturers on Dadaism and subse-
quently presented themselves on the granite steps of the mad-
house with shaven heads and harlequin speech of suicide,
demanding instantaneous lobotomy,
and who were given instead the concrete void of insulin metrasol
electricity hydrotherapy psychotherapy occupational therapy
pingpong & amnesia,
who in humorless protest overturned only one symbolic pingpong table,
resting briefly in catatonia,
returning years later truly bald except for a wig of blood, and tears and
fingers, to the visible madman doom of the wards of the mad-
towns of the East,
Pilgrim State's Rockland's and Greystone's foetid halls, bickering with
the echoes of the soul, rocking and rolling in the midnight
solitude-bench dolmen-realms of love, dream of life a nightmare, bodies turned to stone as heavy as the moon,                  70

with mother finally°°°°°°, and the last fantastic book flung out of the
    tenement window, and the last door closed at 4 AM and the last
    telephone slammed at the wall in reply and the last furnished
    room emptied down to the last piece of mental furniture, a
    yellow paper rose twisted on a wire hanger in the closet, and
    even that imaginary, nothing but a hopeful little bit of hallu-
    cination—
ah, Carl, while you are not safe I am not safe, and now you're really
    in the total animal soup of time—
and who therefore ran through the icy streets obsessed with a sudden
    flash of the alchemy of the use of the ellipse the catalog the
    meter & the vibrating plane,
who dreamt and made incarnate gaps in Time & Space through images
    juxtaposed, and trapped the archangel of the soul between 2
    visual images and joined the elemental verbs and set the noun
    and dash of consciousness together jumping with sensation of
    Pater Omnipotens Aeterna Deus
to recreate the syntax and measure of poor human prose and stand
    before you speechless and intelligent and shaking with shame,
    rejected yet confessing out the soul to conform to the rhythm of
    thought in his naked and endless head,                   75
the madman bum and angel beat in Time, unknown, yet putting down
    here what might be left to say in time come after death,
and rose reincarnate in the ghostly clothes of jazz in the goldhorn
    shadow of the band and blew the suffering of America's naked
    mind for love into an eli eli lamma lamma sabacthani saxophone
    cry that shivered the cities down to the last radio
with the absolute heart of the poem of life butchered out of their own
    bodies good to eat a thousand years.

1955

JOHN DONNE

## Love's Alchemy

Some that have deeper digged love's mine than I,
Say, where his centric happiness doth lie.
    I have loved, and got, and told,
But should I love, get, tell, till I were old,
I should not find that hidden mystery.              5
    Oh, 'tis imposture all:
And as no chemic yet th' elixir got
    But glorifies his pregnant pot,
    If by the way to him befall
Some odoriferous thing, or medicinal,              10
    So lovers dream a rich and long delight,
    But get a winter-seeming summer's night.

Our ease, our thrift, our honor, and our day,
Shall we for this vain bubble's shadow pay?
    Ends love in this, that my man              15
Can be as happy as I can, if he can
Endure the short scorn of a bridegroom's play?
    That loving wretch that swears

'Tis not the bodies marry, but the minds,
    Which he in her angelic finds,           20
    Would swear as justly that he hears,
In that day's rude hoarse minstrelsy, the spheres.
    Hope not for mind in women; at their best
Sweetness and wit they're but *Mummy*, possessed.

                  1633

HOWARD NEMEROV

## The Second-Best Bed

Consider now that Troy has burned
—Priam is dead, and Hector dead,
And great Aeneas long since turned
Away seaward with his gods
To find, found or founder, against frightful odds.     5

And figure to yourselves the clown
Who comes with educated word
To illustrate in mask and gown
King Priam's most illustrious son
And figure forth his figure with many another one     10

Of that most ceremented time
In times have been or are to be
Inhearsed in military rime;
And will recite of royal fates
Until, infamonized among those potentates     15

By a messenger from nearer home,
His comedy is compromised
And he must leave both Greece and Rome
Abuilding but not half begun,
To play the honest Troyan to a girl far gone.     20

The wench lived on, if the son died—
All Denmark wounded in one bed
Cried vengeance on the lusty bride,
Who could not care that there would follow,
After the words of Mercury, songs of Apollo.     25

                  1950

# JOHN KEATS

## To One Who Has Been Long in City Pent

To one who has been long in city pent,
'Tis very sweet to look into the fair
And open face of heaven—to breathe a prayer
Full in the smile of the blue firmament.
Who is more happy, when, with heart's content,          5
Fatigued he sinks into some pleasant lair
Of wavy grass, and reads a debonair
And gentle tale of love and languishment?
Returning home at evening, with an ear
Catching the notes of Philomel[1]—an eye          10
Watching the sailing cloudlet's bright career,
He mourns that day so soon has glided by:
E'en like the passage of an angel's tear
That falls through the clear ether silently.

1816

## On the Grasshopper and the Cricket

The poetry of earth is never dead:
When all the birds are faint with the hot sun,
And hide in cooling trees, a voice will run
From hedge to hedge about the new-mown mead;
That is the grasshopper's—he takes the lead          5
In summer luxury—he has never done
With his delights; for when tired out with fun
He rests at ease beneath some pleasant weed.
The poetry of earth is ceasing never:
On a lone winter evening, when the frost          10
Has wrought a silence, from the stove there shrills
The cricket's song, in warmth increasing ever,
And seems to one in drowsiness half lost,
The grasshopper's among some grassy hills.

December 30, 1816

## On Seeing the Elgin Marbles[2]

My spirit is too weak—mortality
Weighs heavily on me like unwilling sleep,
And each imagined pinnacle and steep
Of godlike hardship tells me I must die
Like a sick eagle looking at the sky.          5
Yet 'tis a gentle luxury to weep
That I have not the cloudy winds to keep
Fresh for the opening of the morning's eye.

1. The nightingale.
2. Figures and friezes from the Athenian Parthenon, purchased from the Turks by Lord Elgin and then sold to the British Museum, where Keats saw them.

Such dim-conceived glories of the brain
Bring round the heart an indescribable feud;                    10
So do these wonders a most dizzy pain,
That mingles Grecian grandeur with the rude
Wasting of old Time—with a billowy main—
A sun—a shadow of a magnitude.

1817

## *from* Endymion ( Book I )[1]

A thing of beauty is a joy for ever:
Its loveliness increases; it will never
Pass into nothingness; but still will keep
A bower quiet for us, and a sleep
Full of sweet dreams, and health, and quiet breathing.          5
Therefore, on every morrow, are we wreathing
A flowery band to bind us to the earth,
Spite of despondence, of the inhuman dearth
Of noble natures, of the gloomy days,
Of all the unhealthy and o'er-darkened ways                    10
Made for our searching: yes, in spite of all,
Some shape of beauty moves away the pall
From our dark spirits. Such the sun, the moon,
Trees old, and young sprouting a shady boon
For simple sheep; and such are daffodils                       15
With the green world they live in; and clear rills
That for themselves a cooling covert make
'Gainst the hot season; the mid forest brake,[2]
Rich with a sprinkling of fair musk-rose blooms:
And such too is the grandeur of the dooms[3]                   20
We have imagined for the mighty dead;
All lovely tales that we have heard or read:
An endless fountain of immortal drink,
Pouring unto us from the heaven's brink.
    Nor do we merely feel these essences                       25
For one short hour; no, even as the trees
That whisper round a temple become soon
Dear as the temple's self, so does the moon,
The passion poesy, glories infinite,
Haunt us till they become a cheering light                     30
Unto our souls, and bound to us so fast,
That, whether there be shine, or gloom o'ercast,
They always must be with us, or we die.

1817

## When I Have Fears

When I have fears that I may cease to be
Before my pen has gleaned my teeming brain,

1. Keats's long poem about the myth of    2. Thicket.
a mortal (Endymion) loved by the goddess    3. Judgments.
of the moon.

Before high-piléd books, in charact'ry,
Hold like rich garners the full-ripened grain;
When I behold, upon the night's starred face,                    5
Huge cloudy symbols of a high romance,
And think that I may never live to trace
Their shadows, with the magic hand of chance;
And when I feel, fair creature of an hour!
That I shall never look upon thee more,                          10
Never have relish in the faery power
Of unreflecting love!—then on the shore
Of the wide world I stand alone, and think
Till Love and Fame to nothingness do sink.

1818

# What the Thrush Said

O thou[1] whose face hath felt the Winter's wind,
Whose eye has seen the snow-clouds hung in mist,
And the black elm tops 'mong the freezing stars,
To thee the Spring will be a harvest-time.
O thou, whose only book has been the light                       5
Of supreme darkness which thou feddest on
Night after night when Phœbus[2] was away,
To thee the spring shall be a triple morn.
O fret not after knowledge—I have none,
And yet my song comes native with the warmth.                    10
O fret not after knowledge—I have none,
And yet the Evening listens. He who saddens
At thought of idleness cannot be idle,
And he's awake who thinks himself asleep.

1818

# On Visiting the Tomb of Burns[1]

The town, the churchyard, and the setting sun,
The clouds, the trees, the rounded hills all seem,
Though beautiful, cold—strange—as in a dream,
I dreamed long ago, now new begun.
The short-lived, paly Summer is but won                          5
From Winter's ague, for one hour's gleam;
Though sapphire-warm, their stars do never beam:
All its cold Beauty; pain is never done:
For who has mind to relish, Minos-wise,[2]
The Real of Beauty, free from that dead hue                      10
Sickly imagination and sick pride
Cast wan upon it? Burns! with honor due
I oft have honored thee. Great shadow, hide
Thy face; I sin against thy native skies.

1818

1. The thrush addresses the poet.
2. The sun.
1. Scots poet (1759–1796).

2. In Greek legend, Minos was king and
lawgiver of Crete who at death became the
supreme judge of the underworld.

# The Eve of St. Agnes[1]

### I

St. Agnes' Eve—Ah, bitter chill it was!
The owl, for all his feathers, was a-cold;
The hare limped trembling through the frozen grass,
And silent was the flock in woolly fold:
Numb were the Beadsman's[2] fingers, while he told                5
His rosary, and while his frosted breath,
Like pious incense from a censer old,
Seemed taking flight for heaven, without a death,
Past the sweet Virgin's picture, while his prayer he saith.

### II

His prayer he saith, this patient, holy man;                10
Then takes his lamp, and riseth from his knees,
And back returneth, meager, barefoot, wan,
Along the chapel aisle by slow degrees:
The sculptured dead, on each side, seem to freeze,
Emprisoned in black, purgatorial rails:                15
Knights, ladies, praying in dumb orat'ries,[3]
He passeth by; and his weak spirit fails
To think[4] how they may ache in icy hoods and mails.

### III

Northward he turneth through a little door,
And scarce three steps, ere Music's golden tongue                20
Flattered[5] to tears this aged man and poor;
But no—already had his deathbell rung:
The joys of all his life were said and sung:
His was harsh penance on St. Agnes' Eve:
Another way he went, and soon among                25
Rough ashes sat he for his soul's reprieve,
And all night kept awake, for sinners' sake to grieve.

### IV

That ancient Beadsman heard the prelude soft;
And so it chanced, for many a door was wide,
From hurry to and fro. Soon, up aloft,                30
The silver, snarling trumpets 'gan to chide:
The level chambers, ready with their pride,[6]
Were glowing to receive a thousand guests:
The carvéd angels, ever eager-eyed,
Stared, where upon their heads the cornice rests,                35
With hair blown back, and wings put cross-wise on their breasts.

### V

At length burst in the argent revelry,[7]
With plume, tiara, and all rich array,

1. Martyred early in the fourth century at the age of 13, St. Agnes became the patron saint of virgins. According to popular belief, if a virgin performed the proper ritual on St. Agnes' Eve (January 20), she would dream of her future husband.
2. Someone paid to pray for the soul of another. "told": counted his beads.
3. Silent chapels inside the larger chapel.
4. When he thinks. "mails": suits of armor.
5. Coaxed, beguiled.
6. Splendor.
7. Silver-clad revelers.

Numerous as shadows haunting fairily
The brain, new stuffed, in youth, with triumphs gay        40
Of old romance. These let us wish away,
And turn, sole-thoughted, to one Lady there,
Whose heart had brooded, all that wintry day,
On love, and winged St. Agnes' saintly care,
As she had heard old dames full many times declare.        45

### VI

They told her how, upon St. Agnes' Eve,
Young virgins might have visions of delight,
And soft adorings from their loves receive
Upon the honeyed middle of the night,
If ceremonies due they did aright;        50
As, supperless to bed they must retire,
And couch supine their beauties, lily white;
Nor look behind, nor sideways, but require
Of Heaven with upward eyes for all that they desire.

### VII

Full of this whim was thoughtful Madeline:        55
The music, yearning like a God in pain,
She scarcely heard: her maiden eyes divine,
Fixed on the floor, saw many a sweeping train
Pass by—she heeded not at all: in vain
Came many a tiptoe, amorous cavalier,        60
And back retired; not cooled by high disdain,
But she saw not: her heart was otherwhere:
She sighed for Agnes' dreams, the sweetest of the year.

### VIII

She danced along with vague, regardless eyes,
Anxious her lips, her breathing quick and short:        65
The hallowed hour was near at hand: she sighs
Amid the timbrels,[8] and the thronged resort
Of whisperers in anger, or in sport;
'Mid looks of love, defiance, hate, and scorn,
Hoodwinked with faery fancy; all amort,[9]        70
Save to St. Agnes and her lambs unshorn,[1]
And all the bliss to be before tomorrow morn.

### IX

So, purposing each moment to retire,
She lingered still. Meantime, across the moors,
Had come young Porphyro, with heart on fire        75
For Madeline. Beside the portal doors,
Buttressed[2] from moonlight, stands he, and implores
All saints to give him sight of Madeline,
But for one moment in the tedious hours,
That he might gaze and worship all unseen;        80
Perchance speak, kneel, touch, kiss—in sooth such things have been.

8. Small hand drums or tambourines.
9. Deadened: oblivious.
1. At the feast of St. Agnes the next day, lamb's wool was traditionally offered; later, nuns wove it into cloth (lines 115–17).
2. Shaded by the wall supports.

### X

He ventures in: let no buzzed whisper tell:
All eyes be muffled, or a hundred swords
Will storm his heart, Love's fev'rous citadel:
For him, those chambers held barbarian hordes,                    85
Hyena foemen, and hot-blooded lords,
Whose very dogs would execrations howl
Against his lineage:[3] not one breast affords
Him any mercy, in that mansion foul,
Save one old beldame,[4] weak in body and in soul.                 90

### XI

Ah, happy chance! the aged creature came,
Shuffling along with ivory-headed wand,[5]
To where he stood, hid from the torch's flame,
Behind a broad hall-pillar, far beyond
The sound of merriment and chorus bland:[6]                       95
He startled her; but soon she knew his face,
And grasped his fingers in her palsied hand,
Saying, "Mercy, Porphyro! hie thee from this place;
They are all here tonight, the whole blood-thirsty race!

### XII

Get hence! get hence! there's dwarfish Hildebrand;               100
He had a fever late, and in the fit
He curséd thee and thine, both house and land:
Then there's that old Lord Maurice, not a whit
More tame for his gray hairs—Alas me! flit!
Flit like a ghost away."—"Ah, Gossip[7] dear,                     105
We're safe enough; here in this arm-chair sit,
And tell me how"—"Good Saints! not here, not here;
Follow me, child, or else these stones will be thy bier."

### XIII

He followed through a lowly archéd way,
Brushing the cobwebs with his lofty plume,                        110
And as she muttered "Well-a—well-a-day!"
He found him in a little moonlight room,
Pale, latticed, chill, and silent as a tomb.
"Now tell me where is Madeline," said he,
"O tell me, Angela, by the holy loom                              115
Which none but secret sisterhood may see,
When they St. Agnes' wool are weaving piously."

### XIV

"St. Agnes! Ah! it is St. Agnes' Eve—
Yet men will murder upon holy days:
Thou must hold water in a witch's sieve,                          120
And be liege-lord of all the Elves and Fays,
To venture so:[8] it fills me with amaze
To see thee, Porphyro!—St. Agnes' Eve!

---

3. Because of the feud between his
family and Madeline's.
4. Old, usually ugly, woman.
5. Walking stick, cane.

6. Soothing.
7. Old friend.
8. I.e., Porphyro would need to be a
magician to take such chances.

God's help! my lady fair the conjuror plays[9]
This very night: good angels her deceive!                              125
But let me laugh awhile, I've mickle[1] time to grieve."

### XV

Feebly she laugheth in the languid moon,
While Porphyro upon her face doth look,
Like puzzled urchin on an aged crone
Who keepeth closed a wond'rous riddle-book,                            130
As spectacled she sits in chimney nook.
But soon his eyes grew brilliant, when she told
His lady's purpose; and he scarce could brook[2]
Tears, at the thought of those enchantments cold
And Madeline asleep in lap of legends old.                             135

### XVI

Sudden a thought came like a full-blown rose,
Flushing his brow, and in his painéd heart
Made purple riot: then doth he propose
A stratagem, that makes the beldame start:
"A cruel man and impious thou art:                                     140
Sweet lady, let her pray, and sleep, and dream
Alone with her good angels, far apart
From wicked men like thee. Go, go!—I deem
Thou canst not surely be the same that thou didst seem."

### XVII

"I will not harm her, by all saints I swear,"                          145
Quoth Porphyro: "O may I ne'er find grace
When my weak voice shall whisper its last prayer,
If one of her soft ringlets I displace,
Or look with ruffian passion in her face:
Good Angela, believe me by these tears;                                150
Or I will, even in a moment's space,
Awake, with horrid shout, my foemen's ears,
And beard[3] them, though they be more fanged than wolves and bears."

### XVIII

"Ah! why wilt thou affright a feeble soul?
A poor, weak, palsy-stricken, churchyard thing,                        155
Whose passing-bell[4] may ere the midnight toll;
Whose prayers for thee, each morn and evening,
Were never missed."—Thus plaining,[5] doth she bring
A gentler speech from burning Porphyro;
So woeful, and of such deep sorrowing,                                 160
That Angela gives promise she will do
Whatever he shall wish, betide her weal or woe.[6]

### XIX

Which was, to lead him, in close secrecy,
Even to Madeline's chamber, and there hide

9. In trying to evoke the image of her lover.
1. Plenty of.
2. Hold back.
3. Defy, affront.
4. Bell that rings for death.
5. Complaining.
6. Whatever happens to her, good or bad.

Him in a closet, of such privacy 165
That he might see her beauty unespied,
And win perhaps that night a peerless bride,
While legioned fairies paced the coverlet,
And pale enchantment held her sleepy-eyed.
Never on such a night have lovers met, 170
Since Merlin paid his Demon all the monstrous debt.[7]

#### XX

"It shall be as thou wishest," said the Dame:
"All cates[8] and dainties shall be storéd there
Quickly on this feast-night: by the tambour frame[9]
Her own lute thou wilt see: no time to spare, 175
For I am slow and feeble, and scarce dare
On such a catering trust my dizzy head.
Wait here, my child, with patience; kneel in prayer
The while: Ah! thou must needs the lady wed,
Or may I never leave my grave among the dead." 180

#### XXI

So saying, she hobbled off with busy fear.
The lover's endless minutes slowly passed;
The dame returned, and whispered in his ear
To follow her; with agéd eyes aghast
From fright of dim espial. Safe at last, 185
Through many a dusky gallery, they gain
The maiden's chamber, silken, hushed, and chaste;
Where Porphyro took covert, pleased amain.[1]
His poor guide hurried back with agues in her brain.

#### XXII

Her falt'ring hand upon the balustrade, 190
Old Angela was feeling for the stair,
When Madeline, St. Agnes' charméd maid,
Rose, like a missioned spirit,[2] unaware:
With silver taper's light, and pious care,
She turned, and down the agéd gossip led 195
To a safe level matting. Now prepare,
Young Porphyro, for gazing on that bed;
She comes, she comes again, like ring dove frayed[3] and fled.

#### XXIII

Out went the taper as she hurried in;
Its little smoke, in pallid moonshine, died: 200
She closed the door, she panted, all akin
To spirits of the air, and visions wide:
No uttered syllable, or, woe betide!
But to her heart, her heart was voluble,
Paining with eloquence her balmy side; 205
As though a tongueless nightingale should swell
Her throat in vain, and die, heart-stifled, in her dell.

7. Merlin was a powerful magician in the Arthurian legends; the incident referred to here has not been identified.
8. Delicacies.
9. Embroidery frame.
1. Greatly.
2. Angel on a mission.
3. Frightened.

## XXIV

A casement[4] high and triple-arched there was,
All garlanded with carven imag'ries
Of fruits, and flowers, and bunches of knot-grass,                210
And diamonded with panes of quaint device,
Innumerable of stains and splendid dyes,
As are the tiger moth's deep-damasked wings;
And in the midst, 'mong thousand heraldries,
And twilight saints, and dim emblazonings,                         215
A shielded scutcheon blushed with blood of queens and kings.

## XXV

Full on this casement shone the wintry moon,
And threw warm gules[5] on Madeline's fair breast,
As down she knelt for heaven's grace and boon;[6]
Rose-bloom fell on her hands, together pressed,                    220
And on her silver cross soft amethyst,
And on her hair a glory,[7] like a saint:
She seemed a splendid angel, newly dressed,
Save wings, for heaven—Porphyro grew faint:
She knelt, so pure a thing, so free from mortal taint.             225

## XXVI

Anon his heart revives: her vespers done,
Of all its wreathéd pearls her hair she frees;
Unclasps her warméd jewels one by one;
Loosens her fragrant bodice; by degrees
Her rich attire creeps rustling to her knees:                      230
Half-hidden, like a mermaid in sea-weed,
Pensive awhile she dreams awake, and sees,
In fancy, fair St. Agnes in her bed,
But dares not look behind, or all the charm is fled.

## XXVII

Soon, trembling in her soft and chilly nest,                       235
In sort of wakeful swoon, perplexed she lay,
Until the poppied warmth of sleep oppressed
Her soothéd limbs, and soul fatigued away;
Flown, like a thought, until the morrow-day;
Blissfully havened both from joy and pain;                         240
Clasped like a missal where swart Paynims[8] pray;
Blinded alike from sunshine and from rain,
As though a rose should shut, and be a bud again.

## XXVIII

Stol'n to this paradise, and so entranced,
Porphyro gazed upon her empty dress,                               245
And listened to her breathing, if it chanced
To wake into a slumberous tenderness;
Which when he heard, that minute did he bless,

---

4. Window, in which are stained-glass
representations of many kinds, including a
royal coat of arms (line 216).
5. Heraldic red.

6. Gift, blessing.
7. Halo.
8. Pagans.

And breathed himself: then from the closet crept,
Noiseless as fear in a wide wilderness,                                   250
And over the hushed carpet, silent, stepped,
And 'tween the curtains peeped, where, lo!—how fast she slept.

### XXIX

Then by the bedside, where the faded moon
Made a dim, silver twilight, soft he set
A table, and, half anguished, threw thereon                               255
A cloth of woven crimson, gold, and jet—
O for some drowsy Morphean amulet![9]
The boisterous, midnight, festive clarion,[1]
The kettledrum, and far-heard clarinet,
Affray his ears, though but in dying tone—                                260
The hall door shuts again, and all the noise is gone.

### XXX

And still she slept an azure-lidded sleep,
In blanchéd linen, smooth, and lavendered,
While he from forth the closet brought a heap
Of candied apple, quince, and plum, and gourd;                            265
With jellies soother than the creamy curd,
And lucent syrups, tinct with cinnamon;
Manna[2] and dates, in argosy[3] transferred
From Fez; and spicéd dainties, every one,
From silken Samarcand to cedared Lebanon.                                 270

### XXXI

These delicates he heaped with glowing hand
On golden dishes and in baskets bright
Of wreathéd silver: sumptuous they stand
In the retired quiet of the night,
Filling the chilly room with perfume light.                               275
"And now, my love, my seraph[4] fair, awake!
Thou art my heaven, and I thine eremite:
Open thine eyes, for meek St. Agnes' sake,
Or I shall drowse beside thee, so my soul doth ache."

### XXXII

Thus whispering, his warm, unnervéd arm                                   280
Sank in her pillow. Shaded was her dream
By the dusk curtains:—'twas a midnight charm
Impossible to melt as icéd stream:
The lustrous salvers in the moonlight gleam;
Broad golden fringe upon the carpet lies:          ,                      285
It seemed he never, never could redeem
From such a steadfast spell his lady's eyes;
So mused awhile, entoiled[5] in wooféd fantasies.

---

9. A charm of Morpheus, god of sleep.
1. Trumpet.
2. Sweet gum.
3. Merchant ships. Fez, Samarcand, and
Lebanon are in Morocco, central Asia, and
the Levant, respectively.
4. The highest order of angel. "eremite":
devotee.
5. Entangled. "wooféd": woven.

### XXXIII

Awakening up, he took her hollow lute—
Tumultuous—and, in chords that tenderest be,                    290
He played an ancient ditty, long since mute,
In Provence called, "La belle dame sans merci": [6]
Close to her ear touching the melody—
Wherewith disturbed, she uttered a soft moan.
He ceased—she panted quick—and suddenly                         295
Her blue affrayéd eyes wide open shone:
Upon his knees he sank, pale as smooth-sculptured stone.

### XXXIV

Her eyes were open, but she still beheld,
Now wide awake, the vision of her sleep:
There was a painful change, that nigh expelled                  300
The blisses of her dream so pure and deep,
At which fair Madeline began to weep,
And moan forth witless words with many a sigh;
While still her gaze on Porphyro would keep;
Who knelt, with joinéd hands and piteous eye,                   305
Fearing to move or speak, she looked so dreamingly.

### XXXV

"Ah, Porphyro!" said she, "but even now
Thy voice was at sweet tremble in mine ear,
Made tunable with every sweetest vow;
And those sad eyes were spiritual and clear:                    310
How changed thou art! how pallid, chill, and drear!
Give me that voice again, my Porphyro,
Those looks immortal, those complainings dear!
Oh leave me not in this eternal woe,
For if thou diest, my Love, I know not where to go."            315

### XXXVI

Beyond a mortal man impassioned far
At these voluptuous accents, he arose,
Ethereal, flushed, and like a throbbing star
Seen mid the sapphire heaven's deep repose
Into her dream he melted, as the rose                           320
Blendeth its odor with the violet—
Solution sweet: meantime the frost-wind blows
Like Love's alarum pattering the sharp sleet
Against the windowpanes; St. Agnes' moon hath set.

### XXXVII

'Tis dark: quick pattereth the flaw-blown[7] sleet:             325
"This is no dream, my bride, my Madeline!"
'Tis dark: the icéd gusts still rave and beat:
"No dream, alas! alas! and woe is mine!
Porphyro will leave me here to fade and pine.
Cruel! what traitor could thee hither bring?                    330
I curse not, for my heart is lost in thine,

---

6. "The beautiful lady without pity,"     medieval Provence.
the kind of love song played or sung in     7. Gust-blown.

Though thou forsakest a deceivéd thing—
A dove forlorn and lost with sick prunéd wing."

### XXXVIII

"My Madeline! sweet dreamer! lovely bride!
Say, may I be for aye[8] thy vassal blest?                     335
Thy beauty's shield, heart-shaped and vermeil[9] dyed?
Ah, silver shrine, here will I take my rest
After so many hours of toil and quest,
A famished pilgrim—saved by miracle.
Though I have found, I will not rob thy nest                   340
Saving of thy sweet self; if thou think'st well
To trust, fair Madeline, to no rude infidel.

### XXXIX

"Hark! 'tis an elfin-storm from faery land,
Of haggard[1] seeming, but a boon indeed:
Arise—arise! the morning is at hand—                          345
The bloated wassailers[2] will never heed—
Let us away, my love, with happy speed;
There are no ears to hear, or eyes to see—
Drowned all in Rhenish and the sleepy mead:[3]
Awake! arise! my love, and fearless be,                       350
For o'er the southern moors I have a home for thee."

### XL

She hurried at his words, beset with fears,
For there were sleeping dragons all around,
At glaring watch, perhaps, with ready spears—
Down the wide stairs a darkling way they found.               355
In all the house was heard no human sound.
A chain-drooped lamp was flickering by each door;
The arras,[4] rich with horseman, hawk, and hound,
Fluttered in the besieging wind's uproar;
And the long carpets rose along the gusty floor.              360

### XLI

They glide, like phantoms, into the wide hall;
Like phantoms, to the iron porch, they glide;
Where lay the Porter, in uneasy sprawl,
With a huge empty flagon by his side:
The wakeful bloodhound rose, and shook his hide,              365
But his sagacious eye an inmate[5] owns:
By one, and one, the bolts full easy slide—
The chains lie silent on the footworn stones—
The key turns, and the door upon its hinges groans.

### XLII

And they are gone: ay, ages long ago                          370
These lovers fled away into the storm.

8. Forever.
9. Vermilion: bright red.
1. Wild.
2. Drunken revelers.
3. Liquor made from honey. "Rhenish":
rhine wine.
4. Tapestry.
5. Member of the household. "owns": recognizes.

That night the Baron dreamt of many a woe,
And all his warrior-guests, with shade and form
Of witch, and demon, and large coffin-worm,
Were long be-nightmared. Angela the old                    375
Died palsy-twitched, with meager face deform;
The Beadsman, after thousand aves[6] told,
For aye unsought for slept among his ashes cold.

1819

## Bright Star

Bright star! would I were steadfast as thou art—
    Not in lone splendor hung aloft the night
And watching, with eternal lids apart,
    Like nature's patient, sleepless Eremite,[7]
The moving waters at their priestlike task           5
    Of pure ablution round earth's human shores,
Or gazing on the new soft fallen mask
    Of snow upon the mountains and the moors—
No—yet still steadfast, still unchangeable,
    Pillowed upon my fair love's ripening breast,      10
To feel for ever its soft fall and swell,
    Awake for ever in a sweet unrest,
Still, still to hear her tender-taken breath,
And so live ever—or else swoon to death.

1819

## La Belle Dame sans Merci[1]

### A Ballad
(original version)

O what can ail thee, knight-at-arms,
    Alone and palely loitering?
The sedge has withered from the lake,
    And no birds sing.

O what can ail thee, knight-at-arms,                    5
    So haggard and so woe-begone?
The squirrel's granary is full,
    And the harvest's done.

I see a lily on thy brow,
    With anguish moist and fever dew,                   10
And on thy cheeks a fading rose
    Fast withereth too.

I met a lady in the meads,[2]
    Full beautiful—a faery's child,

6. Ave Maria's: Hail Mary's.
7. Religious hermit.
1. "The beautiful lady without pity."
The title (but not the subject matter) derives from a medieval poem by Alain
Chartier.
2. Meadows.

Her hair was long, her foot was light,    15
    And her eyes were wild.

I made a garland for her head,
    And bracelets too, and fragrant zone;[3]
She looked at me as she did love,
    And made sweet moan.    20

I set her on my pacing steed,
    And nothing else saw all day long,
For sidelong would she bend, and sing
    A faery's song.

She found me roots of relish sweet,    25
    And honey wild, and manna dew,
And sure in language strange she said,
    "I love thee true."

She took me to her elfin grot,
    And there she wept, and sighed full sore,    30
And there I shut her wild wild eyes
    With kisses four.

And there she lulléd me asleep,
    And there I dreamed—Ah! woe betide!
The latest[4] dream I ever dreamed    35
    On the cold hill side.

I saw pale kings and princes too,
    Pale warriors, death-pale were they all;
They cried—"La Belle Dame sans Merci
    Hath thee in thrall!"    40

I saw their starved lips in the gloam,
    With horrid warning gapéd wide,
And I awoke and found me here,
    On the cold hill's side.

And this is why I sojourn here,    45
    Alone and palely loitering,
Though the sedge has withered from the lake,
    And no birds sing.

April, 1819

# La Belle Dame sans Merci
(revised version)[1]

Ah, what can ail thee, wretched wight,
    Alone and palely loitering;
The sedge is withered from the lake,
    And no birds sing.

3. Girdle.
4. Last.
1. Most critics consider this inferior to the original version, one of the few instances in which Keats's revisions failed to improve his work.

Ah, what can ail thee, wretched wight,                 5
   So haggard and so woe-begone?
The squirrel's granary is full,
   And the harvest's done.

I see a lily on thy brow,
   With anguish moist and fever dew;         10
And on thy cheek a fading rose
   Fast withereth too.

I met a lady in the meads
   Full beautiful, a fairy's child;
Her hair was long, her foot was light,         15
   And her eyes were wild.

I set her on my pacing steed,
   And nothing else saw all day long;
For sideways would she lean, and sing
   A fairy's song.                         20

I made a garland for her head,
   And bracelets too, and fragrant zone:
She looked at me as she did love,
   And made sweet moan.

She found me roots of relish sweet,           25
   And honey wild, and manna dew;
And sure in language strange she said,
   "I love thee true."

She took me to her elfin grot,
   And there she gazed and sighéd deep,      30
And there I shut her wild sad eyes—
   So kissed to sleep.

And there we slumbered on the moss,
   And there I dreamed, ah woe betide,
The latest dream I ever dreamed                35
   On the cold hill side.

I saw pale kings, and princes too,
   Pale warriors, death-pale were they all;
Who cried—"La belle Dame sans merci
   Hath thee in thrall!"                     40

I saw their starved lips in the gloom
   With horrid warning gapéd wide,
And I awoke, and found me here
   On the cold hill side.

And this is why I sojourn here                 45
   Alone and palely loitering,
Though the sedge is withered from the lake,
   And no birds sing.

# To Sleep

O soft embalmer of the still midnight,
Shutting, with careful fingers and benign,
Our gloom-pleased eyes, embowered from the light,
Enshaded in forgetfulness divine;
O soothest[1] Sleep! if so it please thee, close,  5
In midst of this thine hymn, my willing eyes,
Or wait the amen, ere thy poppy[2] throws
Around my bed its lulling charities;
Then save me, or the passéd day will shine
Upon my pillow, breeding many woes;  10
Save me from curious[3] conscience, that still lords
Its strength for darkness, burrowing like a mole;
Turn the key deftly in the oiléd wards,[4]
And seal the hushéd casket of my soul.

April, 1819

# On Fame

*"You cannot eat your cake and have it too."—Proverb.*

How fevered is the man, who cannot look
Upon his mortal days with temperate blood,
Who vexes all the leaves of his life's book,
And robs his fair name of its maidenhood;
It is as if the rose should pluck herself,  5
Or the ripe plum finger its misty bloom,
As if a Naiad,[1] like a meddling elf,
Should darken her pure grot with muddy gloom;
But the rose leaves herself upon the briar,
For winds to kiss and grateful bees to feed,  10
And the ripe plum still wears its dim attire,
The undisturbéd lake has crystal space;
Why then should man, teasing the world for grace,
Spoil his salvation for a fierce miscreed?[2]

April, 1819

# Ode to Psyche[1]

O Goddess! hear these tuneless numbers, wrung
  By sweet enforcement and remembrance dear,
And pardon that thy secrets should be sung
  Even into thine own soft-conchéd[2] ear:

1. Softest.
2. Because opium derives from it, the poppy was associated with sleep.
3. Scrupulous. "lords": marshals.
4. Ridges in a lock that distinguish proper from improper keys.
1. Water nymph.
2. The false doctrine that ambition is divinely approved.
1. In Apuleius' *Golden Ass* (second century) Psyche is a beautiful maiden beloved by Cupid, the "wingéd" (line 21) son of Venus. Cupid forbids Psyche to look at his face, and when she disobeys, he flees; she then wanders far and wide in search of him, finally being reunited with him and becoming immortal. In Greek, *psyche* means both "breath" and "soul."
2. Shaped like a seashell.

Surely I dreamt today, or did I see                                    5
    The wingéd Psyche with awakened eyes?
I wandered in a forest thoughtlessly,
    And, on the sudden, fainting with surprise,
Saw two fair creatures, couchéd side by side
    In deepest grass, beneath the whisp'ring roof       10
    Of leaves and trembled blossoms, where there ran
        A brooklet, scarce espied:

'Mid hushed, cool-rooted flowers, fragrant-eyed,
    Blue, silver-white, and budded Tyrian,[3]
They lay calm-breathing on the bedded grass;           15
    Their arms embracéd, and their pinions[4] too;
    Their lips touched not, but had not bade adieu,
As if disjoinéd by soft-handed slumber,
And ready still past kisses to outnumber
    At tender eye-dawn of aurorean[5] love:             20
        The wingéd boy I knew;
But who wast thou, O happy, happy dove?
        His Psyche true!

O latest born and loveliest vision far
    Of all Olympus' faded hierarchy![6]                 25
Fairer than Phœbe's[7] sapphire-regioned star,
    Or Vesper,[8] amorous glow-worm of the sky;
Fairer than these, though temple thou hast none,
        Nor altar heaped with flowers;
Nor virgin choir to make delicious moan                30
        Upon the midnight hours;
No voice, no lute, no pipe, no incense sweet
        From chain-swung censer teeming;
No shrine, no grove, no oracle, no heat
        Of pale-mouthed prophet dreaming.               35

O brightest! though too late for antique vows,
        Too, too late for the fond believing lyre,
When holy were the haunted forest boughs,
        Holy the air, the water, and the fire;
Yet even in these days so far retired                  40
        From happy pieties, thy lucent fans,[9]
        Fluttering among the faint Olympians,
I see, and sing, by my own eyes inspired.
So let me be thy choir, and make a moan
        Upon the midnight hours;                        45
Thy voice, thy lute, thy pipe, thy incense sweet
        From swingéd censer teeming;
Thy shrine, thy grove, thy oracle, thy heat
        Of pale-mouthed prophet dreaming.

3. Purple or crimson, like the dye made in ancient Tyre from shellfish.
4. Wings.
5. Dawning.
6. Mt. Olympus was the home of the gods. In a letter of April 30, 1819, Keats wrote: "You must recollect that Psyche was not embodied as a goddess before the time of Apuleius . . . and consequently . . . never worshiped or sacrificed to with any of the ancient fervor. . . ."
7. Diana's, as goddess of the moon.
8. Venus, the evening star.
9. Shining wings.

Yes, I will be thy priest, and build a fane[1]                    50
In some untrodden region of my mind,
Where branchéd thoughts, new grown with pleasant pain,
Instead of pines shall murmur in the wind:
Far, far around shall those dark-clustered trees
Fledge[2] the wild-ridgéd mountains steep by steep;          55
And there by zephyrs,[3] streams, and birds, and bees,
The moss-lain Dryads[4] shall be lulled to sleep;
And in the midst of this wide quietness
A rosy sanctuary will I dress
With the wreathed trellis of a working brain,                    60
With buds, and bells, and stars without a name,
With all the gardener Fancy e'er could feign,
Who breeding flowers, will never breed the same:
And there shall be for thee all soft delight
That shadowy thought can win,                                          65
A bright torch, and a casement ope at night,
To let the warm Love[5] in!

April, 1819

# Ode to a Nightingale

### I

My heart aches, and a drowsy numbness pains
My sense, as though of hemlock[1] I had drunk,
Or emptied some dull opiate to the drains
One minute past, and Lethe-wards[2] had sunk:
'Tis not through envy of thy happy lot,                              5
But being too happy in thine happiness,
That thou, light-wingéd Dryad[3] of the trees,
In some melodious plot
Of beechen green, and shadows numberless,
Singest of summer in full-throated ease.                          10

### II

O, for a draught of vintage! that hath been
Cooled a long age in the deep-delvéd earth,
Tasting of Flora[4] and the country green,
Dance, and Provençal song,[5] and sunburnt mirth!
O for a beaker full of the warm South,                           15
Full of the true, the blushful Hippocrene,[6]
With beaded bubbles winking at the brim,
And purple-stainéd mouth;
That I might drink, and leave the world unseen,
And with thee fade away into the forest dim:                  20

1. Temple.
2. Stand like thick layers of feathers.
3. Breezes.
4. In classical mythology, tree nymphs.
5. Cupid.
1. A poisonous drug.
2. Toward the river of forgetfulness (Lethe) in Hades.

3. Wood nymph.
4. Roman goddess of flowers.
5. The medieval troubadors of Provence (in southern France) were famous for their love songs.
6. The fountain of the Muses on Mt. Helicon, whose waters bring poetic inspiration.

### III

Fade far away, dissolve, and quite forget
    What thou among the leaves hast never known,
The weariness, the fever, and the fret
    Here, where men sit and hear each other groan;
Where palsy shakes a few, sad, last gray hairs,                    25
    Where youth grows pale, and specter-thin, and dies;
        Where but to think is to be full of sorrow
            And leaden-eyed despairs,
    Where Beauty cannot keep her lustrous eyes,
        Or new Love pine at them beyond tomorrow.              30

### IV

Away! away! for I will fly to thee,
    Not charioted by Bacchus and his pards,[7]
But on the viewless wings of Poesy,
    Though the dull brain perplexes and retards:
Already with thee! tender is the night,                              35
    And haply the Queen-Moon is on her throne,
        Clustered around by all her starry Fays;[8]
            But here there is no light,
    Save what from heaven is with the breezes blown
        Through verdurous glooms and winding mossy ways.      40

### V

I cannot see what flowers are at my feet,
    Nor what soft incense hangs upon the boughs,
But, in embalméd[9] darkness, guess each sweet
    Wherewith the seasonable month endows
The grass, the thicket, and the fruit-tree wild;                    45
    White hawthorn, and the pastoral eglantine;[1]
        Fast fading violets covered up in leaves;
            And mid-May's eldest child,
    The coming musk-rose, full of dewy wine,
        The murmurous haunt of flies on summer eves.          50

### VI

Darkling[2] I listen; and, for many a time
    I have been half in love with easeful Death,
Called him soft names in many a muséd rhyme,
    To take into the air my quiet breath;
Now more than ever seems it rich to die,                            55
    To cease upon the midnight with no pain,
        While thou art pouring forth thy soul abroad
            In such an ecstasy!
    Still wouldst thou sing, and I have ears in vain—
        To thy high requiem become a sod.                         60

### VII

Thou wast not born for death, immortal Bird!
    No hungry generations tread thee down;

7. The Roman god of wine was sometimes portrayed in a chariot drawn by
leopards. "viewless": invisible.
8. Fairies.

9. Fragrant, aromatic.
1. Sweetbriar or honeysuckle.
2. In the dark.

The voice I hear this passing night was heard
  In ancient days by emperor and clown:
Perhaps the selfsame song that found a path                    65
  Through the sad heart of Ruth,³ when, sick for home,
    She stood in tears amid the alien corn;
      The same that ofttimes hath
Charmed magic casements, opening on the foam
  Of perilous seas, in faery lands forlorn.                    70

### VIII

Forlorn! the very word is like a bell
  To toll me back from thee to my sole self!
Adieu! the fancy cannot cheat so well
  As she is famed to do, deceiving elf.
Adieu! adieu! thy plaintive anthem fades                       75
  Past the near meadows, over the still stream,
    Up the hillside; and now 'tis buried deep
      In the next valley-glades:
Was it a vision, or a waking dream?
  Fled is that music:—Do I wake or sleep?                      80
May, 1819

# Ode on a Grecian Urn

### I

Thou still unravished bride of quietness,
  Thou foster-child of silence and slow time,
Sylvan¹ historian, who canst thus express
  A flowery tale more sweetly than our rhyme:
What leaf-fringed legend haunts about thy shape                5
  Of deities or mortals, or of both,
    In Tempe or the dales of Arcady?²
What men or gods are these? What maidens loath?
  What mad pursuit? What struggle to escape?
    What pipes and timbrels? What wild ecstasy?               10

### II

Heard melodies are sweet, but those unheard
  Are sweeter; therefore, ye soft pipes, play on;
Not to the sensual³ ear, but, more endeared,
  Pipe to the spirit ditties of no tone:
Fair youth, beneath the trees, thou canst not leave           15
  Thy song, nor ever can those trees be bare;
    Bold Lover, never, never canst thou kiss,
Though winning near the goal—yet, do not grieve;
  She cannot fade, though thou hast not thy bliss,
    For ever wilt thou love, and she be fair!                 20

---

3. A virtuous Moabite widow who, according to the Old Testament *Book of Ruth*, found a husband while gleaning in the wheat fields of Judah.
  1. Rustic. The urn depicts a woodland scene.
  2. Arcadia. Tempe is a beautiful valley near Mt. Olympus in Greece, and the valley ("dales") of Arcadia a picturesque section of the Peloponnesus; both came to be associated with the pastoral ideal.
  3. Of the senses, as distinguished from the "ear" of the spirit or imagination.

### III

Ah, happy, happy boughs! that cannot shed
    Your leaves, nor ever bid the Spring adieu;
And, happy melodist, unweariéd,
    For ever piping songs for ever new;
More happy love! more happy, happy love!          25
    For ever warm and still to be enjoyed,
        For ever panting, and for ever young;
All breathing human passion far above,
    That leaves a heart high-sorrowful and cloyed,
        A burning forehead, and a parching tongue.   30

### IV

Who are these coming to the sacrifice?
    To what green altar, O mysterious priest,
Lead'st thou that heifer lowing at the skies,
    And all her silken flanks with garlands dressed?
What little town by river or sea shore,            35
    Or mountain-built with peaceful citadel,
        Is emptied of this folk, this pious morn?
And, little town, thy streets for evermore
    Will silent be; and not a soul to tell
        Why thou art desolate, can e'er return.      40

### V

O Attic[4] shape! Fair attitude! with brede[5]
    Of marble men and maidens overwrought,
With forest branches and the trodden weed;
    Thou, silent form, dost tease us out of thought
As doth eternity: Cold Pastoral!                   45
    When old age shall this generation waste,
        Thou shalt remain, in midst of other woe
Than ours, a friend to man, to whom thou say'st,
    Beauty is truth, truth beauty[6]—that is all
        Ye know on earth, and all ye need to know.    50

May, 1819

## Ode on Melancholy

### I

No, no, go not to Lethe,[1] neither twist
    Wolfsbane, tight-rooted, for its poisonous wine;[2]
Nor suffer thy pale forehead to be kissed
    By nightshade, ruby grape of Proserpine;
Make not your rosary of yew-berries,[3]             5

4. Attica was the district of ancient Greece surrounding Athens.
5. Woven pattern. "overwrought": ornamented all over.
6. In some texts of the poem "Beauty is truth, truth beauty" is in quotation marks and in some texts it is not, leading to critical disagreements about whether the last line and a half are also inscribed on the urn or spoken by the poet.
1. The river of forgetfulness in Hades.
2. Like nightshade (line 4), wolfsbane is a poisonous plant. "Proserpine": Queen of Hades.
3. Which often grow in cemeteries and which are traditionally associated with death.

Nor let the beetle, nor the death-moth be
Your mournful Psyche,[4] nor the downy owl
A partner in your sorrow's mysteries;
For shade to shade will come too drowsily,
And drown the wakeful anguish of the soul.                          10

## II

But when the melancholy fit shall fall
Sudden from heaven like a weeping cloud,
That fosters the droop-headed flowers all,
And hides the green hill in an April shroud;
Then glut thy sorrow on a morning rose,                            15
Or on the rainbow of the salt sand-wave,
Or on the wealth of globéd peonies;
Or if thy mistress some rich anger shows,
Emprison her soft hand, and let her rave,
And feed deep, deep upon her peerless eyes.                        20

## III

She[5] dwells with Beauty—Beauty that must die;
And Joy, whose hand is ever at his lips
Bidding adieu; and aching Pleasure nigh,
Turning to poison while the bee-mouth sips:
Ay, in the very temple of Delight                                  25
Veiled Melancholy has her sov'reign shrine,
Though seen of none save him whose strenuous tongue
Can burst Joy's grape against his palate fine;[6]
His soul shall taste the sadness of her might,
And be among her cloudy trophies hung.[7]                          30
May, 1819

# To Autumn

## I

Season of mists and mellow fruitfulness,
    Close bosom-friend of the maturing sun;
Conspiring with him how to load and bless
    With fruit the vines that round the thatch-eves run;
To bend with apples the mossed cottage-trees,                      5
    And fill all fruit with ripeness to the core;
        To swell the gourd, and plump the hazel shells
With a sweet kernel; to set budding more,
And still more, later flowers for the bees,
Until they think warm days will never cease,                       10
    For Summer has o'er-brimmed their clammy cells.

4. *Psyche* means both "soul" and "breath," and sometimes it was anciently represented by a moth leaving the mouth at death. Owls and beetles were also traditionally associated with darkness and death.
5. The goddess Melancholy, whose chief place of worship ("shrine") is described in lines 25–26.
6. Sensitive, discriminating.
7. The ancient Greeks and Romans hung trophies in their gods' temples.

## II

Who hath not seen thee oft amid thy store?
  Sometimes whoever seeks abroad may find
Thee sitting careless on a granary floor,
  Thy hair soft-lifted by the winnowing wind;[1]                15
Or on a half-reaped furrow sound asleep,
  Drowsed with the fume of poppies, while thy hook[2]
    Spares the next swath and all its twinèd flowers:
And sometimes like a gleaner thou dost keep
  Steady thy laden head across a brook;                        20
  Or by a cider-press, with patient look,
    Thou watchest the last oozings hours by hours.

## III

Where are the songs of Spring? Ay, where are they?
  Think not of them, thou hast thy music too—
While barrèd clouds bloom the soft-dying day,                  25
  And touch the stubble-plains with rosy hue;
Then in a wailful choir the small gnats mourn
  Among the river sallows,[3] borne aloft
    Or sinking as the light wind lives or dies;
And full-grown lambs loud bleat from hilly bourn;[4]           30
  Hedge-crickets sing; and now with treble soft
  The red-breast whistles from a garden-croft;[5]
    And gathering swallows twitter in the skies.
September 19, 1819

## *from* Letter to Benjamin Bailey, November 22, 1817[1]

\* \* \* I am certain of nothing but of the holiness of the Heart's affections and the truth of Imagination—What the imagination seizes as Beauty must be truth—whether it existed before or not—for I have the same Idea of all our Passions as of Love they are all in their sublime, creative of essential Beauty \* \* \* The Imagination may be compared to Adam's dream[2]—he awoke and found it truth. I am the more zealous in this affair, because I have never yet been able to perceive how any thing can be known for truth by consequitive reasoning—and yet it must be—Can it be that even the greatest Philosopher ever when arrived at his goal without putting aside numerous objections—However it may be, O for a Life of Sensations rather than of Thoughts! It is "a Vision in the form of Youth" a Shadow of reality to come—and this consideration has further conv[i]nced me for it has come as auxiliary to another favorite Speculation of mine, that we shall enjoy ourselves here after by having what we called happiness on Earth repeated in a finer tone and so repeated—And yet such a fate can only befall those who delight in sensation rather than hunger as you do after Truth— Adam's dream will do here and seems to be a conviction that Imagination and its empyreal reflection is the same as human Life and its spiritual repetition. But as I was saying—the simple imaginative Mind

1. Which sifts the grain from the chaff.
2. Scythe or sickle.
3. Willows.
4. Domain.

5. An enclosed garden near a house.
1. Keats's private letters, often carelessly written, are reprinted uncorrected.
2. In *Paradise Lost*, VIII, 460–90.

may have its rewards in the repeti[ti]on of its own silent Working coming continually on the spirit with a fine suddenness—to compare great things with small—have you never by being surprised with an old Melody—in a delicious place—by a delicious voice, fe[l]t over again your very speculations and surmises at the time it first operated on your soul—do you not remember forming to yourself the singer's face more beautiful that [*for* than] it was possible and yet with the elevation of the Moment you did not think so—even then you were mounted on the Wings of Imagination so high—that the Prototype must be here after—that delicious face you will see—What a time! I am continually running away from the subject—sure this cannot be exactly the case with a complex Mind—one that is imaginative and at the same time careful of its fruits—who would exist partly on sensation partly on thought—to whom it is necessary that years should bring the philosophic Mind—such an one I consider your's and therefore it is necessary to your eternal Happiness that you not only ~~have~~ drink this old Wine of Heaven which I shall call the redigestion of our most ethereal Musings on Earth; but also increase in knowledge and know all things. * * *

## *from* Letter to George and Thomas Keats, December 21, 1817

* * * I spent Friday evening with Wells[1] & went the next morning to see *Death on the Pale horse.*[2] It is a wonderful picture, when West's age is considered; But there is nothing to be intense upon; no women one feels mad to kiss, no face swelling into reality. the excellence of every Art is its intensity, capable of making all disagreeables evaporate, from their being in close relationship with Beauty & Truth— Examine King Lear & you will find this examplified throughout; but in this picture we have unpleasantness without any momentous depth of speculation excited, in which to bury its repulsiveness—The picture is larger than Christ rejected—I dined with Haydon the sunday after you left, & had a very pleasant day, I dined too (for I have been out too much lately) with Horace Smith & met his two Brothers with Hill & Kingston & one Du Bois,[3] they only served to convince me, how superior humour is to wit in respect to enjoyment—These men say things which make one start, without making one feel, they are all alike; their manners are alike; they all know fashionables; they have a mannerism in their very eating & drinking, in their mere handling a Decanter—They talked of Kean[4] & his low company—Would I were with that company instead of yours said I to myself! I know such like acquaintance will never do for me & yet I am going to Reynolds, on wednesday—Brown & Dilke walked with me & back from the Christmas pantomime. I had not a dispute but a disquisition with Dilke, on various subjects; several things dovetailed in my mind, & at once it struck me, what quality went to form a Man of Achievement especially in Literature & which Shakespeare posessed so enormously—I mean

1. Charles Wells (1800–1879), an author.
2. By Benjamin West (1738–1820), American painter and president of the Royal Academy; "Christ Rejected" (mentioned below) is also by West.

3. Thomas Hill (1760–1840), a book collector, and Edward duBois (1774–1850), a journalist.
4. Edmund Kean, a famous Shakespearean actor.

*Negative Capability,* that is when man is capable of being in uncertainties, Mysteries, doubts, without any irritable reaching after fact & reason—Coleridge, for instance, would let go by a fine isolated verisimilitude caught from the Penetralium of mystery, from being incapable of remaining content with half knowledge. This pursued through Volumes would perhaps take us no further than this, that with a great poet the sense of Beauty overcomes every other consideration, or rather obliterates all consideration.

## *from* Letter to John Hamilton Reynolds, February 3, 1818

\* \* \* It may be said that we ought to read our Contemporaries. that Wordsworth &c should have their due from us. but for the sake of a few fine imaginative or domestic passages, are we to be bullied into a certain Philosophy engendered in the whims of an Egotist—Every man has his speculations, but every man does not brood and peacock over them till he makes a false coinage and deceives himself—Many a man can travel to the very bourne of Heaven, and yet want confidence to put down his halfseeing. Sancho[1] will invent a Journey heavenward as well as any body. We hate poetry that has a palpable design upon us—and if we do not agree, seems to put its hand in its breeches pocket. Poetry should be great & unobtrusive, a thing which enters into one's soul, and does not startle it or amaze it with itself but with its subject.—How beautiful are the retired flowers! how would they lose their beauty were they to throng into the highway crying out, "admire me I am a violet! dote upon me I am a primrose!["] Modern poets differ from the Elizabethans in this. Each of the moderns like an Elector of Hanover governs his petty state, & knows how many straws are swept daily from the Causeways in all his dominions & has a continual itching that all the Housewives should have their coppers well scoured: the antients were ~~Emperors of large~~ Emperors of vast Provinces, they had only heard of the remote ones and scarcely cared to visit them.—I will cut all this—I will have no more of Wordsworth or Hunt in particular—Why should we be of the tribe of Manasseh, when we can wander with Esau? why should we kick against the Pricks, when we can walk on Roses? Why should we be owls, when we can be Eagles? Why be teased with "nice Eyed wagtails," when we have in sight "the Cherub Contemplation"?[2]—Why with Wordsworths "Matthew with a bough of wilding in his hand" when we can have Jacques "under an oak &c"[3]—The secret of the Bough of Wilding will run through your head faster than I can write it—Old Matthew spoke to him some years ago on some nothing, & because he happens in an Evening Walk to imagine the figure of the old man—he must stamp it down in black & white, and it is henceforth sacred—I don't mean to deny Wordsworth's grandeur & Hunt's merit, but I mean to say we need not be teazed with grandeur & merit—when we can have them uncontaminated & unobtrusive. \* \* \*

1. Don Quixote's squire.
2. The phrases are from Leigh Hunt ("The Nymphs," ii, 170) and Milton (*Il Penseroso,* line 54) respectively.

3. The phrases are from Wordsworth ("The Two April Mornings," lines 57–60) and Shakespeare (*As You Like It,* Act II, sc. i, 31).

# Letter to John Hamilton Reynolds, February 19, 1818

I have an idea that a Man might pass a very pleasant life in this manner—let him on any certain day read a certain Page of full Poesy or distilled Prose and let him wander with it, and muse upon it, and reflect from it, and bring home to it, and prophesy upon it, and dream upon it—untill it becomes stale—but when will it do so? Never— When Man has arrived at a certain ripeness in intellect any one grand and spiritual passage serves him as a starting post towards all "the two-and-thirty Pallaces"[1] How happy is such a "voyage of conception," what delicious diligent Indolence! A doze upon a Sofa does not hinder it, and a nap upon Clover engenders ethereal finger-pointings—the prattle of a child gives it wings, and the converse of middle age a strength to beat them—a strain of musick conducts to "an odd angle of the Isle",[2] and when the leaves whisper it puts a "girdle round the earth",[3] Nor will this sparing touch of noble Books be any irreverance to their Writers—for perhaps the honors paid by Man to Man are trifles in comparison to the Benefit done by great Works to the "Spirit and pulse of good" by their mere passive existence. Memory should not be called knowledge—Many have original minds who do not think it— they are led away by Custom—Now it appears to me that almost any Man may like the Spider spin from his own inwards his own airy Citadel—the points of leaves and twigs on which the Spider begins her work are few and she fills the Air with a beautiful circuiting: man should be content with as few points to tip with the fine Webb of his Soul and weave a tapestry empyrean—full of Symbols for his spiritual eye, of softness for his spiritual touch, of space for his wandering of distinctness for his Luxury—But the Minds of Mortals are so different and bent on such diverse Journeys that it may at first appear impossible for any common taste and fellowship to exist ~~bettween~~ between two or three under these suppositions—It is however quite the contrary— Minds would leave each other in contrary directions, traverse each other in Numberless points, and all [*for* at] last greet each other at the Journeys end—An old Man and a child would talk together and the old Man be led on his Path, and the child left thinking—Man should not dispute or assert but whisper results to his neighbor, and thus by every germ of Spirit sucking the Sap from mould ethereal every human might become great, and Humanity instead of being a wide heath of Furse[4] and Briars with here and there a remote Oak or Pine, would become a grand democracy of Forest Trees. It has been an old Comparison for our urging on—the Bee hive—however it seems to me that we should rather be the flower than the Bee—for it is a false notion that more is gained by receiving than giving—no, the receiver and the giver are equal in their benefits—The f[l]ower I doubt not receives a fair guer-don from the Bee—its leaves blush deeper in the next spring—and who shall say between Man and Woman which is the most delighted? Now it is more noble to sit like Jove that [*for* than] to fly like Mer-cury—let us not therefore go hurrying about and collecting honey bee like, buzzing here and there impatiently from a knowledge of what is

1. "Places of delight" in Buddhism.
2. *The Tempest*, Act I, sc. ii, 223.
3. The phrase is from *Midsummer*
*Night's Dream*, Act II, sc. i, 175.
4. *The Tempest*, Act I, sc. i, 68–69.

to be arrived at; but let us open our leaves like a flower and be passive and receptive—budding patiently under the eye of Apollo and taking hints from every noble insect that favors us with a visit—sap will be given us for Meat and dew for drink—I was led into these thoughts, my dear Reynolds, by the beauty of the morning operating on a sense of Idleness—I have not read any Books—the Morning said I was right —I had no Idea but of the Morning, and the Thrush said I was right— seeming to say—

> O thou whose face hath felt the Winter's wind,
> Whose eye has seen the snow-clouds hung in mist,
> And the black elm tops 'mong the freezing stars,
> To thee the spring will be a harvest-time.
> O thou, whose only book has been the light
> Of supreme darkness which thou feddest on
> Night after night when Phœbus was away,
> To thee the spring shall be a triple morn.
> O fret not after knowledge—I have none,
> And yet my song comes native with the warmth.
> O fret not after knowledge—I have none,
> And yet the Evening listens. He who saddens
> At thought of idleness cannot be idle,
> And he's awake who thinks himself asleep.

Now I am sensible all this is a mere sophistication, however it may neighbor to any truths, to excuse my own indolence—so I will not deceive myself that Man should be equal with jove—but think himself very well off as a sort of scullion-Mercury, or even a humble Bee—It is not [*for* no] matter whether I am right or wrong either one way or another, if there is sufficient to lift a little time from your Shoulders.

## *from* Letter to John Taylor, February 27, 1818

* * * It is a sorry thing for me that any one should have to overcome Prejudices in reading my Verses—that affects me more than any hypercriticism on any particular Passage. In *Endymion* I have most likely but moved into the Go-cart from the leading strings. In Poetry I have a few Axioms, and you will see how far I am from their Centre. 1st I think Poetry should surprise by a fine excess and not by Singularity—it should strike the Reader as a wording of his own highest thoughts, and appear almost a Remembrance—2nd Its touches of Beauty should never be half way therby making the reader breathless instead of content: the rise, the progress, the setting of imagery should like the Sun come natural natural too him—shine over him and set soberly although in magnificence leaving him in the Luxury of twilight—but it is easier to think what Poetry should be than to write it—and this leads me on to another axiom. That if Poetry comes not as naturally as the Leaves to a tree it had better not come at all. However it may be with me I cannot help looking into new countries with "O for a Muse of fire to ascend!"[1]—If Endymion serves me as a Pioneer perhaps I ought to be content. I have great reason to be content, for thank God I can read

---

1. Shakespeare, *Henry V*, Prologue, 1.

and perhaps understand Shakspeare to his depths, and I have I am sure many friends, who, if I fail, will attribute any change in my Life and Temper to Humbleness rather than to Pride—to a cowering under the Wings of great Poets rather than to a Bitterness that I am not appreciated. I am anxious to get Endymion printed that I may forget it and proceed. * * *

## *from* the Preface to *Endymion,* dated April 10, 1818

The imagination of a boy is healthy, and the mature imagination of a man is healthy; but there is a space of life between, in which the soul is in a ferment, the character undecided, the way of life uncertain, the ambition thick-sighted: thence proceeds mawkishness, and all the thousand bitters which those men I speak of must necessarily taste in going over the following pages.

I hope I have not in too late a day touched the beautiful mythology of Greece, and dulled its brightness: for I wish to try once more, before I bid it farewell.

## *from* Letter to James Augustus Hessey, October 8, 1818

* * * Praise or blame has but a momentary effect on the man whose love of beauty in the abstract makes him a severe critic on his own Works. My own domestic criticism has given me pain without comparison beyond what Blackwood or the ~~Edinburgh~~ Quarterly[1] could possibly inflict. and also when I feel I am right, no external praise can give me such a glow as my own solitary reperception & ratification of what is fine. J. S.[2] is perfectly right in regard to the slip-shod Endymion. That it is so is no fault of mine.—No!—though it may sound a little paradoxical. It is as good as I had power to make it—by myself—Had I been nervous about its being a perfect piece, & with that view asked advice, & trembled over every page, it would not have been written; for it is not in my nature to fumble—I will write independantly.—I have written independently *without Judgment.*—I may write independently & *with judgment* hereafter.—The Genius of Poetry must work out its own salvation in a man: It cannot be matured by law & precept, but by sensation & watchfulness in itself—That which is creative must create itself—In Endymion, I leaped headlong into the Sea, and thereby have become better acquainted with the Soundings, the quicksands & the rocks, than if I had ~~stayed~~ stayed upon the green shore, and piped a silly pipe, and took tea & comfortable advice.—I was never afraid of failure; for I would sooner fail than not be among the greatest—But I am nigh getting into a rant. * * *

---

1. *Endymion* was violently attacked by reviewers in *Blackwood's Edinburgh Magazine* and *The Quarterly Review.*

2. Whose letter to the *Morning Chronicle* defended Keats.

# ADRIENNE RICH
## A Clock in the Square

This handless clock stares blindly from its tower,
Refusing to acknowledge any hour.
But what can one clock do to stop the game
When others go on striking just the same?
Whatever mite of truth the gesture held,                    5
Time may be silenced but will not be stilled,
Nor we absolved by any one's withdrawing
From all the restless ways we must be going
And all the rings in which we're spun and swirled,
Whether around a clockface or a world.                       10

1951


## Aunt Jennifer's Tigers

Aunt Jennifer's tigers prance across a screen,
Bright topaz denizens of a world of green.
They do not fear the men beneath the tree;
They pace in sleek chivalric certainty.

Aunt Jennifer's fingers fluttering through her wool         5
Find even the ivory needle hard to pull.
The massive weight of Uncle's wedding band
Sits heavily upon Aunt Jennifer's hand.

When Aunt is dead, her terrified hands will lie
Still ringed with ordeals she was mastered by.              10
The tigers in the panel that she made
Will go on prancing, proud and unafraid.

1951


[In When We Dead Awaken: Writing as Re-Vision, *a talk[1] given in December, 1951, the author said of* Aunt Jennifer's Tigers: "In writing this poem, composed and apparently cool as it is, I thought I was creating a portrait of an imaginary woman. But this woman suffers from the opposition of her imagination, worked out in tapestry, and her life style, 'ringed with ordeals she was mastered by.' It was important to me that Aunt Jennifer was a person as distinct from myself as possible—distanced by the formalism of the poem, by its objective, observant tone— even by putting the woman in a different generation. In those years formalism was part of the strategy—like asbestos gloves, it allowed me to handle materials I couldn't pick up bare-handed."]


## Storm Warnings

The glass has been falling all the afternoon,
And knowing better than the instrument

1. At the Women's Forum of the Modern Language Association.

What winds are walking overhead, what zone
Of gray unrest is moving across the land,
I leave the book upon a pillowed chair    5
And walk from window to closed window, watching
Boughs strain against the sky

And think again, as often when the air
Moves inward toward a silent core of waiting,
How with a single purpose time has traveled    10
By secret currents of the undiscerned
Into this polar realm. Weather abroad
And weather in the heart alike come on
Regardless of prediction.

Between foreseeing and averting change    15
Lies all the mastery of elements
Which clocks and weatherglasses cannot alter.
Time in the hand is not control of time,
Nor shattered fragments of an instrument
A proof against the wind; the wind will rise,    20
We can only close the shutters.

I draw the curtains as the sky goes black
And set a match to candles sheathed in glass
Against the keyhole draught, the insistent whine
Of weather through the unsealed aperture.    25
This is our sole defense against the season;
These are the things that we have learned to do
Who live in troubled regions.

         1951

# Ideal Landscape

We had to take the world as it was given:
The nursemaid sitting passive in the park
Was rarely by a changeling prince accosted.
The mornings happened similar and stark
In rooms of selfhood where we woke and lay    5
Watching today unfold like yesterday.

Our friends were not unearthly beautiful,
Nor spoke with tongues of gold, our lovers blundered
Now and again when most we sought perfection,
Or hid in cupboards when the heavens thundered.    10
The human rose to haunt us everywhere,
Raw, flawed, and asking more than we could bear.

And always time was rushing like a tram
Through streets of a foreign city, streets we saw
Opening into great and sunny squares    15
We could not find again, no map could show—
Never those fountains tossed in that same light,
Those gilded trees, those statues green and white.

         1955

## The Diamond Cutters

However legendary,
The stone is still a stone,
Though it had once resisted
The weight of Africa,
The hammer-blows of time                    5
That wear to bits of powder
The mountain and the pebble—
But not this coldest one.

Now, you intelligence
So late dredged up from dark                 10
Upon whose smoky walls
Bison took fumbling form
Or flint was edged on flint—
Now, careful arriviste,[1]
Delineate at will                            15
Incisions in the ice.

Be serious, because
The stone may have contempt
For too-familiar hands,
And because all you do                       20
Loses or gains by this:
Respect the adversary,
Meet it with tools refined,
And thereby set your price.

Be hard of heart, because                    25
The stone must leave your hand.
Although you liberate
Pure and expensive fires
Fit to enamour Shebas,
Keep your desire apart.                       30
Love only what you do,
And not what you have done.

Be proud, when you have set
The final spoke of flame
In that prismatic wheel,                      35
And nothing's left this day
Except to see the sun
Shine on the false and the true,
And know that Africa
Will yield you more to do.                    40

1955

---

1. Opportunist, upstart.

# Snapshots of a Daughter-in-Law

### 1
You, once a belle in Shreveport,
with henna-colored hair, skin like a peachbud,
still have your dresses copied from that time,
and play a Chopin prelude
called by Cortot: *"Delicious recollections*          5
*float like perfume through the memory."*

Your mind now, mouldering like wedding-cake,
heavy with useless experience, rich
with suspicion, rumor, fantasy,
crumbling to pieces under the knife-edge          10
of mere fact. In the prime of your life.

Nervy, glowering, your daughter
wipes the teaspoons, grows another way.

### 2
Banging the coffee-pot into the sink
she hears the angels chiding, and looks out          15
past the raked gardens to the sloppy sky.
Only a week since They said: *Have no patience.*

The next time it was: *Be insatiable.*
Then: *Save yourself; others you cannot save.*[1]
Sometimes she's let the tapstream scald her arm,          20
a match burn to her thumbnail,

or held her hand above the kettle's snout
right in the woolly steam. They are probably angels,
since nothing hurts her any more, except
each morning's grit blowing into her eyes.          25

### 3
A thinking woman sleeps with monsters.
The beak that grips her, she becomes. And Nature,
that sprung-lidded, still commodious
steamer-trunk of *tempora* and *mores*[2]
gets stuffed with it all:          the mildewed orange-flowers,          30
the female pills, the terrible breasts
of Boadicea[3] beneath flat foxes' heads and orchids.

Two handsome women, gripped in argument,
each proud, acute, subtle, I hear scream
across the cut glass and majolica          35
like Furies[4] cornered from their prey:

1. According to *Matthew* 27:42, the chief priests, scribes, and elders mocked the crucified Jesus by saying, "He saved others; himself he cannot save."
2. Times and customs.
3. Queen of the ancient Britons. When her husband died, the Romans seized the territory he ruled and scourged Boadicea; she then led a heroic but ultimately unsuccessful revolt.
4. In Roman mythology, the three sisters were the avenging spirits of retributive justice.

The argument *ad feminam*,[5] all the old knives
that have rusted in my back, I drive in yours,
*ma semblable, ma soeur!*[6]


4

Knowing themselves too well in one another:                     40
their gifts no pure fruition, but a thorn,
the prick filed sharp against a hint of scorn . . .
Reading while waiting
for the iron to heat,
writing, *My Life had stood—a Loaded Gun*—[7]            45
in that Amherst pantry while the jellies boil and scum,
or, more often,
iron-eyed and beaked and purposed as a bird,
dusting everything on the whatnot every day of life.


5

*Dulce ridens, dulce loquens,*[8]                             50
she shaves her legs until they gleam
like petrified mammoth-tusk.


6

When to her lute Corinna sings[9]
neither words nor music are her own;
only the long hair dipping                                      55
over her check, only the song
of silk against her knees
and these
adjusted in reflections of an eye.


Poised, trembling and unsatisfied, before                       60
an unlocked door, that cage of cages,
tell us, you bird, you tragical machine—
is this *fertilisante douleur?*[1] Pinned down
by love, for you the only natural action,
are you edged more keen                                         65
to prise the secrets of the vault? has Nature shown
her household books to you, daughter-in-law,
that her sons never saw?


7

*"To have in this uncertain world some stay*
*which cannot be undermined, is*                                70
*of the utmost consequence."*[2]
                                        Thus wrote

---

5. The *argumentum ad hominem* (literally, argument to the man) is (in logic) an argument aimed at a person's individual prejudices or special interests.

6. "My mirror-image (or 'double'), my sister." Baudelaire, in the prefatory poem to *Les Fleurs du Mal*, addresses (and attacks) his "hypocrite reader" as "mon semblable, mon frère" (my double, my brother).

7. " 'My Life had stood—a Loaded Gun' [Poem No. 754], Emily Dickinson, *Complete Poems*, ed. T. H. Johnson, 1960, p. 369." (Rich's note)

8. "Sweet (or winsome) laughter, sweet chatter." The phrase concludes Horace's *Ode*, 1, 22, describing the appeal of a mistress.

9. The opening line of a famous Elizabethan lyric (by Thomas Campion) in which Corinna's music is said to control totally the poet's happiness or despair.

1. Enriching pain.

2. " '. . . is of the utmost consequence,' from Mary Wollstonecraft, *Thoughts on the Education of Daughters*, London, 1787." (Rich's note)

a woman, partly brave and partly good,
who fought with what she partly understood.
Few men about her would or could do more,
hence she was labeled harpy, shrew and whore.      75

8

"You all die at fifteen," said Diderot,[3]
and turn part legend, part convention.
Still, eyes inaccurately dream
behind closed windows blankening with steam.
Deliciously, all that we might have been,      80
all that we were—fire, tears,
wit, taste, martyred ambition—
stirs like the memory of refused adultery
the drained and flagging bosom of our middle years.

9

*Not that it is done well, but*      85
*that it is done at all?*[4] Yes, think
of the odds! or shrug them off forever.
This luxury of the precocious child,
Time's precious chronic invalid,—
would we, darlings, resign it if we could?      90
Our blight has been our sinecure:
mere talent was enough for us—
glitter in fragments and rough drafts.

Sigh no more, ladies.
                    Time is male
and in his cups drinks to the fair.      95
Bemused by gallantry, we hear
our mediocrities over-praised,
indolence read as abnegation,
slattern thought styled intuition,
every lapse forgiven, our crime      100
only to cast too bold a shadow
or smash the mould straight off.

For that, solitary confinement,
tear gas, attrition shelling.
Few applicants for that honor.

10
Well,      105
she's long about her coming, who must be
more merciless to herself than history.[5]

3. " 'Vous mourez toutes à quinze ans,' from the *Lettres à Sophie Volland*, quoted by Simone de Beauvoir in *Le Deuxième Sexe*, vol. II, pp. 123–4." (Rich's note) Editor of the *Encyclopédie* (the central document of the French Enlightenment), Diderot became disillusioned with the traditional education of women and undertook an experimental education for his own daughter.

4. Samuel Johnson's comment on women preachers: "Sir, a woman's preaching is like a dog's walking on his hinder legs. It is not done well, but you are surprised to find it done at all." (Boswell's *Life of Johnson*, ed. Birbeck-Hill, I, 463)

5. "Cf. *Le Deuxième Sexe*, vol. II, p. 574: '. . . elle arrive du fond des ages, de Thèbes, de Minos, de Chichen Itza; et elle est aussi le totem planté au coeur de la brousse africaine; c'est un helicoptère et c'est un oiseau; et voilà la plus grande merveille: sous ses cheveux peints le bruissement des feuillages devient une pensée et des paroles s'échappent de ses seins.' " (Rich's note)

Her mind full to the wind, I see her plunge
breasted and glancing through the currents,
taking the light upon her                                110
at least as beautiful as any boy
or helicopter,
           poised, still coming,
her fine blades making the air wince

but her cargo
no promise then:                                         115
delivered
palpable
ours.
1958–60


[*In* When We Dead Awaken, *Rich described her consciousness during the time she was writing this poem:* "Over two years I wrote a 10-part poem called 'Snapshots of A Daughter-in-Law,' in a longer, looser mode than I've ever trusted myself with before. It was an extraordinary relief to write that poem. It strikes me now as too literary, too dependent on allusion; I hadn't found the courage yet to do without authorities, or even to use the pronoun 'I'—the woman in the poem is always 'she.' One section of it, #2, concerns a woman who thinks she is going mad; she is haunted by voices telling her to resist and rebel, voices which she can hear but not obey."]


# Double Monologue

To live illusionless, in the abandoned mine-
      shaft of doubt, and still
mime illusions for others? A puzzle
      for the maker who has thought
once too often too coldly.                               5

Since I was more than a child
      trying on a thousand faces
I have wanted one thing: to know
      simply as I know my name
at any given moment, where I stand.                      10

How much expense of time and skill
      which might have set itself
to angelic fabrications! All merely
      to chart one needle in the haymow?
Find yourself and you find the world?                    15

Solemn presumption! Mighty Object
      no one but itself has missed,
what's lost, if you stay lost? Someone
      ignorantly loves you—will that serve?
Shrug that off, and presto!—                             20

the needle drowns in the haydust.
    Think of the whole haystack—
a composition so fortuitous
    it only looks monumental.
There's always a straw twitching somewhere.       25

Wait out the long chance, and
    your needle too could get nudged up
to the apex of that bristling calm.
    Rusted, possibly. You might not want
to swear it was the Object, after all.       30

Time wears us old utopians.
    I now no longer think
"truth" is the most beautiful of words.
    Today, when I see "truthful"
written somewhere, it flares       35

like a white orchid in wet woods,
    rare and grief-delighting, up from the page.
Sometimes, unwittingly even,
    we have been truthful.
In a random universe, what more       40

exact and starry consolation?
    Don't think I think
facts serve better than ignorant love.
    Both serve, and still
our need mocks our gear.       45

1960

# Necessities of Life

Piece by piece I seem
to re-enter the world: I first began

a small, fixed dot, still see
that old myself, a dark-blue thumbtack

pushed into the scene,       5
a hard little head protruding

from the pointillist's[1] buzz and bloom.
After a time the dot

begins to ooze. Certain heats
melt it.
       Now I was hurriedly       10
blurring into ranges
of burnt red, burning green,

---

1. Post-impressionist painters (Seurat, for example) who fused small dots of paint with brush strokes.

whole biographies swam up and
swallowed me like Jonah.

Jonah! I was Wittgenstein,[2]                              15
Mary Wollstonecraft, the soul

of Louis Jouvet, dead
in a blown-up photograph.

Till, wolfed almost to shreds,
I learned to make myself                                  20

unappetizing. Scaly as a dry bulb
thrown into a cellar

I used myself, let nothing use me.
Like being on a private dole,

sometimes more like kneading bricks in Egypt.[3]         25
What life was there, was mine,

now and again to lay
one hand on a warm brick

and touch the sun's ghost
with economical joy,                                      30

now and again to name
over the bare necessities.

So much for those days. Soon
practice may make me middling-perfect, I'll

dare inhabit the world                                    35
trenchant in motion as an eel, solid

as a cabbage-head. I have invitations:
a curl of mist steams upward

from a field, visible as my breath,
houses along a road stand waiting                         40

like old women knitting, breathless
to tell their tales.

1962

2. Ludwig Wittgenstein (1889–1951), Austrian-born philosopher. His early thought heavily influenced logical positivism, and his later work expressed such strong skepticism about the reliability of language that he ultimately resigned his chair of philosophy lest his ideas be misunderstood or misinterpreted. Mary Wollstonecraft, an early feminist, wrote *Vindication of the Rights of Women* (1792). Louis Jouvet (1887–1951), innovative French actor and producer.

3. According to *Exodus* 5, one of the most oppressive tasks imposed on the Israelites during their Egyptian bondage was the making of bricks.

# Orion

Far back when I went zig-zagging
through tamarack pastures
you were my genius, you
my cast-iron Viking, my helmed
lion-heart king in prison.                                              5
Years later now you're young

my fierce half-brother, staring
down from that simplified west
your breast open, your belt dragged down
by an oldfashioned thing, a sword                                      10
the last bravado you won't give over
though it weighs you down as you stride

and the stars in it are dim
and maybe have stopped burning.
But you burn, and I know it;                                           15
as I throw back my head to take you in
an old transfusion happens again:
divine astronomy is nothing to it.

Indoors I bruise and blunder,
break faith, leave ill enough                                          20
alone, a dead child born in the dark.
Night cracks up over the chimney,
pieces of time, frozen geodes
come showering down in the grate.

A man reaches behind my eyes                                           25
and finds them empty
a woman's head turns away
from my head in the mirror
children are dying my death
and eating crumbs of my life.                                          30

Pity is not your forte.
Calmly you ache up there
pinned aloft in your crow's nest,
my speechless pirate!
You take it all for granted                                            35
and when I look you back

it's with a starlike eye
shooting its cold and egotistical spear
where it can do least damage.
Breathe deep! No hurt, no pardon                                       40
out here in the cold with you
you with your back to the wall.

1965

[*In* When We Dead Awaken, *Rich described* Orion *as* "a poem of reconstruction with a part of myself I had felt I was losing—the active
principle, the energetic imagination, the 'half-brother' whom I pro-
jected, as I had for many years, into the constellation Orion. It's no accident that the words 'cold and egotistical' appear in this poem, and are
applied to myself. The choice still seemed to be between 'love'—
womanly, maternal love, altruistic love—a love defined and ruled by
the weight of an entire culture—and egotism—a force directed by men
into creation, achievement, ambition, often at the expense of others,
but justifiably so. For weren't they men, and wasn't that their destiny
as womanly love was ours? I know now that the alternatives are false
ones—that the word 'love' is itself in need of re-vision."]

# Planetarium

(*Thinking of Caroline Herschel, 1750–1848,
astronomer, sister of William; and others*)

A woman in the shape of a monster
a monster in the shape of a woman
the skies are full of them

a woman          "in the snow
among the Clocks and instruments          5
or measuring the ground with poles"

in her 98 years to discover
8 comets

she whom the moon ruled
like us          10
levitating into the night sky
riding the polished lenses

Galaxies of women, there
doing penance for impetuousness
ribs chilled          15
in those spaces          of the mind

An eye,
          "virile, precise and absolutely certain"
from the mad webs of Uranisborg
                    encountering the NOVA

every impulse of light exploding          20
from the core
as life flies out of us

          Tycho[1] whispering at last
          "Let me not seem to have lived in vain"

1. Tycho Brahe (1546–1601), Danish astronomer whose cosmology tried to fuse the
Ptolemaic and Copernican systems. He discovered and described (*De Nova Stella*, 1573)
a new star in what had previously been considered a fixed star-system. Uraniborg (line
19) was Tycho's famous and elaborate palace-laboratory-observatory.

What we see, we see                                                    25
and seeing is changing

the light that shrivels a mountain
and leaves a man alive

Heartbeat of the pulsar
heart sweating through my body                                         30

The radio impulse
pouring in from Taurus
       I am bombarded yet      I stand

I have been standing all my life in the
direct path of a battery of signals                                    35
the most accurately transmitted most
untranslatable language in the universe
I am a galactic cloud so deep      so invo-
luted that a light wave could take 15
years to travel through me      And has                      40
taken      I am an instrument in the shape
of a woman trying to translate pulsations
into images      for the relief of the body
and the reconstruction of the mind.
1968

[*Rich described this poem, in* When We Dead Awaken, *as a* "companion poem to 'Orion,' " *above:* "at last the woman in the poem and
the woman writing the poem become the same person. . . . It was written after a visit to a real planetarium, where I read an account of the
work of Caroline Herschel, the astronomer, who worked with her
brother William, but whose name remained obscure, as his did not."]

# I Dream I'm the Death of Orpheus[1]

I am walking rapidly through striations of light and dark thrown under
      an arcade.
I am a woman in the prime of life, with certain powers
and those powers severely limited
by authorities whose faces I rarely see.
I am a woman in the prime of life                                       5
driving her dead poet in a black Rolls-Royce
through a landscape of twilight and thorns.
A woman with a certain mission
which if obeyed to the letter will leave her intact.
A woman with the nerves of a panther                                   10

1. A legendary Greek poet whose music could charm even inanimate objects and who
once briefly secured—by the power of his music—the release of his wife, Eurydice, from
Hades. But when she returned to Hades, he was overcome with grief, and his prolonged
wailing enraged Bacchanalian orgiasts, who tore him to pieces. Later the fragments of
his body, except for the head, were collected by the Muses and buried at the foot of
Mt. Olympus. The poem derives from Cocteau's version of the myth in his film *Orphée;*
in this version a modern poet goes to the underworld (which looks like a bombed-out
city) and confronts Death, a handsome middle-aged lady whose car is escorted by two
men on motorcycles (see line 11). Rich points out that the poem assumes the perspective of Death who, in the film, comes and goes through a mirror.

a woman with contacts among Hell's Angels
a woman feeling the fullness of her powers
at the precise moment when she must not use them
a woman sworn to lucidity
who sees through the mayhem, the smoky fires                    15
of these underground streets
her dead poet learning to walk backward against the wind
on the wrong side of the mirror
1968

# Leaflets

1
The big star, and that other
lonely on black glass
overgrown with frozen
lesions, endless night
the Coal Sack gaping                                            5
black veins of ice on the pane
spelling a word:
            Insomnia
not manic but ordinary
to start out of sleep
turning off and on                                              10
this seasick neon
vision, this
division

the head clears of sweet smoke
and poison gas                                                  15

life without caution
the only worth living
love for a man
love for a woman
love for the facts                                              20
protectless

that self-defense be not
the arm's first motion

memory not only
cards of identity                                               25

*that I can live half a year*
*as I have never lived up to this time—*[1]

Chekhov coughing up blood almost daily
the steamer edging in toward the penal colony

---

1. Quoted from a letter by Anton Chekhov to I. L. Scheglov, March 22, 1890, explaining his forthcoming visit to Saghalien, an island penal colony. Chekhov (1860–1904), the Russian playwright and short story writer, had contracted tuberculosis at age 23 (see line 28).

chained men dozing on deck 30
five forest fires lighting the island

lifelong that glare, waiting.

        2
Your face
      stretched like a mask
             begins to tear
as you speak of Che Guevara[2]
Bolivia, Nanterre 35
I'm too young to be your mother
you're too young to be my brother

your tears are not political
they are real water, burning
as the tears of Telemachus 40
burned

Over Spanish Harlem the moon
swells up, a fire balloon
fire gnawing the edge
of this crushed-up newspaper 45

                 now
the bodies come whirling
coal-black, ash-white
out of torn windows
and the death columns blacken
          whispering 50
*Who'd choose this life?*

We're fighting for a slash of recognition,
a piercing to the pierced heart.
*Tell me what you are going through*—[3]

but the attention flickers 55
        and will flicker
a matchflame in poison air
a thread, a hair of light
        sum of all answer
to the *Know that I exist!* of all existing things. 60

        3
If, says the Dahomeyan devil,[4]
someone has courage to enter the fire
the young man will be restored to life.

---

2. Cuban revolutionary theorist and an early leader in the Castro regime. Guevara was killed in the abortive Bolivian revolution in 1967. Nanterre: site of the French student uprising.

3. "Simone Weil: 'The love of a fellow-creature in all its fullness consists simply in the ability to say to him: "What are you going through" '—*Waiting For God*." (Rich's note)

4. Legba the trickster.

If, the girl whispers,
I do not go into the fire                                            65
I will not be able to live with my soul.

(Her face calm and dark as amber
under the dyed butterfly turban
her back scarified in ostrich-skin patterns.)


                          4
Crusaders' wind glinting                                            70
off linked scales of sea
ripping the ghostflags
galloping at the fortress
Acre, bloodcaked, lionhearted
raw vomit curdling in the sun                                       75
gray walkers walking
straying with a curbed intentness
in and out the inclosures
the gallows, the photographs
of dead Jewish terrorists, aged 15                                  80
their fading faces wide-eyed
and out in the crusading sunlight
gray strayers still straying
dusty paths
the mad who live in the dried-up moat                               85
of the War Museum

what are we coming to
what wants these things of us
who wants them


                          5
The strain of being born                                            90
        over and over has torn your smile into pieces
Often I have seen it broken
        and then re-membered
and wondered how a beauty
        so anarch, so ungelded                                      95
will be cared for in this world.
        I want to hand you this
leaflet streaming with rain or tears
        but the words coming clear
something you might find crushed into your hand                     100
        after passing a barricade
and stuff in your raincoat pocket.
        I want this to reach you
who told me once that poetry is nothing sacred
        —no more sacred that is                                     105
than other things in your life—
        to answer yes, if life is uncorrupted
no better poetry is wanted.

        I want this to be yours
in the sense that if you find and read it                           110
        it will be there in you already

and the leaflet then merely something
    to leave behind, a little leaf
in the drawer of a sublet room.
    What else does it come down to                                  115
but handing on scraps of paper
    little figurines or phials
no stronger than the dry clay they are baked in
    yet more than dry clay or paper
because the imagination crouches in them.                              120
    If we needed fire to remind us
that all true images
    were scooped out of the mud
where our bodies curse and flounder
    then perhaps that fire is coming                               125
to sponge away the scribes and time-servers
    and much that you would have loved will be lost as well
before you could handle it and know it
    just as we almost miss each other
in the ill cloud of mistrust, who might have touched          130
    hands quickly, shared food or given blood
for each other. I am thinking how we can use what we have
    to invent what we need.
Winter–Spring 1968

## *from* Ghazals: Homage to Ghalib

7/12/68
*for Sheila Rotner*

The clouds are electric in this university.
The lovers astride the tractor burn fissures through the hay.

When I look at that wall I shall think of you
and of what you did not paint there.

Only the truth makes the pain of lifting a hand worthwhile:          5
the prism staggering under the blows of the raga.

The vanishing-point is the point where he appears.
Two parallel tracks converge, yet there has been no wreck.

To mutilate privacy with a single foolish syllable
is to throw away the search for the one necessary word.          10

When you read these lines, think of me
and of what I have not written here.

7/13/68

The ones who camped on the slopes, below the bare summit,
saw differently from us, who breathed thin air and kept walking.

Sleeping back-to-back, man and woman, we were more conscious          15
than either of us awake and alone in the world.

These words are vapor-trails of a plane that has vanished;
by the time I write them out, they are whispering something else.

Do we still have to feel jealous of our creations?
Once they might have outlived us; in this world, we'll die together.    20

Don't look for me in the room I have left;
the photograph shows just a white rocking-chair, still rocking.

7/14/68: i

In Central Park we talked of our own cowardice.
How many times a day, in this city, are those words spoken?

The tears of the universe aren't all stars, Danton;    25
some are satellites of brushed aluminum and stainless steel.

He, who was temporary, has joined eternity;
he has deserted us, gone over to the other side.

In the Theater of the Dust no actor becomes famous.
In the last scene they all are blown away like dust.    30

"It may be if I had known them I would have loved them."
You were American, Whitman, and those words are yours.

7/14/68: ii

Did you think I was talking about my life?
I was trying to drive a tradition up against the wall.

The field they burned over is greener than all the rest.    35
You have to watch it, he said, the sparks can travel the roots.

Shot back into this earth's atmosphere
our children's children may photograph these stones.

In the red wash of the darkroom, I see myself clearly;
when the print is developed and handed about, the face is nothing to me.    40

For us the work undoes itself over and over:
the grass grows back, the dust collects, the scar breaks open.

                    ❁   ❁   ❁

7/23/68

When your sperm enters me, it is altered;
when my thought absorbs yours, a world begins.

If the mind of the teacher is not in love with the mind of the student,    75
he is simply practicing rape, and deserves at best our pity.

To live outside the law! Or, barely within it,
a twig on boiling waters, enclosed inside a bubble.

Our words are jammed in an electronic jungle;
sometimes, though, they rise and wheel croaking above the treetops.     80

An open window; thick summer night; electric fences trilling.
What are you doing here at the edge of the death-camps, Vivaldi?

### 7/24/68: i

The sapling springs, the milkweed blooms: obsolete Nature.
In the woods I have a vision of asphalt, blindly lingering.

I hardly know the names of the weeds I love.     85
I have forgotten the names of so many flowers.

I can't live at the hems of that tradition—
will I last to try the beginning of the next?

Killing is different now: no fingers round the throat.
No one feels the wetness of the blood on his hands.     90

When we fuck, there too are we remoter
than the fucking bodies of lovers used to be?

How many men have touched me with their eyes
more hotly than they later touched me with their lips.

### 7/24/68: ii

The friend I can trust is the one who will let me have my death.     95
The rest are actors who want me to stay and further the plot.

At the drive-in movie, above the PanaVision,
beyond the projector beams, you project yourself, great Star.

The eye that used to watch us is dead, but open.
Sometimes I still have a sense of being followed.     100

How long will we be waiting for the police?
How long must I wonder which of my friends would hide me?

Driving at night I feel the Milky Way
streaming above me like the graph of a cry.

### 7/26/68: i

Last night you wrote on the wall: Revolution is poetry.     105
Today you needn't write; the wall has tumbled down.

We were taught to respect the appearance behind the reality.
Our senses were out on parole, under surveillance.

A pair of eyes imprisoned for years inside my skull
is burning its way outward, the headaches are terrible.     110

I'm walking through a rubble of broken sculpture, stumbling
here on the spine of a friend, there on the hand of a brother.

All those joinings! and yet we fought so hard to be unique.
Neither alone, nor in anyone's arms, will we end up sleeping.

❂ ❂ ❂

8/4/68
*for Aijaz Ahmad*

If these are letters, they will have to be misread.
If scribblings on a wall, they must tangle with all the others.    150

Fuck reds      Black Power      Angel loves Rosita
—and a transistor radio answers in Spanish: *Night must fall.*

Prisoners, soldiers, crouching as always, writing,
explaining the unforgivable to a wife, a mother, a lover.

Those faces are blurred and some have turned away    155
to which I used to address myself so hotly.

How is it, Ghalib, that your grief, resurrected in pieces,
has found its way to this room from your dark house in Delhi?

When they read this poem of mine, they are translators.
Every existence speaks a language of its own.    160

8/8/68: i

From here on, all of us will be living
like Galileo turning his first tube at the stars.

Obey the little laws and break the great ones
is the preamble to their constitution.

Even to hope is to leap into the unknown,    165
under the mocking eyes of the way things are.

There's a war on earth, and in the skull, and in the glassy spaces,
between the existing and the non-existing.

I need to live each day through, have them and know them all,
though I can see from here where I'll be standing at the end.    170

8/8/68: ii
*for A.H.C.*

A piece of thread ripped-out from a fierce design,
some weaving figured as magic against oppression.

I'm speaking to you as a woman to a man:
when your blood flows I want to hold you in my arms.

How did we get caught up fighting this forest fire,                    175
we, who were only looking for a still place in the woods?

How frail we are, and yet, dispersed, always returning,
the barnacles they keep scraping from the warship's hull.

The hairs on your breast curl so lightly as you lie there,
while the strong heart goes on pounding in its sleep.                  180

[*In her volume* Leaflets, *published in* 1969, *Rich wrote the following introduction to the* ghazals: "This poem began to be written after I read Aijaz Ahmad's literal English versions of the work of the Urdu poet Mirza Ghalib, 1797–1869. While the structure and metrics used by Ghalib are much stricter than mine, I have adhered to his use of a minimum five couplets to a *ghazal*, each couplet being autonomous and independent of the others. The continuity and unity flow from the associations and images playing back and forth among the couplets in any single *ghazal*. My *ghazals* are personal and public, American and twentieth-century; but they owe much to the presence of Ghalib in my mind: a poet self-educated and profoundly learned, who owned no property and borrowed his books, writing in an age of political and cultural break-up. I have left the *ghazals* dated as I wrote them."]

[*In a letter to Aijaz Ahmad, Rich described her reactions to translating Ghalib:* "The marvelous thing about these *ghazals* is precisely (for me) their capacity for both concentration and a gathering, cumulative effect. . . . I needed a way of dealing with very complex and scattered material which was demanding a different kind of unity from that imposed on it by the isolated, single poem: in which certain experiences needed to find both their intensest rendering and to join with other experiences not logically or chronologically connected in any obvious way. I've been trying to make the couplets as autonomous as possible and to allow the unity of the *ghazal* to emerge from underneath, as it were, through images, through associations, private and otherwise. . . . For me, the couplets work only when I can keep them from being too epigrammatic; what I'm trying for, not always successfully, is a clear image or articulation behind which there are shadows, reverberations, reflections of reflections. In other words, something that will *not* remind the Western reader of *haiku* or any other brief, compact form, such as Pope's couplet in English, or *The Greek Anthology.*"]

# A Valediction Forbidding Mourning[1]

My swirling wants. Your frozen lips.
The grammar turned and attacked me.
Themes, written under duress.
Emptiness of the notations.

They gave me a drug that slowed the healing of wounds.                 5

1. The title of a poem by John Donne.

I want you to see this before I leave:
the experience of repetition as death
the failure of criticism to locate the pain
the poster in the bus that said:
*my bleeding is under control.*                                      10

A red plant in a cemetery of plastic wreaths.

A last attempt: the language is a dialect called metaphor.
These images go unglossed: hair, glacier, flashlight.
When I think of a landscape I am thinking of a time.
When I talk of taking a trip I mean forever.                         15
I could say: those mountains have a meaning
but further than that I could not say.

To do something very common, in my own way.
1970


# Trying to Talk with a Man

Perhaps my life is nothing but an image of this kind; perhaps I am doomed to retrace my
steps under the illusion that I am exploring, doomed to try and learn what I should
simply recognize, learning a mere fraction of what I have forgotten.
—ANDRE BRETON, *Nadja*[1]


Out in this desert we are testing bombs.

That's why we came here.

Sometimes I feel an underground river
forcing its way between deformed cliffs
an acute angle of understanding                                      5
moving itself like a locus of the sun
into this condemned scenery.

What we've had to give up to get here!
Whole lp collections, the films we starred in
playing in the neighborhoods, bakery windows                         10
full of dry, chocolate-filled Jewish cookies,
the language of love-letters, of suicide notes,
afternoons on the riverbank
pretending to be children

Coming out                                                           15
to this desert we meant to change the face of
driving among dull-green succulents
walking at noon in the ghost-town
surrounded by a silence

1. Bretón (1896–1968), a French poet and critic, was one of the founders of both
Dadaism and Surrealism. His novel *Nadja* was published in 1928.

that sounds like the silence of the place    20
except that it came with us
and is familiar
and everything we were saying until now
was an effort to blot it out
Coming out here we are up against it    25

Out here I feel more helpless
with you than without you.
You mention the danger
and list the equipment
we talk of people caring for each other
in emergencies—laceration, thirst—
but you look at me like an emergency

Your dry heat feels like power
your eyes are stars of a different magnitude
they reflect lights that spell out EXIT
when you get up and pace the floor

talking of the danger
as if it were not ourselves
as if we were testing anything else.

p. 1971

## The Mirror in Which Two Are Seen as One

"The situation can be changed only by the patient changing herself. Nothing can be
changed in the mother, for she is dead. And the friend cannot be nagged into changing.
If she wants to change, that is her own affair."                    —C. G. Jung

1

She is the one you call sister.
Her simplest act has glamor,
as when she scales a fish the knife
flashes in her long fingers
no motion wasted or when    5
rapidly talking of love
she steel-wool-burnishes
the battered kettle

Love-apples cramp you sideways
with sudden emptiness    10
the cereals glutting you, the grains
ripe clusters picked by hand
Love: the refrigerator
with open door
the ripe steaks bleeding    15
their hearts out in plastic film
the whipped butter, the apricots
the sour leftovers

A crate is waiting in the orchard
for you to fill it    20

Adrienne Rich

your hands are raw with scraping
the sharp bark, the thorns
of this succulent tree
Pick, pick, pick
this harvest is a failure                                          25
the juice runs down your cheekbones
like sweat or tears


                              2
She is the one you call sister
you blaze like lightning about the room
flicker around her like fire                                       30
dazzle yourself in her wide eyes
listing her unfelt needs
thrusting the tenets of your life
into her hands

She moves through a world of India print                           35
her body dappled
with softness, the paisley swells at her hip
walking the street in her cotton shift
buying fresh figs because you love them
photographing the ghetto because you took her there               40

Why are you crying dry up your tears
we are sisters
words fail you in the stare of her hunger
you hand her another book
scored by your pencil                                              45
you hand her a record
of two flutes in India reciting


                              3
Late summer night the insects
fry in the yellowed lightglobe
your skin burns gold in its light                                  50
In this mirror, who are you? Dreams of the nunnery
with its discipline, the nursery
with its nurse, the hospital
where all the powerful ones are masked
the graveyard where you sit on the graves                          55
of women who died in childbirth
and women who died at birth

Dreams of your sister's birth
your mother dying in childbirth over and over
not knowing how to stop                                            60
bearing you over and over
your mother dead and you unborn
your two hands grasping your head
drawing it down against the blade of life
your nerves the nerves of a midwife                                65
learning her trade

## Diving into the Wreck

First having read the book of myths,
and loaded the camera,
and checked the edge of the knife-blade,
I put on
the body-armor of black rubber                                    5
the absurd flippers
the grave and awkward mask.
I am having to do this
not like Cousteau with his
assiduous team                                                   10
aboard the sun-flooded schooner
but here alone.

There is a ladder.
The ladder is always there
hanging innocently                                               15
close to the side of the schooner.
We know what it is for,
we who have used it.
Otherwise
it is piece of maritime floss                                    20
some sundry equipment.

I go down.
Rung after rung and still
the oxygen immerses me
the blue light                                                   25
the clear atoms
of our upper air.
I go down.
My flippers cripple me,
I crawl like an insect down the ladder                           30
and there is no-one
to tell me when the ocean
will begin.

First the air is blue and then
it is bluer and then green and then                              35
black I am blacking out and yet
my mask is powerful
it pumps my blood with power.
The sea is another story
the sea is not a question of power                               40
I have to learn alone
to turn my body without force
in the deep element.

And now: it is easy to forget
what I came for                                                  45
among so many who have always
lived here
swaying their crenellated fans

between the reefs
and besides                                              50
you breathe differently down here.

I came to explore the wreck.
The words are purposes.
The words are maps.
I came to see the damage that was done              55
and the treasures that prevail.
I stroke the beam of my lamp
slowly along the flank
of something more permanent
than fish or weed                                        60

the thing I came for:
the wreck and not the story of the wreck
the thing itself and not the myth
the drowned face always staring
towards the sun                                          65
the evidence of damage
worn by salt and sway into this threadbare beauty
the ribs of the disaster curving their assertion
among the tentative haunters.

This is the place.                                       70
And I am here, the mermaid whose dark hair
streams black, the merman in his armored body.
We circle silently
about the wreck
we dive into the hold.                                   75
I am she:      I am he

whose drowned face sleeps with open eyes
as figurehead
whose breasts still bear the stress
whose silver, copper, golden cargo lies              80
obscurely inside barrels
half-wedged and left to rot
we are the half-destroyed instruments
that once held to a course
the water-eaten log                                      85
the fouled compass

We are, I am, you are
by cowardice or courage
the one who find our way
back to this scene                                       90
carrying a knife, a camera,
a book of myths
in which
our names do not appear.

p. 1972

# *from* Talking with Adrienne Rich[1]

* * * I think of myself as using poetry as a chief means of self-exploration—one of several means, of which maybe another would be dreams, really thinking about, paying attention to dreams, but the poem, like the dream, does this through images and it is in the images of my poems that I feel I am finding out more about my own experience, my sense of things. But I don't think of myself as having a position or a self-description which I'm then going to present in the poem.

* * *

When I started writing poetry I was tremendously conscious of, and very much in need of, a formal structure that could be obtained from outside, into which I could pour whatever I had, whatever I thought I had to express. But I think that was a part of a whole thing that I see, now as a teacher, very much with young writers, of using language more as a kind of façade than as either self-revelation or as a probe into one's own consciousness. I think I would attribute a lot of the change in my poetry simply to the fact of growing older, undergoing certain kinds of experiences, realizing that formal metrics were not going to suffice me in dealing with those experiences, realizing that experience itself is much more fragmentary, much more sort of battering, much ruder than these structures would allow, and it had to find its own form.

* * *

I have a very strong sense about the existence of poetry in daily life and poetry being part of the world as it is, and that the attempt to reduce poetry to what is indited on a page just limits you terribly. . . . The poem is the poetry of things lodged in the innate shape of the experience. My saying "The moment of change is the only poem" is the kind of extreme statement you feel the need to make at certain times if only to force someone to say, "But I always thought a poem is something written on a piece of paper," you know, and to say: "But look, how did those words get on that piece of paper." There had to be a mind; there had to be an experience; the mind had to go through certain shocks, certain stresses, certain strains, and if you're going to carry the poem back to its real beginnings it's that moment of change. I feel that we are always writing.

* * *

When I was in my twenties * * * I was going through a very sort of female thing—of trying to distinguish between the ego that is capable of writing poems, and then this other kind of being that you're asked to be if you're a woman, who is, in a sense, denying that ego. I had great feelings of split about that for many years actually, and there are a lot of poems I couldn't write even, because I didn't want to confess to having that much aggression, that much ego, that much sense of myself. I had always thought of my first book as being a book of very well-tooled poems of a sort of very bright student, which I was at that time, but poems in which the unconscious things never got to the surface. But there's a poem in that book about a woman who sews a

1. A transcript of a conversation recorded March 9, 1971, and printed in *The Ohio Review*, Fall, 1971.

tapestry and the tapestry has figures of tigers on it. But the woman is represented as being completely—her hand is burdened by the weight of the wedding band, and she's meek, and she's fearful, and the only way in which she can express any other side of her nature is in embroidering these tigers. Well, I thought of that as almost a formal exercise, but when I go back and look at that poem I really think it's saying something about what I was going through. And now that's lessened a great deal for all sorts of reasons—that split.

## *from* An Interview with Adrienne Rich[1]

I would have said ten or fifteen years ago that I would not even want to identify myself as a woman poet. That term *has* been used pejoratively; I just don't think it can be at this point. You know, for a woman the act of creation is prototypically to produce children, while the act of creating with language—I'm not saying that women writers haven't been accepted; certainly, more have been accepted than women lawyers or doctors. Still, a woman writer feels, she is going against the grain—or there has been this sense until very recently (if there isn't still). Okay, it's all right to be a young thing and write verse. But a friend of mine was telling me about meeting a noted poet at a cocktail party. She'd sent him a manuscript for a contest he was judging. She went up to him and asked him about it, and he looked at her and said, "Young girls *are* poems; they shouldn't write them." This attitude toward women poets manifests itself so strongly that you are made to feel you are becoming the thing you are not.

✿ ✿ ✿

If a man is writing, he's gone through all the nonsense and said "Okay, I am a poet and I'm still a man. They don't cancel each other out or, if they do, then I'll opt to be a poet." He's not writing for a hostile sex, a breed of critics who by virtue of their sex are going to look at his language and pass judgment on it. That does happen to a woman. I don't know why the woman poet has been slower than the woman novelist in taking risks though I'm very grateful that this is no longer so. I feel that I dare to think further than I would have dared to think ten years ago—and *that* certainly is going to affect my writing. And I now dare to entertain thoughts and speculations that then would have seemed unthinkable.

✿ ✿ ✿

Many of the male writers whom I very much admire—Galway Kinnell, James Wright, W. S. Merwin—are writing poetry of such great desolation. They come from different backgrounds, write in different ways, and yet all seem to write out of a sense of doom, as if we were fated to carry on these terribly flawed relationships. I think it's expressive of a feeling that "we, the masters, have created a world that's impossible to live in and that probably may not be livable in, in a very literal sense. What we thought, what we'd been given to think is our privilege, our right, and our sexual prerogative has led to this, to our doom." I guess a lot of women—if not a lot of women poets—

1. By David Kalstone, in *The Saturday Review*, April 22, 1972.

are feeling that there has to be some other way, that human life is messed-up but that it doesn't have to be *this* desolate.

✿   ✿   ✿

Today, much poetry by women is charged with anger and uses voices of rage and anger that I don't think were ever used in poetry before. In poets like Sylvia Plath and Diane Wakoski, say, those voices are so convincing that it is impossible to describe them by using those favorite adjectives of phallic criticism—shrill and hysterical. Well, Sylvia Plath is dead. I always maintained from the first time I read her last poems that her suicide was not necessary, that she could have gone on and written poems that would have given us even more insight into the states of anger and willfulness, even of self-destructiveness, that women experience. She didn't need literally to destroy herself in order to reflect and express those things. Diane Wakoski is a young woman. She's changing a lot and will continue to change. What I admire in her, besides her energy and dynamism and quite a beautiful gift for snatching the image that she wants out of the air, is her honesty. No woman has written before about her face and said she hated it, that it had served her ill, that she wished she could throw acid in it. That's very shocking. But I think all women, even the most beautiful women, at times have felt that in a kind of self-hatred. Because the *face* is supposed to be the *woman*.

✿   ✿   ✿

A lot of poetry is becoming more oral. Certainly, it's true of women and black poets. Reading black poetry on the printed page gives no sense of the poem, if you're going to look at that poetry the way you look at poems by Richard Wilbur. Yet you can hear these poets read and realize it's the oldest kind of poetry.

✿   ✿   ✿

I think the energy of language comes somewhat from the pressure and need and unbearableness of what's being done to you. It's not the same energy you find in the blues. The blues are a grief language, a lost language, and a cry of pain, usually in a woman's voice, which is interesting. For a long time you sing the blues, and then you begin to say, "I'm tired of singing the blues. I want something else." And that's what you're hearing now. There seems to be a connection between an oppressed condition and having access to certain kinds of energy, vitality, and subjectivity. For women as well as blacks. Though I don't feel there is a necessary cause-and-effect relationship; what seems to happen is that being on top, being in a powerful position leads to a divorce between one's unruly, chaotic, revolutionary sensitivity and one's reason, sense of order and of maintaining a hold. And, therefore, you have at the bottom of the pile, so to speak, a kind of churning energy that gets lost up there among the administrators.

✿   ✿   ✿

I don't know how or whether poetry changes anything. But neither do I know how or whether bombing or even community organizing changes anything when we are pitted against a massive patriarchal system armed with supertechnology. I believe in subjectivity—that a lot of male Left leaders have turned into Omnipotent Administrators, because their "masculinity" forced them to deny their subjectivity. I believe in dreams and visions and "the madness of art." And at moments I can conceive of a women's movement that will show the way to humanizing technology and fusing dreams and skills and visions and reason to begin the healing of the human race. But I don't want women to take over the world and run it the way men have, or to take on—yet again!—the burden of carrying the subjectivity of the race. Women are a vanguard now, and I believe will increasingly become so, because we have—Western women, Third World women, all women—known and felt the pain of the human condition most consistently. But in the end it can't be women alone.

## *from* When We Dead Awaken: Writing as Re-Vision

Most, if not all, human lives are full of fantasy—passive daydreaming which need not be acted on. But to write poetry or fiction, or even to think well, is not to fantasize or to put fantasies on paper. For a poem to coalesce, for a character or an action to take shape, there has to be an imaginative transformation of reality which is in no way passive. And a certain freedom of the mind is needed—freedom to press on, to enter the currents of your thought like a glider pilot, knowing that your motion can be sustained, that the buoyancy of your attention will not be suddenly snatched away. Moreover, if the imagination is to transcend and transform experience it has to question, to challenge, to conceive of alternatives, perhaps to the very life you are living at that moment. You have to be free to play around with the notion that day might be night, love might be hate; nothing can be too sacred for the imagination to turn into its opposite or to call experimentally by another name. For writing is re-naming.

Now, to be maternally with small children all day in the old way, to be with a man in the old way of marriage, requires a holding back, a putting aside of that imaginative activity, and seems to demand instead a kind of conservatism. I want to make it clear that I am *not* saying that in order to write well, or think well, it is necessary to become unavailable to others, or to become a devouring ego. This has been the myth of the masculine artist and thinker; and, I repeat, I do not accept it. But to be a female human being trying to fulfill traditional female functions in a traditional way *is* in direct conflict with the subversive function of the imagination. The word "traditional" is important here. There must be ways, and we will be finding out more and more about them, in which the energy of creation and the energy of relation can be united. But in those earlier years I always felt the conflict as a failure of love in myself. I had thought I was choosing a full life: the life available to most men, in which sexuality, work and parenthood could coexist. But I felt, at 29, guilt toward the people closest to me, and guilty toward my own being.

I wanted, then, more than anything, the one thing of which there was never enough: time to think, time to write. The '50s and early '60s were years of rapid revelations: the sit-ins and marches in the South, the Bay of Pigs, the early antiwar movement, raised large questions—questions for which the masculine world of the academy around me seemed to have expert and fluent answers. But I needed desperately to think for myself—about pacifism and dissent and violence, about poetry and society, and about my own relationship to all these things. For about ten years I was reading in fierce snatches, scribbling in notebooks, writing poetry in fragments; I was looking desperately for clues, because if there were no clues then I thought I might be insane. I wrote in a notebook about this time:

> Paralyzed by the sense that there exists a mesh of relationships —e.g. between my anger at the children, my sensual life, pacifism, sex (I mean sex in its broadest significance, not merely sexual desire)—an interconnectedness which, if I could see it, make it valid, would give me back myself, make it possible to function lucidly and passionately. Yet I grope in and out among these dark webs.

I think I began at this point to feel that politics was not something "out there" but something "in here" and of the essence of my condition.

In the late '50s I was able to write, for the first time, directly about experiencing myself as a woman. The poem was jotted in fragments during children's naps, brief hours in a library, or at 3 A.M. after rising with a wakeful child. I despaired of doing any continuous work at this time. Yet I began to feel that my fragments and scraps had a common consciousness and a common theme, one which I would have been very unwilling to put on paper at an earlier time because I had been taught that poetry should be "universal," which meant, of course, non-female. Until then I had tried very much *not* to identify myself as a female poet.

# The Elements of Poetry

## 1. ARGUMENT, MEANING, AND THEME

Most readers would agree with Archibald MacLeish that "a poem should not mean but be," but discovering what a poem "is" often involves identifying what it contains. Poets often used to provide an **argument** for their poems, a prose summary of what "happens"; now they seldom provide such a convenience, but to begin interpretation and experience of a poem readers often find it useful to **paraphrase,** put into prose exactly what the poem says, line by line, in words that are different but as nearly equivalent as possible. Such a method will usually clarify the situation and setting of the poem and help to characterize the speaker (see §3), leading to a definition of a poem's attitude toward its subject and to more careful distinctions about its ideas. A poem's **meaning** involves more than the **statement** it makes, more than a prose summary of its idea or ideas. Recognizing the ideas and seeing how they are articulated in the poem is an important early step toward experiencing the poem in its full meaning, which includes the implications of its statement.

Some of the terms used to describe a poem's ideas are often used interchangeably, but it is useful to distinguish among them. The **subject,** or **topic,** of a poem is its general or specific area of concern, usually something categorical such as death (or the death of a particular person), war (or a specific war, or specific battle), suffering, love, rejection, or the simple life. Most poems make statements about a subject and define the degree and kind of their interest in it; a poem about war, for example, may ultimately be more concerned to say something about the nature of man or about honor or about peace than about war itself. Subjects offer a great variety of **themes:** that death is a release from pain, or a gateway to immortality, that war is senseless, or brutal, or a necessary evil, or a heroic quest for justice. A poem's theme is the statement it makes about its subject; summarizing a paraphrase in one or two sentences often yields the theme. A poem also may be said to use a **motif** (plural, motifs or motives): a recurrent device, formula, or situation which deliberately connects the poem with common patterns of previous thought. One common motif, occurring in such poems as Waller's "Go, lovely rose" (p. 399) or Marvell's *To His Coy Mistress* (p. 405), is that of **carpe diem.** The phrase literally means "seize the day," and *carpe diem* poems inevitably remind us of the shortness of life and beauty and the necessity to take advantage of the present. Such recurring situations as temptations in the garden are also motifs; one might speak of the "garden motif" or "temptation motif" in Louise Bogan's *The Crossed Apple* (p. 111) or the journey motif in Tennyson's *Ulysses* (p. 245).

The **meaning** of every poem, like the "being" of the poem, is finally unique, but a poem's subject, theme, and motif relate it to other poems with similar ideas and attitudes. An **explication**, or **exegesis**, explains how all of the elements in an individual poem or passage work; in explication, a critic analyzes the various component parts in order to interpret the poem's statement. Explication takes a step beyond paraphrase in attempting to discover a poem's meaning. The terms **message** and **moral**, once used to summarize the poem's meaning, are now usually considered outmoded and misleading because they tend to oversimplify and confuse statement with meaning. Similarly objec‿ tionable to many is the term **hidden meaning**, which implies that a poem is a puzzle or that the author is deliberately obscuring his or her point; a poem may use complicated methods to achieve its clarity and emotional impact, but a good poem does not value obscurity or even difficulty purely for its own sake. **Meaning** is the poem's combination of motifs, themes, and statements about a subject or series of subjects *and* the emotions that it artfully evokes toward them by means of poetic devices and strategies. But meaning—however well defined and articulated—is never the precise equivalent of the poem itself.

## 2. AUDIENCE

Even poems which seem personal, confessional, and private are influenced by a poet's sense of who he or she is writing for and who will ultimately read the poem. Because poems are meant to be read and experienced by someone besides the poet, they are more than simple records of an event, or idea, or state of mind. Poets fictionalize or imagine circumstances and reflections, and they usually try to communicate by evoking in the reader a particular attitude or emotion.

The means by which poems generate an effect are usually called **poetic** (or **artistic**) **devices** or **strategies**. Even when the precise effect of a poem is difficult to determine (as it often is, unless one uses a purely mechanical criterion), the efforts to obtain an effect can usually be isolated. Almost everything in a poem is in some sense (but not a bad sense) a device: the choice of one word rather than another one, the use of metaphor, of certain sounds and rhythms, of allusions, conventions, forms—all contribute to a total effect. Most poets depend upon some version of the poetic tradition (§9) and use standard poetic conventions as short cuts for projecting an attitude or gaining an impact; even highly unusual or eccentric poems use strategies that have proved effective in the past or invent new strategies which will produce a predictable response. Often poets depend upon a reader's recognition of a tradition, conventions, or standard poetic devices to produce a knowing response, but often too there is a kind of friendly deception involved, an attempt to persuade by using some means which will move readers without their consent, or even against their will. The **rhetoric** of a poem is the sum of the persuasive devices used to affect readers, with or without their consent.

Many of the most important **rhetorical devices** (or **rhetorical figures**) date from classical antiquity, and some of these are so common in ordinary life that we scarcely recognize them as devices, even in a poem. **Comparison** and **contrast** may clarify the identity and properties of a person, place, or thing, but persuasive values may also be built in, depending on what is being compared with what. **Acceptance by association** is as common as **guilt by association**; naming admired names may lull a reader into easy submission or be part of a complex web of interrelationships in which an author places his or her values among things certain to be admired, or expected to be admired among readers of a certain kind. Or vice versa. Ginsberg's *Howl* (p. 448) achieves many of its most persuasive effects by listing cultural villains his audience is likely to agree about, and then inserting in the list forces that to most of his audience might ordinarily seem neutral. An **allusion** is a reference to something outside the poem (in history, perhaps, or in another poem) which has built-in emotional associations; in *Sunday Morning* (p. 160) Stevens alludes to the Crucifixion to suggest a tradition of use of Sunday mornings, and in *The Love Song of J. Alfred Prufrock* (p. 133) Eliot alludes to Polonius (in *Hamlet*) to help establish the manner of his "hero." **Example** is simply the giving of a specific instance to back up a generalization, and many whole poems are built upon the principle, directly or indirectly; sometimes, as in Pound's *The Garden* (p. 214), the whole poem presents the example, and the generalization for which the example stands is left unstated.

Several classic figures of speech, though not restricted to poetry, are often found in poems. **Hyperbole** (or extravagant **exaggeration**) may be serious or comic or both at the same time, pushing something so far toward absurdity that its ordinary manifestation may seem normal and acceptable, as in Marvell's *To His Coy Mistress*. **Meiosis** (or **understatement**) consciously underrates something or portrays it as lesser than it is usually thought to be; its psychology is to bring the reader instinctively to the defense of the thing being undervalued. It is closely related to **irony** (§3), especially in one of its forms, **litotes,** which affirms something by denying its opposite, as in colloquial expressions such as "He's no Einstein." **Periphrasis** (or **circumlocution**) is deliberate avoidance of the obvious, writing which circles its subject and refuses to take the simplest route toward clear meaning. **Synechdoche** is using a part of something to signify the whole (as in "hired hands" for "workmen"), and **metonymy** is naming something associated with what is being talked about rather than the thing itself, as in the use of "crown" for "king." **Hyperbaton** is the rearrangement of sentence elements for special effects; Milton, in *Paradise Lost,* for example, often uses extreme instances of the figure, as in the sentence beginning in line 44 of Book I. **Prolepsis** is the **foreshadowing** of a future event as if it were already influencing the present, as in Eliot's *Journey of the Magi* (p. 231) when the wise men on their way to Bethlehem see objects suggestive of the Crucifixion.

Some writers, especially during the Renaissance and 18th century, have deliberately used these rhetorical devices and hosts of others, but even more common is use of them without deliberation, for the terms themselves try to describe and categorize standard ways in which words may affect psychological processes. Many kinds of attempts to persuade—sermons, political speeches, TV commercials, informal conversations—use some version of such devices, though often in more simple and less subtle ways than good poetry. Identifying the devices is only a way of discovering what a poem advocates, how it tries to develop emotional energy, and whether its methods are effective. Being able to identify the devices is useful but only as a means to a more important end.

Poems which openly and directly advocate a particular ideology, argue for a specific cause, or try to teach us something are called **didactic** poems. Critics sometimes distinguish between didactic poems and **mimetic** (or **imaginative**) poems, which are more concerned to present than to persuade. But the distinction is one of degree, for most poems mean at the very least to make their attitudes, their vision, their presentation of reality plausible and attractive. Poems which openly and explicitly have designs upon their readers have been out of fashion since the 18th century, and some modern critics use the term "didactic" pejoratively to suggest that an author is too blatant, unsubtle, and moralistic in approach. The term **propaganda** is almost always used pejoratively, to suggest that a writer's main aim is to arouse readers toward immediate action in a specific situation; poems so specifically and narrowly directed are usually assumed to be ephemeral, though good "occasional poems" and "satires" (see §6 and §10) often transcend their occasions.

### 3. AUTHOR, SPEAKER, AND TONE

It has become traditional to distinguish between the person who wrote the poem and the person who speaks in a poem, for an author often deliberately chooses to speak through a **character** quite different from his real self. Poets thus sometimes create a fictional person as a **speaker,** just as playwrights create a character who is then obliged to say things in a characteristic way, that is, a way appropriate to the character as created. In Robert Browning's *Soliloquy of the Spanish Cloister* (p. 148), for example, the speaker is a disagreeable, vindictive monk pursuing a vendetta against a fellow monk, and he is not much like Browning, who was not a monk and not necessarily disagreeable and vindictive; Browning allows the character to reveal himself through his own words and in doing so to clarify what Browning thinks of such attitudes. In many poems the speaker is very like the author himself, or very like what the author wishes to think he or she is like. Between the speaker who is a fully distinct character and the author speaking honestly and directly are many degrees of detachment. Many critics and teachers prefer that the person speaking the words of a poem always be called a speaker, but others find it unnecessary to make the distinction when the author is clearly speaking in his own person; the difficulty usually lies in deciding what "clearly" means.

The term **persona** is often used synonymously with speaker, especially in satire, where the author usually speaks in a voice very like his own except that he often pretends to be more innocent, more earnest, and more pure than he knows himself to be. Such a **pose** (or **posture,** or **mask**) is not really dishonest any more than the creation of a character in a play or story is dishonest; it is part of the author's strategy of making a point effectively and persuasively. It is often useful to compare several poems by the same author; such a procedure helps identify the speaker in individual poems and points up similarities in attitude and strategy that run through an author's work.

Defining the attitude which a poem takes toward a certain subject or theme or situation is often a matter of being clear about the poem's speaker, situation, and setting. In poems that tell a story or present a clearly defined dramatic situation, the circumstances under which someone speaks affect the way we receive and interpret what is being said. **Setting** (either as place or time) may also affect interpretation, just as in a story or play—as, for example, in Bogan's *Crossed Apple* or Stevens' *Sunday Morning.*

When the author's attitude is different from that of the speaker (as in Browning's *Soliloquy*) the poem is said to be ironic, though the term **irony** also means several other things. Irony is not only saying one thing and meaning its opposite; it is also any manner of being oblique rather than straightforward and often involves exaggeration or understatement. A whole poem may be said to be ironic (or to have **structural irony**) when its total effect is to reverse the attitude presented by the speaker, but poems which are not wholly ironic may use ironic words and phrases (**verbal irony**) to generate a more complex statement or attitude. When irony is stark, simple, snide, exactly inverted—that is, when what is said is exactly the opposite of what is meant—it is called **sarcasm.** The term "irony," qualified in various ways, may indicate almost any kind of discrepancy between what is apparent in a literary work and what someone else knows to be so. **Dramatic irony** (which may be used in a poem as well as in a play) occurs when the speaker is unaware of something about himself or his situation but the reader is not, as in Henry Reed's *Lessons of the War* (p. 10) or Jonson's *Come, My Celia* (p. 403). In **socratic irony,** the speaker poses as an innocent and ignorant person who then provokes a revelation through his apparently naive assumptions or questions, as in Chaucer's *Canterbury Tales* and many satires.

The terms **tone** and **voice** represent attempts to be still more precise about the author's attitude toward what his or her poem literally says. Descriptions of tone try to characterize the way the words of the poem are (or should be) spoken when one sensitively reads the poem aloud. The concept of tone recognizes that meaning is often adjusted in human speech by the way one says words, for by subtle modulation one can change the meaning of words completely, and by stress, rhythm, and volume, one regulates emphases which the syntax may not by itself make clear. Tone literally tries to describe the vocal sounds which a poem seems to demand, and one may speak of the tone of an individual word or phrase, of a longer passage, or of a whole poem. Words such as "ironic," "comic," "playful," "sincere," and "straight-

forward" may sometimes accurately describe tone, as may more particular adjectives such as "boisterous," "boastful," "taunting," "apologetic,"
"plaintive," or "bemused." Sometimes, when the speaker's attitude
toward what he says is different from that of the author, the term
"voice" is used to describe the prevailing sense of the author's presence.
In Browning's *Soliloquy of the Spanish Cloister*, for example, the
speaker's tone may be described as "gruff," "resentful," "vindictive,"
"sadistic," but the voice disapproves of these tones. The interrelation-
ship between voice and tone is sometimes called **mood**, that total
**atmosphere** which pervades the work and gives the reader a sense of
what to expect. In some poems, of course, the tone, voice, and mood
may be identical, but the reader is always well advised to examine the
situation and speaker carefully as a means of testing the emotional
charge of words, phrases, and larger units of expression.

4. FIGURATIVE LANGUAGE

Most nouns, verbs, adjectives, and adverbs not only **denote** a thing,
action, or attribute, but also **connote** feelings and associations suggested by it. A horse is literally a four-legged, whinnying, rideable,
workable animal, but the word "horse" connotes to most people
strength, vitality, vigor. To speak of a horse that is not strong and
vigorous, one either qualifies the term in some way ("drawhorse" or
"bedraggled horse" or "sorry horse") or uses a synonym such as
"nag"—which literally denotes the same animal but which implies
(connotes) different qualities. To be even more emphatic about its
vigor and strength and to imply wildness as well, one might call it a
steed or stallion. To the extent that the **connotations** of a word are
generally agreed on, a writer may use the word to indicate a whole
range of attitudes. In *Still to Be Neat* (p. 172) Ben Jonson uses words
with heavily moral connotations ("sound," "adulteries") to question
the fears behind a woman's fastidiousness and to help create a preference for women who are more casually dressed and made up, less
powdered and more natural; in *Delight in Disorder* (p. 172) Robert
Herrick expresses the same preference, but the praising words he uses
are joyous and carefree, suggesting that the preference is based on
sensual, not moral grounds—even implying that the carefree, informally clad woman is apt not to be chaste.

Not all words have clear, universally accepted connotations built
into them, and writers often use the more elaborate devices of metaphor and symbolism to build a specific set of associations and values
into the words and combinations of words that they use. By building
visual patterns or self-contained systems out of individual words, a
poet may control more accurately and more complexly the emotional
value and suggestion of individual words and develop a more satis-
fying total effect. How this is done in an individual poem depends
upon the particular requirements of the subject and theme as well as
upon the talents, style, and artistic choices of an individual poet; one
can, however, distinguish among different kinds of methods, and it is
useful to have a set of distinguishing terms firmly in mind. Many of

the most popular terms are used differently by different critics; uniformity of terminology—even if considered ideal—is not really possible, but all readers of poetry should take care that they themselves use whatever terms they use consistently, carefully, and unambiguously.

**Imagery** is used by different critics to mean three related but distinct things: (1) the mental pictures suggested by the verbal descriptions in a poem; (2) the visual descriptions in the poem itself; or (3) the figurative language (including metaphors, similes, and analogies) in the poem. In all three uses, imagery is technically a visual term, though other sense impressions are sometimes included under its large umbrella; imagery which mingles different sense impressions (sound or touch, for example, with sight, as in Roethke's *I Knew a Woman*, p. 102) is said to be **synesthetic imagery.**

The first definition of imagery is the least precise one, for it tries to describe the effect of the poem in the reader; effects may be predicated generally, but because each reader's response is likely to be a little different from every other reader's, critics usually find it safer and more precise to articulate the poem's efforts to create the effect; the second and third definitions of imagery are attempts to describe these efforts, the *means* of bringing about a certain effect. The third definition is the most common one, and it has the advantage of greater precision in describing different indirect ways that a poem may use to translate words into less abstract sense experience. Critics who use the term "imagery" in this third way may refer to nonfigurative description simply as description and to the presumed effect on the reader of both description and imagery as **visual impressions** or **sense impressions.** Imagery is the collective term for a group of individual **images.** One may speak of an **image cluster** (a group of similar images concentrated in a short passage), of a **controlling image** (when a single image seems to dominate a passage or even a whole poem, making other images subservient to it), or of an **image pattern** (when one or more images recur in a passage or poem). Sometimes it is convenient to speak of **kinds of imagery** ("animal imagery" or "architectural imagery") as well as to define individual images in greater detail.

Imagery defined in the third way includes the use of simile, metaphor, analogy, and personification. A **simile** is a direct, explicit comparison of one thing to another and usually uses "like" or "as" in drawing the connection. In *A Red, Red Rose* (p. 408) Burns explicitly compares his friend to a rose, detailing in the poem itself in what different ways she is like a rose. A simile may **extend** throughout a poem and be elaborated (it is then called an **analogy**) or be used to make a brief comparison in only one specified sense.

A **metaphor** pretends that one thing is something else, thus making an implicit comparison between the things. Even more than similes, metaphors are often **extended** because, in describing a thing in terms of something else, a metaphor often implies a detailed and complex resemblance between the two, one which may not be obvious at first glance. When a metaphor compares things which seem radically unlike, but which can be developed into a striking parallel, it is called a conceit; the "metaphysical poets" of the 17th century specialized in finding surprising likenesses in things usually considered unlike, and their poems often elaborate a single **metaphysical conceit**, as in Donne's *Love's Alchemy* (p. 452) or Herbert's *The Collar* (p. 151). The terms **tenor** and **vehicle** are often used to distinguish the primary object of attention from the thing being used to clarify that object. In Shakespeare's *That Time of Year* (p. 177) the primary object of attention (**tenor**) is the aging speaker, and late autumn is the **vehicle** which in the first few lines clarifies his aging. Metaphors are often said to be **extended metaphors** or **controlling metaphors** (in the same sense I have described above for images) when they dominate or organize a passage or poem. Because the central thrust of metaphor is to provide a new experience of something by letting us see it in terms of something else, metaphor is often said to be the soul of poetry itself, and whole poems are sometimes said to be metaphors for an action, or feeling, or state of mind which they attempt to explore and communicate.

A **mixed metaphor** is one in which terms from one metaphor are incorporated into another one, usually by mistake. A **dead metaphor** is one that has passed into such common usage as to have obscured its origins: we speak of a "leg" of a chair or the "heart" of the problem without remembering that the terms are metaphors implying a comparison to living bodies. When language, metaphorical or not, becomes unnecessarily specialized and self-consciously unavailable to an outsider, it is **jargon**. When such language is used mindlessly, it is called **cant**. When it is slangy and lives the short life of fashion among a select in-group, it is called **argot**. A **cliché** is any expression or idea which, through repeated use, has become commonplace, tiresome, and trite.

**Personification** (or **prosopopeia**) is the strategy of giving human qualities to abstract concepts or inanimate things: Beauty, Honor, Cruelty, Death, flowers and various aspects of the natural landscape have been personified in various ages, but the strategy has been largely out of favor except for specialized and comic uses in the 20th century. Closely related is the strategy of ascribing to nature emotions which reflect human happenings, as when "universal Nature did lament" the death of Milton's Lycidas.

A **symbol** is many things to many people, and often it means no more than that the person using the term is dealing with something he doesn't know how to describe or think about precisely. The term is difficult to define and be precise about, but it can be used quite sensibly. A symbol is, put simply, something which stands for something else. The everyday world is full of simple examples; a flag, a peace sign, a star, or a skull and crossbones all suggest things beyond themselves, and everyone is likely to understand what their display is meant to signify, even though the viewer may not necessarily share the commitment which the object represents. In common usage a prison is a symbol of confinement, constriction, and loss of freedom, and in specialized traditional usage a cross may symbolize oppression, cruelty, suffering, death, resurrection, triumph, or the intersection of two separate things, traditions, ideas, etc. The specific symbolic significance is controlled by the context; a reader may often decide by looking at contiguous details in the poem and by examining the poem's attitude toward a particular tradition or body of beliefs; a star means one kind of thing to a Jewish poet and something else to a Christian poet, still something else to a Nazi or to someone whose religion is surfing. Too easy categorization, though, is dangerous, for a Christian poet may use the star of David in a traditional Jewish way (as in Marianne Moore's *The Hero*, p. 292), and a nonbeliever may draw upon the fund of traditional symbolic values without implying commitment to a particular religious system that lies behind them.

In a very literal sense, words themselves are all symbols (they stand for an object, action, or quality, not just for letters or sounds), but symbols in poetry are said to be those words and groups of words which have a range of reference beyond their literal denotation. The word "rose" simply denotes a kind of flower, but in poetry over the years it has come to symbolize youth, beauty, perfection, and shortness of youth and life. When a poem pervasively uses symbols as a major strategy and when the poem is more committed to the things which the symbols represent than to everyday reality, it is called a **symbolic poem** and is said to use **symbolism.** Poems, like everyday conversation, may use symbols occasionally and casually without being called symbolic.

**Allegory** is another slippery term closely related to symbol. In allegory, the action of the poem consistently and systematically describes another order of things beyond the obvious one. Spenser's *The Faerie Queene* is allegorical on several levels at the same time; the narrative action makes literal sense as a story, but the characters and actions also stand for political happenings, religious events, and moral values. *The Faerie Queene* is thus said to be a political, religious, and moral allegory. Allegory need not however, operate on more than one level beyond the literal one.

Poets sometimes develop a highly specialized and personal set of **private symbols**—words, objects, and phrases which take on specific meanings as a result of repeated use by the poet in poem after poem. Yeats, for example, developed a highly complex symbolic system, and so did Blake; their poems are largely accessible without specialized knowledge of their "systems," but the experienced reader of each soon discovers that the meanings of individual poems resonate in the context of other poems and in the reader's expanding knowledge of special symbols.

At the opposite extreme from private symbols are those which are universally shared within a defined culture. The framework of such shared symbols is called a **myth,** and the myth may include characters, events, and recurrent patterns of experience which the culture recognizes as, on some deep level, true. Poets often draw heavily upon the myth or myths of their culture; poets such as Milton or Eliot draw as heavily upon the Christian myth as ancient Greek and Roman poets upon classical myth. Poets sometimes too use particulars of a myth no longer literally or generally accepted; many English poets, for example, allude to classical myths in which neither they nor their audience believe in a truly mythic sense, but the wide recognition of standard myths allows writers to employ examples either in or out of their full mythic context. In recent years, critics have been heavily influenced by **myth criticism**, which may mean a great many things but which usually signifies an attempt to discover **archetypes**, patterns of experience and action which are similar in different nations and cultures. In this sense, myth is not restricted to a single system, but rather attempts to transcend the particulars of time and place and locate fundamental recurrent patterns in human nature and human history. Myth is also sometimes used in a very general sense to include a closed or self-defining system; in this sense, Yoknapatawpha County in Faulkner's novels is a myth, the ideals and goals of a culture (the American dream or frontierism or progress) are myths, and the framework which supports an individual poet's private symbols may be called his private or personal myth.

### 5. FORM AND STRUCTURE

The terms **form** and **structure** are among the most frequently used and abused in literary criticism. Almost everyone agrees that both terms describe organizing principles in a literary work and that meaning is finally inseparable from form and structure, but the particular values associated with each term vary widely. It is useful, though, to distinguish between the two, taking advantage of the spatial basis of the terms.

The **form** of a poem has to do with its appearance, just as does the form of a building, and one can describe that form in many different ways, just as a description of the form of a building depends upon the angle of vision (from the ground or from the air), the distance of the viewer, and to what other buildings the building is being compared. The simplest sense of poetic form involves the literal appearance on the page, the poem's shape seen physically, conceived literally. On the page most traditional poems look regular—that is, they are either divided into regular "stanzas" (§8) or they flow continually down the page in lines of more or less equal length. The breaks between stanzas, when they occur, usually reinforce divisions of meaning, much as do paragraph breaks in prose, though sometimes the break in meaning and break in form contradict each other, or operate in tension, for a particular purpose. Modern poems tend to be less regular and thus to look more scattered and fragmented on the page, reflecting a general modern attitude that poetic meaning accumulates in a less regular and less programmed way. Sometimes the appearance on the page reflects a visual attempt to capture oral patterns or speech rhythms (in the alternately bunched and scattered words of cummings's *chanson innocente*, p. 259 or *portrait*, p. 32; sometimes the appearance tries to reflect the action described (as in cummings's *l(a* in which the fall of a leaf is described and depicted). Occasionally the words are even shaped like a particular object, as in Renaissance **emblem poetry** (or **carmen figuratum** or **shaped verse**) such as Herbert's *Easter Wings* (p. 375) or recent **concrete poetry** such as Richard Kostelanetz's *A Tribute to Henry Ford* (p. 381) or Robert Hollander's *You Too? Me Too—Why Not* (p. 377) which resemble a freeway and a Coke bottle, respectively. Concrete poetry involves experiments with eye appeal, attempting to supplement (or replace) verbal meanings with devices from painting and sculpture. The idea is an old one; Theodoric in ancient Greece is credited with inventing **technopaegnia**—that is, constructing poems with visual appeal. The **acrostic,** a crossword-puzzle type of poem in which the first letter of each line spells words when read down as well as across, similarly counts on visual impact (see Carroll's *Acrostic,* p. 378). Such experimentation was once thought to have mystical significance, but it now survives only as playful exercise.

More enduring, more significant, and more complex senses of form involve less easily seeable ways of classifying external characteristics. Poetry is itself a sort of **formal** classification as distinguished from drama or fiction, and one can also distinguish between kinds of poetry (elegy, for example, or epigram) on the basis of subject matter, tone, conventions, etc. (see §6). Stanza varieties and rhythmic patterns (see §8 and §7) are also formal matters, for each involves external patterns which may be described relative to other poems. If one diagrams such matters as rhyme and accent, the patterns are readily visible, though the unpracticed eye might not discover them without help, just as casual viewers may need to have the Doric or Attic lines of a building pointed out to them.

As in a building, **structure** supports form and makes it possible. Many organizational elements enter into considerations of structure, and there are countless ways to speak of structure. The order and arrangement of all of a poem's constituent parts—words, images, figures of speech, ideas, everything—involve structure, and the ways of discussing the relationship between parts vary from matters of word arrangement (grammar, syntax) to the development and presentation of ideas. Structure enables the form; the planning and craft of poetry are all, finally, structural matters.

The distinction I have made between form and structure corresponds to distinctions that some critics make between **external** and **internal** form (or external and internal structure). Another frequent distinction is that between **organic** structure or form and **architechtonic** structure or form (those who make this distinction do not necessarily use the terms "form" and "structure" as they have been explained above). Things organic are said to take their shape from natural forces, like living organisms, and things architechtonic to have shape artificially imposed upon them from without; a strong bias is usually implied toward the former, for the distinction implies the livingness, wholeness, and uniqueness of an individual poem.

Some works are shaped by other works which they **imitate** or **parody.** An **imitation** which makes fun of another work is a **burlesque** or **parody** of it, exaggerating its distinctive features and holding them up to ridicule; it is a parody if its attitude is one of gentle teasing, a burlesque if it is harsh and vicious. Imitation may also be a kind of flattery, honoring the methods, values, and meanings of another work and expropriating them into the new one. Imitation is sometimes considered an inferior, unoriginal way of constructing a poem, but many great poems have their basis in imitation (*The Aeneid,* for example, imitates *The Iliad*), and a good imitation—even though it may borrow major features from its original—is never a simple copy, and it often derives major effects from its similarities to and differences from the original.

Finally, questions of form and structure are related to questions about the integrity and autonomy of individual poems. For many years, critics were reluctant to deal with **parts** of a poem, insisting that as self-existent **wholes** poems deserved to be dealt with **holistically,** as creations having their own laws. More recently, criticism has dealt more directly with parts of poems, admitting that they too have organizational principles and facing squarely the difficulty that knowing whether a poem is whole or not is, even for the author, very nearly a mystical matter. Besides, an individual poem is often part of a larger **sequence** or **cycle**—that is, a group of poems which have significant features in common: they may be about a similar subject, tell a story progressively, or be calculated to produce a particular effect. Some ages have emphasized the possibilities of such sequences (see §10), and in the early 17th century poets such as Herbert and Herrick arranged poems in their volumes very carefully toward a total effect; and some poets (Stevens and Ammons, for example) have insisted that all their poems are really only parts of the larger poem which is their total work or even their life. Almost all poets themselves arrange the poems in their individual volumes, and it is often useful and revealing to read individual poems in the context of these volumes.

## 6. GENRES AND KINDS

The word **genre** signifies an attempt to classify literary works in a way similar to biological classification, but there has never been a very precise agreement as to how that classification should be done. Different poems are said to belong to different groups, classified according to subject matter, level of language, mode of presentation, shape of plot, prose or verse form, etc., and often all of these ways of classifying are lumped together as **genre** classifications. But it is useful to distinguish among different ways of classifying literary works; here we use the term **genre** to indicate the traditional classroom distinction between fiction, poetry, and drama. Other less inclusive terms may then be used for subdividing genres and for different ways of classifying literary works according to characteristics they have in common.

A **mode** is, literally, a way of doing something; as a literary term it may most usefully be employed to indicate basic literary patterns of organizing experience. The **narrative mode** tells a story and organizes experience along a time continuum. The **dramatic mode** presents a change, usually an abrupt one, and organizes experience emotionally according to the rise and fall of someone's fortunes. The **lyric mode** reflects upon an experience or an idea and organizes experience irrespective of time and space, though it may describe a particular time or specific place. These traditional modes represent basic ways of viewing experience and have been around for a very long time. They obviously influenced the development of genres, which represent a somewhat artificial stiffening or rigidification of the narrative, dramatic, and lyric modes.

One may also think of modes in terms of the conclusions they draw about experience or the dominant emotions they arouse in their presentations of experience. Such a use of the term "mode" also has the sanction of time, and four such divisions are popularly used. **Tragedy,** or the **tragic mode,** describes someone's downfall, usually in stately language; and tragedy may exist in poetry (see, for example, *Sir Patrick Spens*, p. 194) as well as in drama. **Comedy,** or the **comic mode,** describes in more common language someone's triumph or the successful emergence of some order which encompasses and mutes all disorderly forces. **Romance,** or the **romantic mode,** describes the ideal, or what ought to be, often in terms of nostalgia or fantasy or longing. **Satire,** or the **satiric mode,** attacks the way things are and usually distributes the blame. In *The Anatomy of Criticism,* Northrup Frye argues that these modes correspond to the **myths** of the four seasons (comedy—spring; romance—summer; tragedy—autumn; satire—winter) and thus considers them universal ways of organizing experience.

Poetry considered as a genre may also be subdivided into **kinds** (or **types,** or **subgenres**). In the 17th century, French neoclassical critics believed poetry to consist of specific kinds that corresponded to absolute categories in the nature of things, though they never agreed on exactly what the kinds were. Even if one does not believe in kinds as such absolutes, knowing the characteristics of major kinds can be useful to readers in letting them know what to expect of a poem which consciously defines itself as of a certain kind. Over the years there has been general agreement about some of these kinds and their characteristics. The **epic,** or **heroic poetry,** was traditionally regarded as the highest in a hierarchy of kinds because it described the great deeds of mighty heroes and heroines, usually in founding a nation or developing a distinctive culture, and used elevated language and a grand, high style. **Pastoral poetry,** on the other hand, describes the simple life of country folk, usually shepherds who live a timeless, painless (and sheepless) life in a world that is full of beauty, music, and love, and that remains forever green. (Most pastoral poetry was, of course, written by city poets who used the kind nostalgically and self-consciously as fantasy; see, for example, Ralegh's *Nymph's Reply* to Marlowe's *Passionate Shepherd to His Love,* p. 78). The pastoral poem is also sometimes called an **eclogue,** a **bucolic,** or an **idyll.** The **elegy** was, in classical times, a poem on any subject written in "elegiac" meter, but since the Renaissance the term has usually indicated a formal lament for the death of a particular person; a **dirge,** or **threnody,** is similar but less formal and is supposed to be sung. A dirge or elegy supposed to be sung by one person is called a **monody.** Many elegies are **pastoral** elegies in which the dead person is imagined to be a shepherd (as in Milton's *Lycidas*); many of the conventions of pastoral carry over to the pastoral elegy, except that here time and death have invaded the simple world and destroyed its joyful, carefree spirit. An **epigram** was originally any poem carved in stone (on tombstones, buildings, gates, etc.), but in modern usage it denotes a very short, usually witty verse with a quick turn at the end; it is often, but not always, comic, as the group of epigrams in this anthology demonstrates. Several epigrams on pages 341–342 attempt to define the kind. The **epitaph** is a variety of epigram in which the poem is supposed to be carved on someone's tombstone, but many epitaphs are comic, written about people not yet dead, and of course not really intended for engraving.

A **verse epistle** is ostensibly a letter from the poet to someone, usually a good friend (for example, Jonson's *Inviting a Friend to Supper*, p. 227), and it uses the tone of a familiar letter; its themes are usually the joys of friendship and the pleasures of civilized conversation, but sometimes (as in Pope's *Epistle to Dr. Arbuthnot*, p. 50) the traditional materials are turned to satiric use. A **georgic,** or **didactic-descriptive poem,** is a how-to-do-it poem, often mixing moral instruction with practical advice about homely matters; georgics often contain long descriptive passages about natural phenomena or processes. If a georgic describes a particular place in detail, it is called **topographical poetry,** which has several variations. **House poems,** very popular in the Renaissance, describe the residence and estate of someone who is directly characterized by the account of his tastes in ambience (Waller's *On St. James's Park,* for example, p. 330). **Prospect poems** (such as Denham's *Cooper's Hill,* p. 363) describe in receding detail toward infinity the land visible from some specific vista, and they often unite a temporal (historical) with a spatial description of the place. (Some of the changes in topographical poetry over the years may be seen by comparing Waller's poem with Tomlinson's *At Barstow,* p. 337.)

A **mock poem** uses the conventions of one of the standard kinds in order to attack something; the thing attacked may be the kind itself, the artificiality of its conventions, or a real situation which does not measure up to the quality of life usually represented in the kind. **Mock-epic,** or **mock-heroic,** poems (*The Dunciad,* for example) commonly attack conditions in the present which do not measure up to the presumed heroism in epical accounts of the past.

A **lyric** is a short poem in which a speaker expresses intense personal emotion rather than telling a story or anecdote; Blake's *The Lamb* (p. 310) and *The Tiger* (p. 311), Roethke's *My Papa's Waltz* (p. 113), Wordsworth's *Tintern Abbey* (p. 289), and Elizabeth Barrett Browning's *How Do I Love Thee* (p. 304) suggest the range of poems which are properly called lyrics, and sometimes the term is used even more broadly for *any* short poem. The lyric is considered by many to be the essence of poetry itself as distinguished from the other genres (note its relation to the term "lyrical mode"). Originally the term "lyric" designated poems meant to be sung to the accompaniment of the lyre, and the names of several other kinds also specify their original connection with music. Many **songs** (whose words are usually called lyrics) are poems which have been set to music. During the Renaissance music and poetry were especially closely related. Many of the best Renaissance short poems were written specifically for music or were later set to music by professional musicians, and in recent years an increasing number of song writers are serious poets whose lyrics are poems of some quality. A **ballad** is a narrative poem which is, or originally was, meant to be sung (*Sir Patrick Spens*, for example). Characterized by much repetition and often by a repeated **refrain** (recurrent phrase or series of phrases), ballads were originally a folk creation, transmitted orally from person to person and age to age. Once **folk ballads** began to be written down (in the 18th century), **literary ballads** in imitation of folk ballads began to be created by individual authors. A **hymn** is a song of praise, usually in praise of God but sometimes of abstract qualities. A **chanson** (which in French simply means "song") was originally a song written in "couplets" (§8), but the term now describes any simple song; poems such as cummings' *chanson innocente* or Donne's *Song* (p. 150) make use of the expectations aroused by the claim to simplicity. The **madrigal**, a short poem, usually about love, set to music for unaccompanied voices, was very popular in Renaissance England. A **rhapsody**, like its counterpart in music, is a medley of extravagant utterances, usually in praise of something. An **epithalamium** or **epithalamion** is a marriage song or a song in praise of the bride; Spenser's *Prothalamion* (p. 386) is a variation which concentrates on events before the ceremony itself. An **aubade** is a morning song in which the coming of dawn is either celebrated or denounced as a nuisance (Donne's *The Sun Rising*, p. 163, for example). An **aube** is a more rigidly defined morning poem; the speaker of an aube is the woman in a love triangle, and she expresses regret that dawn is coming so that she and her lover must part, as in *Crabbed Age and Youth*, (p. 392). In a **complaint** a lover bemoans his sad condition as a result of neglect by his mistress (the speaker in Marvell's *To His Coy Mistress* mentions such a complaint, line 7). A **litany** (Nashe's *A Litany in Time of Plague*, p. 27) is a ritualistic invocational prayer, related to responsive readings in church liturgy. The **debate** is an old medieval kind in which two allegorical figures dispute; Randall's *Booker T. and W.E.B.* (p. 144) is a modern example of the debate kind. In a **palinode**, an author recants his previous attitude toward something, often apologizing for his earlier poetry, which he now claims to have been trifling. The **confessional poem** is a relatively new (or at least only recently defined) kind in which the speaker describes his confused chaotic state, which becomes a metaphor for the state of the world around him (as in Robert Lowell's *Skunk Hour*, p. 327). A **meditation** is a contemplation of some physical object as a way of reflecting upon some larger truth, often (but not necessarily) a spiritual one.

Many other ways of grouping poetry are less categorical, and some of them consciously overlap with other groupings. Debates are, for example, **dialogues** (that is, they have two speakers); and many of the kinds (confessional, complaint, aube, and many others) are traditionally **monologues** (one clearly distinguishable speaker does all the speaking). Monologues are sometimes called **interior monologues** (as in fiction) if the speaker seems to be thinking thoughts rather than speaking to someone. A monologue set in a specific situation and spoken to someone (but not necessarily anyone in particular) is often called a **soliloquy** or **dramatic monologue** (Browning's *Soliloquy of the Spanish Cloister* and *My Last Duchess*, p. 201). **Light verse** encompasses many poems in many kinds; it is not necessarily trivial, but its speaker takes or affects a whimsical, twitting attitude toward his or her subject, as in most epigrams or poems such as Armour's *Hiding Place* (p. 438). Light verse that deals with the manners and mores of polite society is called **vers de société**. And some terms which properly describe a kind also properly describe some other sort of grouping. If **satire**, for example, is in one sense a mode, it is also a kind, for there is **formal verse satire** which attacks a specific vice in the manner of a verse essay. And the term "satire" also describes an attitude toward experience and a tone; as the opposite of **panegyric** (poetry praising something) satire attacks something, usually by analyzing, specifying, and naming names. Satire which is mild, civilized, and gentle is called **Horatian satire** (named after the Roman poet Horace); vicious, violent, loud satire is **Juvenalian satire** (named after Juvenal), or **invective;** **Menippean satire** (named after Menippus) mixes poetry and prose (Wakoski's *The Buddha Inherits 6 Cars on His Birthday*, p. 219, is a modern instance of this tradition). A satire which attacks a specific person is a **lampoon.**

It is also difficult to distinguish certain poetic kinds from stanza forms. The **sonnet**, for example, is in a sense a kind, for it has certain conventions and usually treats specified subjects in a traditional way. But its conventions include a specified stanza, metrical pattern, and rhyme scheme, and I have described it (as well as the **ode** and **haiku**) under "Stanza and Verse Forms" (§8). The sonnet, ode, and haiku may properly be called either kinds or verse forms.

7. PROSODY

Prosody is the study of sound and rhythm in poetry. It is not a very exact science, but properly used it can be an aid to reading and *hearing* poems more fully. Poetry is more than a collection of sounds in a particular sequence, but poetry has a historical and primal relationship to music, and the audial aspects of poetry are basic to more complex matters involving words and arrangement. The sounds of poetry often clarify meaning, sometimes extend it, and nearly always provide tonal controls and gauges. A careful student of prosody may discover nuances and subtleties unavailable to a more casual hearer and may often gain insights into a poet's craft, but the most important function of prosody for most readers is to develop a sense of how poetry should be read aloud and, when it is read aloud, heard in its full subtlety and resonance.

The **rhythm** of a passage—in prose or poetry—is the pattern of sound pulsations in the voice as one reads it. Almost all spoken language has some kind of rhythm, however irregular, and simply listening to a human voice reciting, reading, or talking informally reveals recurrent systems of **stress** or **accent**. Stress is a relative matter (and this fact is a major difficulty for prosodic analysis), but in listening to the human voice we can always hear that some words and syllables are **stressed** (accented), and that others are, relatively, **unstressed** (**unaccented**). When the stress recurs at quite regular intervals—that is, when the rhythm has a pattern—the result is **meter**. The systematic analysis of patterns of stress, syllable by syllable, sound unit by sound unit, is called **scansion**; a reader who can **scan** a poem will discern the poem's basic rhythmic pattern (meter) and may then notice variations in the pattern or departures from it. These variations are often the most interesting metrical characteristics of the poem (and it is here that prosody is the least dull). But to discover variations one must see how patterns are formed and what the basic ones are.

According to pronouncing dictionaries, all words bear a stress on one or more syllables, and it is this syllable stress that forms the basis of any meter. But when words are put together into a sentence, or even a phrase, other regulators of stress are added. Monosyllabic words (words of one syllable) all have, according to a pronouncing dictionary, the same stress, but in a sentence or phrase the sameness of stress disappears; nouns and verbs generally receive stress while prepositions, articles, and conjunctions do not, but meaning governs where the stresses fall. In the sentence,

Throw the ball to me

stresses "naturally" fall on "throw," "ball," and "me," but another context of meaning might considerably alter the stress pattern:

I said, throw the ball to me, not over my head.

Stress here would likely fall on "to," and there might be some other "unusual" stresses, provided by the demands of meaning in particular instances or by particular speakers. When a sentence or phrase appears in a certain rhythmic context (in, for example, a poem written in a certain meter), the sound context also affects it, tending to bend it (or "wrench" it) toward the basic pattern in the surrounding passage. There are, then, three factors which determine stress: (1) the "natural" stress or stresses of each word; (2) meaning and emphasis in a sentence or phrase; and (3) the patterns of stress in the surrounding context.

Meter is measured in feet; a **foot** normally consists of a stressed syllable and one or more unstressed syllables. In the following line, in which stressed syllables are marked "–" and unstressed syllables "˘," the division into five feet is indicated by a **virgule**, or **slash mark** (/):

$$\overset{\smallsmile}{A} \; \overset{-}{lit}/\overset{\smallsmile}{tle} \; \overset{-}{lear}/\overset{\smallsmile}{ning} \; \overset{-}{is}/ \; \overset{\smallsmile}{a} \; \overset{-}{dang}/\overset{\smallsmile}{'rous} \; \overset{-}{thing}$$

Each of its feet is an **iambic** foot—that is, it has an unstressed syllable followed by a stressed one. Iambic meter is the most common one in English poetry, but three other meters are of some importance:

*Trochaic* (a stressed syllable followed by an unstressed one):

Tēll mĕ/ nōt ĭn/ mōurn fŭl/ nŭm bĕrs

*Anapestic* (two unstressed syllables followed by a stressed one):

'Twăs thĕ nīght/ bĕ fŏre Chrīst/ măs ănd āll/ thrŏugh thĕ hōuse

*Dactylic* (a stressed syllable followed by two unstressed ones):

Hīg glĕ dў/ pīg glĕ dў/ Āl frĕd Lŏrd/ Tēn nў sŏn.

Most English poems use one of these meters as their basic meter, but not with absolute regularity. An iambic poem will often contain trochaic feet (for emphasis, perhaps, or just for change), and some variation is almost a requirement if a poem is not to lull the ear into total dull deafness. Besides the standard meters, there are special feet used for variations.

Here is a table of the basic metrical feet and the most frequent variations:

| ADJECTIVAL FORM OF THE NAME | NOUN FORM | PATTERN |
|---|---|---|
| *iambic* | *iamb* (or *iambus*) | ˘ ‒ |
| *trochaic* | *trochee* | ‒ ˘ |
| *anapestic* | *anapest* | ˘ ˘ ‒ |
| *dactylic* | *dactyl* | ‒ ˘ ˘ |
| *spondaic* | *spondee* | ‒ ‒ |
| *pyrrhic* | *pyrrhic* | ˘ ˘ |
| *amphibrachic* | *amphibrach* (or *amphibrachys* or *rocking foot*) | ˘ ‒ ˘ |
| *amphimacric* | *amphimacer* (or *amphimac* or *cretic*) | ‒ ˘ ‒ |

Coleridge's *Metrical Feet* (p. 355) exemplifies most of them.

The most common line length in English poetry is pentameter, five feet. Here is a table of the most common line lengths:

| | |
|---|---|
| *monometer* | one foot |
| *dimeter* | two feet |
| *trimeter* | three feet |
| *tetrameter* | four feet |
| *pentameter* | five feet |
| *hexameter* | six feet |
| *heptameter* | seven feet |
| *octameter* | eight feet |

Iambic and anapestic meters are sometimes called **rising rhythms** (or **rising meters**) because their basic movement is from unstressed to stressed syllables; and trochaic and dactylic meters are called **falling rhythms** (or **falling meters**). When a foot lacks a syllable it is called **catalectic**; the first foot of anapestic lines is often catalectic, and the final foot of most trochaic lines is catalectic because lines that end with an unstressed syllable are usually thought to "sound funny"; such lines usually occur only in comic poetry. Lines that rhyme by using an unstressed final syllable are said to have **feminine rhyme**. Certain meters are also said to incline toward comic effects; anapestic rhythm tends to produce comic effects, though the examples on pages 355–360 demonstrate that anapests may also produce serious, even lofty, tones. Iambic tetrameter also seems more liable than most meters to comic effects, though it also has been used (as in Marvell's *To His Coy Mistress*) for great varieties of tone. The number and length of pauses in a line affect the speed with which the line is read and, indirectly, the tone in any meter, for a slow-paced line seems less emphatic in its rhythm than a rapid-paced one. Almost all lines contain one or more natural pauses, some very short and some fairly long; any significant pause within a line is called a **caesura,** and in scansion it is indicated by a double virgule (//).

I have been pretending that metrical matters can be dealt with categorically and with great certainty, but the whole question is much more approximate (and often uncertain) than I have let on. The distinction between stressed and unstressed is, for example, not a very precise one, for many degrees of stress are possible, and even an untrained ear can usually hear great variety of stress in the reading of a single line from a single poem. Division into feet is sometimes arbitrary, for there is often more than one way to count the number of feet, even assuming that the stresses are all accurately marked. Students often get bogged down in the technicalities of such matters and lose sight of the point of metrical analysis—which is to *hear* poems more accurately and notice those surprising places when the poem departs from its basic pattern. Often (but not always) a sharp departure from rhythmic expectations which the poem builds up signals something special going on. Note, for example, the variations from the basic iambic pattern in Dryden's *To the Memory of Mr. Oldham* (p. 367); some are for emphasis, others indicate structural breaks, and some mimic or echo the action or sounds of action which the poem describes.

Not all English poetry uses meter in the traditional senses I have described. Much modern poetry is in **free verse**, which avoids regularized meter and has no significant recurrent stress rhythms, though it may use other repetitive patterns—of words, phrases, structures—as Whitman often does. (**Free verse** should not be confused with **blank verse**, which is unrhymed but is by definition written in iambic pentameter.) So-called **prose poems** (such as Ginsberg's *A Supermarket in California*, p. 294) avoid even the appearance of traditional line divisions and lengths. Many modern poems that may appear unpatterned are, however, very tightly controlled metrically; the absence of rhyme does not mean the absence of metrical pattern, and many untraditional-looking modern poems use traditional meter in traditional ways. Many poems, old as well as new, experiment with meter too, trying odd combinations within the definitions I have given or using different principles altogether. The **sprung rhythm** used by Gerard Manley Hopkins avoids the usual distinctions about kinds of feet and only counts the numbers of stressed syllables; each foot begins with a stressed syllable, but any number of unstressed syllables may follow before the next foot begins, so that traditional scansion would make the pattern seem unpatterned. **Quantitative verse,** imitating the metrical principles used by Latin and Greek poets, has been attempted in almost every age, but seldom with success. Unlike stress meters of any kind, quantitative verse determines pattern by the duration of sounds and sets up various meters in combinations of long and short syllables. Some modern experimenters have fused quantitative and stress patterns, and still others have tried patterns based on the number of sounds (see the discussion of syllabic verse in §8), on the kind of sounds used rather than either duration or stress, or on attempts at precise distinctions in the *amount* of stress in stressed syllables.

Until recently **rhyme** has been nearly as important as meter to most poetry, and there are still some poets and critics who regard rhyme as a requirement for poetry. Robert Frost, paraphrasing a 17th-century French poet, used to say that writing a poem without rhyme was like playing tennis without a net. Proponents of rhyme usually argue along similar lines, emphasizing craft and discipline; opponents insist that rhyme requirements wrench and distort natural, effective expression.

Rhyme is based on the duplication of the vowel sound and all sounds after the vowel in the relevant words. Most rhyme is **end-rhyme** (that is, the near-duplication of sound takes place at the ends of the lines), but other patterns are possible. **Internal rhyme** involves rhyming sounds within the same line; in **beginning rhyme,** the first word or syllable rhymes in two or more lines. Not-quite rhyme is often used to vary strict rhyme schemes; the most common form is **slant rhyme** (or **half rhyme**) in which the relevant words have similar but not exactly rhyming sounds because either the vowel or consonant varies slightly (as in backs/box, bent/want, or web/step). **Visual** (or **eye**) **rhyme** uses words with identical endings but different pronunciations (bead/tread), and **rime riche** uses words that sound exactly the same but have different spellings and meanings (knight/night; lead/led; him/hymn). The variations of rhyme possibility are many, and it is surprising how many of the possibilities have actually been given names—on the basis of whether the vowel or consonant varies, which vowel or consonant sounds are used, how many syllables are rhymed, and whether a word is partly carried over into another line so that rhyme will work. Most of the more extreme variations are used for comic effect, though almost all have been used seriously at one time or another. In poetry of earlier ages, one needs to watch, too, for **historical rhyme**—rhyme that was perfect when the poem was written but, because of historical changes in pronunciation, is no longer so; tea/day and join/divine were once good rhymes in the easiest and simplest sense.

Sound effects not involving rhyme continue to be important to poetry, and many of them are (like rhyme and meter) based on the ordering principle of **repetition**. **Alliteration** is the repetition of sounds in nearby words; usually alliteration involves the initial consonant sounds of words (and sometimes internal consonants in stressed syllables). Such insistence of a single sound may reinforce meaning or imitate a sound relevant to what the words are describing; sometimes, too, alliteration is used to link certain words within a line or in close-by lines, implying connections not strictly logical. Satirists, for example, often invent damaging alliterative patterns for their objects of attack. **Assonance** is a repetition of vowel sounds in a line or series of lines; assonance often affects pace (by unbalancing short and long vowel patterns) and the way words included in the pattern tend to seem underscored. **Consonance** involves a repeated sequence of consonants but with varied vowels (as in stop/step, rope/reap, or hip/hop).

**Onomatopoeia** is the attempt to imitate or echo sounds being described. Some words are in themselves **onomatopoeic** (buzz, fizz, murmur), and others suggest action or qualities related to their literal meaning (slippery, lull). Passages may use rhythms and vocal sounds for onomatopoeic purposes, as in Shakespeare's *Like as the Waves* (p. 361) or Hart Crane's "The nasal whine of power" (p. 364). Sometimes the term onomatopoeia is used rather loosely to describe any sound effects correlated to the meaning of the poem; the famous "Sound and Sense" passage by Pope exemplifies many of the possibilities of sound to produce imitative, harmonious, or cacophonous effects.

## 8. STANZA AND VERSE FORMS

Most poems of more than a few lines are divided into **stanzas,** groups of lines with a specific cogency of their own and usually set off from one another by a space. Traditionally, stanzas are linked by a common **rhyme scheme** (pattern of rhyme words) or by a common pattern of rhythms; modern poems which are divided into stanzas often, however, lack such patterns. Stanza lengths vary considerably, and so do the patterns and complexity of rhyme. Poets often invent distinctive patterns of their own—sometimes for novelty, sometimes to generate a particular effect—but over the years some stanza patterns have proved quite durable.

The **ballad stanza** is one of the oldest; it consists of four lines, the second and fourth of which are iambic trimeter and rhyme with each other. The first and third lines, in iambic tetrameter, do not rhyme. Letters of the alphabet are usually used to indicate the rhyme scheme, as in this stanza from *Sir Patrick Spens*:

> The king sits in Dumferling toune,  a
> Drinking the blude-reid wine:  b
> "O where will I get guid sailor  c
> To sail this ship of mine?"  b

The ballad stanza moves quickly, and combines some rhyme with relative structural freedom; it is easy to memorize (an important quality in folk poetry, which was transmitted orally), for both the simplicity and the rhyme are **mnemonic** (memory) devices. Rhyme, repetition, and other memorable sound combinations are almost always features of primitive poetry.

The **elegiac stanza** consists of four lines of iambic pentameter, rhymed abab; it takes its name from the use of it in Gray's once famous and influential *Elegy Written in a Country Churchyard* (p. 70). **Terza rima** is the three-line stanza in which Dante wrote *The Divine Comedy;* each iambic pentameter stanza (aba) interlocks with the next (bcb, cdc, ded, etc.), and English poets (even those translating Dante) have generally found its rhyme needs too demanding for English, which is usually regarded as a "rhyme-poor" language because of its wholesale adoption of words from many languages rather than home growth of parallel endings. Still, some important poems, such as Shelley's *Ode to the West Wind* (p. 287), have used terza rima. Among longer stanza forms are **rime royal**, seven iambic pentameter lines which rhyme ababbcc, used by Chaucer and Shakespeare and revived in the 19th century; **ottava rima**, an Italian form adapted to English as eight lines of iambic pentameter rhyming abababcc and used especially by Byron (in *Don Juan*, for example); and the **Spenserian stanza,** the nine-line form Spenser invented for his *Faerie Queene* (eight lines of iambic pentameter and a ninth line of iambic hexameter, called an **alexandrine**, rhymed ababbcbcc). There are, of course, many varieties possible in the rhythms, lengths of lines, and rhymes in stanzas of all lengths, and many popular combinations have remained nameless. Stanzas with no official names are simply designated by the number of lines; a three-line stanza is called a **tristich, triplet,** or **tercet** (the latter is also a term for part of the sonnet—see the discussion below); a four-line stanza is a **quatrain;** a five-line stanza is a **quintain** or **quintet;** a six-line stanza is a **sextain** or **sixain.**

The modern rebellion against rhyme and traditional meters has brought many experiments with new ways of generating and justifying breaks within poems. Many modern poems are divided according to breaks in syntax, meaning, or tone, and the individual characteristics of a particular poem may dictate such breaks; some spatial breaks produce a special effect; some breaks represent merely capriciousness or convenience. Some experiments have also produced patterns as demanding in their own way as rhyme-based stanzas. **Syllabic verse,** for example, requires that the number of syllables in each line of the first stanza be duplicated in each subsequent stanza; stanzas (and lines within them) may thus be of any length, but the poet commits himself to a pattern in the first stanza and thereafter sticks to it. Many early- to mid-20th-century poets worked seriously in the form; see, for example, Marianne Moore's *The Hero* (p. 292). In a **rhopalic stanza,** which may theoretically be of any length, each line has one more (or one less) foot than the preceding line, and in a **rhopalic poem** each stanza has one more (or less) line than the preceding one.

The **couplet** is a rather special case among stanza forms. It consists of two lines (of any specifiable length or rhythm) which rhyme with one another, and seldom is one couplet divided by space from another one. Larger divisions within couplet verse are usually indicated (as in blank verse) by indentation, and the units are called **verse paragraphs,** which may or may not be separated by space. The **heroic couplet,** rhyming lines of iambic pentameter, has been the most popular and durable of couplet forms; it dominated English poetry during much of the 17th and 18th centuries and has been used successfully by many earlier and later poets. When the syntax of one couplet carries over into the next couplet, the couplets are said to be **open** or **enjambed; enjambment** is the continuation of syntax beyond the borders of a single couplet. **Closed** (or **end-stopped**) **couplets** are—as far as the technicalities of syntax are concerned—complete in themselves. Couplets written in iambic tetrameter tend to be used for comic effect because of the emphatic regularity of the rhythms and the abrupt underscoring of the rhyme. Not to be confused with the couplet is the **distich,** a two-line unit of verse in which both lines are structurally similar but do not rhyme. The **ghazal,** an Eastern stanza form, contains at least five couplets unified imagistically or associationally.

In some stanza forms (most notably the **sonnet** and **ode**) the overlapping with poetic kind (§6) is obvious. A sonnet is a poetic kind in the sense that it usually deals with certain subjects, bears a tradition of attitudes and tones, and has many conventions; but it also (unlike most poetic kinds) makes specific rhythmic and rhyme demands. A **sonnet** is a 14-line poem in iambic pentameter; its divisions and rhyme scheme depend upon whether it is an **Italian sonnet** or an **English sonnet.** An Italian sonnet has a two-part division; the first eight lines, or **octave** (sometimes divided into two four-line sections or **quatrains**) forms one unit of meaning. The octave's statement or question is qualified, balanced, or answered in the second, six-line part, or **sestet** (sometimes divided into two three-line sections called **tercets**). The Italian sonnet (it is also sometimes called a **Petrarchan sonnet**) is especially suited to dramatic contrasts; its rhyme scheme is usually abbaabba cdecde, but that of the sestet sometimes varies widely. The English sonnet (sometimes called the **Shakespearean sonnet** after its most famous practitioner but not because he invented it) is divided into three four-line sections (quatrains) and a final couplet; its rhyme scheme is abab cdcd efef gg. Usually the English sonnet contains a progression by steps in an argument or situation, and the couplet summarizes (or sometimes reverses) what has developed or what has been proved. Both Italian and English sonnets traditionally deal with love and private emotions, but their compact, tight form and the resulting intensity have sometimes made them attractive to satirists and political poets. As a form (and kind), the sonnet is very demanding, but many poets have found its rigidities useful for discipline, for organizing and controlling intense feelings, and for discussing themes of limitation and confinement (as in Wordsworth's *Nuns Fret Not,* p. 309).

The **ode** is an ancient and dignified kind; it treats an exalted theme in an elevated style and usually praises something or somebody. Its stanzaic demands result from the traditional following of two ancient models, Pindar and Horace. The **Pindaric ode** consists of an indefinite number of three-stanza units. Each unit contains a **strophe** (or **turn**), an **antistrophe** (**counterturn**), and **epode** (**stand**); the strophe and antistrophe are equal in length, for the Pindaric ode was originally an attempt to imitate the chorus in Greek drama (the strophe was to be chanted as the chorus moved to the left, the antistrophe as they returned, and the epode as they stood still). The **Horatian ode** consists of a series of **homostrophic** (regular) stanzas (as in Marvell's *Horatian Ode*, p. 311). The **irregular ode**, introduced in the 17th century, is closer to Pindar, but its often complex stanzas have no rigid pattern; the form resulted from a lack of understanding of Pindar's principles.

Several **fixed poetic forms** (which contain a certain number of stanzas organized in a determined way) have been popular, from time to time, with English poets. Most of them were introduced by French troubadours in Provence, some of them as early as the 12th century. The **villanelle** contains five three-line stanzas and a final four-line stanza; only two rhymes are permitted, and the first and third lines of the first stanza are repeated, alternately, as the third line of subsequent stanzas throughout the poem until the last stanza. In the last stanza the repeating lines become the final two lines of the poem, as in Empson's *Missing Dates* (p. 296). The **sestina** is even more complex; it contains six six-line stanzas and a final three-line stanza, all unrhymed; but the final word in each line of the first stanza then becomes the final word in other stanzas (but in a different specified pattern); the final stanza uses these words again in a specified way, one in each half line. Sidney's *Farewell, O Sun* (p. 295) exemplifies the pattern (and difficulty) of the form; Justice's *Here in Katmandu* (p. 183) is a modern example with several innovative puns. Some poets have even written **double** and **triple sestinas,** in which the demands increase geometrically. The **rondel** contains two four-line stanzas and a final five-line stanza and has only two rhymes (as in Henley's *Rondel,* p. 295). Like the villanelle it also repeats whole lines in a specified way, as indicated here by capital letters: ABba abAB abbaA; sometimes a 14th line is added, repeating the second (B) line. Repetition (probably originally for mnemonic purposes) is a major feature in each of these forms and in other fixed forms: the **rondeau,** the **virelay,** the **pantoum,** the **triolet,** the **chant royal,** and the **ballade** (not to be confused with the ballad). Many fixed poetic forms conclude with an **envoi,** or postscript stanza, which may summarize the poem, imply a wider significance, dedicate the poem to someone, or send it into the world with a specific commission or set of directions. An envoi, or **commission,** may also be appended to any poem or book of poems, sometimes assuming a length and form quite different from what precedes it. An **epigraph** (or **motto**) is a brief quotation which prefaces a poem, often to set up its subject or tone.

Several single-stanza forms also exist. They include the **limerick,** five lines in anapestic rhythms (the first, second, and fifth lines in trimeter, the third and fourth in dimeter), rhymed aabba, always comic, often obscene, and usually purporting to present the exploits of a fictional person; the **haiku,** a three-line poem with five syllables each in the first and third lines and seven syllables in the middle line, used primarily to describe a momentary sensation or impression which seems to characterize a specific season of the year; and several other highly technical forms (including the tanka and double dactyl) not exemplified in this anthology.

## 9. TRADITION AND CONVENTION

Tradition is seldom listed or defined in glossaries of literary terms, perhaps because it is so pervasive, persistent, complex, and controversial. In its most inclusive sense, **tradition** is the influence—deliberate or not—of any previous event, technique, or consciousness upon subsequent ways of thought and action. Poetic tradition may involve an influence in ideas, or style, or both. Poets may deliberately seek to follow, refine, or respond to previous thinkers and poets, or they may find themselves conditioned by the past in ways over which they have no control. An awareness of continuity (from one time to another or from one poet to another) is essential to tradition, but the continuity need not be obvious to the persons and times involved; sometimes the awareness of continuity is only available to observers after the fact, when the tradition is no longer operable. But often poets write with a **sense of tradition;** that is, they deliberately attempt to confront the past and turn it to their own purposes. Such a sense may involve the accumulated characteristics of a whole culture or, more narrowly, the expectations of a poetic kind, a verse form, or any particular literary device.

Poetry, perhaps more than drama or fiction, is subject to the characteristic habits and limitations of a particular language, and it is common practice to speak of **the English tradition** (or **the English poetic tradition,** or simply **the tradition**), meaning all of the recurrent tendencies over the years, including many which oppose, modify, or contradict other tendencies. The poetry of Pound or cummings, for example, is as surely a part of the tradition as that of Milton or Tennyson, for the tradition is not something which once and for all defines itself but rather consists of a continuity marked by continual modification. Participation in the tradition is not always easy to recognize or predict, for some of the English tradition's brightest lights (Shakespeare, Swift, Shelley, and Eliot are examples) at first seemed to their contemporaries most untraditional—in the sense of the tradition then understood. Tradition continually redefines itself to comprehend rebellious sons and daughters born into its line and intent on the old rituals of father-killing and mansion-burning. Sometimes the tradition is defined as if it were already complete, but it is more useful to consider it a living, changing thing which will, by definition, ultimately render any definition incomplete. Much (perhaps most) of what seems new and innovative does not, of course, last long enough in the public memory or evoke a substantial enough response in its audience to become part of the tradition. Contemporary with Shakespeare, for example, were many poets whose innovations did not "catch on" or whose distinctive appeal did not prove to be permanent; it is so in every age, and the process of developing a tradition is a perpetual matter of experimenting and sorting.

Within a language tradition are **national** and **regional traditions** as well; one may speak, for example, of a Canadian tradition, an Irish tradition, or a New England tradition. Such divisions have partly to do with local variations in linguistic usage, but they also relate to ideological concerns, cultural assumptions, and social, political, and economic movements. The same sort of division may be broadened, reaching beyond language barriers to comprehend the **European tradition** or the **Western tradition**. The latter term is often used nearly synonymously with the English tradition; such usage is not entirely precise, but many of the most characteristic features of English poetry do have origins or counterparts in ancient Greece or Rome or in more recent Continental cultures, especially those of France, Italy, and Germany.

Besides definitions based on linguistic, national, and cultural boundaries, there are other, more narrow senses of tradition in common use. Tradition may describe the history and accumulated characteristics of a literary kind or a stanza form (one might speak of the epic tradition, the sonnet tradition, the couplet tradition, or the tradition of free verse), the recurrent appearances of a motif or theme (the **carpe diem** tradition), the characteristics of a thought or value pattern (the Puritan tradition or the metaphysical tradition), or characteristics associated with a particular time or age (the Elizabethan tradition). Any device that recurs (metaphor, alliteration, a particular rhyme scheme or rhythmic pattern) tends to develop a tradition of usage that affects every new user. All of these senses represent a tendency for a poet to do things in a way related to how they have been done before, and they all represent a series of expectations he can count on in his readers. Readers who have read many sonnets have an idea of what to expect in a new one; they will know the conventions (see below), the ranges of possibility, the presumed limits. A new sonneteer may not stay within the presumed limits and may actually extend the range of possibility, but having the tradition to begin from offers a firm sense of where the frontiers are and provides an initial common ground with the reader.

Tradition may, of course, be an enemy as well as a friend, and many poets feel hostile toward the limitations which they believe tradition places upon them, and others feel intimidated by past accomplishments which seem to crowd present possibilities. Some of the uses and liabilities of tradition are not necessarily deliberate or conscious; there is an important sense in which poets are stuck with their traditions just as they are stuck with their genes, their bodies, and, after a while, with their personal habits and mannerisms. Few poets learn a new language well enough to make it their own for poetry, and perhaps even fewer fully become part of a new culture, with other institutions, histories, and expectations—though they may use information from another culture and try to translate values from it. The most deliberate uses of traditions—whether to praise, denounce, or modify them—may be said to involve awareness of one's own hereditary plight within them. Recent attempts by black poets to recover a part of their past in Africa—even though removed from it by generations, centuries, and attempts to suppress mere memory of it—suggest the deep attraction to felt lineage. And the recurrent attempts by many Westerners to engraft new life from the East finally comes down to a sense of strengths and weaknesses, real or imaginary, in one's own traditions.

A **convention** is any characteristic which over a period of time has come to be expected in poetry or in a poem of a certain sort. There are conventions of subject matter and conventional ways of using the standard poetic devices, but conventions are especially associated with the older poetic kinds. In pastoral, for example, it is a convention that shepherds sing and are happy and cheerful; this does not mean that the poet thinks that all shepherds are musical and jolly—or that *any* are, or that the poet knows anything about real shepherds—but simply that the poet, wishing to accomplish something in pastoral poetry or through it, has followed the conventions of his chosen poetic kind. Following the standard conventions is usually less significant than not following them; when a poem ignores or contradicts a convention, a reader can be pretty sure that the convention is missing or altered for a specific reason. Conventions at their best are shortcuts in communication; they tell a reader what to look for and establish a beginning rapport between poet and reader; what happens as the expectations are satisfied or surprised is then up to the poet.

The function of conventions is, of course, lost on the reader who does not know the conventions, and sometimes, too, conventions diminish their own effects by overuse or by continued mechanical use after their function has disappeared. Most conventions originated in the doctrine of **decorum,** which insists on appropriateness in all things: every poetic kind, for example, was assumed to require a certain level of language and persons and incidents of a specific level of dignity. Conventions almost always begin in a need to accomplish a specific thing in a specific way; pastorals contain happy shepherds because writers of pastoral were consciously creating a never-never land as a contrast to the worlds they themselves lived in, and they meant to project imaginatively what it would be like to live in a world without time pressures, death, disharmony, failures, and disappointments—a world which lacked the stench, pollution, and crowding of the city and in which no one felt winter cold or lacked the ability to carry a tune. New poetic kinds have conventions too, but they are more difficult to see because they seem, in the beginning, to be "natural" characteristics. Confessional poems, for example, are written in the first person, express a sense of personal disorientation, and describe a perception which links individual experience with a larger social or cosmic disorder. But many of the classic confessional poems imaginatively participate in such situations and strategies rather than deriving from a specific real experience; they assume the posture of the first person and use the conventions of the kind. As a kind takes shape, becomes known, and gets defined, it channels (for better or worse) subject matter and strategies into conventional molds, some useful, some not. Most conventions begin in necessity, flourish when they are recognizable to a large number of readers, and linger on simply as decoration, a memory of past needs. When specific conventions totally lose their use and force, they become merely ornamental, and sometimes seem amusing or absurd. This is why mechanical repetition of what is expected is often said to be "conventional" (or "merely conventional") in a negative sense. Sensible use of conventions involves taking advantage of the technical solutions and shortcuts they provide, but it involves too the personalized touch of an individual poet. No great poet leaves a convention exactly as he found it.

A list of even the major conventions would exhaust the reader before it exhausted the possibilities. Here instead are brief definitions of some of the major conventions of one poetic kind, the epic; the passages from Milton's *Paradise Lost* and Pope's *Dunciad* exemplify most of them. The **invocation of the muse**, at the beginning of an epic poem, asks for supernatural help for the poet, usually from one of the nine muses which classical poets celebrated as the source of poetic inspiration; Calliope, the muse of heroic poetry, is usually the muse invoked in epics. The action of an epic traditionally begins **in medias res**— that is, in the middle of things; rather than beginning with a careful exposition of the situation, epics move quickly to action and conflict and save background explanations for later. **Epic similes** are lengthy and detailed comparisons of a person, place, or thing to something else; in epic they are frequent and likely to occur even at the height of the action. **Epic epithets** are descriptive phrases repeatedly used to recall the traits of a particular character; **epic catalogues** give long lists of things often peripheral to the action, providing a sense of detail, completeness, and range of involvement. The **epic hero** is usually many times life-size and seems superhuman in his power and strength of character; his majesty and grandeur match the huge scope or **magnitude** of the action (which usually involves the history and destiny of a whole people) and the **grand style** considered appropriate to the recounting of great actions. It is also conventional in epic to have supernatural interventions, gigantic battles, and a clearly defined **theme** which involves universal human issues.

In the hands of a shrewd craftsman, tradition and convention may be innovative and exciting; in the hands of a mindless ape of the past, they are nearly always dull and deadly. There are, of course, poets and critics who take a far more uncompromising view. Some say that any attempt to engage or use tradition in any way dooms originality and creativity, others that any departures from the tried ways of the past deprive poetry of shared values and leave a poet undernourished, incomplete, and alone. The two writers whose poems are grouped at the end of this book—Keats and Rich—by no means represent these extremes, but they do provide a strong contrast in their attitudes toward the uses of tradition.

10. WIDER CONTEXTS

No poem is altogether self-existent. In a sense, every poem creates a world all its own, but every poem also reflects aspects of a larger world from which it derives. Often it is important—and sometimes it is crucial—for a reader to recognize **context**, the circumstances that surrounded the making of the poem. The most obvious and compelling contexts are in poems that refer explicitly to some historical event or situation; poems such as Milton's *On the New Forcers of Conscience Under the Long Parliament* (p. 443) or Joni Mitchell's *Woodstock* (p. 85) require knowledge of the central event they describe and of the whole cultural ambience surrounding and influencing that event. A poem written about a specific event or occasion is called an **occasional poem;** the occasion may be a well known public one (as in Berryman's *1 September 1939* (p. 441) or a private one as in Swift's *On Stella's Birthday, 1719* (p. 218) or Rich's *Planetarium* (p. 492). In poems which celebrate, attack, or reflect upon an event likely to seem obscure to most readers, editors often provide footnotes as a guide to the context, but footnotes are at best a pathetic attempt to mention facts about the context, and they can only begin to suggest the complex of emotions and attitudes from which a poem may begin. In Shelley's *England in 1819* (p. 128), for example, the political facts, though important, are only a small part of the total context; also important, but less easily specified, are the surrounding climate of political and cultural opinion, the tide of antimonarchic feeling, the frustration of reformers, the winds of change on the continent, the weight of English tradition, and Romantic ideas about poetry and its relation to public and political issues. All of these matters make up the **referential context** of the poem; they specify and explain the events and situations to which the poem refers. Such matters are easier to recover for newer poems, but the poems themselves may be just as demanding contextually. Ginsberg's *Howl* (p. 448), for example, requires a sense of the 1950s as much as specific facts about people, places, and terminology; Snodgrass's *Campus on the Hill* (p. 137) and Worley's *De Gustibus* (p. 32) make similar demands. Often, of course, a reader may be able to share the poem's intensity of feeling without substantial factual knowledge (as in Milton's *On the Late Massacre in Piedmont,* p. 304), and contextual knowledge may explain details and extend the range of effects.

Even when they do not refer to a specific event or situation, poems are very much influenced by the times and circumstances in which they were written. All poems, even those that may seem "timeless" or "universal", have a **historical present**—that is, they depend upon the ideological and esthetic resources available to the poet in his or her society. Linguistic patterns and tendencies, philosophical and social assumptions, and ideas about practically everything change from age to age, and how poets write—as well as what they write about—is to an extent dependent on the when and where of their lives. All matters of time and circumstance that might affect either the conception or execution are part of the poem's **historical** or **cultural context.** It is not always easy to determine exactly which factors are relevant to a poem and which are not; deciding just what information is necessary and how to use it once acquired is one of the most delicate tasks in good interpretation. The needs of historical context vary from minute details to broad generalizations about a nation or an era; to read Snyder's *Not Leaving the House* (p. 82) accurately one needs to know a great deal about American social patterns and the youth culture of the late 1960s and early 1970s, but for Davies' *Orchestra* (p. 427) and Whitaker's *Leaving the Dance* (p. 432) one needs the larger cultural assumptions about order in the Renaissance and the 20th century.

Literary historians often designate **periods** in which cultural and esthetic assumptions are more or less shared, speaking for example of the Elizabethan period (literally, 1558–1603, the reign of Queen Elizabeth in England) or the Romantic period (approximately 1790–1830) to describe certain common tendencies in a given historical era. The terminal dates in such periods are not meant to be taken too literally, and poets who outlive a period or whose lives span two or more periods continually offer problems in placement that may affect the interpretation of individual poems. Sensibly applied, period designations may provide convenient shortcuts for contextual description, but they always run the risk of oversimplifying and stereotyping, and like any generalizations they have limited applications. The poems on pages 383–398, for example, were all written within about 20 years of one another near the end of the Elizabethan period. Reading them in a group may provide some sense of the period, and knowledge of the period will, in turn illuminate each poem, but some of the poems will challenge generalizations about the period just as others will confirm them.

Another kind of context involves individual traits of the authors themselves. Reading a group of poems by an author usually clarifies every individual poem, for the reader can develop a sense of the poet's distinctive style, strategies, and ideas. The total work of an author is called a **canon;** one may speak of the Milton canon or the Eliot canon. But even a sampling of a poet's work often leads a reader to expect certain procedures and attitudes, enabling a more exact and intense response. In its broadest sense, the **authorial context** may include biographical detail, psychological analysis, and specific facts about the conditions under which a poem was created, as well as dominant characteristics or tendencies in poems by a certain author. Like other contexts, the authorial context needs to be applied to interpretation with care and good sense; a poet is not necessarily always concerned with immortality or revolutionary politics just because several poems show that concern. And poets do change their techniques as well as their ideas. Still, intensive reading of an author often isolates characteristics not visible (or not so easily visible) in an individual poem, and the use of such authorial contexts may clarify or intensify an experience of an individual poem.

Closely related to the authorial context is the problem of **parts** and **wholes.** Many short poems are actually parts of larger wholes (songs in a play, for example) or part of a sequence of poems. Very popular in the Elizabethan period were **sonnet sequences,** groups of a hundred or more sonnets which, when read consecutively, told a kind of story which supplemented the effects of individual poems. When a poem is part of some larger work, the **internal context** of the larger work (that is, the situation, action, and tone in the surrounding passages) influences the meaning of the poem. Jonson's *Come, My Celia* (p. 403), for example, is sung by a villain in the play in which it appears, and most of Sidney's sonnets are from a sonnet sequence in which the speaker is portrayed as ignorant, awkward, bumbling—the very antithesis of the courtier Sir Philip Sidney. Questions of completeness and integrity become very difficult in cases where the poet has conceived the poem doubly, both as a part of a larger unit of meaning and as a whole in itself. Reading passages from a long poem is a similar but not identical problem, for here it is the reader (or editor) who asserts the ability of the passage to stand alone. Some critics adamantly insist that no work should be excerpted or considered in part, but they still have to face the difficult question of how to construe those poems which are wholes and parts at the same time. When a poem is part of something larger— a play, a novel, a long poem, a sequence or cycle of poems, or even a book of poems put together by the author—it is best to consider that larger internal context when interpreting the poem.

What kind of contextual knowledge and how much of it a poem requires varies, of course, from poem to poem; many poems are readily accessible without deliberate pursuit of historical, intellectual, or authorial background, but the range and intensity of experience available through a poem is almost always enhanced by more knowledge. The group of poems on pages 441–453 has been left unannotated so that readers may test for themselves various kinds of contextual problems and textual needs. Some of these poems need footnotes only to supplement fundamental clarity or to explain a small point, but a poem such as Nemerov's *The Second-Best Bed* (p. 453) is not likely to make any sense at all to a reader who does not know that Shakespeare, in his will, bequeathed the "second best bed" to his wife.

# List of Terms Defined

# Index of Titles and First Lines

# Index of Authors